STUDENT'S SOLUTIONS MANUAL

David Lund
University of Wisconsin - Eau Claire

Introductory Statistics

Sixth Edition

NEIL A. WEISS

Boston San Francisco New York
London Toronto Sydney Tokyo Singapore Madrid
Mexico City Munich Paris Cape Town Hong Kong Montreal

Reproduced by Addison-Wesley from camera-ready copy supplied by the author.

Printed in the United States of America.

ISBN 0-201-73711-6

1 2 3 4 5 6 7 8 9 10 VG 04 03 02 01

PREFACE

Student's Solutions Manual is designed to be used with the text *Introductory Statistics, Sixth Edition* by Neil A. Weiss. It provides complete solutions to all (686) of the odd-numbered exercises and all 366 review problems in Chapters 1-16 of the text. The solutions are more than answers--intermediary steps in the process of solving the exercises are also provided.

New to this edition of the text are 609 supplementary exercises which are on the Weiss Stats CD supplied with the text. In this manual, we have also provided the answers to all 310 of the odd-numbered supplementary exercises and complete solutions for some of them.

Note: Many of the numerical answers presented here were obtained by using computer software and the original set of data. If you solve problems by hand and do some intermediate rounding or use the summary statistics which are provided in the text for many of the exercises, your answers may differ slightly from the ones given in this manual. In a few instances, the solutions provided here may also differ slightly from the answers provided in Appendix B of the text, but we are not aware of any instances in which the differences are significant enough to alter the conclusions reached. As noted by the author, you should retain intermediate results in your calculator or on your computer and delay any rounding until the end of your calculations.

My thanks go to a number of people. Completing a work as large as this has required the understanding, assistance, patience, stamina, and tolerance of Neil and the staff at Addison Wesley, especially Rachel Reeve, who have been such a great help in completing this project. It has been an excellent exercise in cooperation and teamwork. I would also like to thank Vivien Freund and Lindsay Packer for their excellent work in checking all of the solutions in this manual. Finally, I want to express my thanks to my wife, Judy, for her support and encouragement throughout this project.

D.R.L.
Eau Claire, WI

CONTENTS

CHAPTER 1 ANSWERS

Exercises 1.1

1.1 (a) The *population* is the collection of all individuals, items, or data under consideration in a statistical study.

(b) A *sample* is that part of the population from which information is collected.

1.3 Descriptive methods are used for organizing and summarizing information and include graphs, charts, tables, averages, measures of variation, and percentiles.

1.5 This study is inferential. Data from a sample of Americans are used to make an estimate of (or an inference about) average TV-viewing time for all Americans.

1.7 This study is inferential. Data from a 10% sampling of all 1997 U.S. death certificates are used to make a estimates of (or inferences about) rates of the leading causes of death.

1.9 This study is descriptive. It is a summary of the final closing values of the Dow Jones Industrial Average at the end of December for the years 1994-1999.

1.11 (a) This statement is descriptive since it only tells what was said by those who were surveyed.

(b) Then the statement would be inferential since the data would have been used to provide an estimate of what all Americans would choose.

Exercises 1.3

1.13 A census is generally time consuming, costly, frequently impractical, and sometimes impossible.

1.15 The sample should be representative so that it reflects as closely as possible the relevant characteristics of the population under consideration.

1.17 Dentists form a high-income group whose incomes are not representative of the incomes of Seattle residents in general.

1.19 (a) Probability sampling uses a randomizing device to decide which members of the population will constitute the sample. This can involve tossing a coin or die, or consulting a random number table.

(b) False. It is possible for the randomizing device to randomly produce a sample which is not representative.

(c) Probability sampling eliminates unintentional bias, permits the researcher to control the chance of obtaining a nonrepresentative sample, and guarantees that the techniques of inferential statistics can be applied.

1.21 Simple random sampling.

1.23 (a) GLS, GLA, GLT, GSA, GST, GAT, LSA, LST, LAT, SAT.

(b) There are 10 samples, each of size three. Each sample has a one in ten chance of being selected. Thus, the probability that a sample of three salaries is the first sample on the list presented in part (a) is 1/10. The same is true for the second sample and for the tenth sample.

1.25 (a)

E,M,P,L	E,M,L,F	E,P,B,F	M,P,B,F
E,M,P,B	E,M,B,F	E,L,B,F	M,L,B,F
E,M,P,F	E,P,L,B	M,P,L,B	P,L,B,F
E,M,L,B	E,P,L,F	M,P,L,F	

(b) One procedure for obtaining a random sample of four representatives from the six is to write the initials of the representatives on six separate pieces of paper, place the six slips of paper into a box, and then, while blindfolded, pick four of the slips of paper. Or, number the representatives 1-6, and use a table of random numbers or a random-number generator to select four different numbers between 1 and 6.

(c) P(E, F, L, and B) = 1/15; P(P, B, M and F) = 1/15

1.27 I am using Table I to obtain a list of 10 random numbers between 1 and 500 as follows. First, I pick a random starting point by closing my eyes and putting my finger down on the table.

My finger falls on the three digits located at the intersection of line number 00 with columns 34, 35, and 36. The selected digits are 356. This is my starting point.

I now go down the table and record the three-digit numbers appearing directly beneath 356. Since I want numbers between 1 and 500 only, I throw out numbers between 501 and 999, inclusive. I also discard the number 000.

After 356, I skip 876, record 351, skip 717, record 239, 455, 431, 008, skip 900, 721, record 259, 068, 156, skip 570, 540, 937, 989, and record 047.

I've finished recording the 10 random numbers. In summary, these are:

356	239	431	259	156
351	455	008	068	047

1.29 (a) The possible samples of size one are G L S A T

(b) There is no difference between obtaining a simple random sample of size one and selecting one official at random.

1.31 Set a range of 1 to 500 integers and have a random-number generator generate 10 numbers in this range. Match these numbers to a numbered list of the 500 firms.

<u>Exercises 1.4</u>

1.33 (a) Answers will vary, but here is the procedure: (1) Divide the population size, 500, by the sample size, 10, and round down to the nearest whole number if necessary; this gives 50. (2) Use a table of random numbers (or a similar device) to select a number at random between 1 and 50, call it k. (3) List every 50th number, starting with k, until 10 numbers are obtained; thus the first number on the required list of 10 numbers is k, the second is $k+50$, the third is $k+100$, and so forth (e.g., if $k=6$, then the numbers on the list are 6, 56, 106, ...).

(b) Systematic random sampling is easier.

(c) The answer may depend on the purpose of the sampling. If the purpose of sampling is not related to the size of the sales outside the U.S., systematic sampling may work. However, since the listing is a ranking by amount of sales, if the first number chosen is low (say 2), then the sample will contain firms that, on the average, have higher sales outside the U.S. than the population as a whole. If the first number is high, say 49, then the sample will contain firms that, on the average, have lower sales than the population as a whole. In either of those cases, the sample would not be representative of the population in regard to the amount of sales outside the U.S.

1.35 (a) Number the suites from 1 to 48, use a table of random numbers to randomly select three of the 48 suites, and take as the sample the 24 dormitory residents living in the three suites obtained.

(b) Probably not, since friends are more likely to have similar opinions than are strangers.

(c) There are 384 students in total. Freshman make up 1/3 of them. Sophomores make up 7/24 of them, Juniors 1/4, and Seniors 1/8. Multiplying each of these fractions by 24 yields the proportional allocation which dictates that the number of freshmen, sophomores, juniors, and seniors selected be, respectively, 8, 7, 6, and 3. Thus a stratified sample of 24 dormitory residents can be obtained as follows: Number the freshmen dormitory residents from 1 to 128 and use a table of random numbers to randomly select 8 of the 128 freshman dormitory residents; number the sophomore dormitory residents from 1 to 112 and use a table of random numbers to randomly select 7 of the 112 sophomore dormitory residents; and so forth.

1.37 From the information about the sample, we can conclude that the population of interest consists of all adults in the continental U.S. The sample size was 2010 except that for questions about politics, only registered voters were considered part of the sample. The sample size for those questions was 1,637.

The overall procedure for drawing the sample was multistage sampling (actually, three stages were used): the first stage was to randomly select 520 geographic points in the continental U.S.; then proportional sampling was used to randomly sample a number of households with telephones from each of the 520 regions in proportion to its population; finally, once each household was selected, a randomizing procedure was used to ensure that the correct numbers of adult male and female respondents were included in the sample.

The last paragraph indicates the confidence that the poll-takers had in the results of the survey, that is, that there is a 95% chance that the sample results will not differ by more than 2.2 percentage points in either direction from the true percentage that would have been obtained by surveying all adults in the actual population, or by more than 2.5 percentage points in either direction from the true percentage that would have been obtained by surveying all registered voters in the population. The last sentence says that smaller samples have a larger "margin of error," an explanation for the difference in the maximum error for all adults and the maximum error for registered voters.

Exercises 1.5

1.39 Observational studies can reveal only association, whereas designed experiments can help establish cause and effect.

1.41 Here is one of several methods that could be used: Number the women from 1 to 4753; use a table of random numbers or a random-number generator to obtain 2376 different numbers between 1 and 4753; the 2376 women with those numbers are in one group, the remaining 2377 women are in the other group.

1.43 Designed experiment. The researchers did not simply observe the two groups of children, but instead randomly assigned children to receive the Salk vaccine or to receive a placebo.

1.45 (a) Experimental units are the individuals or items on which the experiment is performed.

(b) When the experimental units are humans, we call them subjects.

1.47 (a) Experimental units: the twenty flashlights

(b) Response variable: battery lifetime in a flashlight

(c) Factors: one factor - battery brand

(d) Levels of the factor: the four brands of batteries

(e) Treatments: the four brands of batteries

1.49 (a) Experimental units: the product being sold

(b) Response variable: the number of units of the product sold

(c) Factors: two factors - display type and pricing scheme

(d) Levels of each factor: the three different types of display and the three different pricing schemes

(e) Treatments: the nine different combinations of display type and price which result from testing each of the three pricing schemes with each of the three display types

1.51 This is a completely randomized design since all the flashlights were randomly assigned to the different battery brands.

1.53 Double-blinding guards against bias, both in the evaluations and in the responses. In the Salk-vaccine experiment, double-blinding ensured that a doctor's evaluation would not be influenced by knowing which treatment (vaccine or placebo) a patient received; it also ensured that a patient's response to the treatment from would not be influenced by knowing which treatment he or she received.

1.55 Minitab is a comprehensive statistical software package which contains features used for random sampling. Using Minitab, we wish to randomly select 2376 different numbers from the set of numbers 1 to 4753. To do this,

- From the pull-down menu, choose **Calc ▶ Make Patterned Data ▶ Simple Set of Numbers...**
- Type NUMBERS in the **Store patterned data in** text box.
- Select the **Patterned sequence** option button
- Click in the **From first value** text box and type 1
- Click in the **To last value** text box and type 4753
- Click **OK**
- Now choose **Calc ▶ Random Data ▶ Sample From Columns...**
- Type 2376 in the small text box after **Sample**
- Click in the **Sample ☐ rows from column(s)** text box and specify NUMBERS
- Click in the **Store Samples in** text box and type SRS
- Click **OK**

To print the numbers now in the SRS column, we choose **Manip ▶ Display Data...**, specify SRS in the **Columns, Constants, and Matrices to display** text box, and then click **OK**. Results are shown in the Session window and can be printed from there.

REVIEW TEST FOR CHAPTER 1

1. Student exercise.

2. Descriptive statistics are used to display and summarize the data to be used in an inferential study. Preliminary descriptive analysis of a sample often reveals features of the data that determine the choice of the appropriate inferential analysis procedure.

3. Descriptive study. The scores are merely reported.

4. Descriptive study. The paragraph describes the results of a survey of thousands of students.

5. A literature search should be made before planning and conducting a study.

6. (a) A representative sample is one which reflects as closely as possible the relevant characteristics of the population under consideration.

   (b) Probability sampling involves the use of a randomizing device to determine which members of the population will make up the sample. This can involve tossing a coin or die, using a random number table, or using computer software which generates random numbers

   (c) Simple random sampling is a sampling procedure in which all possible samples of a given size are equally likely to be the actual sample selected.

7. Since Yale is a highly selective and expensive institution, it is very unlikely that the students at Yale are representative of the population of all college students or that their parents are representative of the population of parents of all college students.

8. (a) This method does not involve probability sampling. No randomizing device is being used and people who do not visit the campus have no chance of being included in the sample.

   (b) The dart throwing is a randomizing device which makes all samples of size 20 equally likely. This is probability sampling.

9. (a) SW,AA,DL SW,AA,US SW,AA,AK SW,DL,US SW,DL,AK

   SW,US,AK AA,DL,US AA,DL,AK AA,US,AK DL,US,AK

   (b) Since each of the 10 samples of size three is equally likely, there is a 1/10 chance that the sample chosen is the first sample in the list, a 1/10 chance that it is the second sample in the list, and a 1/10 chance that it is the tenth sample in the list.

10. (a) Table I can be employed to obtain a sample of 15 different random numbers between 1 and 100 as follows. First, I pick a random starting point by closing my eyes and putting my finger down on the table.

    My finger falls on three digits located at the intersection of a line with three columns. (Notice that the first column of digits is labeled "00" rather than "01"). This is my starting point.

    I now go down the table and record all three-digit numbers appearing directly beneath the first three-digit number which are between 001 and 100 inclusive. I throw out numbers between 101 and 999, inclusive. I also discard the number 0000. When the bottom of the column is reached, I move over to the right to the next sequence of three digits and work my way back up the table. Continue in this manner. When 10 distinct three-digit numbers have been recorded, the sample is complete.

    (b) Starting in row 10, columns 7-9, we skip 484, 797, record 082, skip 586, 653, 452, 552, 155, record 008, skip 765, move to the right and record 016, skip 534, 593, 964, 667, 452, 432, 594, 950, 670, record 001, skip 581, 577, 408, 948, 807, 862, 407, record 047, skip 977, move to the right, skip 422 and all of the rest of the numbers in that column, move to the right, skip 732, 192, record 094, skip 615 and all of the rest of the numbers in that column, move to the right, record 097, skip 673, record 074, skip 469, 822, record 052, skip 397, 468, 741, 566, 470, record 076, 098, skip 883, 378, 154, 102, record 003, skip 802, 841, move to the right, skip 243, 198, 411, record 089, skip 701, 305, 638, 654, record 041, skip 753, 790, record 063.

The final list of numbers is

082, 008, 016, 001, 047, 094, 097, 074, 052, 076, 098, 003, 089, 041, 063.

11. (a) The procedure for systematic random sampling is as follows: first we divide the population size by the sample size and round the result down to the next integer, say k. Then we select one random number, say r, between 1 and k inclusive. That number will be the first member of the sample. The remaining members of sample will be those numbered r+k, r+2k, r+3k, ... until a sample of the desired size n has been chosen. Systematic sampling will yield results similar to simple random sampling as long as there is nothing systematic about the way the members of the population were assigned their numbers.

(b) In cluster sampling, clusters of the population (such as blocks, precincts, wards, etc.) are chosen at random from all such possible clusters. Then every member of the population belonging to the chosen clusters is sampled. This method of sampling is particularly convenient when members of the population are widely scattered and is appropriate when the members of each cluster are representative of the entire population.

(c) In stratified random sampling with proportional allocation, the population is first divided into subpopulations, called strata, and simple random sampling is done within each stratum. Proportional allocation means that the size of the sample from each stratum is proportional to the size of the stratum.

12. (a) Answers will vary, but here is the procedure: (1) Divide the population size, 100, by the sample size 15, and round down to the nearest whole number; this gives 6. (2) Use a table of random numbers (or a similar device) to select a number between 1 and 6, call it *k*. (3) List every 6th number, starting with *k*, until 15 numbers are obtained; thus the first number on the required list of 15 numbers is *k*, the second is *k*+6, the third is *k*+12, and so forth (e.g., if *k*=4, then the numbers on the list are 4, 10, 16, ...).

(b) Yes, unless for some reason there is some kind of trend or a cyclical pattern in the listing of the athletes.

13. (a) The number of full professors should be (205/820) x 40 = 10. Similarly, proportional allocation dictates that 16 associate professors, 12 assistant professors, and 2 instructors be selected.

(b) The procedure is as follows: Number the full professors from 1 to 205, and use Table I to randomly select 10 of the 205 full professors; number the associate professors from 1 to 328, and use Table I to randomly select 16 of the 328 associate professors; and so on.

14. The statement under the vote is a disclaimer as to the validity of the survey. Since the vote reflects only the responses of volunteers who chose to vote, it cannot be regarded as representative of the public in general, some of whom do not use the Internet, nor as representative of Internet users since the sample was not chosen at random from either group.

15. (a) In an observational study, researchers simply observe characteristics and take measurements. In a designed experiment, researchers impose treatments and controls and *then* observe characteristics and take measurements.

(b) An observational study can only reveal associations between variables, whereas a designed experiment can help to establish cause and effect relationships.

16. This is an observational study. The researchers at the University of Michigan simply observed the poverty status and IQs of the children.

17. (a) This is a designed experiment.

(b) The treatment group consists of the 158 patients who took AVONEX. The control group consists of the 143 patients who were given a placebo. The treatments were the AVONEX and the placebo.

18. The three basic principles of experimental design are control, randomization, and replication. Control refers to methods for controlling factors other than those of primary interest. Randomization means randomly dividing the subjects into groups in order to avoid unintentional selection bias in constituting the groups. Replication means using enough experimental units or subjects so that groups resemble each other closely and so that there is a good chance of detecting differences among the treatments when such differences actually exist.

19. (a) Experiment units: the doughnuts

(b) Response variable: amount of fat absorbed

(c) Factor(s): fat type

(d) Levels of the factor: four types of fat

(e) Treatments: four types of fat

20. (a) Experiment units: tomato plants

(b) Response variable: yield of tomatoes

(c) Factor(s): tomato variety and density of plants

(d) Levels of each factor: These are not given, but tomato varieties tested would be the levels of variety and the different densities of plants would be the levels of density.

(e) Treatments: Each treatment would be one of the combinations of a tomato and a given plant density.

21. (a) This is a completely randomized design since all 24 cars were randomly assigned to the 4 brands of gasoline.

(b) This is a randomized block design. The four different gasoline brands are randomly assigned to the four cars separately within each of the six car model groups. The blocks are the six groups of four identical cars.

(c) If the purpose is learn about the mileage rating of one particular car model with each of the four gasolines, then the completely randomized design is appropriate. But if the purpose is to learn about the performance of the gasolines across a variety of cars (and this seems more reasonable), then the randomized block design is more appropriate and will allow the researcher to determine the effect of car model as well as of gasoline type on the mileage obtained.

24. (a) Student Exercise. This can be done easily in Minitab or Excel. In Excel, type the expression <u>=INT(100*RAND()+1)</u> in cell A1. This will produce a random integer between 1 and 100 inclusive. Then copy this expression into cells A2:A15. The result will be a sample of 15 numbers. If there are duplicates, copy the expression into enough cells to yield 15 different values.

CHAPTER 2 ANSWERS

Exercises 2.1

2.1 (a) Answers may vary. Eye color and model of car are qualitative variables.

(b) Answers may vary. Number of eggs in a nest, number of cases of flu, and number of employees are discrete, quantitative variables.

(c) Weight and voltage are examples of quantitative continuous variables.

2.3 (a) Qualitative data are obtained by observing the characteristics described by a qualitative variable such as color or shape.

(b) Discrete, quantitative data are numerical data that are obtained by observing values, usually by counting, of a discrete variable whose values form a finite or countably infinite set of numbers.

(c) Continuous, quantitative data are numerical data that are obtained by observing values of a continuous variable. They are usually the result of measuring something such as temperature which can take any value in a given interval.

2.5 Of qualitative and quantitative (discrete and continuous) types of data, only qualitative involves non-numerical data.

2.7 (a) The second column consists of *quantitative, discrete* data. This column provides the ranks of the cities according to their highest temperatures.

(b) The third column consists of *quantitative, continuous* data. This column provides the highest temperature on record in each of the listed cities.

(c) The information that Phoenix is in Arizona is qualitative data since it is non-numeric.

2.9 (a) The third column consists of *quantitative, discrete* data. Although the data are presented to one decimal point, the data represent the number of albums sold in millions, which can only be whole numbers.

(b) The information that *Supernatural* was performed by Santana is qualitative data since it is non-numerical.

Exercises 2.2

2.11 One of the main reasons for grouping data is that it often makes a rather complicated set of data easier to understand.

2.13 When grouping data, the three most important guidelines in choosing the classes are: (1) the number of classes should be small enough to provide an effective summary, but large enough to display the relevant characteristics of the data; (2) each piece of data must belong to one, and only one, class; and (3) whenever feasible, all classes should have the same width.

2.15 If the two data sets have the same number of data values, either a frequency distribution or a relative-frequency distribution is suitable. If, however, the two data sets have different numbers of data values, relative-frequency distributions should be used because the total of each set of relative frequencies is 1, putting both distributions on the same basis.

2.17 In the first method for depicting classes we used the notation **a<b** to mean values that are greater than or equal to **a** and up to, but not including **b.** So, for example, 30<40 represents a range of values greater than or equal to 30, but strictly less than 40. In the alternate method, we used the notation **a-b** to indicate a class that extends from **a** to **b,** including both endpoints. For example, 30-39 is a class that includes both 30 and 39. The alternate method is especially appropriate when all of the data values are integers. If the data include values like 39.7 or 39.93, the first method is preferable since the cutpoints remain integers whereas in the alternate method, the upper limits for each class would have to be expressed in decimal form such as 39.9 or 39.99.

2.19 When grouping data using classes that each represent a single possible numerical value, the midpoint of any given class would be the same as the value for that class. Thus listing the midpoints would be redundant.

2.21 The first class is 52<54. Since all classes are to be of equal width 2, the classes are presented in column 1. The last class is 74<76, since the largest data value is 75.3. Having established the classes, we tally the speed figures into their respective classes. These results are presented in column 2, which lists the frequencies. Dividing each frequency by the total number of observations, which is 35, results in each class's relative frequency. The relative frequencies are presented in column 3. By averaging the lower and upper class cutpoints for each class, we arrive at the class midpoints which are presented in column 4.

Speed (MPH)	Frequency	Relative Frequency	Midpoint
52<54	2	0.057	53
54<56	5	0.143	55
56<58	6	0.171	57
58<60	8	0.229	59
60<62	7	0.200	61
62<64	3	0.086	63
64<66	2	0.057	65
66<68	1	0.029	67
68<70	0	0.000	69
70<72	0	0.000	71
72<74	0	0.000	73
74<76	1	0.029	75
	35	1.001	

Note that the relative frequencies sum to 1.01, not 1.00, due to round-off errors in the individual relative frequencies.

2.23 The first class is 52-53.9. Since all classes are to be of equal width, the second class has limits of 54 and 55.9. The classes are presented in column 1. The last class is 74-75.9 since the largest data value is 75.3. Having established the classes, we tally the speed figures into their respective classes. These results are presented in column 2, which lists the frequencies. Dividing each frequency by the total number of observations, 35, results in each class's relative frequency which is presented in column 3. By averaging the lower limit for each class with the upper limit of the same class, we arrive at the class mark for each class. The class marks are presented in column 4.

Speed (MPH)	Frequency	Relative Frequency	Class Mark
52-53.9	2	0.057	52.95
54-55.9	5	0.143	54.95
56-57.9	6	0.171	56.95
58-59.9	8	0.229	58.95
60-61.9	7	0.200	60.95
62-63.9	3	0.086	62.95
64-65.9	2	0.057	64.95
66-67.9	1	0.029	66.95
68-69.9	0	0.000	68.95
70-71.9	0	0.000	70.95
72-73.9	0	0.000	72.95
74-75.9	1	0.029	74.95
	35	1.001	

Note that the relative frequencies sum to 1.01, not 1.00, due to round-off errors in the individual relative frequencies.

2.25 Since the data values range from 3 to 12, we could construct a table with classes based on a single value or on two values. We will choose classes with a single value because one of the classes based on two values would have contained almost half of the data. The resulting table is shown below.

Number of Pups	Frequency	Relative Frequency
3	2	0.0250
4	5	0.0625
5	10	0.1250
6	11	0.1375
7	17	0.2125
8	17	0.2125
9	11	0.1375
10	4	0.0500
11	2	0.0250
12	1	0.0125
	80	1.0000

2.27

Network	Frequency	Relative Frequency
ABC	5	0.25
CBS	8	0.40
NBC	7	0.35
	20	1.00

2.29 (a) The first class is 1<2. Since all classes are to be of equal width 1, the second class is 2<3. The classes are presented in column 1. Having established the classes, we tally the volume figures into their respective classes. These results are presented in column 2, which lists the frequencies. Dividing each frequency by the total number of observations, which is 30, results in each class's relative frequency. The relative frequencies are presented in column 3. By averaging the lower and upper class cutpoints for each class, we arrive at the class midpoint for each class. The class midpoints are presented in column 4.

Volume (100sh)	Frequency	Relative Frequency	Midpoint
1<2	4	0.13	1.5
2<3	4	0.13	2.5
3<4	2	0.07	3.5
4<5	6	0.20	4.5
5<6	3	0.10	5.5
6<7	1	0.03	6.5
7<8	2	0.07	7.5
8<9	3	0.10	8.5
9<10	1	0.03	9.5
10 & Over	4	0.13	
	30	0.99	

Note that the relative frequencies sum to 0.99, not 1.00, due to round-off errors in the individual relative frequencies.

(b) Since the last class has no upper cutpoint, the midpoint cannot be computed.

2.31 (a) The classes are presented in column 1. With the classes established, we then tally the exam scores into their respective classes. These results are presented in column 2, which lists the frequencies. Dividing each frequency by the total number of exam scores, which is 20, results in each class's relative frequency. The relative frequencies are presented in column 3. By averaging the lower and upper cutpoints for each class, we arrive at the class mark for each class. The class marks are presented in column 4.

Score	Frequency	Relative Frequency	Class Mark
30-39	2	0.10	34.5
40-49	0	0.00	44.5
50-59	0	0.00	54.5
60-69	3	0.15	64.5
70-79	3	0.15	74.5
80-89	8	0.40	84.5
90-100	4	0.20	95.0
	20	1.00	

(b) The first six classes have width 10; the seventh class has width 11.

(c) Answers will vary, but one choice is to keep the first six classes the same and make the next two classes 90-99 and 100-109.

2.33 In Minitab, place the cheetah speed data in a column named SPEED and put the *WeissStats* CD in the CD drive. Assuming that the CD drive is drive D, then type in Minitab's session window after the MTB> prompt the command

%D:\IS6\Minitab\Macro\group.mac 'SPEED' and press the **ENTER** key. We are given three options for specifying the classes. Since we want the first class to have lower cutpoint 52 and a class width of 2, we select the third option

(3) by entering 3 after the DATA> prompt, press the **ENTER** key, and then type 52 2 when prompted to enter the cutpoint and class width of the first class.

Press the **ENTER** key again. The resulting output is

Grouped-data table for SPEED N = 35

Row	LowerCut	UpperCut	Freq	RelFreq	Midpoint
1	52	54	2	0.057	53
2	54	56	5	0.143	55
3	56	58	6	0.171	57
4	58	60	8	0.229	59
5	60	62	7	0.200	61
6	62	64	3	0.086	63
7	64	66	2	0.057	65
8	66	68	1	0.029	67
9	68	70	0	0.000	69
10	70	72	0	0.000	71
11	72	74	0	0.000	73
12	74	76	1	0.029	75

2.35 In Minitab, with the data from the Network column in a column named NETWORK,

- Choose **Stat ▶ Tables ▶ Tally...**
- Click in the **Variables** text box and select NETWORK
- Click in the **Counts** and **Percents** boxes under **Display**
- Click **OK.** The results are

NETWORK	Count	Percent
ABC	5	25.00
CBS	8	40.00
NBC	7	35.00
N=	20	

Exercises 2.3

2.37 A frequency histogram shows the actual frequencies on the vertical axis whereas the relative frequency histogram always shows proportions (between 0 and 1) or percentages (between 0 and 100) on the vertical axis.

2.39 Since a bar graph is used for qualitative data, we separate the bars from each other to emphasize that there is no numerical scale and no special ordering of the classes; if the bars were to touch, some viewers might infer an ordering and common values for adjacent bars.

2.41 (a) Each rectangle in the frequency histogram would have a height equal to the number of dots in the dot diagram.

(b) If the classes for the histogram were based on multiple values, there would not be one rectangle corresponding to each column of dots (there would be fewer rectangles than columns of dots). The height of a given rectangle would be equal to the total number of dots between its cutpoints. If the classes were constructed so that only a few columns of dots corresponded to each rectangle, the general shape of the distribution should remain the same even though the details may differ.

2.43 (a) The frequency histogram in Figure (a) is constructed using the frequency distribution presented in this exercise; i.e., columns 1 and 2. The lower class limits of column 1 are used to label the horizontal axis of the frequency histogram. Suitable candidates for vertical-axis units in the frequency histogram are the integers 0 through 8, since these are representative of the magnitude and spread of the frequencies presented in column 2. The height of each bar in the frequency histogram matches the respective frequency in column 2.

(b) The relative-frequency histogram in Figure (b) is constructed using the relative-frequency distribution presented in this exercise; i.e., columns 1 and 3. It has the same horizontal axis as the frequency histogram. We notice that the relative frequencies presented in column

3 range in size from 0.000 to 0.229. Thus, suitable candidates for vertical axis units in the relative-frequency histogram are increments of 0.05 (or 5%), starting with zero and ending at 0.25 (or 25%). The height of each bar in the relative-frequency histogram matches the respective relative frequency in column 3.

(a) (b)

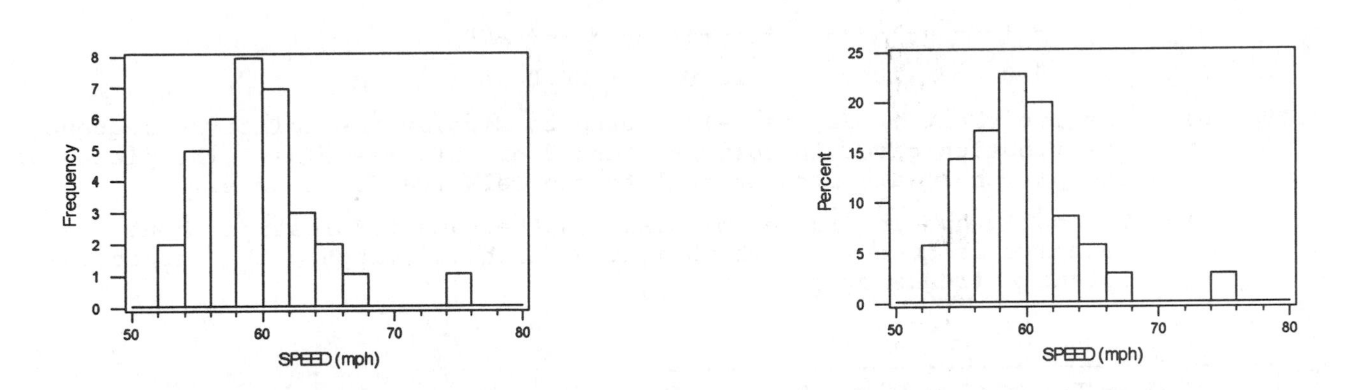

2.45 (a) The frequency histogram in Figure (a) is constructed using the frequency distribution presented in this exercise; i.e., columns 1 and 2. Column 1 demonstrates that the data are grouped using classes based on a single value. These single values in column 1 are used to label the horizontal axis of the frequency histogram. Suitable candidates for vertical-axis units in the frequency histogram are the even integers within the range 0 through 20, since these are representative of the magnitude and spread of the frequencies presented in column 2. When classes are based on a single value, the middle of each histogram bar is placed directly over the single numerical value represented by the class. Also, the height of each bar in the frequency histogram matches the respective frequency in column 2.

(b) The relative-frequency histogram in Figure (b) is constructed using the relative-frequency distribution presented in this exercise; i.e., columns 1 and 3. It has the same horizontal axis as the frequency histogram. We notice that the relative frequencies presented in column 3 range in size from 0.013 to 0.213. Thus, suitable candidates for vertical-axis units in the relative-frequency histogram are increments of 0.05 (5%), starting with zero and ending at 0.25 (25%). The middle of each histogram bar is placed directly over the single numerical value represented by the class. Also, the height of each bar in the relative-frequency histogram matches the respective relative frequency in column 3.

(a)

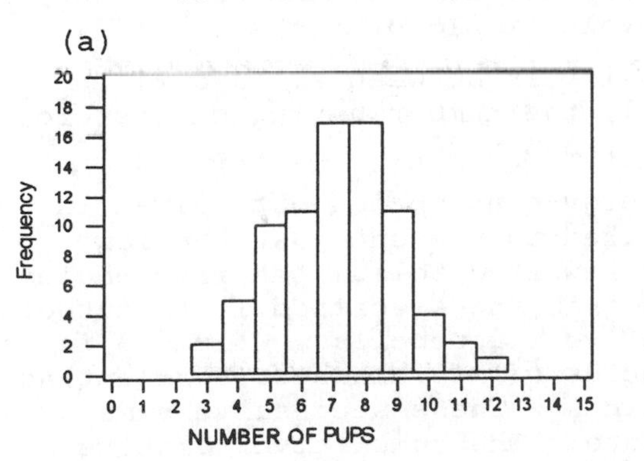

(b)

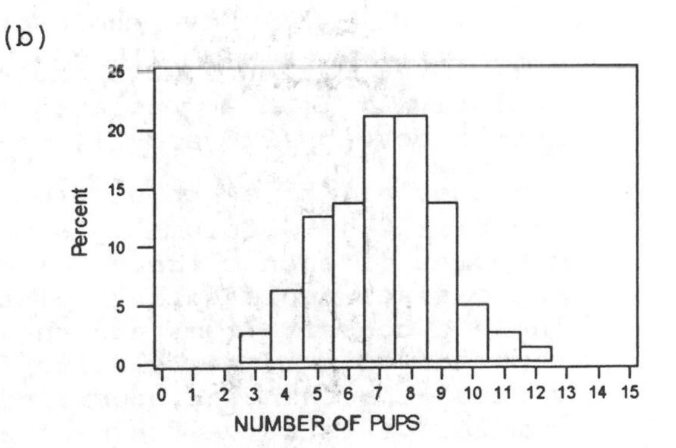

2.47 The horizontal axis of this dotplot displays a range of possible ages. To complete the dotplot, we go through the data set and record each age by placing a dot over the appropriate value on the horizontal axis.

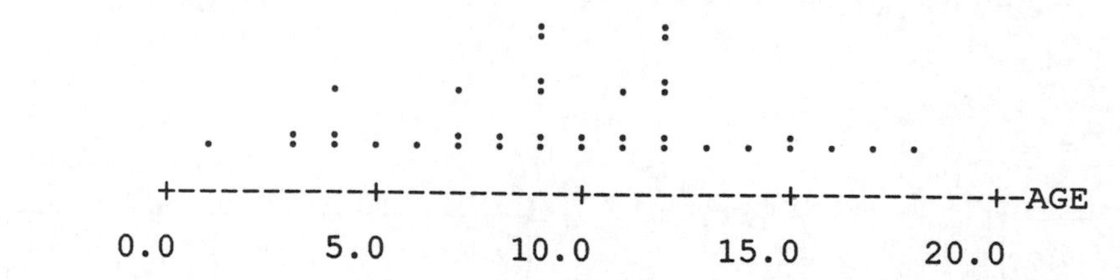

2.49 (a) The pie chart in Figure (a) is used to display the relative-frequency distribution given in columns 1 and 3 of this exercise. The pieces of the pie chart are proportional to the relative frequencies.

(b) The bar graph in Figure (b) displays the same information about the relative frequencies. The height of each bar matches the respective relative frequency.

(a)

All-time Top TV Programs by Rating

NBC 35%

ABC 25%

CBS 40%

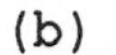

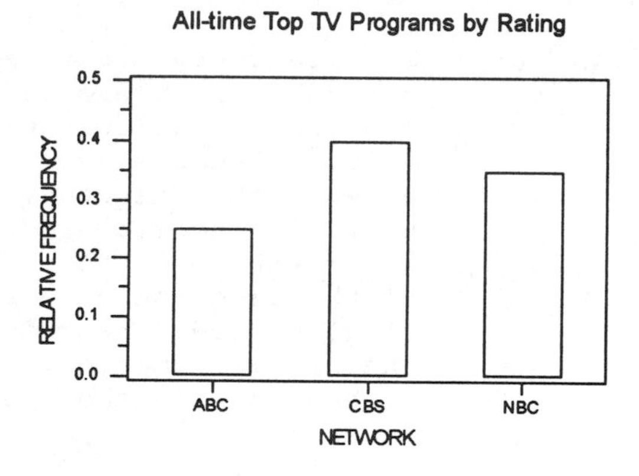

2.51 The graph indicates that:

(a) 20% of the patients have cholesterol levels between 205 and 209, inclusive.

(b) 20% are between 215 and 219; and 5% are between 220 and 224. Thus, 25% (i.e., 20% + 5%) have cholesterol levels of 215 or higher.

(c) 35% of the patients have cholesterol levels between 210 and 214, inclusive. With 20 patients in total, the number having cholesterol levels between 210 and 214 is 7 (i.e., 35% x 20).

2.53 (a) Consider all three columns of the energy-consumption data given in Exercise 2.42. Column 1 is now reworked to present just the lower cutpoint of each class. Column 2 is reworked to sum the frequencies of all classes representing values less than the specified lower cutpoint. These successive sums are the cumulative frequencies. Column 3 is reworked to sum the relative frequencies of all classes representing values less than the specified cutpoints. These successive sums are the cumulative relative frequencies. (Note: The cumulative relative frequencies can also be found by dividing the corresponding cumulative frequency by the total number of pieces of data.)

Less than	Cumulative Frequency	Cumulative Relative Frequency
40	0	0.00
50	1	0.02
60	8	0.16
70	15	0.30
80	18	0.36
90	24	0.48
100	34	0.68
110	39	0.78
120	43	0.86
130	45	0.90
140	48	0.96
150	48	0.96
160	50	1.00

(b) Pair each class limit in the reworked column 1 with its corresponding cumulative relative frequency found in the reworked column 3. Construct a horizontal axis, where the units are in terms of the cutpoints and a vertical axis where the units are in terms of cumulative relative frequencies. For each cutpoint on the horizontal axis, plot a point whose height is equal to the corresponding cumulative relative frequency. Then join the points with connecting lines. The result, presented in Figure (b), is an ogive based on cumulative relative frequencies. (Note: A similar procedure could be followed using cumulative frequencies.)

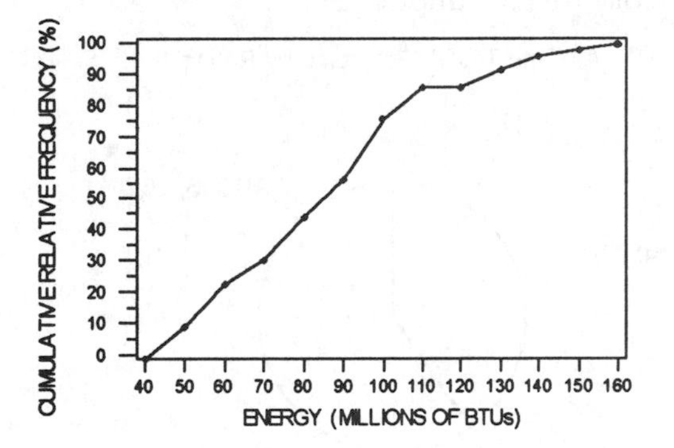

2.55 In Minitab, with the raw, ungrouped data from Exercise 2.25 in a column named PUPS,

- Choose **Graph ▶ Histogram...** from the pull-down menu
- Select PUPS for **Graph1** for the **X Variable**
- Click on the **Options** button and select **Frequency** for the **Type of histogram.**
- Select **Midpoint** for the **Type of Intervals**

- Click on the **Midpoint/Cutpoint positions** button and type 3:12/7 in the **Midpoint/Cutpoint positions** text box
- Click **OK**
- Click **OK**

Then repeat the above process selecting **Percents** instead of **Frequency** for the **Type of Histogram**. The resulting histograms follow.

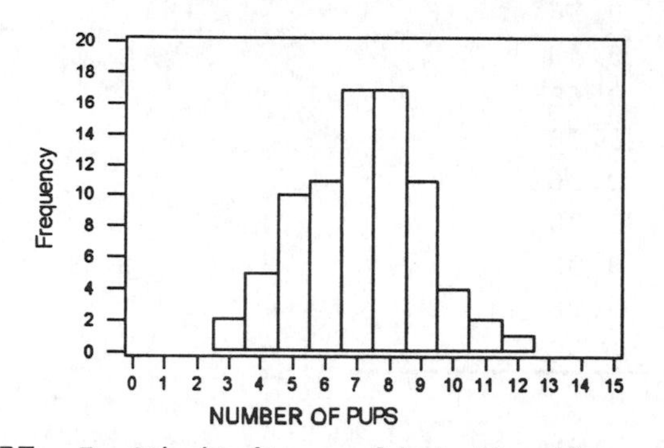

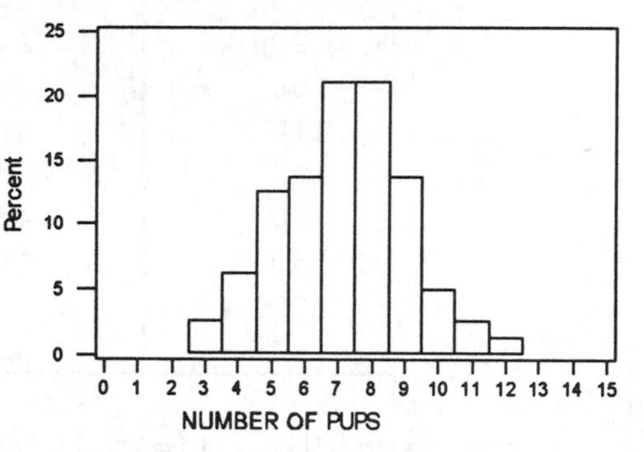

2.57 In Minitab, we list the three networks in a column titled NETWORK and the frequencies in a second column labeled FREQ. Then

- Choose Graph ▶ Pie Chart
- Click on **Chart Table**
- Specify NETWORK in the **Categories in:** text box
- Specify FREQ in the **Frequencies in:** text box.
- Type a title for your graph in the **Title** text box.
- Click **OK** The computer output is

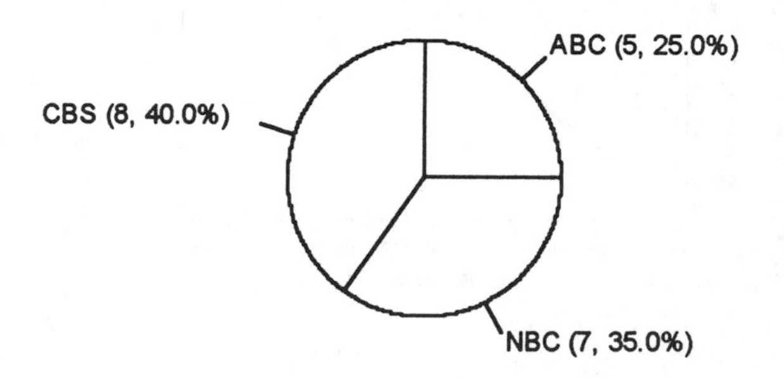

Now

- Choose **Graph** ▶ **Chart**
- Click on the **Function** down-arrow and select **Sum**
- Specify FREQ in the **Y** column of **Graph1** text box

- Specify NETWORK in the **X** column of **Graph1** text box.
- Click on the **Annotations** down-arrow, select **Title,** and then enter your title in the first text box.
- Click **OK** The computer output is shown below.

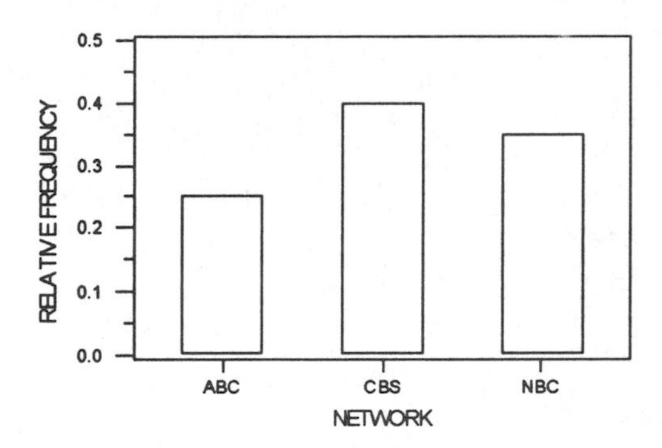

Exercises 2.4

2.59 For data sets with many values, a frequency histogram is more suitable for displaying the data since the vertical axis can be scaled appropriately for any number of data values. With very large sets of data, the stem-and-leaf plot would likely be much too large for display purposes unless the font size were made very small, which would render the plot nearly useless.

2.61 Depending on how 'compact' the data is, each of the original stems can be divided into either 2 or 5 stems to increase the number of stems and make the diagram more useful.

2.63 (a) Construction of a stem-and-leaf diagram for the heart rate data begins with a vertical listing of the numbers comprising the stems. These numbers are 5, 6, 7, and 8. To the right of this listing is a vertical line which serves as a demarcation between the stems and leaves that are about to be added. Each leaf will be the right-most digit -- the units digit -- of a number presented in the data set. The completed stem-and-leaf diagram is presented below.

5	2734459
6	730308466384
7	477637113
8	042

(b) The ordered stem-and-leaf is created from the diagram in part (a) by ordering the leaves in each stem numerically as shown below.

5	2344579
6	003334466788
7	113346777
8	024

(c) With two lines per stem, the leaf digits 0-4 are placed in the first of the two lines and the leaf digits 5-9 are placed in the second line.

The completed stem-and-leaf diagram is presented followed by the ordered stem-and-leaf diagram.

5	2344
5	579
6	3030434
6	78668
7	43113
7	7767
8	042

Ordered stem-and-leaf

5	2344
5	579
6	0033344
6	66788
7	11334
7	6777
8	024

2.65 (a) Construction of a stem-and-leaf diagram for the crime data begins with a vertical listing of the numbers comprising the stems. These numbers are 2, 3, 4, ..., 7. To the right of this listing is a vertical line which serves as a demarcation between the stems and leaves that are about to be added. Each leaf will be the right-most digit -- the units digit -- of a number presented in the data set. The completed stem-and-leaf diagram is shown below with ordered leaves.

2	5678
3	11247778999
4	0113445566778999
5	1125555789
6	0001349
7	23

(b) With two lines per stem, the leaf digits 0-4 are placed in the first of the two lines and the leaf digits 5-9 are placed in the second line. The completed stem-and-leaf diagram follows with the leaves ordered.

2	5678
3	1124
3	7778999
4	011344
4	5566778999
5	112
5	5555789
6	000134
6	9
7	23

(c) With five lines per stem, the leaf digits 0-1 are placed in the first of the five lines, 2-3 are placed in the second line, and so on. The completed stem-and-leaf diagram is presented below as an ordered stem-and-leaf.

2	5
2	67
2	8
3	11
3	2
3	4
3	777
3	8999
4	011
4	3
4	4455
4	6677
4	8999
5	11
5	2
5	5555
5	7
5	89
6	0001
6	3
6	4
6	
6	9
7	
7	23

(d) Two lines per stem seems to be the most useful for visualizing the shape of this set of data. Five lines per stem produces a graph that is too spread out with several "holes" and numerous lines with only one leaf. One line per stem is acceptable, but concentrates about two-thirds of the data in the second, third, and fourth lines. All of the diagrams show the near symmetry of the data.

2.67 (a) The data rounded to the nearest 10 ml with the terminal 0 dropped are shown at the left with a 5-line stem-and-leaf plot at the right (with data ending in '5' rounded to the nearest even 10 ml).

102	98	102	98	98
99	96	96	103	96
99	91	101	99	103
99	100	98	97	102
106	103	99	100	100
100	101	95	100	99

```
 9 | 1
 9 |
 9 | 5
 9 | 6 6 6 7
 9 | 8 8 8 9 9 9 9 8 9 9
10 | 1 0 0 0 0 1 0
10 | 2 2 3 3 2 3
10 |
10 | 6
```

(b) The data with the units digits truncated are shown at the left in the following table and the stem-and-leaf plot is on the right.

102	97	101	97	97
99	95	95	103	96
98	91	101	98	102
98	100	98	97	101
106	103	99	99	99
99	101	94	99	98

```
 9 | 1
 9 |
 9 | 5 5 4
 9 | 7 7 7 6 7
 9 | 9 8 8 8 8 9 9 9 9 9 8
10 | 1 1 0 1 1
10 | 2 3 3
10 | 4
10 | 6
```

(c) While the values of a number of the leaves are different in the two diagrams and some of them change from one stem to another, the general shape of the data is virtually the same in both diagrams, with the diagram in (b) looking slightly more symmetric. Comparing with the diagram in Exercise 2.62, we see that both of the current diagrams are missing the "hole" that appeared in the 100 stem previously. Otherwise, the general shape is the same.

2.69 (a) With the data in a column named CRIME,

- Choose **Graph ▶ Stem and Leaf...**
- Select CRIME in the **Variables** text box
- Click on the **Increment** text box and type 10 to produce one line per stem.
- Click **OK.**

The result is

```
Stem-and-leaf of CRIME      N  = 50
Leaf Unit = 1.0

   4    2 5678
  15    3 11247778999
 (16)   4 0113445566778999
  19    5 1125555789
   9    6 0001349
   2    7 23
```

(b) Follow the same procedure used in part (a), except type 5 for the interval. The result is

```
Stem-and-leaf of CRIME      N  = 50
Leaf Unit = 1.0

      4     2 5678
      8     3 1124
     15     3 7778999
     21     4 011344
    (10)    4 5566778999
     19     5 112
     16     5 5555789
      9     6 000134
      3     6 9
      2     7 23
```

(c) Follow the same procedure used in part (a), except type 2 for the interval. The result is

```
Stem-and-leaf of CRIME      N  = 50
Leaf Unit = 1.0

      1     2 5
      3     2 67
      4     2 8
      6     3 11
      7     3 2
      8     3 4
     11     3 777
     15     3 8999
     18     4 011
     19     4 3
     23     4 4455
     (4)    4 6677
     23     4 8999
     19     5 11
     17     5 2
     16     5 5555
     12     5 7
     11     5 89
      9     6 0001
      5     6 3
      4     6 4
      3     6
      3     6 9
      2     7
      2     7 23
```

Exercises 2.5

2.71 (a) The distribution of a data set is a table, graph, or formula that gives the values of the observations and how often each one occurs.

(b) Sample data is data obtained by observing the values of a variable for a sample of the population.

(c) Population data is data obtained by observing the values of a variable for all of the members of a population.

(d) Census data is the same as population data, a complete listing of all data values for the entire population.

(e) A sample distribution is a distribution of sample data.

(f) A population distribution is a distribution of population data.

(g) A distribution of a variable is the same as a population distribution, a distribution of population data.

2.73 A large sample from a bell-shaped distribution would be expected to have roughly a bell shape.

2.75 Three distribution shapes that are symmetric are bell-shaped, triangular, and rectangular, shown in that order below. It should be noted that there are others as well.

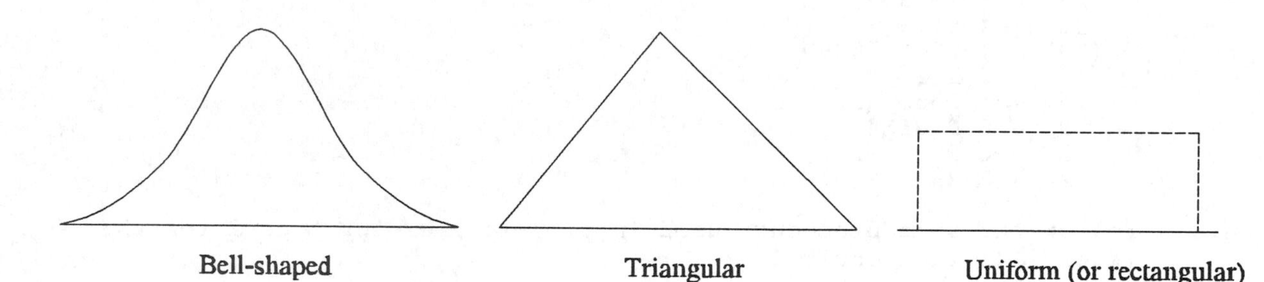

2.77 (a) The overall shape of the distribution of the number of white shark pups is roughly *bell-shaped.*

(b) The distribution is roughly *symmetric.*

2.79 (a) The distribution of cholesterol levels of high-level patients is *left skewed. Note*: The answer *bell-shaped* is also acceptable.

(b) The shape of the distribution of cholesterol levels of high-level patients is *left skewed. Note*: The answer *symmetric* is also acceptable.

2.81 (a) The distribution of the lengths of stay in Europe and the Mediterranean of the 36 U.S. residents is *right skewed.*

(b) The shape of the distribution of the lengths of stay in Europe and the Mediterranean of the 36 U.S. residents is *right skewed.*

2.83 The precise answers to this exercise will vary from class to class or individual to individual. Thus your results are likely to differ from our results shown below.

(a) We obtained 50 random digits from a table of random numbers. The digits were

4 5 4 6 8 9 9 7 7 2 2 2 9 3 0 3 4 0 0 8 8 4 4 5 3

9 2 4 8 9 6 3 0 1 1 0 9 2 8 1 3 9 2 5 8 1 8 9 2 2

(b) Since each digit is equally likely in the random number table, we expect that the distribution would be roughly rectangular.

(c) Using single value classes, the frequency distribution is given by the following table. The histogram is shown below.

Value	Frequency	Relative-Frequency
0	5	.10
1	4	.08
2	8	.16
3	5	.10
4	6	.12
5	3	.06
6	2	.04
7	2	.04
8	7	.14
9	8	.16

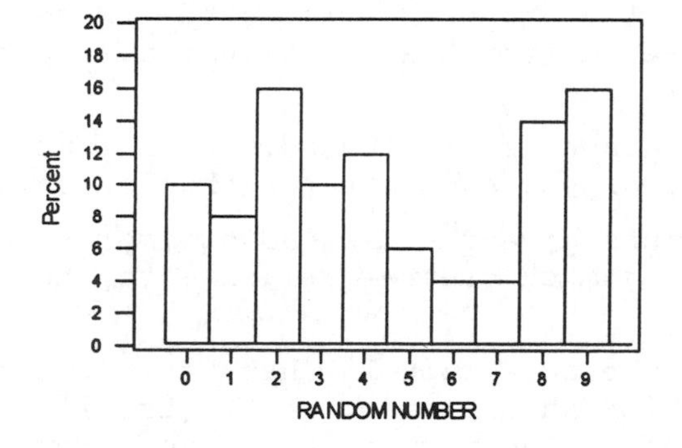

We did not expect to see this much variation.

(d) We would have expected a histogram that was a little more 'even', more like a rectangular distribution, but when the sample size is so small, there can be considerable variation from what is expected.

(e) We should be able to get a more evenly distributed set of data if we choose a larger set of data.

(f) Class project.

2.85 (a) Your results will differ from the ones below which were obtained using Minitab. Choose **Calc ▶ Random Data ▶ Normal...**, type <u>3000</u> in the **Generate rows of data** text box, click in the **Store in column(s)** text box and type <u>STDNORM</u>, and click **OK**. Then choose **Graph ▶ Histogram**, enter <u>STDNORM</u> in the **Graph 1** text box under **X**, and click **OK**.

(b)

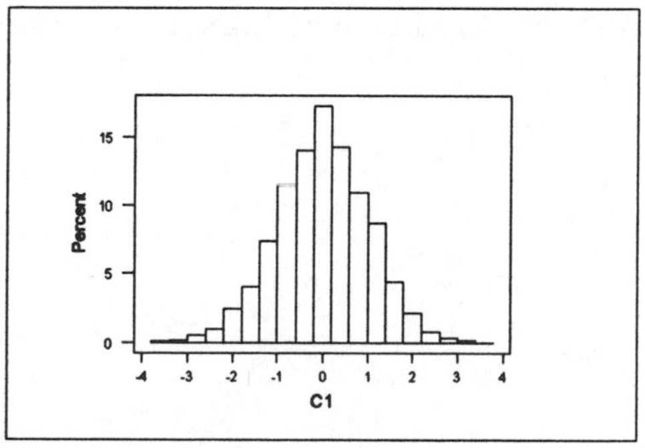

(c) The histogram in part (b) is bell-shaped. The sample of 3000 is representative of the population from which the sample was taken. This suggests that the standard normal distribution is bell-shaped.

Exercises 2.6

2.87 (a) A truncated graph is one for which the vertical axis starts at a value other than its natural starting point, usually zero.

(b) A legitimate motivation for truncating the axis of a graph is to place the emphasis on the ups and downs of the graph rather than on the actual height of the graph.

(c) To truncate a graph and avoid the possibility of misinterpretation, one should start the axis at zero and put slashes in the axis to indicate that part of the axis is missing.

2.89 (a) A good portion of the graph is eliminated. When this is done, differences between district and national averages appear greater than in the original figure.

(b) Even more of the graph is eliminated. Differences between district and national averages appear even greater than in part (a).

(c) The truncated graphs give the misleading impression that, in 1993, the district average is much greater relative to the national average than it actually is.

2.91 (a) The problem with the bar graph is that it is truncated. That is, the vertical axis, which should start at \$0 (trillions), starts with \$3.05 (trillions) instead. The part of the graph from \$0 (trillions) to \$3.05 (trillions) has been cut off. This truncation causes the bars to be out of correct proportion and hence creates the misleading impression that the money supply is changing more than it actually is.

(b) A version of the bar graph with a nontruncated and unmodified vertical axis is presented in Figure (a). Notice that the vertical axis starts at \$0.00 (trillions). Increments are in halves of a trillion dollars. In contrast to the original bar graph, this one illustrates that the changes in money supply from week to week are very small. However, the "ups" and "downs" are not as easy to spot as in the original, truncated bar graph.

(c) A version of the bar graph in which the vertical axis is modified in an acceptable manner is presented in Figure (b). Notice that the special symbol "//" is used near the base of the vertical axis to indicate that the vertical axis has been modified. Thus, with this version of the bar graph, not only are the "ups" and "downs" easy to spot, but the reader is also aptly warned that part of the vertical axis between \$0.00 (trillions) and \$3.05 (trillions) has been removed.

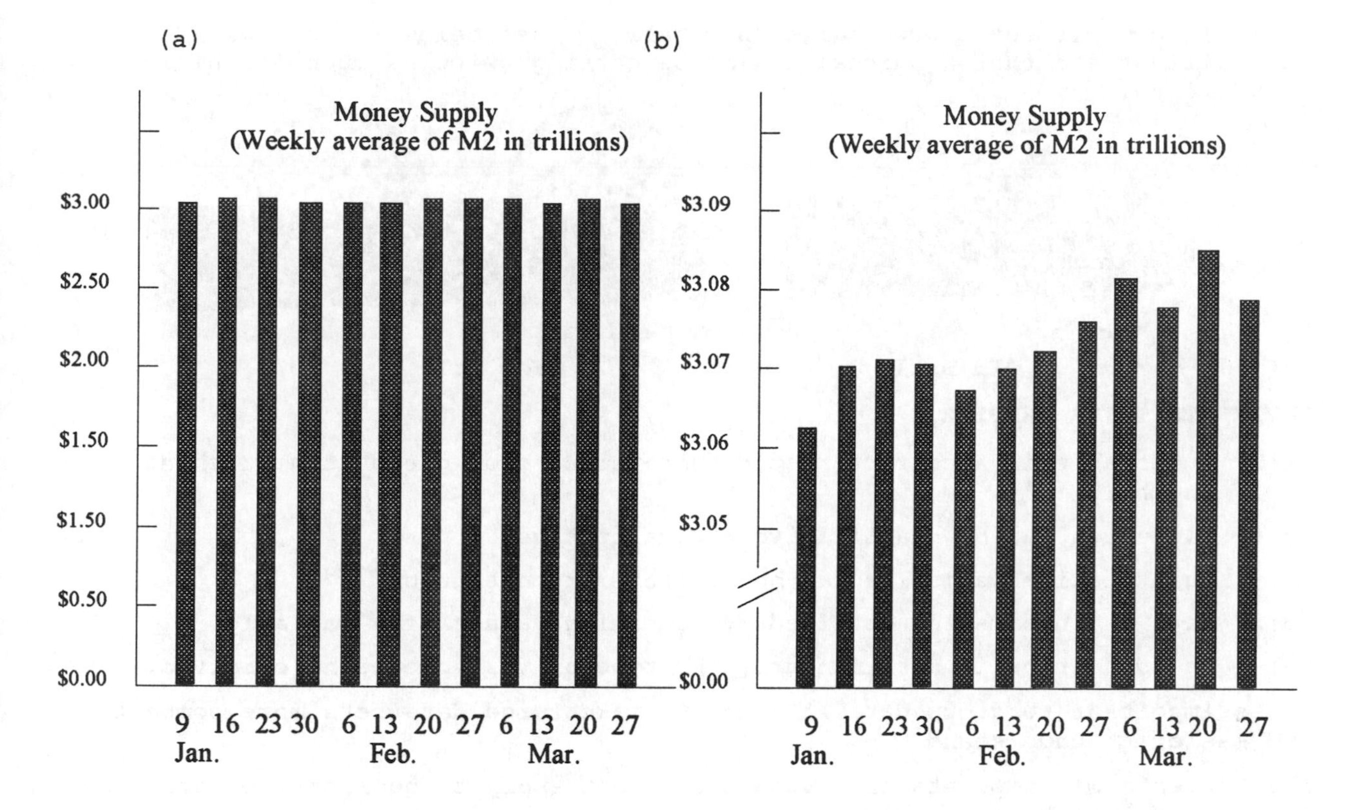

2.93 (a) The brochure shows a "new" ball with twice the radius of the "old" ball. The intent is to give the impression that the "new" ball lasts roughly twice as long as the "old" ball. Pictorially, the "new" ball dwarfs the "old" ball. From the perspective of measurement, if the "new" ball has twice the radius of the "old" ball, it will have eight times the volume of the "old" ball (since the volume of a sphere is proportional to the cube of its radius. Thus, the scaling is improper because it gives the impression that the "new" ball lasts roughly eight times as long as the "old" ball.

Old Ball

New Ball

(b) One possible way for the manufacturer to illustrate that the "new" ball lasts twice as long as the "old" ball is to present a picture of two balls, side by side, each of the same magnitude as the "old" ball and to label this set of two balls "new ball". (See below.) This will illustrate that a purchaser will be getting twice as much for his or her money.

Old Ball **New Ball**

REVIEW TEST FOR CHAPTER 2

1. (a) A variable is a characteristic that varies from one person or thing to another.

   (b) Variables can be quantitative or qualitative.

   (c) Quantitative variables can be discrete or continuous.

   (d) Data is information obtained by observing values of a variable.

   (e) The data type is determined by the type of variable being observed.

2. It is important to group data in order to make large data sets more compact and easier to understand.

3. The concepts of midpoints and cutpoints do not apply to qualitative data since the data do not take numerical values.

4. (a) The midpoint is halfway between the cutpoints. Since the class width is 8, the cutpoints are 6 and 14.

   (b) The class width is also the distance between consecutive midpoints. Therefore the second midpoint is 10 + 8 = 18.

   (c) The sequence of cutpoints is 6, 14, 22, 30, 38, ... Therefore the lower and upper cutpoints of the third class are 22 and 30.

   (d) An observation of 22 would go into the third class since that class contains data greater than or equal to 22 and strictly less than 30.

5. (a) The common class width is the distance between consecutive cutpoints, which is 15 - 5 = 10.

   (b) The midpoint of the second class is halfway between the cutpoints 15 and 25, and is therefore 20.

   (c) The sequence of cutpoints is 5, 15, 25, 35, 45, ... Therefore the lower and upper cutpoints of the third class are 25 and 35.

6. Single value grouping is appropriate when the data is discrete with relatively few distinct observations.

7. (a) The vertical edges of the bars will be aligned with the cutpoints.

   (b) Each bar is centered over its midpoint.

8. The two main types of graphical displays for qualitative data are the bar chart and the pie chart.

9. A histogram is better than a stem-and-leaf diagram for displaying large quantitative data sets since it can always be scaled appropriately and the individual values are of less interest than the overall picture of the data.

10. Bell-shaped Right skewed Reverse J shaped Uniform

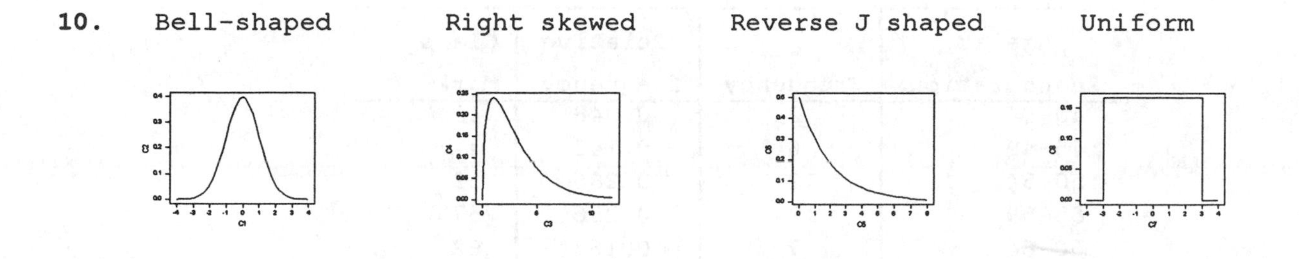

11. (a) Slightly skewed to the right. Assuming that the most typical heights are around 5'10", there are likely to be more heights above 6'4" than below 5'4". An answer of roughly bell-shaped is also acceptable.

(b) Skewed to the right. High incomes extend much further above the mean income than low incomes extend below the mean.

(c) Skewed to the right. While most full-time college students are in the 17-22 age range, there are very few below 17 while there are many above 22.

(d) Skewed to the right. The main reason for the skewness to the right is that those students with GPAs below fixed cutoff points have been suspended before they become seniors.

12. (a) The distribution of the sample will reflect the distribution of the population, so it should be left-skewed as well.

(b) No. The randomness in the samples will almost certainly produce different sets of observations resulting in nonidentical shapes.

(c) Yes. We would expect both of the samples to reflect the shape of the population and to be left-skewed if the samples are reasonably large.

13. (a) The first column ranks the hydroelectric plants. Thus, it consists of *quantitative, discrete* data.

(b) The fourth column provides measurements of capacity in megawatts. Thus, it consists of *quantitative, continuous* data.

(c) The third column provides non-numerical information. Thus, it consists of *qualitative* data.

14. (a) The first class is 40-44. Since all classes are to be of equal width, and the second class begins with 45, we know that the width of all classes is 45 - 40 = 5. The classes are presented in column 1 of the grouped-data table below. The last class is 65-69, since the largest data value is 69. Having established the classes, we tally the ages into their respective classes. These results are presented in column 2, which lists the frequencies. Dividing each frequency by the total number of observations, which is 42, results in each class's relative frequency. The relative frequencies for are presented in column 3.

By averaging the lower and upper limits for each class, we arrive at the class mark for each class. The class marks are presented in column 4.

Age at inauguration	Frequency	Relative frequency	Class mark
40-44	2	0.048	42
45-49	6	0.143	47
50-54	12	0.286	52
55-59	12	0.286	57
60-64	7	0.167	62
65-69	3	0.071	67
	42	1.001	

(b) The lower cutpoint for the first class is 40. The upper cutpoint for the first class is 45 since that is the samllest value that can go into the second class.

(c) The common class width is 45 - 40 = 5.

(d) The following frequency histogram is constructed using the frequency distribution presented above; i.e., columns 1 and 2. Notice that the lower cutpoints of column 1 are used to label the horizontal axis of the frequency histogram. Suitable candidates for vertical-axis units are the even integers in the range 0 through 12, since these are representative of the magnitude and spread of the frequencies. The height of each bar in the frequency histogram matches the respective frequency in column 2.

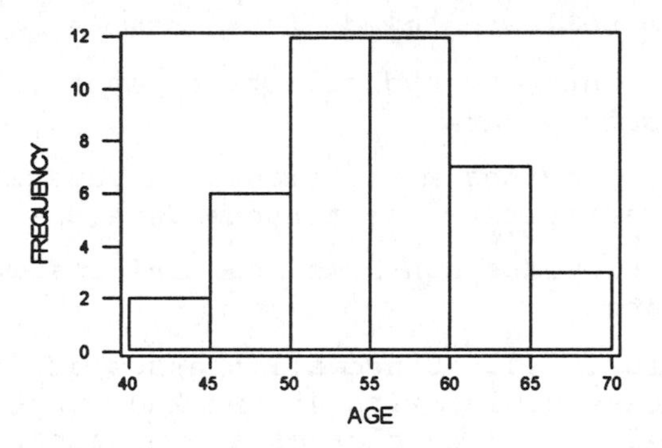

15. The horizontal axis of this dotplot displays a range of possible ages for the 42 Presidents of the United States. To complete the dotplot, we go through the data set and record each age by placing a dot over the appropriate value on the horizontal axis.

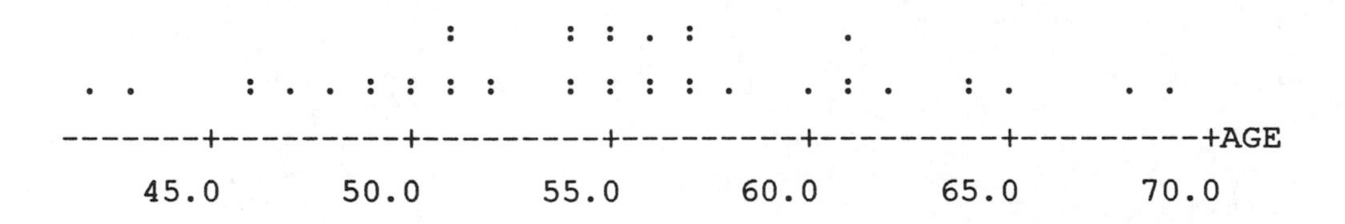

16. (a) Using *one* line per stem in constructing the ordered stem-and-leaf diagram means vertically listing the numbers comprising the stems *once* only. The ordered leaves are then placed with their respective stems. The ordered stem-and-leaf diagram using one line per stem is presented in Figure (a).

(b) Using *two* lines per stem in constructing the ordered stem-and-leaf diagram means vertically listing the numbers comprising the stems *twice*. If a leaf is one of the digits 0 through 4, it is ordered and placed with the first of the two stem lines. If a leaf is one of the digits 5 through 9, it is ordered and placed with the second of the two stem lines. The ordered stem-and-leaf diagram using two lines per stem is presented in Figure (b).

(a)

```
4 | 2 3 6 6 7 8 9 9
5 | 0 0 1 1 1 1 2 2 4 4 4 4 5 5 5 5 6 6 6 7 7 7 7 8
6 | 0 1 1 1 2 4 4 5 8 9
```

(b)

```
4 | 2 3
4 | 6 6 7 8 9 9
5 | 0 0 1 1 1 1 2 2 4 4 4 4
5 | 5 5 5 5 6 6 6 7 7 7 7 8
6 | 0 1 1 1 2 4 4
6 | 5 8 9
```

(c) The stem-and-leaf diagram with two lines per stem corresponds to the frequency distribution in Problem 14(a) as it groups the data in the same classes, names 40-44, 45-49, ... 65-69.

17. (a) The grouped-data table presented below is constructed using classes based on a single value. Since each data value is one of the integers 0 through 6, inclusive, the classes will be 0 through 6, inclusive. These are presented in column 1. Having established the classes, we tally the number of busy tellers into their respective classes. These results are presented in column 2, which lists the frequencies. Dividing each frequency by the total number of observations, which is 25, results in each class's relative frequency. The relative frequencies are presented in column 3. Since each class is based on a single value, it is not necessary to give midpoints.

Number busy	Frequency	Relative frequency
0	1	0.04
1	2	0.08
2	2	0.08
3	4	0.16
4	5	0.20
5	7	0.28
6	4	0.16
	25	1.00

(b) The following relative-frequency histogram is constructed using the relative-frequency distribution presented in part (a); i.e., columns 1 and 3. Column 1 demonstrates that the data are grouped using classes based on a single value. These single values are used to label the horizontal axis of the relative-frequency histogram. We notice that the relative frequencies presented in column 3 range in size from 0.04 to

0.28 (4% to 28%). Thus, suitable candidates for vertical axis units are increments of 0.05, starting with zero and ending at 0.30. Each histogram bar is centered over the single numerical value represented by its class. Also, the height of each bar in the relative-frequency histogram matches the respective relative frequency in column 3.

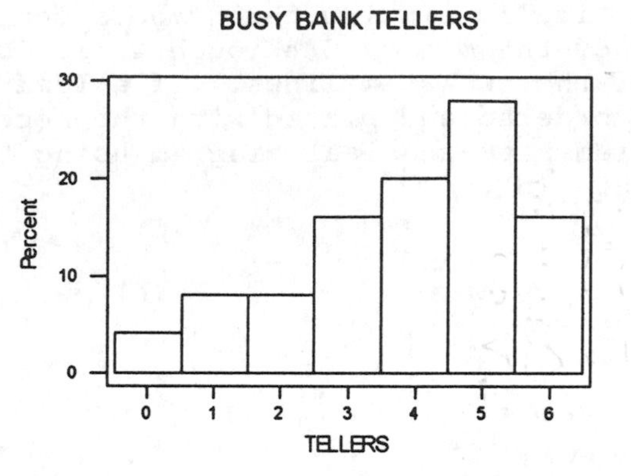

18. (a) The table below shows both the frequency distribution and the relative frequency distribution. If each frequency is divided by the total number of students, which is 40, we obtain the relative frequency (or percentage) of the class.

Class	Frequency	Relative Frequency
Fr	6	0.150
So	15	0.375
Ju	12	0.300
Se	7	0.175

(b) The following pie chart displays the percentage of students at each class level.

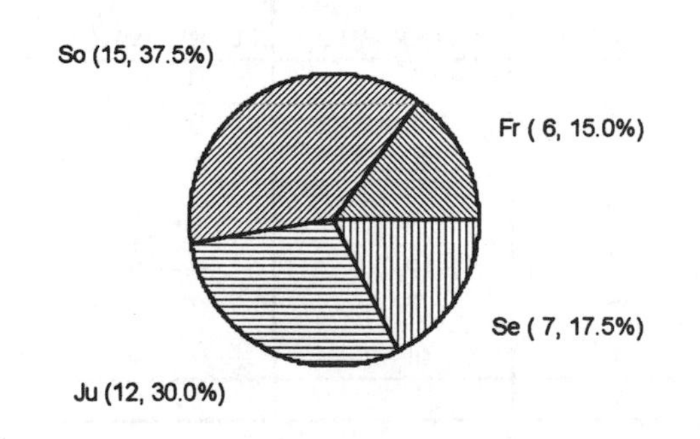

(c) The following bar graph also displays the relative frequencies of each class.

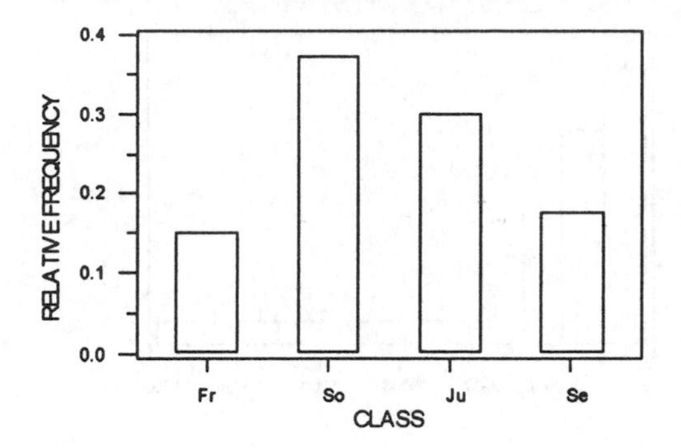

19. (a) The first class is 0<1000. Since all classes are to be of equal width, we know that the width of all classes is 1000 - 0 = 1000. The classes are presented in column 1 of Figure (a) below. The last class is 11,000<12,000, since the largest data value is 11,568.80. Having established the classes, we tally the highs into their respective classes. These results are presented in column 2, which lists the frequencies. Dividing each frequency by the total number of observations, which is 36, results in each class's relative frequency. The relative frequencies are presented in column 3. By averaging the lower and upper cutpoints for each class, we obtain the midpoint for each class. The midpoints are presented in column 4.

High	Freq.	Relative Frequency	Midpoint
0<1000	13	0.361	500
1000<2000	10	0.278	1500
2000<3000	4	0.111	2500
3000<4000	4	0.111	3500
4000<5000	0	0.000	4500
5000<6000	1	0.028	5500
6000<7000	1	0.028	6500
7000<8000	0	0.000	7500
8000<9000	1	0.028	8500
9,000<10,000	1	0.028	9500
10,000<11,000	0	0.000	10,500
11,000<12,000	1	0.028	11,500
	36	1.001	

(b) The following relative-frequency histogram is constructed using the relative-frequency distribution presented above; i.e., columns 1 and 3. The lower cutpoints of column 1 are used to label the horizontal axis. We notice that the relative frequencies presented in column 3 range in size from 0.000 to 0.361 (0 to 36.1%). Thus, suitable candidates for vertical axis units in the relative-frequency histogram are increments of 0.05 (5%), starting with 0.00 (0%) and ending at 0.40 (40%). The height of each bar in the relative-frequency histogram matches the respective relative frequency in column 3.

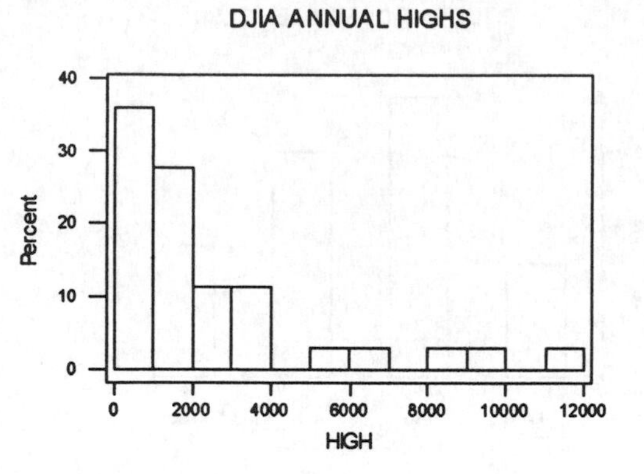

20. (a) The shape of the distribution of the inauguration ages of the first 42 presidents of the United States is roughly *bell-shaped.*

(b) The shape of the distribution of the number of tellers busy with customers at Prescott National Bank during 25 spot checks is *left skewed.*

21. Answers will vary, but here is one possibility:

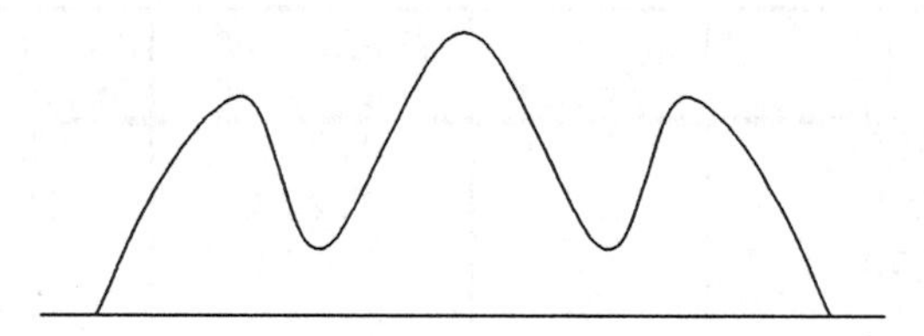

22. (a) Covering up the numbers on the vertical axis totally obscures the percentages.

(b) Having followed the directions in part (a), we might conclude that the percentage of women in the labor force for 2000 is about three and one-third times that for 1960.

(c) Using the vertical scale, we find that the percentage of women in the labor force for 2000 is about 1.8 times that for 1960.

(d) The graph is potentially misleading because it is truncated. Notice that vertical axis units begin at 30 rather than at zero.

(e) To make the graph less potentially misleading, we can start it at zero instead of at 30.

23. (a) In Minitab, first store the data in a column named AGE. Then

■ Choose **Graph ▶ Histogram...**

- Specify AGE in the **X** text box for **Graph 1.**
- Click the **Options...** button
- Select the **Cutpoint** option button from the **Type of Intervals** field
- Select the **Midpoint/cutpoint positions** text box and type 40:70/5
- Click **OK**
- Click **OK**

To print the result at the right from the Graph window, choose

File ▶ Print Window... .

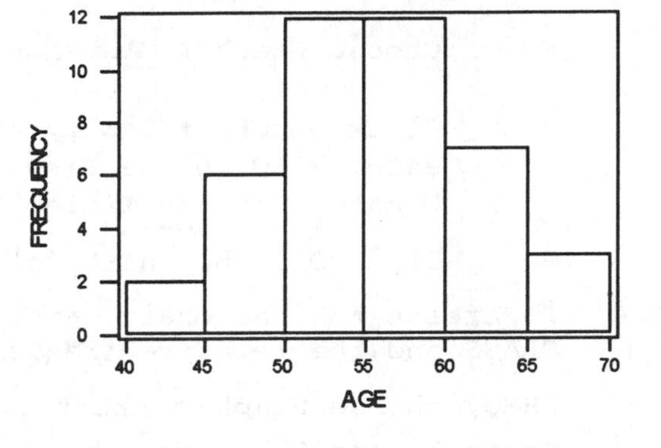

(b) With the data already stored in the column name AGE,

- Choose **Graph ▶ Character Graphs ▶ Dotplot...**
- Specify AGE in the **Variables** text box.
- Click **OK**

The computer output shown in the Session window is:

```
Character Dotplot

                   :     : : . :       .
 . .     : . . : : : :   : : : : .   . : .   : .     . .
-------+---------+---------+---------+---------+---------AGE
    45.0      50.0      55.0      60.0      65.0      70.0
```

(c) With the data already stored in the column named AGES,

- Choose **Graph ▶ Stem-and-Leaf...**
- Specify AGE in the **Variables** text box.
- Click on the **Intervals** text box and type 5
- Click **OK**

The computer output is:

```
Stem-and-leaf of AGE      N = 42
Leaf Unit = 1.0
   2    4  23
   8    4  667899
  20    5  001111224444
 (12)   5  555566677778
  10    6  0111244
   3    6  589
```

24. (a) Using Minitab to create the pie chart and bar chart, enter the student class level in a column named CLASS and the frequency in a column named FREQ. Then

- Choose **Graph ▶ Pie Chart...**
- Click on **Chart Table,** enter CLASS in **Categories in** text box and enter FREQ in the **Frequencies in** text box. Enter 'Pie Chart of Classes' in the **Titles** text box.
- Click **OK.** The chart follows after part (b).

(b) To create the bar chart, enter the class abbreviations in a column named CLASS and the relative frequencies from Problem 18 in a column named REL FREQ, choose **Graph ▶ Chart...,** select REL FREQ for the **Y variable** in **Graph 1,** and CLASS for the X variable. Click **OK.**

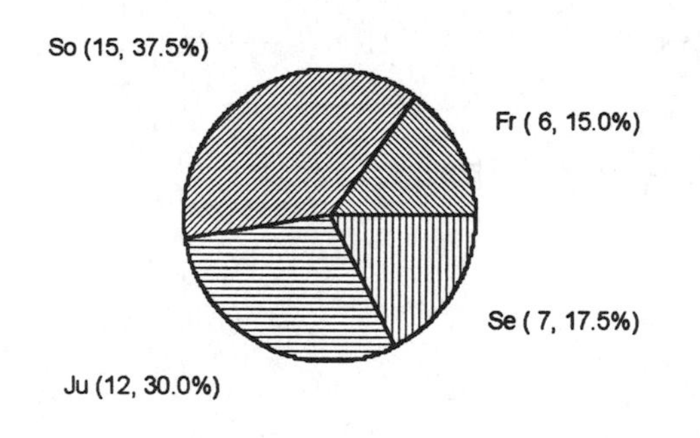

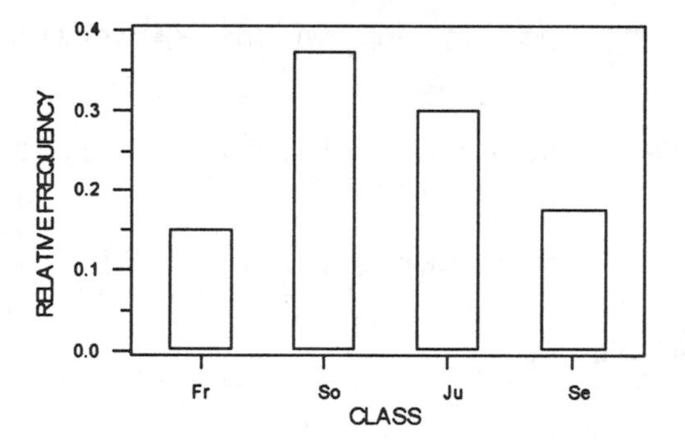

CHAPTER 3 ANSWERS

Exercises 3.1

3.1 The purpose of a measure of center is to indicate where the center or most typical value of a data set lies.

3.3 Of the mean, median, and mode, only the mode is appropriate for use with qualitative data.

3.5 (a) The mean is the sum of the values (45) divided by n (9). The result is 5. The median is the middle value in the ordered list and thus is 5.

(b) The mean is the sum of the values (135) divided by n (9). The result is 15. The median is the middle value in the ordered list and thus is 5, as before. The median is more typical of most of the data than is the mean and thus works better here.

(c) The mean does not have the property of being resistant to the influence of extreme observations.

3.7 The median is more appropriate as a measure of central tendency than the mean because, unlike the mean, the median is not affected strongly by the relatively few homes that have extremely large or small areas.

3.9 The mean number of volumes is calculated first by summing all seven values presented, which results in 1351 thousand volumes, and then dividing this by 7. Thus, the mean is 193 thousand volumes. Carrying this last figure to one more decimal place than the original data provides a mean of 193.0 thousand volumes.

Calculating the median requires ordering the data from the smallest to the largest values. Since the number of data values is odd, the median will be the observation exactly in the middle of this ordering, i.e., in the fourth ordered position. Thus, the median number of volumes is 79.0 thousand.

The mode is the most frequently occurring data value or values. In this exercise, there is no mode because none of the data values occurs more than once.

3.11 The mean number of tornado touchdowns is calculated by first summing all 12 data values presented, which results in 1417, and then dividing this sum by 12. Thus, the mean is 118.1. This figure is already rounded to one more decimal place than the original data.

Calculating the median requires ordering the data from the smallest to the largest values (6, 25, 47, 60, 72, **72**, **82**, 86, 104, 182, 308, 373). Since the number of data values is even, the median will be the mean of the two middle data values in the ordered list. The two middle values are the sixth and seventh ordered observations, or 72 and 82. Thus, the median age is found as (72 + 82)/2 = 77.0.

The mode is the most frequently occurring data value or values. In this exercise, 72 is the only value that occurs more than once, so 72 is the mode.

3.13 (a) The mode is defined as the data value or values that occur most frequently. In this exercise, the data values are the three different networks. During the period January, 1961 to January, 1997, CBS had the all-time top television program eight times, NBC seven times, and ABC five times. Since CBS is the data value that occurs most frequently, it is the mode.

(b) Again, the data values are the three networks. There is no way to compute a mean or median for such data. Thus, it would not be appropriate to use either the mean or median here. In general, the mode is the only measure of center that can be used for qualitative data.

3.15 (a) The mean of the ratings is 2.5. This is derived by summing the 14 individual ratings, which yields 35, and dividing by 14.

(b) The median of the data is the average of the two observations appearing in the middle position after ordering the data from the smallest to the largest values (1, 1, 2, 2, 2, 2, **2**, **2**, 3, 3, 3, 4, 4, 4). The median is the average of the seventh and eighth ordered observations, or (2 + 2)/2 = 2.

(c) In this case, the median provides a better descriptive summary of the data than does the mean. Notice that six of the fourteen values are 2s and these are more in line with the median 2 than with the mean 2.5. Furthermore, the data are not actually measurements, but reflect the opinions of the participants, each of whom must decide what a '2' or a '3' really means.

3.17 Spreadsheets, such as Excel, provide a simple and effective way of finding the mean and the median. To compute the mean, simply enter the 12 data values in any order in the cells A1, A2, ..., A12. In another cell, say A14, type the expression <u>=AVERAGE(A1:A12)</u>, hit the ENTER key and the mean, 118.1, will appear in cell A14. To compute the median, type the expression <u>=MEDIAN(A1:A12)</u> in A15, hit the ENTER key, and the median, 77, will appear in A15.

3.19 While we could use Excel again as in Exercise 3.17, we will use Minitab for this exercise. In Minitab, open the worksheet for Exercise 3.19 from the *WeissStats* CD. This will enter the 93 data values in column C1 under the name BODYTEMP. From the pull-down menu, choose **Stat ▶ Basic Statistics ▶ Display Descriptive Statistics**, enter <u>BODYTEMP</u> in the **Variables** text box, click **OK**. The output appears in the Session Window as

Variable	N	Mean	Median	TrMean	StDev	SE Mean
BODYTEMP	93	98.124	98.200	98.129	0.647	0.067

Variable	Minimum	Maximum	Q1	Q3
BODYTEMP	96.700	99.400	97.650	98.600

From the output, we see that the mean is 98.124 and the median is 98.2.

<u>Exercises 3.2</u>

3.21 Mathematical notation allows us to express mathematical definitions and other mathematical relationships more concisely.

3.23 For a given population, the population mean is not a variable; it is a parameter, a constant. The sample mean will vary from sample to sample and thus is considered to be a variable.

3.25 (a) $\Sigma x = 12 + 8 + 9 + 17 = 46$

(b) n = number of observations = 4

(c) $\bar{x} = \Sigma x/n = 46/4 = 11.5$

3.27 (a) $\Sigma x = 23.3$

(b) n = number of observations = 10

(c) $\bar{x} = \Sigma x/n = 23.3/10 = 2.33$, which is given to two decimal places.

3.29 (a) $\bar{x} = \Sigma x/n = 405/5 = 81.0$

(b)

x	x^2	$x-\bar{x}$	$(x-\bar{x})^2$
78	6084	-3	9
79	6241	-2	4
82	6724	1	1
81	6561	0	0
85	7225	4	16
405	32835	0	30

From the bottom row, $\Sigma x^2 = 32835$, $\Sigma(x-\bar{x}) = 0$, and $\Sigma(x-\bar{x})^2 = 30$.

3.31 The expression Σxy represents the sum of products of the pairs of data; that is,

$$\Sigma xy = x_1y_1 + x_2y_2 + \ldots + x_ny_n.$$

The expression $\Sigma x\Sigma y$ represents the product of the sums of the two data sets; that is,

$$\Sigma x\Sigma y = (x_1 + x_2 + \ldots + x_n)\ (y_1 + y_2 + \ldots + y_n).$$

To show that these two quantities are generally unequal, consider three observations on x and three observations on y as presented in the first two columns of the following table:

x	y	xy
1	2	2
3	4	12
5	6	30
9	12	44

Consider also a third column which is the product of x and y, appropriately labeled xy. From the bottom row, we see that $\Sigma x = 9$, $\Sigma y = 12$, and $\Sigma xy = 44$.

From this simple example, it is obvious that Σxy does not equal $\Sigma x\Sigma y$, since $\Sigma xy = 44$ and $\Sigma x\Sigma y = (9)(12) = 108$.

Exercises 3.3

3.33 The purpose of a measure of variation is to show the amount of variation in a data set. By itself, any value of central tendency does not adequately characterize the elements of a data set. Central tendency merely describes the center of the observations but does not show how observations differ from each other. A measure of dispersion is intended to capture the degree to which observations differ among themselves.

3.35 When we use the standard deviation as a measure of variation, the reference point is the mean since all deviations are computed using that value.

3.37 (a) The mean of this data set is 5. Thus

$$\Sigma(x-\bar{x})^2 = (-4)^2 + (-3)^2 + (-2)^2 + (-1)^2 + 0^2 + 1^2 + 2^2 + 3^2 + 4^2 = 60$$

Dividing by $n - 1 = 8$, $s^2 = 60/8 = 7.5$. The standard deviation, s, is the square root of 7.5, or 2.739.

(b) The mean of this data set is 15. Thus
$\Sigma(x-\bar{x})^2 = (-14)^2 + (-13)^2 + (-12)^2 + (-11)^2 + (-10)^2 + (-9)^2 + (-8)^2 + (-7)^2 + 84^2 = 7980$

Dividing by n - 1 = 8, $s^2 = 7980/8 = 997.5$. The standard deviation, s, is the square root of 997.5, or 31.583.

(c) Changing the 9 to 99 greatly increases the standard deviation, illustrating that it lacks the property of resistance to the influence of extreme data values.

3.39 (a) The defining formula for *s* is $s = \sqrt{\dfrac{\sum (x-\bar{x})^2}{n-1}}$.

The first three columns of the following table present the calculations that are needed to compute *s* by the defining formula:

x	$x-\bar{x}$	$(x-\bar{x})^2$	x^2
110	-4.2	17.64	12,100
122	7.8	60.84	14,884
132	17.8	316.84	17,424
107	-7.2	51.84	11,449
101	-13.2	174.24	10,201
97	-17.2	295.84	9,409
115	0.8	0.64	13,225
91	-23.2	538.24	8,281
125	10.8	116.64	15,625
142	27.8	772.84	20,164
1,142	0	2,345.60	132,762

With n = 10 and using the bottom figure of column 1, we find that $\bar{x} = \Sigma x/n = 1{,}142/10 = 114.2$. This value is needed to construct the differences presented in column 2. Column 3 squares these differences. The figure presented at the bottom of column 3 is the computation needed for the numerator of the defining formula for *s*. Thus,

$$s = \sqrt{\frac{2345.6}{10-1}} = 16.14$$

b. The computing formula for s is

$$s = \sqrt{\frac{\sum x^2 - (\sum x)^2/n}{n-1}}$$

The computing formula for s with figures used from the bottom of Columns 1 and 4 of the previous table yields

$$s = \sqrt{\frac{132762 - 1142^2/10}{10-1}} = 16.14$$

(c) The computing formula was a time-saver since only one column of intermediate numbers needs to calculated, whereas the defining formula requires three additional columns.

3.41 (a) The range is 516 - 15 = 501.

(b) The defining formula for *s* is $s=\sqrt{\dfrac{\sum(x-\bar{x})^2}{n-1}}$

The first three columns of the following table present the calculations that are needed to compute *s* by the defining formula:

x	$x-\bar{x}$	$(x-\bar{x})^2$	x^2
79	-114	12,996	6,241
516	323	104,329	266,256
24	-169	28,561	576
265	72	5,184	70,225
41	-152	23,104	1,681
15	-178	31,684	225
411	218	47,524	168,921
1,351	0	253,382	514,125

With n = 7 and using the bottom figure of column 1, we find that $\bar{x} = \Sigma x/n = 1351/7 = 193$. This value is needed to construct the differences presented in column 2. Column 3 squares these differences. The figure presented at the bottom of column 3 is the computation needed for the numerator of the defining formula for *s*. Thus,

$$s=\sqrt{\frac{253382}{7-1}}=205.5$$

c. The computing formula for s is $s=\sqrt{\dfrac{\sum x^2-(\sum x)^2/n}{n-1}}$

d. Columns 1 and 4 of the previous table present the calculations needed to compute *s* by the computing formula. Using the figures presented at the bottom of each of these columns and substituting into the formula itself, we get:

$$s=\sqrt{\frac{514125-1351^2/7}{7-1}}=205.5$$

(d) The computing formula was easier to use. It required both fewer and easier column manipulations.

3.43 (a) The range of a data set is defined to be the difference between the largest and smallest data values in the data set. The largest number of tornado touchdowns is 373. The smallest number is 6. The range is 373 - 6 = 367.

(b) The defining formula for *s* is $s=\sqrt{\dfrac{\sum(x-\bar{x})^2}{n-1}}$.

The first three columns of the following table present the calculations that are needed to compute *s* by the defining formula:

x	$x-\bar{x}$	$(x-\bar{x})^2$	x^2
47	-71.1	5055.21	2209
72	-46.1	2125.21	5184
72	-46.1	2125.21	5184
182	63.9	4083.21	33124
308	189.9	36062.01	94864
373	254.9	64974.01	139129
82	-36.1	1303.21	6724
60	-58.1	3375.61	3600
104	-14.1	198.81	10816
86	-32.1	1030.41	7396
25	-93.1	8667.61	625
6	-112.1	12566.41	36
1417	-0.2	141566.92	308891

With n = 12 and using the bottom figure of column 1, we find that $\bar{x} = \Sigma x/n = 1417/12 = 118.1$. This value is needed to construct the differences in column 2. Column 3 squares the differences presented in column 2. The figure presented at the bottom of column 3 is the computation needed for the numerator of the defining formula *s*. Thus,

$$s = \sqrt{\frac{141566}{12-1}} = 113.44$$

(c) The computing formula for *s* is

$$s = \sqrt{\frac{\sum x^2 - (\sum x)^2 / n}{n-1}}$$

Columns 1 and 4 of the previous table present the calculations needed to compute *s* by the computing formula. Using the figures presented at the bottom of each of these columns and substituting into the formula itself, we get:

$$s = \sqrt{\frac{308891 - 1417^2 / 12}{12-1}} = 113.44$$

(d) The computing formula was easier to use. It required both fewer and easier column manipulations.

3.45 (a) We will compute *s* for each data set using the computing formula. The computing formula requires the following column manipulations.

Data Set I

x	x^2
0	0
0	0
10	100
12	144
14	196
14	196
14	196
15	225
15	225
15	225
16	256
17	289
23	529
24	576
189	3,157

Data Set II

x	x^2
10	100
12	144
14	196
14	196
14	196
15	225
15	225
15	225
16	256
17	289
142	2,052

For each data set, the calculations for *s* are presented in column 2 of the following table.

Data Set	s	Range
I	$\sqrt{\frac{3157-189^2/14}{14-1}}=6.8$	24
II	$\sqrt{\frac{2052-142^2/10}{10-1}}=2.0$	7

(b) The range for Data Set I is 24 - 0 = 24. The range for Data Set II is 17 - 10 = 7. These are recorded in column 3 of the previous table.

(c) Outliers increase the variation in a data set; in other words, removing the outliers from a data set results in a decrease in the variation.

3.47 (a) We create a table with columns headed by x, f, xf, $(x-\bar{x})$, $(x-\bar{x})^2$, and $(x-\bar{x})^2f$ to estimate the sample mean and standard deviation of the days-to-maturity data.

Midpoint x	Frequency f	xf	$x-\bar{x}$	$(x-\bar{x})^2$	$f(x-\bar{x})^2$
35	3	105	-33.5	1122.25	3366.75
45	1	45	-23.5	552.25	552.25
55	8	440	-13.5	182.25	1458.00
65	10	650	-3.5	12.25	122.50
75	7	525	6.5	42.25	295.75
85	7	595	16.5	272.25	1905.75
95	4	380	26.5	702.25	2809.00
	40	2740			10510.00

The mean $\overline{x}$ = 2740/40 =68.5. This is subtracted from each of the midpoints in column 1 to get the entries in column 4. The grouped data formula yields the following estimate of the standard deviation:

$$s = \sqrt{\frac{\sum (x - \overline{x})^2 f}{n-1}} = \sqrt{\frac{10510}{40-1}} = 16.4$$

(b) The estimated mean and standard deviation are both very close to the actual values. The small discrepancies occur because, in the grouped data formulas, every actual data value in a given class is replaced by the class midpoint even though most values in the class are not equal to the midpoint. For example, every data value in the first class is represented by the midpoint 35, but the three data values are 36, 38, and 39, all of them larger than the midpoint. This introduces a small error in each difference between an observation and the mean. It is unlikely that all of these small errors will cancel each other out and thus both the mean and the standard deviation will exhibit small errors.

3.49 We will use Excel to compute the range and sample standard deviation of the hospital stay data. Enter the 9 data values in cells A1 through A9. In A12, type the expression =MAX(A1:A9)-MIN(A1:A9). The result in A2 will be the range, 52. In A13, type the expression =STDEV(A1:A9). The result will be the standard deviation, 16.1.

3.51 (a) We will use Minitab to compute the range and sample standard deviation of the Sex and Direction data. In Minitab, open the worksheet for Exercise 3.51 from the WeissStats CD. This will enter the 60 data values in columns C1 and C2 under the names MALE and FEMALE. From the pull-down menu, choose **Stat ▶ Basic Statistics ▶ Display Descriptive Statistics**, enter MALE FEMALE in the **Variables** text box, and click **OK.** The output appears in the Session Window as

Variable	N	Mean	Median	TrMean	StDev	SE Mean
MALE	30	37.60	22.50	31.73	38.49	7.03
FEMALE	30	55.80	35.00	52.08	48.26	8.81

Variable	Minimum	Maximum	Q1	Q3
MALE	3.00	167.00	10.75	59.25
FEMALE	3.00	176.00	14.75	95.50

Minitab does not compute the range directly, but you can obtain the ranges by subtracting the Minimums from the Maximums, 167 - 3 = 164 for the males and 176 - 3 = 173 for the females. The standard deviations are listed in the output as StDev = 38.49 for the males and 48.26 for the females.

(b) By both measures of variation, there is greater variation in the data for females than there is in the data for males.

Exercises 3.4

3.53 The median and interquartile range have the advantage over the mean and standard deviation that they are not sensitive to a few extreme values; they are said to be resistant.

3.55 An extreme observation may be an outlier, but it may also be an indication of skewness.

3.57 (a) The interquartile range is a descriptive measure of variation.

(b) It measures the spread of the middle two quarters (50%) of the data.

3.59 A modified boxplot will be the same as an ordinary boxplot when the maximum and minimum values lie inside the upper and lower limits, respectively. In other words, the maximum and minimum values are also the adjacent values.

3.61 First arrange the 16 data values in increasing order and note the two middle values:

13 16 18 21 22 23 28 **29 30** 30 31 35 38 38 44 51

The median (second quartile) is the average of the two middle values, 29 and 30, and thus equals (29 + 30)/2 = 29.5.

The first quartile Q_1 is the median of the lower half of the ordered data set 13 16 18 **21 22** 23 28 29 and thus is the average of the fourth and fifth values, 21 and 22. $Q_1 = (21 + 22)/2 = 21.5$

The third quartile Q_3 is the median of the upper half of the ordered data set 30 30 31 **35 38** 38 44 51 and thus is the average of the fourth and fifth values, 35 and 38. $Q_3 = (35 + 38)/2 = 36.5$

3.63 First arrange the data in increasing order:

1 1 3 3 4 4 5 6 6 7 **7** 9 9 10 12 12 13 15 18 23 55

Since this data set has on odd number of values (21), the median is the middle value (11th) in the ordered list. Thus the median, or second quartile, is 7.

The first quartile Q_1 is the median of the lower half of the ordered data set (including the median) 1 1 3 3 4 **4** 5 6 6 7 7. Since this data set has an odd number of values (11), Q_1 is the sixth value, so $Q_1 = 4$.

The third quartile Q_3 is the median of the upper half of the ordered data set (including the median) 7 9 9 10 12 **12** 13 15 18 23 55. Since this data set has an odd number of values (11), Q_3 is the sixth value, so $Q_3 = 12$.

3.65 (a) The interquartile range is $IQR = Q_3 - Q_1 = 36.5 - 21.5 = 15.0$.

(b) Min = 13, $Q_1 = 21.5$, Median = 29.5, $Q_3 = 36.5$, Max = 51

(c) By constructing the lower and upper limits, you can determine if there are any potential outliers.

Lower limit = $Q_1 - 1.5(IQR) = 21.5 - 1.5(15) = -1.0$

Upper limit = $Q_3 + 1.5(IQR) = 36.5 + 1.5(15) = 59.0$

Since there are no values below -1.0 or above 59.0, there are no potential outliers.

(d)

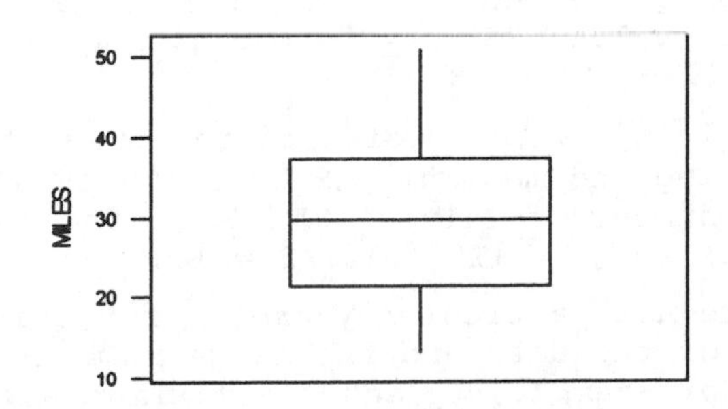

The preceding figure is the boxplot for the miles traveled by the 18 salmon. Note that the two boxes in the boxplot indicate the spread of the two middle quarters of the data and that the two whiskers indicate the spread of the first and fourth quarters. Thus, we see that there is a little more variation in the top quarter of the data than in the bottom three quarters, but that, overall, the distribution is fairly symmetric. Since there are no potential outliers, a modified boxplot would be identical to the plot shown.

3.67 (a) The interquartile range is IQR = $Q_3 - Q_1$ = 12 - 4 = 8.

(b) Min = 1, Q_1 = 4, Median = 7, Q_3 = 12, Max = 55

(c) By constructing the lower and upper limits, you can determine if there are any potential outliers.

Lower limit = Q_1 - 1.5(IQR) = 4 - 1.5(8) = -8

Upper limit = Q_3 + 1.5(IQR) = 12 + 1.5(8) = 24

Since 55 lies outside the limits, it is a potential outlier.

(d) 

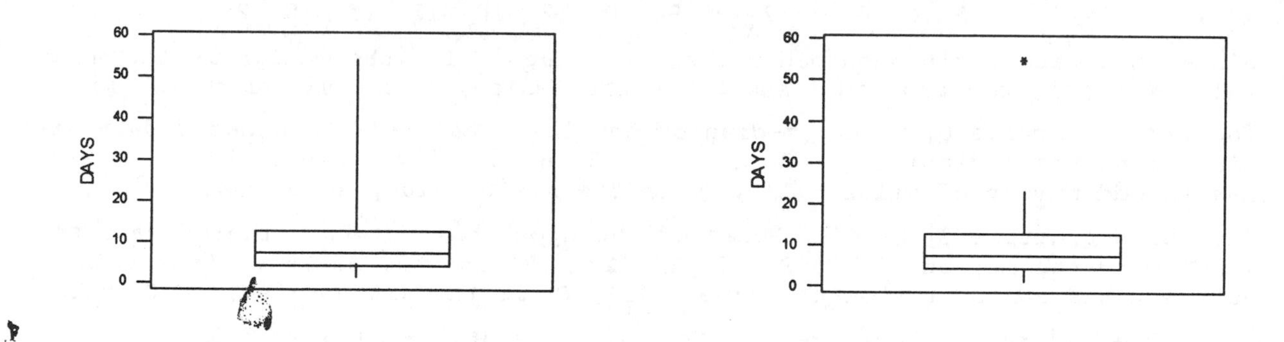

The figures above are the boxplot and modified boxplot for the lengths of stay in short-term hospitals by 21 randomly selected patients. Note that the potential outlier of 55 is denoted in the modified boxplot.

3.69 (a) First, arrange the data in increasing order

6 7 8 8 8 8 9 **9** 9 10 10 10 10 10 10

Since there is an odd number of data values (15), the median is the middle (8th) value. Thus the median is 9.

The first quartile Q_1 is the median of the lower half of the ordered data set (including the median) 6 7 8 **8** **8** 8 9 9. Since this data set has an even number of values (8), Q_1 is the average of the fourth and fifth values, so Q_1 = (8 + 8)/2 = 8.

The third quartile Q_3 is the median of the upper half of the ordered data set (including the median) 9 9 10 **10** **10** 10 10 10. Since this data set has an even number of values (8), Q_3 is the average of the fourth and fifth values, so Q_3 = (10 + 10)/2 = 10.

The quartiles are not particularly useful for this set of data due to the small range of the data and the large numbers of identical values at 8, 9, and 10. For example, Q_3 and the maximum are equal as a result of the highest six values all being 10.

3.71 The center of the distribution of weight loss, as measured by the median, is very similar for the two groups. However, group 1 has less variation of weight loss. Group 2 has a larger range than group 1. The distribution of weight loss for both groups is approximately symmetric.

3.73 The central box is divided into equal parts by the median. The two whiskers will be the same length, although they may not necessarily be the same length as each part of the central box.

3.75 (a) Using Minitab, we store the unemployment check amounts data in a column named AMOUNT. To obtain a modified boxplot, we

- Now choose **Graphs ▶ Boxplot...**
- Select AMOUNT in the **Y** text box for **Graph 1.** Leave the **X** text box blank.
- Click **OK**

(b) To determine the smallest and largest data values and the quartiles of the data, we

- Choose **Stat ▶ Basic Statistics ▶ Display Descriptive Statistics...**
- Select AMOUNT in the **Variables** text box
- Click **OK**

The output for part (a) as shown in the Graph Window and that for part (b) shown in the Sessions Window are, respectively:

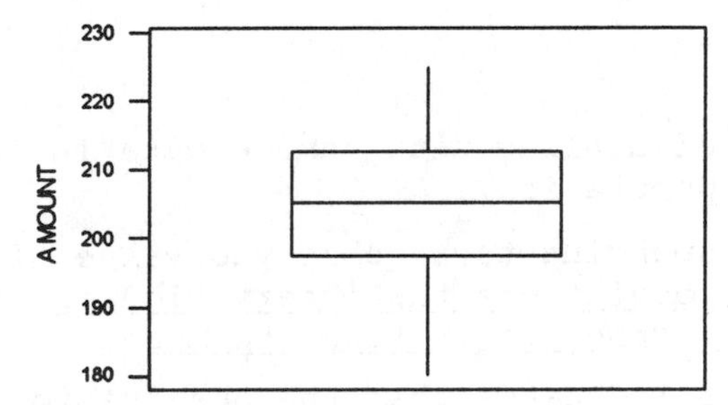

Variable	N	Mean	Median	TrMean	StDev	SE Mean
AMOUNT	14	204.79	205.00	205.17	11.95	3.19

Variable	Minimum	Maximum	Q1	Q3
AMOUNT	180.00	225.00	197.25	212.75

Thus, the five-number summary of the data is

Minimum = 180, Q_1 = 197.25, Median = 205, Q_3 = 212.75, Maximum = 225

3.77 (a) Using Minitab, we store the sex and direction data in 2 columns, MALE and FEMALE. To obtain modified side-by-side boxplots, we

- Now choose **Graphs ▶ Boxplot...**
- Select MALE in the **Y** text box for **Graph 1** and FEMALE in the **Y** text box for **Graph 2.** Leave the **X** text boxes blank.
- Click on the **Frame** button and select **Multiple Graphs.** Then select **Overlay graphs on the same page** and click **OK.**
- Click **OK**

The output as shown in the Graph Window is

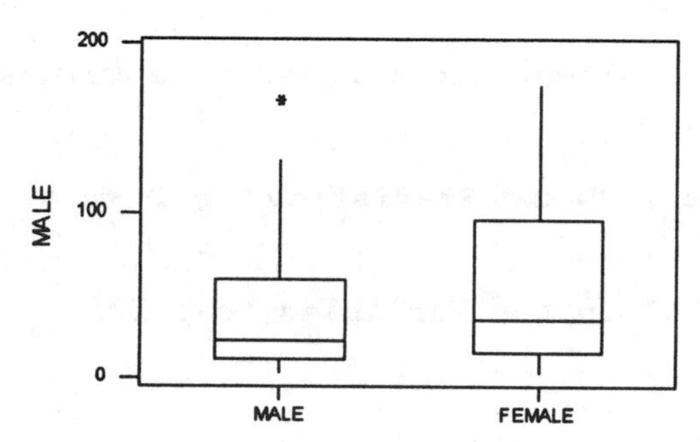

(b) The graph shows that while the overall range of values for males and females is about the same and the minimums and maximums are about the same, the two quartiles and the median are lower for the males than for the females.

<u>**Exercises 3.5**</u>

3.79 The ultimate objective of dealing with sample data in inferential studies is to describe the entire population.

3.81 (a) The z-score corresponding to an observed value of a variable tells us <u>how many standard deviations the observation is from the mean and, by its sign, what direction it is from the mean.</u>

(b) A positive z-score indicates that the observation is <u>greater than</u> the mean, whereas a negative z-score indicates that the observation is <u>less than</u> the mean.

3.83 The number 134.75 is a parameter since it is the mean of the entire population of players on the 1999 U.S. Women's World Cup soccer team.

3.85 We first create a table of values necessary to compute the mean and the standard deviation.

Wind Speed x	$x - \mu$	$(x - \mu)^2$
60	-45.4	2061.16
140	34.6	1197.16
140	34.6	1197.16
105	-.4	.16
50	-55.4	3069.16
155	49.6	2460.16
150	44.6	1989.16
60	-45.4	2061.16
110	4.6	21.16
100	-5.4	29.16
40	-65.4	4277.16
155	49.6	2460.16
1265		20822.92

(a) From the total in column 1, the mean is $\mu = \frac{\sum x}{N} = \frac{1265}{12} = 105.4 \text{ mph}$. This is subtracted from each value in column 1 to get the values in column 2.

(b) The values in column 2 are squared and entered in column 3. The total in column 3 is the numerator in the defining formula for σ.

$$\sigma = \sqrt{\frac{\sum (x-\mu)^2}{N}} = \sqrt{\frac{20822.92}{12}} = 41.7 \text{ mph}$$

(c) To obtain the median, we first arrange the data in increasing order.

40 50 60 60 100 **105 110** 140 140 150 155 155

Since there is an even number of values (12), the median is the average of the middle two (7th and 8th) and is (105 + 110)/2 = 107.5.

(d) The mode is that number which occurs most often. In this case, there are three modes, 60, 140, and 155, each of which occurs twice.

(e) To obtain the IQR, we need the first and third quartiles. The first quartile Q_1 is the median of the lower half of the ordered list of data:

40 50 **60 60** 100 105

Since this set has an even number of values (6), $Q_1 = (60 + 60)/2 = 60$.

The third quartile Q_3 is the median of the upper half of the ordered list of data:

110 140 **140 150** 155 155

Since this set has an even number of values (6), $Q_3 = (140 + 150)/2 = 145$.

Finally, the IQR = $Q_3 - Q_1 = 145 - 60 = 85$

3.87 (a) The standardized version of x is $z = (x - 16.3)/17.9$.

(b) The mean and standard deviation of z are 0 and 1 respectively.

(c) For x = 64.7, the z score is $(64.7 - 16.3)/17.9 = 2.70$

For x = 4.2, the z score is $(4.2 - 16.3)/17.9 = -0.68$

(d) The value 64.7 is 2.70 standard deviations above the mean 16.3.

The value 4.2 is 0.68 standard deviations below the mean 16.3.

(e)

$\bar{x}-3s$	$\bar{x}-2s$	$\bar{x}-s$	$\bar{x}$	$\bar{x}+s$	$\bar{x}+2s$	$\bar{x}+3s$	
-37.4	-19.5	-1.6	16.3	34.2	52.1	70.0	x
-3	-2	-1	0	1	2	3	z

3.89 Your z-score is $(350 - 280)/20 = 70/20 = 3.50$; i.e., your score is 3.50 standard deviations above the mean for the class, a very good score.

3.91 The formulas used here to compute s and σ are

$$s = \sqrt{\frac{\sum (x - \bar{x})^2}{n-1}} \quad \text{and} \quad \sigma = \sqrt{\frac{\sum (x - \mu)^2}{N}}$$

For each data set, the relevant calculations are:

Data Set	Number of observations	$\Sigma(\text{x-mean})^2$	s	σ
1	4	14.00	2.16	1.87
2	7	24.86	2.04	1.88
3	10	36.40	2.01	1.91

(a) The sample standard deviations are found in the fourth column of the previous table.

(b) The population standard deviations are found in the fifth column of the previous table.

(c) Comparing s and σ for a given data set, the two measures will tend to be closer together if the data set is large.

3.93 (a) Using Excel, we enter the 20 data values in cells A1 through A20. The data values in inches are

68	63	66	67	64	67	65	65	65	70
66	71	64	65	66	62	71	69	67	69

To obtain the mean, in cell A22 we type =AVERAGE(A1:A20) and the result is 66.5 inches.

To obtain the population standard deviation directly, in cell A23 we type =STDEVP(A1:A20). This yields the value 2.48 inches.

REVIEW TEST FOR CHAPTER 3

1. (a) Descriptive measures are numbers used to describe data sets.

   (b) Measures of center indicate where the center or most typical value of a data set lies.

   (c) Measures of variation indicate how much variation or spread the data set has.

2. The two most commonly used measures of center for quantitative data are the mean and the median. The mean uses all of the data, but can be influenced by the presence of a few outliers. The median is computed from the one or two center values in an ordered list of the data. It does not make use of all of the data, but it has the advantage that it is not influenced by the presence of a few outliers.

3. The only measure of center, among those we discussed, that is appropriate for qualitative data is the mode.

4. (a) standard deviation

   (b) interquartile range

5. (a) $\bar{x}$ (b) s (c) μ (d) σ

6. (a) Not necessarily true.

   (b) This is necessarily true.

7. Almost all of the observations in any data set lie within 3 standard deviations of the mean.

8. (a) The components of the five-number summary are the minimum, Q_1, median, Q_3, and the maximum.

   (b) The median is a measure of the center. The interquartile range which is found as $Q_3 - Q_1$, and the range, which is the difference between the maximum and the minimum are measures of variation.

   (c) The boxplot is based on the five-number summary.

9. (a) An outlier is an observation that falls well outside the overall pattern of the data.

   (b) First compute the interquartile range $IQR = Q_3 - Q_1$. Then compute two 'fences' as $Q_1 - 1.5IQR$ and $Q_3 + 1.5IQR$. Observations which are lower than the first fence or higher than the second fence are potential outliers and require further study.

10. (a) A z-score for an observation x is obtained by subtracting the mean of the data set from x and then dividing the result by the standard deviation; i.e., $z = (x - \mu)/\sigma$ for population data or $z = (x - \bar{x})/s$ for sample data.

    (b) A z-score indicates how many standard deviations an observation is below or above the mean of the data set.

    (c) An observation with a z-score of 2.9 is likely to be greater than all or almost all of the other data values.

11. (a) The mean is calculated as $\bar{x} = \Sigma x/n$. For the sample of 20 guests, $\bar{x} = 47/20 = 2.35$ alcoholic drinks.

The median is found by ordering the observations from lowest to highest and finding the average of the two observations in the middle. The list is

0 0 1 1 1 1 1 2 2 **2** **2** 2 3 3 4 4 4 4 5 5

The median is the average of the 10th and 11th values, and is therefore (2 + 2)/2 = 2.

The mode is the value that occurs the most times. In this data set, 1 and 2 both occur 5 times, and so the modes are 1 and 2.

(b) If the purpose is to help in estimating the cost of the party, the mean is the best since it takes into account the drinking practices of all of the guests. If the purpose is to describe the average guest, the median is more typical of the list of values. The mode is less useful for this data since there are two modes.

12. Many more marriages are characterized as being of short duration than other durations. Since the median is ordinarily preferred for data sets that have exceptional (very large or small) values, the median is more appropriate than the mean as a measure of central tendency for data on the duration of marriages.

13. Regarding death certificates, we are interested in the most frequent cause of death. Causes of death are qualitative. There is no way to compute a mean or median for such data. The mode is the only measure of central tendency that can be used for qualitative data.

14. (a) $\bar{x} = \frac{\sum x}{n} = \frac{457}{10} = 45.7$ kilograms

(b) range = 54 - 37 = 17 kilograms

(c) $s = \sqrt{\frac{\sum x^2 - (\sum x)^2/n}{n-1}} = \sqrt{\frac{21109 - 457^2/10}{9}} = 5.0$ kilograms.

15. (a)

$\bar{x}-3s$	$\bar{x}-2s$	$\bar{x}-s$	$\bar{x}$	$\bar{x}+s$	$\bar{x}+2s$	$\bar{x}+3s$
18.3	31.7	45.1	58.5	71.9	85.3	98.7

(b) Almost all of the ages of the 36 millionaires are between 18.3 and 98.7 years old.

16. (a) The first quartile is the median of the lower half of the ordered list. Since there is a total of 36 ages, the first 18 are in the lower half and the median of these is the average of the middle two, the 9th and 10th values. Thus Q_1 = (48 + 48)/2 = 48.

The second quartile is the median of the entire data set. The number of pieces of data is 36, and so the position of the median is (36 + 1)/2 = 18.5, halfway between the eighteenth and nineteenth data value. Thus the median of the entire data set is (59 + 60)/2 = 59.5. That is, Q_2 = 59.5.

The third quartile is the median of the upper half of the ordered list. Since there is a total of 36 ages, the last 18 are in the upper half and the median of these is the average of the middle two, the 9th and 10th values. Thus $Q_3 = (68 + 69)/2 = 68.5$.

Interpreting our results, we conclude that 25% of the ages are less than 48 years; 25% of the ages are between 48 and 59.5 years; 25% of the ages are between 59.5 and 68.5 years; and 25% of the ages are greater than 68.5 years.

(b) The IQR = $Q_3 - Q_1 = 68.5 - 48 = 20.5$. Thus, the middle 50% of the ages has a range of 20.5 years.

(c) Min = 31, $Q_1 = 48$, $Q_2 = 59.5$, $Q_3 = 68.5$, Max = 79

(d) The limits are given by:

Lower limit = $Q_1 - 1.5(\text{IQR}) = 48.0 - 1.5(20.5) = 17.25$

Upper limit = $Q_3 + 1.5(\text{IQR}) = 68.5 + 1.5(20.5) = 99.25$

(e) There are no values below 17.25 or above 99.25, so there are no potential outliers.

(f) A boxplot is constructed easily using the information in part (a).

(i) low data value = 31 years

(ii) high data value = 79 years

(iii) Q_1 = 48.0 years

(iv) Q_3 = 68.5 years

(v) median = Q_2 = 59.5 years.

These values are used to construct the boxplot as follows:

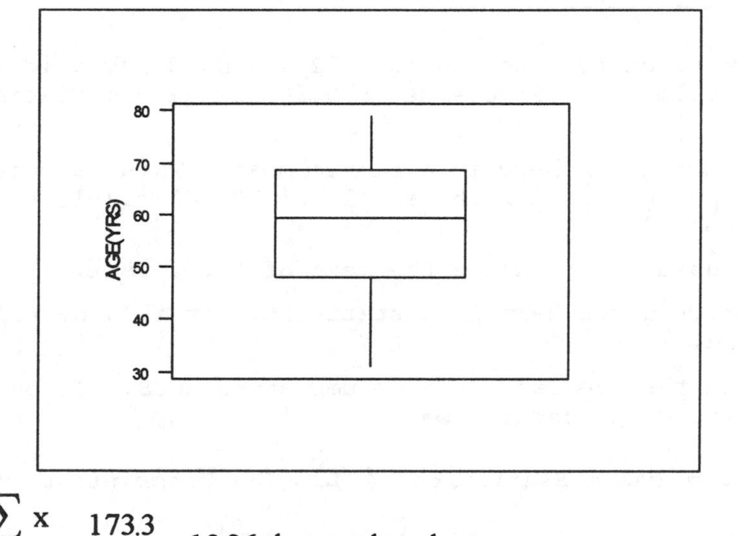

17. (a) $$\mu = \frac{\sum x}{N} = \frac{173.3}{9} = 19.26 \text{ thousand students}$$

(b) Squaring each data value and then summing, we find that

$\sum x^2 = 4172.6$. Then the population standard deviation is

$$\sigma = \sqrt{\frac{\sum x^2 - (\sum x)^2 / N}{N}} = \sqrt{\frac{4172.6 - 173.3^2/9}{9}} = 9.64 \text{ thousand students}$$

(c) $z = (x - \mu)/\sigma = (x - 19.26)/9.64$

(d) The mean of z is 0, and the standard deviation of z is 1. All standardized variables have mean 0 and standard deviation 1.

(e)

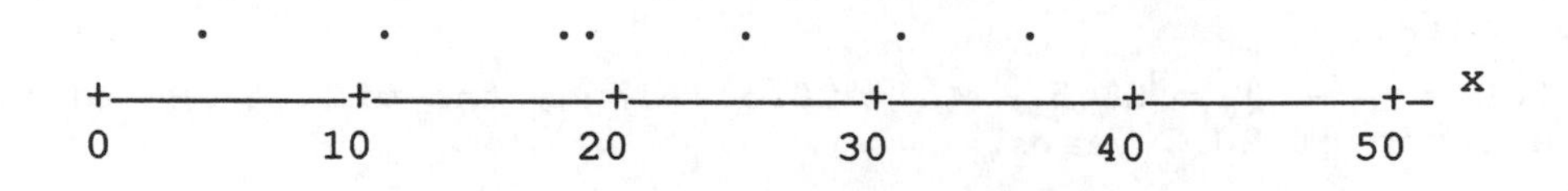

Converting each x value to its corresponding z-score results in the dotplot below.

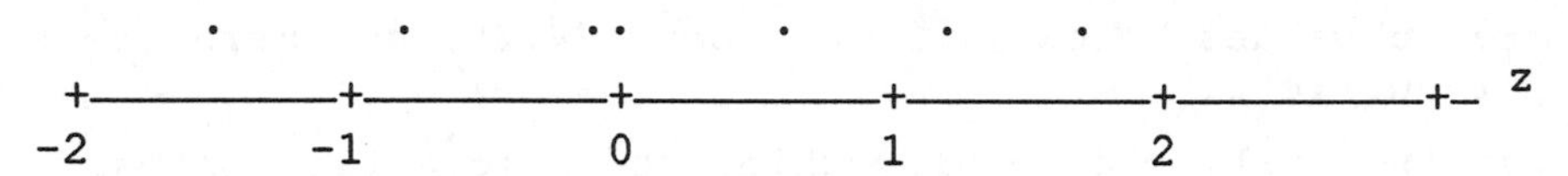

The relative positions of the points in the two plots are the same, but the scales are different.

(f)

x	$z = (x - \mu)/\sigma$
35.8	(35.8 - 19.26)/9.64 = 1.72
10.6	(10.6 - 19.26)/9.64 = -0.90

The enrollment at Los Angeles is 1.72 standard deviations above the mean and the enrollment at Riverside is 0.90 standard deviation below the mean.

18. (a) The mean price given here is a sample mean. This is because it is the mean price per gallon for the sample of 10,000 gasoline service stations.

(b) The letter used to designate the mean of $1.51 is $\bar{x}$.

(c) The mean price given here is a statistic. It is a descriptive measure for a sample.

19. To begin, we store the age data in a column named AGES. To employ Minitab's Descriptive statistics procedure, we

- Choose **Stat ▶ Basic Statistics ▶ Display Descriptive Statistics...**
- Select AGES in the **Variables** text box
- Click **OK**

The results are shown in the Sessions window as

Descriptive Statistics

Variable	N	Mean	Median	TrMean	StDev	SEMean
AGES	36	58.53	59.50	58.75	13.36	2.23

Variable	Min	Max	Q1	Q3
AGES	31.00	79.00	48.00	68.75

(a) Mean = 58.53

(b) Median = 59.50

(c) Range = Max - Min = 79.00 - 31.00 = 48.00

(d) Sample standard deviation = 13.36

20. (a) With the age data already stored in a column named AGES, we

- Choose **Graph ▶ Boxplot...**
- Select AGES in the **Y** text box for **Graph 1**
- Click **OK**

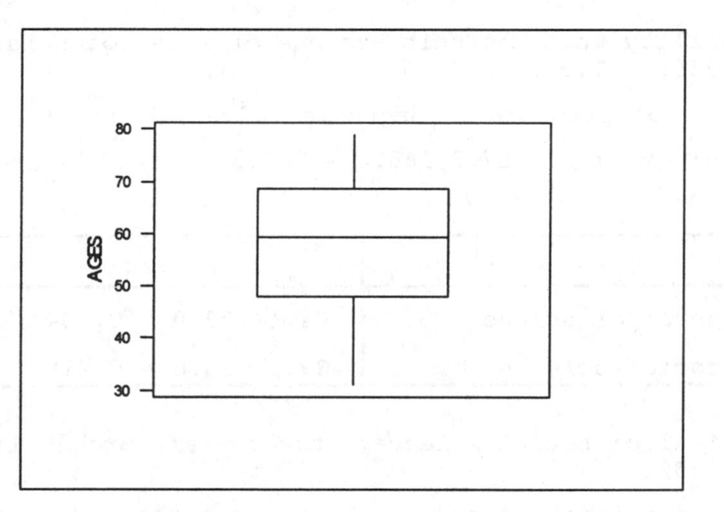

(b) The five-number summary may be obtained from the descriptive statistics printout in Problem 19.

Minimum = 31.0, Q_1 = 48.0, Median = 59.5, Q_3 = 68.75, Maximum = 79.0

21. (a) The least variation occurs in the third quarter of the age data, the next least in the fourth quarter, the next least in the second quarter, and the greatest in the first quarter. Also, minimum ≈ 31, maximum ≈ 79, Q_1 ≈ 48, Median = Q_2 ≈ 60, Q_3 ≈ 69.

(b) There are no potential outliers in the data.

CHAPTER 4 ANSWERS

Exercises 4.1

4.1 An experiment is an action the result of which cannot be predicted with certainty. An event is a specified result that may or may not occur when the experiment is performed.

4.3 There is no difference.

4.5 The frequentist interpretation of probability is that the probability of an event is the proportion of times the event occurs in a large number of repetitions of the experiment.

4.7 The following could not possibly be probabilities:

(b) -0.201: A probability cannot be negative.

(e) 3.5: A probability cannot exceed 1.

4.9 The total number of units (in thousands) is N = 112,356.

(a) The probability that the unit has 4 rooms is f/N = 23,468/112,356 = 0.209 (to three decimal places).

(b) The probability that the unit has more than 4 rooms is f/N = (24476 + 21327 + 13782 + 15647)/112356 = 75232/112356 = 0.670.

(c) The probability that the unit has 1 or 2 rooms is f/N = (471 + 1470)/112356 = 1941/112356 = 0.017.

(d) The probability that the unit has fewer than one room is f/N = 0/112356 = 0.000.

(e) The probability that the unit has one or more rooms is f/N = 112356/112356 = 1.000.

4.11 The total number of graduate students is 180.0 (thousand).

(a) For psychology, f/N = 27.3/180.0 = 0.152.

(b)

Type	f/N
physical science	24.1/180.0 = 0.134
social science	39.3/180.0 = 0.218

For "physical or social science," the overall probability is 0.134 + 0.218 = 0.352.

(c) For computer science, f = 7.6. Thus the total for "not computer science" is 180.0 - 7.6 = 172.4. The probability of "not computer science" is 172.4/180.0 = 0.958.

4.13 (a) Five of the 36 possible outcomes have sums of 6. Thus, f/N = 5/36 = 0.139.

(b) Eighteen of the 36 possible outcomes provide a sum that is even. Thus, f/N = 18/36 = 0.500.

(c) Six of the 36 possible outcomes have a sum of 7, and two have a sum of 11. Thus, f/N = (6 + 2)/36 = 0.222.

(d) One of the 36 possible outcomes has a sum of 2, two have a sum of 3, and one has a sum of 12. Thus, f/N = (1 + 2 + 1)/36 = 0.111.

4.15 The event in part (d), that the housing unit has fewer than one room, is impossible. The event in part (e), that the housing unit has one or more rooms, is a certainty.

4.17 The frequentist interpretation construes the probability of an event to be the proportion of times the event occurs in a <u>large number of repetitions</u> of the experiment. Some 'experiments' can not be run more than once under identical conditions - a horse race, a World Series, a super Bowl football game - so it makes no sense to think about a large number of repetitions of the experiment. For these experiments, the frequentist interpretation cannot be used, and therefore it cannot be used as an overall definition of probability.

4.19 If p is the probability that a randomly selected adult woman believes that a "cyber affair" is cheating, then $p = 0.75$. The odds <u>against</u> selecting such a woman are in the ratio of 1-p to p, or 0.25 to 0.75. This is normally expressed in integers as 1 to 3.

<u>Exercises 4.2</u>

4.21 Venn diagrams are useful for portraying events and relationships between events.

4.23 Two events are mutual exclusive if they cannot occur at the same time, i.e., they have no outcomes in common. Three events are mutually exclusive if no two of them can occur at the same time, i.e., no pair of the events has any outcomes in common.

4.25 A = {2, 4, 6}; B = {4, 5, 6}; C = {1, 2}; D = {3}

4.27 (a) (not A) = {1, 3, 5} = the event the die comes up odd.

(b) (A & B) = {4, 6} = the event the die comes up four or six.

(c) (B or C) = {1, 2, 4, 5, 6} = the event the die does *not* come up three.

4.29 (a) (not A) is the event that the unit has more than 4 rooms. There are 24,476 + 21,327 + 13,782 + 15,647 = 75,232 (thousand) such units.

(b) (A&B) is the event that the unit has at most 4 rooms and at least 2 rooms, i.e., has 2 or 3 or 4 rooms. There are 1,470 + 11,715 + 23,468 = 36,653 (thousand) such units.

(c) The event (C or D) is the event that the unit has between 5 and 7 rooms inclusive or more than seven rooms, i.e., has 5 or more rooms. This is the same as the event (not A) and therefore there are 75,232 (thousand) such units.

4.31 (a) Events A and B are not mutually exclusive. They have outcomes four and six in common.

(b) Events B and C are mutually exclusive. They have no outcomes in common.

(c) Events A, C, and D are not mutually exclusive. The outcome two is common to A and C.

(d) Among A, B, C, and D, there are three mutually exclusive events. These are B, C, and D. Among B, C, and D, there are no outcomes in common. There are not, however, four mutually exclusive events. The outcome two is common to A and C, and the outcomes four and six are common to A and B.

4.33 The groups that are mutually exclusive are A and C; A and D; C and D; and A, C, and D.

4.35 Below is a Venn diagram portraying four mutually exclusive events.

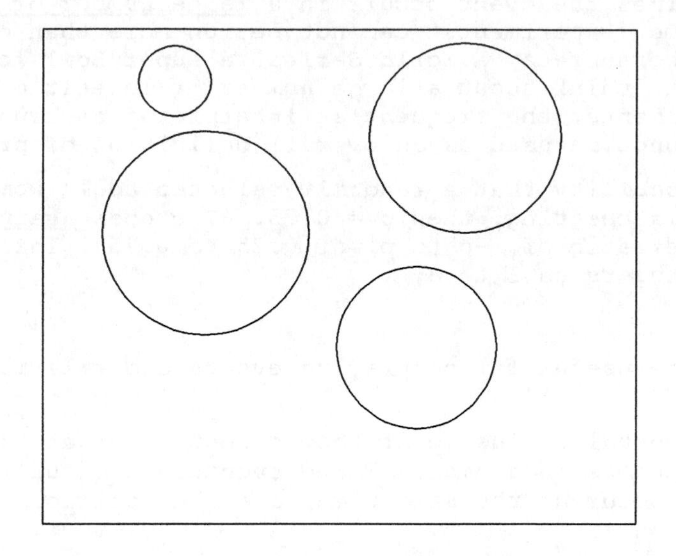

4.37 To say that A, B, and C do not all occur simultaneously does not necessarily imply that A, B, and C are mutually exclusive. In the following diagram, C does not touch A or B. That is, we have a situation where A, B, and C do not occur simultaneously. However, these three events clearly are not mutually exclusive.

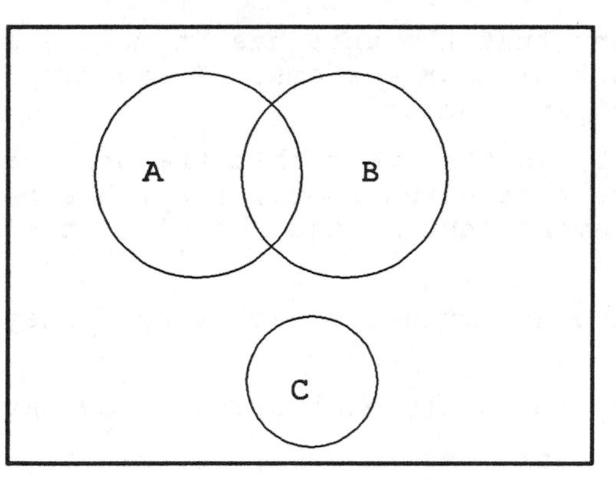

Exercises 4.3

4.39 (a) P(S) = f/N = (1 + 14 + 41)/100 = 0.56.

(b) S = (A or B or C)

(c) P(A) = 1/100 = 0.01; P(B) = 14/100 = 0.14;

P(C) = 41/100 = 0.41.

(d) P(S) = P(A or B or C) = P(A) + P(B) + P(C) = 0.01 + 0.14 + 0.41 = 0.56. This result is identical to the one found in part (a).

4.41 (a) P(Spill occurs in an ocean) = P(Atlantic Ocean or Pacific Ocean) = P(Atlantic Ocean) + P(Pacific Ocean) = 0.011 + 0.059 = 0.070. That is, 7.0% of the spills occur in an ocean.

(b) P(Spill occurs in a lake or harbor) = P(Great Lakes or Other lakes or Harbors) = P(Great Lakes) + P(Other lakes) + P(Harbors)

= 0. 018 + 0.003 + 0.099 = 0.120. That is, 12.0% of the spills occur in a lake or harbor.

(c) P(Spill does not occur in a lake, ocean, river, or canal) = P(Gulf of Mexico or Bays and Sounds or Harbors or Other) = P(Gulf of Mexico) + P(Bays and Sounds) + P(Harbors) + P(Other) = 0.271 + 0.094 + 0.099 + 0.234 = 0.698. That is, 69.8% of the spills do not occur in a lake, ocean, river, or canal.

4.43 (a) P(senator is at least 40) = $=\frac{14}{100}+\frac{41}{100}+\frac{27}{100}+\frac{17}{100}=\frac{99}{100}=0.99$.

This is accomplished more easily using the complementation rule:

P(senator is at least 40) = 1 - P(senator is under 40) $=1-\frac{1}{100}=0.99$.

(b) P(senator is under 60) $=\frac{1}{100}+\frac{14}{100}+\frac{41}{100}=\frac{56}{100}=0.56$.

This is accomplished more easily using the complementation rule:

P(senator is under 60) = 1 - P(senator is at least 60)

$$=1-\left(\frac{27}{100}+\frac{17}{100}\right)=1-\frac{44}{100}=\frac{56}{100}=0.56.$$

4.45 (a) $P(A)=\frac{6}{36}=0.167$ $P(B)=\frac{2}{36}=0.056$ $P(C)=\frac{1}{36}=0.028$ $P(D)=\frac{2}{36}=0.056$

$P(E)=\frac{1}{36}=0.028$ $P(F)=\frac{5}{36}=0.139$ $P(G)=\frac{6}{36}=0.167$

(b) P(7 or 11)= P(A) + P(B) = 0.167 + 0.056 = 0.223.

(c) P(2 or 3 or 12) = P(C or D or E) = P(C) + P(D) + P(E)

= 0.028 + 0.056 + 0.028 = 0.112

(d) P(8 or doubles): Using Figure 4.1: $\frac{10}{36}=0.278$

(e) P(8) + P(doubles) - P(8 & doubles) = 0.139 + 0.167 - 0.028 = 0.278.

4.47 (a) For A and B to be mutually exclusive, P(A & B) must equal zero. Recalling the general addition rule and making the appropriate substitutions, we have:

P(A or B) = P(A) + P(B) - P(A & B)

or

1/2 = 1/4 + 1/3 - P(A & B).

Rearranging terms and solving for P(A & B), we find:

P(A & B) = 1/4 + 1/3 - 1/2 = 3/12 + 4/12 - 6/12 = 1/12.

Thus, A and B are not mutually exclusive because P(A & B) = 1/12 ≠ 0.

(b) From part (a), P(A & B) = 1/12 = 0.083.

4.49 (a) P(A or B) = P(A) + P(B)

(b) Since A and B are mutually exclusive, P(A&B) = 0. Therefore P(A or B) = P(A) + P(B) - P(A&B) = P(A) + P(B) - 0 = P(A) + P(B)

Exercises 4.4

4.51 The total number of observations of bivariate data can be obtained from the frequencies in a contingency table by summing the counts in the cells, summing the row totals, or summing the column totals.

4.53 (a) Data obtained by observing values of one variable of a population are called univariate data.

(b) Data obtained by observing values of two variables of a population are called bivariate data.

4.55 (a) This contingency table has twelve cells.

(b) The total number of players on the New England Patriots as of May 24, 2000 is 94.

(c) There are 42 rookies.

(d) There are 54 players who weigh between 200 and 300 pounds.

(e) There are 22 rookies who weigh between 200 and 300 pounds.

4.57 (a) To fill in the five empty cells, we first determine the A_2 total as 57,959 - 22,180 - 11,025 = 24,754 and the S_3 total as 57,959 - 15467 - 30,501 - 478 = 11,513. Then the number in the A_2S_2 cell is 24,754 - 6,797 - 4,857 - 262 = 12,838 and the number in the A_3S_2 cell is 30,501 - 11,799 - 12,838 = 5864. The last number in A_3S_3 can be determined from the S3 total as 11,513 - 4,454 - 4,857 = 2,202. The final result can be checked by showing that the A_3 total is 11,025. Thus the table is now

		Under 35 A_1	35-44 A_2	45 and over A_3	Total
Family practice	S_1	5,842	6,797	2,828	15,467
Internal medicine	S_2	11,799	12,838	5,864	30,501
Obstetrics/gynecology	S_3	4,454	4,857	2,202	11,513
Plastic Surgery	S_4	85	262	131	478
Total		22,180	24,754	11,025	57,959

(b) The number between 35 and 44 years old is 24,754.

(c) The number of plastic surgeons under 35 is 85.

(d) The number who are either plastic surgeons or who are under 35 is 478 + 22,180 - 85 = 22,573.

(e) The event of being neither a plastic surgeon nor under 35 is the complement of the event in part (d). Thus the number of such female physicians can be found as 57,959 - 22,573 = 35,386.

(f) The number not in family practice is 57,959 - 15,467 = 42,492.

4.59 (a) Y_3 is the event that the player has 6-10 years of experience. W_2 is the event that the player weighs between 200 and 300 pounds. $W_1\&Y_2$ is the event that the player has between 1 and 5 years of experience and weighs under 200 pounds.

(b) $P(Y_3) = 8/94 = 0.085$; $P(W_2) = 54/94 = 0.574$; $P(W_1\&Y_2) = 9/94 = 0.096$. Thus 8.5% of the players have 6-10 years of experience; 57.4% of the players weigh between 200 and 300 pounds; and 9.6% of the players have 1-5 years of experience and weigh under 200 pounds.

(c)

		Rookie Y_1	1-5 Y_2	6-10 Y_3	10+ Y_4	Total
Under 200	W_1	0.096	0.096	0.021	0.011	0.223
200-300	W_2	0.234	0.266	0.053	0.021	0.574
Over 300	W_3	0.117	0.074	0.011	0.000	0.202
Total		0.447	0.436	0.085	0.032	1.000

(d) The sum of each row and column of joint probabilities equals the marginal probability to within 0.001.

4.61 (a) S_2 is the event the physician is an internist; A_3 is the event the physician is 45 or over; and $S_1\&A_1$ is the event that the physician is in family practice and under 35.

(b) $P(S_2) = 30501/57959 = 0.526$; $P(A_3) = 11025/57959 = 0.190$; $P(S_1\&A_1) = 5842/57959 = 0.101$.

(c) Percentage Distribution

		Under 35 A_1	35-44 A_2	45 and over A_3	Total
Family practice	S_1	10.1	11.7	4.9	26.7
Internal medicine	S_2	20.4	22.2	10.1	52.6
Obstetrics/gynecology	S_3	7.7	8.4	3.8	19.9
Plastic Surgery	S_4	0.1	0.5	0.2	0.8
Total		38.3	42.7	19.0	100.0

4.63 (a) A member of the population (or sample) that belongs to category R_1 must also belong to one of the categories $C_1, C_2, \ldots, C_n$.

(b) The events $(R_1 \& C_1)$, $(R_1 \& C_2)$, ..., $(R_1 \& C_n)$ are mutually exclusive since no member of the population (or sample) can belong to more than one of the categories $C_1, C_2, \ldots, C_n$.

(c) We can conclude that this equation holds because of the special addition rule.

Exercises 4.5

4.65 (a) P(B) = 4/52 = 0.077; the probability of selecting a king from an ordinary deck of 52 playing cards is 0.077.

(b) P(B|A) = 4/12 = 0.333; given that the selection is made from among (the 12) face cards, the probability of selecting a king is 0.333.

(c) P(B|C) = 1/13 = 0.077; given that the selection is made from among (the 13) hearts, the probability of selecting a king is 0.077.

(d) P(B|(not A)) = 0/40 = 0; given that the selection is made from among (the 40) non-face cards, the probability of selecting a king is 0.

(e) P(A) = 12/52 = 0.231; the probability of selecting a face card from an ordinary deck of 52 playing cards is 0.231.

(f) P(A|B) = 4/4 = 1; given that the selection is made from among (the four) kings, the probability of selecting a face card is 1.

(g) P(A|C) = 3/13 = 0.231; since the selection is made from among (the 13) hearts, the probability of selecting a face card is 0.231.

(h) P(A|(not B)) = 8/48 = 0.167; given that the selection is made from among (the 48) non-kings, the probability of selecting a face card is 0.167.

4.67 (a) P(Rookie) = 42/94 = 0.447 (b) P(Over 300 pounds) = 19/94 = 0.202

(c) P(Rookie|Over 300 pounds) = 11/19 = 0.579

(d) P(Weighs over 300 pounds|Rookie) = 11/42 = 0.262

(e) Of the players, 44.7% are rookies and 20.2% weigh over 300 lbs; 57.9% of players who weigh over 300 lbs are rookies; 26.2% of the rookies weigh over 300 lbs.

4.69 (a) $P(L_2)$ = P(lives with spouse) = 0.529

(b) $P(A_4)$ = P(over 64) = 0.153

(c) $P(L_2 \& A_4)$ = P(lives with spouse and is over 64) = 0.084

(d) $P(L_2 | A_4)$ = P(lives with spouse|over 64) = $P(L_2 \& A_4)/P(A_4)$ = 0.084/0.153 = 0.549.

(e) $P(A_4 | L_2)$ = P(over 64|lives with spouse) = $P(L_2 \& A_4)/P(L_2)$ = 0.084/0.529 = 0.159

(f) Parts (a) - (e) are interpreted, respectively, as follows:

(a) the probability is 0.529 that the person selected lives with a spouse;

(b) the probability is 0.153 that the person selected is over 64;

(c) the probability is 0.084 that the person selected lives with a spouse and is over 64;

(d) the probability is 0.549 that the person selected lives with a spouse if the person is over 64;

(e) the probability is 0.159 that the person selected is over 64 if the person lives with a spouse.

4.71 (a) Answers will vary, but any experiment in which all possible outcomes are equally likely and can be counted will be included. For example, if two cards are dealt from a standard deck, P(two kings|at least one king) can be computed both directly and using the conditional probability rule.

(b) Answers will vary, but for any experiment in which outcomes are not equally likely or cannot be counted, only the conditional probability rule can be used. For example, P(Fleetfeet will win a horse race|Fleetfeet will finish third or better) cannot be computed directly since the possible outcomes are not equally likely.

Exercises 4.6

4.73 (a) General multiplication rule: P(A&B) = P(A)· P(B|A)

Conditional-probability rule: P(B|A) = P(A&B)/P(A)

(b) Multiplying both sides of the conditional probability rule by P(A) results in the general multiplication rule.

(c) When the marginal and conditional probabilities are known, we can use the general multiplication rule to obtain a joint probability. When the joint and marginal probabilities are known, we can use the conditional probability rule to obtain conditional probabilities.

4.75 The information given can be expressed as P(Regular User) = 0.36; P(Reduced Social Contact|Regular User) = 0.25; Let U = Regular User and R = Reduced Social Contact. We want to find

P(U & R) = P(R|U)P(U) = 0.25 x 0.36 = 0.09

In other words, 9% of Americans with Internet access are regular users who feel that the Web has reduced their social contact.

4.77 Let: D_i = Democrat on selection i, where i = 1, 2;

R_i = Republican on selection i, where i = 1,2;

I_i = Independent on selection i, where i = 1,2.

(a) $P(R_1 \& D_2) = (31/50)(17/49) = 0.2152$.

(b) $P(R_1 \& R_2) = (31/50)(30/49) = 0.380$.

(c)

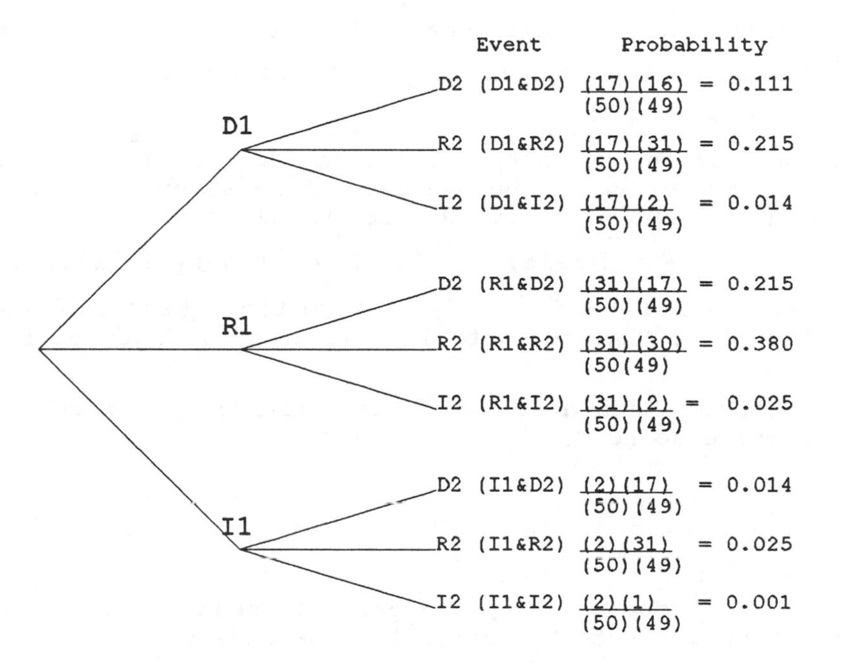

(d) The probability that both governors selected belong to the same party is

$P(R_1 \& R_2) + P(D_1 \& D_2) + P(I_1 \& I_2)$

$= [(31)(30) + (16)(16) + (2)(1)]/(50)(49) = 0.491.$

(e) P(one governor is Republican and one is Democrat)

$= P(R_1 \& D_2) + P(D_1 \& R_2) = 0.215 + 0.215 = 0.430$

4.79 (a) $P(A) = 18/36 = 0.5$; $P(B) = 18/36 = 0.5$;

$P(C) = 3/36 = 0.083$; $P(D) = 18/36 = 0.5$.

(b) $P(B|A) = 9/18 = 0.5$.

(c) Events A and B are independent because $P(B|A) = P(B)$.

(d) $P(C|A) = 2/18 = 0.111$

(e) Events A and C are not independent because $P(C|A) \neq P(C)$.

(f) $P(D|A) = 9/18 = 0.5$.

(g) Events A and D are independent because $P(D|A) = P(D)$.

4.81 Let A_i = draw an ace on selection i, where i = 1,2.

(a) If the first card is replaced before the second card is drawn:

$P(A_1 \& A_2) = (4/52)(4/52) = 0.006$.

(b) If the first card is not replaced before the second card is drawn:

$P(A_1 \& A_2) = (4/52)(3/51) = 0.005$.

4.83 Let:

$\overline{F}_i$ = non-failure of "criticality 1" item i, where i = 1, 2, ..., 748;

F_i = failure of "criticality 1" item i, where i = 1, 2, ..., 748.

Also, $P(\overline{F}_i) = 0.9999$ and $P(F_i) = 0.0001$.

(a) The probability that none of the "criticality 1" items would fail is

$P(\overline{F}_1)\cdot(P(\overline{F}_2)\cdot \ldots \cdot P(\overline{F}_{748}) = (0.9999)^{748} = 0.928$.

(b) The probability that at least one "criticality 1" item would fail is

1 - P(none of the "criticality 1" items would fail)

= 1 - 0.928 = 0.072.

(c) There was a 7.2% chance that at least one "criticality 1" item would fail. In other words, on the average, at least one "criticality 1" item will fail in 7.2 out of every 100 such missions.

4.85 Let: M = male; F = female; L = activity limitation.

Also, $P(L|M) = 0.136$ and $P(L|F) = 0.144$. Note that these probabilities are different. This means that activity limitation is influenced by a person's gender.

If gender and activity limitation were statistically independent, the following would have to hold:

$P(L|M) = P(L)$

and

$P(L|F) = P(L)$.

But P(L) is different depending upon a person's gender. Thus, gender and activity limitation are not statistically independent.

4.87 Four events A, B, C, and D are said to be independent if all of the following conditions hold:

P(A & B) = P(A)P(B)	P(A & B & C) = P(A)P(B)P(C)
P(A & C) = P(A)P(C)	P(A & B & D) = P(A)P(B)P(D)
P(A & D) = P(A)P(D)	P(A & C & D) = P(A)P(C)P(D)
P(B & C) = P(B)P(C)	P(B & C & D) = P(B)P(C)P(D)
P(B & D) = P(B)P(D)	
P(C & D) = P(C)P(D)	P(A & B & C & D) = P(A)P(B)P(C)P(D)

Four events A, B, C, and D are said to be independent if the special multiplication rule holds for all four events, all sets of three events, and all pairs of events.

4.89 We have

$$P(A) = \frac{8}{16} = \frac{1}{2} \quad P(B) = \frac{8}{16} = \frac{1}{2} \quad P(C) = \frac{4}{16} = \frac{1}{4}$$
$$P(A\&B) = \frac{4}{16} = \frac{1}{4} \quad P(A\&C) = \frac{2}{16} = \frac{1}{8} \quad P(B\&C) = \frac{2}{16} = \frac{1}{8}$$
$$P(A\&B\&C) = \frac{1}{16}$$

Therefore,

$$P(A\&B) = \frac{1}{4} = \frac{1}{2}\cdot\frac{1}{2} = P(A)P(B)$$
$$P(A\&C) = \frac{1}{8} = \frac{1}{2}\cdot\frac{1}{4} = P(A)P(C)$$
$$P(B\&C) = \frac{1}{8} = \frac{1}{2}\cdot\frac{1}{4} = P(B)P(C)$$

and
$$P(A\&B\&C) = \frac{1}{16} = \frac{1}{2}\cdot\frac{1}{2}\cdot\frac{1}{4} = P(A)P(B)P(C)$$

Consequently, the events A, B, and C are independent.

Exercises 4.7

4.91 (a) $P(R_3)$

(b) $P(S|R_3)$

(c) $P(R_3|S)$

4.93 (a) P(believe in aliens) = 0.54 · 0.48 + 0.33 · 0.52 = 0.431, so 43.1% of U.S. adults believe in aliens

(b) P(believe in aliens|woman) = 0.33; so 33% of women believe in aliens.

(c) P(woman|believe in aliens) = (0.33· 0.52)/.431 = 0.398; so 39.8% of adults who believe in aliens are women.

4.95 Let: M = sell more than projected P(M) = 0.10 P(R|M) = 0.70

C = sell close to projected P(C) = 0.30 P(R|C) = 0.50

L = sell less than projected P(L) = 0.60 P(R|L) = 0.20

R = revised for a second edition

(a) $P(R) = P(M)\cdot P(R|M) + P(C)\cdot P(R|C) + P(L)\cdot P(R|L)$

$= (0.10 \cdot 0.70) + (0.30 \cdot 0.50) + (0.60 \cdot 0.20) = 0.34$ or 34%

(b) $$P(L|R) = \frac{P(L\&R)}{P(R)} = \frac{P(L)P(R|L)}{P(R)} = \frac{(0.60)(0.20)}{0.34} = 0.353 \text{ or } 35.3\%$$

4.97 Let: 0B = zero broken eggs P(0B) = 0.785

1B = one broken egg P(1B) = 0.192

2B = two broken eggs P(2B) = 0.022

3B = three broken eggs P(3B) = 0.001

1SB = the one egg selected is found to be broken

$$P(1B|1SB) = \frac{P(1B)P(1SB|1B)}{P(0B)P(1SB|0B) + P(1B)P(1SB|1B) + P(2B)P(1SB|2B) + P(1B)P(1SB|1B)}$$

$$= \frac{(0.192)(0.083)}{(0.785)(0.000) + (0.192)(1/12) + (0.022)(2/12) + (0.001)(3/12)} = 0.803$$

4.99 Let: J = people interviewed that enjoy their job

P = people interviewed that enjoy their personal life

P(not J & not P) = 0.15 P(J & not P) = 0.80 P(J & P) = 0.04

(a) P(J) = P(J & P) + P(J & not P) = 0.04 + 0.80 = 0.84

84% of the people interviewed enjoy their jobs.

(b) P(P|J) = P(J & P)/P(J) = 0.04/0.84 = 0.048

4.8% of the people interviewed who enjoy their jobs also enjoy their personal lives.

4.101 (a) The diagram below shows three events that are mutually exclusive, but not exhaustive.

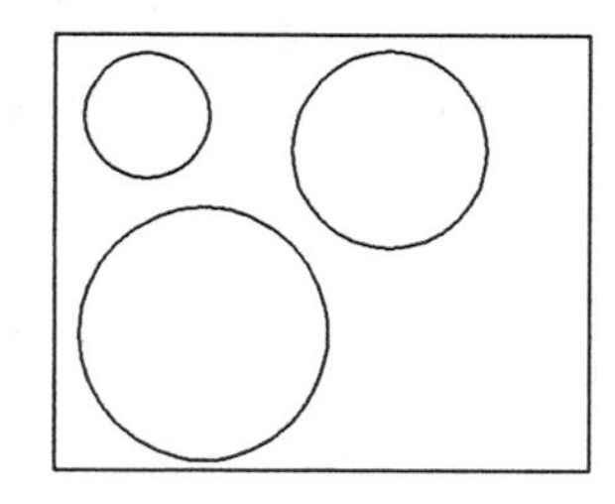

(b) In baseball, in one time at bat, a batter might strike out, get a base on balls, or get a hit. These are mutually exclusive, but not exhaustive since there are other things that could happen such as being hit by a pitch, getting on base on an error or a fielder's choice, or executing a sacrifice.

(c) The diagram below shows three events that are exhaustive, but not mutually exclusive. Event C overlaps both A and B (A is the left half of the rectangle and B is the right half.).

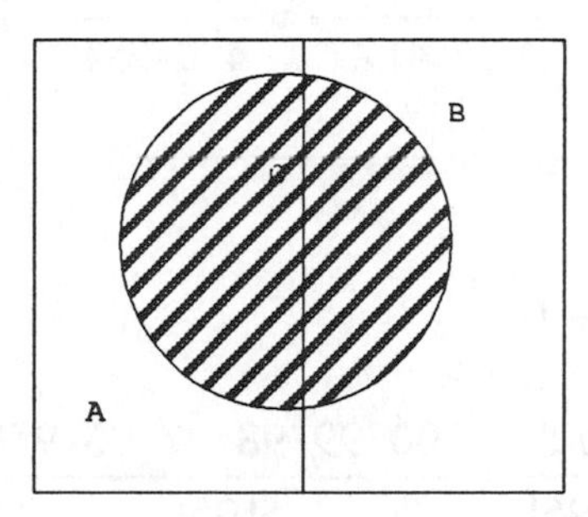

(d) A person selected at random could be male, female, or statistician. These are exhaustive, but since a statistician is either male or female, they are not mutually exclusive.

Exercises 4.8

4.103 The BCR is often referred to as the multiplication rule because the total number of possibilities in a multi-step process is the product of the numbers of ways each action can be carried out (as long as the number of ways for each action is constant and not dependent on how other actions are performed).

4.105 (a)

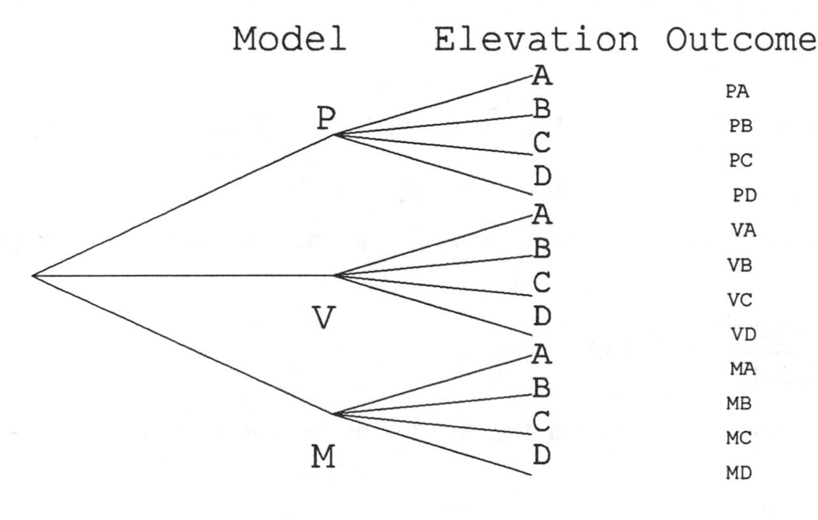

(b) There are 12 choices for the selection of a home.

(c) There are 3 ways to choose the model and 4 ways to choose the elevation, so there are $3 \cdot 4 = 12$ ways to choose the model and elevation.

4.107 There are $6 \cdot 8 \cdot 5 \cdot 19 \cdot 16 \cdot 14 = 1{,}021{,}440$ possibilities for answering all six questions.

4.109 There are $30 \cdot 29 \cdot 28 \cdot 27 = 657{,}720$ ways to make the four investments.

4.111 (a) $_7C_3 = \dfrac{7!}{3!(7-3)!} = \dfrac{7!}{3!4!} = \dfrac{7 \cdot 6 \cdot 5 \cdot 4!}{3!4!} = \dfrac{7 \cdot 6 \cdot 5}{3 \cdot 2 \cdot 1} = 35$

(b) $_5C_2 = \dfrac{5!}{2!(5-2)!} = \dfrac{5!}{2!3!} = \dfrac{5 \cdot 4 \cdot 3!}{2!3!} = \dfrac{5 \cdot 4}{2 \cdot 1} = 10$

(c) $_8C_4 = \dfrac{8!}{4!(8-4)!} = \dfrac{8!}{4!4!} = \dfrac{8\cdot7\cdot6\cdot5\cdot4!}{4!4!} = \dfrac{8\cdot7\cdot6\cdot5}{4\cdot3\cdot2\cdot1} = 70$

(d) $_6C_0 = \dfrac{6!}{0!(6-0)!} = \dfrac{6!}{0!6!} = 1$

(e) $_9C_9 = \dfrac{9!}{9!(9-9)!} = \dfrac{9!}{9!0!} = 1$

4.113 (a) $_{100}C_5 = \dfrac{100!}{5!(100-5)!} = \dfrac{100!}{5!95!} = \dfrac{100\cdot99\cdot98\cdot97\cdot96\cdot95!}{5!95!} = \dfrac{100\cdot99\cdot98\cdot97\cdot96}{5\cdot4\cdot3\cdot2\cdot1} = 75{,}287{,}520$

(b) $_{50}C_5 \cdot 2^5 = \dfrac{50!}{5!(50-5)!}\cdot 32 = 67{,}800{,}320$

(c) The probability that no state will have both of its senators on the committee is the answer in part (b) divided by the answer in part (a), which is 67,800,320/75,287,520 = 0.901.

4.115 You have eight tries to find the right key. Each try has the same probability of occurrence.

(a) The probability that you get the right key on the first try is 1/8.

(b) The probability that you get the key right on the last try is 1/8.

$$P(F_1F_2F_3F_4F_5F_6F_7S_8) = \frac{7\cdot6\cdot5\cdot4\cdot3\cdot2\cdot1\cdot1}{8\cdot7\cdot6\cdot5\cdot4\cdot3\cdot2\cdot1} = \frac{1}{8}$$

(c) The probability that you get the right key on or before the fifth try is 5(1/8) = 5/8.

P(S) + P(FS) + P(FFS) + P(FFFS) + P(FFFFS) = 5(1/8) = 5/8.

4.117 Given 365 days in a year and 38 students, the probability that no two students have the same birthday is

$$\frac{365!}{(365-38)!}/365^{38} = \frac{3.1655642\text{x}10^{96}}{23.287820\text{x}10^{96}} = 0.1359$$

The probability that at least two students in the class have the same birthday is then 1- 0.1359 = 0.8641.

4.119 There are 15 true-false questions.

(a) The probability of getting at least one question correct is

$$1-\frac{_{15}C_0}{2^{15}} = 1-\frac{1}{32768} = 0.99997$$

(b) Getting a 60% or better on the exam means getting nine or more questions correct. The required calculations are

$_{15}C_9 / 32768 = 0.1527$ $\quad$ $_{15}C_{13} / 32768 = 0.0032$

$_{15}C_{10} / 32768 = 0.0916$ $\quad$ $_{15}C_{14} / 32768 = 0.0005$

$_{15}C_{11} / 32768 = 0.0417$ $\quad$ $_{15}C_{15} / 32768 = 0.0000$

$_{15}C_{12} / 32768 = 0.0139$

The probability of a 60% or better is the sum of the seven items above, or 0.304.

4.121 Given 365 days in a year and N students, the probability that at least two students have the same birthday is

$$1-\left[\frac{365!}{(365-N)!}/365^N\right]$$

4.123 If the values for N = 2, 3, ..., 70 are successively substituted into the formula in Exercise 4.121, we obtain a table giving the probability that at least two of the students in the class have the same birthday, for N = 2, 3, ..., 70.

N	Probability	N	Probability	N	Probability
2	0.003	25	0.569	48	0.961
3	0.008	26	0.598	49	0.966
4	0.016	27	0.627	50	0.970
5	0.027	28	0.654	51	0.974
6	0.040	29	0.681	52	0.978
7	0.056	30	0.706	53	0.981
8	0.074	31	0.730	54	0.984
9	0.095	32	0.753	55	0.986
10	0.117	33	0.775	56	0.988
11	0.141	34	0.795	57	0.990
12	0.167	35	0.814	58	0.992
13	0.194	36	0.832	59	0.993
14	0.223	37	0.849	60	0.994
15	0.253	38	0.864	61	9.995
16	0.284	39	0.878	62	0.996
17	0.315	40	0.891	63	0.997
18	0.347	41	0.903	64	0.997
19	0.379	42	0.914	65	0.998
20	0.411	43	0.924	66	0.998
21	0.444	44	0.933	67	0.998
22	0.476	45	0.941	68	0.999
23	0.507	46	0.948	69	0.999
24	0.538	47	0.955	70	0.999

REVIEW TEST FOR CHAPTER 4

1. Probability theory enables us to control and evaluate the likelihood that a statistical inference is correct, and it provides the mathematical basis for statistical inference.

2. (a) The equal-likelihood model is used for computing probabilities when an experiment has N possible outcomes, all equally likely.

   (b) If an experiment has N equally likely possible outcomes and an event can occur in f ways, then the probability of the event is f/N.

3. In the frequentist interpretation of probability, the probability of an event is the relative frequency of the event in a large number of repetitions of the experiment.

4. The numbers (b) -0.047 and (c) 3.5 cannot be probabilities because probabilities must always be between 0 and 1.

5. The Venn diagram is a common graphical technique used for portraying events and relationships between events.

6. Two or more events are mutually exclusive if no two of the events have any outcomes in common, i.e., no two of the events can occur at the same time.

7. (a) P(E)

   (b) P(E) = 0.436

8. (a) False. For any two events, the probability that one or the other occurs equals the sum of the two individual probabilities minus the probability that both events occur.

   (b) True. Either the event occurs or it doesn't. Therefore, the probability that the event occurs plus the probability that it doesn't occur equals 1. Thus the probability that it occurs is 1 minus the probability that it doesn't occur.

9. Frequently, it is quicker to compute the probability of the complement of an event than it is to compute the probability of the event itself. The complement rule allows one to use the probability of the complement to obtain the probability of the event itself.

10. (a) Data obtained by observing values of one variable of a population are called <u>univariate</u> data.

    (b) Data obtained by observing values of two variables of a population are call <u>bivariate</u> data.

    (c) A frequency distribution for bivariate data is call a <u>contingency table</u>.

11. The sum of the joint probabilities in a row or column of a joint probability distribution equals the <u>marginal</u> probability in that row or column.

12. (a) P(B|A)

    (b) A

13. Conditional probabilities can sometimes be computed directly as f/N or by using the formula P(B|A) = P(A&B)/P(A).

14. The joint probability of two independent events is the product of their marginal probabilities.

15. If two or more events have the property that at least one of them must occur when the experiment is performed, then the events are said to be <u>exhaustive</u>.

16. If r actions are to be performed in a definite order and there are m_1 possibilities for the first action, m_2 possibilities for the second action, ..., and m_r possibilities for the rth action, then there are $m_1 \, m_2 \, m_3 \ldots m_r$

possibilities altogether for the r actions.

17. (a) ABC ACB BAC BCA CAB CBA

ABD ADB BAD BDA DAB DBA

ACD ADC CAD CDA DAC DCA

BCD BDC CBD CDB DBC DCB

(b) ABC ABD ACD BCD

(c) ${}_4P_3 = 24$ ${}_4C_3 = 24$

(d) ${}_4P_3 = 4!/(4-1)! = 24$ ${}_4C_3 = 4!/3!(4-3)! = 4$

18. (a) $P(A) = \dfrac{28269}{122423} = 0.231$

(b) $\text{P(D or E or F)} = \text{P(D)} + \text{P(E)} + \text{P(F)} = \dfrac{12967 + 9788 + 21635}{122423} = \dfrac{44390}{122423} = 0.363$

(c)

Event	Probability
A	0.231
B	0.201
C	0.147
D	0.106
E	0.080
F	0.177
G	0.059

19. (a) (not J) is the event that the return selected shows an adjusted gross income of at least $100,000. There are 7,186 thousand such returns.

(b) (H & I) is the event that the return selected shows an adjusted gross income of between $20,000 and $50,000. There are 40,765 thousand such returns.

(c) (H or K) is the event that the return selected shows an adjusted gross income of at least $20,000. There are 69,586 thousand such returns.

(d) (H & K) is the event that the return selected shows an adjusted gross income of between $50,000 and $100,000. There are 21,635 thousand such returns.

20. (a) Events H and I are not mutually exclusive. They have events C, D, and E in common.

(b) Events I and K are mutually exclusive. They have no events in common.

(c) Events H and (not J) are mutually exclusive. They have no events in common.

(d) Events H, (not J), and K are not mutually exclusive. While H and (not J) have no events in common, a part of K (i.e., event F) is common to event H, and the other part of K (i.e., event G) is common to event (not J).

21. (a)

$$P(H) = \frac{18010 + 12967 + 9788 + 21635}{122423} = \frac{62400}{122423} = 0.510$$

$$P(I) = \frac{28269 + 24568 + 18010 + 12967 + 9788}{122423} = \frac{93602}{122423} = 0.765$$

$$P(J) = \frac{122423 - 7186}{122423} = \frac{115237}{122423} = 0.941$$

$$P(K) = \frac{21635 + 7186}{122423} = \frac{28821}{122423} = 0.235$$

(b) H = (C or D or E or F)

I = (A or B or C or D or E)

J = (A or B or C or D or E or F)

K = (F or G)

(c) P(H) = P(C) + P(D) + P(E) + P(F) = 0.147 + 0.106 + 0.080 + 0.177 = 0.510

P(I) = P(A) + P(B) + P(C) + P(D) + P(E) = 0.231 + 0.201 + 0.147 + 0.106 + 0.080 = 0.765

P(J) = P(A) + P(B) + P(C) + P(D) + P(E) + P(F) = 0.231 + 0.201 + 0.147 + 0.106 + 0.080 + 0.177 = 0.942

P(K) = P(F) + P(G) = 0.177 + 0.059 = 0.236

22. (a)

$$P(\text{not } J) = \frac{7186}{122423} = 0.059$$

$$P(H \& I) = \frac{40765}{122423} = 0.333$$

$$P(H \text{ or } K) = \frac{69586}{122423} = 0.568$$

$$P(H \& K) = \frac{21635}{122423} = 0.177$$

(b) P(J) = 1 - P(not J) = 1 - 0.059 = 0.941

(c) P(H or K) = P(H) + P(K) - P(H & K) = 0.510 + 0.235 - 0.177 = 0.568.

(d) The answer in (c) agrees with that in (a).

23. (a) The contingency table has six cells.

(b) There are 14,903 thousand students in high school.

(c) There are 59,066 thousand students in public schools.

(d) There are 3,263 thousand students in private colleges.

24. (a) (i) L_3 = the student selected is in college;

(ii) T_1 = the student selected attends a public school;

(iii) (T_1 & L_3) = the student selected attends a public college.

(b)

$$P(L_3) = \frac{14889}{68335} = 0.218$$

$$P(T_1) = \frac{59066}{68335} = 0.864$$

$$P(T_1 \& L_3) = \frac{11626}{68335} = 0.170$$

The interpretation of each result above as a percentage is as follows: 21.8% of students attend college, 86.4% attend public schools, and 17.0% attend public colleges.

(c)

Level	Type: Public T_1	Private T_2	$P(L_i)$
Elementary L_1	0.496	0.068	0.564
High School L_2	0.198	0.020	0.218
College L_3	0.170	0.048	0.218
$P(T_j)$	0.864	0.136	1.000

(d) $P(T_1 \text{ or } L_3) = (33903 + 13537 + 11626 + 3263)/68335 = 0.912$

(e) $P(T_1 \text{ or } L_3) = P(T_1) + P(L_3) - P(T_1 \& L_3) = 0.864 + 0.218 - 0.170 = 0.912$.

25. (a) $P(L_3|T_1) = \frac{11626}{59066} = 0.197$

19.7% of students attending public schools are in college.

(b) $P(L_3|T_1) = \frac{P(L_3 \& T_1)}{P(T_1)} = \frac{0.170}{0.864} = 0.197$

26. (a) $P(T_2) = \frac{9269}{68335} = 0.136$; $P(T_2|L_2) = \frac{1366}{14903} = 0.092$

(b) For L_2 and T_2 to be independent, $P(T_2|L_2)$ must equal $P(T_2)$. From part (a), however, we see that this is not the case. In terms of percentages, these probabilities, respectively, indicate that 9.2% of high school students attend private schools, whereas 13.6% of all students attend private schools.

(c) Events L_2 and T_2 are not mutually exclusive. From Table 4.170 we see that both events can occur simultaneously. There are 1,366 thousand students who attend a private high school.

(d) Let: L_1 = a student is in elementary school;

T_1 = a student attends public school.

For L_1 and T_1 to be independent, $P(L_1|T_1)$ must equal $P(L_1)$. But, $P(L_1) = 0.564$ and $P(L_1|T_1) = 0.496/0.864 = 0.574$. Since $P(L_1|T_1) \neq P(L_1)$, the event that a student is in elementary school is *not* independent of the event that a student attends public school.

27. Let MA1, MP1, and MS1 denote, respectively, the events that the first student selected received a master of arts, a master of public administration, and a master of science; and let MA2, MP2, and MS2 denote, respectively, the events that the second student selected received a master of arts, a master of public administration, and a master of science.

(a) $P(\text{MA1\& MS2}) = \frac{3}{50} \cdot \frac{19}{49} = 0.023$

(b) $P(\text{MP1\& MP2}) = \frac{28}{50} \cdot \frac{27}{49} = 0.309$

(c)

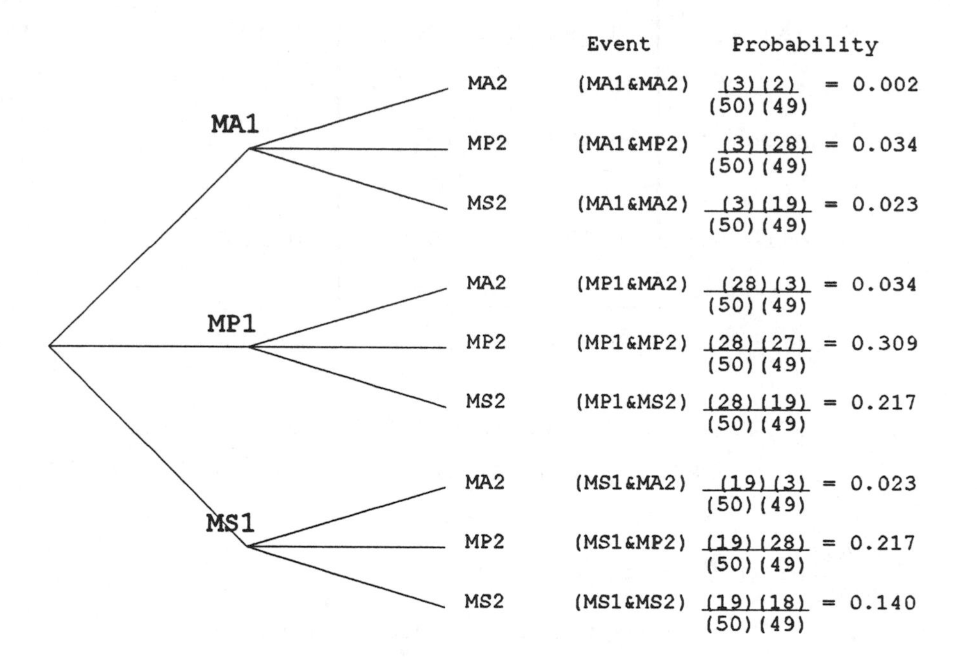

(d) P(MA1 & MA2) + P(MP1 & MP2) + P(MS1 & MS2)

= 0.002 + 0.309 + 0.140 = 0.451 .

28. Let F = event that pairs raised their offspring to the Fledgling stage, and D = event that pairs divorced. The given information is

P(D) = 0.63, P(D|F) = 0.81, P(D|not F) = 0.43.

(a) We are trying to find P(Offspring died) = P(not F). The total probability rule states that

P(D) = P(D|F)P(F) + P(D|not F)P(not F) or

P(D) = P(D|F)P(F) + P(D|not F)[1 - P(F)]. Substituting known values,

0.63 = (0.81)P(F) + (0.43)[1 - P(F)] or

0.20 = 0.38 P(F). Thus

P(F) = 0.20/0.38 = 0.526. Therefore P(not F) = 1 - 0.526 = 0.474.

(b) We can use the multiplication rule to find

P(D & not F) = P(D|not F)P(not F) = (0.43)(1 - 0.20/0.38) = 0.203684

Thus 20.4% divorced and had offspring that died.

(c) P(not F|D) = P(D & not F)/P(D) = (0.203684)/(0.63) = 0.323

Thus, among those that divorced, 32.3% had offspring that died.

29. (a) Let C_i be the event that the ith man selected is color blind.

P(none color blind) = P{(not C_1) & (not C_2) & (not C_3) & (not C_4)} =

P(not C_1)P(not C_2)P(not C_3)P(not C_4) = 0.91^4 = 0.686

(b) P{(not C_1)& (not C_2)& (not C_3)& (C_4)} =

P(not C_1)P(not C_2)P(not C_3)P(C_4) = 0.91· 0.91· 0.91· 0.09 = 0.068

(c) There are four sequences like the one in part (b) in which one of the men is color blind. The others have the first man color blind and the others not; the second color blind and the others not; and the third color blind and the others not. Each sequence has the same probability as the one in part (b). Thus P(exactly one man is color blind) is

4 · 0.91· 0.91· 0.91· 0.09 = 0.271

30. (a) No. A&B has a probability of 0.2. Thus A and B can occur together.

(b) Yes. P(A&B) = P(A)P(B).

31. Let: A1 = Driver is 16-20 years old

A2 = Driver is 21-24 years old

A3 = Driver is 25-34 years old

A4 = Driver is 35-44 years old

A5 = Driver is 45-64 years old

A6 = Driver is 65 years old or older

B = Driver has BAC of 0.10% or greater

(a) P(B|A2) = 0.278

(b)

$$P(B) = \sum P(B|A_i)P(A_i)$$
$$= (0.127)(0.141) + (0.278)(0.114) + \ldots + (0.050)(0.114) = 0.192$$

(c) P(A2|B) = P(A2&B)/P(B) = P(B|A2)P(A2)/P(B) = (0.278)(0.114)/0.192 = 0.165

(d) Thus 27.8% of drivers aged 21-24 at fault in fatal crashes had a BAC of 0.10% or greater; 19.2% of all drivers at fault in fatal crashes had a BAC of 0.10% or greater; and of those drivers at fault in fatal crashes with a BAC of 0.10% or greater, 16.5% were in the 21-24 age group.

(e) The probabilities in parts (a) and (b) are prior; the probability in part (c) is posterior because it represents the probability that the person selected was in the 21-24 age group **after** knowing that the person has a BAC over 0.10%.

32. (a) $_{12}C_2 = \frac{12!}{2!10!} = \frac{12 \cdot 11}{2 \cdot 1} = 66$

(b) $_{12}P_3 = \dfrac{12!}{(12-3)!} = 12 \cdot 11 \cdot 10 = 1320$

(c) (i) $_8C_2 = \dfrac{8!}{2!6!} = \dfrac{8 \cdot 7}{2 \cdot 1} = 28$

(ii) $_8P_3 = \dfrac{8!}{(8-3)!} = 8 \cdot 7 \cdot 6 = 336$

33. (a) $_{52}C_{13} = \dfrac{52!}{13!(52-13)!} = 635{,}013{,}559{,}600$

(b)
$$\frac{_4C_2 \, _{48}C_{11}}{_{52}C_{13}} = \frac{\dfrac{4!}{2!(4-2)!} \cdot \dfrac{48!}{11!(48-11)!}}{\dfrac{52!}{13!(52-13)!}} = 0.213$$

(c) With four choices for the eight-card suit, three choices for the four-card suit, and two choices for the one-card suit, the probability of being dealt an 8-4-1 distribution is

$$4 \cdot 3 \cdot 2 \cdot \frac{_{13}C_8 \cdot {}_{13}C_4 \cdot {}_{13}C_1 \cdot {}_{13}C_0}{_{52}C_{13}} = 24 \cdot \frac{\dfrac{13!}{8!(13-8)!} \cdot \dfrac{13!}{4!(13-4)!} \cdot \dfrac{13!}{1!(13-1)!} \cdot \dfrac{13!}{0!(13-0)!}}{635{,}013{,}559{,}600}$$
$$= 24 \cdot \frac{1287 \cdot 715 \cdot 13 \cdot 1}{635{,}013{,}559{,}600} = 24 \cdot \frac{11{,}962{,}665}{635{,}013{,}559{,}600} = 0.00045$$

(d) Initially, two suits from among the four are to be selected, from each of which five cards are drawn. From the remaining two suits, one is to be selected from which two cards are drawn. Finally, only one suit remains from which to draw the final card. The probability of being dealt a 5-5-2-1 distribution is

$$_4C_2 \cdot {}_2C_1 \cdot {}_1C_1 \cdot \frac{_{13}C_5 \cdot {}_{13}C_5 \cdot {}_{13}C_2 \cdot {}_{13}C_1}{_{52}C_{13}} = 12 \cdot \frac{\dfrac{13!}{5!(13-5)!} \cdot \dfrac{13!}{5!(13-5)!} \cdot \dfrac{13!}{2!(13-2)!} \cdot \dfrac{13!}{1!(13-1)!}}{635{,}013{,}559{,}600}$$
$$= 12 \cdot \frac{1287 \cdot 1287 \cdot 78 \cdot 13}{635{,}013{,}559{,}600} = 12 \cdot \frac{1{,}679{,}558{,}166}{635{,}013{,}559{,}600} = 0.032$$

(e) The probability of being dealt a hand void in a specified suit is

$$\frac{_{39}C_{13} \cdot {}_{13}C_0}{_{52}C_{13}} = \frac{\dfrac{39!}{13!(39-13)!} \cdot \dfrac{13!}{0!(13-0)!}}{\dfrac{52!}{13!(52-13)!}} = 0.013$$

CHAPTER 5 ANSWERS

Exercises 5.1

5.1 (a) probability

(b) probability

5.3 The notation {X=3} denotes the event that occurs when a student has three siblings. P(X=3) denotes the probability of the event that the student will have three siblings. Another way of thinking about the difference is that the first is a set and the second is a number between zero and one.

5.5 This table will resemble the probability distribution of the random variable.

5.7 (a) X = 2, 3, 4, 5, 6, 7, 8

(b) {X = 7}

(c) P(X = 4) = 2/96 = 0.021

2.1% of the shuttle crews consist of exactly four people.

(d)

Size of Crew x	Probability P(X=x)
2	0.042
3	0.010
4	0.021
5	0.375
6	0.188
7	0.344
8	0.021

(e)

5.9 (a) {X = 4} (b) $\{X \geq 2\}$ (c) {X < 5} (d) $\{2 \leq X < 5\}$

(e) P(X = 4) = 0.212

(f) $P(X \geq 2)$ = P(X = 2) + P(X = 3) + P(X = 4) + P(X = 5) + P(X = 6)

= 0.078 + 0.155 + 0.212 + 0.262 + 0.215 = 0.922

(g) P(X < 5) = P(X = 0) + P(X = 1) + P(X = 2) + P(X = 3) + P(X = 4)

= 0.029 + 0.049 + 0.078 + 0.155 + 0.212 = 0.523

(h) $P(2 \leq X < 5)$ = P(X = 2) + P(X = 3) + P(X = 4)

= 0.078 + 0.155 + 0.212 = 0.445

5.11 $P(Z \leq 1.96) + P(Z > 1.96) = 1$.

Since $P(Z > 1.96) = 0.025$,

$P(Z \leq 1.96) + 0.025 = 1$, or

$P(Z \leq 1.96) = 1 - 0.025 = 0.975$.

5.13 (a) $P(X \leq c) + P(X > c) = 1$.

Since $P(X > c) = \alpha$,

$P(X \leq c) + \alpha = 1$, or

$P(X \leq c) = 1 - \alpha$.

(b) $P(Y < -c) + P(-c \leq Y \leq c) + P(Y > c) = 1$.

Since $P(Y < -c) = P(Y > c) = \alpha/2$,

$\alpha/2 + P(-c \leq Y \leq c) + \alpha/2 = 1$, or

$P(-c \leq Y \leq c) = 1 - \alpha/2 - \alpha/2 = 1 - \alpha$.

(c) $P(T < -c) + P(-c \leq T \leq c) + P(T > c) = 1$.

Since $P(-c \leq T \leq c) = 1 - \alpha$,

$P(T < -c) + (1 - \alpha) + P(T > c) = 1$, or

$P(T < -c) + P(T > c) = 1 - 1 + \alpha = \alpha$.

Since $P(T < -c) = P(T > c)$,

$2 \cdot [P(T > c)] = \alpha$ or $P(T > c) = \alpha/2$.

Exercises 5.2

5.15 The mean of a discrete random variable generalizes the concept of a population mean.

5.17 The required calculations are

x	P(X=x)	xP(X=x)	x^2	x^2 P(X=x)
2	0.042	0.084	4.000	0.168
3	0.010	0.030	9.000	0.090
4	0.021	0.084	16.000	0.336
5	0.375	1.875	25.000	9.375
6	0.188	1.128	36.000	6.768
7	0.344	2.408	49.000	16.856
8	0.021	0.168	64.000	1.344
		5.777		34.937

(a) $\mu_x = \Sigma xP(X=x) = 5.777$. The average number of persons in a shuttle crew is about 5.8.

(b) $\sigma_x = \sqrt{\sum x^2 P(X=x) - \mu_x^2} = \sqrt{34.937 - 5.777^2} = 1.250$

(c)

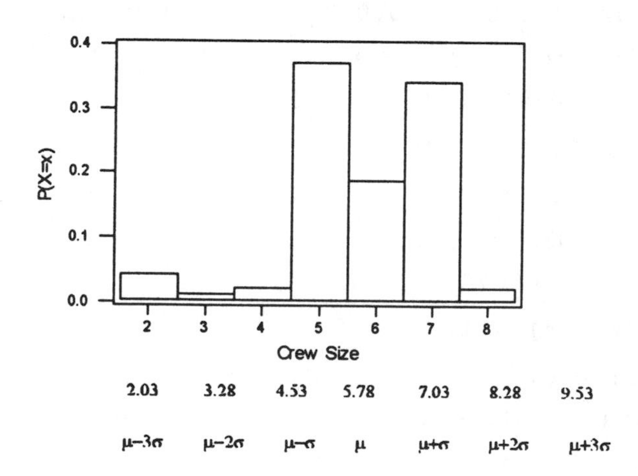

5.19 (a)

$$P(X=1)=\frac{18}{38}=0.474$$

$$P(X=-1)=\frac{20}{38}=0.526;\ \ 0.474+0.526=1.000$$

(b) $\mu = \Sigma x \cdot P(X=x) = (1)(0.474) + (-1)(0.526) = -0.052$

(c) On the average, you will lose 5.2¢ per play.

(d) If you bet $1 on red 100 times, you can expect to lose 100 · 0.052 = $5.20. If you bet $1 on red 1000 times, you can expect to lose $52.00.

(e) Roulette is not a profitable game for a person to play. Parts (c) and (d) demonstrate that, no matter how much you play, you can expect to lose. Also, part (a) shows that a higher probability is associated with losing rather than winning.

5.21

w	P(W=w)	w·P(w)	w^2	w^2·P(W=w)
0	0.80	0.00	0	0.00
1	0.15	0.15	1	0.15
2	0.05	0.10	4	0.20
		0.25		0.35

(a)

$$\mu_w=\sum wP(W=w)=0.25$$

$$\sigma_w=\sqrt{\sum w^2P(W=w)-\mu_w^2}=\sqrt{0.35-(0.25)^2}=\sqrt{0.2875}=0.536.$$

(b) On the average, there are 0.25 breakdowns per day.

(c) Assuming 250 work days per year, the number of breakdowns expected per year is (0.25)(250) = 62.5.

5.23

500w	P(500w)	500w·P(500w)	$(500w)^2$	$(500w)^2$·P(500w)
0	0.80	0.00	0	0
500	0.15	75.00	250,000	37500
1000	0.05	50.00	1,000,000	50000
		125.00		87500

(a) Columns 1 and 2 comprise the probability distribution of the random variable 500W. We have used P(500y) for P(500Y = 500y) in the table headings.

(b) Column 3 of the previous table provides the calculations for the mean: μ_{500w} = $125.00.

(c) $\mu_{500w} = 500\mu_w$

(d) Columns 4 and 5 of the previous table provide the calculations for the standard deviation.

$$\sigma_{500w} = \sqrt{87500 - 125^2} = 268.1 = 500(0.536)$$

(e) $\sigma_{500W} = 500\sigma_W$.

(f) The mean of a constant times a random variable equals the constant times the mean of the random variable. The standard deviation of a constant times a random variable equals the absolute value of the constant times the standard deviation of the random variable.

Exercises 5.3

5.25 (1) Randomly selected pieces of identical rope are tested by subjecting each to a 1000 pound force. Each rope either breaks or it doesn't. (2) People are selected at random by ticket numbers at a large convention and their gender is noted. Each is either male or female.

5.27 $3! = 3 \cdot 2 \cdot 1 = 6$; $7! = 7 \cdot 6 \cdot 5 \cdot 4 \cdot 3 \cdot 2 \cdot 1 = 5{,}040$;

$8! = 8 \cdot 7 \cdot 6 \cdot 5 \cdot 4 \cdot 3 \cdot 2 \cdot 1 = 40{,}320$; $9! = 9 \cdot 8 \cdot 7 \cdot 6 \cdot 5 \cdot 4 \cdot 3 \cdot 2 \cdot 1 = 362{,}880$

5.29 (a) $\binom{5}{3} = \frac{5!}{3!(5-3)!} = \frac{5 \cdot 4 \cdot 3 \cdot 2 \cdot 1}{3 \cdot 2 \cdot 1 \cdot 2 \cdot 1} = 10$

(b) $\binom{10}{0} = \frac{10!}{0!(10-0)!} = \frac{10 \cdot 9 \cdot 8 \cdot 7 \cdot 6 \cdot 5 \cdot 4 \cdot 3 \cdot 2 \cdot 1}{1 \cdot 10 \cdot 9 \cdot 8 \cdot 7 \cdot 6 \cdot 5 \cdot 4 \cdot 3 \cdot 2 \cdot 1} = 1$

(c) $\binom{10}{10} = \frac{10!}{10!(10-10)!} = \frac{10 \cdot 9 \cdot 8 \cdot 7 \cdot 6 \cdot 5 \cdot 4 \cdot 3 \cdot 2 \cdot 1}{10 \cdot 9 \cdot 8 \cdot 7 \cdot 6 \cdot 5 \cdot 4 \cdot 3 \cdot 2 \cdot 1 \cdot 1} = 1$

(d) $\binom{9}{5} = \frac{9!}{5!(9-5)!} = \frac{9 \cdot 8 \cdot 7 \cdot 6 \cdot 5 \cdot 4 \cdot 3 \cdot 2 \cdot 1}{5 \cdot 4 \cdot 3 \cdot 2 \cdot 1 \cdot 4 \cdot 3 \cdot 2 \cdot 1} = 126$

5.31 (a) $p = 0.2$

(b)

Outcome	Probability
ssss	(0.2)(0.2)(0.2)(0.2)=0.0016
sssf	(0.2)(0.2)(0.2)(0.8)=0.0064
ssfs	(0.2)(0.2)(0.8)(0.2)=0.0064
ssff	(0.2)(0.2)(0.8)(0.8)=0.0256
sfss	(0.2)(0.8)(0.2)(0.2)=0.0064
sfsf	(0.2)(0.8)(0.2)(0.8)=0.0256
sffs	(0.2)(0.8)(0.8)(0.2)=0.0256
sfff	(0.2)(0.8)(0.8)(0.8)=0.1024
fsss	(0.8)(0.2)(0.2)(0.2)=0.0064
fssf	(0.8)(0.2)(0.2)(0.8)=0.0256
fsfs	(0.8)(0.2)(0.8)(0.2)=0.0256
fsff	(0.8)(0.2)(0.8)(0.8)=0.1024
ffss	(0.8)(0.8)(0.2)(0.2)=0.0256
ffsf	(0.8)(0.8)(0.2)(0.8)=0.1024
fffs	(0.8)(0.8)(0.8)(0.2)=0.1024
ffff	(0.8)(0.8)(0.8)(0.8)=0.4096

(c)

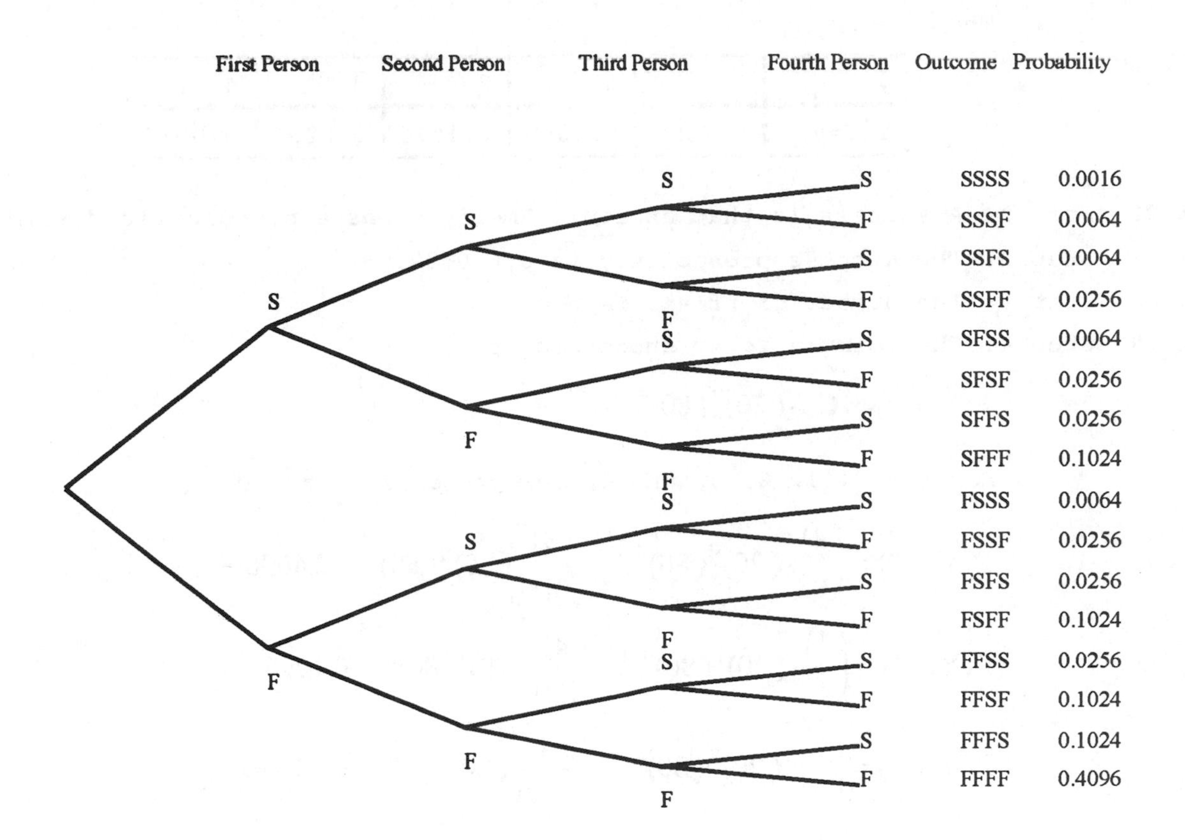

(d) **The outcomes in which exactly three of the four people have a psychiatric disorder are sssf, ssfs, sfss, and fsss.**

(e) **Each outcome in part (d) has probability 0.0064. This probability is the same for each outcome because each probability is obtained by multiplying three success probabilities of 0.2 and one failure probability of 0.8.**

(f) P(exactly three have a psychiatric disorder)

= P(sssf)+ P(ssfs)+ P(sfss)+ P(fsss)

= 0.0064 + 0.0064 + 0.0064 + 0.0064 = 0.0256

(g) P(exactly zero have a psychiatric disorder) = P(ffff) = 0.4096

P(exactly one has a psychiatric disorder)

= P(fffs)+ P(ffsf)+ P(fsff)+ P(sfff)

= 0.1024 + 0.1024 + 0.1024 + 0.1024 = 0.4096

P(exactly two have a psychiatric disorder)

= P(ssff) + P(sfsf) + P(sffs) + P(fssf) + P(fsfs) + P(ffss)

= 0.0256 + 0.0256 + 0.0256 + 0.0256 + 0.0256 + 0.0256 = 0.1536

P(exactly four have a psychiatric disorder) = P(ssss) = 0.0016

Thus

y	0	1	2	3	4
P(Y=y)	0.4096	0.4096	0.1536	0.0256	0.0016

5.33 Step 1: A success is that an adult American has a psychiatric disorder.

Step 2: The success probability is p = 0.20.

Step 3: The number of trials is n = 4.

Step 4: The formula for y successes is

$$P(Y=y)={}_4C_y \cdot (.20)^y (.80)^{4-y} .$$

For y = 0, 1, 2, 3, and 4, the probabilities are

$$P(Y=0)=\binom{4}{0}\cdot(.20)^0(.80)^{4-0}=\frac{4!}{0!4!}(.20)^0(.80)^4=0.4096$$

$$P(Y=1)=\binom{4}{1}\cdot(.20)^1(.80)^{4-1}=\frac{4!}{1!3!}(.20)^1(.80)^3=0.4096$$

$$P(Y=2)=\binom{4}{2}\cdot(.20)^2(.80)^{4-2}=\frac{4!}{2!2!}(.20)^2(.80)^2=0.1536$$

$$P(Y=3)=\binom{4}{3}\cdot(.20)^3(.80)^{4-3}=\frac{4!}{3!1!}(.20)^3(.80)^1=0.0256$$

$$P(Y=4)=\binom{4}{4}\cdot(.20)^4(.80)^{4-4}=\frac{4!}{4!0!}(.20)^4(.80)^0=0.0016$$

5.35 The calculations required to answer all parts of this exercise are

$$P(0)=\binom{5}{0}\cdot(.67)^0(.33)^5=0.004 \quad P(3)=\binom{5}{3}\cdot(.67)^3(.33)^2=0.328$$

$$P(1)=\binom{5}{1}\cdot(.67)^1(.33)^4=0.040 \quad P(4)=\binom{5}{4}\cdot(.67)^4(.33)^1=0.332$$

$$P(2)=\binom{5}{2}\cdot(.67)^2(.33)^3=0.161 \quad P(5)=\binom{5}{5}\cdot(.67)^5(.33)^0=0.135$$

(a) P(2) = 0.161 (b) P(4) = 0.332

(c) $P(X \geq 4)$ = P(4) + P(5) = 0.332 + 0.135 = 0.467.

(d) $P(2 \leq X \leq 4)$ = P(2) + P(3) + P(4) = 0.161 + 0.328 + 0.332 = 0.821

(e)

x	P(X=x)
0	0.004
1	0.040
2	0.161
3	0.328
4	0.332
5	0.135

(f) Left skewed since $p > 0.5$

(g)

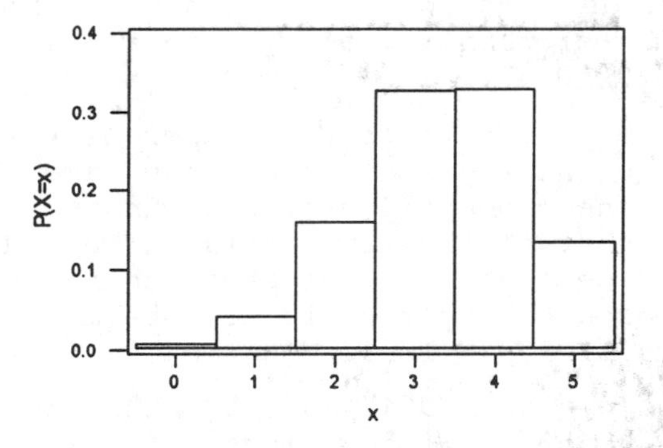

(h)

x	P(X=x)	xP(X=x)	x^2	x^2P(X=x)
0	0.004	0.000	0	0.000
1	0.040	0.040	1	0.040
2	0.161	0.322	4	0.644
3	0.328	0.984	9	2.952
4	0.332	1.328	16	5.312
5	0.135	0.675	25	3.375
		3.349		12.323

$\mu = 3.349$

$\sigma^2 = 12.323 - 3.349^2 = 1.107$; $\sigma = \sqrt{1.107} = 1.052$

(i) $\mu = np = 5(0.67) = 3.35$

$\sigma^2 = np(1-p) = 5(0.67)(0.33) = 1.1055$

$\sigma = \sqrt{1.1055} = 1.051$

(j) Out of any five races, the average number of favorites that finish in the money is 3.35.

5.37 $n = 10$; $p = 0.40$

(a) $P(5) = {}_{10}C_5 \cdot 0.4^5 0.6^5 = 0.201$

(b)

$$P(3 \le x \le 5) = P(3) + P(4) + P(5)$$
$$= \binom{10}{3} \cdot 0.4^3 0.6^7 + \binom{10}{4} \cdot 0.4^4 0.6^6 + \binom{10}{5} \cdot 0.4^5 0.6^5 = 0.215 + 0.251 + 0.201 = 0.667$$

(c) Twenty percent of 10 females surveyed is 2 females. Less than 20% is therefore 0 or 1.

$$P(\text{Under } 20\%) = P(0) + P(1)$$
$$= \binom{10}{0} \cdot 0.4^0 0.6^{10} + \binom{10}{1} \cdot 0.4^1 0.6^9 = 0.0060 + 0.0403 = 0.0463$$

(d) $P(X > 1) = 1 - P(X \le 1) = 1 - 0.0463 = 0.9537$

5.39 (a) Summing the probabilities for 3, 4, 5, and 6 winning numbers, we determine that the probability of winning a prize (based upon purchasing one ticket) is 0.0290647.

(b) If an individual buys one *Lotto* ticket per week for a year, the probability of winning a prize remains the same from week to week. Notice also that the probability of not winning a prize is 1 - 0.0290647 = 0.9709353, and that the weekly trials of purchasing a ticket are identical and independent. All of these characteristics permit the use of the binomial probability formula to determine the probability that an individual wins a prize at least once in the 52 tries.

From the above, we have p = 0.0290647, n = 52, and the possible numbers of successes are X = 0, 1, 2, 3, ..., 52. Thus,

$$P(X \ge 1) = 1 - P(X = 0) = 1 - \binom{52}{0}(0.0290647)^0(0.9709353)^{52}$$

$$= 1 - 0.215722 = 0.784278$$

5.41 (a) If sampling is done with replacement, the trials are independent because the results of one trial have no effect on the probabilities of the outcomes of any other trial. The success probability remains the same from trial to trial because it always represents the proportion of the population having the 'success' attribute.

(b) If sampling is without replacement, the trials are not independent because the outcome of one trial changes the probabilities of the possible outcomes in succeeding trials. Those probabilities vary from trial to trial because the proportion of successes left in the population changes whenever one of the outcomes in the population, whether it be a success or failure, is removed from the population.

5.43 (a) $p = 0.0290647;\ P(X = x) = 0.0290647(0.9709353)^{x-1}$

which is the probability that a person will first win a prize in week **x**.

(b) $P(3) = 0.0290647(0.9709353)^2 = 0.0274$

$P(X \le 3) = P(1) + P(2) + P(3) = 0.0291 + 0.0282 + 0.0274 = 0.0847$

$P(X \ge 3) = 1 - P(X \le 2) = 1 - [0.0291 + 0.0282] = 1 - 0.0573 = 0.9427$

(c) On the average, it will take $\mu = 1/p = 1/0.0290647 = 34.4$ weeks until you win a prize.

5.45 In Minitab, first store the possible values for X (0, 1, 2, 3, 4, 5) in a column named x. Then choose **Calc ▶ Probability distributions ▶ Binomial...**, select the **Probability** option button to get individual probabilities, type 5 in the **Number of trials** text box, type .67 in the **Probability of success** text box, select the **Input column** option button, click in the **Input column** text box and specify x, and click **OK**. The result is

Binomial with n = 5 and p = 0.670000

x	P(X = x)
0.00	0.0039
1.00	0.0397
2.00	0.1613
3.00	0.3275
4.00	0.3325
5.00	0.1350

(c) P(2) = 0.1613 (b) P(4) = 0.3325

(c) $P(X \geq 4) = 0.3325 + 0.1350 = 0.4675$

(d) $P(2 \leq X \leq 4) = 0.1613 + 0.3275 + 0.3325 = 0.8213$

(e) The distribution is presented previous to part (a).

Exercises 5.4

5.47 Two uses of Poisson distributions would be (1) to model the frequency with which a specified event occurs during a particular period of time, and (2) to approximate the binomial distribution.

5.49 (a) $P(0) = \dfrac{e^{-0.7}(0.7)^0}{0!} = 0.497$

(b)

$$P(X \leq 2) = P(0) + P(1) + P(2)$$

$$= e^{-0.7}\frac{(0.7)^0}{0!} + e^{-0.7}\frac{(0.7)^1}{1!} + e^{-0.7}\frac{(0.7)^2}{2!} = 0.966$$

(c)

$$P(1 \leq X \leq 3) = P(1) + P(2) + P(3)$$

$$= e^{-0.7}\frac{(0.7)^1}{1!} + e^{-0.7}\frac{(0.7)^2}{2!} + e^{-0.7}\frac{(0.7)^3}{3!} = 0.498$$

5.51 (a) $\mu_X = 0.7$; on the average 0.7 wars began during the calendar year.

(b) $\sigma_x = \sqrt{0.7} = 0.837$

5.53 (a) We would expect $\mu = np = (10000)(1/1500) = 6.667$ to have Fragile X Syndrome.

(b) First, we note that $n \geq 100$ and $np \leq 10$. Then we use the Poisson probability formula to obtain the probabilities for X = 0 through 10. The required calculations are

$$p(X=0)=e^{-6.67}\frac{(6.67)^0}{0!}=0.0013 \qquad p(X=1)=e^{-6.67}\frac{(6.67)^1}{1!}=0.0085$$

$$p(X=2)=e^{-6.67}\frac{(6.67)^2}{2!}=0.0282 \qquad p(X=3)=e^{-6.67}\frac{(6.67)^3}{3!}=0.0627$$

$$p(X=4)=e^{-6.67}\frac{(6.67)^4}{4!}=0.1046 \qquad p(X=5)=e^{-6.67}\frac{(6.67)^5}{5!}=0.1395$$

$$p(X=6)=e^{-6.67}\frac{(6.67)^6}{6!}=0.1551 \qquad p(X=7)=e^{-6.67}\frac{(6.67)^7}{7!}=0.1478$$

$$p(X=8)=e^{-6.67}\frac{(6.67)^8}{8!}=0.1232 \qquad p(X=9)=e^{-6.67}\frac{(6.67)^9}{9!}=0.0913$$

$$p(X=10)=e^{-6.67}\frac{(6.67)^{10}}{10!}=0.0609$$

The probabilities that more than 7 of the males have Fragile X Syndrome and that at most 10 of the males have Fragile X Syndrome are (from the preceding calculations)

$$\begin{aligned}P(X>7) &= 1-P(X\le 7)=1-(P(0)+P(1)+\ldots+P(7))\\ &= 1-0.0013-0.0085-0.0282-0.0627-0.1046-0.1395-0.1551-0.1478\\ &= 1-0.6477=0.3523\end{aligned}$$

$$P(X\le 10)=0.0013+0.0085+\ldots+0.0609=0.9231$$

5.55 If there is a Poisson distribution which provides a good approximation to the binomial distribution, the one with the same mean is a likely candidate since it will be 'centered' at the same place as the binomial distribution. Given that we only use this approximation when n is large and p is near zero, it will also be the case that 1-p is near one, and therefore $np(1-p)$ will be near np which we set equal to λ. Since λ is the variance of the Poisson distribution and $np(1-p)$ is the variance of the binomial distribution, the Poisson distribution with $\lambda = np$ also has approximately the same variance (and hence standard deviation) as the binomial distribution it is approximating. With both the mean and standard deviation being approximately the same for both distributions, the approximating Poisson distribution should be very similar to the binomial distribution.

5.57 (a) In Minitab, we choose **Calc ▶ Probability distributions ▶ Poisson...** Then we select **Probability**, type .7 in the **Mean** text box, select **Input constant**, and type 0 to indicate that we want the probability for x = 0. Finally, click on **OK**. The output shown in the Sessions window is

```
Probability Density Function
Poisson with μ = .7000
        x         P( X = x)
     0.00          0.4966
```

(b) We choose **Calc ▶ Probability distributions ▶ Poisson...** Then we select **Cumulative Probability**, type .7 in the **Mean** text box, select **Input**

constant, and type <u>2</u> to indicate that we want the probability for $X \le 2$. Finally, click on **OK.** The output shown in the Sessions window is

```
Cumulative Distribution Function

Poisson with μ = .7000

        x        P( X <= x)

     2.00          0.9659
```

(c) First name two columns x and P(X=x). Then enter 1, 2, and 3, in the x column. Choose **Calc ▶ Probability distributions ▶ Poisson...** Then we select **Probability,** type <u>.7</u> in the **Mean** text box, click on **Input column** and select X in the text box, select P(X=x) for **Optional storage** and click on **OK.** The probabilities will now show in the P(X=x) column of the Data window. To get the sum of these probabilities, we choose **Calc ▶ Column statistics...,** click on **Sum,** and select P(X=x) for the **Input variable.** The output shown in the Sessions window is

```
Column Sum

   Sum of P(X=x)     =      0.49766
```

An alternative way of computing this probability is to use the cumulative probability procedure to find $P(X \le 3) - P(X \le 0)$.

5.59 In Excel, enter 10000 in cell A1 and type the expression <u>=1/1500</u> in B1. Then enter 0, 1,...,10 in A3 through A13. In B3, type the expression <u>=BINOMDIST(A3,A1,B1,0)</u> and copy the contents of B3 into B4 through B13. Then type the expression <u>=10000/1500</u> in cell C1 and type in C3 the expression <u>=Poisson(A3,C1,0)</u>. Copy the contents of B3 into B4 through B13. The cells B3 through B13 will contain the binomial probabilities that X = 0 through 10, respectively. The cells C3 through C13 will contain the approximating Poisson probabilities. After adding headings in cells A2, B2, and C2, and formatting Columns B and C to display 4 decimal places, the resulting table is

x	Binomial Probability	Poisson Approximation
0	0.0013	0.0013
1	0.0085	0.0085
2	0.0283	0.0283
3	0.0628	0.0628
4	0.1047	0.1047
5	0.1397	0.1397
6	0.1552	0.1552
7	0.1478	0.1478
8	0.1232	0.1232
9	0.0912	0.0912
10	0.0608	0.0608

For n = 10,000 and p = 1/1500, the binomial probabilities and their Poisson approximations are identical to 4 decimal places for all values of X from 0 through 10.

REVIEW TEST FOR CHAPTER 5

1. (a) random variable

   (b) finite (or countably infinite)

2. A probability distribution of a discrete random variable gives us a listing of the possible values of the random variable and their probabilities; or a formula for the probabilities.

3. Probability histogram

4. 1

5. (a) P(X = 2) = 0.386

   (b) 38.6%

   (c) 50(0.386) = 19.3 or about 19; 500(0.386) = 193

6. 3.6

7. X is more likely to take a value close to its mean because it has less variation.

8. The trials must have two possible outcomes (success and failure) per trial, must be independent, and have a probability of success p that remains constant for all trials.

9. The binomial distribution is a probability distribution for the number of successes in a sequence of n Bernoulli trials.

10. $\binom{10}{3} = \frac{10!}{3!7!} = \frac{10(9)(8)}{3(2)(1)} = 120$

11. Definition 5.4 for the mean and Definition 5.5 for the standard deviation are applied to the binomial and Poisson distribution. For example, in Definition 5.4, the formula for the binomial probability function is substituted for P(X = x) to get the mean.

12. (a) Binomial distribution

    (b) Hypergeometric distribution

    (c) The hypergeometric distribution may be approximated by the binomial distribution when the sample size does not exceed 5% of the population size. When this condition holds, the probability of a success does not change much from trial to trial.

13. (a) X = 1, 2, 3, 4 (b) {X = 3}

    (c) P(X = 3) = 8,141/32,310 = 0.252.

    25.2% of the undergraduates at this university are juniors.

    (d) (e)

Class level x	Probability P(X=x)
1	0.191
2	0.210
3	0.252
4	0.347

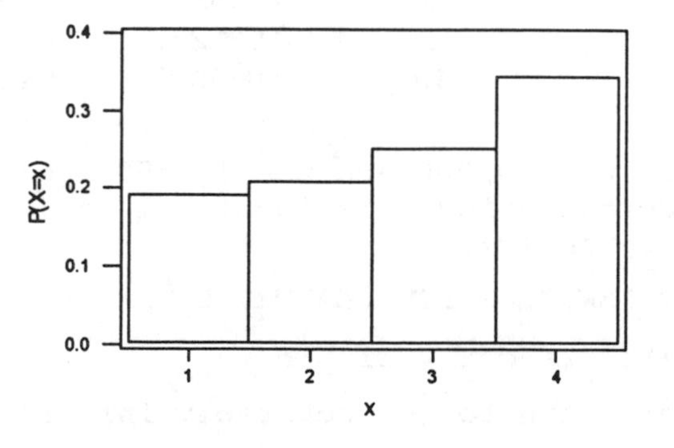

14. (a) $\{Y = 4\}$

(b) $\{Y \geq 4\}$

(c) $\{2 \leq Y \leq 4\}$

(d) $\{Y \geq 1\}$

(e) $P(Y = 4) = 0.174$

(f) $P(Y \geq 4) = P(4) + P(5) + P(6) = 0.174 + 0.105 + 0.043 = 0.322$

(g) $P(2 \leq Y \leq 4) = P(2) + P(3) + P(4) = 0.232 + 0.240 + 0.174 = 0.646$

(h) $P(Y \geq 1) = 1 - P(Y \leq 0) = 1 - 0.052 = 0.948$

15. The required calculations are

y	P(Y=y)	yP(Y=y)	y^2	y^2P(Y=y)
0	0.052	0.000	0	0.000
1	0.154	0.154	1	0.154
2	0.232	0.464	4	0.928
3	0.240	0.720	9	2.160
4	0.174	0.696	16	2.784
5	0.105	0.525	25	2.625
6	0.043	0.258	36	1.548
		2.817		10.199

(a) $\mu_Y = \Sigma yP(Y=y) = 2.817.$

(b) On the average, the number of busy lines is about 2.8.

(c)

$$\sigma_y = \sqrt{(Y-\mu_y)^2 P(Y=y)} = \sqrt{2.2635} = 1.50, \text{ or}$$

$$\sigma_y = \sqrt{Y^2 P(Y=y) - \mu_y{}^2} = \sqrt{10.199 - 2.817^2} = 1.50$$

(d)

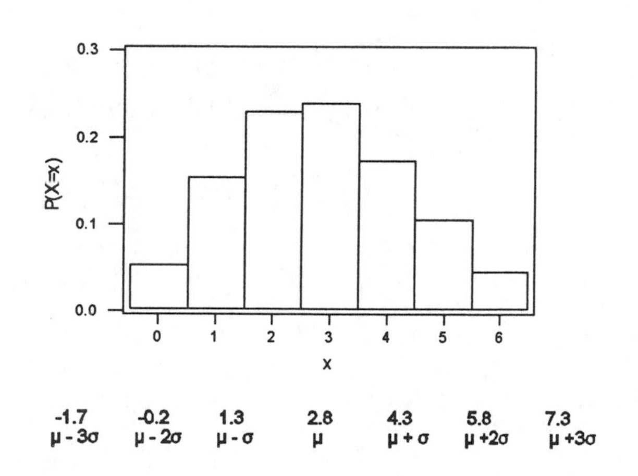

16. $0! = 1$ $\quad 3! = 3\cdot2\cdot1 = 6$ $\quad 4! = 4\cdot3\cdot2\cdot1 = 24$ $\quad 7! = 7\cdot6\cdot5\cdot4\cdot3\cdot2\cdot1 = 5040$

17.

(a) $\binom{8}{3} = \dfrac{8!}{3!5!} = 56$ (b) $\binom{8}{5} = \dfrac{8!}{5!3!} = 56$

(c) $\binom{6}{6} = \dfrac{6!}{6!0!} = 1$ (d) $\binom{10}{2} = \dfrac{10!}{2!8!} = 45$

(e) $\binom{40}{4} = \dfrac{40}{4!36!} = 91390$ (f) $\binom{100}{0} = \dfrac{100!}{0!100!} = 1$

18. (a) $p = 0.40$

(b)

Outcome	Probability
sss	(0.4)(0.4)(0.4) = 0.064
ssf	(0.4)(0.4)(0.6) = 0.096
sfs	(0.4)(0.6)(0.4) = 0.096
sff	(0.4)(0.6)(0.6) = 0.144
fss	(0.6)(0.4)(0.4) = 0.096
fsf	(0.6)(0.4)(0.6) = 0.144
ffs	(0.6)(0.6)(0.4) = 0.144
fff	(0.6)(0.6)(0.6) = 0.216

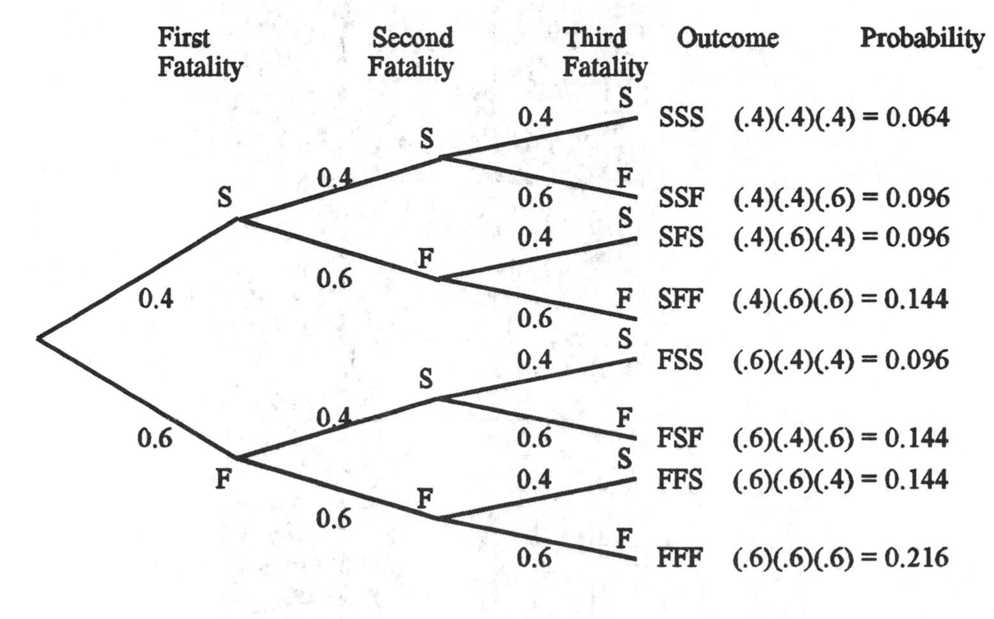

(d) The outcomes in which the driver is a drinker two out of the three times are ssf, sfs, and fss.

(e) Each outcome in part (d) has probability 0.096. The probabilities are equal for each outcome because each probability is obtained by multiplying two success probabilities of 0.4 and one failure probability of 0.6.

(f) P(2 drinkers) = P(ssf) + P(sfs) + P(fss) = 0.096 + 0.096 + 0.096
= 0.288

(g) P(0 drinkers) = P(fff) = 0.216

P(1 drinker) = P(sff) + P(fsf) + P(ffs) = 0.144 + 0.144 + 0.144
= 0.432

P(3 drinkers) = P(sss) = 0.064

y	P(Y=y)
0	0.216
1	0.432
2	0.288
3	0.064

(h) Binomial distribution with parameters n = 3 and p = 0.4

19. The calculations required to answer all parts of this exercise are

$$P(0)=\binom{4}{0}\cdot(0.6)^0(0.4)^4=0.0256 \qquad P(1)=\binom{4}{1}\cdot(0.6)^1(0.4)^3=0.1536$$

$$P(2)=\binom{4}{2}\cdot(0.6)^2(0.4)^2=0.3456 \qquad P(3)=\binom{4}{3}\cdot(0.6)^3(0.4)^1=0.3456$$

$$P(4)=\binom{4}{4}\cdot(0.6)^4(0.4)^0=0.1296$$

(a) P(3) = 0.3456

(b) $P(X \geq 3)$ = P(3) + P(4) = 0.3456 + 0.1296 = 0.4752

(c) $P(X \leq 3)$ = P(0) + P(1) + P(3) + P(4)
= 0.0256 + 0.1536 + 0.3456 + 0.3456 = 0.8704

(d)

Number with Pets x	Probability P(X=x)
0	0.0256
1	0.1536
2	0.3456
3	0.3456
4	0.1296

(e) Left skewed, since p > 0.5.

(f)

(f)

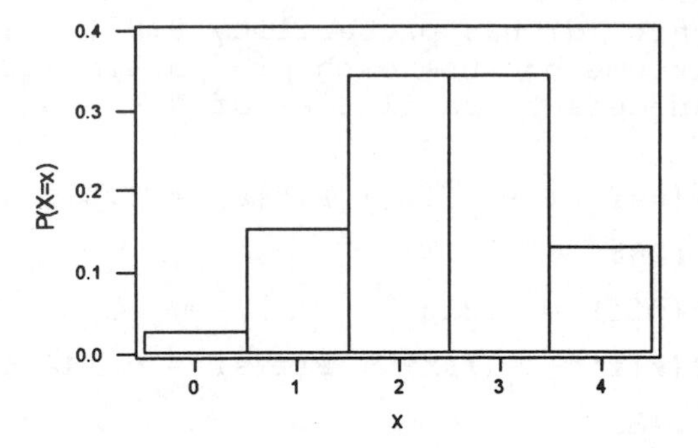

(g) The distribution is only approximate for two reasons: the actual distribution is hypergeometric, based on sampling without replacement; and the success probability p = 0.60 is probably based on a sample.

(h) $\mu = np = 4(.6) = 2.4$; On the average, 2.4 out of 4 households have one or more pets.

(i) $\sigma^2 = np(1-p) = 4(.6)(.4) = 0.96$; $\sigma = \sqrt{0.96} = 0.98$

20. (a) $p > 0.5$ since left skewed (b) $p = 0.5$ since symmetric

21. (a) $P(X=2) = e^{-1.75}\dfrac{1.75^2}{2!} = 0.266$

(b) $P(4 \le X \le 6) = e^{-1.75}\dfrac{1.75^4}{4!} + e^{-1.75}\dfrac{1.75^5}{5!} + e^{-1.75}\dfrac{1.75^6}{6!}$
$= 0.068 + 0.024 + 0.007 = 0.099$

(c) $P(X \ge 1) = 1 - P(0) = 1 - e^{-1.75}\dfrac{1.75^0}{0!} = 1 - 0.174 = 0.826$

(d) (e)

x	P(X=x)
0	0.174
1	0.304
2	0.266
3	0.155
4	0.068
5	0.024
6	0.007
7	0.002
8	0.000

(f) The distribution is right skewed. Yes, this is typical of Poisson distributions.

22. (a) $\mu = \lambda = 1.75$; on the average, there are 1.75 calls to a wrong number per minute.

(b) $\sigma = \sqrt{\lambda} = \sqrt{1.75} = 1.323$

23. Step 1: Determine n and p; n = 10,000 and p = 0.00024.

Step 2: Check if $n \geq 100$ and $np \leq 10$.

From part (a), we conclude that n = 10,000 and np = 2.4.

Thus $n \geq 100$ and $np \leq 10$.

Step 3: Use the Poisson probability formula.

(a) $\mu = np = 2.4$; you would expect to be dealt four of a kind roughly 2.4 times.

(b) $$P(2) = \frac{e^{-2.4}(2.4)^2}{2!} = 0.2613$$

(c)

$$P(X \geq 2) = 1 - P(X < 2) = 1 - [P(0) + P(1)]$$

$$= 1 - [e^{-2.4}(\frac{2.4^0}{0!} + \frac{2.4^1}{1!})] = 0.6916$$

24. (a) In Minitab, name three columns x, P(X=x), and CLASS. In the X column, enter the numbers 1, 2, 3, and 4. In the P(X=x) column, enter the probabilities .191, .210, .252, and .347. Now choose **Calc ▶ Random Data ▶ Discrete...**, type 2500 in the **Generate rows of data** text box, click in the **Store in column[s]** text box and type CLASS, click in the **Values in** text box and specify x, click in the **Probabilities in** text box and specify P(X=x), and click **OK**. The numbers of the classes obtained in 2500 observations are now stored in CLASS.

(b) Choose **Stat ▶ Tables ▶ Tally**, select CLASS in the **Variables** text box, check the **Counts** and **Percents Display** boxes, and click **OK**.

Our result is

Class	Count	Percent
1	491	19.64
2	498	19.92
3	638	25.52
4	873	34.92
N=	2500	

The proportions for the 2500 simulated class levels are very close to the probabilities in the probability distribution.

(c)

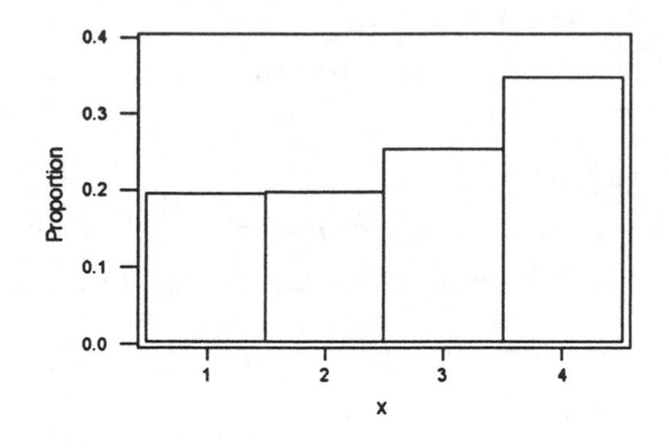

(d) Parts (b) and (c) illustrate that samples tend to reflect the populations from which they are drawn.

25. (a) In Minitab, name three columns Y, P(Y), and NUMLINE. In the Y column, enter the numbers 0, 1, 2, 3, 4, 5, and 6. In the P(Y) column, enter the probabilities .052, .154, .232, .240, .174, .105, and .043. Now choose **Calc ▶ Random Data ▶ Discrete...**, type 200 in the **Generate rows of data** text box, click in the **Store in column[s]** text box and type NUMLINE, click in the **Values in** text box and specify Y, click in the **Probabilities in** text box and specify P(Y), and click **OK.** The numbers of busy lines obtained in 200 observations are now stored in NUMLINE.

(b) To obtain the mean for the numbers of busy lines, we choose **Calc ▶ Column statistics...**, click on the **Mean** button and specify NUMLINE in the **Input Variable** text box, and click **OK.**

Our output was (yours may be different)

MEAN = 2.8600

The average value of the 200 observation was 2.86 which is quite close to the mean, μ_y = 2.817.

(c) Part (b) is illustrating that samples tend to reflect the properties of the populations from which they are drawn.

26. (a) Choose **Calc ▶ Probability Distributions ▶ Binomial...** Then click in the **Number of trials** text box and type 4, click in the **Probability** text box and type .6, click on the **Input constant** button, click in its text box, and type 3. Finally, click **OK.** The output shown in the Sessions window is

x	P(X = x)
3.00	0.3456

(b) Choose **Calc ▶ Probability Distributions ▶ Binomial...** Then click in the **Number of trials** text box and type 4, click on the **Cumulative probability** button, click in the **Probability of success** text box and type .6, click on the **Input constant** button, click in its text box, and type 3. Finally, click **OK.** The output shown in the Sessions window is

x	P(X <= x)
3.00	0.8704

(c) One way to find $P(X \geq 3)$ is by finding $1 - P(X \leq 2)$. $P(X \leq 2)$ is found using the cumulative probability for 2. We choose **Calc ▶ Probability Distributions ▶ Binomial...** Then click in the **Number of trials** text box and type 4, click on the **Cumulative probability** button, click in the **Probability of success** text box and type .6, click on the **Input constant** button, click in its text box, and type 2. Finally, click **OK**. The output shown in the Sessions window is

Cumulative Distribution Function

Binomial with n = 4 and p = 0.600000

x	P(X <= x)
2.00	0.5248

The desired probability is 1 - 0.5248 = 0.4752

(d) Name two columns x and P(X=x). In the x column, enter the numbers 0, 1, 2, 3, and 4. Then we choose **Calc ▶ Probability Distributions ▶ Binomial...** Click in the **Number of trials** text box and type 4, click on the **Probability** button, click in the **Probability of success** text box and type .6, click on the **Input column** button, click in its text box and select X. Leave the **Option storage** text box empty and click **OK**. The output shown in the Sessions window is

Binomial with n = 4 and p = 0.600000

x	P(X = x)
0.00	0.0256
1.00	0.1536
2.00	0.3456
3.00	0.3456
4.00	0.1296

27. In Minitab, name two columns x and P(X=x). In the x column, enter the numbers 0, 1, 2, 3, 4, 5, 6, 7, and 8. Then we choose **Calc ▶ Probability Distributions ▶ Poisson...** Click in the **Mean** text box and type 1.75, click on the **Probability** button, click on the **Input column** button, click in its text box and select x. Leave the **Option storage** text box empty and click **OK**. The output shown in the Sessions window is

Poisson with μ = 1.75000

x	P(X = x)
0.00	0.1738
1.00	0.3041
2.00	0.2661
3.00	0.1552
4.00	0.0679
5.00	0.0238
6.00	0.0069
7.00	0.0017
8.00	0.0004

(a) $P(2) = 0.2661$

(b) $P(4 \leq X \leq 6) = 0.0679 + 0.0238 + 0.0069 = 0.0986$

(c) $P(X \geq 1) = 1 - P(0) = 1 - 0.1738 = 0.8262$

(d) See table previous to part (a).

CHAPTER 6 ANSWERS

Exercises 6.1

6.1 The histogram will be roughly bell-shaped.

6.3 Their distributions are identical. The mean and standard deviation completely determine the shape of a normal distribution. Thus if two normally distributed variables have the same mean and standard deviation, they also have the same distribution.

6.5 (a) True. Both normal curves have the same shape because their standard deviations are equal.

(b) False. A normal distribution is centered at its mean μ. Since this parameter is different for the two normal curves, these normal curves are centered at different places.

6.7 The parameters for a normal curve are the mean μ and the standard deviation σ.

6.9 The percentage of all possible observations of a normally distributed variable that lie between 2 and 3 equals the area under the associated normal curve between 2 and 3. If the variable is only approximately normally distributed, the percentage of all possible observations between 2 and 3 is approximately the area under the associated normal curve between 2 and 3.

6.11 (a) The percentage of female students who are between 60 and 65 inches tall is $0.0450 + 0.0757 + 0.1170 + 0.1480 + 0.1713 = 0.5570$ (55.70%).

(b) The area under the normal curve with parameters $\mu = 64.4$ and $\sigma = 2.4$ between 60 and 65 is approximately 0.5570. This is only an estimate because the distribution of heights is only approximately normally distributed.

6.13 (a)

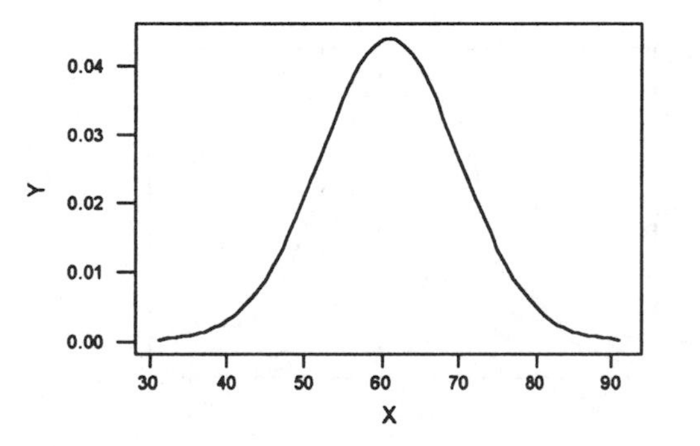

(b) $z = (x - 61)/9$

(c) z has a standard normal distribution ($\mu = 0$ and $\sigma = 1$).

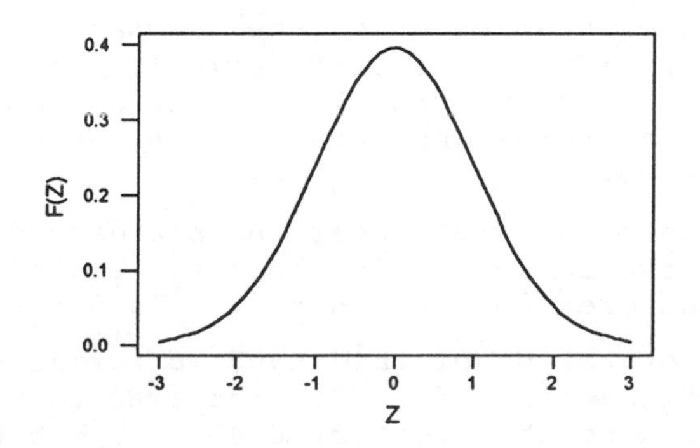

(d) The percentage of finishers in the New York City 10-km run with times between 50 and 70 minutes is equal to the area under the standard normal curve between -1.22 and +1.00.

(e) The percentage of finishers in the New York city 10-km run with times exceeding 75 minutes is equal to the area under the standard normal curve that lies to the right of 1.56.

6.15 The number of chips per bag could not be exactly normally distributed because that number is a discrete random variable, whereas any variable having a normal distribution is a continuous random variable.

6.17 Using Minitab we choose **Calc ▶ Make patterned data ▶ Simple set of numbers...**, enter X in the **Store patterned data** in text box, type -1 in the **From first value** text box, type 11 in the **To last value** text box, type .2 in the **In steps of** text box, and click **OK.** This will provide X values within 3 standard deviations on both sides of the mean. Now choose **Calc ▶ Probability distribution ▶ Normal...**, click on **Probability density**, type 5 in the **Mean** text box and 2 in the **Standard deviation** text box, click in the **Input column** text box and select X, click in the **Optional storage** text box and type P(X), and click **OK.** Now choose **Graph ▶ Plot...**, select P(X) in the **Y** column for **Graph1** and X for the **X** column. In the **Data display** area, click on the arrow to the right of **Display** and select **Connect.** Click **OK.**

The result is

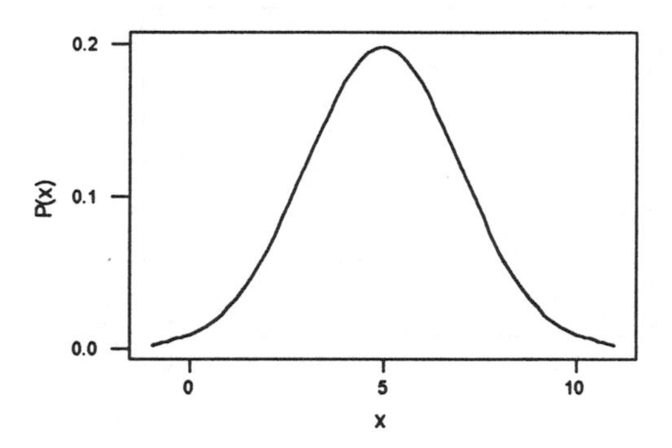

Exercises 6.2

6.19 Finding areas under the standard normal curve is important because for any normally distributed variable, we can obtain the percentage of all possible observations that lie within any specified range by first converting x values to z-scores and then finding the corresponding area under the standard normal curve.

6.21 The total area under the standard normal curve is 1, and the standard normal curve is symmetric about 0. Therefore, the area to the left of 0 is 0.5, and the area to the right of 0 is 0.5.

6.23 The area under the standard normal curve to the right of 0.43 is 1 - the area to the left of 0.43. The area to the left of 0.43 is 0.6664. Therefore, the area to the right of 0.43 is 1 - 0.6664 = 0.3336.

6.25 The area to the left of z = 3.00 is 0.9987 and the area to the left of -3.00 is 0.0013. Therefore the area between -3.00 and 3.00 is 0.9987 - 0.0013 =

0.9974. The percentage of the area between -3.00 and 3.00 is 99.74%.

6.27 (a) Locate the row (tenths digit) and column (hundredths digit) of the specified z-score. The corresponding table entry is the area under the standard normal curve that lies to the left of the z-score.

(b) The area that lies under the standard normal curve to the right of a specified z-score is 1 - (area to the left of the z-score).

(c) The area that lies under the standard normal score between two specified z-scores, say *a* and *b*, where a < b, is found be subtracting the area to the left of *a* from the area to the left of *b*.

6.29 (a)

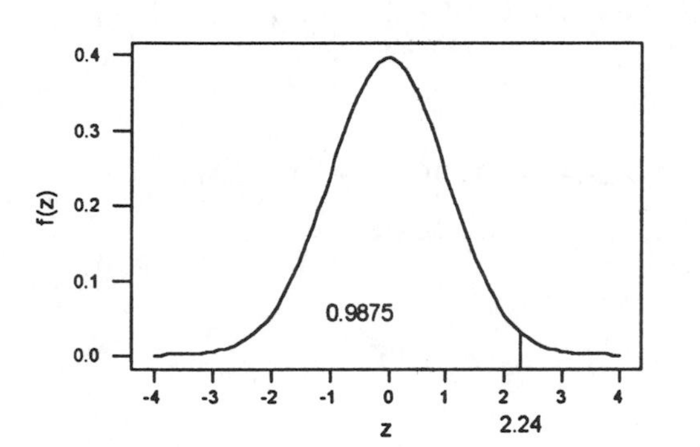

Area = 0.9875

(b)

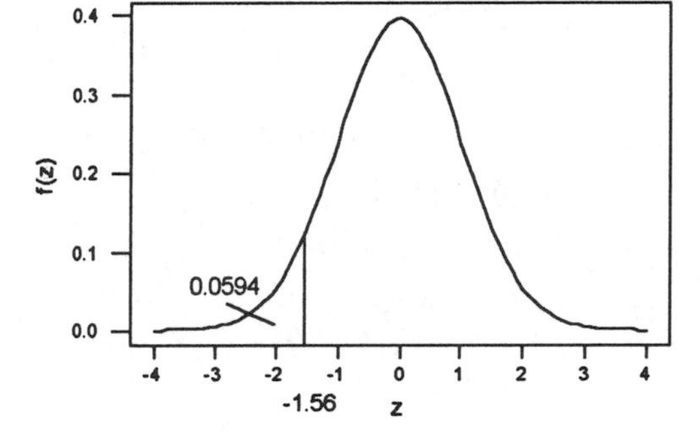

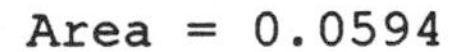
Area = 0.0594

(c)

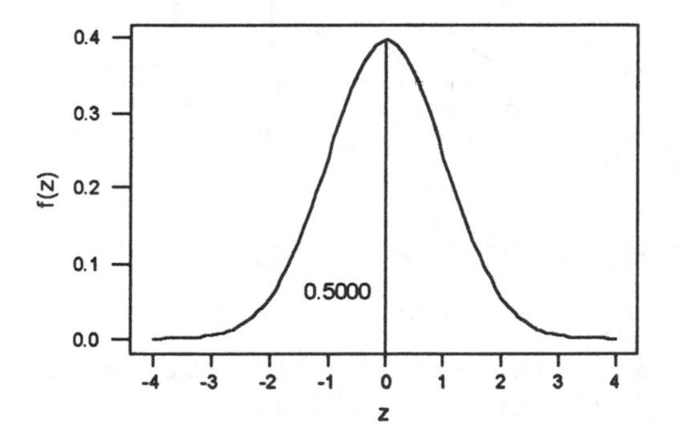

Area = 0.5000

(d)

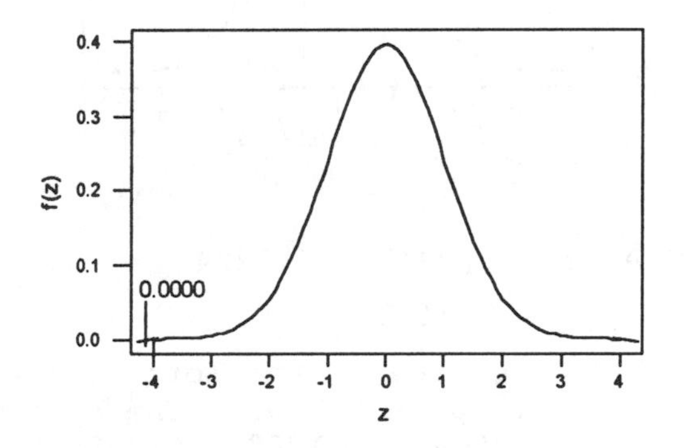

Area = 0.0000

6.31 (a)

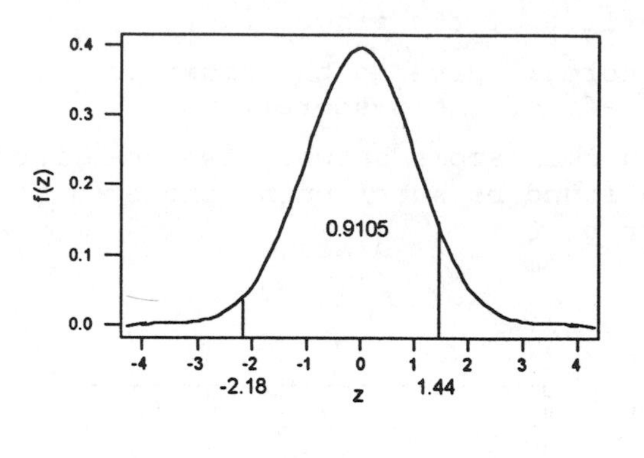

Area = 0.9251 - 0.0146
= 0.9105

(b)

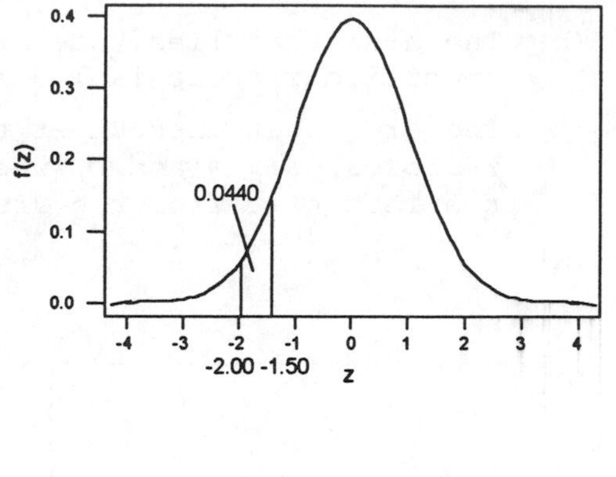

Area = 0.0668 - 0.0228
= 0.0440

(c)

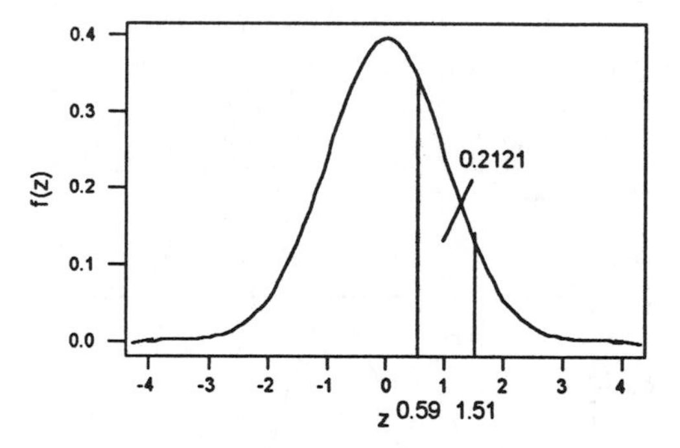

Area = 0.9345 - 0.7224
= 0.2121

(d)

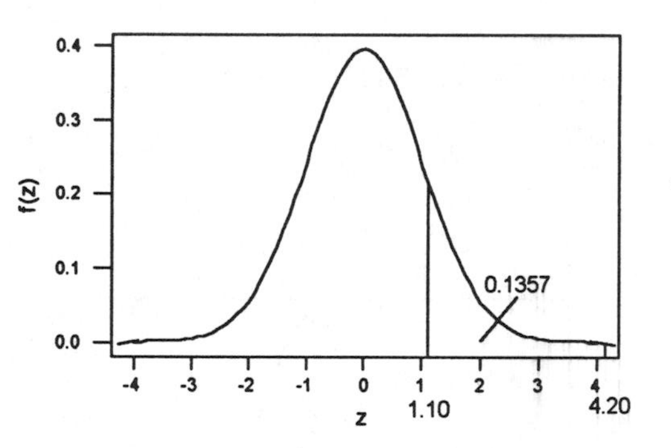

Area = 1.0 - 0.8643
= 0.1357

6.33 (a) The area to the left of z = 1.28 is 0.8997. The area to the left of z = -1.28 is 0.1003. The area between z = -1.28 and z = 1.28 is 0.8997 - 0.1003 = 0.7994.

(b) The area to the left of z = 1.64 is 0.9495. The area to the left of z = -1.64 is 0.0505. The area between z = -1.64 and z = 1.64 is 0.9495 - 0.0505 = 0.8990.

(c) The area to the left of z = -1.96 is 0.0250. The area to the right of z = 1.96 is 1.0000 - 0.9750 = 0.0250. The area either to the left of z = -1.96 or to the right of z = 1.96 is 0.0250 + 0.0250 = 0.0500.

(d) The area to the left of z = -2.33 is 0.0099. The area to the right of z = 2.33 is 1.0000 - 0.9901 = 0.0099. The area either to the left of z = -2.33 or to the right of z = 2.33 is 0.0099 + 0.0099 = 0.0198.

6.35 (a) and (b)

Region	Area	Percentage of total area
$-\infty$ to -3	0.0013	0.13
-3 to -2	0.0228 - 0.0013 = 0.0215	2.15
-2 to -1	0.1587 - 0.0228 = 0.1359	13.59
-1 to 0	0.5000 - 0.1587 = 0.3413	34.13
0 to 1	0.8413 - 0.5000 = 0.3413	34.13
1 to 2	0.9772 - 0.8413 = 0.1359	13.59
2 to 3	0.9987 - 0.9722 = 0.0215	2.15
3 to ∞	1.0000 - 0.9987 = 0.0013	0.13
	1.0000	100.00

6.37

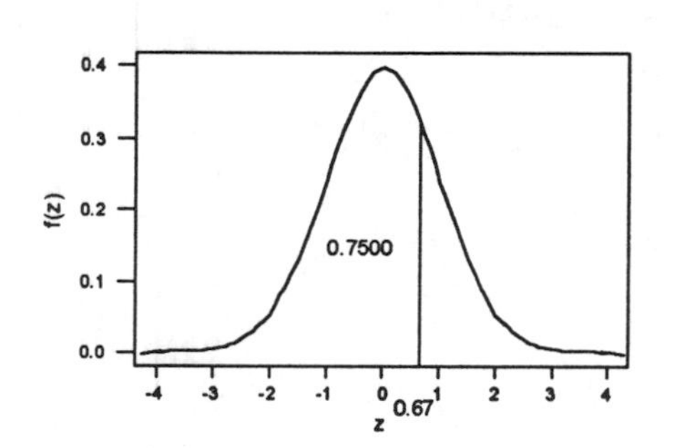

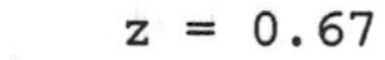
$z = 0.67$

6.39

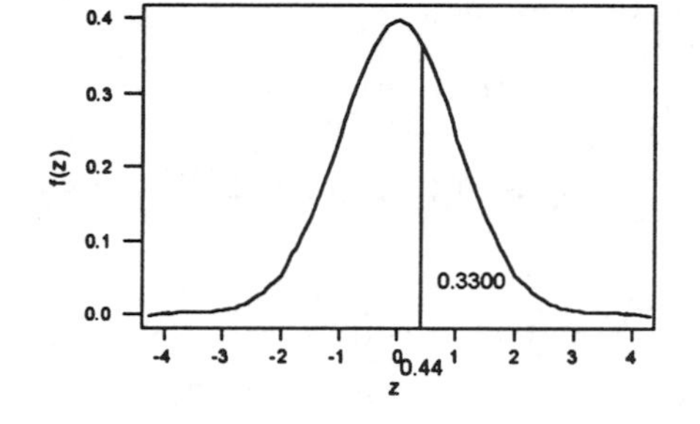

$z = 0.44$

6.41

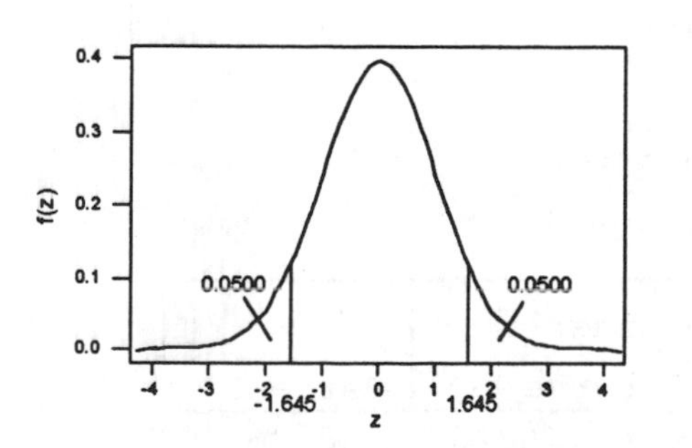

$z = \pm\ 1.645$

6.43 The area under any curve representing the distribution of a variable is equivalent to probability. Since the total probability for all of the values of any variable is 1, the total area under the curve representing the probability distribution of any variable is also 1.

Exercises 6.3

6.45 Sketch the normal curve for the variable, shade the region of interest and locate the pertinent x-values, compute the z-scores corresponding to those x values, and use Table II to obtain the area under the standard normal curve delimited by those z-scores.

6.47 (a) For x = 260 and 280, the z-values are

$$z = \frac{260 - 272.2}{8.12} = -1.50 \text{ and } z = \frac{280 - 272.2}{8.12} = 0.96$$

The area to the left of z = -1.50 is 0.0668 and the area to the left of z = 0.96 is 0.8315. Therefore the area between z = -1.50 and z = 0.96 is 0.8315 - 0.0668 = 0.7647. Thus the percentage of tee shots that went between 260 and 280 years is 76.47%.

(b) For x = 300, the z-value is

$z = \frac{300 - 272.2}{8.12} = 3.42$. The area to the left of z = 3.42 is 0.9997.

Thus the area to the right of z = 3.42 is 1 - 0.9997 = 0.0003, implying that only 0.03% of tee shots went more than 300 yards.

6.49 (a) P(X > 75):

z-score computation:	Area to the left of z:
$x = 75 \rightarrow z = \frac{75-61}{9} = 1.56$	0.9406

Total area = 1.0000 - 0.9406 = 0.0594

(b) P(X < 50 or X > 70):

z-score computations:	Area to the left of z:
$x = 50 \rightarrow z = \frac{50-61}{9} = -1.22$	0.1112
$x = 70 \rightarrow z = \frac{70-61}{9} = 1.00$	0.8413

Total area = 0.1112 + (1.0000 - 0.8413) = 0.2699

6.51

Part	Standard deviations to either side of the mean	Area under normal curve	Percent
(a)	1	0.3413 x 2 = 0.6826	68.26
(b)	2	0.4772 x 2 = 0.9544	95.44
(c)	3	0.4987 x 2 = 0.9974	99.74

6.53 (a) Q_1 = 272.2 + (-0.67)(8.12) = 266.76

Q_2 = 272.2 + (0)(8.12) = 272.2

Q_3 = 272.2 + (0.67)(8.12) = 277.64

(b) P_{95} = 272.2 + (1.645)(8.12) = 285.56

(c) P_{30} = 272.2 + (−0.52)(8.12) = 267.98

(d) Of the driving distances, 25% were less than 266.76 yards, 25% were between 266.76 and 272.2 yards, 25% were between 272.2 and 277.64 yards, 95% were less than 285.56 yards, and 30% were less than 267.98 yards.

6.55 (a) 95% of the population values lie within 1.96 standard deviations to either side of the mean.

(b) 89.9% of the population values lie within 1.64 standard deviations to either side of the mean.

6.57 (a) Exact percentage between 62 and 63 inches is 0.1170 (11.70%).

z-score computations:	Area to the left of z:
$x = 62 \rightarrow z = \frac{62-64.4}{2.4} = -1.00$	0.1587
$x = 63 \rightarrow z = \frac{63-64.4}{2.4} = -0.58$	0.2810

Area between x-values = 0.2810 − 0.1587 = 0.1223 (12.23%)

The two percentages are quite close.

(b) Exact percentage between 65 and 70 = 0.1575 + 0.1100 + 0.0735 + 0.0374 + 0.0199 = 0.3983 (39.83%)

z-score computations:	Area to the left of z:
$x = 65 \rightarrow z = \frac{65-64.4}{2.4} = 0.25$	0.5987
$x = 70 \rightarrow z = \frac{70-64.4}{2.4} = 2.33$	0.9901

Area between x-values = 0.9901 − 0.5987 = 0.3914 (39.14%)

The two percentages are quite close.

6.59 (a) $Q_1 = \mu - 0.67\sigma$

$Q_2 = \mu$

$Q_3 = \mu + 0.67\sigma$

(b) $P_k = \mu + z_{(1-k/100)}\sigma$

6.61 We will use Excel to solve for the probabilities in Exercise 6.50. First, enter the mean 6.1 in cell A1 and the standard deviation 1.3 in cell A2. Enter the x values 3, 5, and 7 in cells A3, A4, and A5. In cell B3, type the expression =NORMDIST(A3,A1,B1,1). Copy the contents of B3 into cells B4 and B5. Cells B3 through B5 now contain the probabilities that X will be less than the values in A3 through A5, respectively. Then $P(X < 3) = 0.0085$, and $P(5 < X < 7)$ = B5 − B4 = 0.7556 − 0.1987 = 0.5569. These two results differ slightly from our previous results because in Exercise 6.50, the z-values were rounded to two decimal places, whereas in Excel they were not rounded.

Exercises 6.4

6.63 A normal probability plot is particularly useful when sample sizes are small; these are situations in which histograms, stem-and-leaf diagrams, and dotplots are less useful in determining the shape of the distribution.

6.65 (a)

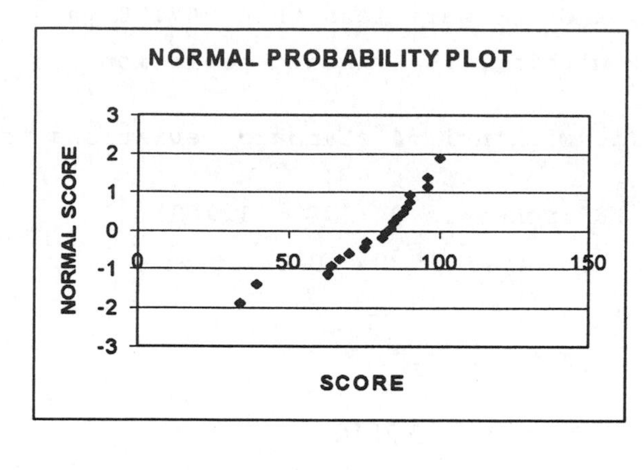

Exam Score x	Normal Score y
34	-1.87
39	-1.40
63	-1.13
64	-0.92
67	-0.74
70	-0.59
75	-0.45
76	-0.31
81	-0.19
82	-0.06
84	0.06
85	0.19
86	0.31
88	0.45
89	0.59
90	0.74
90	0.92
96	1.13
96	1.40
100	1.87

(b) Based on the probability plot, there appear to be two outliers in the sample: 34 and 39.

(c) Based on the probability plot, the sample does not appear to come from a normally distributed population.

6.67 (a)

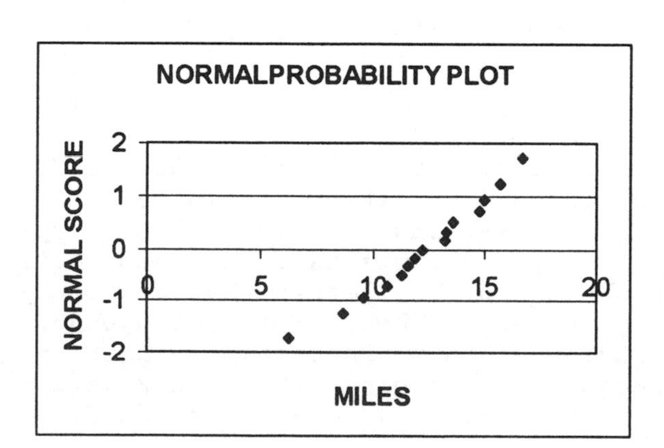

Miles driven x	Normal Score y
6.3	-1.74
8.7	-1.24
9.6	-0.94
10.7	-0.71
11.3	-0.51
11.6	-0.33
11.9	-0.16
12.2	0.0
13.2	0.16
13.3	0.33
13.6	0.51
14.8	0.71
15.0	0.94
15.7	1.24
16.7	1.74

(b) Based on the probability plot, there do not appear to be any outliers in the sample.

(c) Based on the probability plot, the sample appears to be from an approximately normally distributed population.

6.69 Using Minitab and assuming that the data are in a column named SCORES, choose **Calc ▶ Calculator...**, type NSCORE in the **Store result in variable** text box, scroll down to **Normal scores** in the **Functions** list box, click on the **Select** button, specify NSCORES for **number** in the **Expression** text box by double-clicking on it, and click **OK.** Now choose **Graph ▶ Plot...**, select NSCORE for the **Y** variable for **Graph 1** and SCORES for the **X** variable for **Graph 1,** and click **OK.** The output in the Graph window follows.

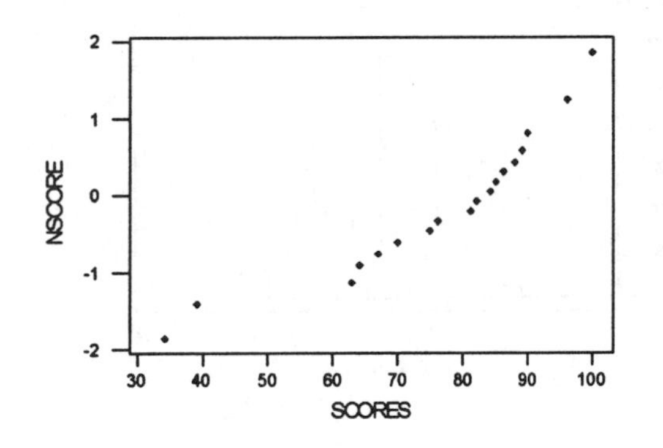

6.71 (a) Using Minitab and assuming that the data are in a column named 'FAT GRAMS', choose **Calc ▶ Calculator...**, type NSCORES in the **Store result in variable** text box, scroll down to **Normal scores** in the **Functions** list box, click on the **Select** button, specify 'FAT GRAMS' for **number** in the **Expression** text box by double-clicking on it, and click **OK.** Now choose **Graph ▶ Plot...**, select NSCORES for the **Y** variable for **Graph 1** and 'FAT GRAMS' for the **X** variable for **Graph 1,** and click **OK.** The output in the Graph window follows.

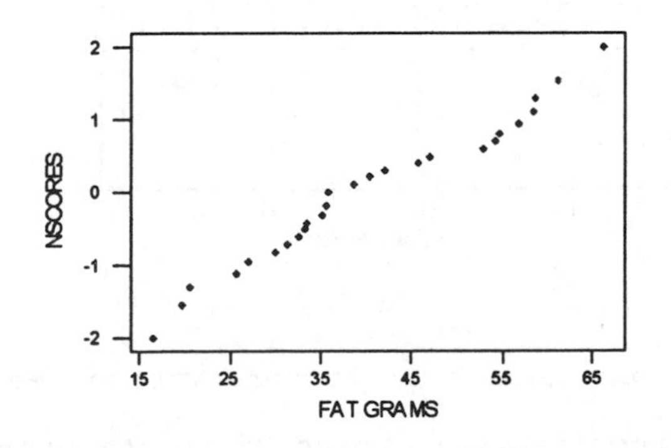

(b) There do not appear to be any outliers in this data.

(c) Since the plot follows a fairly straight line, normality of the fat consumption data seems to be a reasonable assumption.

6.73 (a) Minitab has the capability of producing a histogram and a normal probability plot from grouped data. Enter the midpoints from 9.5 to 13.4 in a column named LENGTH and enter the corresponding frequencies in a column named FREQ. To create the histogram using these two columns, select **Graph ▶ Chart,** then enter FREQ in the **Y** column for **Graph 1** and LENGTH in the **X** column for **Graph 1.** Click on the **Edit Attributes** button and select a bar width of 1.0. Click **OK** and then click **OK** again. The graph is shown below and looks very much like a normal distribution.

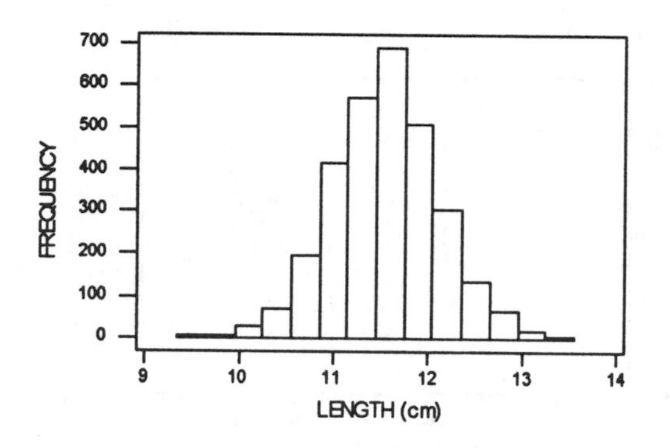

(d) To produce the normal probability plot, select **Graph ▶ Probability Plot,** then enter LENGTH in the **Variables** box and FREQ in the **Frequency Columns** box. Click **OK.** The resulting plot follows and is very close to a straight line, indicating that normality is a reasonable assumption for this set of data.

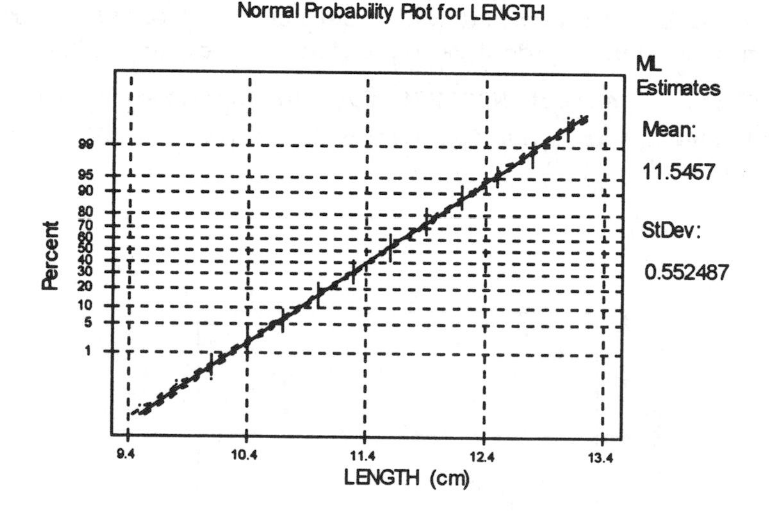

6.75 (a) We will generate four columns of 75 observations each by choosing **Calc ▶ Random data ▶ Exponential...,** typing <u>75</u> in the **Generate rows of data**

text box, clicking in the **Store in column(s)** text box and typing C1-C4, clicking in the **Mean** text box and typing 8.7, and clicking **OK**. Now click in the worksheet column title row and name the four columns TIME1, TIME2, TIME3, and TIME4.

(b) Next we create a column with the normal scores for the first sample (TIME1) and then create the normal probability plot. To do this, we choose **Calc ▶ Calculator...**, type NSCORE1 in the **Store result in variable** text box, scroll down to **Normal scores** in the **Functions** list box, click on the **Select** button, specify TIME1 for **number** in the **Expression** text box by double-clicking on it, and click **OK**. Now choose **Graph ▶ Plot...**, select NSCORE1 for the **Y** variable for **Graph 1** and TIME1 for the **X** variable for **Graph 1**, and click **OK**. Repeat this process for TIME2 and NSCORE2, TIME3 and NSCORE3, and TIME4 and NSCORE4. Our results are shown. Yours will difer from ours.

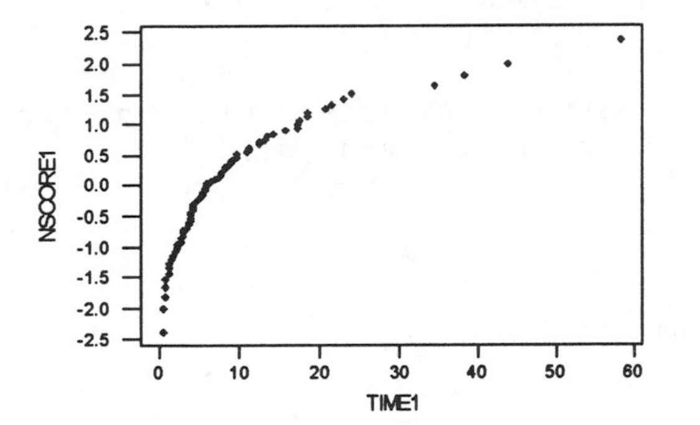

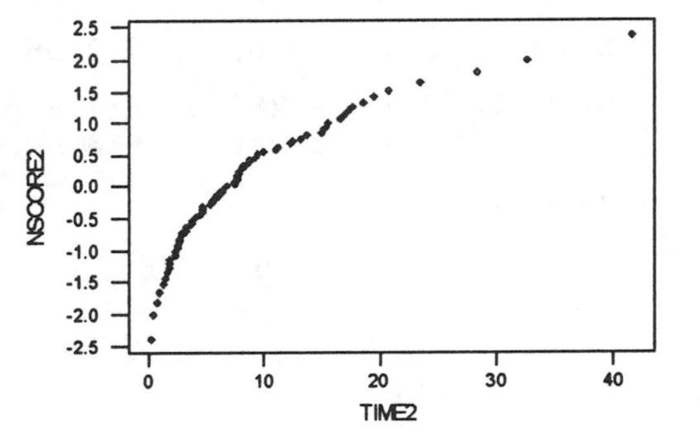

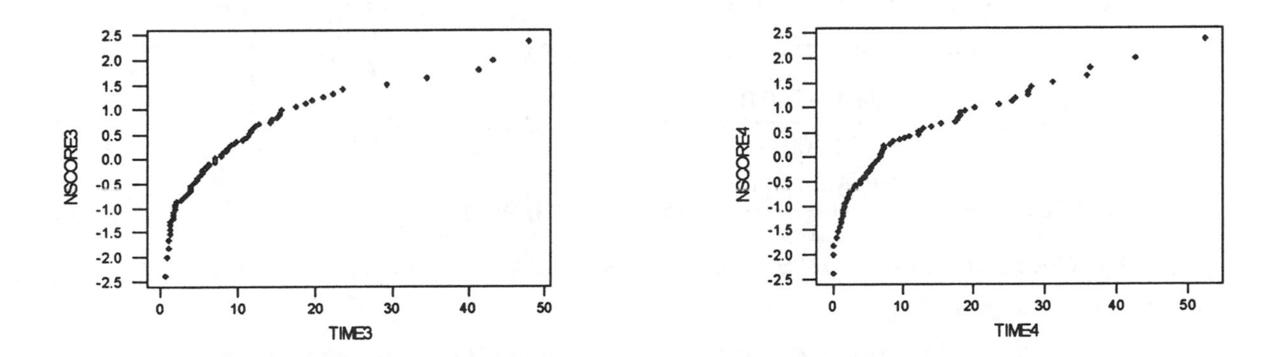

(c) Since the data were generated from a non-normal reverse J-shaped distribution, we should expect the plots to be non-linear as they are.

Exercises 6.5

6.76 It is not practical to use the binomial probability formula when the number of trials, *n*, is large.

6.77 A binomial distribution with *p* not equal to 0.5 is skewed for small *n*; the skewness is enough to preclude using a normal approximation. However, as *n* increases, the skewness decreases and the binomial distribution becomes sufficiently bell-shaped to permit a normal approximation. On the other hand, a binomial distribution with *p* equal to 0.5 is symmetric, regardless of the number of trials.

6.79 If n = 30 and p remains 0.5,

$$\mu_x = np = 30(0.5) = 15$$

$$\sigma_x = \sqrt{np(1-p)} = \sqrt{30(0.5)(0.5)} = 2.74$$

Thus, the normal curve used to approximate probabilities for the number of correct guesses is that with parameters $\mu = 15$ and $\sigma = 2.74$.

6.81 For parts (a), (b), and (c), steps 1-3 are as follows:

Step 1: n = 500; p = 0.56

Step 2: np = 280.0; n(1 - p) = 220.0. Since both np and n(1 - p) are at least 5, the normal approximation can be used.

Step 3:

$$\mu_x = np = 500(0.56) = 280.0$$

$$\sigma_x = \sqrt{np(1-p)} = \sqrt{500(0.56)(0.44)} = 11.100$$

(a) P(x = 300):

Step 4: x = 299.5 and x = 300.5

z-score computations:	Area to the left of z:
$x = 299.5 \rightarrow z = \dfrac{299.5 - 280.0}{11.100} = 1.76$	0.9608
$x = 300.5 \rightarrow z = \dfrac{300.5 - 280.0}{11.100} = 1.85$	0.9678

Required area = 0.9678 - 0.9608 = 0.0070

(b) Step 4: x = 274.5 and x = 300.5

z-score computations:	Area to the left of z:
$x = 274.5 \rightarrow z = \dfrac{274.5 - 280.0}{11.100} = -0.50$	0.3085
$x = 300.5 \rightarrow z = \dfrac{300.5 - 280.0}{11.100} = 1.85$	0.9678

Required area = 0.9678 - 0.3085 = 0.6593

(c) Step 4: x = 299.5

z-score computation:	Area to the left of z:
$x = 299.5 \rightarrow z = \dfrac{299.5 - 280.0}{11.100} = 1.76$	0.9608

Required area = 1.0000 - 0.9608 = 0.0392

6.83 For parts (a), (b), and (c), steps 1-3 are as follows:

Step 1: $n = 300$; $p = 0.26$

Step 2: $np = 78$; $n(1 - p) = 222$. Since both $n(1 - p)$ and np are at least 5, the normal approximation can be used.

Step 3:

$$\mu_x = np = 300(0.26) = 78$$
$$\sigma_x = \sqrt{np(1-p)} = \sqrt{300(0.26)(0.74)} = 7.60$$

(a) 26% of 300 is 78. $P(X = 78)$:

Step 4: $x = 77.5$ and $x = 78.5$

z-score computations:	Area to the left of z:
$x = 77.5 \rightarrow z = \frac{77.5 - 78.0}{7.60} = -0.07$	0.4721
$x = 78.5 \rightarrow z = \frac{78.5 - 78.0}{7.60} = 0.07$	0.5279

Required area = 0.5279 - 0.4721 = 0.0558

(b) Step 4: $x = 78.5$

z-score computations:	Area to the left of z:
$x = 78.5 \rightarrow z = \frac{78.5 - 78.0}{7.60} = 0.07$	0.5279

Required area = 0.5279

(c) Step 4: $x = 77.5$

z-score computation:	Area to the left of z:
$x = 77.5 \rightarrow z = \frac{77.5 - 78.0}{7.60} = -0.07$	0.4721

Required area = 1.000 - 0.4721 = 0.5279

6.85 Battery lifetime (x) is normally distributed with $\mu = 30$ hours and $\sigma = 5$ hours. Also, $n = 500$. Initially, we need to find the "success" probability associated with any one battery lasting longer than 25 hours. This success probability is calculated as follows:

z-score computation:	Area to the left of z:
$x = 25 \rightarrow z = \frac{25 - 30}{5} = -1.00$	0.1587

Required area = 1.0000 - 0.1587 = 0.8413

We now calculate the probability that at least 80% of the batteries last longer than 25 hours. We do this by using the normal approximation to the binomial. Since 80% of 500 is 400, we can find $P(X \geq 400)$ as follows:

Step 1: $n = 500$; $p = 0.8413$

Step 2: $np = 420.65$; $n(1-p) = 79.35$. Since both np and $n(1-p)$ are at least 5, the normal approximation can be used.

Step 3:

$$\mu_x = np = 500(0.8413) = 420.65$$

$$\sigma_x = \sqrt{np(1-p)} = \sqrt{500(0.8413)(0.1587)} = 8.17$$

Step 4: x = 399.5

z-score computation: Area to the left of z:

$$x = 399.5 \rightarrow z = \frac{399.5 - 420.65}{8.17} = -2.59 \qquad 0.0048$$

Required area = 1.0000 - 0.0048 = 0.9952

Thus, the probability that at least 80% of the batteries will last longer than 25 hours is 0.9952.

REVIEW TEST FOR CHAPTER 6

1. Two primary reasons for studying the normal distribution are that

   (a) it is often appropriate to use the normal distribution as the distribution of a population or random variable.

   (b) the normal distribution is frequently employed in inferential statistics.

2. (a) A variable is normally distributed if its distribution has the shape of a normal curve.

   (b) A population is normally distributed if a variable of the population is normally distributed and it is the only variable under consideration.

   (c) The parameters for a normal curve are the mean μ and the standard deviation σ.

3. (a) False. There are many different distributions that could have the same mean and standard deviation.

   (b) True. The mean and standard deviation completely determine a normal distribution, so if two normal distributions have the same mean and standard deviation, then those two distributions are identical.

4. For a normally distributed variable, percentages and corresponding areas under the normal curve (expressed as a percentage) are identical.

5. The distribution of the standardized version of a normally distributed variable is the standard normal distribution, that is, a normal distribution with a mean of 0 and standard deviation of 1.

6. (a) True.

   (b) True.

7. (a) The (second) curve with σ = 6.2 has the largest spread.

   (b) The first and second curves are both centered at μ = 1.5.

   (c) The first and third curves have the same shape because σ is the same for both.

   (d) The third curve is centered farthest to the left because it has the smallest value of μ.

   (e) The fourth curve is the standard normal curve because μ = 0 and σ = 1.

8. Key fact 6.2.

9. (a) The table entry corresponding to the specified z-score is the area to the left of that z-score.

(b) The area to the right of a specified z-score is found by subtracting the table entry from 1.

(c) The area between two specified z-scores is found by subtracting the table entry for the smaller z-score from the table entry for the larger z-score.

10. (a) Find the table entry that is closest to the specified area. The z-score determined by locating the corresponding marginal values is the z-score that has the specified area to its left.

(b) Subtract the specified area from 1. Find the entry in the table that is closest to the result of the subtraction. The z-score determined by locating the corresponding marginal values is the z-score that has the specified area to its right.

11. The value z_α is the z-score that has area α to its right under the standard normal curve.

12. The 68.26-95.44-99.74 rule states that for a normally distributed variable: 68.26% of all possible observations lie within one standard deviation to either side of the mean; 95.44% of all possible observations lie within two standard deviations to either side of the mean; 99.74% of all possible observations lie within three standard deviations to either side of the mean.

13. The normal scores for a sample of observations are the observations we would expect to get for a sample of the same size for a variable having the standard normal distribution.

14. If we observe the values of a normally distributed variable for a sample, then a normal probability plot should be roughly <u>linear</u>.

15.

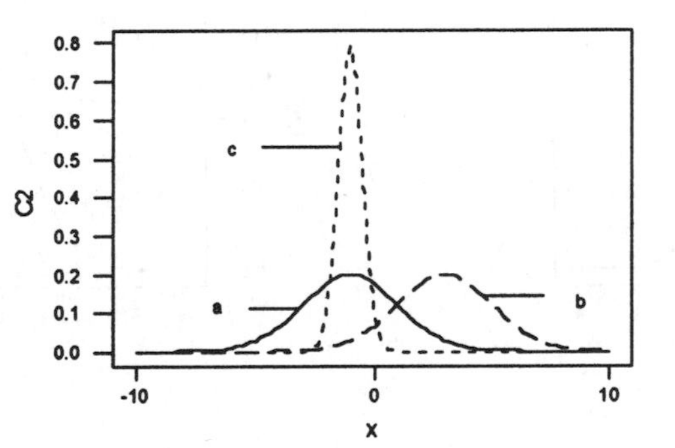

16. (a)

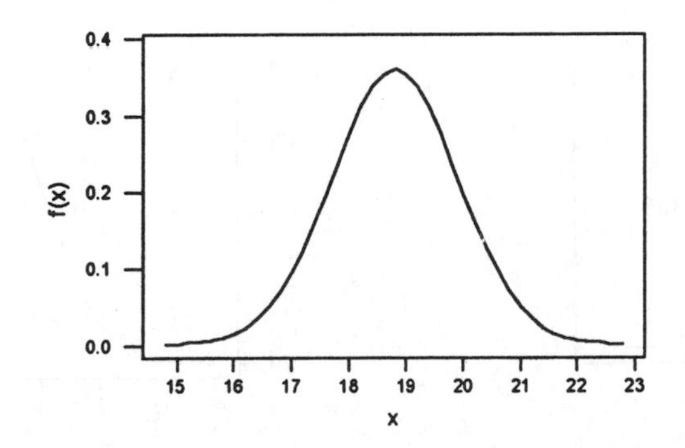

(b) $z = (x - 18.8)/1.1$

(c)

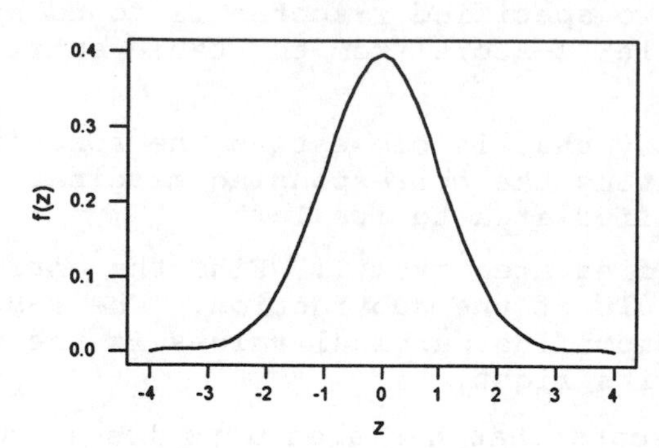

(d) $P(17 \leq X \leq 20) = 0.8115$

(e) The percentage of men who have forearm lengths less than 16 inches equals the area under the standard normal curve that lies to the <u>left</u> of <u>-2.55</u>.

17. (a) The area to the right of 1.05 is 1 - 0.8531 = 0.1469.

(b) The area to the left of -1.05 is 0.1469 (by symmetry).

(c) The area between -1.05 and 1.05 is 0.8531 - 0.1469 = 0.7062.

18. (a) Area = 0.0013

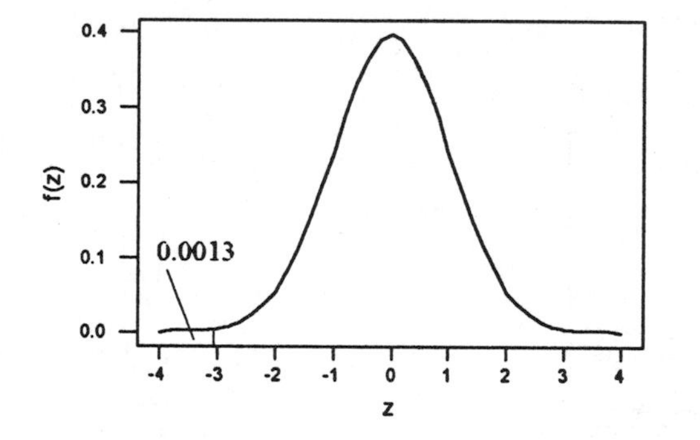

(b) Area = 1 - 0.7291 = 0.2709

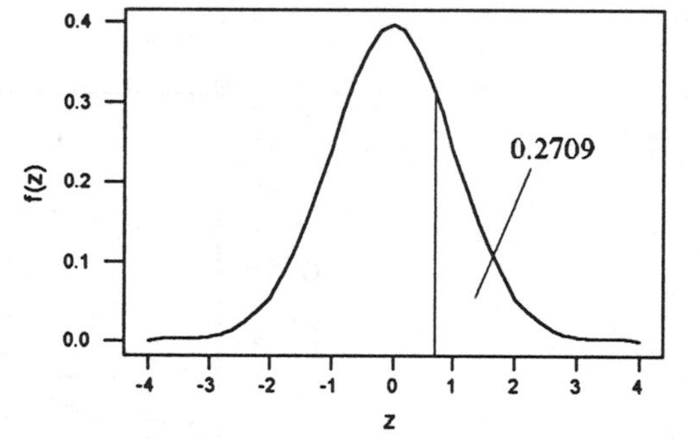

(c) Area = 0.9970 - 0.8665 = 0.1305

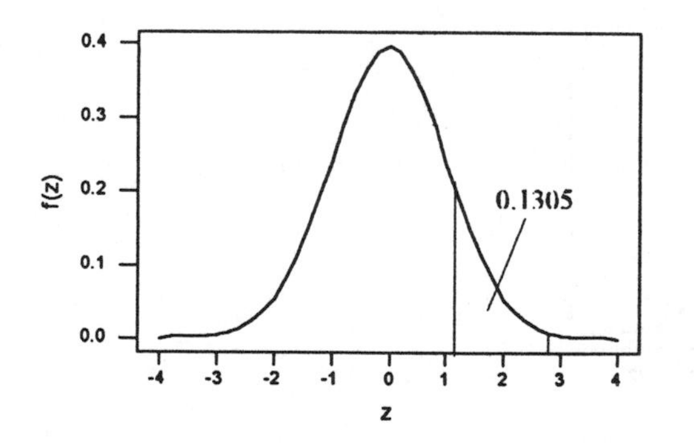

(d) Area = 1.000 - 0.0197 = 0.9803

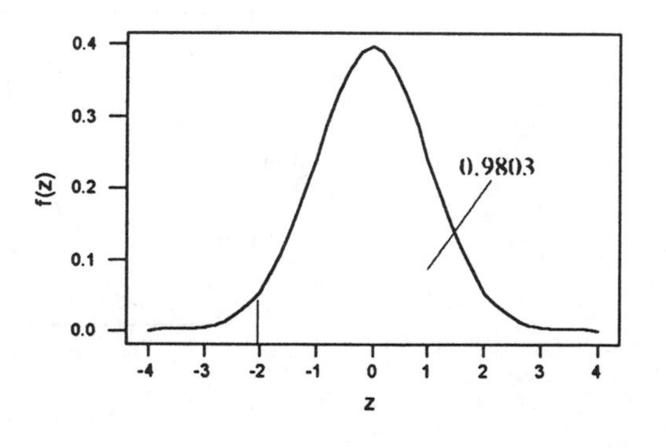

(e) Area = 0.0668 - 0.0000 = 0.0668 (f) Area = 0.8413 + (1 - 0.9987) = 0.8426

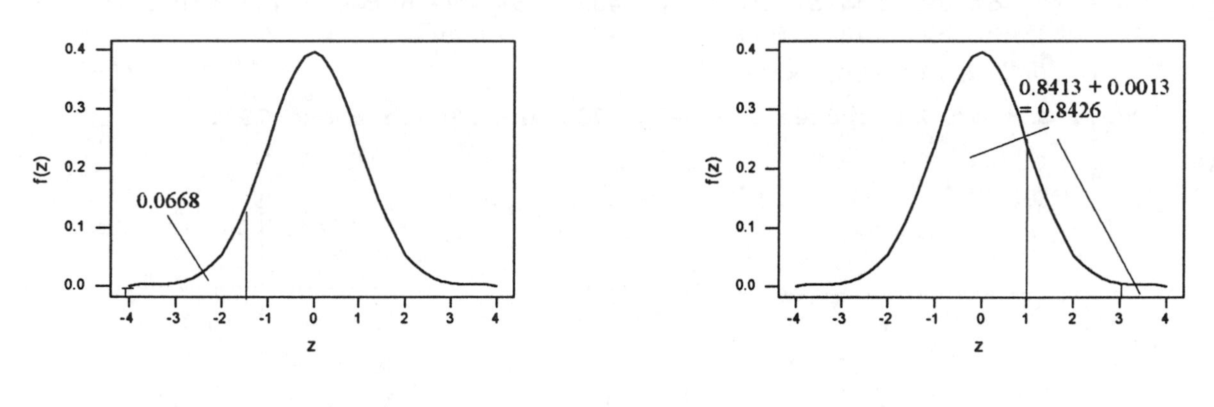

19. (a) z = -0.52

(b) z will have 0.9 to its left: z = 1.28

(c) $z_{0.025}$ = 1.96; $z_{0.05}$ = 1.645; $z_{0.01}$ = 2.33; $z_{0.005}$ = 2.575

(d) -2.575 and +2.575

20. (a) Between 350 and 625:

z-score computations: Area to the left of z:

$$x = 350 \rightarrow z = \frac{350-500}{100} = -1.50 \qquad 0.0668$$

$$x = 625 \rightarrow z = \frac{625-500}{100} = 1.25 \qquad 0.8944$$

Required area = 0.8944 - 0.0668 = 0.8276 = 82.76%

(b) 375 or greater:

z-score computation: Area to the left of z:

$$x = 375 \rightarrow z = \frac{375-500}{100} = -1.25 \qquad 0.1056$$

Required area = 1.0000 - 0.1056 = 0.8944 = 89.44%

(c) Below 750:

z-score computation: Area to the left of z:

$$x = 750 \rightarrow z = \frac{750-500}{100} = 2.50 \qquad 0.9938$$

Required area = 0.9938 = 99.38%

21.

Part	Percent	Lower bound	Upper bound
(a)	68.26	500 - 1(100) = 400	500 + 1(100) = 600
(b)	95.44	500 - 2(100) = 300	500 + 2(100) = 700
(c)	99.74	500 - 3(100) = 200	500 + 3(100) = 800

22. (a) $Q_1 = 500 + (-0.67)(100) = 433$

$Q_2 = 500 + (0)(100) = 500$

$Q_3 = 500 + (0.67)(100) = 567$

Thus 25% of GRE scores are below 433, 25% are between 433 and 500, 25% are between 500 and 567, and 25% are above 567.

(b) $P_{99} = 500 + 2.33(100) = 733$

Thus, 99% of GRE scores are below 733 and 1% are above 733.

23. (a)

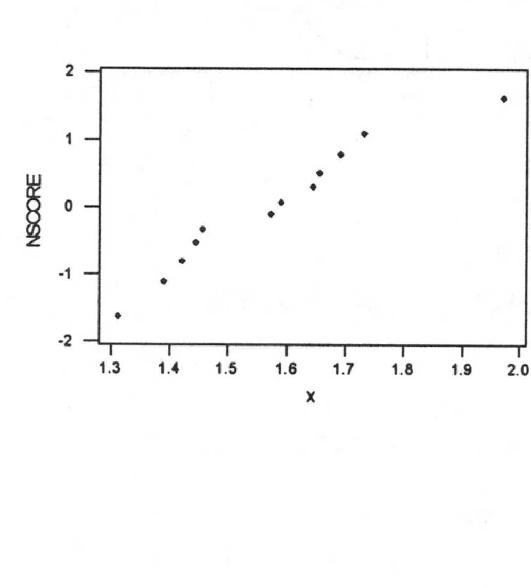

Gas Price x	Normal Score y
1.31	-1.64
1.39	-1.11
1.42	-0.79
1.445	-0.53
1.455	-0.31
1.57	-0.10
1.59	0.10
1.645	0.31
1.655	0.53
1.69	0.79
1.73	1.11
1.97	1.64

(b) Based on the probability plot, there do not appear to be any outliers in the sample.

(c) Based on the probability plot, the sample appears to be from an approximately normally distributed population.

24. For parts (a), (b), and (c), steps 1-3 are as follows:

Step 1: n = 1500; p = 0.80

Step 2: np = 1200; n(1 - p) = 300. Since both np and n(1 - p) are at least 5, the normal approximation can be used.

Step 3:

$$\mu_x = np = 1500(0.8) = 1200$$

$$\sigma_x = \sqrt{np(1-p)} = \sqrt{1500(0.8)(0.2)} = 15.49$$

(a) P(X = 1225):

Step 4: x = 1224.5 and x = 1225.5

z-score computations:	Area to the left of z:
$x = 1224.5 \rightarrow z = \dfrac{1224.5 - 1200}{15.49} = 1.58$	0.9429
$x = 1225.5 \rightarrow z = \dfrac{1225.5 - 1200}{15.49} = 1.65$	0.9505

Required area = 0.9505 - 0.9429 = 0.0076

(b) $P(X \geq 1175)$:

Step 4: x = 1174.5

z-score computation: Area to the left of z:

$$x = 1174.5 \rightarrow z = \frac{1174.5 - 1200}{15.49} = -1.65 \qquad 0.0495$$

Required area = 1.0000 - 0.0495 = 0.9505

(c) $P(1150 \leq X \leq 1250)$:

Step 4: x = 1149.5 and x = 1250.5

z-score computations: Area to the left of z:

$$x = 1149.5 \rightarrow z = \frac{1149.5 - 1200}{15.49} = -3.26 \qquad 0.0006$$

$$x = 1250.5 \rightarrow z = \frac{1250.5 - 1200}{15.49} = 3.26 \qquad 0.9994$$

Required area = 0.9994 - 0.0006 = 0.9988

25. (a)

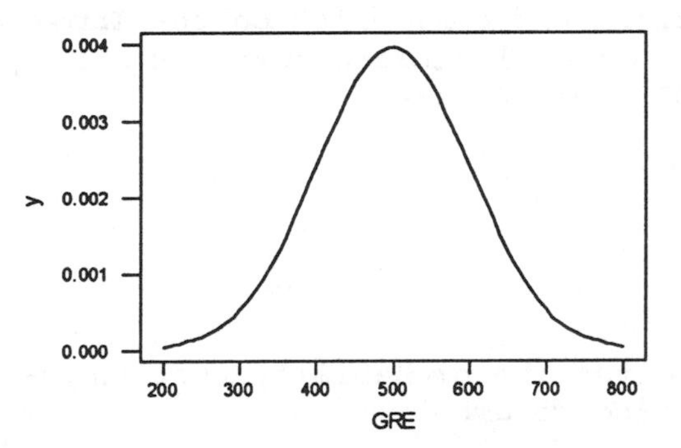

(b) We will generate a column of 1000 observations by choosing **Calc ▶ Random data ▶ Normal...**, typing 1000 in the **Generate rows of data** text box, clicking in the **Store in column(s)** text box and typing GRE, clicking in the **Mean** text box and typing 500, clicking in the **Standard deviation** text box and typing 100, and clicking **OK.** Your results will differ from ours.

(c) We would expect the sample mean to be about 500 and the sample standard deviation to be about 100 since the sample is expected to reflect the characteristics of the population from which it is drawn.

(d) Choose **Calc ▶ Column statistics...**, click on the **Mean** button, and select GRE in the **Input variable:** text box , and click **OK.** Then repeat the process, clicking on the **Standard deviation** button. The results are

Mean of GRE = 500.69

Standard deviation of GRE = 96.739

(e) The histogram of the 1000 GRE scores should look roughly like a bell-shaped curve centered at 500 and most of the observations should be between 200 and 800.

(f) Choose **Graph ▶ Histogram...**, select GRE for **Graph 1** for **X** and click **OK**. The result is (Your results will be different from ours.)

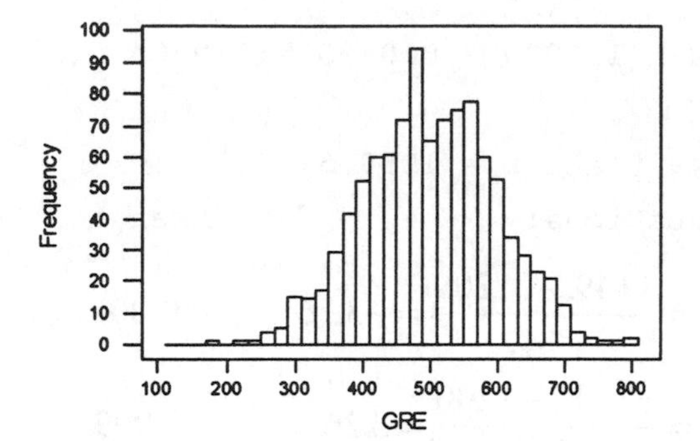

26. Using Minitab, we first enter all of the values in parts a, b, and c of Exercise 20 (350, 625, 375, and 750) in a column (say C23) of the Minitab worksheet. Then choose **Calc ▶ Probability distributions ▶ Normal...**, click on the **Cumulative Probability** button, type 500 in the **Mean** test box, type 100 in the **Standard deviation** text box, click on the **Input column** text box and type C23, click in the **Optional storage** text box and type C24, and click **OK**. The results shown in C23 and C24 are

350 0.066807

625 0.894350

375 0.105650

750 0.993790

The right hand column gives the probability that the GRE score is less than the value in the left hand column.

(a) Thus P(350 ≤ GRE < 625) = 0.894350 - 0.066807 = 0.827543 (82.75%)

(b) P(GRE > 375) = 1 - 0.105650 = 0.894350 (89.435%)

(c) P(GRE < 750) = 0.993790 (99.38%)

27. Using Minitab, we first enter all of the percentile values from parts a and b of Exercise 22 (.25, .5, .75, and .99) in a column (say C25) of the Minitab worksheet. Then choose **Calc ▶ Probability distributions ▶ Normal...**, click on the **Inverse Cumulative Probability** button, type 500 in the **Mean** test box, type 100 in the **Standard deviation** text box, click on the **Input column** text box and type C25, click in the **Optional storage** text box and type C26, and click **OK**. The results shown in C25 and C26 are

0.25 432.551

0.50 500.000

0.75 567.449

0.99 732.635

(a) The first quartile is 432.551, the second quartile is 500, and the third quartile is 567.449. This means that 25% of the observations are below 432.551, 50% are below 500, and 75% are below 567.449.

(b) The 99th percentile is 732.635. This means that 99% of the observations are less than 732.635.

28. Using Minitab with the (unadjusted) data in a column named PRICE, we choose **Calc ▶ Calculator...**, click in the **Store result in variable:** text box and type NSCORE, click in the **Functions** box and select **Normal scores**, then select PRICE for **number**, and click **OK**. Then choose **Graph ▶ Plot...**, select NSCORE for the **Y** variable for **Graph 1** and PRICE for the **X** variable, and click **OK**.

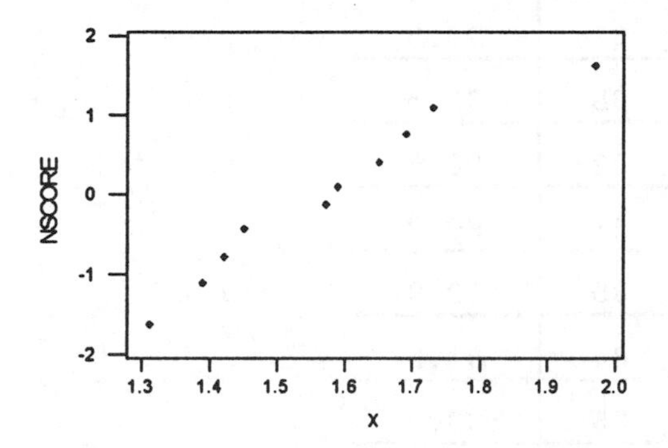

Minitab plots the identical points in the same place so that it appears that only 10 of the 12 data points are present. In the first graph (Exercise 23), the identical mileage values were changed slightly and are plotted with different normal scores.

CHAPTER 7 ANSWERS

Exercises 7.1

7.1 Sampling is often preferable to conducting a census because it is quicker, less costly, and sometimes it is the only practical way to get information.

7.3 (a) $\mu = \Sigma x/N = 405/5 = 81$ inches.

(b)

Sample	Heights	$\bar{x}$
HG,BG	78, 79	78.5
HG,HF	78, 82	80.0
HG,GF	78, 81	79.5
HG,OC	78, 85	81.5
BG,HF	79, 82	80.5
BG,GF	79, 81	80.0
BG,OC	79, 85	82.0
HF,GF	82, 81	81.5
HF,OC	82, 85	83.5
GF,OC	81, 85	83.0

(c)

```
                             o              o
    o          o        o    o    o         o    o         o    o
+---------+---------+---------+---------+---------+---------+---------+
78        79        80        81        82        83        84        85
```

(d) $P(\bar{x} = \mu) = P(\bar{x} = 81) = 0.0$

(e) $P(81 - 1 \leq \bar{x} \leq 81 + 1) = P(80 \leq \bar{x} \leq 82)$

$= P(80 \text{ or } 80.5 \text{ or } 81.5 \text{ or } 82)$

$= 6/10 = 0.6$

If we take a random sample of two heights, there is a 60% chance that the mean of the sample selected will be within one inch of the population mean.

7.5 (b)

Sample	Heights	$\bar{x}$
HG,BG,HF	78,79,82	79.67
HG,BG,GF	78,79,81	79.33
HG,BG,OC	78,79,85	80.67
HG,HF,GF	78,82,81	80.33
HG,HF,OC	78,82,85	81.67
HG,GF,OC	78,81,85	81.33
BG,HF,GF	79,82,81	80.67
BG,HF,OC	79,82,85	82.00
BG,GF,OC	79,81,85	81.67
HF,GF,OC	82,81,85	82.67

(c)

```
                          o         o
             o   o     o  o      o  o   o       o
+---------+---------+---------+---------+---------+---------+---------+
78        79        80        81        82        83        84        85
```

(d) $P(\bar{x} = \mu) = P(\bar{x} = 81) = 0.0$

(e) $P(81 - 1 \le \bar{x} \le 81 + 1) = P(80 \le \bar{x} \le 82)$

$= P(80.33) + P(80.67) + P(81.33) + P(81.67) + P(82.00)$

$= 0.1 + 0.2 + 0.1 + 0.2 + 0.1 = 0.7$

If we take a random sample of three heights, there is a 70% chance that the mean of the sample selected will be within one inch of the population mean.

7.7 (b)

Sample	Salaries	$\bar{x}$
HG,BG,HF,GF,OC	78,79,82,81,85	81.00

(c)

```
                              o
+---------+---------+---------+---------+---------+---------+---------+
78        79        80        81        82        83        84        85
```

(d) $P(\bar{x} = \mu) = P(\bar{x} = 81) = 1.0$

(e) $P(81 - 1 \le \bar{x} \le 81 + 1) = P(80 \le \bar{x} \le 82) = P(81.00) = 1.0$

If we take a random sample of five heights, there is a 100% chance that the mean of the sample selected will be within one inch of the population mean.

7.9 (a) $\mu = \Sigma x/N = 216/6 = 36$ billion

(b)

Sample	Wealths	$\bar{x}$
G,E	60, 47	53.5
G,K	60, 30	45.0
G,A	60, 28	44.0
G,B	60, 28	44.0
G,N	60, 23	41.5
E,K	47, 30	38.5
E,A	47, 28	37.5
E,B	47, 28	37.5
E,N	47, 23	35.0
K,A	30, 28	29.0
K,B	30, 28	29.0
K,N	30, 23	26.5
A,B	28, 28	28.0
A,N	28, 23	25.5
B,N	28, 23	25.5

(c)

```
       o      o                o            o
       o o  o o           o    o o     o    o o                o
+-----+-----+-----+-----+-----+-----+-----+-----+-----+-----+-----+-----+
22    25    28    31    34    37    40    43    46    49    52    55    58
```

(d) $P(\bar{x} = \mu) = P(\bar{x} = 36) = 0/15 = 0.000$

(e) $P(36 - 2 \leq \bar{x} \leq 36 + 2) = P(34 \leq \bar{x} \leq 38)$

$= P(35) + P(37.5) = 1/15 + 2/15$

$= 3/15$

$= 0.2$

If we take a random sample of two rich people, there is a 20% chance that their mean wealth will be within two billion of the population mean wealth.

7.11 (b)

Sample	Wealths	$\bar{x}$
G,E,K	60, 47, 30	45.7
G,E,A	60, 47, 28	45.0
G,E,B	60, 47, 28	45.0
G,E,N	60, 47, 23	43.3
G,K,A	60, 30, 28	39.3
G,K,B	60, 30, 28	39.3
G,K,N	60, 30, 23	37.7
G,A,B	60, 28, 28	38.7
G,A,N	60, 28, 23	37.0
G,B,N	60, 28, 23	37.0
E,K,A	47, 30, 28	35.0
E,K,B	47, 30, 28	35.0
E,K,N	47, 30, 23	33.3
E,A,B	47, 28, 28	34.3
E,A,N	47, 28, 23	32.7
E,B,N	47, 28, 23	32.7
K,A,B	30, 28, 28	28.7
K,A,N	30, 28, 23	27.0
K,B,N	30, 28, 23	27.0
A,B,N	28, 28, 23	26.3

(c)

```
          o          o    o   o   o           o
         oo   o      oo  oo   oo oo       o   oo
+-----+-----+-----+-----+-----+-----+-----+-----+-----+-----+-----+-----+-----+
22    25    28    31    34    37    40    43    46    49    52    55    58    61
```

(d) $P(\bar{x} = \mu) = P(\bar{x} = 36) = 0/20 = 0.00$

(e) $P(36 - 2 \leq \bar{x} \leq 36 + 2) = P(34 \leq \bar{x} \leq 38)$

$= P(34.3) + P(35) + P(37) + P(37.7) = 1/20 + 2/20 + 2/20 + 1/20 = 6/20$

$= 0.30$

If we take a random sample of three wealthy people, there is a 30% chance that their mean wealth will be within two billion of the population mean wealth.

7.13 (b)

Sample	Wealths	$\bar{x}$
G,E,K,A,B	60, 47, 30, 28, 28	38.6
G,E,K,A,N	60, 47, 30, 28, 23	37.6
G,E,K,B,N	60, 47, 30, 28, 23	37.6
G,E,A,B,N	60, 47, 28, 28, 23	37.2
G,K,A,B,N	60, 30, 28, 28, 23	33.8
E,K,A,B,N	47, 30, 28, 28, 23	31.2

(c)

```
                               o
                  o    o      oo o
+-----+-----+-----+-----+-----+-----+-----+-----+-----+-----+-----+-----+-----+
22    25    28    31    34    37    40    43    46    49    52    55    58    61
```

(d) $P(\bar{x} = \mu) = P(\bar{x} = 36) = 0/6 = 0.000$

(e) $P(36 - 2 \leq \bar{x} \leq 36 + 2) = P(34 \leq \bar{x} \leq 38)$

$= P(37.2) + P(37.6) = 1/6 + 2/6 = 3/6 = 0.5$

If we take a random sample of five wealthy people, there is a 50% chance that their mean wealth will be within two billion of the population mean wealth.

7.15 Increasing the sample size tends to reduce the sampling error.

7.17 (a) If a sample of size n = 1 is taken from a population of size N, there are N possible samples.

(b) Since each sample mean is based upon a single observation, the possible $\bar{x}$-values and the population values are the same.

(c) There is no difference between taking a random sample of size n = 1 from a population and selecting a member at random from the population.

Exercises 7.2

7.19 Obtaining the mean and standard deviation of $\bar{x}$ is a first step in approximating the sampling distribution of the mean by a normal distribution because the normal distribution is completely determined by its mean and standard deviation.

7.21 Yes. The spread of the distribution of $\bar{x}$ gets smaller as the sample size increases. Since that spread is measured by the standard deviation of $\bar{x}$, the standard deviation also gets smaller.

7.23 Standard error (SE) of the mean. The standard deviation of $\bar{x}$ determines the amount of sampling error to be expected when a population mean is estimated by a sample mean.

7.25 (a) $\mu = \Sigma x/N = 405/5 = 81.0$

(b)

$\bar{x}$	$P(\bar{x})$	$\bar{x}P(\bar{x})$
78.5	0.1	7.85
79.5	0.1	7.95
80.0	0.2	16.00
80.5	0.1	8.05
81.5	0.2	16.30
82.0	0.1	8.20
83.0	0.1	8.30
83.5	0.1	8.35
		81.00

From the third column, $\mu_{\bar{x}} = \Sigma\bar{x}P(\bar{x}) = 81.00$.

(c) $\mu_{\bar{x}} = \mu = 81.00$

7.27 (b)

$\bar{x}$	$P(\bar{x})$	$\bar{x}P(\bar{x})$
79.33	0.1	7.933
79.67	0.1	7.967
80.33	0.1	8.033
80.67	0.2	16.134
81.33	0.1	8.133
81.67	0.2	16.334
82.00	0.1	8.200
82.67	0.1	8.267
		81.001

From the third column, $\mu_{\bar{x}} = \Sigma\bar{x}P(\bar{x}) = 81.00$. The discrepancy is due to round-off error.

(c) $\mu_{\bar{x}} = \mu = 81.00$

7.29 (b)

$\bar{x}$	$P(\bar{x})$	$\bar{x}P(\bar{x})$
81.0	1.0	81.0
		81.0

From the third column, $\mu_{\bar{x}} = \Sigma\bar{x}P(\bar{x}) = 81.0$.

(c) $\mu_{\bar{x}} = \mu = 81.0$

7.31 (a) The population consists of all babies born in 1991. The variable is the birth weight of the baby.

(b) $\mu_{\bar{x}} = \mu = 3369$ grams; $\sigma_{\bar{x}} = \sigma / \sqrt{n} = 581 / \sqrt{200} = 41.08$ grams

(c) $\mu_{\bar{x}} = \mu = 3369$ grams; $\sigma_{\bar{x}} = \sigma / \sqrt{n} = 581 / \sqrt{400} = 29.05$ grams

7.33 (a) $\mu_{\bar{x}} = \mu = \$43{,}800$; $\sigma_{\bar{x}} = \sigma / \sqrt{n} = \$7200 / \sqrt{50} = \$1018.23$. Thus for samples of size 50, the mean and standard deviation of all possible sample means are respectively, $43,800 and $1018.23.

(b) $\mu_{\bar{x}} = \mu = \$43{,}800$; $\sigma_{\bar{x}} = \sigma / \sqrt{n} = \$7200 / \sqrt{100} = \$720.00$. Thus for samples of size 100, the mean and standard deviation of all possible sample means are respectively, $43,800 and $720.

7.35 (a) Yes. The mean of the sampling distribution of $\bar{x}$ is always μ. A demonstration of this is given in Example 7.2 and in Exercises 7.25 through 7.29.

(b) No. For example, in Example 7.2, the population consists of five observations (76, 78, 79, 81, and 86). The population median is 79. For samples of size 2, the median and mean are identical and therefore have the same sampling distribution. The mean of the sampling distribution of the median equals the mean of the sampling distribution of the mean which is shown to be 80 in the example. Since this is not equal to the population median, it is clear that, in general, the sample median is not an unbiased estimator of the population median.

7.37 (a) Theoretically, the mean of possible sample means is 266 and the standard deviation is $16/\sqrt{9} = 5.33$.

(b) We have Minitab take 2000 random samples of size n = 9 from a normally distributed population with mean 266 and standard deviation 16 by choosing **Calc ▶ Random Data ▶ Normal...**, typing 2000 in the **Generate rows of data** text box, typing C1-C9 in the **Store in column(s)** text box, typing 266 in the **Mean** text box and 16 in the **Standard deviation** text box, and clicking **OK.** These commands tell Minitab to place a total of 18000 observations from the population into columns C1-C9, with 2000 observations in each column. Then, our first random sample of size n = 9 is the first row of columns C1-C9, our second random sample of size n = 9 is the second row of columns C1-C9, and so on.

(c) We compute the sample mean of each of the 2000 samples by choosing **Calc ▶ Row statistics...,** clicking on the **Mean** button, typing C1-C9 in the **Input variables** text box and XBAR in the **Store result in** text box, and clicking **OK.** This command instructs Minitab to compute the means of the 2000 rows of C1-C9 and to place those means in a column named XBAR. Thus, the 2000 $\bar{x}$-values are now in XBAR. (We will not print these values.)

(d) We would expect the mean of the 2000 sample means to be roughly 266 and the standard deviation of the sample means to be about 5.33 since we are taking a sample of 2000 means from a theoretical sampling distribution with mean and standard deviation given in part (a).

(e) The mean is obtained by choosing **Calc ▶ Column statistics...**, clicking on the **Mean** button, selecting XBAR in the **Input variable** text box, and clicking **OK.** The result is

Mean of XBAR = 266.03

Similarly, the standard deviation is obtained by choosing **Calc ▶ Column statistics...**, clicking on the **Standard deviation** button, selecting XBAR in the **Input variable** text box, and clicking **OK.** The result is

Standard deviation of XBAR = 5.2753

Thus, the mean of our 2000 means was 266.03 and the standard deviation was 5.2753.

(f) The answers in part (e) differ from the theoretical values given in part (d) as a result of random error or sampling variability.

Exercises 7.3

7.39 (a) The sampling distribution of the mean is approximately normally distributed with mean

$\mu_{\bar{x}}$ = 100 and standard deviation $\sigma_{\bar{x}} = 28/\sqrt{49} = 4$.

(b) No assumptions were made about the distribution of the population.

(c) Part (a) cannot be answered if the sample size is n = 16. Since the distribution of the population is not specified, we need a sample size of at least 30 to apply Key Fact 7.4.

7.41 (a) The probability distribution of $\bar{x}$ is normal.

(b) The answer to part (a) does not depend on how large the sample size is because the population being sampled is normally distributed.

(c) The mean of $\bar{x}$ is $\mu_{\bar{x}} = \mu$; its standard deviation is $\sigma_{\bar{x}} = \sigma / \sqrt{n}$.

(d) No. Formulas 7.1 and 7.2 apply regardless of the distribution of x.

7.43 (a) All four graphs are centered at the same place because $\mu_{\bar{x}} = \mu$ and because normal curves are centered at their means.

(b) Since $\sigma_{\bar{x}} = \sigma / \sqrt{n}$, we see that $\sigma_{\bar{x}}$ decreases as n increases. This results in a diminishing of the spread, because the spread of a distribution is determined by its σ-parameter. As a consequence, we see that the larger the sample size, the greater the likelihood for small sampling error.

(c) The graphs in Figure 7.6(a) are bell-shaped because, for normally distributed populations, the random variable $\bar{x}$ is normally distributed (regardless of the sample size).

(d) The graphs in Figures 7.6(b) and 7.6(c) become bell-shaped as the sample size increases because of the central limit theorem; the probability distribution of $\bar{x}$ tends to a normal distribution as the sample size increases.

7.45 (a) Because the weights themselves are normally distributed, the sampling distribution for means of samples of size 3 will also be normal and will have mean $\mu_{\bar{x}} = \mu = 1.40$ kg and standard deviation

$\sigma_{\bar{x}} = \sigma / \sqrt{n} = 0.11 / \sqrt{3} = 0.0635$. Thus the distribution of the possible sample means for samples of three brain weights will be normal with mean 1.40 kg and standard deviation 0.0635 kg.

(b) Because the weights themselves are normally distributed, the sampling distribution for means of samples of size 12 will also be normal and will have mean $\mu_{\bar{x}} = \mu = 1.40$ and standard deviation

$\sigma_{\bar{x}} = \sigma / \sqrt{n} = 0.11 / \sqrt{12} = 0.0318$. Thus the distribution of the possible sample means for samples of twelve brain weights will be normal with mean 0.11 kg and standard deviation 0.0318 kg.

(c) To facilitate the comparison of the three graphs, we have overlaid them on one set of axes.

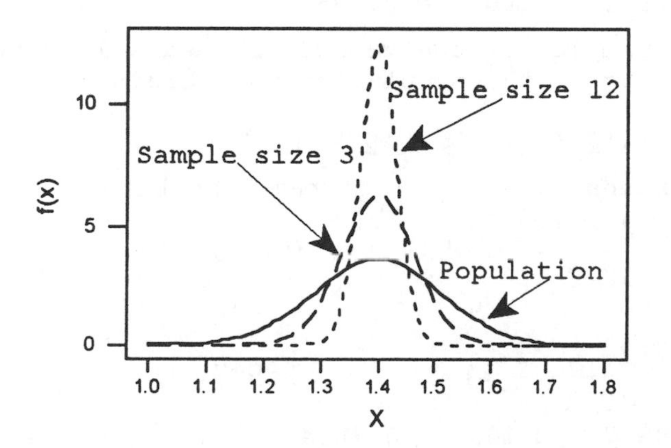

7.47 (a) The sampling distribution of the sample mean for samples of size 100 will be approximately normal with a mean of 272.2 yards and a standard deviation of $\sigma_{\bar{x}} = \sigma / \sqrt{n} = 8.12 / \sqrt{100} = 0.812$ yards. Thus, if all possible sample means for samples of size 100 were found, their distribution would be approximately normal with mean 272.2 yards and standard deviation 0.812 yards.

(b) The sampling distribution of the sample mean for samples of size 100 will be approximately normal with a mean of 272.2 yards and a standard deviation of $\sigma_{\bar{x}} = \sigma / \sqrt{n} = 8.12 / \sqrt{200} = 0.574$ yards. Thus, if all possible sample means for samples of size 200 were found, their distribution would be approximately normal with mean 272.2 yards and standard deviation 0.574 yards.

(c) No. These results follow from the central limit theorem which implies that for large samples ($n \geq 30$), the distribution of the sample mean will be approximately normal regardless of the distribution of the original variable.

7.49 (a) $\sigma_{\bar{x}} = 0.11 / \sqrt{3} = 0.064; P(1.30 \leq x \leq 1.50)$:

z-score computations: Area less than z:

$x = 1.30 \rightarrow z = \dfrac{1.30 - 1.40}{0.064} = -1.56$ 0.0594

$x = 1.50 \rightarrow z = \dfrac{1.50 - 1.40}{0.064} = 1.56$ 0.9406

Total area = 0.9406 - 0.0594 = 0.8812

Thus, 88.12% of samples of three Swedish men will have mean brain wieghts with 0.1 kg of the population mean brain weight of 1.40 kg.

(b) $\sigma_{\bar{x}} = 0.11 / \sqrt{12} = 0.0318; P(1.30 \leq x \leq 1.50)$:

z-score computations: Area less than z:

$x = 1.30 \rightarrow z = \dfrac{1.30 - 1.40}{0.032} = -3.13$ 0.0009

$x = 1.50 \rightarrow z = \dfrac{1.50 - 1.40}{0.032} = 3.13$ 0.9991

Total area = 0.9991 - 0.0009 = 0.9982

Thus, 99.82% of samples of twelve Swedish men will have mean brain weights with 0.1 kg of the population mean brain weight of 1.40 kg.

7.51 (a) $\sigma_{\bar{x}} = 8.12 / \sqrt{100} = 0.812; P(271.2 \leq x \leq 273.2)$:

z-score computations: Area less than z:

$x = 271.2 \rightarrow z = \dfrac{271.2 - 272.2}{0.812} = -1.23$ 0.1093

$x = 273.2 \rightarrow z = \dfrac{273.2 - 272.2}{0.812} = 1.23$ 0.8907

Total area = 0.8907 - 0.1093 = 0.7814

There is a 0.7814 probability that the sampling error will be less than $1000 for samples of size 100.

(b) $\sigma_{\bar{x}} = 8.12/\sqrt{200} = 0.574; P(271.2 \le x \le 273.2)$:

z-score computations: Area less than z:

$x = 271.2 \rightarrow z = \dfrac{271.2 - 272.2}{0.574} = -1.74$ 0.0409

$x = 273.2 \rightarrow z = \dfrac{273.2 - 272.2}{0.574} = 1.74$ 0.9591

Total area = 0.9591 - 0.0409 = 0.9182

There is a 0.9182 probability that the sampling error will be less than \$1000 for samples of size 200.

7.53 $\sigma_{\bar{x}} = 40/\sqrt{250} = 2.53;\ P(|\bar{x} - \mu| \le 5)$

z-score computations: Area less than z:

$\bar{x} = \mu - 5 \rightarrow z = \dfrac{(\mu - 5) - \mu}{2.53} = -1.98$ 0.0239

$\bar{x} = \mu + 5 \rightarrow z = \dfrac{(\mu + 5) - \mu}{2.53} = 1.98$ 0.9761

Required area = 0.9761 - 0.0239 = 0.9522

Thus, there is a 0.9522 probability that the contractor's estimate will be within 5 months of the true mean.

7.55 (a) 68.26 (b) 95.44 (c) 99.74

(c) $100(1 - \alpha)$

7.57 (a) We have Minitab take 2000 random samples of size n = 9 from a normally distributed population with mean 266 and standard deviation 16 by choosing **Calc ▶ Random Data ▶ Normal...**, typing 2000 in the **Generate rows of data** text box, typing C1-C9 in the **Store in column(s)** text box, typing 266 in the **Mean** text box and 16 in the **Standard deviation** text box, and clicking **OK.** These commands tell Minitab to place a total of 18000 observations from the population into columns C1-C9, with 2000 observations in each column. Then, our first random sample of size n = 9 is the first row of columns C1-C9, our second random sample of size n = 9 is the second row of columns C1-C9, and so on.

(b) We compute the sample mean of each of the 2000 samples by choosing **Calc ▶ Row statistics...**, clicking on the **Mean** button, typing C1-C9 in the **Input variables** text box and XBAR in the **Store result in** text box, and clicking **OK.** This command instructs Minitab to compute the means of the 2000 rows of C1-C9 and to place those means in a column named XBAR. Thus, the 2000 $\bar{x}$-values are now in XBAR. (We will not print these values.)

(c) The mean is obtained by choosing **Calc ▶ Column statistics...**, clicking on the **Mean** button, selecting XBAR in the **Input variable** text box, and clicking **OK.** The result is

Mean of XBAR = 266.03

Similarly, the standard deviation is obtained by choosing **Calc ▶ Column statistics...**, clicking on the **Standard deviation** button, selecting XBAR in the **Input variable** text box, and clicking **OK.** The result is

Standard deviation of XBAR = 5.2753

To get a histogram of the 2000 sample means stored in XBAR, choose **Graph ▶ Histogram...**, select XBAR for the **X** variable for **Graph 1**, and click **OK**. The result is

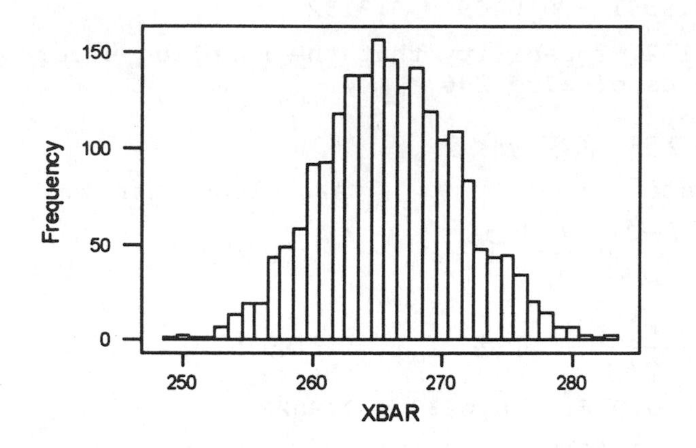

(d) Theoretically, the distribution of all possible sample means for samples of size nine from a normal population should have mean 266 days, standard deviation $\sigma/\sqrt{n} = 16/\sqrt{9} = 5.33$, and a normal distribution.

(e) The histogram is close to bell-shaped, is centered near 266, and most of the data lies within three standard deviations (3 x 5.33 = 16) of 266, i.e. between 250 and 282. The mean of the 2000 sample means is 266.03, very close to 266, and the standard deviation of the sample means is 5.27, very close to 5.33.

REVIEW TEST FOR CHAPTER 7

1. Errors that result from sampling because sampling provides information for only a portion of a population are called sampling errors.

2. The sampling distribution of a statistic is the set of all possible observations of the statistic for a sample of a given size.

3. Two other terms are 'sampling distribution of the mean' and 'the distribution of the variable $\bar{x}$.'

4. The set of possible means exhibits less and less variability as the sample size increases, that is, the set becomes more and more clustered about the population mean. This means that as the sample size increases, there is a greater chance that the value of the sample mean from any sample is close to the value of the population mean.

5. (a) The error results from using the mean income tax, $\bar{x}$, of the 125,000 tax returns sampled as an estimate of the mean income tax, μ, of all 1998 tax returns.

   (b) The sampling error is the difference between $8426 and $8514, or $88.

   (c) No, not necessarily. However, increasing the sample size from 125,000 to 250,000 would increase the likelihood for small sampling error.

   (d) Increase the sample size.

6. (a) $\mu = \$108/6 = \$18$ (thousands)

(b)

Sample	Salaries	$\bar{x}$
A,B,C,D	8, 12, 16, 20	14
A,B,C,E	8, 12, 16, 24	15
A,B,C,F	8, 12, 16, 28	16
A,B,D,E	8, 12, 20, 24	16
A,B,D,F	8, 12, 20, 28	17
A,B,E,F	8, 12, 24, 28	18
A,C,D,E	8, 16, 20, 24	17
A,C,D,F	8, 16, 20, 28	18
A,C,E,F	8, 16, 24, 28	19
A,D,E,F	8, 20, 24, 28	20
B,C,D,E	12, 16, 20, 24	18
B,C,D,F	12, 16, 20, 28	19
B,C,E,F	12, 16, 24, 28	20
B,D,E,F	12, 20, 24, 28	21
C,D,E,F	16, 20, 24, 28	22

(c)

```
                        •
                •   •   •   •   •
        •   •   •   •   •   •   •   •   •
        +---+---+---+---+---+---+---+---+   x̄
       14  15  16  17  18  19  20  21  22
                        μ
```

(d)

$$P(|\bar{x}-\mu| \le 1) = P(\bar{x}=17) + P(\bar{x}=18) + P(\bar{x}=19)$$
$$= 2/15 + 3/15 + 2/15 = 7/15 = 0.4666$$

(e) $\mu_{\bar{x}} = \dfrac{\sum \bar{x}}{N} = \dfrac{270}{15} = 18.0$. The mean of the means of all of the possible samples of size 4 is \$18.0 (thousands).

(f) Yes. The mean of the sampling distribution of $\bar{x}$ is always the same as the mean of the population, which is \$18 thousand in this case.

7. (a) The population consists of all new cars and trucks sold in the U.S. in 1999. The variable under consideration is the amount spent for a new vehicle.

(b) $\mu_{\bar{x}} = \$21022;\ \sigma_{\bar{x}} = \$10200/\sqrt{50} = \$1442.5$

(c) $\mu_{\bar{x}} = \$21022;\ \sigma_{\bar{x}} = \$10200/\sqrt{100} = \$1020.0$

(d) The value of $\sigma_{\bar{x}}$ will be smaller than \$1020 because $\sigma_{\bar{x}} = \sigma/\sqrt{n}$. Thus, the larger the sample size, the smaller the value of $\sigma_{\bar{x}}$.

8. (a) False. By the central limit theorem, the random variable $\bar{x}$ is approximately normally distributed. Furthermore, $\mu_{\bar{x}} = \mu = 45$ and $\sigma_{\bar{x}} = \sigma / \sqrt{n} = 7 / \sqrt{196} = 0.5$. Thus, $P(31 \le \bar{x} \le 59)$ equals the area under the normal curve with parameters $\mu_{\bar{x}} = 45$ and $\sigma_{\bar{x}} = 0.5$ that lies between 31 and 59. Applying the usual techniques, we find that area to be 1.0000 to four decimal places. Hence, there is almost a 100% chance that the mean of the sample will be between 31 and 59.

(b) This is not possible to tell, since we do not know the distribution of the population.

(c) True. Referring to part (a), we see that $P(44 \le \bar{x} \le 46)$ equals the area under the normal curve with parameters $\mu_{\bar{x}} = 45$ and $\sigma_{\bar{x}} = 0.5$ that lies between 44 and 46. Applying the usual techniques, we find that area to be 0.9544. Hence, there is about a 95.44% chance that the mean of the sample will be between 44 and 46.

9. (a) False. Since the population is normally distributed, so is the random variable $\bar{x}$. Furthermore, $\mu_{\bar{x}} = \mu = 45$ and $\sigma_{\bar{x}} = \sigma / \sqrt{n} = 7 / \sqrt{196} = 0.5$. Hence, as in Problem 8(a), we find that there is almost a 100% chance that the mean of the sample will be between 31 and 59.

(b) True. Since the population is normally distributed, percentages for the population are equal to areas under the normal curve with parameters μ = 45 and σ = 7. Applying the usual techniques, we find that the area under that normal curve between 31 and 59 is 0.9544.

(c) True. From part (a), we see that the random variable $\bar{x}$ is normally distributed with $\mu_{\bar{x}} = 45$ and $\sigma_{\bar{x}} = 0.5$. Hence, as in Problem 8(c), we find that there is about a 95.44% chance that the mean of the sample will be between 44 and 46.

10. (a) $\mu = 40$ and $\sigma = 12$

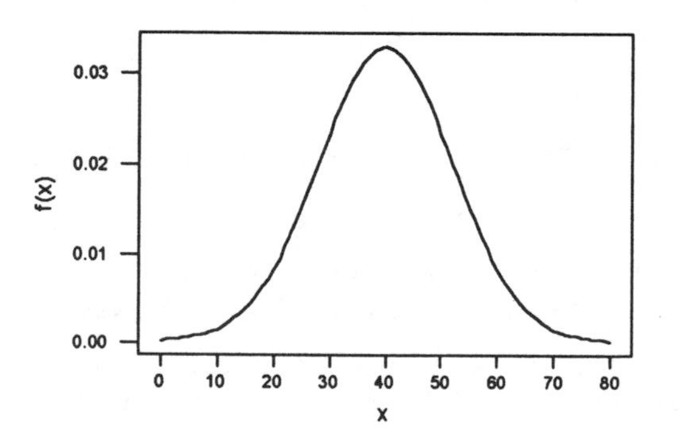

(b) $\mu_{\bar{x}} = 40;\ \ \sigma_{\bar{x}} = 12/\sqrt{4} = 6$

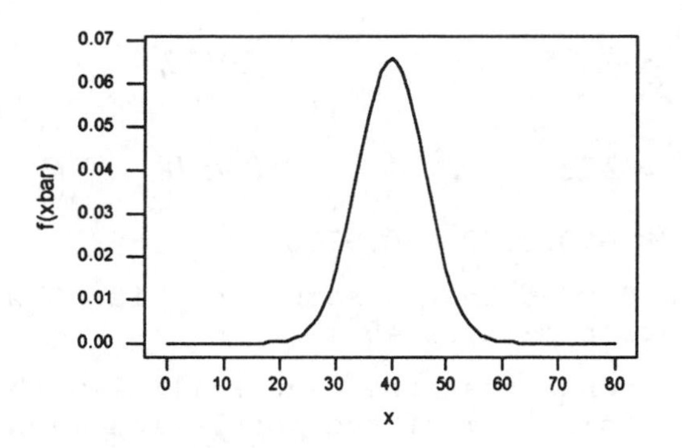

(c) $\mu_{\bar{x}} = 40;\ \ \sigma_{\bar{x}} = 12/\sqrt{9} = 4$

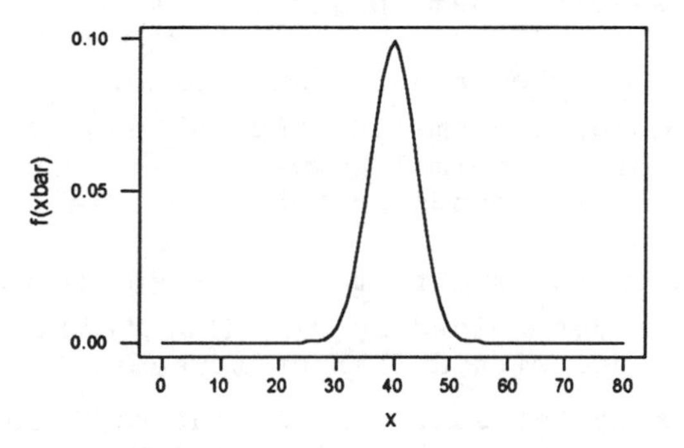

11. $n = 4;\ \ \mu_{\bar{x}} = 40;\ \ \sigma_{\bar{x}} = 12/\sqrt{4} = 6$

(a) $P(31 \le \bar{x} \le 49)$:

z-score computations:	Area less than z:
$\bar{x} = 31 \rightarrow z = \dfrac{31-40}{6} = -1.50$	0.0668
$\bar{x} = 49 \rightarrow z = \dfrac{39-40}{6} = 1.50$	0.9332

Total area = 0.9332 - 0.0668 = 0.8664, or 86.64%.

(b) The probability is 0.8664 that a sample of size four will have a mean within 9 mm of the population mean of 40 mm.

(c) There is an 86.64% chance that the mean krill length $\bar{x}$ of the four krill will be within 9 mm of the population mean krill length of 40 mm.

(d) $n = 9;\ \mu_{\bar{x}} = 40;\ \sigma_{\bar{x}} = 12/\sqrt{9} = 4$

z-score computations:	Area less than z:
$\bar{x} = 31 \rightarrow z = \dfrac{31-40}{4} = -2.25$	0.0122
$\bar{x} = 49 \rightarrow z = \dfrac{49-40}{4} = 2.25$	0.9878

Total area = 0.9878 - 0.0122 = 0.9756 or 97.56%

The probability is 0.9756 that a sample of size 9 will have a mean within 9 mm of the population mean of 40 mm.

There is a 97.56% chance that the mean krill length $\bar{x}$ of the 9 krill obtained will be within 9 mm of the population mean krill length of 40 mm.

12. (a) For a normally distributed population, the random variable $\bar{x}$ is normally distributed, regardless of the sample size. Also, we know that $\mu_{\bar{x}} = \mu$. Consequently, since the normal curve for a normally distributed population or random variable is centered at its μ-parameter, all three curves are centered at the same place.

(b) Curve B corresponds to the larger sample size. Since $\sigma_{\bar{x}} = \sigma/\sqrt{n}$, the larger the sample size, the smaller the value of $\sigma_{\bar{x}}$ and, hence, the smaller the spread of the normal curve for $\bar{x}$. Thus, Curve B, which has the smaller spread, corresponds to the larger sample size.

(c) The spread of each curve is different because $\sigma_{\bar{x}} = \sigma/\sqrt{n}$ and the spread of a normal curve is determined by $\sigma_{\bar{x}}$. Thus, different sample sizes result in normal curves with different spreads.

(d) Curve B corresponds to the sample size that will tend to produce less sampling error. The smaller the value of $\sigma_{\bar{x}}$, the smaller the sampling error tends to be.

(e) When x is normally distributed, $\bar{x}$ always has a normal distribution as well.

13. (a) $n = 500;\ \mu_{\bar{x}} = \mu;\ \sigma_{\bar{x}} = 50{,}900/\sqrt{500} = 2276.32$;

$P(\mu - 2{,}000 \leq \bar{x} \leq \mu + 2{,}000)$:

z-score computations:	Area less than z:
$\bar{x} = \mu - 2000 \rightarrow z = \dfrac{(\mu - 2000) - \mu}{2276.32} = -0.88$	0.1894
$\bar{x} = \mu + 2000 \rightarrow z = \dfrac{(\mu + 2000) - \mu}{2276.32} = 0.88$	0.8106

Total area = 0.8106 - 0.1894 = 0.6212

(b) To answer part (a), it is not necessary to assume that the population is normally distributed because the sample size is large and, therefore, $\bar{x}$ is approximately normally distributed, regardless of the distribution of the population of life insurance amounts.

If the sample size were 20 instead of 500, it would be necessary to assume normality because the sample size is small.

(c) $n = 5000;\ \mu_{\bar{x}} = \mu;\ \sigma_{\bar{x}} = 50{,}900/\sqrt{5000} = 719.83$

z-score computations: Area less than z:

$$\bar{x} = \mu - 2000 \rightarrow z = \frac{(\mu - 2000) - \mu}{709.83} = -2.78 \qquad 0.0027$$

$$\bar{x} = \mu + 2000 \rightarrow z = \frac{(\mu + 2000) - \mu}{709.83} = 2.78 \qquad 0.9973$$

Total area = 0.9973 - 0.0027 = 0.9946

14. (a) $P(x \leq 4.5)$:

z-score computation: Area less than z:

$$x = 4.5 \rightarrow z = \frac{4.5 - 5}{0.5} = -1.00 \qquad 0.1587$$

Total area = 0.1587

If the paint lasts 4.5 years, I would not consider this to be substantial evidence against the manufacturer's claim that the paint will last an average of five years.

Assuming the manufacturer's claim is correct, the probability is 0.1587 that the paint will last 4.5 years or less on a (randomly selected) house painted with the paint. In other words, there is a (fairly high) 15.87% chance that the paint would last 4.5 years or less, if the manufacturer's claim is correct.

(b) $P(\bar{x} \leq 4.5)$:

$n = 10;\ \mu_{\bar{x}} = 5;\ \sigma_{\bar{x}} = 0.5/\sqrt{10} = 0.158$

z-score computation: Area less than z:

$$\bar{x} = 4.5 \rightarrow z = \frac{4.5 - 5}{0.158} = -3.16 \qquad 0.0008$$

Total area = 0.0008

For 10 houses, if the paint lasts an average of 4.5 years, I would consider this to be substantial evidence against the manufacturer's claim that the paint will last an average of five years.

Assuming the manufacturer's claim is correct, the probability is 0.0008 that the paint will last an average of 4.5 years or less for 10 (randomly selected) houses painted with the paint. In other words, there is less than a 0.1% chance that that would occur, if the manufacturer's claim is correct.

(c) $P(\bar{x} \leq 4.9)$:

z-score computation: Area less than z:

$$\bar{x} = 4.9 \rightarrow z = \frac{4.9 - 5}{0.158} = -0.63 \qquad 0.2643$$

Total area = 0.2643

For 10 houses, if the paint lasts an average of 4.9 years, I would not consider this to be substantial evidence against the manufacturer's claim that the paint will last an average of five years.

Assuming the manufacturer's claim is correct, the probability is 0.2643 that the paint will last an average of 4.9 years or less for 10 (randomly selected) houses painted with the paint. In other words, there is a (fairly high) 26.43% chance that that would occur, if the manufacturer's claim is correct.

15. (a) We have Minitab take 1000 random samples of size n = 4 from a normally distributed population with mean 500 and standard deviation 100 by choosing **Calc ▶ Random Data ▶ Normal...**, typing 1000 in the **Generate rows of data** text box, typing C1-C4 in the **Store in column(s)** text box, typing 500 in the **Mean** text box and 100 in the **Standard deviation** text box, and clicking **OK.**

(b) We compute the sample mean of each of the 1000 samples by choosing **Calc ▶ Row statistics...**,clicking on the **Mean** button, typing C1-C9 in the **Input variables** text box and XBAR in the **Store result in** text box, and clicking **OK.** (We will not print these values.)

(c) The mean is obtained by choosing **Calc ▶ Column statistics...**, clicking on the **Mean** button, selecting XBAR in the **Input variable** text box, and clicking **OK.** Our result is

Mean of XBAR = 500.59

Similarly, the standard deviation is obtained by choosing **Calc ▶ Column statistics...**, clicking on the **Standard deviation** button, selecting XBAR in the **Input variable** text box, and clicking **OK.** Our result is

Standard deviation of XBAR = 48.672

To get a histogram of the 1000 sample means stored in XBAR, choose **Graph ▶ Histogram...**, select XBAR for the **X** variable for **Graph 1**, and click **OK.** The result follows.

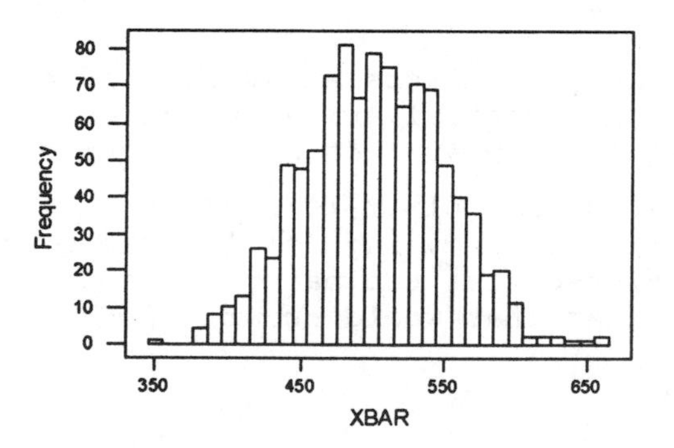

(d) Theoretically, the distribution of all possible sample means for samples of size four from this normal population should have mean 500, standard deviation $\sigma/\sqrt{n} = 100/\sqrt{4} = 50$, and a normal distribution.

(e) The histogram is close to bell-shaped, is centered near 500, and most of the data lies within three standard deviations (3 x 50 = 150) of 500, i.e. between 350 and 650. The mean of the 1000 sample means is 500.59, very close to 500, and the standard deviation of the sample means is 48.672, very close to 50.

16. (a) A uniform distribution between 0 and 1:

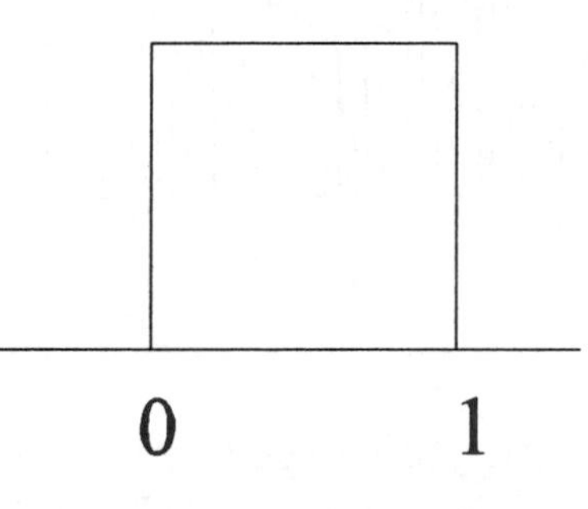

(b) We have Minitab take 2000 random samples of size n = 2 from a uniformly distributed population between 0 and 1 by choosing **Calc ▶ Random Data ▶ Uniform...**, typing 2000 in the **Generate rows of data** text box, typing C1-C2 in the **Store in column(s)** text box, typing 0.0 in the **Lower endpoint** text box and 1.0 in the **Upper endpoint** text box, and clicking **OK.**

(c) We compute the sample mean of each of the 1000 samples by choosing **Calc ▶ Row statistics...**,clicking on the **Mean** button, typing C1-C2 in the **Input variables** text box and XBAR in the **Store result in** text box, and clicking **OK**. (We will not print these values.)

(d) The mean of the sample means is obtained by choosing **Calc ▶ Column statistics...**, clicking on the **Mean** button, selecting XBAR in the **Input variable** text box, and clicking **OK**. Our result is

Mean of XBAR = 0.50454

Similarly, the standard deviation is obtained by choosing **Calc ▶ Column statistics...**, clicking on the **Standard deviation** button, selecting XBAR in the **Input variable** text box, and clicking **OK**. Our result is

Standard deviation of XBAR = 0.20545

(e) Theoretically, the distribution of all possible sample means for samples of size two from this uniform normal population should have mean

(0 + 1)/2 = .5 and standard deviation $\sigma / \sqrt{n} = ((1-0)/\sqrt{12})/\sqrt{2} = 0.2041$. The Minitab simulation results are very close to these theoretical values.

(f) To get a histogram of the 1000 sample means stored in XBAR, choose **Graph**

▶ **Histogram...**, select XBAR for the **X** variable for **Graph 1**, and click **OK**. The result is shown below.

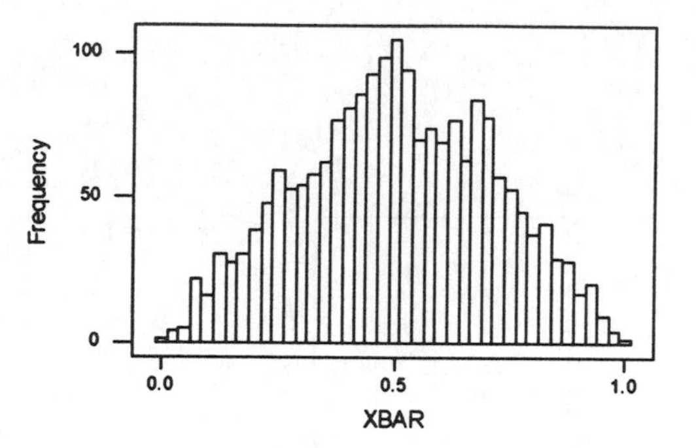

The histogram is more triangle shaped than bell-shaped. Since the population is far from normal and the sample size is only two, we would not expect the sampling distribution to be bell-shaped. In fact, it can be shown using advanced methods that the sum of two uniformly distributed variables has a triangular distribution.

(g) Repeating the process above, but using C1-C35 for the data in each sample, we obtained

Mean of XBAR = 0.49932

Standard deviation of XBAR = 0.049240

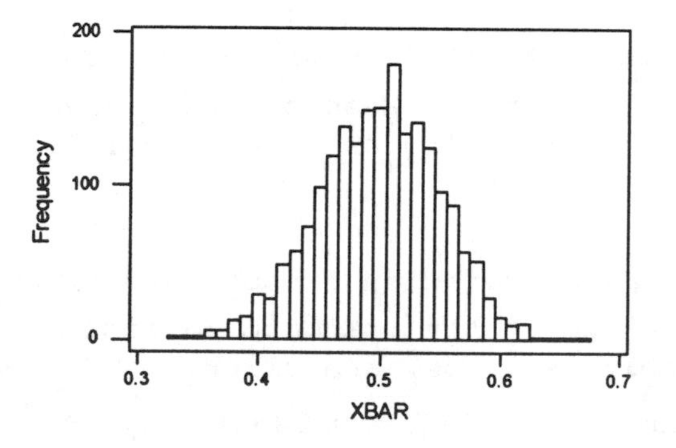

The theoretical distribution of the means has mean 0.5 and standard deviation $\sigma / \sqrt{n} = ((1-0)/\sqrt{12})/\sqrt{35} = 0.0488$. The Minitab simulation values are very close to these. The histogram for the means of the samples of size 35 is shown. It is much more bell-shaped than for samples of size two, as we would expect since n > 30.

CHAPTER 8 ANSWERS

Exercises 8.1

8.1 The value of a statistic that is used to estimate a parameter is called a point estimate of the parameter.

8.3 (a) $\overline{x}$ = \$378,878/20 = \$18,943.90

(b) Since some sampling error is expected, it is unlikely that the sample mean will exactly equal the population mean μ.

8.5 (a) The confidence interval will be

$$\bar{x} - 2\sigma/\sqrt{n} \text{ to } \bar{x} + 2\sigma/\sqrt{n}$$

$$\$18943.90 - 2(\$8100)/\sqrt{20} \text{ to } \$18943.90 + 2(\$8100)/\sqrt{20}$$

$$\$15321.47 \text{ to } \$22566.33$$

(b) Since we know that 95.44% of all samples of 20 wedding costs have the property that the interval from $\bar{x} - \$3622.43$ to $\bar{x} + \$3622.43$ contains μ, we can be 95.44% confident that the interval from \$15321.47 to \$22566.33 contains μ.

(c) We can't be certain that the population mean lies in the interval, but we are 95.44% confident that it does.

8.7 (a) n = 30; $\overline{x}$ = 35,631/30 = 1187.7 miles

(b) The confidence interval will be

$$\bar{x} - 2\sigma/\sqrt{n} \text{ to } \bar{x} + 2\sigma/\sqrt{n}$$

$$1187.7 - 2(450)/\sqrt{30} \text{ to } 1187.7 + 2(450)/\sqrt{30}$$

$$1023.4 \text{ to } 1352.0$$

(c) We could see whether a histogram looked bell-shaped or if a normal probability plot produced a relatively straight line.

(d) It is not necessary that the number of miles traveled per business flight be exactly normally distributed since the sample size 30 is large enough to ensure that the interval obtained is approximately correct.

8.9 Since $P(\bar{x} - 3\sigma/\sqrt{n} < \mu < \bar{x} + 3\sigma/\sqrt{n}) = 0.9974$, we can be 99.74% confident that the interval $\bar{x} - 3\sigma/\sqrt{n}$ and $\bar{x} + 3\sigma/\sqrt{n}$ contains the population mean μ. Since n = 36, $\overline{x}$ = 42.28, and σ = 7.2, the 99.74% confidence interval is (in thousands)

$$\bar{x} - 3\sigma/\sqrt{n} \text{ to } \bar{x} + 3\sigma/\sqrt{n}$$

$$42.28 - 3(7.2)/\sqrt{36} \text{ to } 42.28 + 3(7.2)/\sqrt{36}$$

$$38.68 \text{ to } 45.88$$

We can be 99.74% confident that the interval \$38,860 to \$45,880 contains the value of the mean μ.

Exercises 8.2

8.11 (a) Confidence level = 0.90; α = 0.10

(b) Confidence level = 0.99; α = 0.01

8.13 (a) When x is normally distributed, the sampling distribution of $\overline{x}$ is exactly normally distributed. The confidence interval procedure 8.1 is based on this fact.

(b) When the sample size is large, the sampling distribution of $\bar{x}$ is approximately normal regardless of the shape of the underlying distribution of x itself.

8.15 (a) For use of the z-interval procedure to be appropriate, we must have either a normal population with known standard deviation or a sample size that is large. If the sample size is less than 15, we should be quite certain that the normality assumption is valid; for sample sizes between 15 and 30, the z-procedure is reasonable unless there are outliers or the variable is far from being normally distributed. When there are outliers present, the procedure can still be used provided that their removal can be justified, and removing them results in a data set for which the z-interval is appropriate.

(b) The normality assumption is particularly important when the sample size is small. If the sample size is small and the distribution of the variable under consideration is not normal, then the sampling distribution of the mean may be considerably different from normal. As a result, the true confidence level may differ significantly from the nominal confidence level of $1-\alpha$.

8.17 (a) The z-interval procedure is reasonable since the population is very close to normal.

(b) The z-interval procedure is reasonable since the sample size is very large.

(c) The z-interval procedure is not reasonable with outliers present for such a small sample.

(d) The z-interval procedure is reasonable since the population is roughly normal and the sample size is over 15.

(e) The z-interval procedure is not reasonable since the sample size is too small for a population which is far from normal.

(f) The z-interval procedure is reasonable since the sampling distribution of $\bar{x}$ will be very close to normal for a sample size of 250 even though the population itself is far from normal.

8.19 A 95% confidence interval will give a more precise (shorter interval) estimate of μ.

8.21 $n = 18$; $\bar{x} = 113.97/18 = 6.332$ million; $\sigma = 2.04$ million

(a) Step 1: $\alpha = 0.05$; $z_{\alpha/2} = z_{0.025} = 1.96$

Step 2:

$$\bar{x} - z_{\alpha/2}\sigma/\sqrt{n} \text{ to } \bar{x} + z_{\alpha/2}\sigma/\sqrt{n}$$

$$6.33 - 1.96(2.04)/\sqrt{18} \text{ to } 6.33 + 1.96(2.04)/\sqrt{18}$$

$$5.39 \text{ to } 7.27$$

(b) We can be 95% confident that the mean amount μ of all venture capital investments is somewhere between \$5.39 million and \$7.27 million.

8.23 $n = 30$; $\bar{x} = \$2.27$ million; $\sigma = \$0.5$ million

Step 1: $\alpha = 0.05$; $z_{\alpha/2} = z_{0.025} = 1.96$

Step 2:

$$\bar{x} - z_{\alpha/2}\sigma/\sqrt{n} \text{ to } \bar{x} + z_{\alpha/2}\sigma/\sqrt{n}$$

$$2.27 - 2.575(0.5)/\sqrt{30} \text{ to } 2.27 + 2.575(0.5)/\sqrt{30}$$

$$2.03 \text{ to } 2.51$$

We can be 99% confident that the mean gross earnings, μ, of all Rolling Stones concerts is somewhere between $2.03 and $2.51 million.

8.25 $n = 18$; $\bar{x} = \$6.332$ million; $\sigma = \$2.04$ million

(a) Step 1: $\alpha = 0.20$; $z_{\alpha/2} = z_{0.10} = 1.28$

Step 2:

$$\bar{x} - z_{\alpha/2}\sigma/\sqrt{n} \text{ to } \bar{x} + z_{\alpha/2}\sigma/\sqrt{n}$$
$$6.33 - 1.28(2.04)/\sqrt{18} \text{ to } 6.33 + 1.28(2.04)/\sqrt{18}$$
$$5.72 \text{ to } 6.95$$

(b) The confidence interval in part (a) is shorter than the one in Exercise 8.21 because we have changed the confidence level from 95% in Exercise 8.21 to 80% in this exercise. Notice that decreasing the confidence level from 95% to 80% decreases the $z_{\alpha/2}$-value from 1.96 to 1.28. The smaller z-value, in turn, results in a shorter interval.

(c)

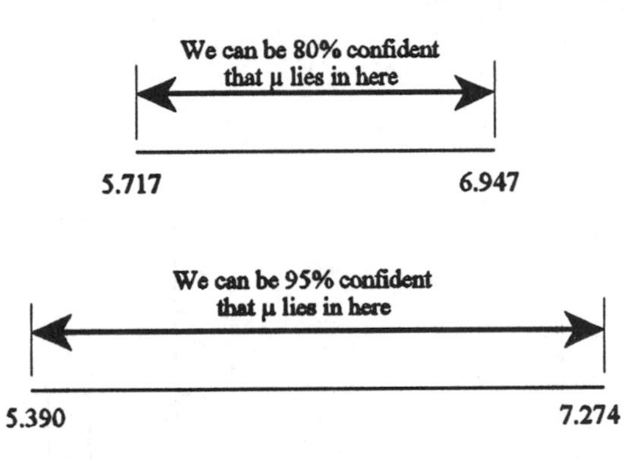

(d) The 80% confidence interval is shorter and therefore provides a more precise estimate of μ.

8.27 (a) To increase the precision (shorten the confidence interval) without reducing the confidence level, we should increase the sample size n.

(b) To increase our level of confidence without reducing the precision, we should increase the sample size n.

8.29 (a) Using Minitab, with the data in a column named INVESTMENT, we first create a column of normal scores. To do this, choose **Calc ▶ Mathematical Expressions...**, type NORMAL in the **Variable (New or Modified):** text box and NSCORES('INVESTMENT') in the **Expression:** text box. Click **OK**. To create the Normal Probability Plot, choose **Graph ▶ Plot..** and select NORMAL for the **Y** variable for **Graph 1** and INVESTMENT for the **X** variable. Click **OK**. For the boxplot, choose **Graph ▶ Boxplot...** and select INVESTMENT for the **Y** variable for **Graph 1**. Click **OK**. For the histogram, choose **Graph ▶ Histogram...** and select INVESTMENT for the **X** variable for **Graph 1**. Click **OK**. For the stem-and-leaf plot, choose **Graph ▶ Character Graphs ▶ Stem-and-leaf...** and select INVESTMENT in the **Variables** text box. Click **OK**. The results are shown below.

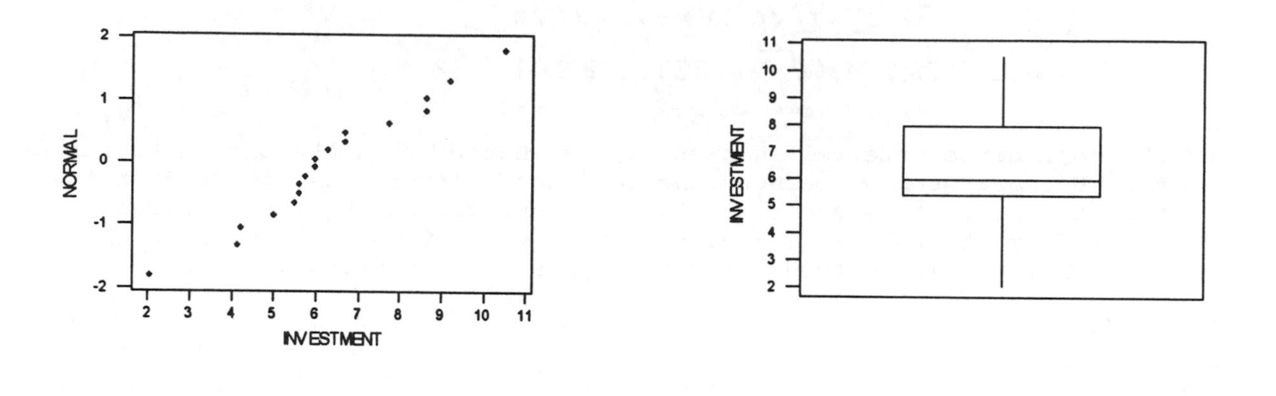


```
Stem-and-leaf of INVESTME  N  = 18
Leaf Unit = 0.10

   1    2 0
   1    3
   4    4 129
 (6)    5 456799
   8    6 266
   5    7 7
   4    8 66
   2    9 2
   1   10 5
```

(b) Choose **Stat ▶ Basic statistics ▶ 1-Sample z...**, specify INVESTMENT in the **Variables** text box, select the **Confidence interval** option button, click in the **Level** text box and type 95, click in the **Sigma** text box and type 2.04, and click **OK**. The result is

The assumed sigma = 2.04

Variable	N	Mean	StDev	SE Mean	95.0 % CI
INVESTME	18	6.332	2.037	0.481	(5.389, 7.274)

(c) There were no potential outliers, the sample size was moderate (more than 15), and the normal probability plot is roughly linear. Therefore there should be no problem with using the z-procedure.

8.31 (a) With the data in a column named CHILDREN, choose **Stat ▶ Basic statistics ▶ 1-Sample z...**, specify CHILDREN in the **Variables** text box, select the

Confidence interval option button, click in the **Level** text box and type 90, click in the **Sigma** text box and type 1.95, and click **OK**. The result is

```
The assumed sigma = 1.95

Variable      N      Mean     StDev  SE Mean        90.0 % C.I.
CHILDREN     22     1.682     1.912    0.416   (  0.998,   2.366)
```

(b) We first create a column of normal scores. To do this, choose **Calc ▶ Mathematical Expressions...**, type NORMAL in the **Variable (New or Modified):** text box and NSCORES('CHILDREN') in the **Expression:** text box. Click **OK**. To create the Normal Probability Plot, choose **Graph ▶ Plot..** and select NORMAL for the **Y** variable for **Graph 1** and CHILDREN for the **X** variable. Click **OK**. For the boxplot, choose **Graph ▶ Boxplot...** and select CHILDREN for the **Y** variable for **Graph 1**. Click **OK**. For the histogram, choose **Graph ▶ Histogram...** and select CHILDREN for the **X** variable for **Graph 1**. Click **OK**. For the stem-and-leaf plot, choose **Graph ▶ Character Graphs ▶ Stem-and-leaf...** and select CHILDREN in the **Variables** text box. Click **OK**. The results are shown below.

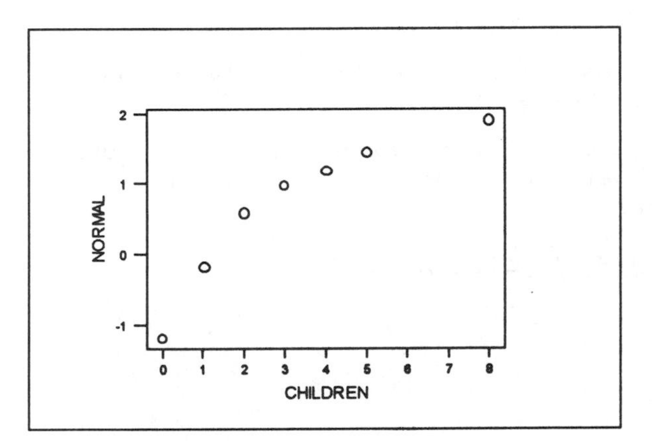

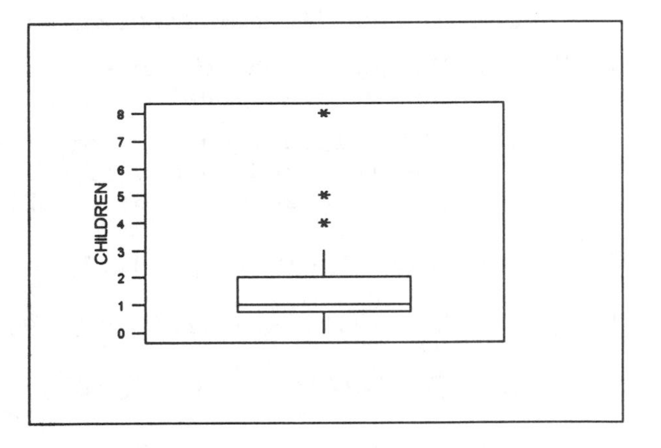


```
Stem-and-leaf of CHILDREN  N  = 22
Leaf Unit = 0.10
    5    0 00000
   (9)   1 000000000
    8    2 0000
    4    3 0
    3    4 0
    2    5 0
    1    6
    1    7
    1    8 0
```

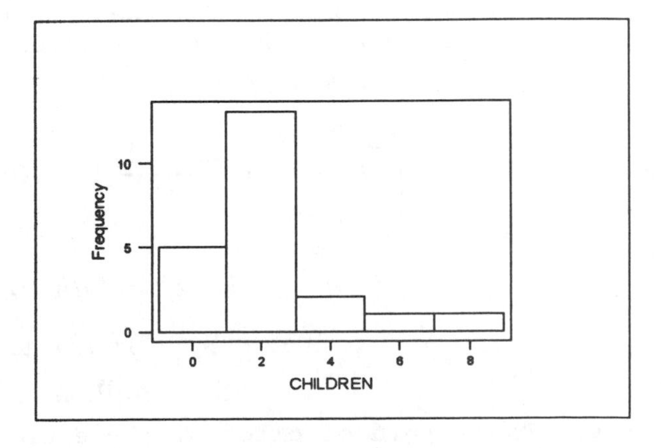

(c) Three observations (4, 5, and 8) are noted as potential outliers (see boxplot). After removing them from the data and repeating part (a), the results are

The assumed sigma = 1.95

Variable	N	Mean	StDev	SE Mean	90.0 % C.I.
CHILDREN	19	1.053	0.848	0.447	(0.328, 1.778)

(d) The mean has changed from 1.682 to 1.053, the standard deviation from 1.912 to 0.848, and the confidence interval from (0.998,2.366) to (0.328,1.778). All of these changes are substantial. It would appear from the graphs that the data may be skewed to the right. Given the moderate sample size of 22, the use of the z-interval procedure is not recommended for these data.

Exercises 8.3

8.33 The margin of error is the standard error of the mean multiplied by $z_{\alpha/2}$.

8.35 (a) Increasing the confidence level while keeping the sample size the same will increase the value of $z_{\alpha/2}$ and hence the length of the confidence interval (thus decreasing the precision of the estimate).

(b) Increasing the sample size while keeping the same confidence level will decrease the margin of error and the length of the confidence interval (thus increasing the precision of the estimate).

8.37 (a) The margin of error is 1/2 the length of the confidence interval; i.e., (1/2) x 20 = 10.

(b) The confidence interval is 60 $\pm$ 10 = 50 to 70.

8.39 (a) We want a whole number because the number of observations to be taken can not be fractional. It must be a whole number.

(b) The original number computed is the smallest value of n that will provide the required margin of error. If we were to round down, the actual sample size would be slightly too small.

8.41 $\alpha = 0.05$; $z_{\alpha/2} = z_{0.025} = 1.96$, so $E = 1.96(20.65/\sqrt{6841}) = \$0.49$.

8.43 (a) $E = (7.27 - 5.39)/2 = \$0.94$ million

(b) $E = 1.96(2.04/\sqrt{18}) = \$0.94$ million

8.45 (a) $E = (2.51 - 2.03)/2 = \$0.24$ million

(b) We can be 99% confident that the maximum error made in using $\bar{x}$ to estimate μ is \$0.24 million.

(c) The margin of error of the estimate is specified to be E = \$0.1 million.

$$n = \left[\frac{z_{\alpha/2}\sigma}{E}\right]^2 = \left[\frac{1.96(0.5)}{0.1}\right]^2 = 96.04 \to 97$$

(d)

$$\bar{x} - z_{\alpha/2}\sigma/\sqrt{n} \text{ to } \bar{x} + z_{\alpha/2}\sigma/\sqrt{n}$$

$$2.35 - 1.96(0.5)/\sqrt{97} \text{ to } 2.35 + 1.96(0.5)/\sqrt{97}$$

$$\$2.25 \text{ million to } \$2.45 \text{ million}$$

8.47 The margin of error of the estimate being \$1,000 does not assure us with 100% certainty that the estimate $\bar{x}$ will be within \$1,000 of the true mean μ. It means only that we can be 100(1-α)% confident that the estimate $\bar{x}$ is within \$1,000 of the true mean μ.

8.49 We have $n = \left[\frac{z_{\alpha/2}\sigma}{E}\right]^2$.

In order to double the precision of the estimate, we must halve the margin of error of the estimate. Replacing E by $E/2$ in the above formula, we obtain

$$n = \left[\frac{z_{\alpha/2}\sigma}{E/2}\right]^2 = 4\left[\frac{z_{\alpha/2}\sigma}{E}\right]^2$$

Thus, we must quadruple the sample size in order to double the precision of the estimate.

Exercises 8.4

8.51 When σ is unknown, the best we can do is to replace it by its estimate, the sample standard deviation s.

8.53 (a) If the population standard deviation is known, use Procedure 8.1.

(b) If the population standard deviation is unknown, use Procedure 8.2.

8.55 The variation in the possible values of the standardized version of $\bar{x}$ is due only to the variation in $\bar{x}$ while the variation in the studentized version results not only from the variation in $\bar{x}$, but also from the variation in the sample standard deviation.

8.57 For df = 6:

(a) $t_{0.10} = 1.440$ (b) $t_{0.025} = 2.447$ (c) $t_{0.01} = 3.143$

8.59 (a) $t_{0.10} = 1.323$ (b) $t_{0.01} = 2.518$

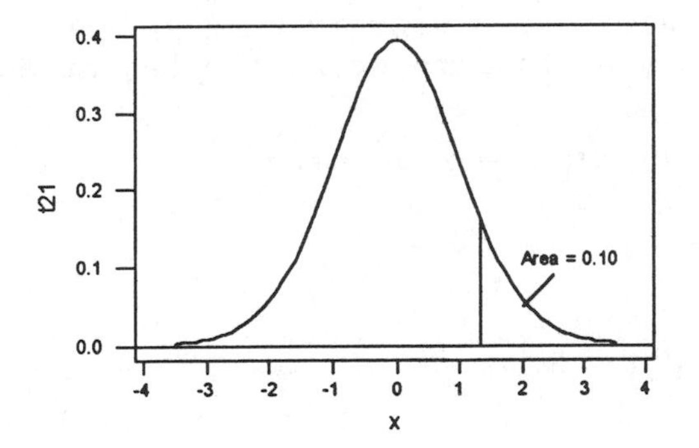

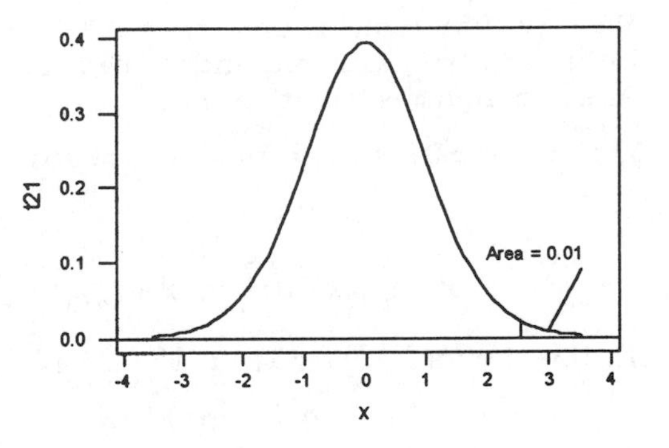

(c) $-t_{0.025} = -2.080$ (d) $\pm t_{0.05} = \pm 1.721$

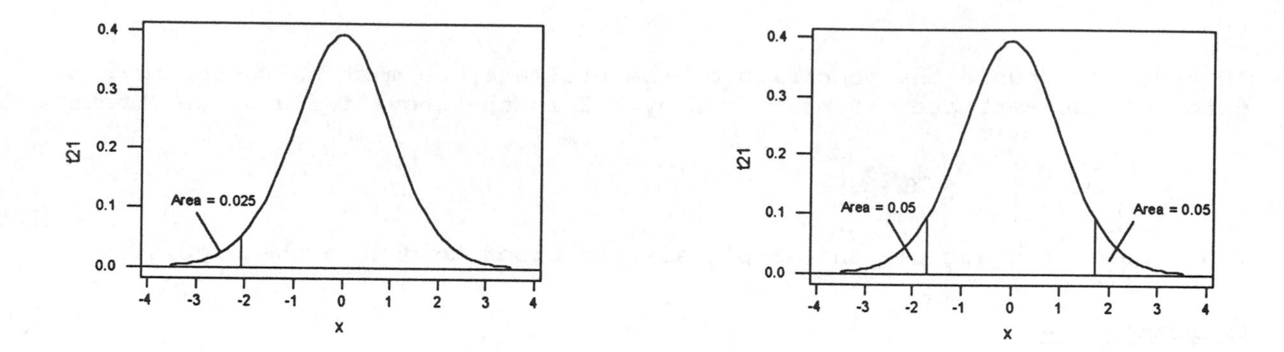

8.61 It is reasonable to use the t-interval procedure since the sample size is large, and for large degrees of freedom (99), the t-distribution is very similar to the standard normal distribution. Another way of expressing this is that the sampling distribution of $\bar{x}$ is approximately normal when n is large regardless of the distribution of the population, so the standardized and studentized versions of $\bar{x}$ are essentially the same.

8.63 $n = 25$; $df = 24$; $t_{\alpha/2} = t_{0.025} = 2.064$; $\bar{x} = \$151.04$; $s = \$22.01$

(a)

$$\bar{x} - t_{\alpha/2} s/\sqrt{n} \text{ to } \bar{x} + t_{\alpha/2} s/\sqrt{n}$$

$$151.04 - 2.064(22.01)/\sqrt{25} \text{ to } 151.04 + 2.064(22.01)/\sqrt{25}$$

$$\$141.95 \text{ to } \$160.13$$

(b) We are 95% confident that the interval \$141.95 to \$160.13 contains the mean, μ, of all expenditures for a family of four to spend the day at an American amusement park.

8.65 $n = 51$; $df = 50$; $t_{\alpha/2} = t_{0.05} = 1.676$; $\bar{x} = 15.05$ cm; $s = 2.50$ cm.

(a)

$$\bar{x} - t_{\alpha/2} s/\sqrt{n} \text{ to } \bar{x} + t_{\alpha/2} s/\sqrt{n}$$

$$15.05 - 1.676(2.50)/\sqrt{51} \text{ to } 15.05 + 1.676(2.50)/\sqrt{51}$$

$$14.46 \text{ to } 15.64$$

(b) We can be 90% confident that the mean, μ, for all burrow depths is somewhere between 14.46 cm and 15.64 cm.

8.67 $n = 22$; $\bar{x} = 25.82$; $s = 7.71$; $df = 21$; $t_{\alpha/2} = t_{0.05} = 1.721$

(a)

$$\bar{x} - t_{\alpha/2} s/\sqrt{n} \text{ to } \bar{x} + t_{\alpha/2} s/\sqrt{n}$$

$$25.82 - 1.721(7.71)/\sqrt{22} \text{ to } 25.82 + 1.721(7.71)/\sqrt{22}$$

$$23.0 \text{ to } 28.6 \text{ minutes}$$

(b) We can be 90% confident that the mean commuting time μ for local bicycle commuters in the city is somewhere between 23.0 and 28.6 minutes.

(c) n=21; $\bar{x}$ = 24.76; s = 6.05; df = 20; $t_{\alpha/2} = t_{0.05}$ = 1.725

$$\bar{x} - t_{\alpha/2} s / \sqrt{n} \text{ to } \bar{x} + t_{\alpha/2} s / \sqrt{n}$$

$$24.76 - 1.725(6.05) / \sqrt{21} \text{ to } 24.76 + 1.725(6.05) / \sqrt{21}$$

$$22.5 \text{ to } 27.0 \text{ minutes}$$

(d) As expected, the mean and standard deviation both decrease when the potential outlier is eliminated from the data. However, the confidence interval has not changed dramatically. If you obtain a normal probability plot of the original data, you will see that the possible deviation from normality caused by the potential outlier is not great. While the sample size is such that one must be alert to the possible influence of outliers, in this instance the use of the t-interval procedure is reasonable.

8.69 The t values approach the z values as the degrees of freedom increase. When the degrees of freedom equal 1000, the bottom five table values differ from the corresponding z values only by amounts ranging from 0.000 to 0.005. Thus if the degrees of freedom are greater than 1000, only a very small error is made by using the z value instead of the t value.

8.71 (a) $t = t_{\alpha}$ (b) $t = -t_{\alpha}$ (c) $t = \pm t_{\alpha/2}$

(d)

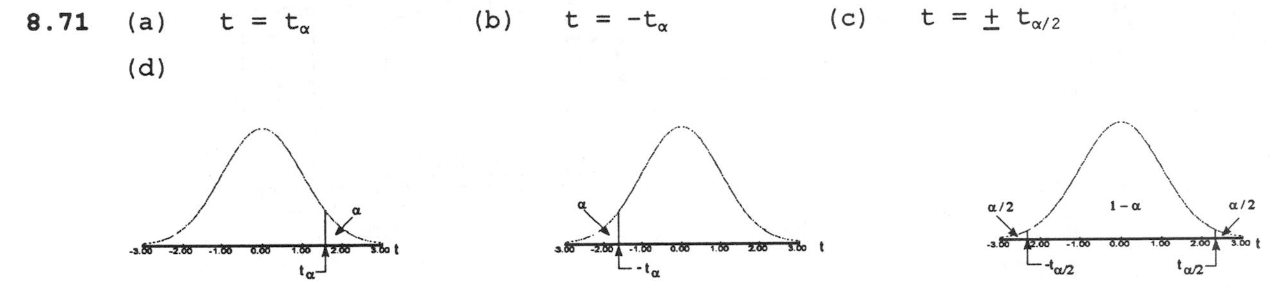

8.73 (a) With the data in a column named COST, first create a column of normal scores. To do this, choose **Calc ▶ Calculator...**,type <u>NORMAL</u> in the **Store result in variable:** text box, select **normal scores** from the function list, select COST to replace **number** in the **Expression:** text box, and click **OK.** To create the Normal Probability Plot, choose **Graph ▶ Plot..** and select NORMAL for the **Y** variable for **Graph 1** and COST for the **X** variable. Click **OK.** For the boxplot, choose **Graph ▶ Boxplot...** and select COST for the **Y** variable for **Graph 1.** Click **OK.** For the histogram, choose **Graph ▶ Histogram...** and select COST for the **X** variable for **Graph 1.** Click **OK.** For the stem-and-leaf plot, choose **Graph ▶ Character Graphs ▶ Stem-and-leaf...** and select COST in the **Variables** text box. Click **OK.**

The results follow.

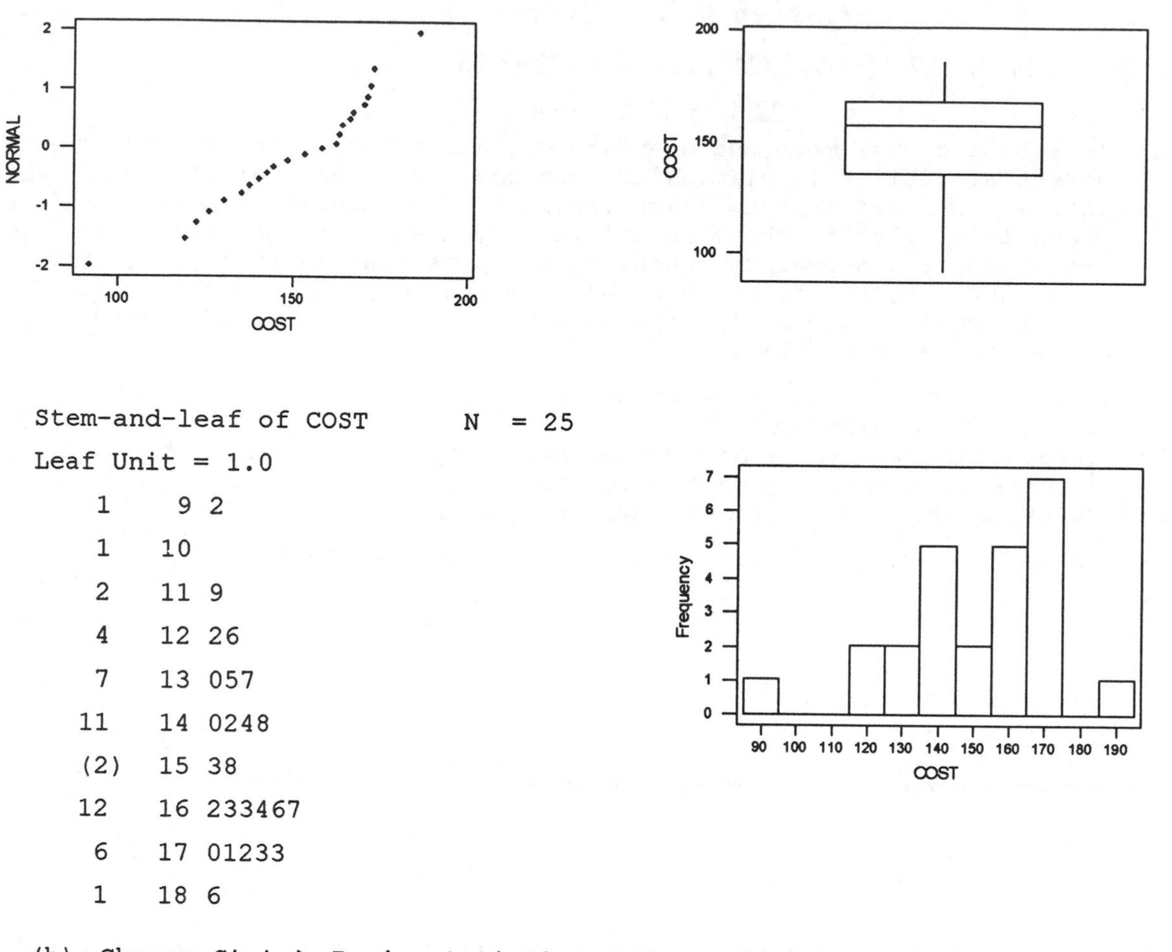


```
Stem-and-leaf of COST       N  = 25
Leaf Unit = 1.0
    1     9 2
    1    10
    2    11 9
    4    12 26
    7    13 057
   11    14 0248
   (2)   15 38
   12    16 233467
    6    17 01233
    1    18 6
```

(b) Choose **Stat ▶ Basic statistics ▶ 1-Sample t...**, specify COST in the **Variables** text box, select the **Confidence interval** option button, click in the **Level** text box and type 95, and click **OK**. The result is

Variable	N	Mean	StDev	SE Mean	95.0 % CI
COST	25	151.04	22.01	4.40	(141.95, 160.13)

(c) Although the graphs indicate a slight skewness to the left, the large sample size and lack of outliers justifies the use of the t-interval procedure.

8.75 (a) Your results will vary. To obtain the 2000 samples using Minitab, Choose **Calc ▶ Random Data ▶ Normal...**, type 2000 in the **Generate rows of data** text box, type C1-C5 in the **Store in Column(s):** text box, type .270 in the **Mean** text box, and type .031 in the **Standard deviation:** text box. Click **OK**.

(b) To find the mean and sample standard deviation in each row (sample), choose **Calc ▶ Row statistics...** and click on **Mean**. Type C1-C5 in the **Input variable(s):** text box and type C6 in the **Store result in:** text box. Repeat this last process, selecting **Standard Deviation** instead of **Mean** and put the results in C7.

(c) To obtain the Standardized version of each $\overline{x}$ in the sample, choose **Calc ▶ Calculator...**, type STANDARD in the **Store results in variable:** text box, type (C6-.270)/(.031/SQRT(5)) in the **Expression:** text box and click **OK**.

(d) Choose **Graph ▶ Histogram...**, select STANDARD as the **X** variable for **Graph 1**. To facilitate a comparison in part (k),. Select the **Frame** button, then **Min and Max...** . Click in the **X minimum** box and type -10 into the text box. Click in the **X maximum** box and type 10 in the text box. Click **OK** and click **OK**. Our graph is shown below, but yours will di[illegible] yet should look similar.

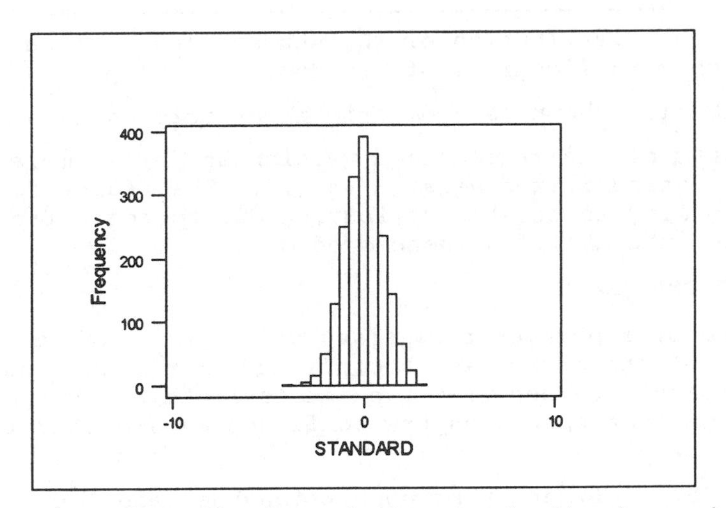

(e) In theory, the distribution of the standardized version of $\overline{x}$ is standard normal.

(f) The histogram in (d) appears to be very close to standard normal. Recall that the distribution is centered at zero and 99.74% of the data should be within 3 standard deviations of the mean. It does appear that this is so for this simulated data.

(g) To obtain the Studentized version of each $\overline{x}$ in the sample, choose **Calc ▶ Calculator...**, type STUDENT in the **Store results in variable:** text box, type (C6-.270)/(C7/SQRT(5) in the **Expression:** text box and click **OK**.

(h) Choose **Graph ▶ Histogram...**, select STUDENT as the **X** variable for **Graph 1** and click **OK**. To facilitate a comparison in part (k),. Select the **Frame** button, then **Min and Max...** . Click in the **X minimum** box and type -10 into the text box. Click in the **X maximum** box and type 10 in the text box. Click **OK** and click **OK**. Your graph should be similar to ours.

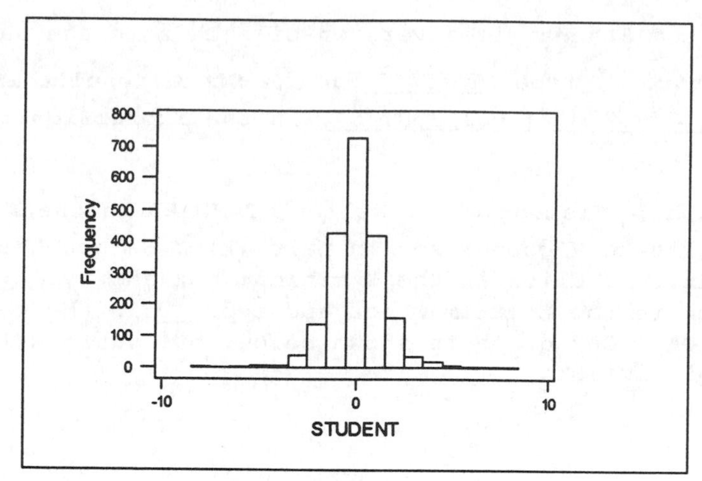

(i) In theory, the distribution of the studentized version of $\bar{x}$ is a t-distribution with 4 degrees of freedom.

(j) The distribution shown is symmetric about zero as is a t-distribution.

(k) The histogram of the studentized version in (h) is more spread out than that of the standardized version in (d). The reason is that there is more variability in the t-distribution due to the extra uncertainty arising from the use of s instead of σ.

REVIEW TEST FOR CHAPTER 8

1. A point estimate of a parameter consists of a single value with no indication of the accuracy of the estimate. A confidence interval consists of an interval of numbers obtained from a point estimate of the parameter together with a percentage that specifies how confident we are that the parameter lies in the interval.

2. False. We are 95% confident that population the mean lies in the interval from 33.8 to 39.0, but about 5% of the time, the procedure will produce an interval that does not contain the population mean. Therefore, we cannot say that the mean must lie in the interval.

3. No. The z-interval procedure can be used almost anytime with large samples because the sampling distribution of $\bar{x}$ is approximately normal for large n. The same is true for the t-interval procedure because when n is large, the t distribution is very similar to the normal distribution. However, when n is small, especially when n is 15 or less, the z-interval and t-interval procedures will not provide reliable estimates if the distribution of the underlying variable is not normal. For sample sizes in the range of 15 to 30, both procedures can be used if the data is roughly normal and has no outliers.

4. Approximately 950 of 1000 95% confidence intervals for a population mean would actually contain the true value of the mean.

5. Before applying a particular statistical inference procedure, we should look at graphical displays of the sample data to see if there appear to be any violations of the conditions required for the use of the procedure.

6. (a) Reducing the sample size from 100 to 50 will reduce the precision of the estimate (will result in a longer confidence interval).

   (b) Reducing the confidence level from .95 to .90 while maintaining the sample size will increase the precision of the estimate (will result in a shorter confidence interval).

7. (a) The length of the confidence interval is twice the margin of error or 2 x 10.7 = 21.4.

(b) The confidence interval will be 75.2 ± 10.7 = 64.5 to 85.9

8. (a) $E = z_{\alpha/2}(\sigma / \sqrt{n}) = 1.645(12/\sqrt{9}) = 6.58$

(b) To obtain the confidence interval, you also need to know $\bar{x}$.

9. (a) The standardized value of $\bar{x}$ is

$$z = \frac{\bar{x}-\mu}{\sigma/\sqrt{n}} = \frac{262.1-266}{16/\sqrt{10}} = -0.77$$

(b) The studentized value of $\bar{x}$ is

$$t = \frac{\bar{x}-\mu}{s/\sqrt{n}} = \frac{262.1-266}{20.4/\sqrt{10}} = -0.605$$

10. (a) standard normal distribution

(b) t distribution with 14 degrees of freedom

11. The curve that looks more like the standard normal curve has the larger degrees of freedom because, as the number of degrees of freedom gets larger, *t*-curves look increasingly like the standard normal curve.

12. (a) The t-interval procedure should be used.

(b) The z-interval procedure should be used.

(c) The z-interval procedure should be used.

(d) Neither procedure should be used.

(e) The z-interval procedure should be used.

(f) Neither procedure should be used.

13. $n = 36$, $\bar{x} = 58.53$, $\sigma = 13.0$, $z_{\alpha/2} = z_{0.025} = 1.96$

$$\bar{x} - z_{\alpha/2}(\sigma/\sqrt{n}) \text{ to } \bar{x} + z_{\alpha/2}(\sigma/\sqrt{n})$$
$$58.53 - 1.96\cdot(13.0/\sqrt{36}) \text{ to } 58.53 + 1.96\cdot(13.0/\sqrt{36})$$
$$54.3 \text{ to } 62.8 \text{ years}$$

14. A confidence-interval estimate specifies how confident we are that an (unknown) parameter lies in the interval. This interpretation is presented correctly by (c). A *specific* confidence interval either will or will not contain the true value of the population mean μ; the *specific* interval is either sure to contain μ or sure not to contain μ. This interpretation is *not* presented correctly by (a), (b), or (d).

15. $n = 461$, $\bar{x} = 11.9$ mm, $\sigma = 2.5$ mm, $z_{\alpha/2} = z_{0.05} = 1.645$

(a)

$$\bar{x} - z_{\alpha/2}\sigma/\sqrt{n} \text{ to } \bar{x} + z_{\alpha/2}\sigma/\sqrt{n}$$
$$11.9 - 1.645(2.5)/\sqrt{461} \text{ to } 11.9 + 1.645(2.5)/\sqrt{461}$$
$$11.7 \text{ to } 12.1$$

(b) We can be 90% confident that the mean length, μ, of N. trivittata is somewhere between 11.1 and 12.1 mm.

(c) Since the sample size is very large, the distribution of sample means will be approximately normal regardless of the shape of the original distribution. It would be nice if the normal probability plot were roughly linear and did not indicate the presence of any extreme outliers, but some non-linearity and a few moderate outliers are not likely to invalidate the use of the z-interval procedure.

16. (a) $E = z_{\alpha/2}\sigma/\sqrt{n} = 1.645(2.5)/\sqrt{461} = 0.2$

(b) We can be 90% confident that the maximum error made in using $\bar{x}$ to estimate μ is 0.2 mm.

(c) The margin of error of the estimate is specified to be E = 0.1 mm.

$$n = \left[\frac{z_{\alpha/2}\,\sigma}{E}\right]^2 = \left[\frac{1.645\,(2.5)}{0.1}\right]^2 = 1691.3 \rightarrow 1692$$

(d)

$$\bar{x} - z_{\alpha/2}\sigma/\sqrt{n} \text{ to } \bar{x} + z_{\alpha/2}\sigma/\sqrt{n}$$

$$12.0 - 1.645(2.5)/\sqrt{1692} \text{ to } 12.0 + 1.645(2.5)/\sqrt{1692}$$

$$11.9 \text{ to } 12.1$$

17. (a) $t_{0.025} = 2.101$

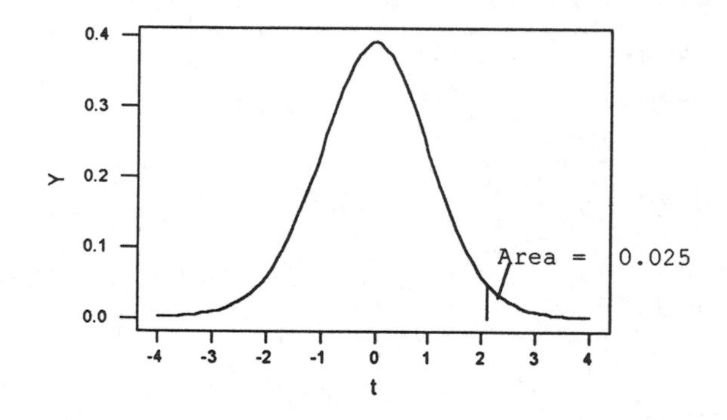

(b) $t_{0.05} = 1.734$

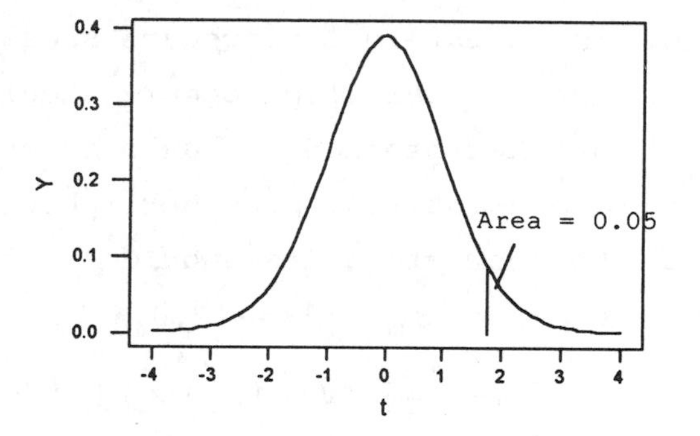

(c) $-t_{0.10} = -1.330$

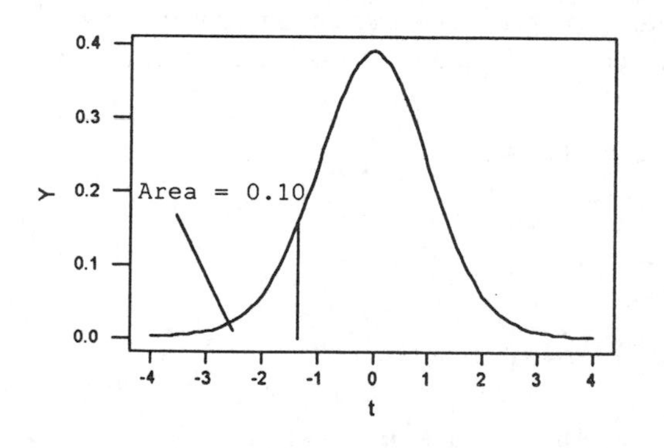

(d) $\pm t_{0.005} = \pm\ 2.878$

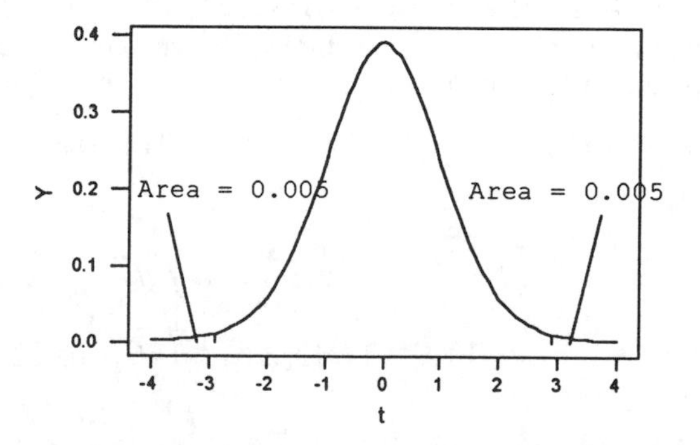

18. n = 16; df = 15; $t_{\alpha/2} = t_{0.025} = 2.131$; $\bar{x} = 86.2$ mm Hg; s = 8.5 mm Hg

(a)

$$\bar{x} - t_{\alpha/2} s/\sqrt{n} \text{ to } \bar{x} + t_{\alpha/2} s/\sqrt{n}$$

$$86.2 - 2.131(8.5)/\sqrt{16} \text{ to } 86.2 + 2.131(8.5)/\sqrt{16}$$

$$81.7 \text{ to } 90.7$$

(b) We can be 95% confident that the mean arterial blood pressure μ of all children of diabetic mothers is somewhere between 81.7 and 90.7 mm Hg.

19. Choose **Stat ▶ Basic statistics ▶ 1-Sample z...**, specify AGES in the **Variables** text box, select the **Confidence interval** option button, click in the **Level** text box and type 95, click in the Σ text box and type 13.0, and click **OK**. The result is

The assumed sigma = 13.0

Variable	N	Mean	StDev	SE Mean	95.0 % C.I.
AGES	36	58.53	13.36	2.17	(54.28, 62.78)

20. (a) With the data in a column named PRESSURE and a second blank column named NORMAL, we choose **Calc ▶ Calculator...**, specify NORMAL in the **Store results in variables** text box, select **normal scores** from the function list, select VIEW to replace **numbers** in the **Expression** text box, and click **OK**. Then choose **Graph ▶ Plot...**, specify NORMAL in the **Y** variable text box for **Graph 1** and PRESSURE in the **X** variable for **Graph 1**, and click **OK**. The result is

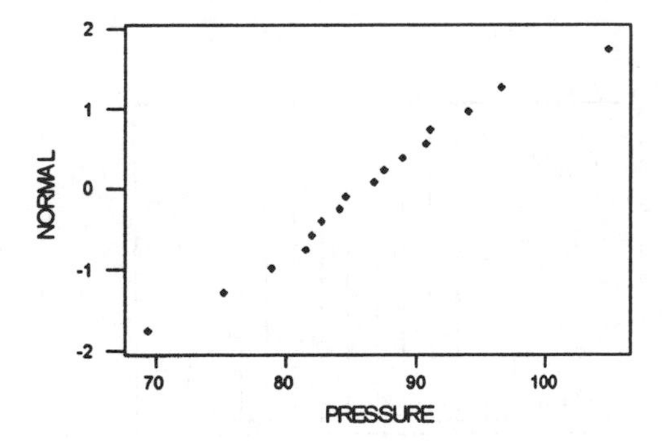

The plot is roughly linear without outliers. With n = 16, it is reasonable to use the t interval procedure.

(b) Choose **Stat ▶ Basic statistics ▶ 1-Sample t...**, specify PRESSURE in the **Variables** text box, select the **Confidence interval** option button, click in the **Level** text box and type 95, and click **OK**. The result is

Variable	N	Mean	StDev	SE Mean	95.0 % CI
PRESSURE	16	86.18	8.49	2.12	(81.66, 90.71)

21. (a) We will import the data into Minitab.

(b) With the data in a column named Duration, first create a column of normal

scores. To do this, choose **Calc ▶ Calculator...**,type NORMAL in the **Store result in variable:** text box, select **normal scores** from the function list, select Duration to replace **number** in the **Expression:** text box, and click **OK.** To create the Normal Probability Plot, choose **Graph ▶ Plot..** and select NORMAL for the **Y** variable for **Graph 1** and Duration for the **X** variable. Click **OK.** For the boxplot, choose **Graph ▶ Boxplot...** and select Duration for the **Y** variable for **Graph 1.** Click **OK.** For the histogram, choose **Graph ▶ Histogram...** and select Duration for the **X** variable for **Graph 1.** Click **OK.** The results follow.

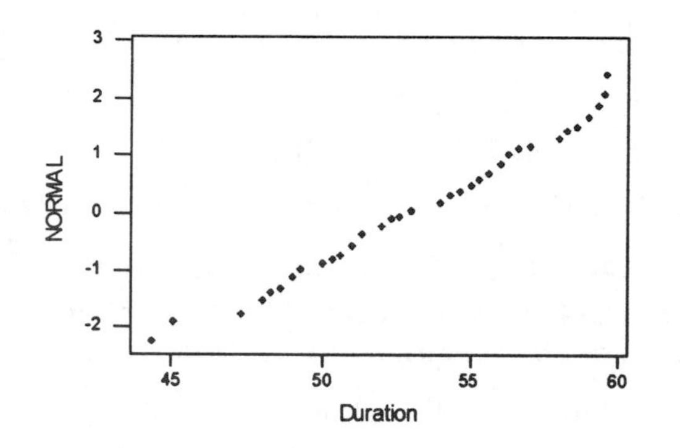

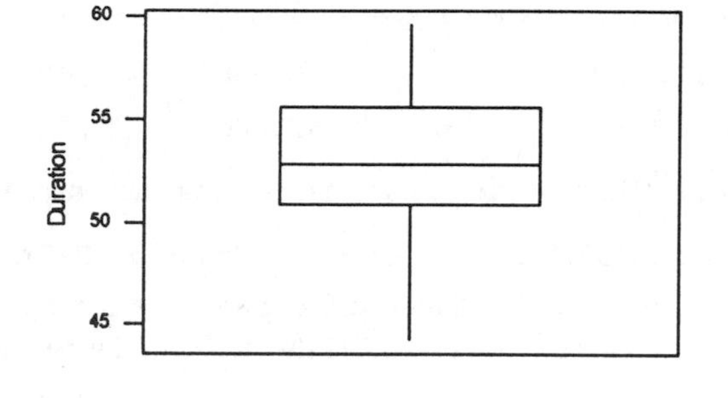

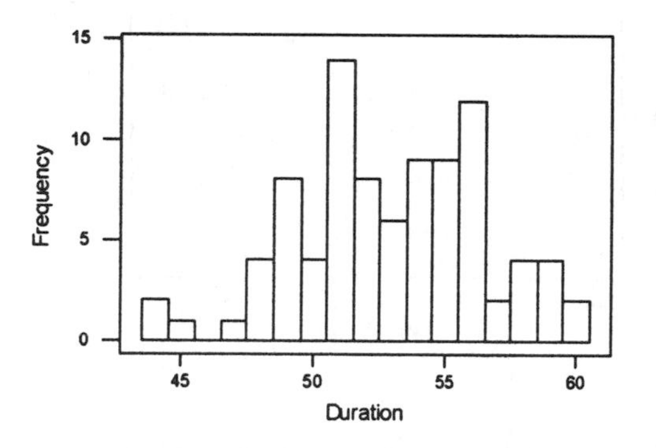

(c) The t-interval procedure is reasonable since the sample size is large (90) and the normal probability plot is quite straight (indicating that the assumption of normality is reasonable). The boxplot does not indicate any potential outliers.

(d) Choose **Stat ▶ Basic statistics ▶ 1-Sample t...**, specify Duration in the **Variables** text box, select the **Confidence interval** option button, click in the **Level** text box and type 99, and click **OK.** The result is

```
Variable      N      Mean     StDev  SE Mean        99.0 % CI
```

Duration 90 52.963 3.479 0.367 (51.998, 53.929)

We can be 99% confident that the population mean larval duration of convict surgeonfish is somewhere between 51.998 and 53.929 days.

22. (a) Your results will vary. To obtain the 3000 samples using Minitab,

Choose **Calc ▶ Random Data ▶ Normal...**, type 3000 in the **Generate rows of data** text box, type C1-C4 in the **Store in Column(s):** text box, type 500 in the **Mean** text box, and type 100 in the **Standard deviation:** text box. Click **OK.**

(b) To find the mean and sample standard deviation in each row (sample),

choose **Calc ▶ Row statistics...** and click on **Mean.** Type C1-C4 in the **Input variable(s):** text box and type C5 in the **Store result in:** text box. Repeat this last process, selecting **Standard Deviation** instead of **Mean** and put the results in C6.

(c) To obtain the Standardized version of each $\overline{x}$ in the sample, choose **Calc**

▶ Calculator..., type STANDARD in the **Store results in variable:** text box, type (C5-500)/(100/SQRT(4)) in the **Expression:** text box and click **OK.**

(d) Choose **Graph ▶ Histogram...**, select STANDARD as the **X** variable for **Graph 1.** To facilitate a comparison in part (k),. Select the **Frame** button, then **Min and Max...** . Click in the **X minimum** box and type -20 into the text box. Click in the **X maximum** box and type 20 in the text box. Click **OK** and click **OK.** Our graph is shown below. Yours will differ, yet should look similar.

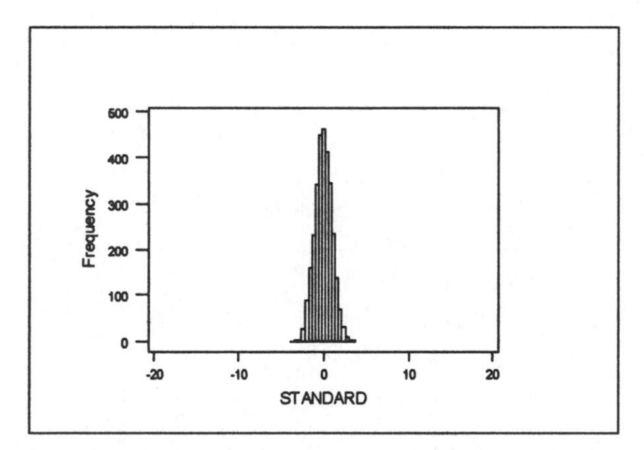

(e) In theory, the distribution of the standardized version of $\overline{x}$ is standard normal.

(f) The histogram in (e) appears to be very close to standard normal. Recall that the distribution is centered at zero and 99.74% of the data should be within 3 standard deviations of the mean. It does appear that this is so for this simulated data.

(g) To obtain the Studentized version of each $\overline{x}$ in the sample, choose **Calc ▶ Calculator...**, type STUDENT in the **Store results in variable** text box, type (C5-500)/(C6/SQRT(4) in the **Expression:** text box and click **OK.**

(h) Choose **Graph ▶ Histogram...**, select STUDENT as the **X** variable for **Graph 1** and click **OK.** To facilitate a comparison in part (k),. Select the **Frame** button, then **Min and Max...** . Click in the **X minimum** box and type -20 into the text box. Click in the **X maximum** box and type 20 in the text box. Click **OK** and click **OK**. Our graph is shown below. Yours will differ, yet should look similar.

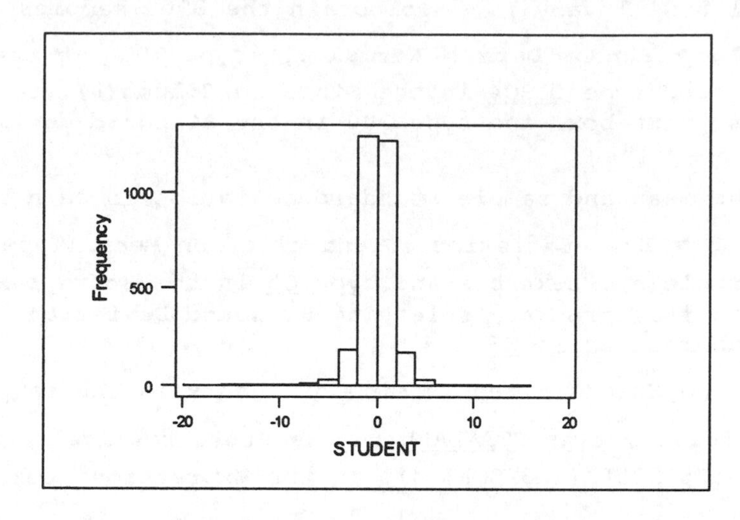

(i) In theory, the distribution of the studentized version of $\bar{x}$ is a t-distribution with 3 degrees of freedom.

(j) The distribution shown is symmetric about zero as is a t-distribution.

(k) The histogram of the studentized version in (h) is much more spread out than that of the standardized version in (d). The reason is that there is more variability in the t-distribution due to the extra uncertainty arising from the use of s instead of σ.

CHAPTER 9 ANSWERS

Exercises 9.1

9.1 A hypothesis is a statement that something is true.

9.3 (a) The population mean μ is equal to some fixed amount μ_0; i.e., $\mu = \mu_0$.

(b) The population mean μ is greater than μ_0; i.e., $\mu > \mu_0$. (Right-tailed)

The population mean μ is less than μ_0; i.e., $\mu < \mu_0$. (Left-tailed)

The population mean μ is unequal to μ_0; i.e., $\mu \neq \mu_0$. (Two-tailed)

9.5 Let μ denote the mean cadmium level in *Boletus pinicola* mushrooms.

(a) H_0: $\mu = 0.5$ ppm (b) H_a: $\mu > 0.5$ ppm (c) right-tailed test

9.7 Let μ denote the mean of last year's customer cell phone use bills.

(a) H_0: $\mu = \$47.70$ (b) H_a: $\mu < \$47.70$

(c) left-tailed test

9.9 Let μ denote the mean annual beer consumption per person in Washington, D.C.

(a) H_0: $\mu = 22.0$ gal. (b) H_a: $\mu \neq 22.0$ gal.

(c) two-tailed test

9.11 (a) H_0: $\mu = 103.6$ million BTU (mean western household energy consumption is the same as all American households)

H_a: $\mu \neq 103.6$ million BTU (mean western household energy consumption differs from that of all American households)

(b) If the sample mean energy consumption $\bar{x}$ differs by too much from 103.6 million BTU, then we should be inclined to reject H_0 and conclude that H_a is true. From the data, we compute $\bar{x} = 79.65$ million BTU. The question is whether the difference of 23.95 million BTU between the sample mean of 79.65 million BTU and the hypothesized population mean of 103.6 million BTU can be attributed to sampling error or whether the difference is large enough to indicate that the population mean is not 103.6 million BTU.

(c) The sampling distribution of $\bar{x}$ will be a normal distribution.

(d) It is quite unlikely that the sample mean $\bar{x}$ will be more than two standard deviations away from the population mean μ. If $\bar{x}$ is more than two standard deviations away from μ, then reject H_0 and conclude that H_a is true. Otherwise, do not reject H_0.

(e) We have $\sigma = 15$, $n = 20$, $\bar{x} = 79.65$, and $\mu = 103.6$ under H_0 true. Thus, $z = (79.72 - 103.6)/(15/\sqrt{20}) = -7.12$. Since $\bar{x}$ is more than two standard deviations away from 103.6 million BTU, we reject H_0 and conclude that H_a is true.

9.13 If the null hypothesis is true, the chance of incorrectly rejecting it is 0.0456 when using the 95.44% part of the 68.26-95.44-99.74 rule.

Exercises 9.2

9.15 A Type I error is made when a true null hypothesis is rejected. The probability of making this error is denoted by α. A Type II error is made when a false null hypothesis is not rejected. We denote the probability of a Type II error by β.

9.17 (a) Rejection region: $z \leq -1.96$ or $z \geq 1.96$

(b) Nonrejection region:

$-1.96 < z < 1.96$

(c) Critical values: $z = \pm1.96$

(d) Significance level: $\alpha = 0.05$

(e) Graph: see below

(f) Two-tailed test

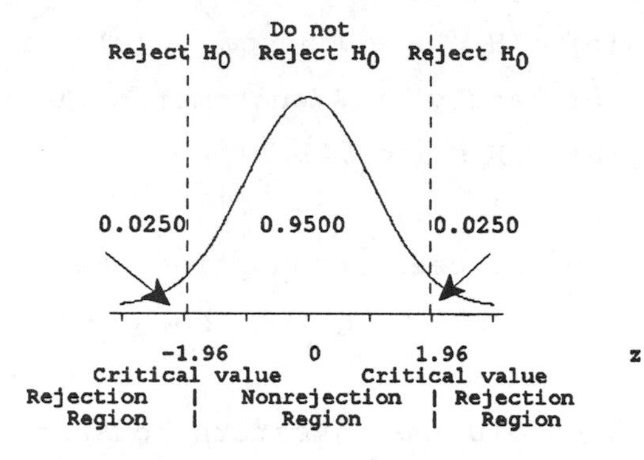

9.19 (a) A Type I error would occur if, in fact, $\mu = 0.5$ ppm, but the results of the sampling lead to the conclusion that $\mu > 0.5$ ppm.

(b) A Type II error would occur if, in fact, $\mu > 0.5$ ppm, but the results of the sampling fail to lead to that conclusion.

(c) A correct decision would occur if, in fact, $\mu = 0.5$ ppm and the results of the sampling do not lead to the rejection of that fact; or if, in fact, $\mu > 0.5$ ppm and the results of the sampling lead to that conclusion.

(d) If, in fact, the mean cadmium level in *Boletus pinicola* mushrooms is equal to 0.5 ppm, and we do not reject the null hypothesis that $\mu = 0.5$ ppm, we made a correct decision.

(e) If, in fact, the mean cadmium level in *Boletus pinicola* mushrooms is greater than to 0.5 ppm, and we do not reject the null hypothesis that $\mu = 0.5$ ppm, we made a Type II error.

9.21 (a) A Type I error would occur if, in fact, $\mu = \$47.70$, but the results of the sampling lead to the conclusion that $\mu < \$47.70$.

(b) A Type II error would occur if, in fact, $\mu < \$47.70$, but the results of the sampling fail to lead to that conclusion.

(c) A correct decision would occur if, in fact, $\mu = \$47.70$ and the results of the sampling do not lead to the rejection of that fact; or if, in fact, $\mu < \$47.70$ and the results of the sampling lead to that conclusion.

(d) If the mean cell phone bill equals the 1996 mean of $47.70, and we do not reject the null hypothesis that $\mu = \$47.70$, we made a correct decision.

(e) If, in fact, the mean cell phone bill is less than the 1996 mean of $47.70, and we do not reject the null hypothesis that $\mu = \$47.70$, we made a Type II error.

9.23 (a) A Type I error would occur if, in fact, $\mu = 22.0$ gal, but the results of the sampling lead to the conclusion that $\mu \neq 22.0$ gal.

(b) A Type II error would occur if, in fact, $\mu \neq 22.0$ gal, but the results of the sampling fail to lead to that conclusion.

(c) A correct decision would occur if, in fact, μ = 22.0 gal and the results of the sampling do not lead to the rejection of that fact; or if, in fact, $\mu \neq$ 22.0 gal and the results of the sampling lead to that conclusion.

(d) If the mean annual beer consumption per person in the nation's capital equals 22.0 gal, and we reject the null hypothesis that μ = 22.0 gal, we made a Type I error.

(e) If, in fact, the annual beer consumption per person in the nation's capital is not equal to 22.0 gal, and we reject the null hypothesis that μ = 22.0 gal, we made a correct decision.

9.25 (a) P(Type I error) = α = 0.

(b) If α = 0, P(Type II error) = β = 1.

9.27 In this exercise, we are told that failing to reject the null hypothesis corresponds to approving the nuclear reactor for use. This action — approving the nuclear reactor — suggests that the null hypothesis must be something like: "The nuclear reactor is safe." This further suggests that the alternative hypothesis is something like: "The nuclear reactor is unsafe." Putting things together, the Type II error in this situation is: "Approving the nuclear reactor for use when, in fact, it is unsafe." This type of error has consequences that are catastrophic. Thus, the property that we want the Type II error probability to have is that it be small.

9.29 (a) The probability of a Type I error is the same as the significance level.

(b) If the mean net weight being packaged is 447 g, then the distribution of $\bar{x}$ is a normal distribution with mean 447 g and standard deviation $\sigma/\sqrt{n}$ = $7.8/\sqrt{25}$ = 1.56 g.

(c) β is the probability of not rejecting the null hypothesis when it is actually false. In this case, β is the probability that $\bar{x}$ falls between 450.88 g and 457.12 g when μ = 447 grams and $\sigma_{\bar{x}}$ = 1.56 g.

Thus

$$\beta = P(450.88 < \bar{x} < 457.12) = P(\frac{450.88 - 447}{1.56} < z < \frac{457.12 - 447}{1.56})$$
$$= \mathrm{P}(2.49 < \mathrm{z} < 6.49) = 1.0000 - 0.9936 = 0.0064$$

(d) The probability of a Type II error is an area between the two critical values of $\bar{x}$ above (i.e., between $\bar{x}_l$ = 450.88 g and $\bar{x}_r$ = 457.12 g) **assuming** that the true mean is any one of the thirteen values of μ presented in this part of the exercise. As a probability statement, this is written P(450.88< $\bar{x}$ < 457.12).

Since the variable x in this exercise is normally distributed, the random variable $\bar{x}$ is normally distributed with mean $\mu_{\bar{x}} = \mu$ and standard deviation $\sigma_{\bar{x}} = \sigma/\sqrt{n}$. Thus, in order to calculate P(450.88 < $\bar{x}$ <457.12), we implement the z-score formulas

$$z = \frac{\bar{x}_l - \mu_a}{\sigma/\sqrt{n}} \text{ and } z = \frac{\bar{x}_r - \mu_a}{\sigma/\sqrt{n}}$$

insert the necessary elements into the right-hand side of each formula itself, and proceed with using Table II to find the appropriate areas.

Notice that $\overline{x}_l = 450.88$ and $\overline{x}_r = 457.12$ and that the standard deviation to be inserted into each formula has already been presented; i.e., $\sigma/\sqrt{n} = 7.8/\sqrt{25} = 1.56$. Most importantly, the value of the population mean to be inserted into each formula is <u>not</u> the value of μ **assuming** that the null hypothesis is true; i.e., it is <u>not</u> $\mu_0 = 454$. It is, instead, an alternative value of μ, as indicated by the symbol μ_a in each of the formulas.

For this part of the exercise, we are given thirteen alternative "true mean" values for μ. This translates into 18 z-scores that need to be computed (i.e., two for each value of the "true mean"). In turn, we calculate the area associated with each pair of z-scores and then use this information to compute β, defined as the probability of a Type II error. The appropriate calculations are:

True mean μ	z-score computation	P(Type II error) β
448	$z = \dfrac{450.88-448}{7.8/\sqrt{25}} = 1.85$ $z = \dfrac{457.12-448}{7.8/\sqrt{25}} = 5.85$	1.0000 - 0.9678 = 0.0322
449	$z = \dfrac{450.88-449}{7.8/\sqrt{25}} = 1.21$ $z = \dfrac{457.12-449}{7.8/\sqrt{25}} = 5.21$	1.0000 - 0.8869 = 0.1131
450	$z = \dfrac{450.12-450}{7.8/\sqrt{25}} = 0.56$ $z = \dfrac{457.12-450}{7.8/\sqrt{25}} = 4.56$	1.0000 - 0.7123 = 0.2877
451	$z = \dfrac{450.88-451}{7.8/\sqrt{25}} = -0.08$ $z = \dfrac{457.12-451}{7.8/\sqrt{25}} = 3.92$	1.0000- 0.4681 = 0.5319
452	$z = \dfrac{450.88-452}{7.8/\sqrt{25}} = -0.72$ $z = \dfrac{457.12-452}{7.8/\sqrt{25}} = 3.28$	0.9995 - 0.2358 = 0.7637

True mean μ	z-score computation	P(Type II error) β
453	$z = \frac{450.88-453}{7.8/\sqrt{25}} = -1.36$ $z = \frac{457.12-453}{7.8/\sqrt{25}} = 2.64$	0.9959 - 0.0869 = 0.9090
455	$z = \frac{450.88-455}{7.8/\sqrt{25}} = -2.64$ $z = \frac{457.12-455}{7.8/\sqrt{25}} = 1.36$	0.9131 - 0.0041 = 0.9090
456	$z = \frac{450.88-456}{7.8/\sqrt{25}} = -3.28$ $z = \frac{457.12-456}{7.8/\sqrt{25}} = 0.72$	0.7642 - 0.0005 = 0.7637
457	$z = \frac{450.88-457}{7.8/\sqrt{25}} = -3.92$ $z = \frac{457.12-457}{7.8/\sqrt{25}} = 0.08$	0.5319 - 0.0000 = 0.5319
458	$z = \frac{450.88-458}{7.8/\sqrt{25}} = -4.56$ $z = \frac{457.12-458}{7.8/\sqrt{25}} = -0.56$	0.2877 - 0.0000 = 0.2877
459	$z = \frac{450.88-459}{7.8/\sqrt{25}} = -5.21$ $z = \frac{457.12-459}{7.8/\sqrt{25}} = -1.21$	0.1131 - 0.0000 = 0.1131

True mean μ	z-score computation	P(Type II error) β
460	$z = \frac{450.88-460}{7.8/\sqrt{25}} = -5.85$ $z = \frac{457.12-460}{7.8/\sqrt{25}} = -1.85$	0.0322 - 0.0000 = 0.0322
461	$z = \frac{450.88-461}{7.8/\sqrt{25}} = -6.49$ $z = \frac{457.12-461}{7.8/\sqrt{25}} = -2.49$	0.0064 - 0.0000 = 0.0064

To summarize this part of the exercise, notice that the answer for each β value is presented in the third column of the previous table.

(e) Consider columns 1 and 3 of the table in part (d). Also consider a graph whose vertical axis is labeled β and whose horizontal axis is labeled μ. Plot the points of β in column 3 of the table versus the respective values of μ in column 1 and then connect the points with a smooth curve. This curve is presented below.

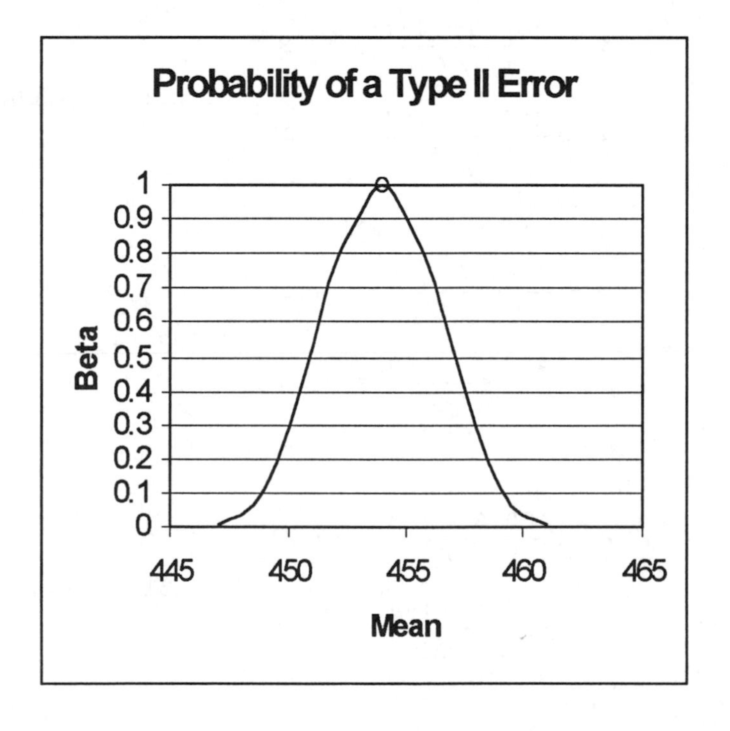

Recall that the value of μ, assuming that the null hypothesis is true, is μ_0 = 454 g. The previous graph tells us that the farther the true value of μ is from the null hypothesis value of 454 g, the smaller is the probability of making a Type II error; i.e., the smaller is β.

All of this is reasonable. We would expect it to be more likely for a false null hypothesis to be detected--and hence β to be small--when the true value of μ is far from the null hypothesis value than when it is close.

Exercises 9.3

9.31 Critical value: $-z_{0.05} = -1.645$

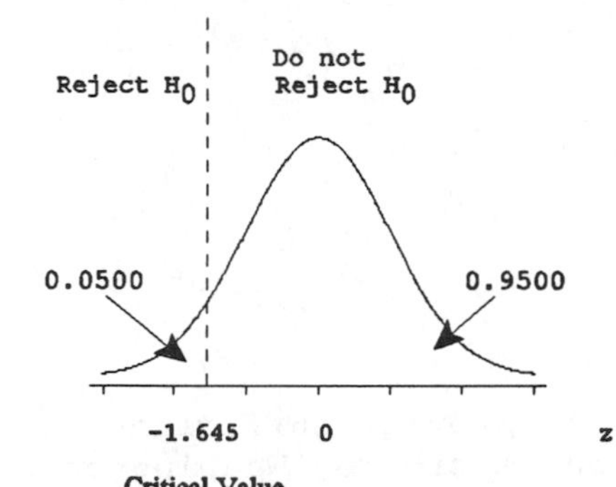

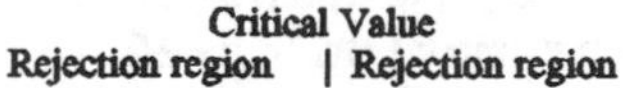

9.33 Critical values: $\pm z_{0.025} = \pm 1.96$

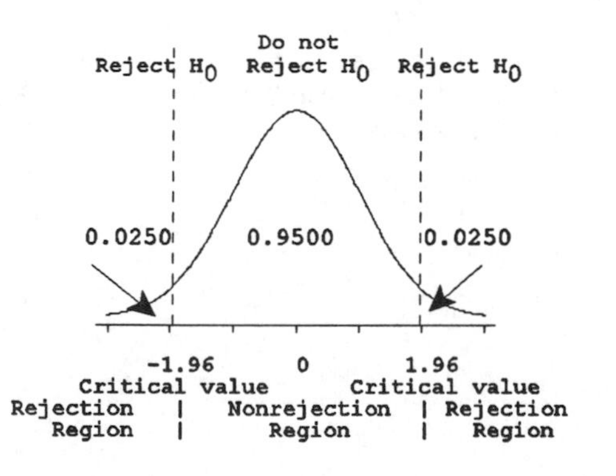

9.35 $n = 12$, $\sigma = 0.37$ ppm, $\bar{x} = 6.31/12 = 0.526$

Step 1: H_0: $\mu = 0.5$ ppm, H_a: $\mu > 0.5$ ppm

Step 2: $\alpha = 0.05$

Step 3: $z = (0.526 - 0.5)/(0.37/\sqrt{12}) = 0.24$

Step 4: Critical value = 1.645

Step 5: Since $0.24 < 1.645$, do not reject H_0.

Step 6: At the 5% significance level, the data do not provide sufficient evidence to conclude that the mean cadmium level μ of *Boletus pinicola* mushrooms is greater than the safety limit of 0.5 ppm.

9.37 $n = 50$, $\bar{x} = \$2069.98/50 = \$41.40$, $\sigma = \$25$

Step 1: H_0: $\mu = \$47.70$, H_a: $\mu < \$47.70$

Step 2: $\alpha = 0.01$

Step 3: $z = (41.40 - 47.70)/(25/\sqrt{50}) = -1.78$

Step 4: Critical value = -2.33

Step 5: Since -1.78 > -2.33, do not reject H_0.

Step 6: At the 1% significance level, the data do not provide sufficient evidence to conclude that the mean cell phone bill has decreased since 1996.

9.39 $n = 300$, $\sigma = 55$, $\bar{x} = 27.8$

Step 1: H_0: $\mu = 22.0$ gal, H_a: $\mu \neq 22.0$ gal

Step 2: $\alpha = 0.10$

Step 3: $z = (27.8 - 22.0)/(55/\sqrt{300}) = 1.83$

Step 4: Critical values = ±1.645

Step 5: Since 1.83 > 1.645, reject H_0.

Step 6: At the 10% significance level, the data do provide sufficient evidence to indicate that annual beer consumption by Washington D.C. residents is different from the national mean consumption of 22.0 gallons.

9.41 (a) The z- test is not appropriate in this case since the sample size is moderate and the population is highly skewed.

(b) The small sample size and the presence of a legitimate outlier observation make it inappropriate to use the z-test.

(c) The mild skewness should present no problems in the use of the z-test when the sample size is 70. The distribution of the sample mean will be approximately normal because of the large sample size.

9.43 (a) The following expressions are equivalent:

$$\bar{x} - z_{\alpha/2} \cdot \frac{\sigma}{\sqrt{n}} < \mu_0 < \bar{x} + z_{\alpha/2} \cdot \frac{\sigma}{\sqrt{n}}$$

$$-z_{\alpha/2} \cdot \frac{\sigma}{\sqrt{n}} < \mu_0 - \bar{x} < z_{\alpha/2} \cdot \frac{\sigma}{\sqrt{n}}$$

$$-z_{\alpha/2} \cdot \frac{\sigma}{\sqrt{n}} < \bar{x} - \mu_0 < z_{\alpha/2} \frac{\sigma}{\sqrt{n}}$$

$$-z_{\alpha/2} < \frac{\bar{x} - \mu_0}{\sigma/\sqrt{n}} < z_{\alpha/2}$$

(b) From part (a) we see that μ_0 lies in the $(1 - \alpha)$-level confidence interval for μ if and only if the test statistic

$$z = \frac{\bar{x} - \mu_0}{\sigma/\sqrt{n}}$$

lies in the nonrejection region.

Exercises 9.4

9.45 (a) A Type I error occurs if the data leads to rejecting the null hypothesis when it is, in fact, true.

(b) A Type II error occurs if the data leads to not rejecting the null hypothesis when it is, in fact, false.

(c) The significance level is the probability associated with the test procedure of rejecting the null hypothesis when it is actually true, i.e., it is the probability of making a Type I error.

9.47 Since μ is unknown, the power curve enables one to evaluate the effectiveness of a hypothesis test for a variety of values of μ.

9.49 If the significance level is decreased without changing the sample size, the rejection region is made smaller (in probability terms). This makes the non-rejection region larger, i.e., β gets larger. This, in turn, makes the power $1 - \beta$ smaller.

9.51 (a) Note: $z = \dfrac{\bar{x} - \mu_0}{\sigma / \sqrt{n}} \Rightarrow \bar{x} = \mu_0 + z \cdot \sigma / \sqrt{n}$

Since this is a right-tailed test, we would reject H_0 if $z \geq 1.645$; or equivalently if $\bar{x} \geq 0.5 + 1.645(0.37)/\sqrt{12} = 0.6757$

So we reject H_0 if $\bar{x} \geq 0.6757$; otherwise do not reject H_0.

(b) $\alpha = 0.05$

(c) Answers may differ from those in text due to intermediate rounding.

True mean μ	z-score computation	P(Type II error) β	Power $1 - \beta$
0.55	$z = \dfrac{0.676 - 0.55}{0.37/\sqrt{12}} = 1.18$	0.8810	0.1190
0.60	$z = \dfrac{0.676 - 0.60}{0.37/\sqrt{12}} = 0.71$	0.7611	0.2389
0.65	$z = \dfrac{0.676 - 0.65}{0.37/\sqrt{12}} = 0.24$	0.5948	0.4052
0.70	$z = \dfrac{0.676 - 0.70}{0.37/\sqrt{12}} = -0.22$	0.4129	0.5871
0.75	$z = \dfrac{0.676 - 0.75}{0.37/\sqrt{12}} = -0.69$	0.2451	0.7549
0.80	$z = \dfrac{0.676 - 0.80}{0.37/\sqrt{12}} = -1.16$	0.1230	0.8770

True mean μ	z-score computation	P(Type II error) β	Power $1 - \beta$
0.85	$z = \dfrac{0.676 - 0.85}{0.37/\sqrt{12}} = -1.63$	0.0516	0.9484

(d)

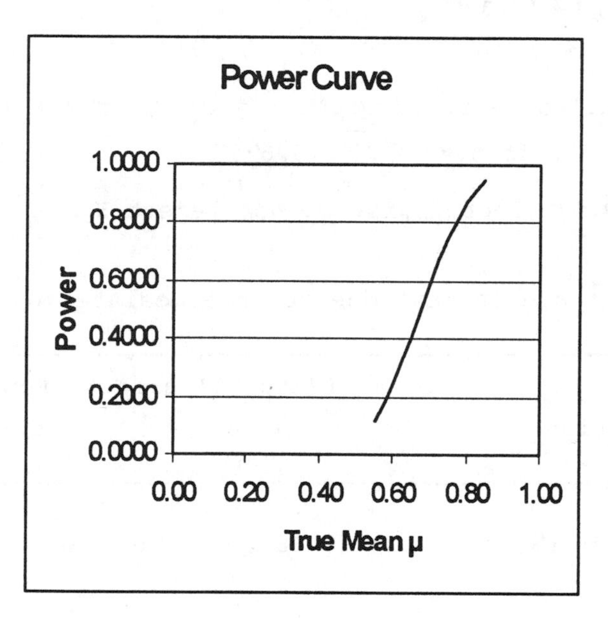

9.53 (a) Note: $z = \dfrac{\bar{x} - \mu_0}{\sigma/\sqrt{n}} \Rightarrow \bar{x} = \mu_0 + z \cdot \sigma/\sqrt{n}$

Since this is a left-tailed test, we would reject H_0 if $z \le -2.33$; or equivalently if $\bar{x} \le 47.70 - 2.33(25)/\sqrt{50} = 39.46$

So reject H_0 if $\bar{x} \le 39.46$; otherwise do not reject H_0.

(b) $\alpha = 0.01$

(c) Answers may differ from those in the text due to intermediate rounding.

True mean μ	z-score computation	P(Type II error) β	Power $1 - \beta$
29	$z = \dfrac{39.46 - 29}{25/\sqrt{50}} = 2.96$	0.0015	0.9985

True mean μ	z-score computation	P(Type II error) β	Power $1-\beta$
32	$z = \dfrac{39.46-32}{25/\sqrt{50}} = 2.11$	0.0174	0.9826
35	$z = \dfrac{39.46-35}{25/\sqrt{50}} = 1.26$	0.1038	0.8962
38	$z = \dfrac{39.46-38}{25/\sqrt{50}} = 0.41$	0.3409	0.6591
41	$z = \dfrac{39.46-41}{25/\sqrt{50}} = -0.44$	0.6700	0.3300
44	$z = \dfrac{39.46-44}{25/\sqrt{50}} = -1.28$	0.8997	0.1003
47	$z = \dfrac{39.46-47}{25/\sqrt{50}} = -2.13$	0.9834	0.0116

(d)

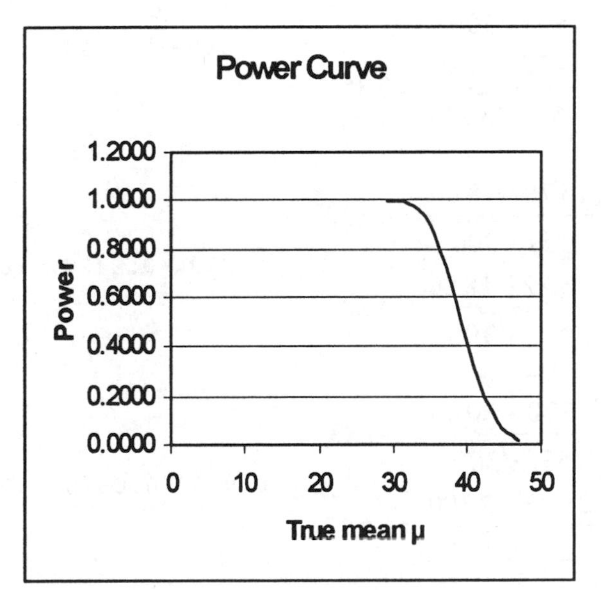

9.55 (a) Note: $z = \dfrac{\bar{x}-\mu_0}{\sigma/\sqrt{n}} \Rightarrow \bar{x} = \mu_0 + z\cdot\sigma/\sqrt{n}$

Since this is a two-tailed test, we would reject H_0 if $|z| \ge 1.96$; or equivalently if $\bar{x} \le 22.0 - 1.96(55)/\sqrt{300} = 15.78$ or

$$\bar{x} \le 22.0 + 1.96(55)/\sqrt{300} = 28.22$$

So reject H_0 if $\bar{x} \le 15.78$ or $\bar{x} \ge 28.22$; otherwise do not reject H_0.

(b) $\alpha = 0.05$

(c) Answers may differ from those in the text due to intermediate rounding.

True mean μ	z-score computation	P(Type II error) β	Power $1 - \beta$
12	$z = \frac{15.78 - 12.00}{55/\sqrt{300}} = 1.19$ $z = \frac{28.22 - 12.00}{55/\sqrt{300}} = 5.11$	1.0000-0.8830 = 0.1170	0.8830
14	$z = \frac{15.78 - 14.00}{55/\sqrt{300}} = 0.56$ $z = \frac{28.22 - 14.00}{55/\sqrt{300}} = 4.48$	1.0000-0.7123 = 0.2877	0.7123
16	$z = \frac{15.78 - 16.00}{55/\sqrt{300}} = -0.07$ $z = \frac{28.22 - 16.00}{55/\sqrt{300}} = 3.85$	0.9999-0.4721 = 0.5278	0.4722
18	$z = \frac{15.78 - 18.00}{55/\sqrt{300}} = -0.70$ $z = \frac{28.22 - 18.00}{55/\sqrt{300}} = 3.22$	0.9994-0.2420 = 0.7574	0.2426
20	$z = \frac{15.78 - 20.00}{55/\sqrt{300}} = -1.33$ $z = \frac{28.22 - 20.00}{55/\sqrt{300}} = 2.59$	0.9952-0.0918 = 0.9034	0.0966
24	$z = \frac{15.78 - 24.00}{55/\sqrt{300}} = -2.59$ $z = \frac{28.22 - 24.00}{55/\sqrt{300}} = 1.33$	0.9082-0.0048 = 0.9034	0.0966

True mean μ	z-score computation	P(Type II error) β	Power $1-\beta$
26	$z=\frac{15.78-26.00}{55/\sqrt{300}}=-3.22$ $z=\frac{28.22-26.00}{55/\sqrt{300}}=0.70$	0.7580-0.0006 = 0.7574	0.2426
28	$z=\frac{15.78-28.00}{55/\sqrt{300}}=-3.85$ $z=\frac{28.22-28.00}{55/\sqrt{300}}=0.07$	0.5279-0.0001 = 0.5278	0.4722
30	$z=\frac{15.78-30.00}{55/\sqrt{300}}=-4.48$ $z=\frac{28.22-30.00}{55/\sqrt{300}}=-0.56$	0.2877-0.0000 = 0.2877	0.7123
32	$z=\frac{15.78-32.00}{55/\sqrt{300}}=-5.11$ $z=\frac{28.22-32.00}{55/\sqrt{300}}=-1.19$	0.1170-0.0000 = 0.1170	0.8830

(d)

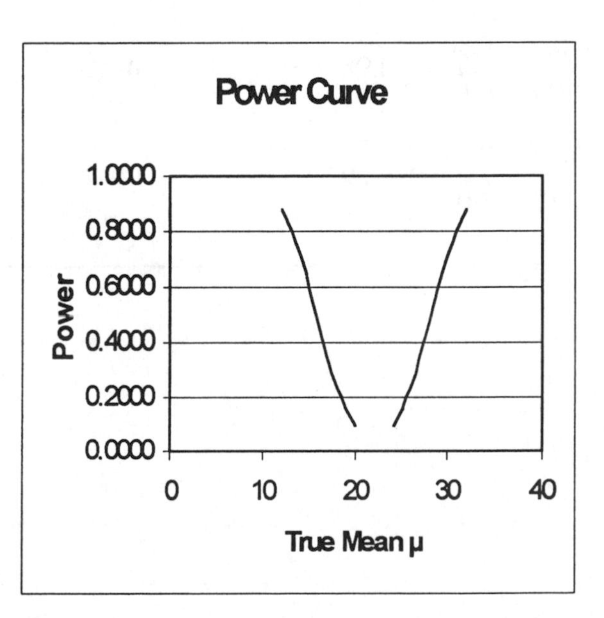

9.57 (a) Note: $z = \dfrac{\bar{x} - \mu_0}{\sigma / \sqrt{n}} \Rightarrow \bar{x} = \mu_0 + z \cdot \sigma / \sqrt{n}$

Since this is a right-tailed test, we would reject H_0 if $z \geq 1.645$; or equivalently if $\bar{x} \geq 0.5 + 1.645(0.37)/\sqrt{20} = 0.636$

So we reject H_0 if $\bar{x} \geq 0.636$; otherwise do not reject H_0.

(b) $\alpha = 0.05$

(c) Answers may differ from those in the text due to intermediate rounding.

True mean μ	z-score computation	P(Type II error) β	Power $1 - \beta$
0.55	$z = \dfrac{0.636 - 0.55}{0.37/\sqrt{20}} = 1.04$	0.8508	0.1492
0.60	$z = \dfrac{0.636 - 0.60}{0.37/\sqrt{20}} = 0.44$	0.6700	0.3300
0.65	$z = \dfrac{0.636 - 0.65}{0.37/\sqrt{20}} = -0.17$	0.4325	0.5675
0.70	$z = \dfrac{0.636 - 0.70}{0.37/\sqrt{20}} = -0.77$	0.2206	0.7794
0.75	$z = \dfrac{0.636 - 0.75}{0.37/\sqrt{20}} = -1.38$	0.0838	0.9162
0.80	$z = \dfrac{0.636 - 0.80}{0.37/\sqrt{20}} = -1.98$	0.0239	0.9761
0.85	$z = \dfrac{0.636 - 0.85}{0.37/\sqrt{20}} = -2.59$	0.0048	0.9952

(d)

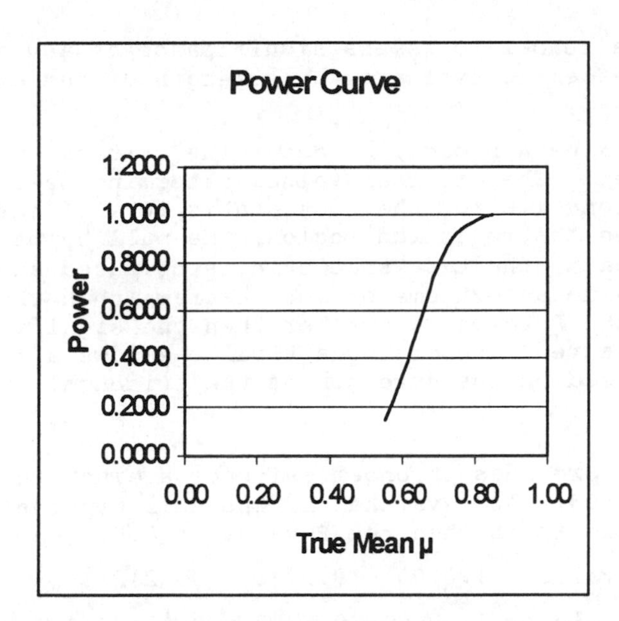

The power curve with n = 20 rises more quickly as the true mean μ increases, resulting in a higher power at any given value of μ than for n = 12. This illustrates the principle that a larger sample size has a higher probability of rejecting the null hypothesis when the null hypothesis is false and the significance level remains the same.

9.59 (a)

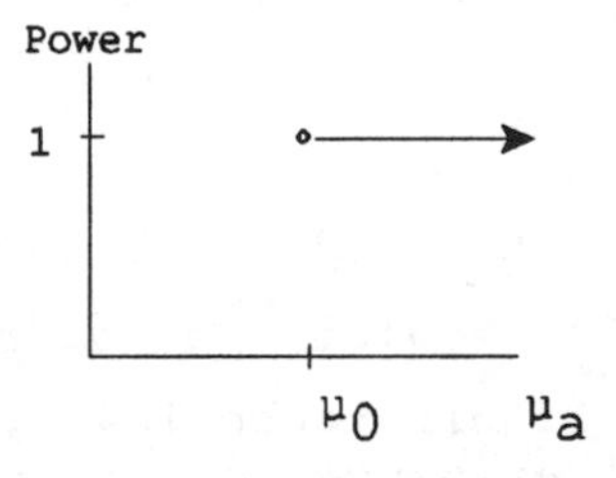

(b) The curve in (a) portrays that, ideally, one desires the value for the power for any given μ_a to be as close to 1 as possible.

9.61 (a)

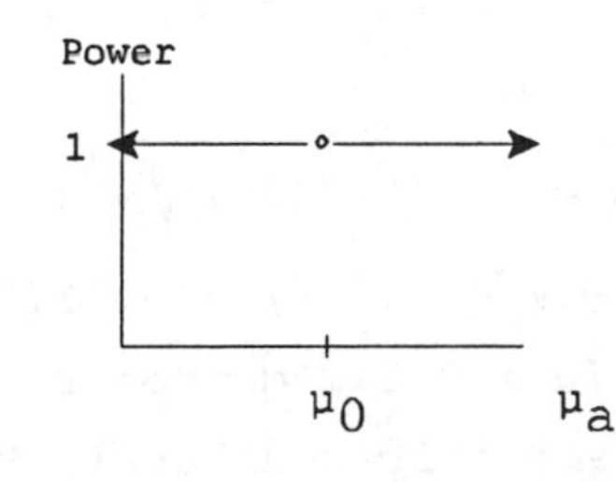

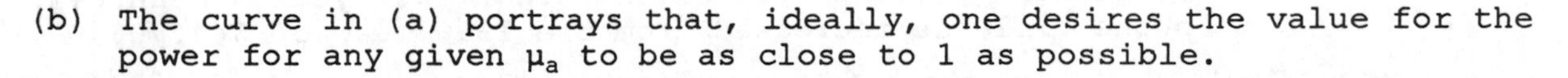

(b) The curve in (a) portrays that, ideally, one desires the value for the power for any given μ_a to be as close to 1 as possible.

Exercises 9.5

9.63 (1) It allows the reader to assess significance at any desired level, and (2) it permits the reader to evaluate the strength of the evidence against the null hypothesis.

9.65 In the **critical value** approach, we determine critical values based on the significance level. The critical values determine where the rejection and nonrejection regions lie for the test statistic. If the value of the test statistic falls in the rejection region, the null hypothesis is rejected. In the **P-value** approach, the test statistic is computed and then the probability of observing a value as extreme or more extreme than the value obtained is determined. If the P-value is smaller than the significance level, the null hypothesis is rejected. Reporting a P-value allows a reader to draw his/her own conclusion based on the strength of the evidence.

9.67 True

9.69 A P-value of 0.02 provides stronger evidence against the null hypothesis than does a value of 0.03. It says that if the null hypothesis is true, the data is less likely than it is when the P-value is 0.03.

9.71 (a) $z = 2.03$, P-value = 1.0000 - 0.9788 = 0.0212

(b) $z = -0.31$, P-value = 1.0000 - 0.3783 = 0.6217

9.73 (a) $z = 3.08$, Right-tail probability = 1.0000 - 0.9990 = 0.0010

P-value = 0.001 x 2 = 0.0020

(b) $z = -2.42$, Left-tail probability = 0.0078

P-value = 0.0078 x 2 = 0.0156

9.75 (See Exercise 9.35 for classical approach results.)

Step 1: H_0: μ = 0.5 ppm, H_a: μ > 0.5 ppm

Step 2: $\alpha = 0.05$

Step 3: $z = 0.24$

Step 4: P-value = $P(z \geq 0.24)$ = 1.0000 - 0.5948 = 0.4052

Step 5: Since 0.4052 > 0.05, do not reject H_0.

Step 6: At the 5% significance level, the data do not provide sufficient evidence to conclude that the mean cadmium level μ of *Boletus pinicola* mushrooms is greater than the safety limit of 0.5 ppm.

Using Table 9.12, we classify the strength of evidence against the null hypothesis as weak or none because P > 0.10.

9.77 (See Exercise 9.37 for classical approach results.)

Step 1: H_0: μ = \$47.70, H_a: μ < \$47.70

Step 2: $\alpha = 0.01$

Step 3: $z = (41.40 - 47.70)/(25/\sqrt{50}) = -1.78$

Step 4: P-value = $P(z \leq -1.78)$ = 0.0375

Step 5: Since 0.0375 > 0.01, do not reject H_0.

Step 6: At the 1% significance level, the data do not provide sufficient evidence to indicate that last year's mean cell phone bill has decreased from the 1996 mean of \$47.70.

Using Table 9.12, we classify the strength of evidence against the null hypothesis as strong because $0.01 < P < 0.05$.

9.79 (See Exercise 9.39 for classical approach results.)

Step 1: H_0: $\mu = 22.0$ gal, H_a: $\mu \neq 22.0$ gal

Step 2: $\alpha = 0.10$

Step 3: $z = (27.8 - 22.0)/(55/\sqrt{300}) = 1.83$

Step 4: P-value = $2P(z > 1.83) = 2(1.0000 - 0.9664) = 0.0672$

Step 5: Since $0.0672 < 0.10$, reject H_0.

Step 6: At the 10% significance level, the data provide sufficient evidence to conclude that the mean annual beer consumption by Washington D.C. residents differs from the national mean of 22.0 gallons.

Using Table 9.12, we classify the strength of evidence against the null hypothesis as moderate because $0.05 < P < 0.10$.

9.81 (a) The P-value is expressed as $P(z \leq z_0)$ if the hypothesis test is left-tailed.

(b) The P-value is expressed as $P(|z| \geq |z_0|)$ if the test is two-tailed.

9.83 Given that x can be transformed to z (and x_0 to z_0), we have:

1. $P(x \geq x_0) = P(z \geq z_0)$, for a right-tailed test
2. $P(x \leq x_0) = P(z \leq z_0)$, for a left-tailed test
3. $2 \cdot \min\{P(x \leq x_0), P(x \geq x_0)\} = 2 \cdot \min\{P(z \leq z_0), P(z \geq z_0)\}$

$$= \begin{cases} 2 \cdot P(z \leq z_0) \text{ if } z_0 < 0 \\ 2 \cdot P(z \geq z_0) \text{ if } z_0 \geq 0 \end{cases}$$

By symmetry $= \begin{cases} 2 \cdot P(z \geq -z_0) \text{ if } z_0 < 0 \\ 2 \cdot P(z \geq z_0) \text{ if } z_0 \geq 0 \end{cases} = 2 \cdot P(z \geq |z_0|)$

By symmetry $= P(z \leq -|z_0|) + P(z \geq |z_0|) = P(|z| \geq |z_0|)$

9.85 With the data in a column named PPM, we choose **Stat ▶ Basic Statistics ▶ 1-Sample z...**, select PPM in the **Variables** text box, click on the **Test mean** button, type 0.5 in the **Test mean** text box, click on the arrow in the **Alternative** text box and select 'greater than,' type 0.37 in the **Sigma** text box, and click **OK**. The result follows.

Test of mu = 0.500 vs mu > 0.500

The assumed sigma = 0.370

Variable	N	Mean	StDev	SE Mean	Z	P
PPM	12	0.526	0.352	0.107	0.24	0.40

The P-value of 0.40 is greater than the significance level of .05, so we conclude that the data do not provide sufficient evidence that the mean Cadmium value is not greater than the safety limit of 0.5 ppm.

9.87 (a) A boxplot will most readily identify outliers. Using Minitab with the data in a column named RENT, we choose **Graph ▶ Boxplot**, select RENT in the **Y** column for **Graph 1**, and click **OK**. The resulting boxplot identifies one potential outlier, the number 289.

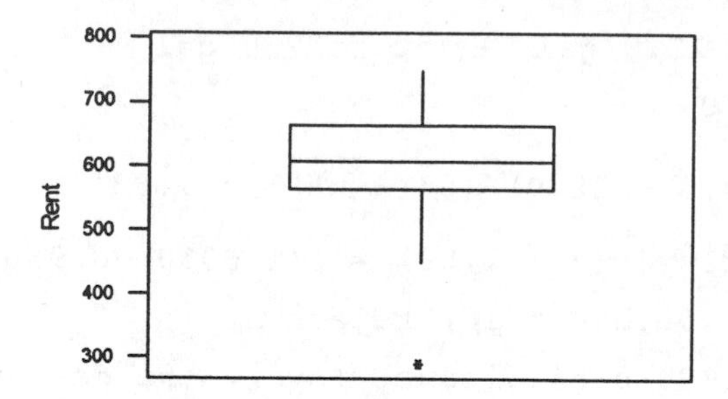

(b) Now choose **Stat ▶ Basic Statistics ▶ 1-Sample z...**, select RENT in the **Variables** text box, click on the **Test mean** button, type 590 in the **Test mean** text box, click on the arrow in the **Alternative** text box and select 'not equal,' type 73.10 in the **Sigma** text box, and click **OK**. The result is

Test of mu = 590.0 vs mu not = 590.0

The assumed sigma = 73.1

Variable	N	Mean	StDev	SE Mean	Z	P
Rent	32	602.3	93.8	12.9	0.95	0.34

The P-value of 0.34 is greater than the significance level of .05, so we conclude that the data do not provide sufficient evidence that the mean monthly rent for two-bedroom units in Maine differs from the FMR of $590.

(c) Delete the value 289 from the data in Minitab and follow the procedure in part (b). The result is

Test of mu = 590.0 vs mu not = 590.0

The assumed sigma = 73.1

Variable	N	Mean	StDev	SE Mean	Z	P
Rent	31	612.4	75.5	13.1	1.71	0.088

The P-value of 0.088 is still greater than the significance level of .05, so we still conclude that the data do not provide sufficient evidence that the mean monthly rent for two-bedroom units in Maine differs from the FMR of $590.

(d) Note that both the z-value and the P-value have changed significantly with the deletion of the number 289, illustrating the effect that the outlier had on the analysis. There is now moderate support for the alternative hypothesis whereas there was no support for it previously.

(e) The conclusion with or without the presence of the outlier is the same, that is, the data do not provide sufficient evidence that the mean monthly rent for two-bedroom units in Maine differs from the FMR of $590. With the outlier deleted, the sample looks very much like what you would expect from a normal distribution. Given that the original sample was barely larger than 30, the outlier should be deleted if the z-test is used. If it found that the value 289 is a legitimate value and should not be deleted, a different type of analysis may be preferable.

Exercises 9.6

9.89 $n = 36$, $df = 35$, $\bar{x} = 1667.11$, $s = 351.69$

Step 1: H_0: $\mu = \$1729$, H_a: $\mu \neq \$1729$

Step 2: $\alpha = 0.05$

Step 3: $t = (1667.11-1729)/(351.69/\sqrt{36}) = -1.056$

Step 4: Critical values = ±2.030

Step 5: Since $-2.030 < -1.056 < 2.030$, do not reject H_0.

Note: For the p-value approach, p-value > 0.20. So, since the p-value > α, do not reject H_0.

Step 6: At the 5% significance level, the data do not provide sufficient evidence to conclude that the 1997 mean apparel and services expenditure μ for households in the Midwest differed from the national average of $1729.

9.91 $n = 10$, $df = 9$, $\bar{x} = 2.5$, $s = 0.14877$

Step 1: H_0: $\mu = 2.3$, H_a: $\mu > 2.3$

Step 2: $\alpha = 0.01$

Step 3: $t = (2.5 - 2.3)/(0.14877/\sqrt{10}) = 4.251$ ($t = 4.245$ is OK)

Step 4: Critical value = 2.821

Step 5: Since $4.251 > 2.821$, reject H_0. Note: For the P-value approach, p-value < 0.005. So, since the p-value < α, reject H_0.

Step 6: At the 1% significance level, the data do provide sufficient evidence to conclude that the mean available limestone in soil treated with 100% MMBL effluent is greater than 2.30%. The practical significance of this result probably depends on what crop is to be grown in the soil.

9.93 $n = 15$, $df = 14$, $\bar{x} = 53.4$, $s = 3.5$

Step 1: H_0: $\mu = 51.0$¢/lb, H_a: $\mu \neq 51.0$¢/lb

Step 2: $\alpha = 0.05$

Step 3: $t = (53.4 - 51.0)/(3.5/\sqrt{15}) = 2.655$

Step 4: Critical values = ±2.145

Step 5: Since $2.655 > 2.145$, reject H_0. Note: For the p-value approach, $0.01 < P < 0.02$. So, since the p-value < α, reject H_0.

Step 6: At the 5% significance level, the data provide sufficient evidence to conclude that the mean retail price μ for bananas now is different from the 1998 mean of 51.0 cents per pound. The practical significance of this result is minimal since the difference is only 2.4¢/lb.

9.95 $n = 40$, $df = 39$, $\bar{x} = 58.40$, $s = 20.42$

(a) Step 1: H_0: $\mu = 64$ lb, H_a: $\mu < 64$ lb

Step 2: $\alpha = 0.05$

Step 3: $t = (58.40 - 64)/(20.42/\sqrt{40}) = -1.734$

Step 4: Critical value = -1.685

Step 5: Since -1.734 < -1.685, reject H_0. Note: For the p-value approach, 0.025 < p-value < 0.05. So, since p-value < α, reject H_0.

Step 6: At the 5% significance level, it appears that last year's mean beef consumption is less than the 1997 mean of 64 lbs. This result would have little practical significance to the individual beef eater, but to beef producers, it would have great practical significance since the apparent decline in consumption by the total population is considerable.

(b) After removing the four potential outliers,

$n = 36$, $df = 35$, $\bar{x} = 64.11$, $s = 11.02$

Step 1: H_0: $\mu = 64$ lb, H_a: $\mu < 64$ lb

Step 2: $\alpha = 0.05$

Step 3: $t = (64.11 - 64)/(11.02/\sqrt{36}) = 0.060$

Step 4: Critical value = -1.690

Step 5: Since 0.060 > -1.690, do not reject H_0. Note: For the p-value approach, p-value > 0.50. So, since p-value > α, do not reject H_0.

Step 6: At the 5% significance level, there is not sufficient evidence to conclude that last year's mean beef consumption is less than the 1997 mean of 64 pounds.

(c) The results in parts (a) and (b) are very different. With the potential outliers included in the data, there appears to be a decrease in the mean beef consumption. With the outliers removed, no such decrease is apparent.

(d) Since the Department of Agriculture's 1997 data would have included the beef consumption of people who ate little or no beef, it is entirely appropriate to include data from such people in last year's sample.

(e) Since the results of the analysis change considerably when the potential outliers are removed, it would be best to increase the size of the sample to reduce the effect of the potential outliers on the results or to use a non-parametric method of analysis which does not assume normality.

9.97 (a) Using Minitab, with the data in a column named EXPEND, to obtain the normal probability plot, we choose **Calc ▶ Calculator...**, type NSCORE in the **Store result in variable** text box, select **Normal scores** from the function list, select EXPEND to replace **numbers** in the **Expression** text box, and click **OK**. We now choose **Graph ▶ Plot...**, select NSCORE for the **Y** variable for **Graph 1** and EXPEND for the **X** variable, and click **OK**. To obtain the boxplot, we choose **Graph ▶ Boxplot...**, select EXPEND for the **Y** variable for **Graph1**, and click **OK**. To obtain the histogram, we choose **Graph ▶ Histogram...**, select EXPEND for the **Y** variable for **Graph1**, and click **OK**. To obtain the stem-and-leaf plot, we choose **Graph ▶ Stem-and-leaf...**, select EXPEND in the **Variables** text box, and click **OK**. The four resulting plots are

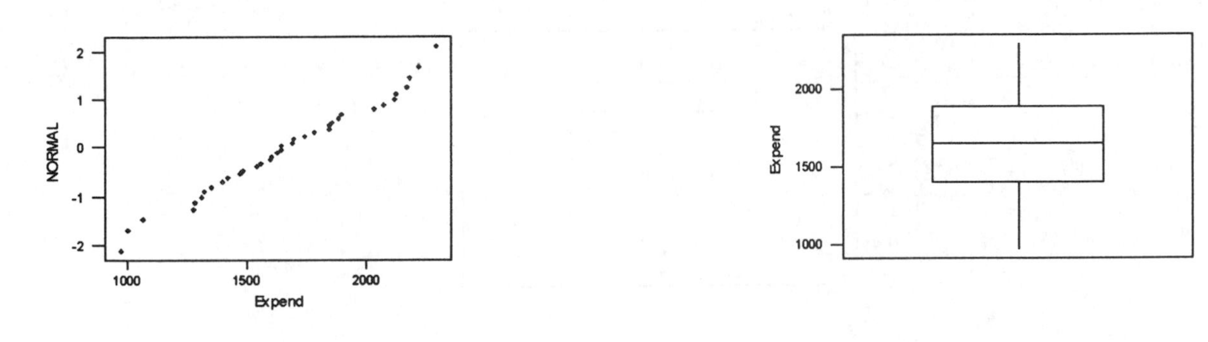


```
Stem-and-leaf of Expend      N  = 36
Leaf Unit = 10
     1     9 7
     3    10 06
     3    11
     5    12 78
     9    13 1259
    12    14 178
    15    15 459
   (6)    16 024499
    15    17 48
    13    18 44589
     8    19
     8    20 37
     6    21 1278
     2    22 29
```

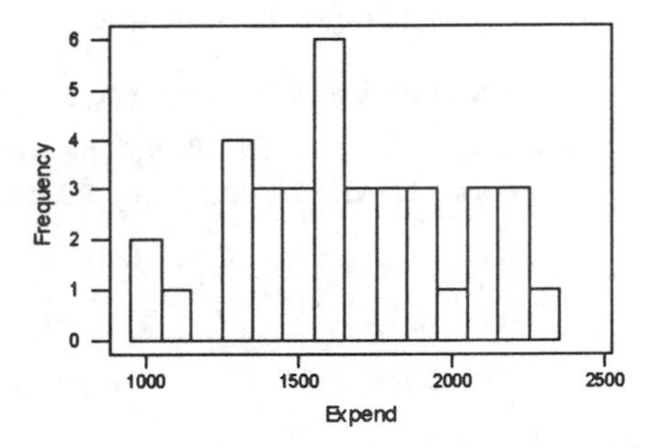

(b) To perform the one-sample t-test, we choose **Stat ▶ Basic statistics ▶ 1-Sample t...**, select EXPEND in the **Variables** text box, click the **Test Mean** button and type 1729 in the **Test mean** text box, select **not equal** in the **Alternative** box, and click **OK**. The results in the Session Window are

Test of mu = 1729.0 vs mu not = 1729.0

Variable	N	Mean	StDev	SE Mean	T	P
Expend	36	1667.1	351.7	58.6	-1.06	0.30

These results are the same as in Exercise 10.89 and do not lead to rejection of the null hypothesis that the mean is $1729.

(c) None of the plots indicate any serious departure from the assumption of normality required for the t-test, so the procedure in part (b) is justified.

9.99 (a) Using Minitab, with the data in a column named BEEFCONSUMP, choose **Graph ▶ Boxplot...**, select BEEFCONSUMP as the **Y** variable for **Graph 1**, and click **OK**. The plot is shown below. Although it appears that there are three potential outliers, there are two observations of zero, and thus there are four potential outliers (0, 0, 8, and 20).

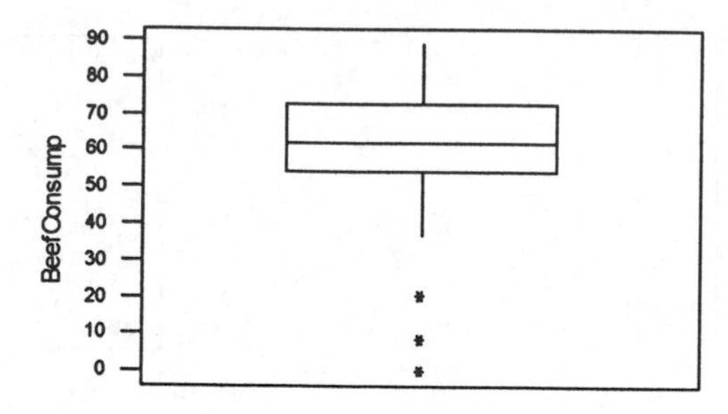

(b) To perform the t-test with the original data, choose **Stat ▶ Basic Statistics ▶ 1-sample t...** and select BEEFCONSUMP in the **Variables** text box, click on **Test mean,** and enter 64 in the **Test mean** text box. Choose **less than** from the **Alternative** text box, and click **OK.** The results are

Test of mu = 64.00 vs mu < 64.00

Variable	N	Mean	StDev	SE Mean	T	P-Value
BEEFCONSUMP	40	58.40	20.42	3.23	-1.73	0.045

(c) Enter the Data window and delete the four data values 0, 0, 8, and 20. Then repeat the process in part (b) above. The results are

Test of mu = 64.00 vs mu < 64.00

Variable	N	Mean	StDev	SE Mean	T	P-Value
BEEFCONSUMP	36	64.11	11.02	1.84	0.06	0.52

(d) Deleting the four low outliers raises the mean, decreases the standard deviation, and changes the P-value from 0.045 to 0.52, from strong evidence against the null hypothesis to weak or no evidence against the null hypothesis. Since the four outliers are presumably legitimate observations, they can not simply be deleted and ignored. Therefore, either the sample size should be increased to reduce the effect of outliers on the result or a non-parametric method of analysis which is not based on the normality assumption should be used.

Exercises 9.7

9.101 The advantages of nonparametric methods are that they do not require normality, they make use of fewer and simpler calculations than do parametric methods, and they are resistant to outliers. The disadvantage of nonparametric methods is that they tend to give less accurate results than parametric methods when the assumptions underlying the parametric methods are actually met.

9.103 It is done because the D-value for such a data value equals 0 and so we cannot attach a sign to the rank of $|D|$.

9.105 (a) Wilcoxon signed-rank test (b) Wilcoxon signed-rank test

(c) Neither

9.107 $\eta_0 = 34.3$, $n = 10$, $\alpha = 0.05$

Step 1: H_0: $\eta = 35.7$, H_a: $\eta > 35.7$

Step 2: $\alpha = 0.01$

Step 3:

x	$x-\eta_0=D$	$\lvert D\rvert$	Rank of $\lvert D\rvert$	Signed Rank R
42	6.3	6.3	3	3
45	9.3	9.3	4	4
62	26.3	26.3	10	10
49	13.3	13.3	6	6
14	-21.7	21.7	8	-8
39	3.3	3.3	2	2
57	21.3	21.3	7	7
11	-24.7	24.7	9	-9
36	0.3	0.3	1	1
26	-9.7	9.7	5	-5

Step 4: W = sum of the + ranks = 33

Step 5: Critical value = 50

Step 6: Since W < 50, do not reject H_0. P-value = 0.305.

Step 7: At the 1% significance level, the data do not provide sufficient evidence to conclude that the median age has increased over the 2000 median age of 35.7 years.

9.109 μ_0 = \$10,735, n = 10, α = 0.10

Step 1: H_0: μ = 10735, H_a: μ < 10735

Step 2: α = 0.10

Step 3:

x	$x-\mu_0=D$	$\lvert D\rvert$	Rank of $\lvert D\rvert$	Signed Rank R
9500	-1235	1235	4	-4
13377	2642	2642	8	8
12250	1515	1515	5	5
10088	-647	647	2.5	-2.5
8497	-2238	2238	7	-7
7877	-2858	2858	10	-10
10088	-647	647	2.5	-2.5
10640	-95	95	1	-1
8900	-1835	1835	6	-6
7900	-2835	2835	9	-9

Step 4: W = sum of the + ranks = 13

Step 5: Critical value = 10(11)/2 - 41 = 14

Step 6: Since W < 14, reject H_0. P-value = 0.077.

Step 7: At the 10% significance level, the data do provide sufficient evidence to conclude that the mean asking price for a 1996 Nissan XE King Cab pickup is less than the *2000 Kelly Blue Book* value.

9.111 μ_0 = 51.0, n = 14, α = 0.05 (The value of 51 was deleted from the original sample.)

(a) Step 1: H_0: μ = 51.0, H_a: $\mu \neq 51.0$

Step 2: α = 0.05

Step 3:

x	$x-\mu_0=D$	$\|D\|$	Rank of $\|D\|$	Signed Rank R
56	5	5	10	10
57	6	6	12	12
50	-1	1	1.5	-1.5
53	2	2	3.5	3.5
58	7	7	14	14
57	6	6	12	12
55	4	4	8	8
54	3	3	5.5	5.5
57	6	6	12	12
53	2	2	3.5	3.5
48	-3	3	5.5	-5.5
51	0	0	---	---
50	-1	1	1.5	-1.5
47	-4	4	8	-8
55	4	4	8	8

Step 4: W = sum of the + ranks = 88.5

Step 5: Critical values = 21, 84 [14(15)/2 - 84 = 21]

Step 6: Since W > 84, reject H_0. P-value = 0.026.

Step 7: At the 5% significance level, the data provide sufficient evidence to conclude that the mean retail price for bananas now is different from the 1996 mean of 51.0 cents per pound.

(b) A Wilcoxon signed-rank test is permissible because a normally distributed population is symmetric.

9.113 $n = 16$, $\bar{x} = 306$, $s = 8.6718$, $\alpha = 0.05$

(a) Step 1: H_0: $\mu = 310$, H_a: $\mu < 310$

Step 2: $\alpha = 0.05$

Step 3: $t = (306 - 310)/(8.6718/\sqrt{16}) = -1.845$

Step 4: Critical value = -1.753

Step 5: Since -1.845 < -1.753, reject H_0. Note: For the p-value approach, $0.025 < P < 0.05$. So, since p-value < α, reject H_0.

Step 6: At the 5% significance level, the data do provide sufficient evidence to conclude that the mean content, μ, is less than the advertised content of 310 ml.

(b) Step 1: H_0: $\mu = 310$, H_a: $\mu < 310$

Step 2: $\alpha = 0.05$

Step 3:

x	$x-\mu_0=D$	$\|D\|$	Rank of $\|D\|$	Signed Rank R
297	-13	13	14	-14
311	1	1	2	2
322	12	12	12.5	12.5
315	5	5	7	7
318	8	8	9	9
303	-7	7	8	-8
307	-3	3	5	-5
296	-14	14	15	-15
306	-4	4	6	-6
291	-19	19	16	-16
312	2	2	4	4
309	-1	1	2	-2
300	-10	10	10.5	-10.5
298	-12	12	12.5	-12.5
300	-10	10	10.5	-10.5
311	1	1	2	2

Step 4: W = sum of the + ranks = 36.5

Step 5: Critical value = (16)(17)/2 - 100 = 36

Step 6: Since W > 36, do not reject H_0.

Step 7: At the 5% significance level, the data do not provide sufficient evidence to conclude that the mean content, μ, is less than the advertised content of 310 ml.

(c) Since the population is normally distributed, the t-test is more powerful than the Wilcoxon signed-rank test; that is, the t-test is more likely to detect a false null hypothesis.

9.115 The distribution of marriage durations is unlikely to be normal, possibly not even symmetric. Given that duration cannot be less than 0 years and there are likely to be some fairly long marriages which might look like outliers, it would be better to use the Wilcoxon signed-rank test which is insensitive to outliers than to use the t-test which assumes normality and is sensitive to outliers.

9.117 (a) If John is not unlucky, he should expect to wait 15 minutes for the train, on the average.

(b) If John is not unlucky, the distribution of the times he waits for the trains should be a uniform distribution over the interval from 0 to 30 minutes.

(c) Step 1: H_0: $\eta = 15$, H_a: $\eta \neq 15$

Step 2: $\alpha = 0.10$

Step 3:

x	$x-\eta_0=D$	$\|D\|$	Rank of $\|D\|$	Signed Rank R
24	9	9	6.5	6.5
26	11	11	9.5	9.5
20	5	5	4	4
4	-11	11	9.5	-9.5
3	-12	12	11	-11
11	-4	4	2.5	-2.5
19	4	4	2.5	4
5	-10	10	8	-8
28	13	13	12	12
16	1	1	1	1
22	7	7	5	5
24	9	9	6.5	6.5

Step 4: W = sum of the + ranks = 48.5

Step 5: Critical values = (15)(16)/2 - 90 = 30, and 90

Step 6: Since 30 < W < 90, do not reject H_0.

Step 7: At the 10% significance level, the data do not provide sufficient evidence to conclude that John waits more than 15 minutes for the train, on the average.

(d) Since the population is uniform (which is symmetric), the Wilcoxon test is appropriate.

(e) Since the population is symmetric and non-normal, the Wilcoxon signed-rank test is more powerful than the t-test and more appropriate than the t-test which assumes normality.

9.119 (a) Step 1: H_0: $\eta = 7.4$ lb, H_a: $\eta \neq 7.4$ lb

Step 2: $\alpha = 0.05$

Step 3: See Step 4 in the solution to Exercise 9.110.

Step 4: From Step 5 in the solution to Exercise 9.110, W = 57.5. Now:

$$z = \frac{W - n(n+1)/4}{\sqrt{n(n+1)(2n+1)/24}} = \frac{57.5 - 13(13+1)/4}{\sqrt{13(13+1)(2\cdot 13+1)24}} = 0.84$$

Step 5: Critical values = ±1.96

Step 6: Since -1.96 < 0.84 < 1.96, do not reject H_0.

Step 7: At the 5% significance level, the data do not provide sufficient evidence to conclude that this year's median birth weight differs from that in 1996.

(b) Neither the Wilcoxon signed-rank test nor the normal approximation led to rejection of the null hypothesis.

9.121 Summing the ranks corresponding to the "+" signs in each row results in a value for W. All sixteen possible values for W are presented in the last column.

(a)

Rank				
1	2	3	4	W
+	+	+	+	10
+	+	+	−	6
+	+	−	+	7
+	+	−	−	3
+	−	+	+	8
+	−	+	−	4
+	−	−	+	5
+	−	−	−	1
−	+	+	+	9
−	+	+	−	5
−	+	−	+	6
−	+	−	−	2
−	−	+	+	7
−	−	+	−	3
−	−	−	+	4
−	−	−	−	0

(b) 1/16 = 0.0625

(c)

W	P(W)
0	0.0625
1	0.0625
2	0.0625
3	0.1250
4	0.1250
5	0.1250
6	0.1250
7	0.1250
8	0.0625
9	0.0625
10	0.0625

(d)

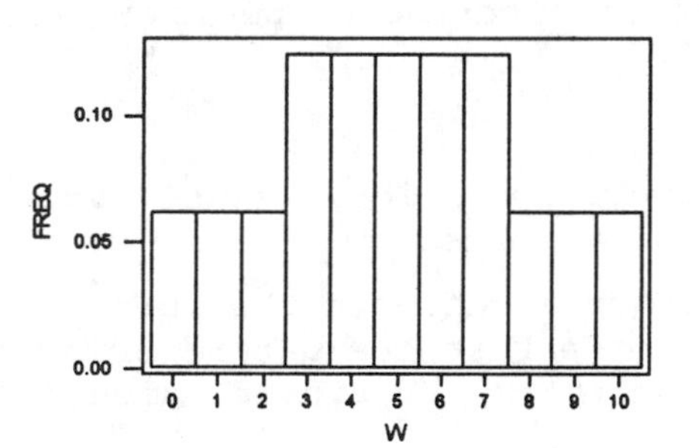

(e) For a left-tailed test with n = 3 and α = 0.125, the critical value W_ℓ equals 1.

9.123 Using Minitab, with the data in a column named PUPrice, we choose **Stat** ▶ **Nonparametrics** ▶ **1-Sample Wilcoxon...**, select PUPrice in the **Variables** text box, click on the **Test median** button and type 10375 in its text box, select 'less than' in the **Alternative** text box, and click **OK.** The result is

Test of median = 10375 versus median < 10375

	N	N for Test	Wilcoxon Statistic	P	Estimated Median
PUPrice	10	10	17.0	0.154	9794

The p-value of 0.154 is larger than the significance level of 0.10 and therefore we conclude that the data do not support the alternative hypothesis that the mean asking price for 1996 XE King Cab pickups in Phoenix is less than the *2000 Kelly Blue Book* value.

Exercises 9.8

9.125 (a) One-sample z-test, One-sample t-test, Wilcoxon signed-rank test

(b) The z-test assumes that σ is known, and that the population is normal or the sample is large. The t-test assumes that σ is unknown, and that the population is normal or the sample is large. The signed-rank test assumes only that the population is symmetric.

(c) $z = (\bar{x} - \mu_0)/(\sigma/\sqrt{n})$ $\quad t = (\bar{x} - \mu_0)/(s/\sqrt{n})$

W = the sum of the positive ranks

9.127 (a) Yes. The t-test can be used when the sample size is large. It is almost equivalent to the z-test in this situation.

(b) Yes. The Wilcoxon signed-rank test can be used when the population distribution is symmetric.

(c) The Wilcoxon signed-rank test is preferable in this situation since it is more powerful (more likely to detect a false null hypothesis) when the population is symmetric, but non-normal.

9.129 Since we have normality and σ is known, use the z-test.

9.131 Since we have a large sample with no outliers and σ is unknown, use the t-test.

9.133 Since we have a symmetric non-normal distribution, use the Wilcoxon signed-rank test.

9.135 The distribution looks skewed and the sample size is not large. Consult a statistician.

REVIEW TEST FOR CHAPTER 9

1. (a) A null hypothesis always specifies a single value for the parameter of a population which is of interest.

(b) The alternative hypothesis reflects the purpose of the hypothesis test which can be to determine that the parameter of interest is greater than, less than, or different from the single value specified in the null hypothesis.

(c) The test statistic is a quantity calculated from the sample, under the assumption that the null hypothesis is true, which is used as a basis for deciding whether or not to reject the null hypothesis.

(d) The rejection region is a set of values of the test statistic which lead to rejection of the null hypothesis.

(e) The nonrejection region is a set of values of the test statistic which lead to not rejecting the null hypothesis.

(f) The critical values are values of the test statistic that separate the rejection region from the nonrejection region.

2. (a) The statement is expressing the fact that there is variability in the net weights of the boxes' content and some boxes may actually contain less than the printed weight on the box. However, the net weights for each day's production will average a bit more than the printed weight.

   (b) To test the truth of this statement, we would use a null hypothesis that stated that the population mean net weight of the boxes was <u>equal</u> to the printed weight and an alternative hypothesis that stated that the population mean net weight of the boxes was <u>greater than</u> the printed weight.

   (c) Null hypothesis: Population mean net weight = 76 oz

   Alternative hypothesis: Population mean net weight > 76 oz

   or

   H_0: $\mu = 76$ oz.

   H_a: $\mu > 76$ oz.

3. (a) Roughly speaking, there is a range of values of the test statistic which one could reasonably expect to occur if the null hypothesis were true. If the value of the test statistic is one which would not be expected to occur when the null hypothesis is true, then we reject the null hypothesis.

   (b) To make this procedure objective and precise, we specify the probability with which we are willing to reject the null hypothesis when it is actually true. This is called the significance level of the test and is usually some small number like 0.05 or 0.01. Specifying the significance level allows us to determine the range of values of the test statistic that will lead to rejection of the null hypothesis. If the computed value of the test statistic falls in this "rejection region," then the null hypothesis is rejected. If it does not fall in the rejection region, then the null hypothesis is not rejected.

4. We would use the alternative hypothesis $\mu \neq \mu_0$ if we wanted to determine whether the population mean were <u>different from</u> the value μ_0 specified in the null hypothesis. We would use the alternative hypothesis $\mu > \mu_0$ if we wanted to determine whether the population mean were <u>greater than</u> the value μ_0 specified in the null hypothesis. We would use the alternative hypothesis $\mu < \mu_0$ if we wanted to determine whether the population mean were <u>less than</u> the value μ_0 specified in the null hypothesis.

5. (a) A Type I error is made whenever the null hypothesis is true, but the value of the test statistic leads us to reject the null hypothesis. A Type II error is made whenever the null hypothesis is false, but the value of the test statistic leads us to not reject the null hypothesis.

   (b) The probability of a Type I error is represented by α and that of a Type II error by β.

   (c) If the null hypothesis is true, the test statistic can lead us to either reject or not reject the null hypothesis. The first is the correct decision, while the latter constitutes a Type I error. Thus a Type I error is the only type of error possible when the null hypothesis is true.

   (d) If the null hypothesis is not rejected, a correct decision has been made if the null hypothesis is, in fact, true. But if the null hypothesis is false, we have made a Type II error. Thus a Type II error is the only type of error possible when the null hypothesis is not rejected.

6. Assuming that the null hypothesis is true, choose the value so that the probability of the test statistic being greater than the specified value is 0.05.

7. (a) If the population standard deviation is known, and the population is normal or the sample size is large, we can use the one-sample z-statistic, $z = (\bar{x} - \mu_0)/(\sigma/\sqrt{n})$.

(b) If the population standard deviation is unknown, and the population is normal or the sample size is large, we can use the one-sample t-statistic, $t = (\bar{x} - \mu_0)/(s/\sqrt{n})$.

(c) If the population is symmetric, we can use the Wilcoxon signed-rank statistic.

8. (a) A hypothesis test is exact if the actual significance level is the same as the one that is stated.

(b) A hypothesis test is approximately correct if the actual significance level is not exactly the one that is stated.

9. A statistically significant result occurs when the value of the test statistic falls in the rejection region. A result has practical significance when it is statistically significant and the result also is different enough from results expected under the null hypothesis to be important to the consumer of the results. By taking large enough sample sizes, almost any result can be made statistically significant due to the increased ability of the test to detect a false null hypothesis, but small differences from the conditions expressed by the null hypothesis may not be important, that is, they may not have practical significance.

10. The probability of a Type II error is increased when the significance level is decreased for a fixed sample size.

11. (a) The power of a hypothesis test is the probability of rejecting the null hypothesis when the null hypothesis is false.

(b) The power of a test increases when the sample size is increased while keeping the significance level constant.

12. (a) The P-value of a hypothesis test is the probability, assuming that the null hypothesis is true, of getting a value of the test statistic that is as extreme or more extreme than the one actually obtained.

(b) True. If the null hypothesis were true, a value of the test statistic with a P-value of 0.02 would be more extreme than one with a P-value of 0.03.

(c) True. If the P-value is 0.74, this means that 74% of the time when the null hypothesis is true, the value of the test statistic would be more extreme than the one actually obtained.

(d) The P-value of a hypothesis test is also called the observed significance level since it represents the lowest possible significance level at which the null hypothesis could have been rejected.

13. In the critical-value approach, the null hypothesis is rejected if the value of the test statistic falls in the rejection region which is determined by the chosen significance level. In the P-value approach, the test statistic is computed and then the probability of obtaining a value as extreme or more extreme than the one actually obtained is found. This is the P-value. The advantages of providing the P-value are that the observed significance level of the test is given and the reader of the results can determine for him/herself whether the results are strong enough evidence against the null hypothesis to reject it.

14. Non-parametric methods have the advantages of involving fewer and simpler calculations than parametric methods and are more resistant to outliers and other extreme values. Parametric methods are preferred when the population is normal or the sample size is large since they are more powerful than non-parametric methods and thus tend to give more accurate results than non-parametric methods under those conditions.

15. Let μ denote last year's mean cheese consumption by Americans.

(a) H_0: μ = 28.0 lb

(b) H_a: μ > 28.0 lb

(c) This is a right-tailed test.

16. (a) Rejection region: $z \geq 1.28$

(b) Nonrejection region: $z < 1.28$

(c) Critical value: $z = 1.28$

(d) Significance level: $\alpha = 0.10$

(e) Graph: see next page

(f) Right-tailed test

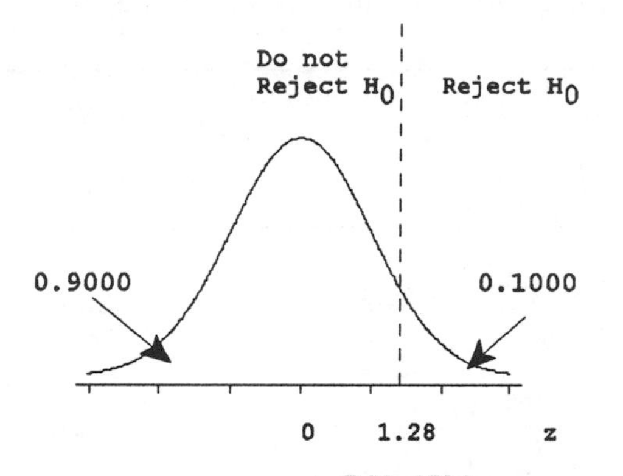

Critical Value
Nonrejection region | Rejection region

17. (a) A Type I error would occur if, in fact, μ = 28.0 lb, but the results of the sampling lead to the conclusion that μ > 28.0 lb.

(b) A Type II error would occur if, in fact, μ > 28.0 lb, but the results of the sampling fail to lead to that conclusion.

(c) A correct decision would occur if, in fact, μ = 28.0 lb and the results of the sampling do not lead to the rejection of that fact; or if, in fact, μ > 28.0 lb and the results of the sampling lead to that conclusion.

(d) If, in fact, last year's mean consumption of cheese for all Americans has not increased over the 1997 mean of 28.0 lb, and we do not reject the null hypothesis that μ = 28.0 lb, we made a correct decision.

(e) If, in fact, last year's mean consumption of cheese for all Americans has increased over the 1997 mean of 28.0 lb, and we fail to reject the null hypothesis that μ = 28.0 lb, we made a Type II error.

18. (a) P(Type I error) = significance level = α = 0.10

(b) The distribution of $\bar{x}$ will be approximately normal with a mean of 28.5 and a standard deviation of $6.9/\sqrt{35} = 1.17$.

(c) Note: $z = \dfrac{\bar{x} - \mu_0}{\sigma / \sqrt{n}} \Rightarrow \bar{x} = \mu_0 + z \cdot \sigma / \sqrt{n}$

Since this is a right-tailed test, we would reject H_0 if $z \geq 1.28$; or equivalently if $\bar{x} \geq 28.00 + 1.28(6.9)/\sqrt{35} = 29.49$.

So reject H_0 if $\bar{x} \geq 29.49$; otherwise do not reject H_0.

If $\mu = 28.50$, then

P(Type II error) $= P(\bar{x} \leq 29.49)$

$= P(z \leq (29.49 - 28.50)/(6.9/\sqrt{35}))$

$= P(z \leq 0.85) = 0.8023$

(d-e) Assuming that the true mean μ is one of the values listed, the distribution of $\bar{x}$ will be approximately normal with that mean and with a standard deviation of 1.166. The computations of β and the power $1 - \beta$ are shown in the table below.

True mean μ	z-score computation	P(Type II error) β	Power $1 - \beta$
28.5	$z = \dfrac{29.49 - 28.50}{6.9/\sqrt{35}} = 0.85$	0.8023	0.1977
29.0	$z = \dfrac{29.49 - 29.00}{6.9/\sqrt{35}} = 0.42$	0.6628	0.3372
29.5	$z = \dfrac{29.49 - 29.50}{6.9/\sqrt{35}} = -0.01$	0.4960	0.5040
30.0	$z = \dfrac{29.49 - 30.00}{6.9/\sqrt{35}} = -0.44$	0.3300	0.6700
30.5	$z = \dfrac{29.49 - 30.50}{6.9/\sqrt{35}} = -0.87$	0.1922	0.8078
31.0	$z = \dfrac{29.49 - 31.00}{6.9/\sqrt{35}} = -1.29$	0.0985	0.9015
31.5	$z = \dfrac{29.49 - 31.50}{6.9/\sqrt{35}} = -1.72$	0.0427	0.9573
32.0	$z = \dfrac{29.49 - 32.00}{6.9/\sqrt{35}} = -2.15$	0.0158	0.9842

(f)

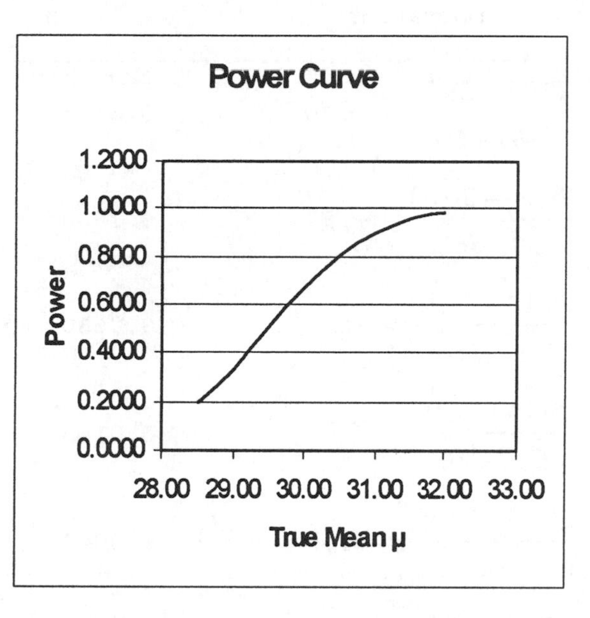

(g) The distribution of $\bar{x}$ will be approximately normal with a mean of 28.5 and a standard deviation of $6.9/\sqrt{60} = 0.891$.

(h) Note: $z = \dfrac{\bar{x} - \mu_0}{\sigma/\sqrt{n}} \Rightarrow \bar{x} = \mu_0 + z \cdot \sigma/\sqrt{n}$

Since this is a right-tailed test, we would reject H_0 if $z \geq 1.28$; or equivalently if $\bar{x} \geq 28.0 + 1.28(6.9)/\sqrt{60} = 29.14$

So reject H_0 if $\bar{x} \geq 29.14$; otherwise do not reject H_0.

If $\mu = 28.5$, then

P(Type II error) $= P(\bar{x} \leq 29.14)$

$= P(z \leq (29.14 - 28.5)/(6.9/\sqrt{60}))$

$= P(z \leq 0.72) = 0.7642$

(i-j) Assuming that the true mean μ is one of the values listed, the distribution of $\bar{x}$ will be approximately normal with that mean and with a standard deviation of 0.891. The computations of β and the power 1 -β are shown in the following table.

True mean μ	z-score computation	P(Type II error) β	Power 1 - β
28.5	$z = \dfrac{29.14 - 28.50}{6.9/\sqrt{60}} = 0.72$	0.7642	0.2358
29.0	$z = \dfrac{29.14 - 29.00}{6.9/\sqrt{60}} = 0.16$	0.5636	0.4364

True mean μ	z-score computation	P(Type II error) β	Power $1 - \beta$
29.5	$z = \frac{29.14 - 29.50}{6.9/\sqrt{60}} = -0.40$	0.3446	0.6554
30.0	$z = \frac{29.14 - 30.00}{6.9/\sqrt{60}} = -0.97$	0.1660	0.8340
30.5	$z = \frac{29.14 - 30.50}{6.9/\sqrt{60}} = -1.53$	0.0630	0.9370
31.0	$z = \frac{29.14 - 31.00}{6.9/\sqrt{60}} = -2.09$	0.0183	0.9817
31.5	$z = \frac{29.14 - 31.50}{6.9/\sqrt{60}} = -2.65$	0.0040	0.9960
32.0	$z = \frac{29.14 - 32.00}{6.9/\sqrt{60}} = -3.21$	0.0007	0.9993

(k)

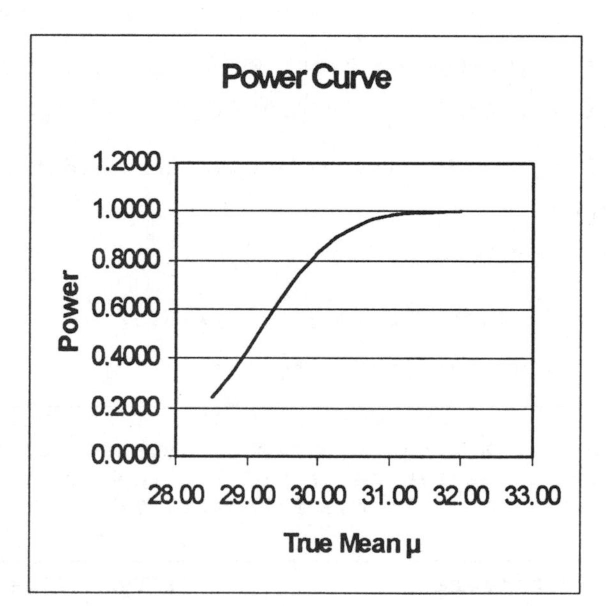

(l) The principle being illustrated is that increasing the sample size for a hypothesis test without changing the significance level increases the power.

19. (a) $n = 35$, $\bar{x} = 1008/35 = 28.8$, $\sigma = 6.9$

Step 1: H_0: $\mu = 28.0$ lb, H_a: $\mu > 28.0$ lb

Step 2: $\alpha = 0.10$

Step 3: $z = (28.8 - 28.0)/(6.9/\sqrt{35}) = 0.69$

Step 4: Critical value = 1.28

Step 5: Since 0.69 < 1.28, do not reject H_0.

Step 6: At the 10% significance level, the data do not provide sufficient evidence to conclude that last year's mean cheese consumption μ for all Americans has increased over the 1997 mean of 28.0 lb.

(b) Given the conclusion in part (a), if an error has been made, it must be a Type II error. This is because, given that the null hypothesis was not rejected, the only error that could be made is the error of not rejecting a false null hypothesis.

20. (a) Step 1: H_0: $\mu = 28.0$, H_a: $\mu > 28.0$

Step 2: $\alpha = 0.10$

Step 3: $z = 0.69$

Step 4: $P = 1 - 0.7549 = 0.2451$

Step 5: Since 0.2451 > 0.10, do not reject H_0.

Step 6: At the 10% significance level, the data do not provide sufficient evidence to conclude that last year's mean cheese consumption μ for all Americans has increased over the 1997 mean of 28.0 lb.

(b) Using Table 9.12 , we classify the strength of evidence against the null hypothesis as weak or none because $P > 0.10$.

21. $n = 12$, $\bar{x} = \$314.10$, $s = \$86.90$

Step 1: H_0: $\mu = \$362$, H_a: $\mu < \$362$

Step 2: $\alpha = 0.05$

Step 3: $t = (314.10 - 362)/(86.90/\sqrt{12}) = -1.909$

Step 4: Critical value = -1.796

Step 5: Since -1.909 < -1.796, reject H_0.

Step 6: At the 5% significance level, the data do provide sufficient evidence to conclude that the mean value lost because of purse snatching has decreased from the 1998 mean of $362.

22. (a) $n = 12$; H_0: $\eta = 362$; H_a: $\eta < 362$; $\alpha = 0.05$

x	$x - \eta_0 = D$	$\lvert D \rvert$	Rank of $\lvert D \rvert$	Signed Rank R
237	-125	125	10	-10
267	-95	95	7	-7
452	90	90	6	6
256	-106	106	9	-9
302	-60	60	3	-3
235	-127	127	11	-11
392	30	30	2	2
378	16	16	1	1
195	-167	167	12	-12
296	-66	66	5	-5
299	-63	63	4	-4
460	98	98	8	8

W = sum of the positive signed ranks = 17

Critical value = 12(13)/2 - 61 = 17

Since W=17 is less than or equal to the critical value of 17, we reject the null hypothesis and conclude that there is evidence that last year's mean value lost to purse snatching has decreased from the 1998 mean.

(b) In performing the Wilcoxon signed-rank test, we are assuming that the distribution of last year's values lost to purse snatching is symmetric.

(c) If the distribution of values lost is, in fact, a normal distribution, it is permissible to use the Wilcoxon test since a normal distribution is also symmetric.

23. If the values lost last year do have a normal distribution, the t-test is the preferred procedure for performing the hypothesis test since it is the more powerful test when the distribution is normal, that is, it has a greater chance of rejecting a false null hypothesis.

24. (a) If the odds-makers are estimating correctly, the mean point-spread error is zero.

(b) It seems reasonable to assume that the distribution of point spread errors is approximately normal. In any case, the sample size of 2109 is very large, so the t-test of H_0: $\mu = 0$ vs. H_a: $\mu \neq 0$ is appropriate. At the 5% significance level, the critical values are ±1.960. Since $t = (-0.2 - 0.0)/(10.9/\sqrt{2109}) = 0.843$, we do not reject H_0. P-value > 0.20.

(c) There is not sufficient evidence to conclude that the mean point-spread is different from zero.

25. Since we have a large sample (n = 50) and σ is known, use the z-test. Some caution is advised since it appears from the probability plot that there may be outliers.

26. Since we have a large sample (n = 37) and σ is unknown, use the t-test even though the variable has a left-skewed distribution. There are no outliers.

27. (a) The Wilcoxon signed-rank test is appropriate in Problem 25 since the distribution is symmetric. It is not appropriate in Problem 26 since the distribution is highly skewed to the left.

(b) The sample size is large (n=50) and the distribution is symmetric in Problem 26, so either the z-test or the Wilcoxon signed-rank test could be used. Since the distribution appears to have outliers, the Wilcoxon test is preferable.

28. (a) Access the *WeissStats CD* and enter the data in Minitab. It will appear in a column named Cheese(lb). Choose **Calc ▶ Calculator**, type NSCORE in the **Store result in variable** text box, select **Normal scores** from the function list and select Cheese(lb) to replace the word number in the **Expression** text box, and click **OK**. Then choose **Graph ▶ Plot**, select NSCORE for the **Y** column of **Graph 1** and Cheese(lb) for the **X** column, and click **OK**. The result is

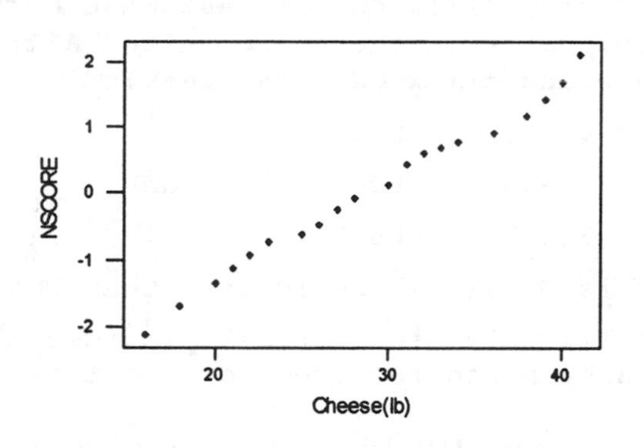

(b) We choose **Stat ▶ Basic Statistics ▶ 1-Sample z...**, select Cheese(lb) in the **Variables** text box, click on the **Test mean** button, type 28.0 in the **Test mean** text box, click on the arrow in the **Alternative** text box and select 'greater than,' type 6.9 in the Σ text box, and click **OK**. The result is

Test of mu = 28.00 vs mu > 28.00

The assumed sigma = 6.90

Variable	N	Mean	StDev	SE Mean	Z	P
Cheese(lb)	35	28.80	6.48	1.17	0.69	0.25

Since the P-value of 0.25 is greater than 0.10, do not reject the null hypothesis.

(c) The sample size is large and the normal probability plot in part (a) provides a fairly straight line, so the normality assumption required for the z-test seems reasonable.

29. (a) Access the *WeissStats CD* and enter the data in Minitab. It will appear in a column named Value. Choose **Calc ▶ Calculator**, type NSCORE in the **Store result in variable** text box, select **Normal scores** from the function list and select Value to replace the word number in the **Expression** text box, and click **OK**. Then choose **Graph ▶ Plot**, select NSCORE for the **Y** column of **Graph 1** and Value for the **X** column, and click **OK**. The result is

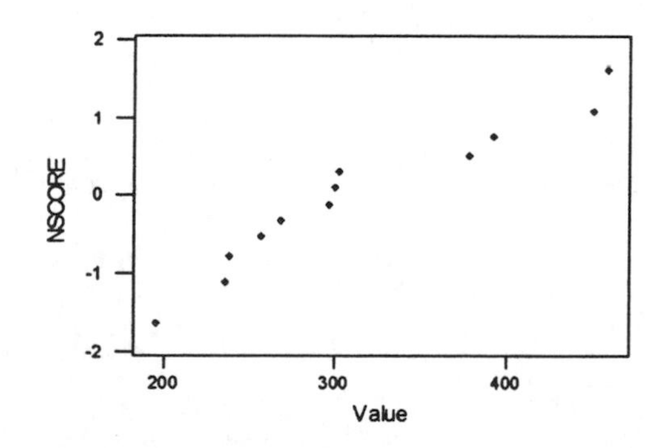

(b) We choose **Stat ▶ Basic Statistics ▶ 1-Sample t...**, select Value(lb) in the **Variables** text box, click on the **Test mean** button, type 362 in the **Test mean** text box, click on the arrow in the **Alternative** text box and select 'less than,' and click **OK**. The result is

Test of mu = 362.0 vs mu < 362.0

Variable	N	Mean	StDev	SE Mean	T	P
Value	12	314.1	86.9	25.1	-1.91	0.041

Since the P-value is 0.041, which is less than 0.05, reject H_0.

(c) The normal probability plot in part (a) provides a fairly straight line, so the normality assumption required for the t-test seems reasonable.

30. With the data in a column named Value, we choose **Stat ▶ Nonparametrics ▶ 1-Sample Wilcoxon...**, select Value in the **Variables** text box, click on the **Test median** button and type 362 in its text box, select 'less than' in the **Alternative** text box, and click **OK**. The result is

Test of median = 362.0 versus median < 362.0

	N	N for Test	Wilcoxon Statistic	P	Estimated Median
Value	12	12	17.0	0.046	307.0

Since the P-value is 0.046, which is less than 0.05, reject H_0.

CHAPTER 10 ANSWERS

Exercises 10.1

10.1 (a) The variable is the age of buyers of new cars.

(b) The two populations are the buyers of new domestic cars and the buyers of new imported cars.

(c) H_0: $\mu_1 = \mu_2$, H_a: $\mu_1 > \mu_2$ where μ_1 = the mean age of buyers of new domestic cars and μ_2 = the mean age of buyers of new imported cars.

10.3 Answers will vary.

10.5 (a) μ_1, σ_1, μ_2, and σ_2 are parameters; $\bar{x}_1$, s_1, $\bar{x}_2$, and s_2 are statistics.

(b) μ_1, σ_1, μ_2, and σ_2 are fixed numbers; $\bar{x}_1$, s_1, $\bar{x}_2$, and s_2 are random variables.

10.7 It is the sampling distribution of the difference of the two sample means that allows us to determine whether the difference of the sample means can be reasonably attributed to sampling error or whether it is large enough for us to conclude that the population means are different.

10.9 (a) The mean of $\bar{x}_1 - \bar{x}_2$ is $\mu_1 - \mu_2 = 40 - 40 = 0$

The standard deviation of $\bar{x}_1 - \bar{x}_2$ is

$$\sigma_{\bar{x}_1-\bar{x}_2} = \sqrt{\frac{\sigma_1^2}{n_1}+\frac{\sigma_2^2}{n_2}} = \sqrt{\frac{12^2}{9}+\frac{6^2}{4}} = 5$$

(b) No. The determination of the mean and standard deviation of $\bar{x}_1 - \bar{x}_2$ is the same regardless of the distributions of the variable on the two populations. The formula for the standard deviation of $\bar{x}_1 - \bar{x}_2$ assumes only that the samples are independent.

(c) No. Since it is not known that the two populations are normally distributed, and since the sample sizes of 9 and 4 are very small, we cannot assume that $\bar{x}_1 - \bar{x}_2$ is normally distributed.

10.11 (a) Population 1: Accounting, $n_1 = 32$, $\bar{x}_1 = 1111.6/32 = 34.74$, $\sigma_1 = 1.73$

Population 2: Liberal arts, $n_2 = 35$, $\bar{x}_2 = 1137.9/35 = 32.51$, $\sigma_2 = 1.82$

Step 1: H_0: $\mu_1 = \mu_2$, H_a: $\mu_1 \neq \mu_2$

Step 2: $\alpha = 0.05$

Step 3: $$z = \frac{34.74 - 32.51}{\sqrt{\frac{1.73^2}{32}+\frac{1.82^2}{35}}} = 5.14$$

Step 4: Critical values = ±1.96

Step 5: Since 5.14 > 1.96, reject H_0.

Step 6: At the 5% significance level, the data provide sufficient evidence to conclude that accounting graduates have a mean starting salary different from that of liberal arts graduates.

For the P-value approach, $P(z < -5.14 \text{ or } z > 5.14) = 0.0000$. Therefore, because the P-value is smaller than the significance level, reject H_0.

(b) The 95% confidence interval for $\mu_1 - \mu_2$ is

$$(34.74 - 32.51) \pm 1.96\sqrt{\frac{1.73^2}{32}+\frac{1.82^2}{35}} = 2.23 \pm 0.85 = (1.38, 3.08)$$

10.13 A hypothesis test of H_0: $\mu_1 = \mu_2$ versus H_a: $\mu_1 \neq \mu_2$ at the significance level α will lead to rejection of the null hypothesis if and only if the number zero does not lie in the $(1 - \alpha)$-level confidence interval for $\mu_1 - \mu_2$.

10.15 (a) We have Minitab take 1000 samples of size 12 observations from a normally distributed population having mean 640 and standard deviation 70 by choosing **Calc ▶ Random Data ▶ Normal...**, typing 1000 in the **Generate rows of data** text box, typing C1-C12 in the **Store in columns** text box, typing 640 in the **Mean** text box and 70 in the **Standard deviation** text box, and clicking **OK**. To get the mean of each row (sample), select **Calc ▶ Row Statistics..**, select The **Mean** button, enter C1-C12 in the **Input Variables:** text box, and type X1BAR in the **Store Result in:** text box. The sample means will be found in C13.

(b) We repeat part (a) for a normally distributed population having mean 715 and standard deviation 150 by choosing **Calc ▶ Random Data ▶ Normal...**, typing 1000 in the **Generate rows of data** text box, typing C14-C28 in the **Store in columns** text box, typing 715 in the **Mean** text box and 150 in the **Standard deviation** text box, and clicking **OK**. To get the mean of each row (sample), select **Calc ▶ Row Statistics..**, select The **Mean** button, enter C14-C28 in the **Input Variables:** text box, and type X2BAR in the **Store Result in:** text box. The sample means will be found in C29.

(c) To find the 1000 differences between X1BAR and X2BAR, select **Calc ▶ Calculator...**, type DIFF in the **Store results in variable** text box, type 'X1BAR' - 'X2BAR' in the **Expression** text box, and click **OK**. The DIFF values will appear in C30.

(d) To get the mean and standard deviation of the DIFF values, select **Stat ▶ Basic Statistics ▶ Display Descriptive statistics...**, and select DIFF in the **Variables** text box. Click **OK**. The results for our simulation were

Variable	N	Mean	Median	TrMean	StDev	SE Mean
DIFF	1000	-75.52	-74.49	-75.47	42.46	1.34

Variable	Minimum	Maximum	Q1	Q3
DIFF	-206.85	55.47	-105.52	-46.99

We see that the simulated mean of $\bar{x}_1 - \bar{x}_2$ is -75.47 and the standard deviation is 42.46. Now select **Graph ▶ Histogram** and enter DIFF in the **X** column for **Graph 1** and click OK. The result is

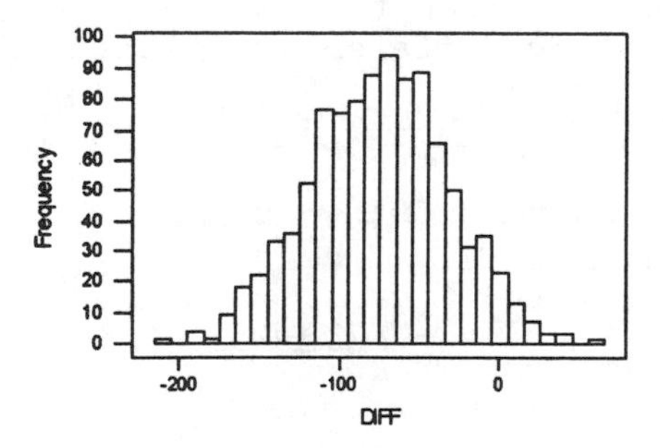

(e) Theoretically, $\bar{x}_1 - \bar{x}_2$ is normally distributed with mean 640 - 715 = -75 and standard deviation $\sqrt{70^2/12 + 150^2/15} = 43.68$.

(f) The histogram looks normal, the simulated mean -75.47 is close to -75, and the simulated standard deviation of 42.46 is very close to 43.68.

Section 10.2

10.17 s_p is called the pooled standard deviation because it combines information about the variability of both samples into one estimate of the common value of the population standard deviations.

10.19 Population 1: Fraud, $n_1 = 10$, $\bar{x}_1 = 10.12$, $s_1 = 4.90$

Population 2: Firearms, $n_2 = 10$, $\bar{x}_2 = 18.78$, $s_2 = 4.64$

$$s_p^2 = \frac{9(4.90)^2 + 9(4.64)^2}{18} = 22.7698$$

Step 1: H_0: $\mu_1 = \mu_2$, H_a: $\mu_1 < \mu_2$

Step 2: $\alpha = 0.05$

Step 3:

$$t = \frac{10.12 - 18.78}{\sqrt{22.7698\left(\frac{1}{10} + \frac{1}{10}\right)}} = -4.058$$

Step 4: df = 18, Critical value = -1.734

Step 5: Since -4.058 < -1.734, reject H_0. P-value < 0.005.

Step 6: At the 5% significance level, the data do provide sufficient evidence to conclude that, on the average, the mean time served for fraud is less than that served for firearms offenses.

10.21 Population 1: 25-34 years, $n_1 = 10$, $\bar{x}_1 = 70.19$, $s_1 = 2.951$

Population 2: 45-54 years, $n_2 = 15$, $\bar{x}_2 = 68.58$, $s_2 = 3.543$

$$s_p^2 = \frac{9(2.951)^2 + 14(3.543)^2}{23} = 11.0485, \text{ df} = (10-1) + (15-1) = 23$$

Step 1: H_0: $\mu_1 = \mu_2$, H_a: $\mu_1 > \mu_2$

Step 2: $\alpha = 0.05$

Step 3: $$t = \frac{70.19 - 68.58}{\sqrt{11.0485\left(\frac{1}{10} + \frac{1}{15}\right)}} = 1.186$$

Step 4: Critical value = 1.714

Step 5: Since 1.186 < 1.714, do not reject H_0.

Step 6: At the 5% significance level, the data do not provide sufficient evidence to conclude that males in the age group 25-34 years are, on the average, taller than those in the age group 45-54 years.

For the P-value approach, $P(t > 1.186) > 0.10$. Therefore, because the P-value is larger than the significance level, do not reject H_0.

10.23 Population 1: Vegetarians, $n_1 = 51$, $\bar{x}_1 = 39.04$, $s_1 = 18.82$

Population 2: Omnivores, $n_2 = 53$, $\bar{x}_2 = 49.92$, $s_2 = 18.97$

$$s_p^2 = \frac{50(18.82)^2 + 52(18.97)^2}{102} = 357.0822, \text{ df} = (51-1)+(53-1) = 102$$

Step 1: H_0: $\mu_1 = \mu_2$, H_a: $\mu_1 \neq \mu_2$

Step 2: $\alpha = 0.01$

Step 3: $$t = \frac{39.04 - 49.92}{\sqrt{357.0822\left(\frac{1}{51}+\frac{1}{53}\right)}} = -2.935$$

Step 4: Critical values = ± 2.626

Step 5: Since $-2.935 < -2.626$, reject H_0.

Step 6: At the 1% significance level, the data provide sufficient evidence to conclude that the mean daily protein intakes of female vegetarians and female omnivores differ.

For the P-value approach, $2\{P(t < -2.935)\} < 2(0.005) = 0.0100$. Therefore, because the P-value is smaller than the significance level, reject H_0.

10.25 From Exercise 10.21, $s_p^2 = 11.0485$, df $= 23$

(a)

$$(70.19 - 68.58) \pm 1.714\sqrt{11.0485\left(\frac{1}{10}+\frac{1}{15}\right)}$$

$$1.61 \pm 2.33$$

$$-0.72 \text{ to } 3.94 \text{ inches}$$

(b) We can be 90% confident that the difference, $\mu_1 - \mu_2$, between the population mean heights of males in the age group 25-34 years and those in the age group 45-54 years is somewhere between -0.72 and 3.94 inches.

10.27 From Exercise 10.23, $s_p^2 = 357.0822$, df $= 102$

(a)

$$(39.04 - 49.92) \pm 2.626\sqrt{357.0822\left(\frac{1}{51}+\frac{1}{53}\right)}$$

$$-10.88 \pm 9.73$$

$$-20.61 \text{ to } -1.15$$

(b) We can be 99% confident that the difference, $\mu_1 - \mu_2$, between the mean daily protein intakes of female vegetarians and of female omnivores is somewhere between -20.61 and -1.15 grams.

10.29 The parameter σ represents the common value of the standard deviations of the two populations. The standard deviation of most populations is unknown, and thus the common standard deviation of the two populations is also likely to be unknown. One argument often given for why the standard deviations are likely to be unknown in this situation is that in order to compute a population standard deviation, the mean μ is needed. In the comparison of means problem, then, both population means would be needed in order to find the common σ. But if both population means are known, the real difference $\mu_1 - \mu_2$ is already known and there is no longer any reason to compute a confidence interval for the difference.

10.31 (a) In Minitab, with the data in columns named OMNI and VEG, we choose **Calc ▶ Functions...**, select OMNI in the **Input Column** text box and type 'NSCORO' in the **Result in** text box, click on the **Normal scores** button, and click **OK**. We now choose **Graph ▶ Plot...**, select NSCORO for the **Y** variable for **Graph 1** and OMNI for the **X** variable, and click **OK**. Then repeat this process with VEG and NSCORV.

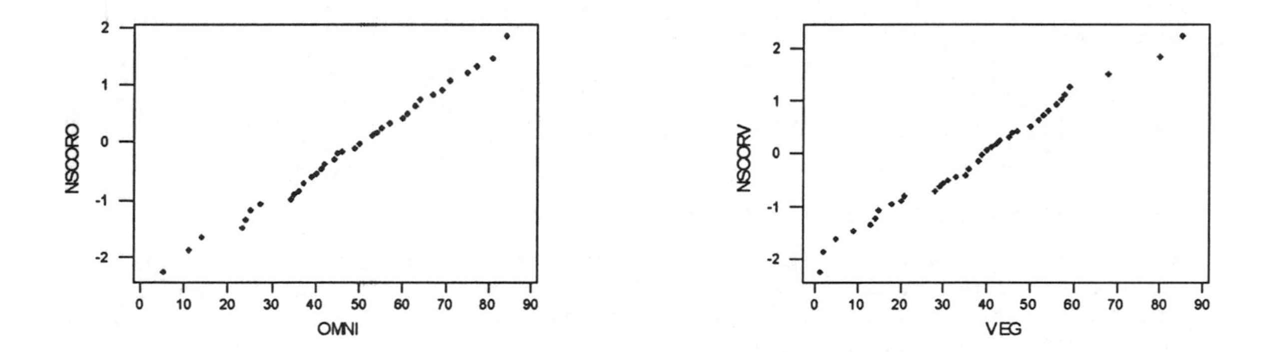

Now choose **Graph ▶ Boxplot...**, select OMNI for **Graph 1** and VEG for **Graph 2**, Then click on the **Frame** down-arrow, select **Multiple Graphs**, click on the **Same X and same Y** button, click **OK**, and click **OK**. The result is shown below.

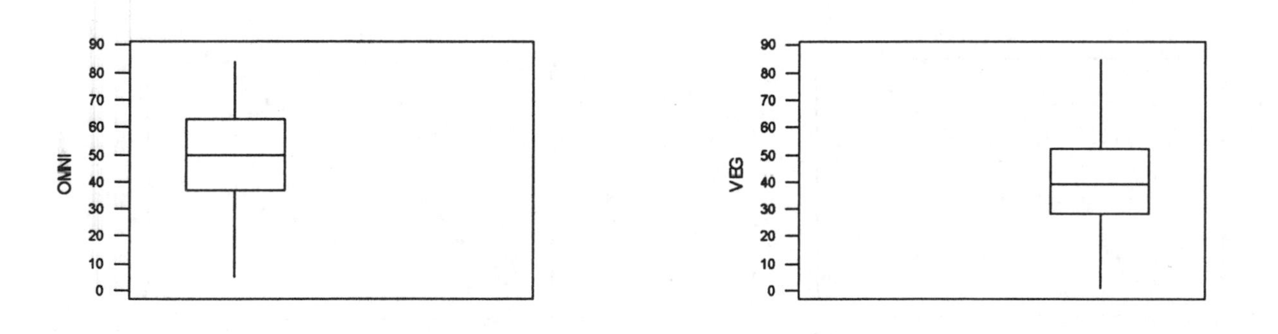

Finally, choose **Calc ▶ Column statistics...**, click on the **Standard deviation** button, select OMNI in the **Input Variables** text box, and click **OK.** Repeat this process with VEG. The results are

Standard deviation of OMNI = 18.968

Standard deviation of VEG = 18.821

(b) To carry out the hypothesis test and obtain a confidence interval for the difference in means, we choose **Stat ▶ Basic Statistics ▶ 2-Sample t...**, click on the **Samples in different columns** option button, select OMNI in the **First** text box and VEG in the **Second** text box, click on **Assume equal variances** so that a ✔ appears in the box, click on the arrow in the **Alternative** text box and select 'not equal', choose 99 for the **Confidence level**, and click **OK.** The results are

Two sample T for OMNI vs VEG

	N	Mean	StDev	SE Mean
OMNI	53	49.9	19.0	2.6
VEG	51	39.0	18.8	2.6

99% CI for mu OMNI - mu VEG: (1.2, 20.6)

T-Test mu OMNI = mu VEG (vs not =): T = 2.94 P = 0.0041 DF = 102

Both use Pooled StDev = 18.9

(c) Based on the graphic displays and sample standard deviations in part (a), it appears reasonable to consider the assumptions for using pooled-t procedures satisfied. Those assumptions are : (1) Independent samples, (2) Normal populations, and (3) Equal population standard deviations.

10.33 (a) In Minitab, with the data in columns named WITHOUT and WITH, we choose **Calc ▶ Functions...**, select WITHOUT in the **Input Column** text box and type 'NSCORWO' in the **Result in** text box, click on the **Normal scores** button, and click **OK.** We now choose **Graph ▶ Plot...**, select NSCORWO for the **Y** variable for **Graph 1** and WITHOUT for the **X** variable, and click **OK.** Then repeat this process with WITH and NSCORW.

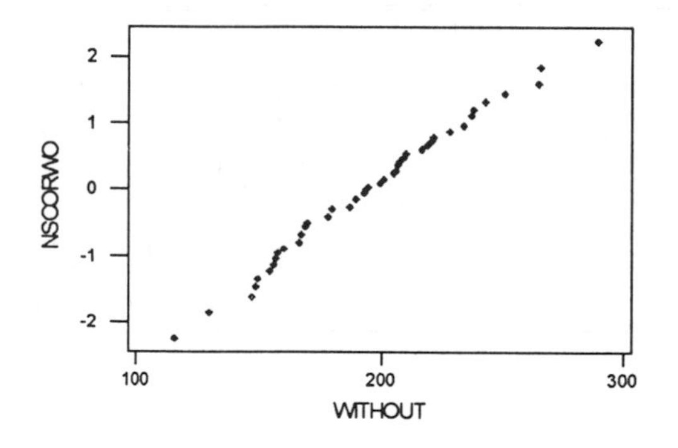

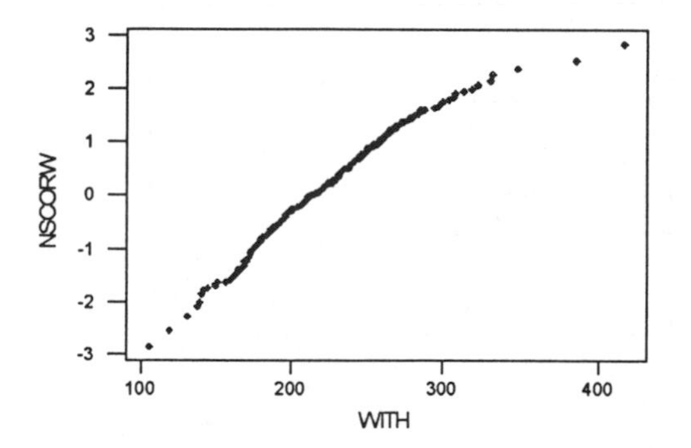

Now choose **Graph ▶ Boxplot...**, select WITHOUT for **Graph 1** and WITH for **Graph 2**, Then click on the **Frame** down-arrow, select **Multiple Graphs**, click on the **Same X and same Y** button, click **OK**, and click **OK**. The result is

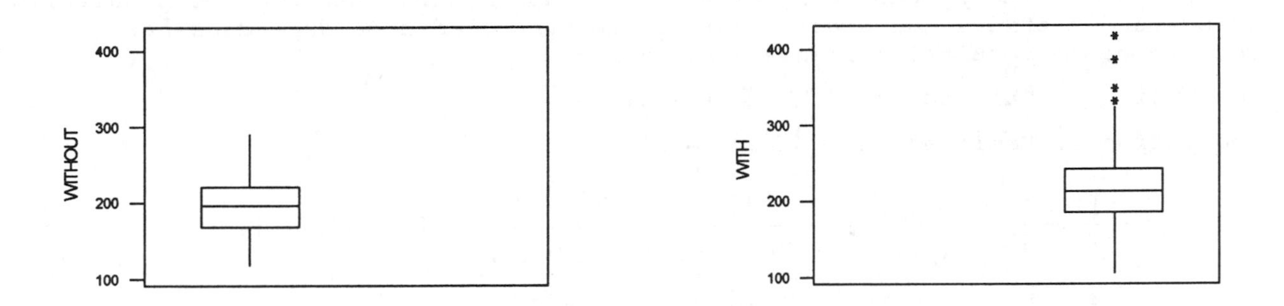

Finally, choose **Calc ▶ Column statistics...**, click on the **Standard deviation** button, select WITHOUT in the **Input Variables** text box, and click **OK**. Repeat this process with WITH. The results are

Standard deviation of WITHOUT = 36.110

Standard deviation of WITH = 43.015

(b-c) To carry out the hypothesis test and obtain a confidence interval for the difference in means, we choose **Stat ▶ Basic Statistics ▶ 2-Sample t...**, click on the **Samples in different columns** option button, select WITHOUT in the **First** text box and WITH in the **Second** text box, click on **Assume equal variances** so that a ✔ appears in the box, click on the arrow in the **Alternative** text box and select 'not equal', choose 99 for the **Confidence level**, and click **OK**. The results are

Two sample T for WITHOUT vs WITH

	N	Mean	StDev	SE Mean
WITHOUT	51	195.3	36.1	5.1
WITH	320	216.2	43.0	2.4

99% CI for mu WITHOUT - mu WITH: (-37.4, -4.5)

T-Test mu WITHOUT = mu WITH (vs not =): T = -3.29 P = 0.0011 DF = 369

Both use Pooled StDev = 42.1

(d) Based on the graphic displays and sample standard deviations in part (a), it appears reasonable to consider the assumptions for using pooled-t procedures satisfied. Those assumptions are : (1) Independent samples, (2) Normal populations, and (3) Equal population standard deviations. Although the WITH sample has four potential outliers, the sample size of 320 is very large and should diminish the effect of the outliers on the analysis.

Exercises 10.3

10.35 The pooled t-test requires the assumption that the two population standard deviations are equal or nearly so. In example 10.6, the two sample standard deviations are 84.7 and 38.2. This is a fairly clear indication that the two population standard deviations are not equal and thus the nonpooled t-test is more appropriate than the pooled t-test.

10.37 Use of the pooled procedure is based on the assumption that the two population standard deviations are equal, whereas the nonpooled procedure does not require equal population standard deviations.

10.39 Population 1: Chronic, $n_1 = 32$, $\bar{x}_1 = 25.8$, $s_1 = 9.2$

Population 2: Remitted, $n_2 = 20$, $\bar{x}_2 = 22.1$, $s_2 = 5.7$

$$\Delta = \frac{[s_1^2/n_1 + s_2^2/n_2]^2}{\frac{(s_1^2/n_1)^2}{n_1 - 1} + \frac{(s_2^2/n_2)^2}{n_2 - 1}} = \frac{[9.2^2/32 + 5.7^2/20]^2}{\frac{(9.2^2/32)^2}{32-1} + \frac{(5.7^2/20)^2}{20-1}} = 49.99995 \rightarrow 49$$

Step 1: H_0: $\mu_1 = \mu_2$, H_a: $\mu_1 \neq \mu_2$

Step 2: $\alpha = 0.10$

Step 3: $$t = \frac{25.8 - 22.1}{\sqrt{\frac{9.2^2}{32} + \frac{5.7^2}{20}}} = 1.791$$

Step 4: Critical value = ± 1.677

Step 5: Since 1.791 > 1.677, we reject H_0.

Step 6: At the 10% significance level, the data do provide sufficient evidence to conclude that there is a difference between the mean ages at arrest of East German prisoners with chronic PTSD and those with remitted PTSD.

For the P-value approach, $0.05 < 2\{P(t > 1.791)\} < 0.10$. Therefore, because the P-value is smaller than the significance level, reject H_0.

10.41 Population 1: Dynamic, $n_1 = 14$, $\bar{x}_1 = 7.36$, $s_1 = 1.22$

Population 2: Static, $n_2 = 6$, $\bar{x}_2 = 10.50$, $s_2 = 4.59$

$$\Delta = \frac{[s_1^2/n_1 + s_2^2/n_2]^2}{\frac{(s_1^2/n_1)^2}{n_1 - 1} + \frac{(s_2^2/n_2)^2}{n_2 - 1}} = \frac{[1.22^2/14 + 4.59^2/6]^2}{\frac{(1.22^2/14)^2}{14-1} + \frac{(4.59^2/6)^2}{6-1}} = 5.305 \rightarrow 5$$

Step 1: H_0: $\mu_1 = \mu_2$, H_a: $\mu_1 < \mu_2$

Step 2: $\alpha = 0.05$

Step 3: $$t = \frac{7.36 - 10.50}{\sqrt{\frac{1.22^2}{14} + \frac{4.59^2}{6}}} = -1.651$$

Step 4: Critical value = -2.015

Step 5: Since $-1.651 > -2.015$, do not reject H_0.

Step 6: At the 5% significance level, the data do not provide sufficient evidence to conclude that the mean number of acute postoperative days in the hospital is smaller with the dynamic system than with the static system.

For the P-value approach, $0.05 < P(t<-1.651) < 0.10$. Therefore, since the P-value is larger than the significance level, do not reject H_0.

10.43 Population 1: Psychotic patients, $n_1 = 10$, $\bar{x}_1 = 0.02426$, $s_1 = 0.00514$

Population 2: Non-psychotic patients, $n_2 = 15$, $\bar{x}_2 = 0.01643$, $s_2 = 0.00470$

Step 1: H_0: $\mu_1 = \mu_2$, H_a: $\mu_1 > \mu_2$

Step 2: $\alpha = 0.01$

$$\Delta = \frac{[s_1^2/n_1 + s_2^2/n_2]^2}{\frac{(s_1^2/n_1)^2}{n_1-1} + \frac{(s_2^2/n_2)^2}{n_2-1}} = \frac{[0.00514^2/10 + 0.00470^2/15]^2}{\frac{(0.00514^2/10)^2}{10-1} + \frac{(0.00470^2/15)^2}{15-1}} = 18.20 \rightarrow 18$$

Step 3: $$t = \frac{0.02426 - 0.01643}{\sqrt{\frac{0.00514^2}{10} + \frac{0.00470^2}{15}}} = 3.860$$

Step 4: Critical value = 2.552 (approximately)

Step 5: Since $3.860 > 2.552$, reject H_0.

Step 6: At the 1% significance level, the data do provide sufficient evidence to conclude that dopamine activity is higher, on average, in psychotic patients than in non-psychotic patients.

For the P-value approach, $P(t > 3.860) < 0.005$. Therefore, since the P-value is smaller than the significance level, reject H_0.

10.45 From Exercise 10.39, $\alpha = 0.10$, df = 49, $t_{0.05,49} = 1.677$

(a)

$$(25.8 - 22.1) \pm 1.677\sqrt{\frac{9.2^2}{32} + \frac{5.7^2}{20}}$$

$$3.7 \pm 3.5$$

0.2 to 7.2

(b) We can be 90% confident that the difference, $\mu_1 - \mu_2$, between the mean ages at arrest of East German prisoners with chronic PTSD and those with remitted PTSD is between 0.2 and 7.2 years.

10.47 From Exercise 10.41, $\alpha = 0.10$, df = 5, $t_{0.05,5} = 2.015$

(a)

$$(7.36 - 10.50) \pm 2.015\sqrt{\frac{1.22^2}{14} + \frac{4.59^2}{6}}$$

$$-3.14 \pm 3.83$$

-6.97 to 0.69

(b) We can be 90% confident that the difference, $\mu_1 - \mu_2$, between the mean numbers of acute postoperative days in the hospital with dynamic and static systems is somewhere between -6.97 and 0.69.

10.49 (a) Population 1: Dynamic, $n_1 = 14$, $\bar{x}_1 = 7.36$, $s_1 = 1.22$

Population 2: Static, $n_2 = 6$, $\bar{x}_2 = 10.50$, $s_2 = 4.59$

Step 1: H_0: $\mu_1 = \mu_2$, H_a: $\mu_1 < \mu_2$

$$s_p^2 = \frac{13(1.22)^2 + 5(4.59)^2}{18} = 6.9272, \text{ df} = (14-1)+(6-1) = 18$$

Step 2: $\alpha = 0.05$

Step 3: $$t = \frac{7.36 - 10.50}{\sqrt{6.9272\left(\frac{1}{14} + \frac{1}{6}\right)}} = -2.445$$

Step 4: Critical value = -1.734

Step 5: Since -2.445 < -1.734, reject H_0.

Step 6: At the 5% significance level, the data do provide sufficient evidence to conclude that the mean number of acute postoperative days in the hospital is smaller with the dynamic system than with the static system.

For the P-value approach, $0.01 < P(t<-2.445) < 0.025$. Therefore, since the P-value is smaller than the significance level, reject H_0.

(b) The pooled t-test resulted in rejecting the null hypothesis while the nonpooled t-test resulted in not rejecting the null hypothesis.

(c) The nonpooled t-test is more appropriate. One sample standard deviation is almost four times as large as the other, making it highly unlikely that the two population standard deviations are equal. The fact that the two sample sizes are also quite different makes it essential that the pooled t-test not be used.

10.51 (a) Pooled t-test. Both populations are normally distributed and the population standard deviations are equal.

(b) Nonpooled t-test. Both populations are normally distributed, but the population standard deviations are unequal.

(c) Neither. Both populations are skewed and it is given that both sample sizes are small.

(d) Neither. Only one population is normally distributed; the other is skewed. Since the sample sizes are small, the non-normality of one population rules out the use of either t-test.

10.53 (a) Using Minitab, with the data in columns named PSYCHO and NOPSYCHO, we

choose **Calc ▶ Calculator...**, type NSCORP in the **Store results in variable** text box, select **Normal scores** from the function list, select PSYCHO to replace **numbers** in the **Expression** text box, and click **OK.**

Repeat this process for NOPSYCHO, using NSCORN. We now choose **Graph ▶ Plot...**, select NSCORP for the **Y** variable for **Graph 1** and PSYCHO for the **X** variable, then select NSCORN for the **Y** variable for **Graph 2** and NOPSYCHO for the **X** variable, and click **OK.** Both graphs will be produced as shown following.

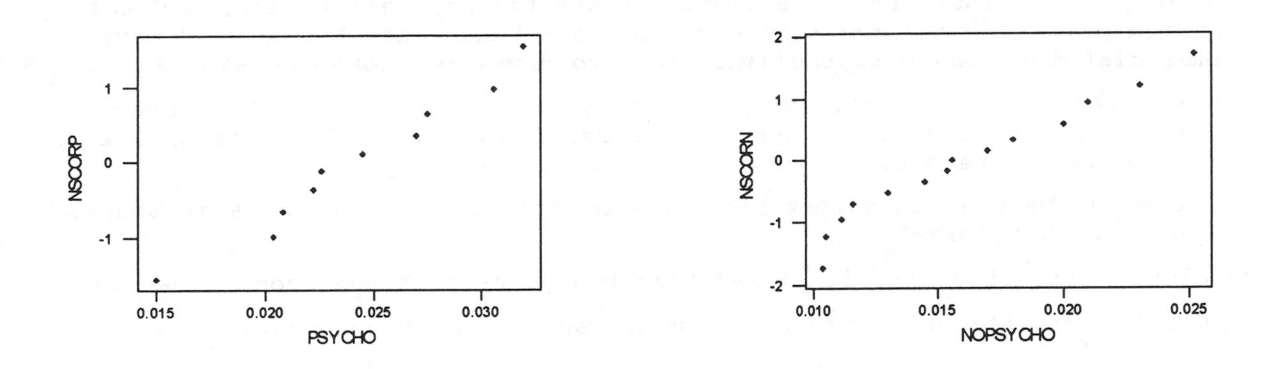

Now choose **Graph ▶ Boxplot...**, select PSYCHO for **Graph 1** and NOPSYCHO for **Graph 2**, click on the **Frame** down-arrow, select **Multiple Graphs**, click on the **Same X and same Y** button, click **OK**, and click **OK**. The result is

(b) To carry out the hypothesis test and obtain a confidence interval for the difference in means, we choose **Stat ▶ Basic Statistics ▶ 2-Sample t...**, click on the **Samples in different columns** option button, select PSYCHO in the **First** text box and NOPSYCHO in the **Second** text box, make certain that no ✔ appears in the **Assume equal variances** box, click on the arrow in the **Alternative** text box and select 'greater than,' choose 99 for the **Confidence level**, and click **OK**. The results are

```
Two sample T for PSYCHO vs NOPSYCHO
              N       Mean     StDev   SE Mean
PSYCHO       10    0.02426   0.00514    0.0016
NOPSYCHO     15    0.01643   0.00470    0.0012
```

(c)
```
99% CI for mu PSYCHO - mu NOPSYCHO: ( 0.0020,  0.0137)
T-Test mu PSYCHO = mu NOPSYCHO (vs >): T = 3.86  P = 0.0006  DF = 18
```

(d) Based on the normal plots in (a) for the two independent samples, it appears reasonable to consider the assumption of normality satisfied; thus, the use of the nonpooled-t procedure.

Exercises 10.4

10.55 All normal distributions are symmetric about the population mean, and the standard deviation determines the spread (and hence the shape). Thus two normal distributions with the same standard deviation have the same shape.

10.57 (a) Use the pooled t-test. It is slightly more powerful than the Mann-Whitney when the conditions for its use (normal distributions with equal variances) are met.

(b) Use the Mann-Whitney test since the distributions have the same shape, but are not normal.

10.59 Population 1: Students with fewer than two years of high-school algebra;

Population 2: Students with two or more years of high-school algebra.

Step 1: H_0: $\mu_1 = \mu_2$, H_a: $\mu_1 < \mu_2$

Step 2: $\alpha = 0.05$

Step 3: Construct a work table based upon the following: First, rank all the data from both samples combined. Adjacent to each column of data as it is presented in the Exercise, record the overall rank. Assign tied rankings the average of the ranks they would have had if there were no ties. For example, the two 81s in the table below are tied for eleventh smallest. Thus, each is assigned the rank (11 + 12)/2 = 11.5.

Fewer Than Two Years of High-School Algebra	Overall Rank	Two or More Years of High-School Algebra	Overall Rank
58	3	84	14
81	11.5	67	7
74	8.5	65	6
61	4	75	10
64	5	74	8.5
43	1	92	15
		83	13
		52	2
		81	11.5

Step 4: The value of the test statistic is the sum of the ranks for the sample data from Population 1:

$$M = 3 + 11.5 + 8.5 + 4 + 5 + 1 = 33.$$

Step 5: We have $n_1 = 6$ and $n_2 = 9$. Since the hypothesis test is left-tailed with $\alpha = 0.05$, we use Table VI to obtain the critical value, which is $M_1 = 6(16)-63 = 33$. Thus, we reject H_0 if $M \leq 33$.

Step 6: Since $M = 33$ equals the critical value, reject H_0.

Step 7: At the 5% significance level, the data provide sufficient evidence to conclude that in this teacher's chemistry courses, students with fewer than two years of high-school algebra have a lower mean semester average than do students with two or more years of high-school algebra.

10.61 Population 1: Volumes held by public colleges and universities;

Population 2: Volumes held by private colleges and universities.

Step 1: H_0: $\eta_1 = \eta_2$, H_a: $\eta_1 > \eta_2$

Step 2: $\alpha = 0.05$

Step 3: Construct a work table based upon the following: First, rank all the data from both samples combined. Adjacent to each column of data as it is presented in the Exercise, record the overall rank.

Private	Overall Rank	Public	Overall Rank
15	1	27	3
24	2	67	5
41	4	113	7
79	6	139	8
265	9	500	11
411	10	603	13
516	12		

Step 4: The value of the test statistic is the sum of the ranks for the sample data from Population 1:

$$M = 1 + 2 + 4 + 6 + 9 + 12 = 44.$$

Step 5: We have $n_1 = 7$ and $n_2 = 6$. Since the hypothesis test is left-tailed with $\alpha = 0.05$, we use Table VI to obtain the critical value, which is $M_r = (13)(14)/2 - 54 = 37$. Thus, we reject H_0 if $M \leq 37$.

Step 6: Since $M > 37$, do not reject H_0.

Step 7: At the 5% significance level, the data do not provide sufficient evidence to conclude that the median number of volumes held by public colleges and universities is less than the median number of volumes held by private colleges and universities.

10.63 Population 1: Time served by prisoners with fraud offenses;

Population 2: Time served by prisoners with firearms offenses.

Step 1: H_0: $\mu_1 = \mu_2$, H_a: $\mu_1 < \mu_2$

Step 2: $\alpha = 0.05$

Step 3: Construct a work table based upon the following: First, rank all the data from both samples combined. Adjacent to each column of data as it is presented in the Exercise, record the overall rank. Assign tied rankings the average of the ranks they would have had if there were no ties. For example, the two 17.9s in the table below are tied for thirteenth smallest. Thus, each is assigned the rank (13 + 14)/2 = 13.5.

Fraud	Overall Rank	Firearms	Overall Rank
3.6	1	10.4	6
5.3	2	13.3	9
5.9	3	16.1	11
7.0	4	17.9	13.5
8.5	5	18.4	15
10.7	7	19.6	16
11.8	8	20.9	17
13.9	10	21.9	18
16.6	12	23.8	19
17.9	13.5	25.5	20

Step 4: The value of the test statistic is the sum of the ranks for the sample data from Population 1:

$$M = 1 + 2 + 3 + 4 + 5 + 7 + 8 + 10 + 12 + 13.5 = 65.5.$$

Step 5: We have $n_1 = 10$ and $n_2 = 10$. Since the hypothesis test is left-tailed with $\alpha = 0.05$, we use Table VI to obtain the critical value, which is $M_1 = 10(21) - 127 = 83$. Thus, we reject H_0 if $M \leq 83$.

Step 6: Since $M < 83$, reject H_0.

Step 7: At the 5% significance level, the data provide sufficient evidence to conclude that the mean time served for fraud offenses is less than the mean time served for firearms offenses.

(b) Normal distributions with the same standard deviations have the same shape, thus the requirement for using the Mann-Whitney test is met. If the distributions are, in fact, normal with equal standard deviations, it is better to use the pooled t-test since it is slightly more powerful than the Mann-Whitney test in this situation.

10.65 (a) Since the populations are normally distributed and have the same shape, use the pooled t-test.

(b) No assumptions are met for any of the tests; therefore, none of these tests can be performed.

(c) Since both samples are large, but the standard deviations are not equal, use the nonpooled t-test.

10.67 Step 1: State the null and alternative hypotheses.

Step 2: Decide on the significance level α.

Step 3: Construct a work table of the form.

Sample from Population 1	Overall Rank	Sample from Population 2	Overall Rank
.	.	.	.
.	.	.	.
.	.	.	.

Step 4: Compute the value of the test statistic

$$z = \frac{M - n_1(n_1 + n_2 + 1)/2}{\sqrt{n_1 n_2 (n_1 + n_2 + 1)/12}}$$

where M is the sum of the ranks for the sample data from Population 1.

Step 5: The critical value(s):

(a) for a two-tailed test are $\pm z_{\alpha/2}$.

(b) for a left-tailed test is $-z_\alpha$.

(c) for a right-tailed test is z_α.

Use Table II to find the critical value(s).

Step 6: If the value of the test statistic falls in the rejection region, reject H_0; otherwise, do not reject H_0.

Step 7: State the conclusion in words.

10.69 (a) (b) 5%

Rank						
1	2	3	4	5	6	M
A	A	A	B	B	B	6
A	A	B	A	B	B	7
A	A	B	B	A	B	8
A	A	B	B	B	A	9
A	B	A	A	B	B	8
A	B	A	B	A	B	9
A	B	A	B	B	A	10
A	B	B	A	A	B	10
A	B	B	A	B	A	11
A	B	B	B	A	A	12
B	A	A	A	B	B	9
B	A	A	B	A	B	10
B	A	A	B	B	A	11
B	A	B	A	A	B	11
B	A	B	A	B	A	12
B	A	B	B	A	A	13
B	B	A	A	A	B	12
B	B	A	A	B	A	13
B	B	A	B	A	A	14
B	B	B	A	A	A	15

M	P(M)
6	0.05
7	0.05
8	0.10
9	0.15
10	0.15
11	0.15
12	0.15
13	0.10
14	0.05
15	0.05

(c) Each row in part (a) has a 1/20 = 0.05 chance of occurring. This results in the probability distribution above at the right for M for the case when $n_1 = 3$ and $n_2 = 3$.

(d) A histogram for the probability distribution of M is shown below for the case when $n_1 = 3$ and $n_2 = 3$.

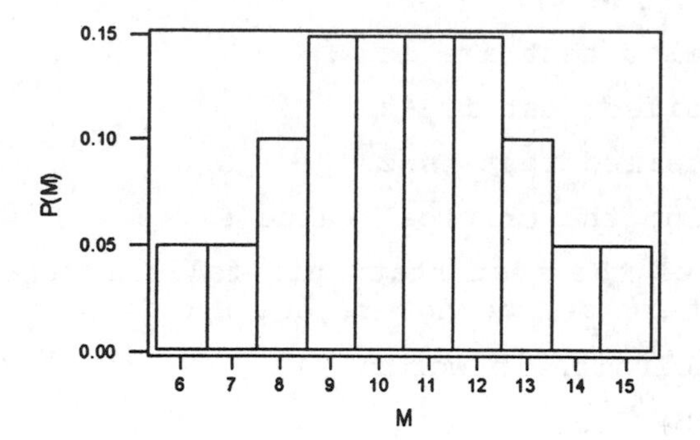

(e) From part (c), we see that $P(M \le 6) = 0.05$ and $P(M \ge 15) = 0.05$. These results correspond with the entries in Table VI for $n_1 = 3$ and $n_2 = 3$. That is, $M_l = 6$ at $\alpha = 0.05$, and $M_r = 15$ at $\alpha = 0.05$.

10.71 With the data in two columns named PUBLIC and PRIVATE, we choose **Stat ▶ Nonparametrics ▶ Mann-Whitney...**, select PUBLIC for **First sample** and PRIVATE for **Second sample**, select 95 for the **Confidence level**, select 'less than' for the **Alternative**, and click **OK**. The results are

```
PUBLIC     N =   7     Median =        79.0
PRIVATE    N =   6     Median =       136.0
Point estimate for ETA1-ETA2 is       -53.0
96.2 Percent C.I. for ETA1-ETA2 is (-459.1,278.1)
W = 44.0
Test of ETA1 = ETA2  vs.  ETA1 < ETA2 is significant at 0.2602
```

Cannot reject at $\alpha = 0.05$

10.73 (a) With the data in columns named UNSEED and SEED, we choose **Graph ▶ Boxplot...**, select UNSEED as the **Y** variable for **Graph1** and SEED as the **Y** variable for **Graph2**, then click on the **Frame** arrow and click on **Multiple graphs**, click on the button for **Overlay graphs on the same page**, click **OK**, and click **OK**. This produces the two boxplots on the same scale in one graph as shown below.

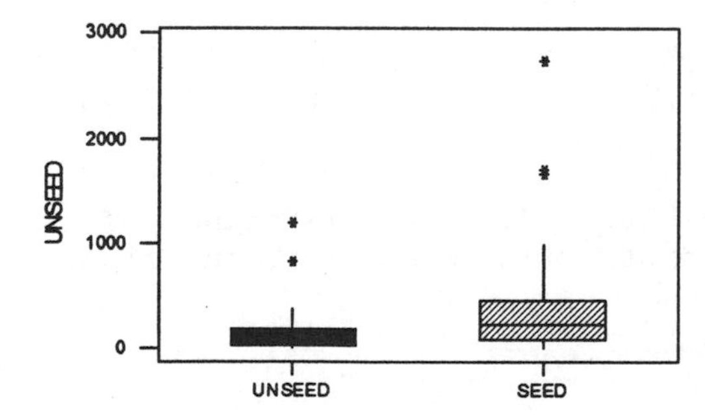

To obtain the normal probability plots, choose **Calc ▶ Calculator...**, type NSCORU in the **Store results in variable** text box, select **Normal scores** from the function list, select UNSEED to replace **numbers** in the **Expression** text box and click **OK**. Then choose **Calc ▶ Calculator...**, type NSCORS in the **Store results in variable** text box, select **Normal scores** from the function list, select SEED to replace **numbers** in the **Expression** text box and click **OK**. Finally, choose **Graph ▶ Plot...**, select NSCORU for the Y variable for Graph1 and UNSEED for the X variable for Graph1, select NSCORS for the Y variable for Graph2 and SEED for the X variable for Graph2, and click **OK**. The results are

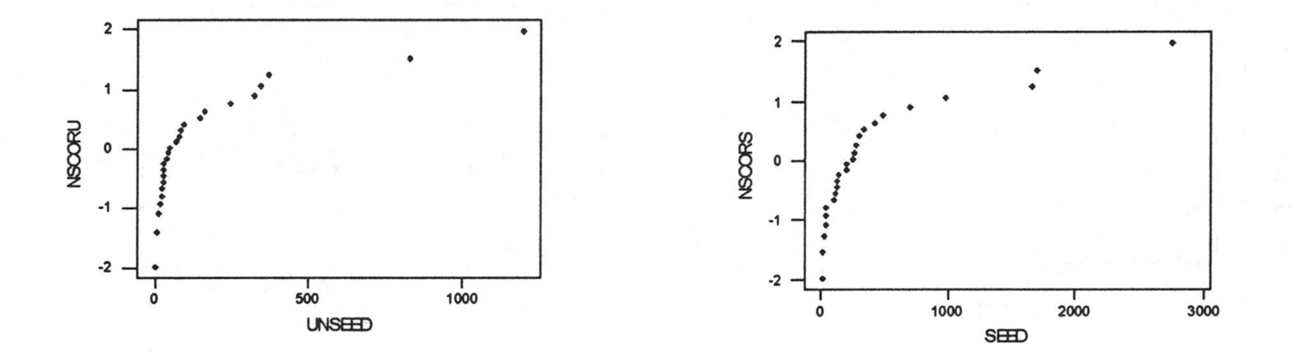

(b) It is not appropriate to use the pooled t-test because the populations are both highly skewed to the right. They are not normally distributed.

(c) It is not appropriate to use the nonpooled t-test because the populations are both highly skewed to the right. They are not normal and the sample sizes are not large.

(d) Although both samples are skewed to the right, they still do not have the same shape. The data for the seeded clouds is more highly skewed than that for the unseeded clouds. Thus it is not appropriate to use the Mann-Whitney test.

(e-f) To transform the data, we choose **Calc ▶ Calculator...**, type LNUNSEED in the **Store result in variable** text box, type LOGE(UNSEED) IN THE **Expression** text box and click **OK**. Proceed in a similar way to logarithmically transform the data for the seeded clouds by typing LNSEED at the second step and LOGE(SEED)at the third step. Then, following the procedure of part (a) for LNUNSEED and LNSEED, we obtain the boxplots and normal probability plots which follow.

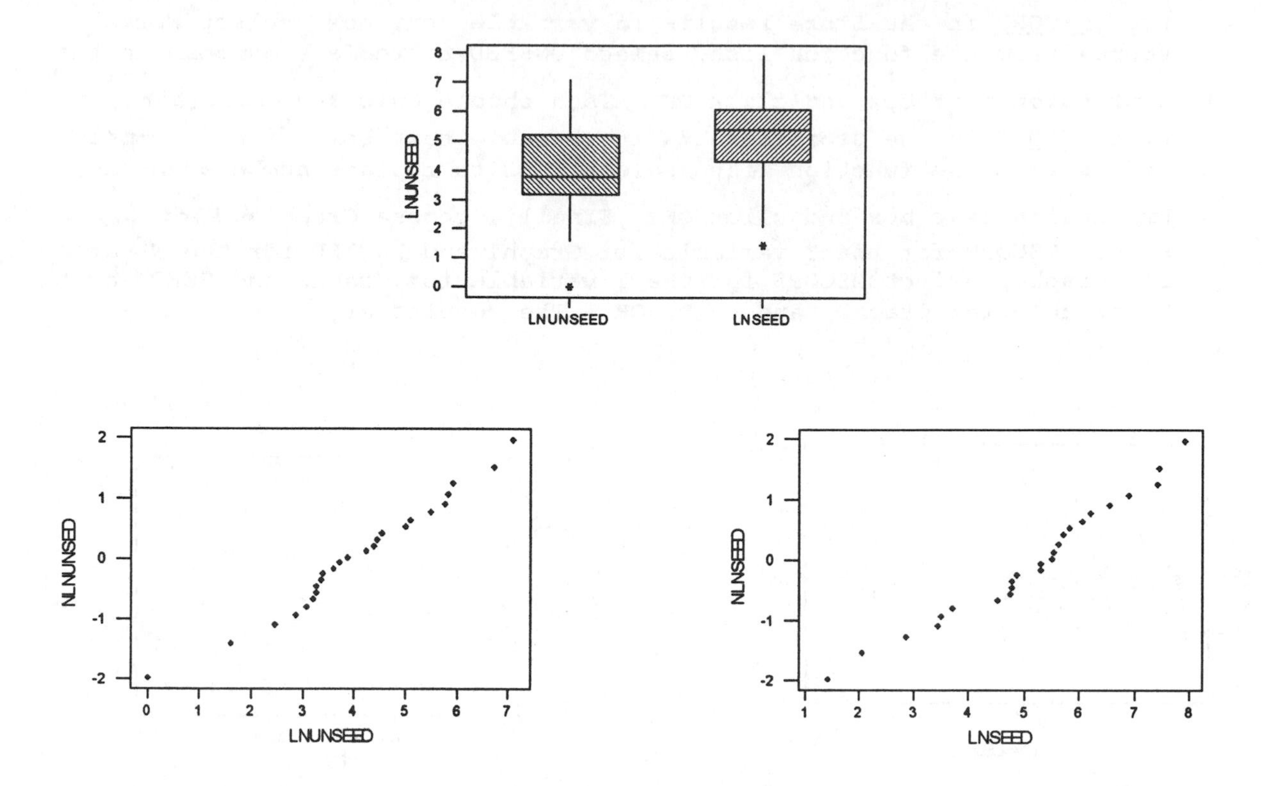

(g) Although the normal probability plots are quite close to linear, the boxplots still indicate a couple of potential outliers. Since the samples are not large, it is possible that the outliers will affect the standard deviations which are not resistant to outliers. We recommend not using the pooled t-test in these circumstances.

(h) The nonpooled t-test is robust to deviations from normality, but can still be affected by the presence of outliers because of their effect on the standard deviations. The nonpooled t-test would be a better choice than the pooled t-test on the transformed data, but it would still be wise to exercise caution in using it.

(i) The two sample boxplots and normal probability plots for the transformed data are not identical in shape, but are reasonably close. The Mann-Whitney test is appropriate in this situation.

(j) Since the presence of the two potential outliers in the transformed data may have an effect on the standard deviations while also raising questions about the normality of the populations, and since the two distributions are close to being the same shape, the Mann-Whitney test is preferred for conducting the hypothesis test for the transformed data.

(k) To perform the Mann-Whitney test on the transformed data, choose **Stat ▶ Nonparametrics ▶ Mann-Whitney..**, specify LNUNSEED in the **First Sample** text box, click in the **Second Sample** text box and specify LNSEED, click the arrow button at the right of the **Alternative** drop-down list box and select **less than**, and click **OK**. The results are

```
LNUNSEED    N =  26     Median =        3.786
LNSEED      N =  26     Median =        5.396
```

```
Point estimate for ETA1-ETA2 is      -1.259
95.1 Percent C.I. for ETA1-ETA2 is (-2.097,-0.282)
W = 554.0
Test of ETA1 = ETA2  vs.  ETA1 < ETA2 is significant at 0.0069
The test is significant at 0.0069 (adjusted for ties)
```

(l) Reject the null hypothesis. The P-value of 0.0069 is very strong evidence that the cloud seeding with silver nitrate increase rainfall. [It may be worth noting that if you had chosen either of the other two tests, you would have arrived at the same conclusion with P-values that are only slightly different.]

Exercises 10.5

10.75 (a) Ages of married people.

(b) Married men and married women.

(c) The pairs are married couples.

(d) The paired difference variable is the difference between the age of the man and the age of the woman in each couple.

10.77 The samples must be paired (this is essential), and the population of all paired differences must be normally distributed or the sample must be large (the procedure works reasonably well even for small or moderate size samples if the paired-difference variable is not normally distributed provided that the deviation from normality is small).

10.79 (a) The variable is the height of the plant.

(b) The two populations are the cross-fertilized plants and the self-fertilized plants.

(c) The paired-difference variable is the difference in heights of the cross-fertilized plants and the self-fertilized plants grown in the same pot.

(d) Yes. They represent difference in heights of two plants grown under the same conditions (same pot), one from each category of plants.

(e) Step 1: H_0: $\mu_1 = \mu_2$, H_a: $\mu_1 \neq \mu_2$

Step 2: $\alpha = 0.05$

Step 3: The paired differences are given.

Step 4: $$t = \frac{\bar{d}}{s_d / \sqrt{n}} = \frac{20.93}{37.74 / \sqrt{15}} = 2.148$$

Step 5: df = 14; critical values = ±2.145

Step 6: Since 2.148 > 2.145, reject H_0. The data do provide sufficient evidence at the 5% significance level that there is a difference between the mean heights of cross-fertilized and self-fertilized plants.

(f) At the 1% significance level, the critical values are ±2.977. Since 2.148 < 2.977, do not reject H_0. The data do not provide sufficient evidence at the 5% significance level that there is a difference between the mean heights of cross-fertilized and self-fertilized plants.

10.81 Population 1: Weights before treatment for anorexia nervosa

Population 2: Weights after treatment for anorexia nervosa

Step 1: H_0: $\mu_1 = \mu_2$, H_a: $\mu_1 < \mu_2$

Step 2: $\alpha = 0.05$

Step 3: The paired differences 'Weight after - Weight before' are
-11.0, -5.5, -9.4, -13.6, 2.9, -10.7, 0.1, -7.4, -21.5, 5.3, 3.8, -11.4, -13.4, -13.1, -9.0, -3.9, -5.7

For these differences, $\sum d = -123.5$ and $\sum d^2 = 1716.85$.

Step 4:

$$\bar{d} = \sum d / n = -123.5/17 = 7.2647$$

$$s_d = \sqrt{\frac{\sum d^2 - \left(\sum d\right)^2 / n}{n-1}} = \sqrt{\frac{1716.85 - 123.5^2/17}{17-1}} = 7.1574$$

$$t = \frac{\bar{d}}{s_d/\sqrt{n}} = \frac{-7.2647}{7.1574/\sqrt{17}} = -4.185$$

Step 5: df = 16; critical value = -1.746

Step 6: Since -4.185 < -1.746, reject H_0. The data do provide sufficient evidence at the 5% significance level that family therapy is effective in helping anorexic young women gain weight.

For the P-value approach, $P(t > 4.181) < 0.005$. Since the P-value is smaller than the significance level, reject H_0.

10.83 Population 1: Corneal thickness in normal eyes

Population 2: Corneal thickness in glaucoma eyes

Step 1: H_0: $\mu_1 = \mu_2$, H_a: $\mu_1 > \mu_2$

Step 2: $\alpha = 0.10$

Step 3: The paired differences, $d = x_1 - x_2$, are
-4, 0 12, 18, -4, -12, 6, 16

For these differences,

$\sum d = 32$ and $\sum d^2 = 936$.

Step 4:

$$\bar{d} = \sum d / n = 32/8 = 4.0$$

$$s_d = \sqrt{\frac{\sum d^2 - \left(\sum d\right)^2 / n}{n-1}} = \sqrt{\frac{936 - 32^2/8}{8-1}} = 10.7438$$

$$t = \frac{\bar{d}}{s_d/\sqrt{n}} = \frac{4.0}{10.7438/\sqrt{8}} = 1.053$$

Step 5: df = 7, Critical value = 1.415

Step 6: Since 1.053 < 1415, do not reject H_0. The data do not provide sufficient evidence at the 10% significance level that the mean corneal thickness is greater in normal eyes than in eyes with glaucoma.

For the P-value approach, $P(t > 1.053) > 0.10$. Since the P-value is larger than the significance level, do not reject H_0.

10.85 From Exercise 10.79, df = 14.

(a)

$$20.933 \pm 2.145 \cdot \frac{37.744}{\sqrt{15}}$$

$$20.933 \pm 20.904$$

0.03 to 41.84 eighths of an inch

We can be 95% confident that the difference, $\mu_1 - \mu_2$, between the mean heights of cross-fertilized and self-fertilized Zea mays is somewhere between 0.03 and 41.84 eighths of an inch.

(b)

$$20.93 \pm 2.977 \cdot \frac{37.74}{\sqrt{15}}$$

$$20.93 \pm 29.01$$

-8.08 to 49.94 eighths of an inch

We can be 99% confident that the difference, $\mu_1 - \mu_2$, between the mean heights of cross-fertilized and self-fertilized Zea mays is somewhere between -8.08 and 49.94 eighths of an inch.

10.87 From Exercise 10.81, df = 16.

$$-7.2647 \pm 1.746 \cdot \frac{7.1574}{\sqrt{17}}$$

$$-7.2647 \pm 3.0309$$

-10.30 to -4.23 pounds

We can be 90% confident that the mean weight gain, $\mu_1 - \mu_2$, resulting from family-therapy treatment by anorexic young women is somewhere between 4.23 and 10.30 pounds.

10.89 Data is obtained from two populations whose members can be naturally paired. By letting d represent the difference between the values in each pair, we can reduce the data set from pairs of numbers to a single number representing each pair. Since the mean of the paired differences is the same as the difference of the two population means, we can test the equality of the two population means by testing to see if the mean of the paired differences is zero (or some other value if appropriate). If the paired differences are normally distributed, then the one-sample t-test can be used to carry out the test.

10.91 A nonparametric test should be used because the outlier will not have as much effect on the results. In general, nonparametric procedures are more resistant to outliers.

10.93 (a) In Minitab, with the differences in a column named DIFF, choose **Calc ▶ Functions...**, select DIFFS in the **Input Column** text box and type NSCORED in the **Result in** text box, click on the **Normal scores** button, and click **OK**. Now choose **Graph ▶ Plot...**, select NSCORED for the **Y** variable for **Graph 1** and DIFF for the **X** variable, and click **OK**.

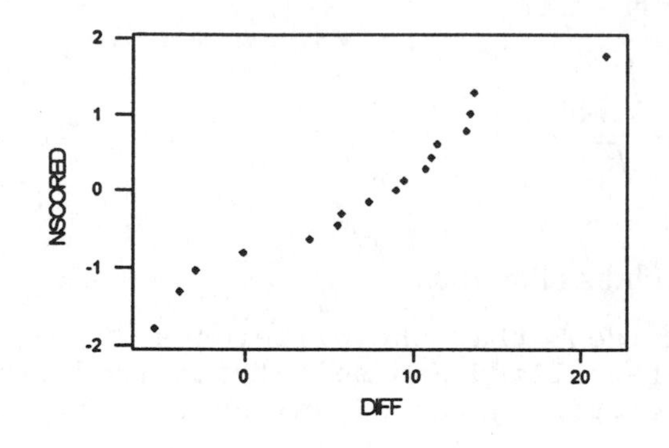

(b) Now choose **Stat ▶ Basic statistics ▶ Paired t...**, select AFTER in the **First Sample** text box, select BEFORE in the **Second Sample** text box , click on the **Options...** button, click in the **Confidence level** text box and type <u>90</u>, click on the **Test Mean** button, click in the **Test mean** text box and type <u>0</u>, select **'greater than'** in the **Alternative** box, click **OK**, and click **OK**. The results are

Paired T for AFTER - BEFORE

	N	Mean	StDev	SE Mean
AFTER	17	90.49	8.48	2.06
BEFORE	17	83.23	5.02	1.22
Difference	17	7.26	7.16	1.74

90% CI for mean difference: (4.23, 10.30)

T-Test of mean difference = 0 (vs > 0): T-Value = 4.18 P-Value = 0.000

(c) The normal probability plot indicates that the assumption of a normal distribution for the difference data is reasonable; therefore the one-sample t-test is appropriate.

10.95 Using Minitab, with the differences in a column named DIFF, choose **Calc ▶ Functions...**, select DIFF in the **Input Column** text box and type <u>NSCOD</u> in the **Result in** text box, click on the **Normal scores** button, and click **OK**. Now choose **Graph ▶ Plot...**, select NSCOD for the **Y** variable for **Graph 1** and DIFF for the **X** variable, and click **OK**. Then choose **Graph ▶ Boxplot**, select DIFF for the **Y** variable for **Graph 1** and click **OK**.

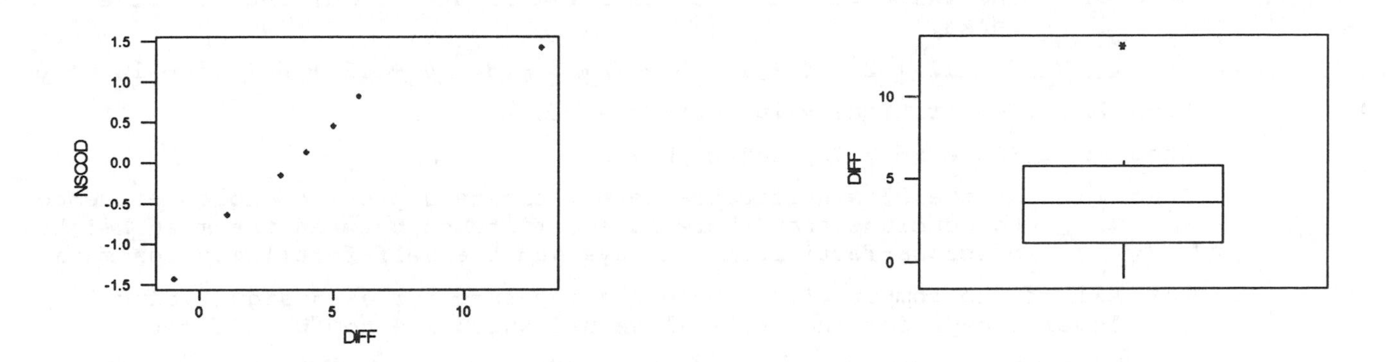

The sample size is very small (8) and there is one outlier (13) in the differences. Since the t-test is not robust to outliers, it is not appropriate for these data.

Exercises 10.6

10.97 (a) Yes. The two requirements for a paired-t test are met, namely that the variable is a paired-difference variable and that it is normally distributed.

(b) Yes. The Wilcoxon signed-rank test requires that the distribution of the differences be symmetrical. The normal distribution is symmetric.

(c) The paired-t test is preferred when the underlying distribution of the differences is normal because it is the more powerful test.

10.99 (a) Population 1: Cross-fertilized;

Population 2: Self-fertilized

Step 1: H_0: $\mu_1 = \mu_2$, H_a: $\mu_1 \neq \mu_2$

Step 2: $\alpha = 0.05$

Step 3:

d	|d|	Rank	Signed-rank
49	49	11	11
-67	67	14	-14
8	8	2	2
16	16	4	4
6	6	1	1
23	23	5	5
28	28	7	7
41	41	9	9
14	14	3	3
29	29	8	8
56	56	12	12
24	24	6	6
75	75	15	15
60	60	13	13
-48	48	10	-10

Step 4: $n = 15$

Step 5: Work table prepared in Step 3.

Step 6: The value of the test statistic is the sum of the positive ranks.

$W = 11 + 2 + 4 + 1 + 5 + 7 + 9 + 3 + 8 + 12 + 6 + 15 + 13 = 96$

Step 7: The critical values are $W_l = 25$, $W_r = 95$

Step 8: Since 96 > 95, reject H_0.

Step 9: At the 5% significance level, the data provide enough evidence to conclude that there is a difference between the mean heights of cross-fertilized Zea mays and the self-fertilized Zea mays.

(b) All of the computations above are the same for a 1% significance level except for the critical values which are now $W_l = 16$ and

$W_r = 104$. Since $W = 96$ is between the two critical values, we do not reject the null hypothesis at the 1% significance level. Thus at the 1% level, the data do not provide enough evidence to conclude that there is a difference between the mean heights of cross-fertilized Zea mays and self-fertilized Zea mays.

10.101 (a) Population 1: Weight before therapy

Population 2: Weight after therapy

Step 1: H_0: $\mu_1 = \mu_2$, H_a: $\mu_1 < \mu_2$

Step 2: $\alpha = 0.05$

Step 3:

d	|d|	Rank	Signed-rank
-11.0	11.0	12	-12
-5.5	5.5	6	-6
-9.4	9.4	10	-10
-13.6	13.6	16	-16
2.9	2.9	2	2
-10.7	10.7	11	-11
0.1	0.1	1	1
-7.4	7.4	8	-8
-21.5	21.5	17	-17
5.3	5.3	5	5
3.8	3.8	3	3
-11.4	11.4	13	-13
-13.4	13.4	15	-15
-13.1	13.1	14	-14
-9.0	9.0	9	-9
-3.9	3.9	4	-4
-5.7	5.7	7	-7

Step 4: $n = 17$

Step 5: Work table prepared in Step 3.

Step 6: The value of the test statistic is the sum of the positive ranks.

$W = 11$

Step 7: The critical value: $W_l = (17)(18)/2 - 112 = 41$

Step 8: Since 11 < 41, reject H_0.

Step 9: At the 5% significance level, the data provide sufficient evidence to conclude that the family therapy is effective in helping anorexic young women gain weight.

10.103 Population 1: Corneal thickness in normal eyes

Population 2: Corneal thickness in eyes with Glaucoma

Step 1: H_0: $\mu_1 = \mu_2$, H_a: $\mu_1 > \mu_2$

Step 2: $\alpha = 0.10$

Step 3:

d	|d|	Rank	Signed-rank
-4	4	1.5	-1.5
0	0	---	---
12	12	4.5	4.5
18	18	7	7
-4	4	1.5	-1.5
-12	12	4.5	-4.5
6	6	3	3
16	16	6	6

Step 4: n = 7

Step 5: Work table prepared in Step 3.

Step 6: The value of the test statistic is the sum of the positive ranks.

$W = 4.5 + 7 + 3 + 6 = 20.5$

Step 7: The critical value: $W_r = 22$

Step 8: Since 20.5 < 22, do not reject H_0.

Step 9: At the 10% significance level, the data do not provide enough evidence to conclude that the mean corneal thickness is greater in normal eyes than in eyes with glaucoma.

10.105 The Wilcoxon paired-sample signed-rank test should be used because the outlier will not have as much effect on the results. In general, nonparametric procedures are more resistant to outliers.

10.107 (a) Because the paired differences have a uniform distribution which is symmetric and nonnormal, use the Wilcoxon paired-sample signed-rank test.

(b) The population of paired differences is neither normal nor symmetric, but the sample size is large. Therefore use the paired t-test.

(c) Because the paired differences are roughly normally distributed, use the paired t-test.

10.109 (a) Using Minitab, with the differences in a column named DIFF, choose **Graph ▶ Stem-and-Leaf...**, select DIFF in the **Variables** text box and click **OK**. Then choose **Graph ▶ Boxplot**, select DIFF for the **Y** variable for **Graph 1** and click **OK**. The results are

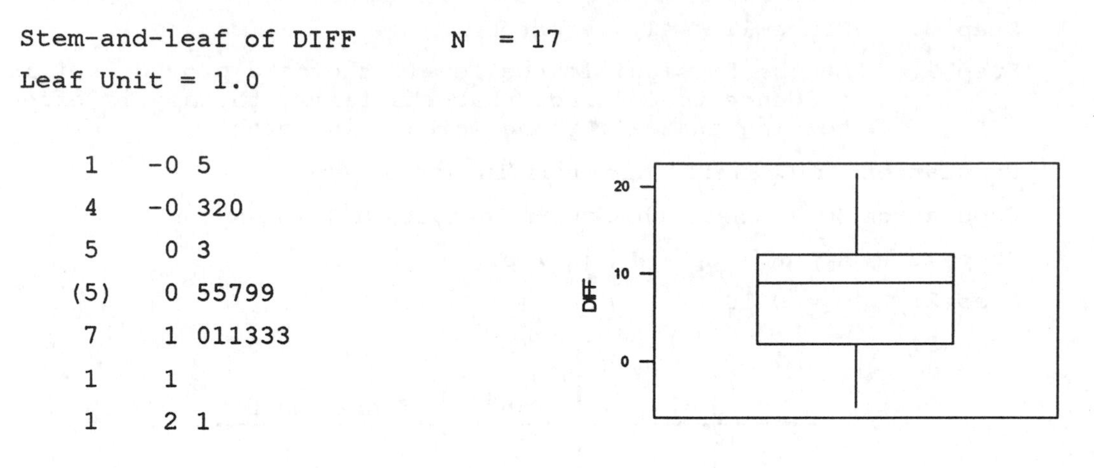

(b) Now choose **Stat ▶ Nonparametrics ▶ 1-Sample Wilcoxon** and select DIFF in the **Variables** text box. Click on the **Test median** button, then of the **Alternative** down arrow, select 'greater than', and click **OK**. The results are

Test of median = 0.000000 versus median > 0.000000

	N	N for Test	Wilcoxon Statistic	P	Estimated Median
DIFF	17	17	142.0	0.001	7.650

(c) Both the Stem-and-Leaf plot and the boxplot in part (a) indicate that the sample of DIFF values is reasonably symmetric. Thus the Wilcoxon signed-rank test is appropriate for these paired data differences.

Since the p-value of 0.001 is less than the 0.05 significance level we reject the null hypothesis and conclude that the therapy program is helpful in helping anorexic young women to gain weight.

10.111 The necessary plots for this exercise were produced in Exercise 10.95. We display them again here.

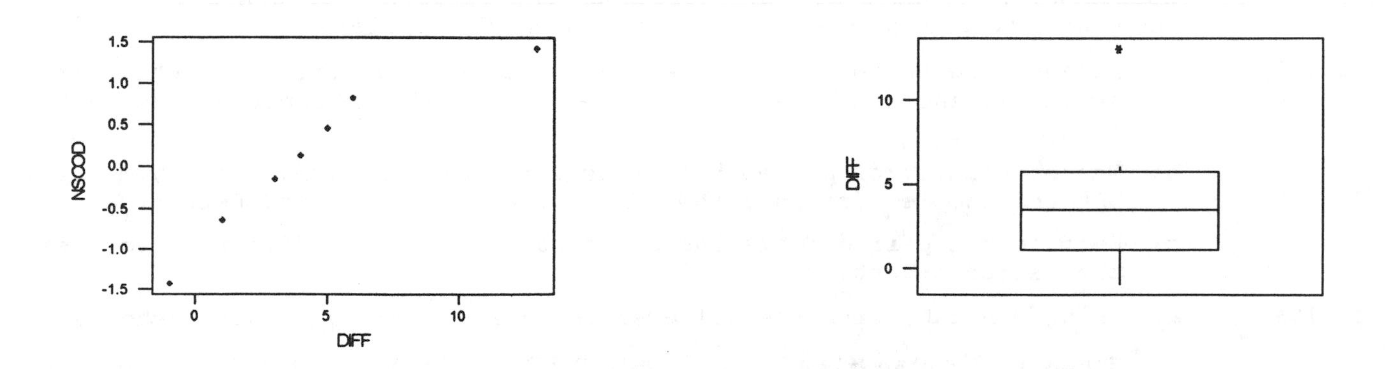

From the boxplot, we see that the distribution of differences is quite symmetric with the exception of the outlier at 13. However, the one-sample Wilcoxon test will be little affected by one outlier since the value of W would be the same if the difference of 13 were in fact a difference of only 7 since the test statistic depends only on the ranks, not on the actual data values. We conclude that the one-sample Wilcoxon test is appropriate for these difference data.

Exercises 10.7

10.113 (a) Pooled t-test, nonpooled t-test, Mann-Whitney test

(b) **Pooled t-test:** Independent samples, normal populations or large samples, and equal population standard deviations

Nonpooled t-test: Independent samples and normal populations or large samples

Mann-Whitney signed-rank test: Independent samples and same shape populations

(c) **Pooled t-test**

$$t = \frac{\bar{x}_1 - \bar{x}_2}{s_p\sqrt{\frac{1}{n_1} + \frac{1}{n_2}}} \text{ where } s_p^2 = \frac{(n_1 - 1)s_1^2 + (n_2 - 1)s_2^2}{n_1 + n_1 - 2}$$

Nonpooled t-test

$$t = \frac{\bar{x}_1 - \bar{x}_2}{\sqrt{\frac{s_1^2}{n_1} + \frac{s_2^2}{n_2}}}$$

where the degrees of freedom are given by

$$\Delta = \frac{[s_1^2 / n_1 + s_2^2 / n_2]^2}{\frac{(s_1^2 / n_1)^2}{n_1 - 1} + \frac{(s_2^2 / n_2)^2}{n_2 - 1}}$$

Mann-Whitney test

M = the sum of the ranks for sample data from Population 1

10.115 (a) One could use the pooled t-test, nonpooled t-test, or Mann-Whitney test.

(b) The pooled t-test is the most appropriate since its conditions are satisfied and it will be the most powerful under these circumstances.

10.117 (a) Because the sample sizes are large, one could use the pooled t-test, nonpooled t-test, or Mann-Whitney test.

(b) Since the populations have the same shape but are not normally distributed, the Mann-Whitney test is the most appropriate since its conditions are satisfied and it will be the most powerful under these circumstances.

10.119 (a) One could use the paired t-test or the paired Wilcoxon signed-rank test (paired W-test).

(b) The paired W-test is the more appropriate test when the distribution is symmetric, but non-normal.

10.121 To determine which procedure should be used to perform the hypothesis test, ask the following questions in sequence according to the flowchart in Figure 10.10:

Question to ask	Answer to question Yes	No
Are the samples paired?		x
Are the populations normal?	x	
Do the populations have equal standard deviations?		x

Since the two independent populations are normal with unequal standard deviations, use the nonpooled t-test.

10.123 To determine which procedure should be used to find the required confidence interval, ask the following questions in sequence according to the flowchart in Figure 10.10:

Question to ask	Answer to question Yes	No
Are the samples paired?		x
Are the populations normal?		x
Are the populations the same shape?		x
Are the samples large?	x	
Do the populations have equal standard deviations?		x

It appears that one of the populations is neither normal nor symmetric, but the sample size is large. Thus, use the nonpooled t-test.

10.125 To determine which procedure should be used to perform the hypothesis test, ask the following questions in sequence according to the flowchart in Figure 10.10:

Question to ask	Answer to question Yes	No
Are the samples paired?	x	
Are the differences normal?		x
Are the differences symmetric?		x
Is the sample large?		x

It appears the paired differences are neither normal nor symmetric. Thus, a statistician must be consulted.

REVIEW TEST FOR CHAPTER 10

1. Randomly sample independently from both populations, compute the means of both samples and reject the null hypothesis of equal population means if the sample means differ by too much. Otherwise, do not reject the null hypothesis.

2. Sample pairs of observations from the two populations, compute the difference of the two observations in each pair, compute the mean of the differences, and reject the null hypothesis of equal population means if the sample mean of the differences differs from zero by too much. Otherwise, do not reject the null hypothesis.

3. (a) The pooled t-test requires that the population standard deviations be equal whereas the nonpooled t-test does not.

   (b) It is absolutely essential that the assumption of independence be satisfied.

   (c) The normality assumption is especially important for both t-tests when the samples are small. With large samples, the Central Limit Theorem applies and the normality assumption is less important.

   (d) Unless we are quite sure that the population standard deviations are equal, the nonpooled t-procedures should be used instead of the pooled t-procedures.

4. (a) No. If the two distributions are normal and have the same shape, then they have the same population standard deviations, and the pooled t-test should be used. If the two distributions are not normal, but have the same shape, the Mann-Whitney test is preferred.

   (b) The pooled t-test is preferred to the Mann-Whitney test if both populations are normally distributed with equal standard deviations.

5. A paired sample may reduce the estimate of the standard error of the mean of the differences, making it more likely that a difference between the population means will be detected when it exists.

6. The paired t-test is preferred to the paired Wilcoxon signed-rank test if the distribution of differences is normal, or if the sample size is large and the distribution of differences is not symmetric.

7. Population 1: Male; $n_1 = 13$, $\bar{x}_1 = 2127$, $s_1 = 513$

   Population 2: Female; $n_2 = 14$, $\bar{x}_2 = 1843$, $s_2 = 446$

   Step 1: H_0: $\mu_1 = \mu_2$, H_a: $\mu_1 > \mu_2$

   Step 2: $\alpha = 0.05$

   Step 3:

$$s_p = \sqrt{\frac{12(513)^2 + 13(446)^2}{25}} = 479.33$$

$$t = \frac{2127 - 1843}{479.33\sqrt{\frac{1}{13} + \frac{1}{14}}} = 1.538$$

   Step 4: df = 25, Critical value = 1.708

   Step 5: Since 1.538 < 1.708, do not reject H_0.

   Step 6: At the 5% significance level, the data do not provide enough evidence to conclude that the mean right-leg strength of males exceeds that of females.

   (b) For the P-value approach, $0.05 < P(t > 1.538) < 0.10$. Therefore, because the P-value is larger than the significance level, do not reject H_0. The evidence against the null hypothesis is moderate.

8.

$$2127 - 1843 \pm 1.708(479.33)\sqrt{\frac{1}{13} + \frac{1}{14}}$$

$$284 \pm 315.3$$

$$-31.3 \text{ to } 599.3$$

We can be 90% confident that the difference, $\mu_1 - \mu_2$, between the mean right-leg strengths of males and females is between -31.3 and 599.3 newtons.

9. Population 1: Florida, $n_1 = 24$, $\bar{x}_1 = 5.4583$, $s_1 = 1.5874$

Population 2: Virginia, $n_2 = 44$, $\bar{x}_2 = 7.5909$, $s_2 = 2.6791$

$$\Delta = \frac{[s_1^2 / n_1 + s_2^2 / n_2]^2}{\frac{(s_1^2 / n_1)^2}{n_1 - 1} + \frac{(s_2^2 / n_2)^2}{n_2 - 1}} = \frac{[1.59^2 / 24 + 2.68^2 / 44]^2}{\frac{(1.59^2 / 24)^2}{24 - 1} + \frac{(2.68^2 / 44)^2}{44 - 1}} = 65.45 \rightarrow 65 = \text{df}$$

Step 1: H_0: $\mu_1 = \mu_2$, H_a: $\mu_1 < \mu_2$

Step 2: $\alpha = 0.01$

Step 3: $$t = \frac{5.4583 - 7.5909}{\sqrt{\frac{1.5874^2}{24} + \frac{2.6791^2}{44}}} = -4.119$$

Step 4: Critical value = -2.385

Step 5: Since -4.119 < -2.385, reject H_0.

Step 6: At the 1% significance level, the data provide sufficient evidence to conclude that the average litter size of cottonmouths in Florida is less than that in Virginia.

For the P-value approach, $P(t < -4.119) < 0.005$. Therefore, because the P-value is smaller than the significance level, reject H_0.

10.

$$(5.46 - 7.59) \pm 2.385\sqrt{\frac{1.59^2}{24} + \frac{2.68^2}{44}}$$

$$-2.13 \pm 1.24$$

$$-3.4 \text{ to } -0.9$$

We can be 98% confident that the average cottonmouth litter sizes in Virginia are somewhere between 0.9 and 3.4 larger than in Florida.

11. Population 1: Home prices in New York City;

Population 2: Home prices in Los Angeles.

Step 1: H_0: $\mu_1 = \mu_2$, H_a: $\mu_1 \neq \mu_2$

Step 2: $\alpha = 0.05$

Step 3: Construct a work table based upon the following: First, rank all the data from both samples combined. Adjacent to each column of data as it is presented in the Exercise, record the overall rank.

NYC	Overall Rank	LA	Overall Rank
149.5	1	160.6	2
162.4	3	163.4	4
175.8	6	165.9	5
177.1	7	186.6	9
186.1	8	188.9	10
190.1	11	196.4	12
212.8	14	199.8	13
219.1	15	274.8	16
280.1	17	349.7	18
424.1	20	394.8	19

Step 4: The value of the test statistic is the sum of the ranks for the sample data from Population 1:

$M = 1 + 3 + 6 + 7 + 8 + 11 + 14 + 15 + 17 + 20 = 102.$

Step 5: Since the populations have the same shape, but are not normal, and since the samples are small, use the Mann-Whitney test. We have $n_1 = 10$ and $n_2 = 10$. Since the hypothesis test is two-tailed with $\alpha = 0.05$, we use Table VI to obtain the critical values, which are $M_l = 10(21) - 131 = 79$ and $M_r = 131$. Thus, we reject H_0 if $M \geq 131$ or $M \leq 79$.

Step 6: Since $79 < M < 131$, do not reject H_0.

Step 7: At the 5% significance level, the data do not provide sufficient evidence to conclude that the mean costs for existing single-family homes differ in New York City and Los Angeles.

12. Step 1: H_0: $\mu_1 = \mu_2$, H_a: $\mu_1 \neq \mu_2$

Step 2: $\alpha = 0.10$

Step 3: Paired differences, $d = x_1 - x_2$:

82	-95	-49	0	-36
-152	49	-38	-43	-118

Step 4:

$$\bar{d} = \frac{-400}{10} = -40; \quad s = \sqrt{\frac{62168 - 400^2/10}{9}} = 71.622$$

$$t = \frac{-40}{71.622/\sqrt{10}} = -1.766$$

Step 5: Critical values = ± 1.833

Step 6: Since $-1.833 < -1.766 < 1.833$, do not reject H_0.

Step 7: At the 10% significance level, the data do not provide sufficient evidence to conclude that there is a difference in mean results for the two speed reading programs.

For the P-value approach, $0.10 < 2\{P(t < -1.766)\} < 0.20$. Therefore, because the P-value is larger than the significance level, do not reject H_0.

13.

$$-40 \pm 1.833 \cdot 71.622/\sqrt{10}$$
$$-40 \pm 41.52$$
$$-81.5 \text{ to } 1.5 \text{ words per minute}$$

We can be 90% confident that the difference, $\mu_1 - \mu_2$, between the mean reading speed of people using Program 1 and the mean reading speed of people using Program 2 is somewhere between -81.5 and 1.5 words per minute.

14. Population 1: South; Population 2: Midwest;

Step 1: H_0: $\mu_1 = \mu_2$, H_a: $\mu_1 > \mu_2$

Step 2: $\alpha = 0.01$

Step 3:

d	|d|	Rank	Signed-rank
20	20	6.5	6.5
23	23	9	9
0	0	---	---
15	15	4.5	4.5
42	42	11	11
-20	20	6.5	-6.5
22	22	8	8
62	62	13	13
8	8	2.5	2.5
32	32	10	10
44	44	12	12
-8	8	2.5	-2.5
-15	15	4.5	-4.5
74	74	14	14
4	4	1	1

Step 4: n = 14

Step 5: Work table shown in Step 3.

Step 6: The value of the test statistic is the sum of the positive ranks.

W = 6.5 + 9 + 4.5 + 11 + 8 + 13 + 2.5 + 10 + 12 + 14 + 1 = 91.5

Step 7: The critical value, $W_r = 89$

Step 8: Since 91.5 > 89, reject H_0.

Step 9: At the 1% significance level, the data do provide sufficient evidence to conclude that the mean monthly rent for renter-occupied housing units in the South exceeds that for those in the Midwest.

15. (a) Choose **Calc ▶ Calculator...**, type NSCORE M in the **Store results in variable** text box, select **Normal scores** from the function list, select MALE to replace **numbers** in the **Expression** text box, and click **OK**. We now choose **Graph ▶ Plot...**, select NSCORE M for the **Y** variable for **Graph 1**

and MALE for the **X** variable, and click **OK**. Next choose **Graph ▶ Stem-and-Leaf...**, select MALE in the **Variables** text box, and click **OK**. Now choose **Graph ▶ Boxplot...**, select MALE for the **Y** Variable for **Graph 1**, and click **OK**. Now choose **Stat ▶ Column statistics...**, click on the **Standard deviation** button, select MALE in the **Input Variables** text box, and click **OK**. Then repeat this entire process for the FEMALE data.

The results for MALES are

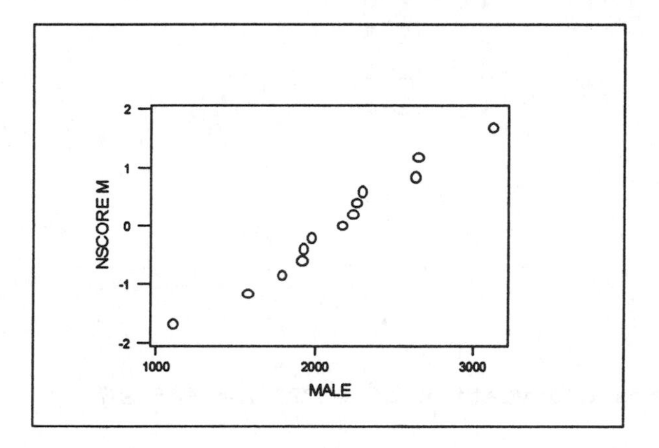


```
Stem-and-leaf of MALE      N  = 13
Leaf Unit = 100
    1    1 1
    1    1
    2    1 5
    3    1 7
    6    1 999
   (1)   2 1
    6    2 222
    3    2
    3    2 66
    1    2
    1    3 1
```

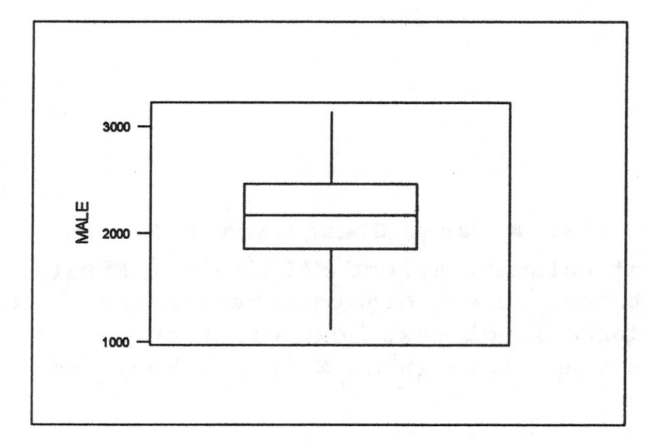

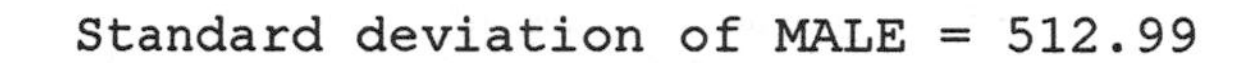
Standard deviation of MALE = 512.99

For the FEMALE data, the results are

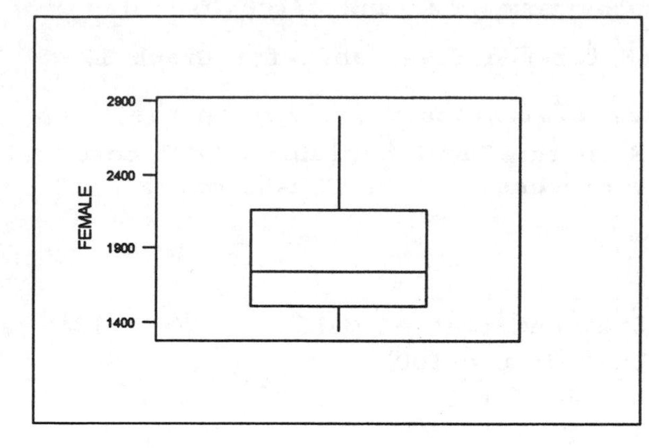


```
Stem-and-leaf of FEMALE    N  = 14
            Leaf Unit = 100

      3    1 333
      5    1 55
    (3)    1 667
      6    1 88
      4    2 0
      3    2 3
      2    2 4
      1    2 7
```

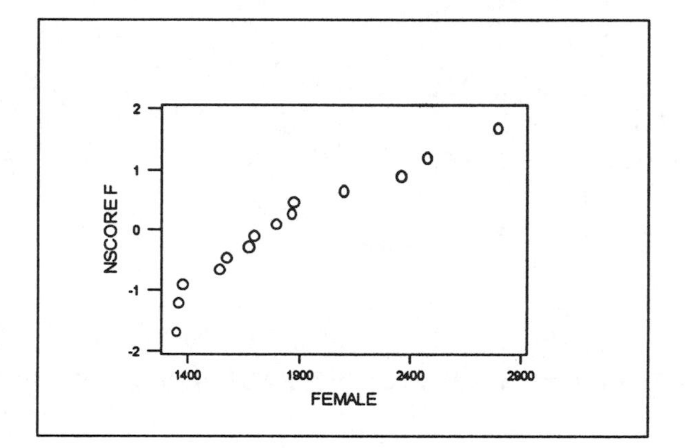

Standard deviation of FEMALE = 445.96

(b) To carry out the pooled t-test, choose **Stat ▶ Basic Statistics ▶ 2-Sample t,** click on **Samples in different columns,** select MALE in the **First** text box and FEMALE in the **Second** text box, select **greater than** in the **Alternative** box, type 90 in the **Confidence level** text box, click on **Assume equal variances** to make certain that there is an **X** in the box, and click **OK.** The results are

```
Twosample T for MALE vs FEMALE

           N       Mean      StDev    SE Mean
MALE      13       2127        513        142
FEMALE    14       1843        446        119


90% C.I. for μ MALE - μ FEMALE: ( -31,  600)
T-Test μ MALE = μ FEMALE (vs >): T= 1.54  P=0.068  DF=  25
Both use Pooled StDev =  479
```

(c) The plots indicate that the distributions are reasonably close to normal with approximately equal standard deviations. Thus the pooled t-test is appropriate.

16. (a) Choose **Calc ▶ Calculator...,** type NSCOREF in the **Store results in**

variable text box, select **Normal scores** from the function list, select FLORIDA to replace **numbers** in the **Expression** text box and click **OK.** We now choose **Graph ▶ Plot...**, select NSCOREF for the **Y** variable for **Graph 1** and FLORIDA for the **X** variable, and click **OK.** Repeat this process with NSCOREV and VIRGINIA. The results are

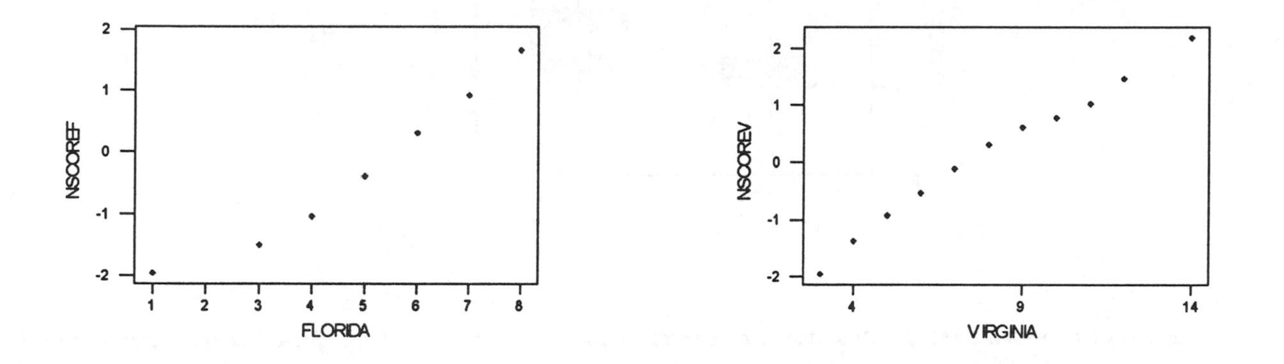

Now choose **Graph ▶ Stem-and-Leaf...**, select FLORIDA in the **Variables** text box, and click **OK.** Repeat this process with VIRGINIA. The resultS are

```
Stem-and-leaf of FLORIDA   N  = 24
Leaf Unit = 0.10

    1    1 0
    1    2
    2    3 0
    5    4 000
   12    5 0000000
   12    6 000000
    6    7 0000
    2    8 00

Stem-and-leaf of VIRGINIA  N  = 44
Leaf Unit = 0.10

    2    3 00
    5    4 000
   10    5 00000
   16    6 000000
   (8)   7 00000000
   20    8 0000000
   13    9 00
   11   10 000
    8   11 000
    5   12 0000
    1   13
    1   14 0
```

Now choose **Graph ▶ Boxplot...**, select FLORIDA for the **Y** Variable for **Graph 1** and VIRGINIA for the **Y** Variable for **Graph 2**, and click **OK**.

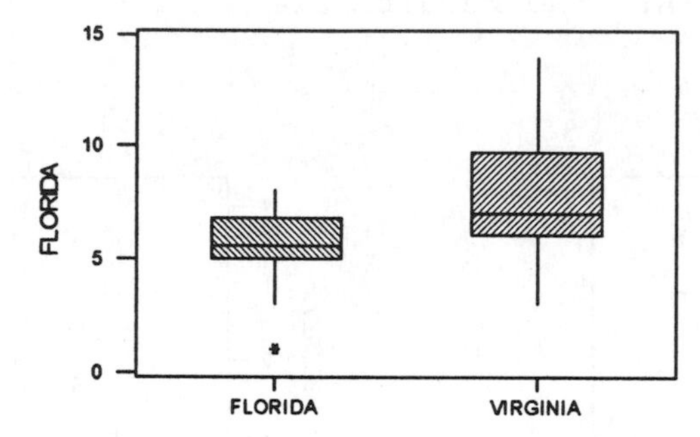

Now choose **Stat ▶ Column statistics...**, click on the **Standard deviation** button, select FLORIDA in the **Input Variables** text box, and click **OK**. Repeat this process for VIRGINIA. The results are

Standard deviation of FLORIDA = 1.5874

Standard deviation of VIRGINIA = 2.6791

(b) Now choose **Stat ▶ Basic Statistics ▶ 2-Sample t...**, click on the **Samples in different columns** button, select FLORIDA in the **First** text box and VIRGINIA in the **Second** text box, select **'less than'** in the **Alternative** text box, type 98 in the **Confidence level** text box, and click **OK**. The result is

Two sample T for FLORIDA vs VIRGINIA

	N	Mean	StDev	SE Mean
FLORIDA	24	5.46	1.59	0.32
VIRGINIA	44	7.59	2.68	0.40

98% CI for mu FLORIDA - mu VIRGINIA: (-3.37, -0.90)

T-Test mu FLORIDA = mu VIRGINIA (vs <): T = -4.12 P = 0.0001 DF = 65

(c) Based on the graphic displays and sample standard deviations in part (a) for two independent samples, it appears reasonable to consider the assumption of normality satisfied, but not the assumption of equal standard deviations; thus, the use of the nonpooled-t procedure.

17. (a) Using Minitab, with the data in columns named NY and LA, choose **Calc ▶ Calculator...**, type 'NSCORENY' in the **Store results in variable** text box, select **Normal scores** from the function list, select NY to replace **numbers** in the **Expression** text box, and click **OK**. Repeat with LA and NSCORELA.

We now choose **Graph ▶ Plot...**, select NSCORENY for the **Y** variable for **Graph 1** and NY for the **X** variable, and click **OK**. Repeat with LA and NSCORELA. Next, choose **Graph ▶ Stem-and-Leaf...**, select NY in the

Variables text box, and click **OK**. Repeat with LA. Then, choose **Graph ▶ Boxplot...**, select NY for the **Y** Variable for **Graph 1** and LA for the **Y** Variable for **Graph 2**, click on the **Frame** down-arrow, select **Multiple graphs**, click on the **Overlay graphs on the same page** button, click **OK**, and click **OK**. Finally, choose **Stat ▶ Column statistics...**, click on the **Standard deviation** button, select NY in the **Input Variables** text box, and click **OK**. Repeat for LA. The results are

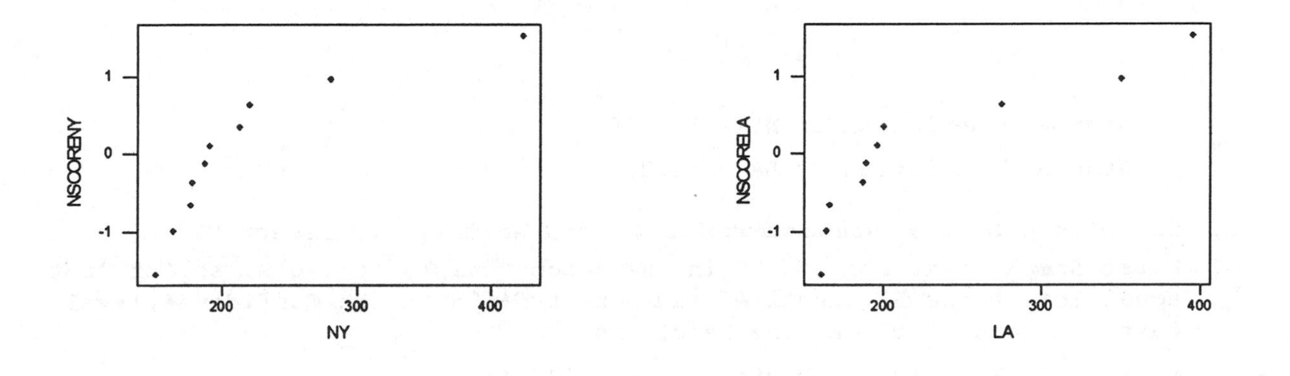


```
Stem-and-leaf of NY        N  = 10
Leaf Unit = 10

    1     1 4
   (5)    1 67789
    4     2 11
    2     2 8
    1     3
    1     3
    1     4 2

Stem-and-leaf of LA        N  = 10
Leaf Unit = 10

   (7)    1 6668899
    3     2
    3     2 7
    2     3 4
    1     3 9
```

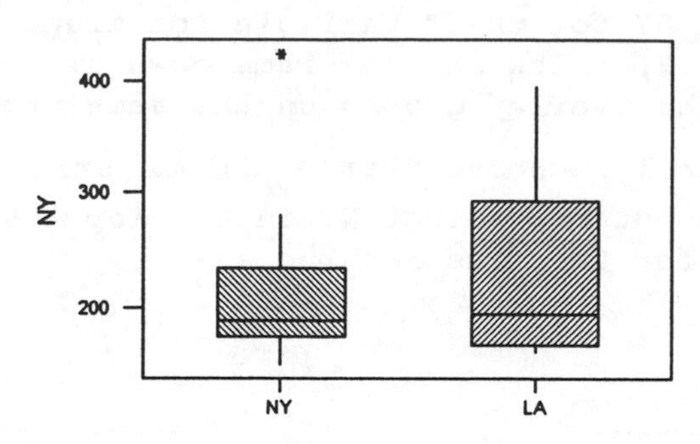

Standard deviation of NY = 81.236

Standard deviation of LA = 83.288

(b) Now choose **Stat ▶ Nonparametrics ▶ Mann-Whitney...**, select NY in the **First Sample** text box and LA in the **Second sample** text box, select 'not equal to' in the **Alternative** text box, type 95 in the **Confidence level** text box, and click **OK**. The result is

```
NY          N =  10     Median =        188.1
LA          N =  10     Median =        192.7
Point estimate for ETA1-ETA2 is          -3.2
95.5 Percent CI for ETA1-ETA2 is (-69.6,30.2)
W = 102.0
Test of ETA1 = ETA2  vs  ETA1 not = ETA2 is significant at 0.8501
Cannot reject at alpha = 0.05
```

(c) Based on the graphic displays and sample standard deviations in part (a), it appears that the two populations are nonnormal; however, they do have the same shape. Thus, the use of the Mann-Whitney test is appropriate.

18. (a) Using Minitab, with the differences in a column named DIFF, choose **Calc ▶ Calculator...**, type NSCODIFF in the **Store results in variable** text box, select **Normal scores** from the function list, select DIFF to replace **numbers** in the **Expression** text box, and click **OK**. We now choose **Graph ▶ Plot...**, select NSCODIFF for the **Y** variable for **Graph 1** and DIFF for the **X** variable, and click **OK**. Next, choose **Graph ▶ Stem-and-Leaf...**, select DIFF in the **Variables** text box, and click **OK**. Then, choose **Graph ▶ Boxplot...**, select DIFF for the **Y** Variable for **Graph 1**, and click **OK**. The results follow.

```
Stem-and-leaf of DIFF      N  = 10
Leaf Unit = 10
    1   -1 5
    2   -1 1
    3   -0 9
   (4)  -0 4433
    3    0 04
    1    0 8
```

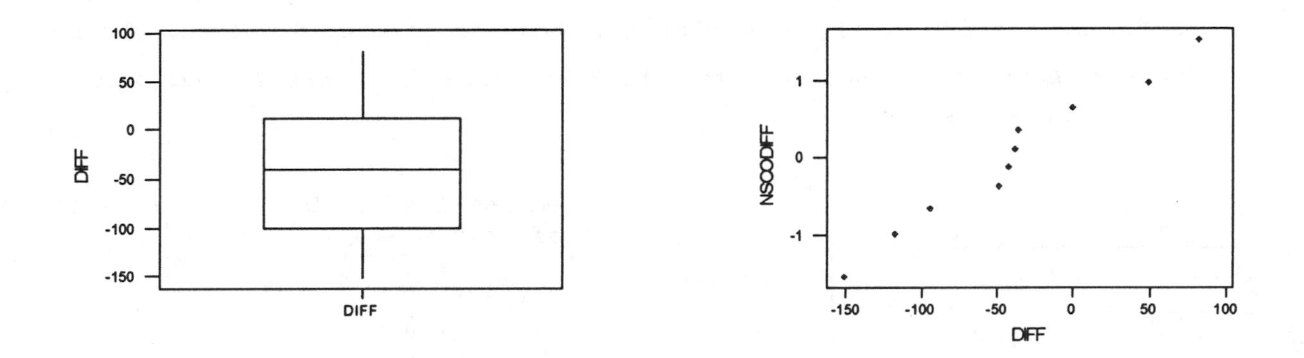

(b) Now choose **Stat ▶ Basic statistics ▶ Paired t...**, select PROGRAM1 in the **First Sample** text box, select PROGRAM2 in the **Second Sample** text box , click on the **Options...** button, click in the **Confidence level** text box and type 90, click on the **Test Mean** button, click in the **Test mean** text box and type 0, select **'not equal to'** in the **Alternative** box, click **OK**, and click **OK**. The results are

Paired T for PROGRAM1 - PROGRAM2

	N	Mean	StDev	SE Mean
PROGRAM1	10	1021.4	80.3	25.4
PROGRAM2	10	1061.4	53.4	16.9
Difference	10	-40.0	71.6	22.6

90% CI for mean difference: (-81.5, 1.5)

T-Test of mean difference = 0 (vs not = 0): T-Value = -1.77 P-Value = 0.111

(c) The graphs in part (a) indicate that the normality assumption is reasonable for the differences, which justifies the use of the paired t-test and paired difference confidence interval.

19. (a) With the data in columns named SOUTH and MIDWEST, choose **Calc ▶ Calculator...**, type D in the Store results in variable ext box, type 'SOUTH' - 'MIDWEST' in the **Expression** text box, and click **OK**. Then

choose **Stat ▶ Nonparametrics ▶ 1-Sample Wilcoxon...**, select D in the **Variables** text box, click on the **Test median** button and type 0 in the **Test median** text box, select **'greater than'** in the **Alternative** box, and click **OK**. The result is

Test of median = 0.000000 versus median > 0.000000

	N	N for Test	Wilcoxon Statistic	P	Estimated Median
D	15	14	91.5	0.008	19.50

(b) Choose **Calc ▶ Calculator...**, type NSCORED in the **Store results in variable** text box, select **Normal scores** from the function list, select D to replace **numbers** in the **Expression** text box, and click **OK**. We now choose **Graph ▶ Plot...**, select NSCORED for the **Y** variable for **Graph 1** and D for the **X** variable, and click **OK**. Next, choose **Graph ▶ Stem-and-Leaf...**, select D in the **Variables** text box, and click **OK**. Then, choose **Graph ▶ Boxplot...**, select D for the **Y** Variable for **Graph 1**, and click **OK**. The results are

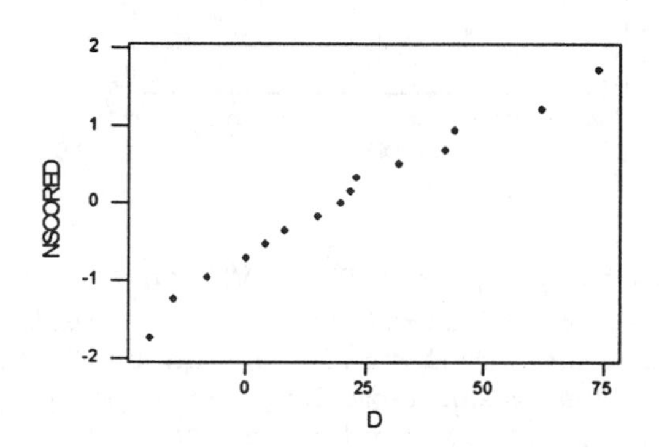


```
Stem-and-leaf of D             N  = 15
Leaf Unit = 1.0
```

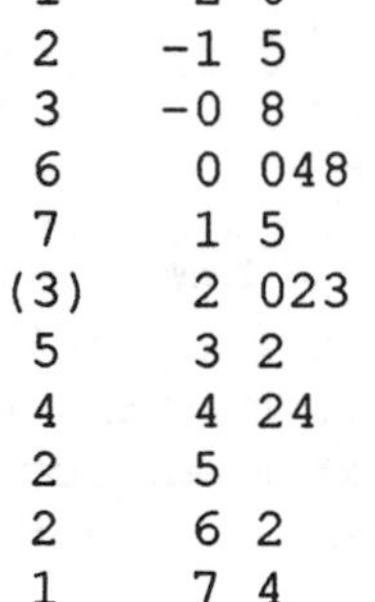

```
  1    -2 0
  2    -1 5
  3    -0 8
  6     0 048
  7     1 5
 (3)    2 023
  5     3 2
  4     4 24
  2     5
  2     6 2
  1     7 4
```

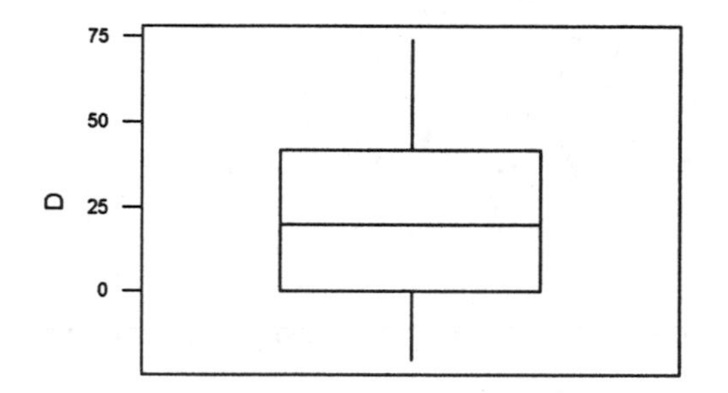

(c) Since the graphs in part (b) indicate that the distribution of differences is symmetric, the conditions for using a paired Wilcoxon signed-rank test are satisfied.

(d) The graphs indicate that the assumption of a normal distribution for the differences is reasonable. Thus the conditions for a paired t-test are satisfied.

(e) Since the conditions for a paired t-test are satisfied, the paired t-test is the preferred test since it is more powerful than the Wilcoxon test when the distribution of differences is normal.

CHAPTER 11 ANSWERS

Exercises 11.1

11.1 A variable has a chi-square distribution if its distribution has the shape of a right-skewed curve called a chi-square curve.

11.3 The curve with 20 degrees of freedom more closely resembles a normal distribution. By Property 4 of Key Fact 11.1, as the degrees of freedom increases, the distributions look increasing like normal distribution curves.

11.5 (a) $\chi^2_{0.025} = 32.852$ (b) $\chi^2_{0.95} = 10.117$

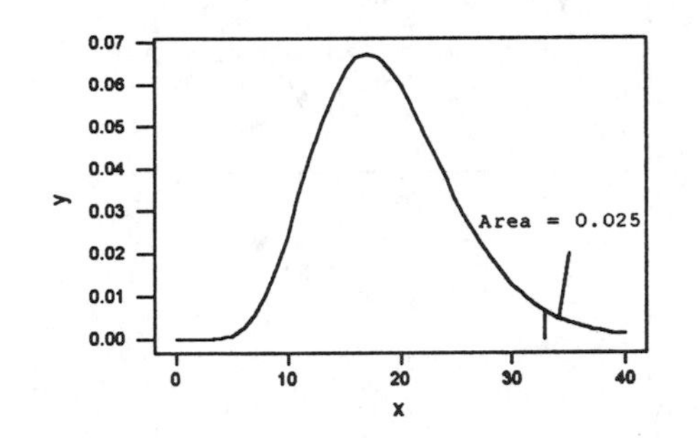

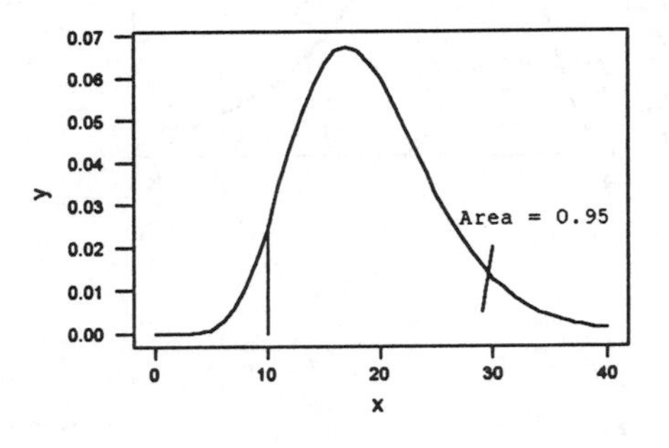

11.7 (a) $\chi^2_{0.05} = 18.305$ (b) $\chi^2_{0.975} = 3.247$

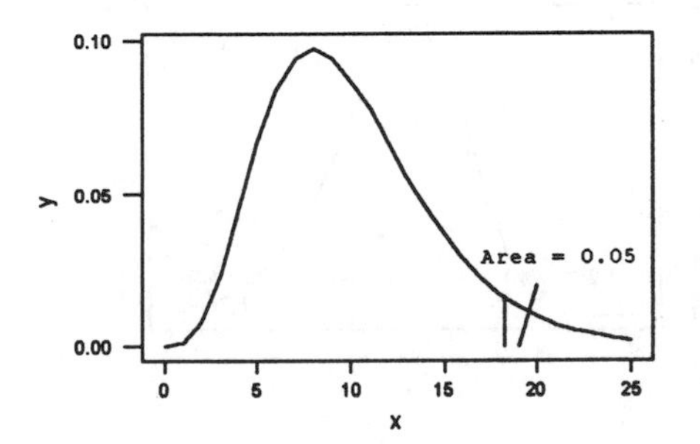

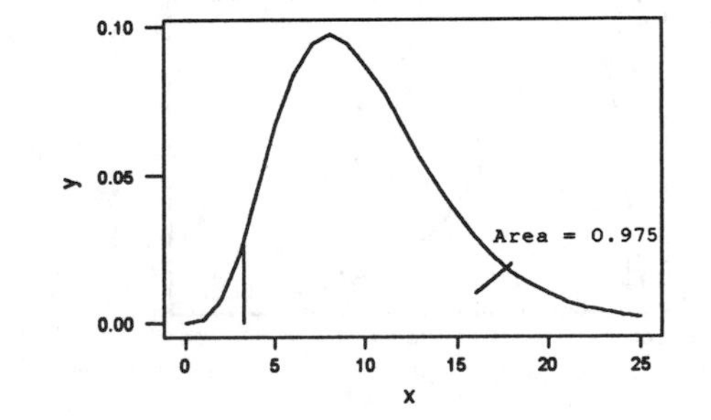

11.9 (a) A left area of 0.01 is equivalent to a right area of 0.99: $\chi^2_{0.99} = 1.646$

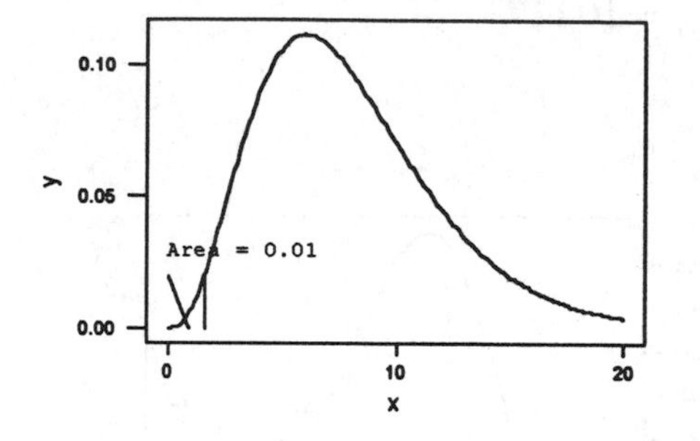

(b) A left area of 0.95 is equivalent to a right area of 0.05: $\chi^2_{0.05} = 15.507$

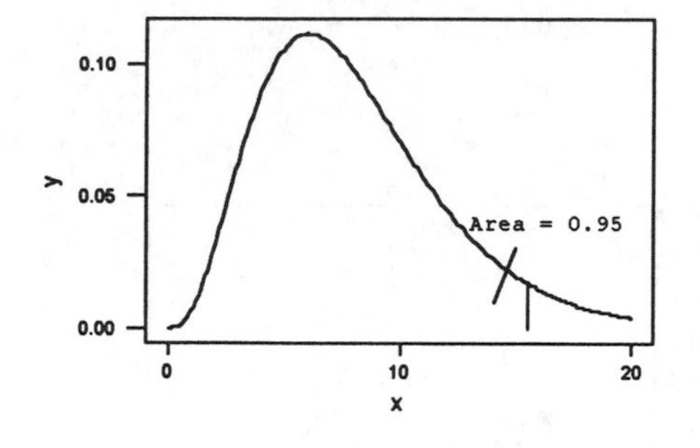

11.11 (a) $\chi^2_{0.975} = 0.831 \quad \chi^2_{0.025} = 12.833$

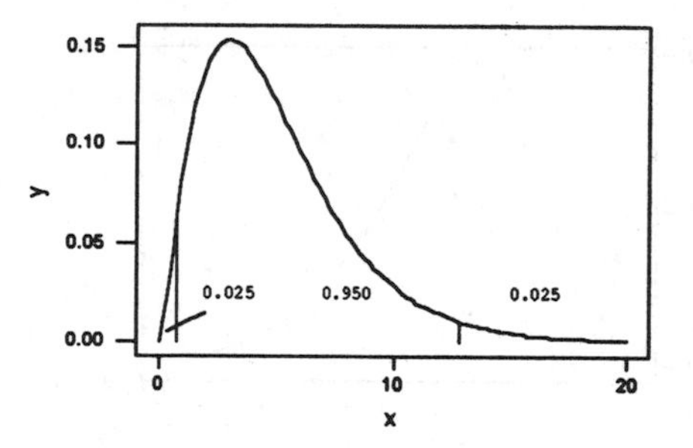

(b)  $\chi^2_{0.975} = 13.844 \quad \chi^2_{0.025} = 41.923$

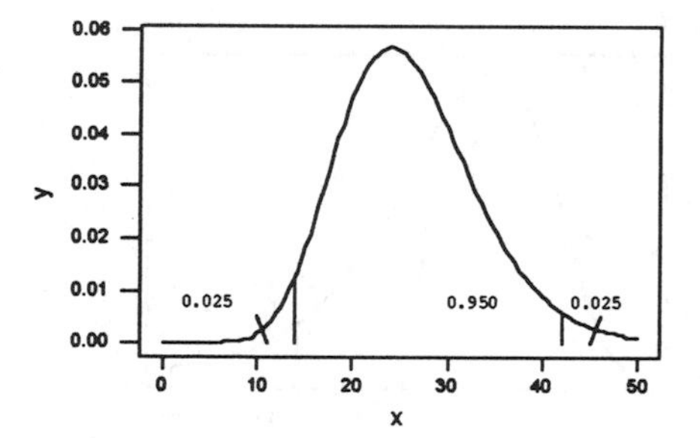

11.13 The chi-square test for one population standard deviation is not robust to moderate violations of the normality assumption.

11.15 Step 1: H_0: $\sigma = 100$ H_a: $\sigma \neq 100$

Step 2: $\alpha = 0.05$

Step 3: $$\chi^2 = \frac{n-1}{\sigma_0^2}s^2 = \frac{24}{100^2}85.492^2 = 17.541$$

Step 4: The critical values with n-1 = 24 degrees of freedom are 12.401 and 39.364.

Step 5: Since 12.401 < 17.541 < 39.364, we do not reject H_0.

Step 6: There is insufficient evidence at the 0.05 level to claim that σ has changed from the 1941 standard of 100. Using Excel, in any cell, type =1-chidist(17.541,24) to obtain $P(\chi^2 < 17.541) = 0.17531$. The P-value is 2(0.17531) = 0.3506.

11.17 Step 1: H_0: $\sigma = 0.27$ H_a: $\sigma > 0.27$

Step 2: $\alpha = 0.01$

Step 3: $\chi^2 = \frac{n-1}{\sigma_0^2} s^2 = \frac{9}{.27^2} 0.75638^2 = 70.631$

Step 4: The critical value with n-1 = 9 degrees of freedom is 21.666.

Step 5: Since 70.631 > 21.666, we reject H_0.

Step 6: There is sufficient evidence at the 0.01 level to claim that the process variation for this piece of equipment exceeds the analytical capability of 0.27. Using Excel, in any cell, type =chidist(70.631,9) to obtain $P(\chi^2 > 70.631) = 1.15 \times 10^{-11}$. The P-value is 1.15×10^{-11}.

11.19 Step 1: H_0: $\sigma = 0.2$ H_a: $\sigma < 0.2$

Step 2: $\alpha = 0.05$

Step 3: $\chi^2 = \frac{n-1}{\sigma_0^2} s^2 = \frac{14}{0.2^2} 0.15416^2 = 8.318$

Step 4: The critical value with n-1 = 14 degrees of freedom is 6.571.

Step 5: Since 8.318 > 6.571, we do not reject H_0.

Step 6: There is insufficient evidence at the 0.05 level to claim that the standard deviation of the amounts dispensed is less than 0.2 fluid ounces. Using Excel, in any cell, type =1-chidist(8.318,14) to obtain $P(\chi^2 < 8.318) = 0.1279$. The P-value is = 0.1279.

11.21 The 95% confidence interval for σ of last year's verbal SAT scores is

$$\left(\sqrt{\frac{n-1}{\chi^2_{.025}}} s, \sqrt{\frac{n-1}{\chi^2_{.975}}} s\right) = \left(\sqrt{\frac{24}{39.364}} 85.5, \sqrt{\frac{24}{12.401}} 85.5\right) = (66.8,\ 118.9)$$

11.23 The 98% confidence interval for the process variation of the piece of equipment under consideration is

$$\left(\sqrt{\frac{n-1}{\chi^2_{.01}}} s, \sqrt{\frac{n-1}{\chi^2_{.99}}} s\right) = \left(\sqrt{\frac{9}{21.666}} 0.756, \sqrt{\frac{9}{2.088}} 0.756\right) = (0.49,\ 1.57)$$

11.25 If the standard deviation is too large, some cups will be filled with too little coffee (making for dissatisfied customers), and some cups may overflow or be in danger of being spilled by the customer. Customers don't appreciate hot coffee spilled on them; in addition, the company loses money (or makes less) if too much coffee is dispensed.

11.27 If the alternative hypothesis is $\sigma < 0.09$, the advantage is that the manufacturer can be quite sure, when the null hypothesis is rejected, that the standard deviation of the bolt diameters is acceptable, that the manufacturing process is "in control." The disadvantage is that σ could actually be smaller than 0.09 (acceptable), but not enough smaller to trigger rejection of the null hypothesis. Without strong evidence that $\sigma < 0.09$, the manufacturer may unnecessarily shut down the manufacturing process to fix a problem that doesn't exist.

If the alternative hypothesis is $\sigma > 0.09$, the advantage is that the manufacturer can be quite sure, when the null hypothesis is rejected, that the standard deviation of the bolt diameters is unacceptable, that the process is "out of control," and that it is worthwhile to shut down the process to fix a problem. The disadvantage is that σ could actually be larger than 0.09 (unacceptable), but not enough larger to trigger rejection of the null hypothesis. Thus the manufacturer may allow the manufacturing process to continue even though the variation is great enough to cause more unacceptable bolts than desired. See the next exercise for information on how to reduce these problems.

11.29 (a) With the data in a column named SATVERB, we choose **Calc ▶ Calculator...**, type NSCORE in the **Store result in variable** text box, select the function NSCOR from the **Function** list, select SATVERB to replace **number** in the **Expression** text box, and click **OK**. Then choose **Graph ▶ Plot...**, select NSCORE in the **Y** column for **Graph1** and SATVERB in the **X** column, and click **OK**. Then choose **Graph ▶ Boxplot...**,select SATVERB in the **Y** column for **Graph1**, and click **OK**. The two graphs are

(b) In Minitab, click in the Sessions Window, and if there is no MTB prompt showing, choose **Editor ▶ Enable command language**. Then with the *WeissStats* CD in drive D, return to the MTB prompt and type %D:\IS6\Minitab\Macro\1stdev.mac 'SATVERB' and press the ENTER key. Then proceed as follows.

1 In response to Do you want to perform a hypothesis test (Y/N)?, type Y and press the ENTER key.

2 In response to Enter the null hypothesis population standard deviation, type 100 and press the ENTER key.

3 In response to Enter 0, 1, or -1, respectively, for a two-tailed, right-tailed, or left-tailed test., type 0 and press the ENTER key.
The output is

```
Test of sigma =     100 vs sigma not =     100
 Row  Variable    n   StDev  Chi-Sq      P
   1   SATVERB   25  85.492  17.541  0.351
```

The macro continues with the confidence-interval procedure.

1 In response to Do you want a confidence interval (Y/N)?, type Y and press the ENTER key.

2 Since we want a 95% confidence interval, type 95 in response to Enter

the confidence level, as a percentage and press the ENTER key. The result is

Row	Variable	n	StDev	Level	CI for sigma
1	SATVERB	25	85.492	95.0%	(66.755, 118.933)

(c) The procedure in (b) depends on the data coming from a normal distribution. The normal probability plot and the box plot indicate that this is a reasonable assumption for the SAT verbal data.

11.31 (a) We will generate the 1000 samples as 1000 rows in Minitab. Choose **Calc ▶ Random data ▶ Normal...**, type 1000 in the **Generate rows of data** text box, type IQ1 IQ2 IQ3 IQ4 in the **Store in columns** text box, type 100 in the **Mean** text box, type 16 in the **Standard deviation** text box, and click **OK.** Now compute the standard deviation of each of the 1000 rows.

(b) Choose **Calc ▶ Calculator**, type SD in the **Store result in variable** text box, click in the **Expression** text box and select **Std. Dev. (Rows)** from the function list, select IQ1, IQ2, IQ3, and IQ4 to replace Number in the function, making sure that the final expression is RSTDEV(IQ1,IQ2,IQ3,IQ4), and click **OK.**

(c) Choose **Calc ▶ Calculator**, type CHI2 in the **Store result in variable** text box, click in the **Expression** text box, type 3*'SD'**2/256, and click **OK.**

(d) Choose **Graph ▶ Histogram...**, select CHI2 for **Graph1** of **X** and click **OK.** The result is

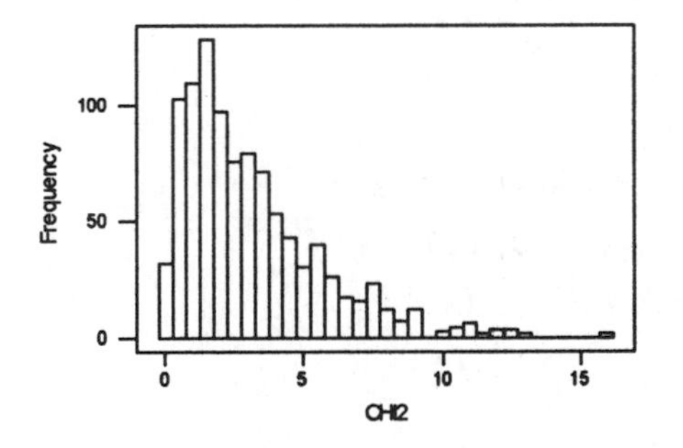

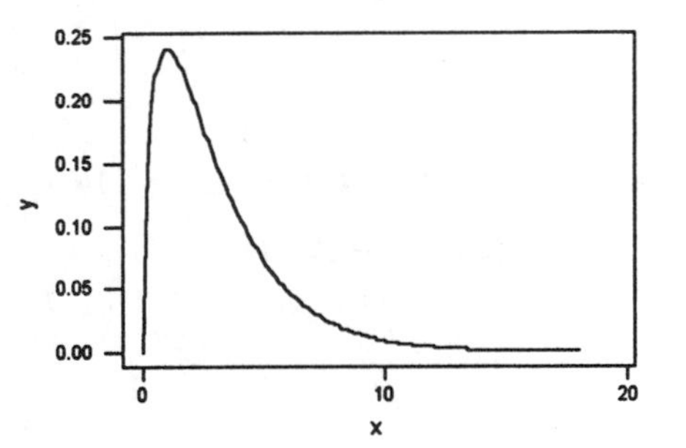

(e) The distribution of the variable in part (c) is a χ^2 distribution with n - 1 = 4 - 1 = 3 degrees of freedom (as shown above right).

(f) A Chi-square distribution with 3 degrees of freedom is very right-skewed. The histogram in part (d) corresponds to such a distribution.

Exercises 11.2

11.33 We identify an F-distribution and its corresponding F-curve by stating its two numbers of degrees of freedom.

11.35 $F_{0.05}$; $F_{0.025}$; F_α

11.37 (a) 12

(b) 7

11.39 (a) $F_{0.05} = 1.89$ (b) $F_{0.01} = 2.47$ (c) $F_{0.025} = 2.14$

11.41 (a) $F_{0.01} = 2.88$ (b) $F_{0.05} = 2.10$ (c) $F_{0.10} = 1.78$

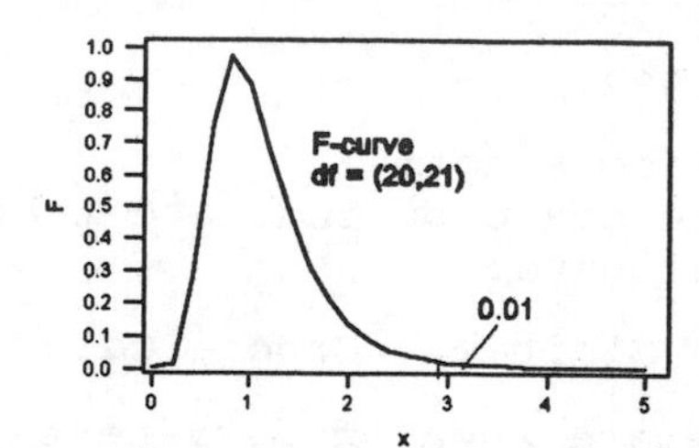

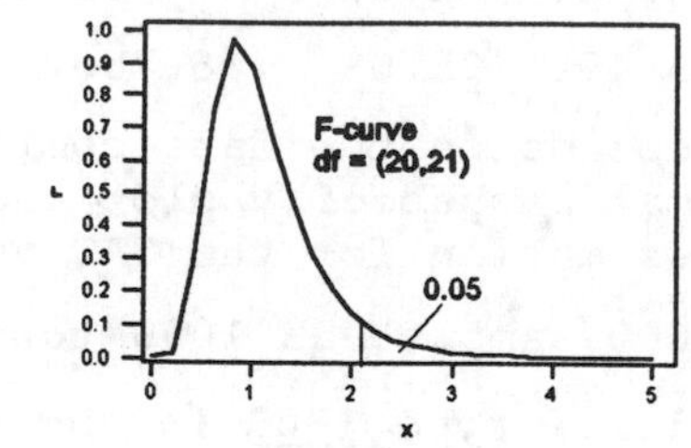

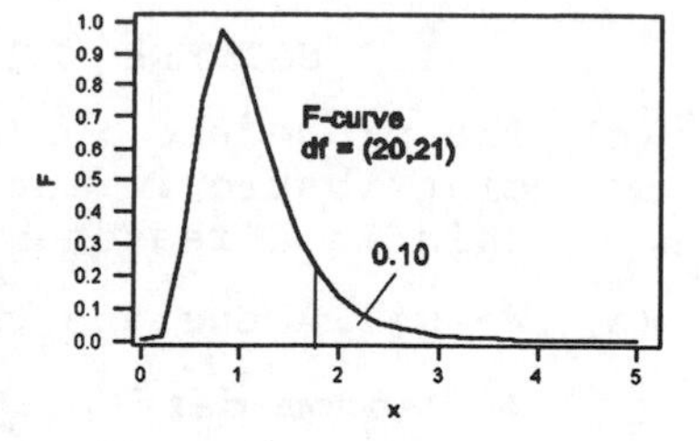

11.43 (a) The F value for a 0.01 left area for df = (6,8) equals 1/F for df = (8,6) for a 0.01 right area. F = 1/8.10 = 0.12

(b) The F Value for a left area of 0.95 equals F for a right area of 0.05 = 3.58

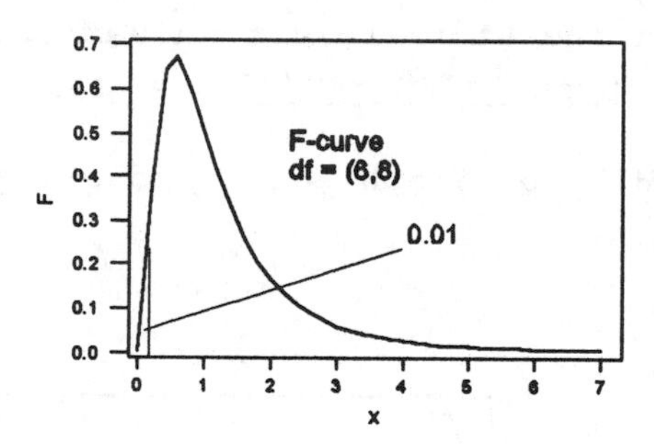

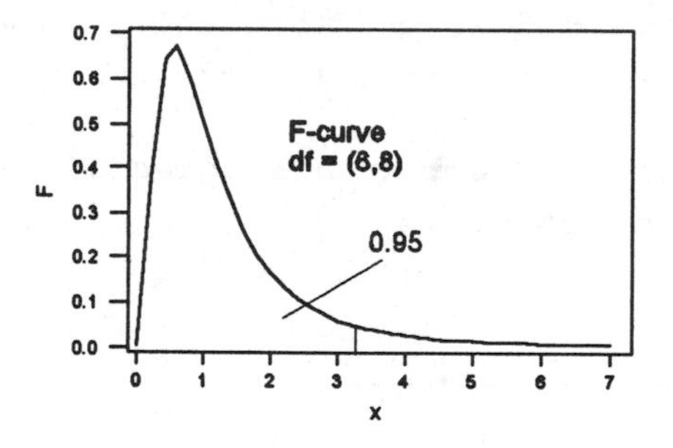

11.45 (a) $F_{0.025} = 9.07; F_{0.975} = 1/F_{0.025}\ (4,7) = 1/5.52 = 0.18$

(b) $F_{0.025} = 2.68; F_{0.975} = 1/F_{0.025}\ (20,12) = 1/3.07 = 0.33$

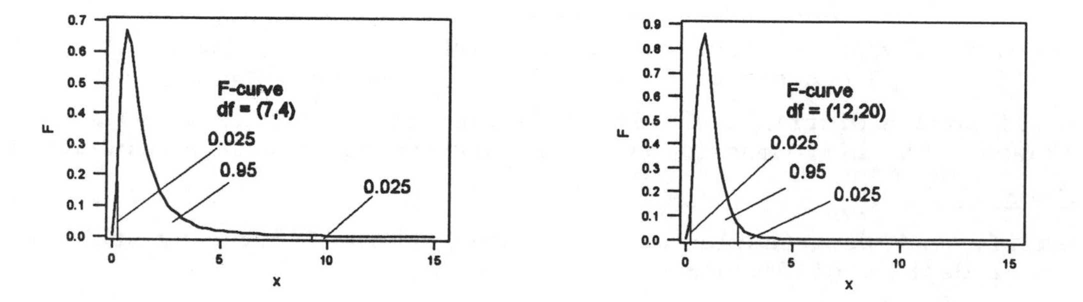

11.47 The F procedures are extremely nonrobust to even moderate violations of the normality assumption for both populations.

11.49 1=Control, 2=Experimental

Step 1: H_0: $\sigma_1 = \sigma_2$ H_a: $\sigma_1 > \sigma_2$

Step 2: $\alpha = 0.05$

Step 3: $F = 7.8134^2/5.2855^2 = 2.1853$

Step 4: The critical value is $F_{0.05}$ with df = (40,19) or 2.03

Step 5: Since 2.1853 > 2.03, we reject the null hypothesis.

Step 6: There is sufficient evidence at $\alpha = 0.05$ to claim that the variation in the control group is greater than that in the experimental group. In Excel, enter =FDIST(2.1853,40,19) in any cell to obtain P(F > 2.1853) = 0.0348. The P-value is 0.0348.

11.51 1=Relaxation tapes, 2=Neutral tapes

Step 1: H_0: $\sigma_1 = \sigma_2$ H_a: $\sigma_1 \neq \sigma_2$

Step 2: $\alpha = 0.10$

Step 3: $F = 10.154^2/9.197^2 = 1.22$

Step 4: The critical values are $F_{0.05}$ with df = (30,24) or 1.94, and $F_{0.95}$ = $1/F_{0.05}$ with df =(24,30) = 1/1.89 = 0.53

Step 5: Since 0.53 < 1.22 < 1.94, we do not reject the null hypothesis.

Step 6: There is not sufficient evidence at the 0.10 significance level to claim that the variation in anxiety test scores for patients seeing videotapes showing progressive relaxation exercises is different from that in patients seeing neutral videotapes. In Excel, in any cell enter =FDIST(1.22,24,30) to obtain P(F > 1.22) = 0.299947. The P-value is 2(0.299947) = 0.59989.

11.53 Step 1: df = (30,24). $F_{0.05}$ is 1.94; $F_{0.95} = 1/F_{0.05}$ for df = (24,30) = 1/1.89 = 0.529.

Step 2: The confidence interval for σ_1/σ_2 is

$$\frac{1}{\sqrt{F_{0.05}}}\cdot\frac{s_1}{s_2} \text{ to } \frac{1}{\sqrt{F_{0.95}}}\cdot\frac{s_1}{s_2} = \frac{1}{\sqrt{1.94}}\frac{10.154}{9.197} \text{ to } \frac{1}{\sqrt{0.529}}\frac{10.154}{9.197} = (0.79,\ 1.52)$$

11.55 The actual value of the F statistic is 0.4128. With df = (9,9) and $\alpha = .20$, the critical values are $F_{0.10} = 2.44$ and $F_{0.90} = 1/F_{0.10} = 1/2.44 = 0.4098$. [Reversing the degrees of freedom results in using the same number for $F_{0.10}$.] Since 0.4098 < 0.4128 < 2.44, the area under the F-curve to the left of 0.4128 is greater than 0.10, and since the test is two-tailed, the P-value is greater than 2(0.10) = 0.20.

11.57 Step 1: df = (40,19). $F_{0.05} = 2.03$. $F_{0.95} = 1/F_{0.05}$ for df = (19,40). $F_{0.05}$ for df = (19,40) will require double linear interpolation since 19 is not in the list for dfn and 40 is not in the list for dfd. First we interpolate between df = (15,30) and (20,30) to estimate $F_{0.05}$ with (19,30) as 2.01 + (4/5)(1.93-2.01) = 1.95; then we interpolate between df = (15,60) and (20,60) to estimate $F_{0.05}$ with (19,60) as 1.84 + (4/5)(1.75-1.84) = 1.77. Finally, we interpolate between df = (19,30) and (19,60) to estimate $F_{0.05}$ with df = (19,40) as 1.95 + (10/30)(1.77-1.95) = 1.89. Thus $F_{0.95} = 1/1.89 = 0.529$.

Step 2: The 90% confidence interval for σ_1/σ_2 is

$$\frac{1}{\sqrt{F_{0.05}}}\cdot\frac{s_1}{s_2} \text{ to } \frac{1}{\sqrt{F_{0.95}}}\cdot\frac{s_1}{s_2} = \frac{1}{\sqrt{2.03}}\frac{7.813}{5.286} \text{ to } \frac{1}{\sqrt{0.529}}\frac{7.813}{5.286} = (1.037, 2.032)$$

11.59 (a) Using Minitab, with the data in columns named RELAX and NEUTRAL, we choose **Calc ▶ Calculator...**, type NRELAX in the **Store result in variable** text box, select the function NSCOR from the **Function** list, select RELAX to replace **number** in the **Expression** text box, and click **OK**. Then choose **Graph ▶ Plot...**, select NRELAX in the **Y** column for **Graph1** and RELAX in the **X** column, and click **OK**. Then choose **Graph ▶ Boxplot...**, select RELAX in the **Y** column for **Graph1**, and click **OK**. Repeat the entire process with NEUTRAL and NNEUTRAL. The four graphs are

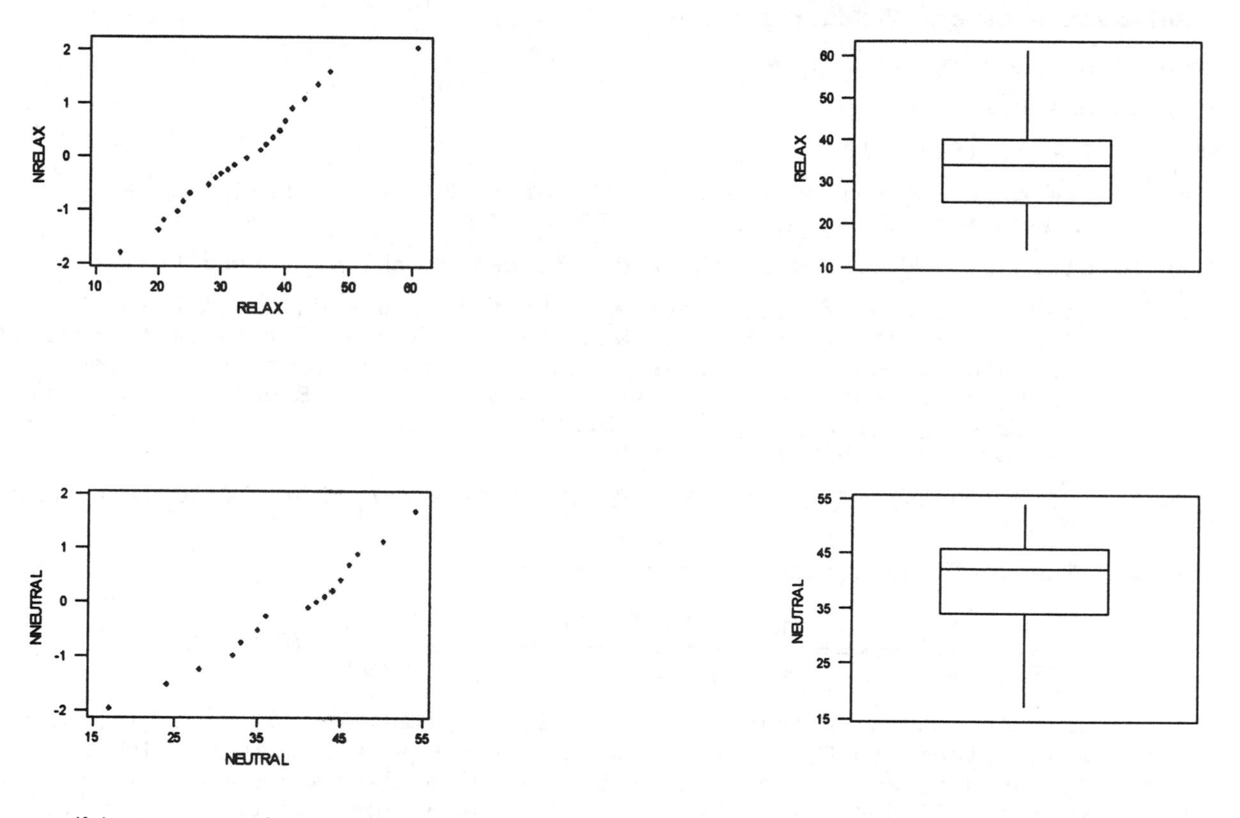

(b) To run the hypothesis test and obtain the confidence interval using the *WeissStats CD* in drive D, we type in the Sessions Window at the MTB> prompt,

%D:\IS6\Minitab\Macro\2stdev.mac 'RELAX' 'NEUTRAL'

and press the ENTER key. Proceed as follows

1 In response to do you want to perform a hypothesis test (Y/N)?, type Y and press the ENTER key.

2 In response to Enter 0, 1, or -1, respectively, for a two-tailed, right-tailed, or left-tailed test., type 0 and press the ENTER key. The output is

```
F-Test of sigma1 = sigma2 (vs not =)
 Row  Variable    n   StDev      F     P
   1   RELAX     31  10.154   1.22  0.624
   2   NEUTRAL   25   9.197
```

Since 0.624 > 0.10, we do not reject the null hypothesis that $\sigma_1 = \sigma_2$. At the 10% significance level, the data do not provide sufficient evidence to conclude that the population standard deviation of anxiety-test scores of patients seeing videotapes showing progressive relaxation exercises is different from that for those seeing neutral videotapes. Continuing with the confidence-interval aspect,

1 In response to Do you want a confidence interval (Y/N)?, type Y and press the ENTER key.

2 Since we want a 90% confidence interval, type 90 in response to Enter the confidence level, as a percentage, and then press the ENTER key. The resulting output is

```
 Row  Variable    n   StDev  Level    CI for ratio
   1   RELAX     31  10.154  90.0%  (0.793, 1.517)
   2   NEUTRAL   25   9.197
```

(c) The graphs in part (a) indicate that the normality assumption is reasonable for both variables. Thus performing the F-procedures is valid.

11.61 Using Minitab, we choose **Calc ▶ Probability distributions... ▶ F**, click on the **Cumulative probability** button, type 9 in the **Numerator degrees of freedom** text box and 9 in the **Denominator degrees of freedom** text box, click on the **Input constant** button and type .41 in the text box, and click **OK**. The result in the Sessions window is

```
F distribution with 9 DF in numerator and 9 DF in denominator
        x      P( X <= x)
   0.4100         0.1001
```

Since the test is two-tailed, the P-value is twice the probability shown in the output, or 0.2002.

11.63 (a) With the data in columns named AML and STANDARD, using the *WeissStats* CD in drive D, we type in the Sessions Window at the MTB> prompt,

```
%D:\IS6\Minitab\Macro\2stdev.mac 'AML' 'STANDARD'
```

and press the ENTER key. Proceed as follows:

1 In response to do you want to perform a hypothesis test (Y/N)?, type Y and press the ENTER key.

2 In response to Enter 0, 1, or -1, respectively, for a two-tailed, right-tailed, or left-tailed test., type 0 and press the ENTER key. The output is

F-Test of sigma1 = sigma2 (vs not =)

Row	Variable	n	StDev	F	P
1	AML	15	778.180	1.99	0.137
2	STANDARD	24	550.960		

Since 0.137 > 0.10, we do not reject the null hypothesis. There is insufficient evidence to conclude that the variation in delivery cost differs for the AML and STANDARD methods of delivery.

(b) We choose **Calc ▶ Calculator...**, type NAML in the **Store result in variable** text box, select the function NSCOR from the **Function** list, select AML to replace **number** in the **Expression** text box, and click **OK**.

Repeat this process for STANDARD and NSTAN. Then choose **Graph ▶ Plot...**, select NAML in the **Y** column for **Graph1** and AML in the **X** column, select NSTAN in the **Y** column for **Graph2** and STANDARD in the **X** column, and click **OK**. The resulting graphs are

(c) Both normal probability plots exhibit a reasonably linear pattern. Thus the test performed in part (a) is reasonable.

REVIEW TEST FOR CHAPTER 11

1. Chi-squared distribution (χ^2)

2. (a) A χ^2-curve is <u>right</u> skewed.

(b) As the number of degrees of freedom becomes larger, a χ^2-curve looks increasingly like a <u>normal</u> curve.

3. The variable must be normally distributed. That assumption is very important because the χ^2 procedures are not robust to moderate violations of the normality assumption.

4. (a) 6.408 (b) 33.409 (c) 27.587 (d) 8.672

(e) 7.564 and 30.191

5. The F distribution is used when making inferences comparing two population standard deviations.

6. (a) An F-curve is <u>right</u>-skewed

(b) <u>reciprocal</u>, <u>(5,14)</u>

(c) 0

7. Both variables must be normally distributed. This is very important since the F procedures are not robust to violations of the normality assumption.

8. (a) 7.01

(b) $F_{0.99} = 1/F_{0.01}$ where $F_{0.01}$ has df = (8,4).

Thus $F_{0.99} = 1/14.80 = 0.068$

(c) 3.84

(d) The F value with 0.05 to its left = $F_{0.95} = 1/F_{0.05}$ where $F_{0.05}$ has df = (8,4).

Thus $F_{0.95} = 1/6.04 = 0.166$

(e) The F value with 0.025 to its left = $F_{0.975} = 1/F_{0.025}$ where $F_{0.025}$ has df = (8,4).

Thus $F_{0.975} = 1/8.98 = \underline{0.111}$; $F_{0.025} = \underline{5.05}$

9. (a) Step 1: H_0: $\sigma = 16$ H_a: $\sigma \neq 16$

Step 2: $\alpha = 0.10$

Step 3: $\chi^2 = \frac{n-1}{\sigma_0^2}s^2 = \frac{24}{16^2}15.006^2 = 21.111$

Step 4: The critical values with n-1 = 24 degrees of freedom are 13.848 and 36.415.

Step 5: Since 13.848 < 21.111 < 36.415, we do not reject H_0.

Step 6: There is insufficient evidence at the 0.10 level to claim that σ for IQs measured on the Stanford revision of the Binet-Simon Intelligence Scale is different from 16. Using Excel, in any cell, type =chidist(21.111,24) to obtain $P(\chi^2 < 21.111) = 0.36783$. The P-value is 2(0.36783) = 0.7357.

(b) Normality is crucial for the hypothesis test in (a) since the procedure is not robust to moderate deviations from the normality assumption.

10. The 90% confidence interval for σ of IQs measured on the Stanford Revision of the Binet-Simon Intelligence Scale is

$$\left(\sqrt{\frac{n-1}{\chi^2_{.05}}}s, \sqrt{\frac{n-1}{\chi^2_{.95}}}s\right) = \left(\sqrt{\frac{24}{36.415}}15.006, \sqrt{\frac{24}{13.848}}15.006\right) = (12.2,\ 19.855)$$

11. (a) F distribution with df = (14,19)

(b) 1=Runners, 2=Others

Step 1: H_0: $\sigma_1 = \sigma_2$ H_a: $\sigma_1 < \sigma_2$

Step 2: $\alpha = 0.01$

Step 3: $F = 1.798^2/6.606^2 = 0.074$

Step 4: For df = (14,19), the critical value is $F_{0.99} = 0.28$

Step 5: Since 0.074 < 0.28, we reject the null hypothesis.

Step 6: There is sufficient evidence at the 0.01 significance level to claim that the variation in skinfold thickness among runners is less than that among others. Enter =1-FDIST(0.074,14,19) in any cell of Excel to obtain P(F < 0.074) = 0.000006. The P-value is 0.000006.

(c) We are assuming that skinfold thickness is a normally distributed variable. This assumption can be checked by looking at a normal probability plot for each set of data. If both plots are linear, the normality assumption is reasonable.

(d) The samples must also be independent.

12. (a) Step 1: df = (14,19). $F_{0.01}$ is 3.19; $F_{0.99}$ = 0.28 from Review Exercise 11.

Step 2: The confidence interval for σ_1/σ_2 is

$$\frac{1}{\sqrt{F_{0.01}}}\cdot\frac{s_1}{s_2}\text{ to }\frac{1}{\sqrt{F_{0.99}}}\cdot\frac{s_1}{s_2}=\frac{1}{\sqrt{3.19}}\frac{1.798}{6.606}\text{ to }\frac{1}{\sqrt{0.28}}\frac{1.798}{6.060}=(0.15,\ 0.51)$$

(b) We can be 98% confident that the ratio of the population standard deviation of skinfold thickness for runners to the standard deviation for others lies between 0.15 and 0.51.

13. Using Minitab, with the data in a column named IQ and with the *WeissStats* CD in drive D, at the MTB> prompt in the Sessions Window, type

%D:\IS6\Minitab\Macro\1stdev.mac 'IQ'

and press the ENTER key. Then proceed as follows.

1 In response to Do you want to perform a hypothesis test (Y/N)?, type Y and press the ENTER key.

2 In response to Enter the null hypothesis population standard deviation, type 16 and press the ENTER key.

3 In response to Enter 0, 1, or -1, respectively, for a two-tailed, right-tailed, or left-tailed test., type 0 and press the ENTER key. The output is

```
Test of sigma =     16 vs sigma not =     16

Row  Variable    n   StDev   Chi-Sq       P
  1        IQ   25  15.006   21.110   0.736
```

Since 0.736 > 0.10, we do not reject the null hypothesis.

The macro continues with the confidence-interval procedure.

1 In response to Do you want a confidence interval (Y/N)?, type Y and press the ENTER key.

2 Since we want a 90% confidence interval, type 90 in response to Enter the confidence level, as a percentage and press the ENTER key. The result is

```
Row  Variable    n   StDev   Level      CI for σ
  1        IQ   25  15.006   90.0%  (12.182, 19.755)
```

14. Using Minitab, to run the hypothesis test and obtain the confidence interval using *WeissStats* CD in drive D, we type in the Sessions Window at the MTB> prompt,

%D:\IS6\Minitab\Macro\2STDEV.MAC 'RUNNERS' 'OTHERS'

and press the ENTER key. Proceed as follows

1 In response to do you want to perform a hypothesis test (Y/N)?, type Y and press the ENTER key.

2 In response to Enter 0, 1, or -1, respectively, for a two-tailed, right-tailed, or left-tailed test., type -1 and press the ENTER key. The output is

F-Test of sigma1 = sigma2 (vs <)

Row	Variable	n	StDev	F	P
1	RUNNERS	15	1.798	0.07	0.000
2	OTHERS	20	6.606		

Since the P-value of 0.000 is less than 0.01, we reject the null hypothesis.

Continuing with the confidence-interval aspect,

1 In response to Do you want a confidence interval (Y/N)?, type Y and press the ENTER key.

2 Since we want a 98% confidence interval, type 98 in response to Enter the confidence level, as a percentage, and then press the ENTER key. The resulting output is

Row	Variable	n	StDev	Level	CI for ratio
1	RUNNERS	15	1.798	98.0%	(0.152, 0.511)
2	OTHERS	20	6.606		

15. We used Minitab to obtain a histogram of each set of data. With the data in columns named GSOD and PSOD, we choose **Graph ▶ Histogram** and select GSOD for **Graph1** in the **X** column and PSOD for **Graph2**. The results are

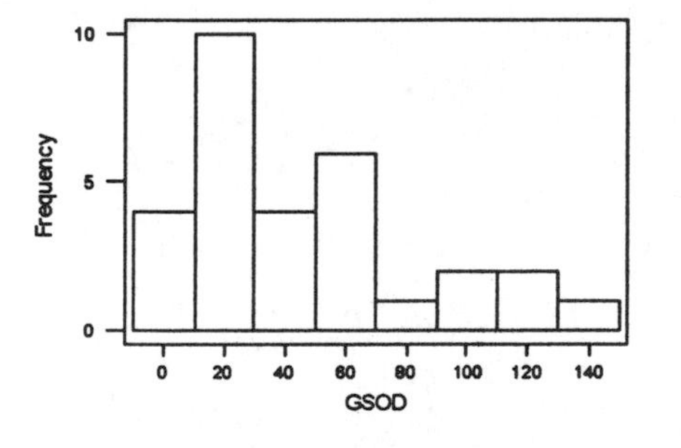

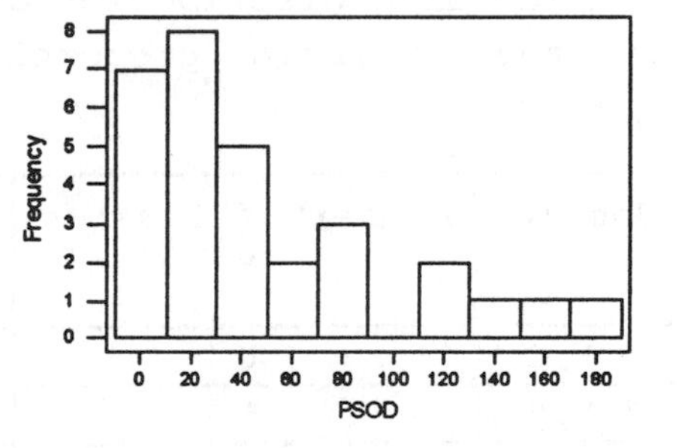

It is clear from both histograms that the data are very right-skewed. Since the F-test is very sensitive to non-normality, the F-test should not be used with these data.

CHAPTER 12 ANSWERS

Exercises 12.1

12.1 Answers will vary.

12.3 A population proportion p is a parameter since it is a descriptive measure for a population. A sample proportion $\hat{p}$ is a statistic since it is a descriptive measure for a sample.

12.5 (a) p = 2/5 = 0.4

(b)

Sample	Number of females x	Sample proportion $\hat{p}$
J,G	1	0.5
J,P	0	0.0
J,C	0	0.0
J,F	1	0.5
G,P	1	0.5
G,C	1	0.5
G,F	2	1.0
P,C	0	0.0
P,F	1	0.5
C,F	1	0.5

(c) The population proportion is marked by the vertical line in the plot at the right.

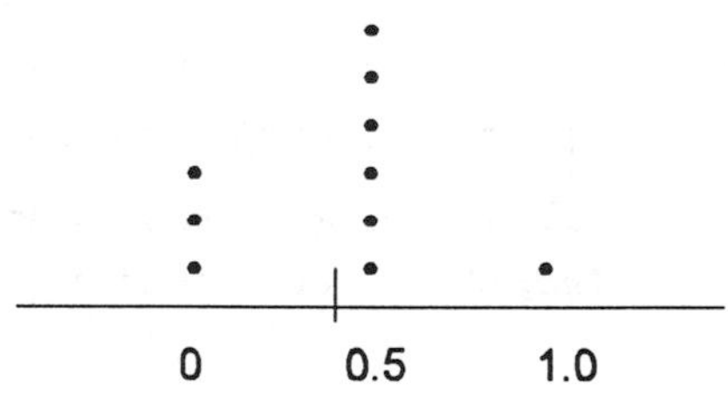

(d) $\mu_{\hat{p}} = (\sum \hat{p})/10 = 4.0/10 = 0.4$

(e) The answers to (a) and (d) are the same. $\hat{p}$ is a sample proportion. The mean of the sampling distribution of $\hat{p}$ is the same as the population proportion which is p.

12.7 (b)

Sample	Number of females x	Sample proportion $\hat{p}$
J,P,C	0	0
J,P,G	1	1/3
J,P,F	1	1/3
J,C,G	1	1/3
J,C,F	1	1/3
J,G,F	2	2/3
P,C,G	1	1/3
P,C,F	1	1/3
P,G,F	2	2/3
C,G,F	2	2/3

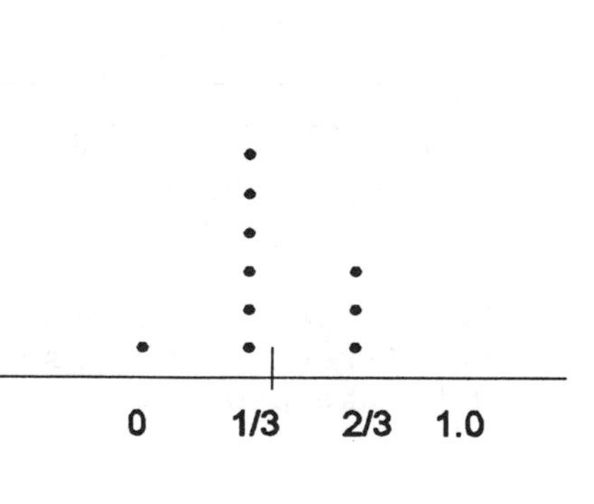

(c) Dot plot at the right of the table above.

(d) $\mu_{\hat{p}} = (\sum \hat{p})/10 = (12/3)/10 = 0.4$

(e) The answers to (a) and (d) are the same. $\hat{p}$ is a sample proportion. The mean of the sampling distribution of $\hat{p}$ is the same as the population proportion which is p.

12.9 (b)

Sample	Number of females x	Sample proportion $\hat{p}$
J,P,C,G,F	2	0.4

(c) The population proportion is marked by the vertical line below.

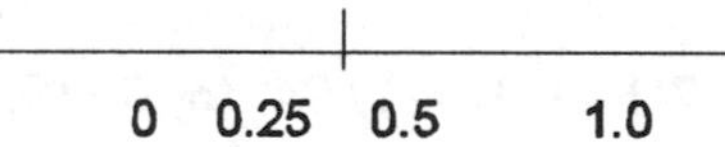

(d) $\mu_{\hat{p}} = (\sum \hat{p})/1 = 0.4/1 = 0.4$

(e) The answers to (a) and (d) are the same. $\hat{p}$ is a sample proportion. The mean of the sampling distribution of $\hat{p}$ is the same as the population proportion which is p.

12.11 (a) The population consists of all #1 NBA draft picks since 1966.

(b) The specified attribute is being a center.

(c) The 45% is a population proportion since all of the #1 picks are known. There is no need to sample this group.

12.13 (a) $\hat{p} = 0.79$; $z_{0.005} = 2.575$; the margin of error is

$$E = z_{0.005} \cdot \sqrt{\hat{p}(1-\hat{p})/n} = 2.575\sqrt{0.79(0.21)/21355} = 0.00718$$

(b) The margin of error will be smaller for a 90% confidence interval. Specifically, 2.575 will be replaced by 1.645 in the formula for E and everything else will stay the same. More generally speaking, in order to attach a higher level of confidence to an interval, one needs to have a wider interval.

12.15 (a) 0.4 (b) 0.5 (c) 0.7 (d) 0.2 (e) 0.5 (f) 0.5

(g) For (a), $0.4 < \hat{p} < 0.6$

For (b), none

For (c), $0.3 < \hat{p} < 0.7$

For (d), $0.2 < \hat{p} < 0.8$

For (e), none

For (f), none

12.17 n = 1,516, x = 985, and n - x = 531. Both x and n - x are at least 5.

$\hat{p}$ = x/n = 985/1,516 = 0.65; $z_{\alpha/2} = z_{0.025} = 1.96$

(a)

$$0.65 - 1.96\sqrt{0.65(1-0.65)/1516} \text{ to } 0.65 + 1.96\sqrt{0.65(1-0.65)/1516}$$
$$0.626 \text{ to } 0.674$$

(b) We can be 95% confident that the percentage of Americans who drink beer, wine, or hard liquor, at least occasionally, is somewhere between 62.6% and 67.4%.

12.19 n = 94, x = 30, and n - x = 64. Both x and n - x are at least 5.

$\hat{p}$ = x/n = 30/94 = 0.3192; $z_{\alpha/2} = z_{0.05} = 1.645$

(a)

$$0.3192 - 1.645\sqrt{0.3192(1-0.3192)/94} \text{ to } 0.3192 + 1.645\sqrt{0.3192(1-0.3192)/94}$$
$$0.240 \text{ to } 0.398 \text{ or } 24.0\% \text{ to } 39.8\%$$

(b) We can be 90% confident that the percentage of Malaysians infected with the Nipah virus who will die from encephalitis is somewhere between 24.0% and 39.8%.

12.21 I didn't do very well. Here, n = 500, $\hat{p}$ = 0.8% = 0.008, x = $\hat{p} \cdot$ n = 4, and n - x = 496. To use Procedure 12.1, both x and n - x must be at least 5. Since x < 5, I should not have used Procedure 12.1.

12.23 $\hat{p}$ = 0.57, E = 0.03

$\hat{p}$ - E to $\hat{p}$ + E

0.57 -0.03 to 0.57 + 0.03 In percentage terms, this is

54.0% to 60.0%

12.25 (a) The confidence interval from Exercise 12.17 was (0.626, 0.674). To find the error, divide the width of the confidence interval by 2. E = (0.674 - 0.626)/2 = 0.024.

(b) E = 0.02; $z_{\alpha/2} = z_{0.025} = 1.96$;

$$n = \hat{p}(1-\hat{p}) \cdot \frac{z_{\alpha/2}^2}{E^2} = 0.5(1-0.5)\frac{1.96^2}{0.02^2} = 2401$$

(c) n = 2401; $\hat{p}$ = 0.63; $z_{\alpha/2} = z_{0.025} = 1.96$

$$0.63 - 1.96\sqrt{0.63(1-0.63)/2401} \text{ to } 0.63 + 1.96\sqrt{0.63(1-0.63)/2401}$$
$$0.611 \text{ to } 0.649$$

(d) The margin of error for the estimate is 0.019, which is less than the margin of error required in part (b).

(e) $\hat{p}_g$ = 0.60; $z_{\alpha/2} = z_{0.025} = 1.96$

part (b) $E = 0.02$, $z_{0.025} = 1.96$; sample size is:

$$n = \hat{p}(1-\hat{p}) \cdot \frac{z_{\alpha/2}^2}{E^2} = 0.6(1-0.6)\frac{1.96^2}{0.02^2} = 2304.96 \rightarrow 2305$$

Thus the required sample size is n = 2305.

part (c)

$$0.63 - 1.96\sqrt{0.63(1-0.63)/2305} \text{ to } 0.63 + 1.96\sqrt{0.63(1-0.63)/2305}$$

$$0.610 \text{ to } 0.650$$

part (d)

The margin of error is 0.020, which is the same as the margin of error specified in part (b).

(f) By employing the guess for $\hat{p}$ in part (d) we can reduce the required sample size (from 2401 to 2305), saving some time and money. Moreover, the margin of error only rises from 0.019 to 0.020. The risk in using the guess 0.60 for $\hat{p}$ is that if the actual value of $\hat{p}$ turns out to be between 0.40 and 0.60, then the achieved margin of error will exceed the specified 0.02.

12.27 (a) The confidence interval from Exercise 12.19 was (24.0%, 39.8%). To find the margin of error, divide the width of the confidence interval by 2. E = (39.8% - 24.0%)/2 = 7.9%.

(b) $E = 0.05$; $z_{\alpha/2} = z_{0.05} = 1.645$;

$$n = \hat{p}(1-\hat{p}) \cdot \frac{z_{\alpha/2}^2}{E^2} = 0.5(1-0.5)\frac{1.645^2}{0.05^2} = 270.60 \rightarrow 271$$

(c) $n = 271$; $\hat{p} = 0.288$; $z_{\alpha/2} = z_{0.05} = 1.645$

$$0.288 - 1.645\sqrt{0.288(1-0.288)/271} \text{ to } 0.288 + 1.645\sqrt{0.288(1-0.288)/271}$$

$$0.243 \text{ to } 0.333$$

(d) The margin of error for the estimate is 0.045, which is less than what is required in part (b).

(e) $\hat{p}_g$ is between 25% and 40%; $z_{\alpha/2} = z_{0.05} = 1.645$

part (b) $E = 0.05$, $z_{0.05} = 1.645$; sample size is:

$$n = \hat{p}(1-\hat{p}) \cdot \frac{z_{\alpha/2}^2}{E^2} = 0.4(1-0.4)\frac{1.645^2}{0.05^2} = 259.78 \rightarrow 260$$

Thus the required sample size is n = 260.

part (c)

$$0.288 - 1.645\sqrt{0.288(1-0.288)/260} \text{ to } 0.288 + 1.645\sqrt{0.288(1-0.288)/260}$$

$$0.242 \text{ to } 0.334$$

part (d) The margin of error is 0.046, which is less than that specified in part (b).

(f) By employing the guess for $\hat{p}$ in part (d) we can reduce the required sample size (from 271 to 260), saving a small amount of time and money. Moreover, the margin of error only rises from 0.045 to 0.046. The risk in using the guess 0.40 for $\hat{p}$ is that if the actual value of $\hat{p}$ turns out to be between 0.40 and 0.60, then the achieved margin of error will exceed the specified 0.05.

12.29 We will assume that both polls used a 95% confidence level. Then at the 95% confidence level, both polls are giving a range of believable values for the true population (Arizonians) proportion that felt Symington should resign. The Research Resources poll gave its range to be 0.531 to 0.629. The Behavior Research Center poll gave its range to be 0.496 to 0.584. We note that both ranges of values have common believable values from 0.531 to 0.584. Thus, it is possible that both of these polls were correct in their conclusions.

12.31 The sample size is directly proportional to the quantity p(1 - p), which takes on its maximum value of 0.25 when p = 0.5. Sample sizes increase as p approaches 0.5 from either above or below. Thus to achieve a sample size adequate for any p in a given range, we should choose the largest sample that could result for any p in the range. This is done by choosing the value of p that is in the range and that is closest to 0.5.

12.33 (a) Np

(b) $\mu_y = \sum yP(Y=y) = 0\cdot(1-p) + 1\cdot p = p$

(c)

$$\sigma_y^2 = \sum y^2 P(Y=y) - \mu_y^2 = [0^2\cdot(1-p) + 1^2\cdot p] - p^2 = p - p^2 = p\cdot(1-p)$$

Therefore, $\sigma_y = \sqrt{p(1-p)}$

(d) In a sample of size n, there are x ones and (n-x) zeros. The ones and zeros are the y values. Therefore the mean of the y values is $\bar{y} = [x\cdot 1 + (n-x)\cdot 0]/n = x/n = \hat{p}$

(e) From Key Fact 7.4, when n is large, the sampling distribution of the mean is approximately normal with mean μ and standard deviation $\sigma/\sqrt{n}$, i.e., $\bar{y}$ has a sampling distribution with mean μ and standard deviation $\sigma/\sqrt{n}$. But here $\bar{y}$ is $\hat{p}$, μ is p, and $\sigma/\sqrt{n}$ is

$$\frac{\sqrt{p(1-p)}}{\sqrt{n}} = \sqrt{\frac{p(1-p)}{n}}.$$

Thus when n is large, the sampling distribution of $\hat{p}$ is approximately normal with mean p and standard deviation $\sqrt{\frac{p(1-p)}{n}}$.

12.35 (a) Choose **Calc ▶ Basic statistics ▶ 1 Proportion...**, select the **Summarized data** option button, click in the **Number of trials** text box and type 1516, click in the **Number of successes** text box and type 985, click the **Options...** button, click in the **Confidence level** text box and type 95, click **OK**, and click **OK**. The resulting output is

```
Test of p = 0.5 vs p not = 0.5

                                            Exact
Sample        X      N  Sample p          95.0 % CI          P-Value
1           985   1516  0.649736  (0.625120, 0.673770)        0.000
```

(b) The confidence interval obtained in Exercise 12.17 was (0.626, 0.674). The discrepancy between that result and this one is due to this one being an exact result based on the binomial distribution while the previous result was based on a normal approximation to the binomial distribution.

Exercises 12.2

12.37 (a) The sample proportion is $\hat{p} = x/n = 459/850 = 0.540$.

(b) $\alpha = 0.05$, $p_0 = 0.50$

$np_o = 850(0.50) = 425$; $n(1 - p_0) = 850(1-0.50) = 425$

Since both are at least 5, we can employ Procedure 12.2.

Step 1: H_0: $p = 0.50$, H_a: $p > 0.50$

Step 2: $\alpha = 0.05$

Step 3: $$z = \frac{0.540 - 0.500}{\sqrt{0.5(1-0.5)/850}} = 2.33$$

Step 4: Since $\alpha = 0.05$, the critical value is $z_\alpha = 1.645$

Step 5: Since $2.33 > 1.645$, reject H_0. Note, for the p-value approach, $P(z > 2.33) = 0.0099$; so the P-value $< \alpha$. Thus we reject H_0.

Step 6: The test results are statistically significant at the 5% level; that is, at the 5% significance level, the data do provide sufficient evidence to conclude that a majority of Generation Y Web users use the Internet to download music.

12.39 The sample proportion is $\hat{p} = x/n = 146/1283 = 0.1138$.

$\alpha = 0.10$, $p_0 = 0.128$

$np_o = 1283(0.128) = 164.2$; $n(1 - p_0) = 1283(1-0.128) = 1118.8$

Since both are at least 5, we can employ Procedure 12.2.

Step 1: H_0: $p = 0.128$, H_a: $p \neq 0.128$

Step 2: $\alpha = 0.10$

Step 3: $$z = \frac{0.1138 - 0.1280}{\sqrt{0.128(1-0.128)/1283}} = -1.52$$

Step 4: Since $\alpha = 0.10$, the critical values are $z_\alpha = \pm 1.645$

Step 5: Since $-1.52 > -1.645$, do not reject H_0. Note, for the p-value approach, $2P(Z < -1.52) = 2(0.0643) = 0.1286$; so the P-value $> \alpha$. Thus we do not reject H_0.

Step 6: The test results are not statistically significant at the 10% level; that is, at the 10% significance level, the data do not provide sufficient evidence to conclude that the percentage of 18-25 year-olds who currently use marijuana or hashish has changed from the 1997 percentage of 12.8%.

12.41 (a) The sample proportion is $\hat{p} = x/n = 909/1515 = 0.600$.

$\alpha = 0.05$, $p_0 = 0.500$

$np_o = 1515(0.500) = 757.5$; $n(1 - p_0) = 1515(1-0.500) = 757.5$

Since both are at least 5, we can employ Procedure 12.2.

Step 1: H_0: $p = 0.500$, H_a: $p > 0.500$

Step 2: $\alpha = 0.05$

Step 3: $z = \dfrac{0.600 - 0.500}{\sqrt{0.5(1-0.5)/1515}} = 7.78$

Step 4: Since $\alpha = 0.05$, the critical value is $z_\alpha = 1.645$

Step 5: Since 7.78 > 1.645, reject H_0. Note, for the p-value approach, $P(Z > 7.78) = 0.0000$; so the P-value < α. Thus we reject H_0.

Step 6: The test results are statistically significant at the 5% level; that is, at the 5% significance level, the data do provide sufficient evidence to conclude that a majority of Americans think that a presidential candidate's position on protecting the environment is very important in deciding how to vote in the next presidential election.

(b) The sample proportion is $\hat{p} = x/n = 909/1515 = 0.600$.

$\alpha = 0.05$, $p_0 = 2/3$

$np_o = 1515(0.667) = 1010$; $n(1 - p_0) = 1515(1-0.667) = 505$

Since both are at least 5, we can employ Procedure 12.2.

Step 1: H_0: $p = 2/3$, H_a: $p < 2/3$

Step 2: $\alpha = 0.05$

Step 3: $z = \dfrac{0.600 - 2/3}{\sqrt{(2/3)(1-2/3)/1515}} = -5.50$

Step 4: Since $\alpha = 0.05$, the critical value is $z_\alpha = -1.645$

Step 5: Since -5.50 < -1.645, reject H_0. Note, for the p-value approach, $P(Z < -5.50) = 0.0000$; so the P-value < α. Thus we reject H_0.

Step 6: The test results are statistically significant at the 5% level; that is, at the 5% significance level, the data do provide sufficient evidence to conclude that less than 2/3 of Americans think that a presidential candidate's position on protecting the environment is very important in deciding how to vote in the next presidential election.

12.43 Choose **Stat ▶ Basic statistics ▶ 1 Proportion...**, select the **Summarized data** option button, click in the **Number of trials** text box and type 1283, click in the **Number of successes** text box and type 146, click the **Options...** button, click in the **Test proportion** text box and type 0.128, click the arrow button at the right of the **Alternative** drop-down list box and select **not equal**, click **OK**, and click **OK.** The resulting output is

Test of p = 0.128 vs p not = 0.128

Sample	X	N	Sample p	95.0 % CI	Exact P-Value
1	146	1283	0.113796	(0.096930, 0.132454)	0.123

Since 0.123 > 0.10, do not reject the null hypothesis.

Exercises 12.3

12.45 For a two-tailed test, we independently sample from the two populations under consideration. Then we compute the sample proportions $\hat{p}_1$ and $\hat{p}_2$. Reject the null hypothesis if the sample proportions differ by too much; otherwise, do not reject the null hypothesis. For a left-tailed test, reject the null hypothesis only if $\hat{p}_1$ is too much smaller than $\hat{p}_2$; for a right-tailed test, reject the null hypothesis only if $\hat{p}_1$ is too much larger than $\hat{p}_2$;

12.47 (a) Using sunscreen before going out in the sun

(b) Teen-age girls and teen-age boys

(c) The two proportions are sample proportions. The reference is specifically to those teen-age girls and boys who were surveyed.

12.49 (a) The parameters are p_1 and p_2. The remaining quantities are statistics.

(b) The fixed numbers are p_1 and p_2. The remaining quantities are variables.

12.51 (a) Population 1: Women who took multivitamins containing folic acid

$\hat{p}_1 = 35/2701 = 0.01296$

Population 2: Women who received only trace elements

$\hat{p}_2 = 47/2052 = 0.02290$

$\hat{p}_p = (35 + 47)/(2,701 + 2,052) = 0.01725$

Step 1: H_0: $p_1 = p_2$, H_a: $p_1 < p_2$

Step 2: $\alpha = 0.01$

Step 3:
$$z = \frac{0.01296 - 0.02290}{\sqrt{0.01725(1-0.01725)}\sqrt{(1/2701)+(1/2052)}} = -2.61$$

Step 4: Since $\alpha = 0.01$, the critical value is $z_\alpha = -2.33$

Step 5: Since $-2.61 < -2.33$, reject H_0. Note: For the p-value approach, $p(z < -2.61) = 0.0045$; so the P-value $< \alpha$. Thus, we reject H_0.

Step 6: The test results are significant at the 1% level; that is, at the 1% significance level, the data do provide sufficient evidence to conclude that the women who take folic acid are at lesser risk of having children with major birth defects.

(b) This is an designed experiment. The researchers decided which women would take daily multivitamins.

(c) Yes. By using the basic principles of design (control, randomization, and replication) the doctors can conclude that a difference in the rates of major birth defects between the two groups not reasonably attributable to chance is likely caused by the folic acid.

12.53 Population 1: Drivers of age 25-34, $\hat{p}_1 = 270/1000 = 0.270$

Population 2: Drivers of age 45-64, $\hat{p}_2 = 330/1100 = 0.300$

$\hat{p}_p = (270 + 330)/(1000 + 1100) = 0.286$

Step 1: H_0: $p_1 = p_2$, H_a: $p_1 \neq p_2$

Step 2: $\alpha = 0.10$

Step 3:
$$z = \frac{0.270 - 0.300}{\sqrt{0.286(1-0.286)}\sqrt{(1/1000)+(1/1100)}} = -1.52$$

Step 4: Since $\alpha = 0.10$, the critical values are $z_{\alpha/2} = \pm 1.645$

Step 5: Since $-1.645 < -1.52 < 1.645$, do not reject H_0. Note: For the P-value approach, $2P(z < -1.52) = 0.1286$; so the P-value > α. Thus, we do not reject H_0.

Step 6: The test results are not significant at the 10% level; that is, at the 10% significance level, the data do not provide sufficient evidence to conclude that there is a difference in seat-belt usage between drivers 25-34 years old and those 45-64 years old.

12.55 Population 1: 1980 American men 20-34 years old, $\hat{p}_1 = 130/750 = 0.17333$

Population 2: 1994 American men 20-34 years old, $\hat{p}_2 = 160/700 = 0.22857$

$$\hat{p}_p = (130 + 160)/(750 + 700) = 0.200$$

Step 1: H_0: $p_1 = p_2$, H_a: $p_1 < p_2$

Step 2: $\alpha = 0.05$

Step 3:
$$z = \frac{0.17333 - 0.22857}{\sqrt{0.200(1-0.200)}\sqrt{(1/700)+(1/750)}} = -2.63$$

Step 4: Since $\alpha = 0.05$, the critical value is $z_\alpha = -1.645$

Step 5: Since $-2.63 < -1.645$, reject H_0. Note: For the P-value approach, $P(z < -2.63) = 0.0043$; so the P-value < α. Thus, we reject H_0.

Step 6: The test results are significant at the 5% level; that is, at the 5% significance level, the data do provide sufficient evidence to conclude that a higher percentage of men 20-34 years old were overweight in 1994 than in 1980.

12.57 (a) From Exercise 12.51,

$$(0.012958 - 0.022904) \pm 2.33\sqrt{\frac{0.012958(1-0.012958)}{2701} + \frac{0.022904(1-0.022904)}{2052}}$$

$$-0.009946 \pm 0.009215$$

$$-0.019161 \text{ to } -0.000731 \text{ or about } -0.019 \text{ to } -0.001$$

(b) We can be 98% confident that the difference $p_1 - p_2$ between the rates of major birth defects for babies born to women who have taken folic acid and those born to women who have not taken folic acid is somewhere between -0.019 and -0.001.

12.59 (a) From Exercise 12.53,

$$(0.270 - 0.300) \pm 1.645\sqrt{\frac{0.270(1-0.270)}{1000} + \frac{0.300(1-0.300)}{1100}}$$

$$-0.0300 \pm 0.0324$$

$$-0.0624 \text{ to } 0.0024$$

(b) We can be 90% confident that the difference $p_1 - p_2$ between the proportions of seat-belt users for drivers in the age groups 25-34 and 45-64 years old is somewhere between -0.0624 and 0.0024.

12.61 The first formula in Key Fact 12.2: $\mu_{\hat{p}_1 - \hat{p}_2} = p_1 - p_2$. This formula says that the mean of $\hat{p}_1 - \hat{p}_2$ is $p_1 - p_2$.

12.63 Using Minitab, choose **Stat ▶ Basic statistics ▶ 2 Proportions...**, select the **Summarized data** option button, click in the **Trials** text box for **First sample** and type 2701, click in the **Successes** text box for **First sample** and type 35, click in the **Trials** text box for **Second sample** and type 2052, click in the **Successes** text box for **Second sample** and type 47, click the **Options...** button, click in the **Confidence level** text box and type 98, click in the **Test difference** text box and type 0, click the arrow button at the right of the **Alternative** drop-down list box and select **less than**, select the **Use pooled estimate of p for test** check box, click **OK**, and click **OK**. The resulting output is

```
Sample        X      N  Sample p
1            35   2701  0.012958
2            47   2052  0.022904

Estimate for p(1) - p(2):  -0.00994632

98% CI for p(1) - p(2):  (-0.0191469, -0.000745697)

Test for p(1) - p(2) = 0 (vs < 0):  Z = -2.61  P-Value = 0.005
```

Note: The slight differences between the solutions here and the solutions in 12.51 and 12.57 are due to rounding the sample proportions to three decimal places in the earlier exercises.

CHAPTER 12 REVIEW TEST

1. (a) Feeling that marijuana should be legalized for medicinal use in patients with cancer and other painful and terminal diseases.

   (b) All Americans

   (c) Proportion of all Americans who feel that marijuana should be legalized for medicinal use in patients with cancer and other painful and terminal diseases.

   (d) Sample proportion. It is the proportion of Americans in the sample who feel that marijuana should be legalized for medicinal use in patients with cancer and other painful and terminal diseases. Clearly the population of all Americans is much larger than 83,957.

2. It is often impossible to take a census of an entire population. It is also expensive and time-consuming.

3. (a) "Number of successes" stands for the number of members of the sample that exhibit the specified attribute.

   (b) "Number of failures" stands for the number of members of the sample that do not exhibit the specified attribute.

4. (a) population proportion

   (b) normal

   (c) number of successes, number of failures, 5

5. The margin of error for the estimate of a population proportion tells us what the maximum difference between the sample proportion and the population proportion is likely to be. It is not an absolute maximum, and the confidence level tells us how likely it is that the difference is not larger than the margin of error.

6. (a) Getting the "holiday blues"

(b) All men and all women

(c) The proportion of men in the population who get the "holiday blues" and the proportion of women in the population who get the "holiday blues"

(d) The proportion of men in the sample who get the "holiday blues" and the proportion of women in the sample who get the "holiday blues"

(e) They are sample proportions since the information came from a poll, not a census. Also, it could not be a population proportion because I was not asked.

7. (a) The mean of all possible differences between the two sample proportions equals the <u>difference of the population proportions</u>.

(b) For large samples, the possible differences between the two sample proportions have approximately a <u>normal</u> distribution.

8. The 95% confidence interval of all young Americans who do not plan to vote in the next presidential election is 46% ± 4.7% or from 41.3% to 50.7%.

9. (a) $n = 0.5 \cdot \dfrac{1.96^2}{0.01^2} = 19{,}208$

(b) $n = [0.75(1-0.75) + 0.75(1-0.75)]\left[\dfrac{1.96}{0.01}\right]^2 = 14{,}406$

10. n = 1218, $\hat{p}$ = 733/1218 = 0.6018, $z_{\alpha/2} = z_{0.025} = 1.96$

$$0.6018 - 1.96\sqrt{0.6018(1-0.6018)/1218} \text{ to } 0.6018 + 1.96\sqrt{0.6018(1-0.6018)/1218}$$

$$0.574 \text{ to } 0.629$$

We can be 95% confident that the proportion, p, of students who expect difficulty finding a job is somewhere between 0.574 and 0.629.

11. (a) The error is found by dividing the width of the confidence interval by 2. So E = (0.6293 - 0.5743)/2 = 0.028.

(b) E = 0.02; $z_{\alpha/2} = z_{0.025} = 1.96$; $\hat{p}_g = 0.50$

$$n = 0.5^2 \cdot \frac{z_{\alpha/2}^2}{E^2} = 0.25 \cdot \frac{1.96^2}{0.02^2} = 2401$$

(c) n = 2401; $\hat{p}$ = 0.587; $z_{\alpha/2} = z_{0.025} = 1.96$

$$0.587 - 1.96\sqrt{0.587(1-0.587)/2401} \text{ to } 0.587 + 1.96\sqrt{0.587(1-0.587)/2401}$$

$$0.567 \text{ to } 0.607$$

(d) The margin of error for the estimate is 0.020 (actually it's 0.0197 to four decimal places), the same as that required in part (b).

(e) $\hat{p}_g = 0.56$; $z_{\alpha/2} = z_{0.025} = 1.96$

part (b) E = 0.02, $z_{0.025} = 1.96$; sample size is

$$n = 0.56(1-0.56) \cdot \frac{z_{\alpha/2}^2}{E^2} = 0.2464 \cdot \frac{1.96^2}{0.02^2} = 2366.42 \rightarrow 2367$$

Thus the required sample size is n = 2367.

part (c)

$$0.587 - 1.96\sqrt{0.587(1-0.587)/2367} \text{ to } 0.587 + 1.96\sqrt{0.587(1-0.587)/2367}$$

$$0.567 \text{ to } 0.607$$

part (d)

The margin of error is 0.020 (actually it's 0.0197 to four decimal places), which is the same as that specified in part (b).

(f) By employing the guess for $\hat{p}$ in part (d) we can reduce the required sample size (from 2401 to 2367), saving a little time and money. Moreover, the margin of error stays almost the same. The risk of using the guess 0.56 for $\hat{p}$ is that if the actual value of $\hat{p}$ turns out to be between .44 and .56, then the achieved margin of error will exceed the specified 0.02.

12. $n = 2512$, $x = 578$, $\alpha = 0.05$, $\hat{p} = 578/2512 = 0.2301$

$np_o = 2512(0.25) = 628$; $n(1 - p_0) = 2512(1 - 0.25) = 1884$

Since both are at least 5, we can employ Procedure 12.2.

(a) Step 1: H_0: $p = 0.25$, H_1: $p < 0.25$

Step 2: $\alpha = 0.05$

Step 3: $$z = \frac{0.2301 - 0.2500}{\sqrt{0.25(1-0.25)/2512}} = -2.30$$

Step 4: Since $\alpha = 0.05$, the critical value is $z_\alpha = -1.645$

Step 5: Since $-2.30 < -1.645$, reject H_0.

Step 6: The test results are statistically significant at the 5% level; that is, at the 5% significance level, the data do provide sufficient evidence to conclude that less than one in four Americans believe that juries "almost always" convict the guilty and free the innocent. $P(z < -2.30) = 0.0107$. Since the P-value $< \alpha$, reject H_0.

(b) The strength of the evidence against the null hypothesis is strong.

13. (a) Observational study. The researchers had no control over any of the factors of the study.

(b) Height may not be the only factor to be considered. Although there does appear to be an association, no causal relationship can be inferred, even though there may be one.

14. Population 1: first poll, $\hat{p}_1 = 0.48$,

Population 2: second poll, $\hat{p}_2 = 0.60$

$$\hat{p}_p = (0.48 + 0.60)/2 = 0.54$$

(a) Step 1: H_0: $p_1 = p_2$, H_a: $p_1 < p_2$

Step 2: $\alpha = 0.01$

Step 3: $$z = \frac{0.48 - 0.60}{\sqrt{0.54(1-0.54)}\sqrt{(1/600)+(1/600)}} = -4.17$$

Step 4: Since $\alpha = 0.01$, the critical value $z_\alpha = -2.33$

Step 5: Since $-4.17 < -2.33$, reject H_0.

Step 6: The test is significant at the 1% level; that is the data do provide sufficient evidence to conclude that the percentage of Maricopa County residents who thought that the state's economy would improve over the next 2 years was less during the time of the first poll than during the time of the second poll.

$P(z < -4.17) = 0.0000$, so the P-value $< \alpha$. Thus, we reject H_0.

(b) The strength of the evidence against the null hypothesis is very strong.

15. (a) From Exercise 14

$$(0.48 - 0.60) \pm 2.326\sqrt{\frac{0.48(1-0.48)}{600} + \frac{0.60(1-0.60)}{600}}$$

$$-0.120 \pm 0.066$$

$$-0.186 \text{ to } -0.054$$

(b) We can be 95% confident that the difference $p_1 - p_2$ between the proportions of Maricopa County residents who thought that the state's economy would improve over the next 2 years during the time of the first poll and during the time of the second poll is somewhere between -0.186 and -0.054.

16. (a) $E = (-0.054 - (-0.186))/2 = 0.066$

We can be 98% confident that the error in estimating the difference between the two population proportions, $p_1 - p_2$, by the difference between the two sample proportions, -0.12, is at most 0.066.

(b) $$E = 2.326\sqrt{\frac{0.48(1-0.48)}{600} + \frac{0.60(1-0.60)}{600}} = 0.066$$

(c) $E = 0.03$, $\alpha = 0.02$

$$n = 0.5 \cdot \frac{2.326^2}{0.03^2} = 3005.715 \rightarrow 3006$$

(d) $n = 3006$, $\hat{p}_1 = 0.475$, $\hat{p}_2 = 0.603$

$$(0.475 - 0.603) \pm 2.326\sqrt{\frac{0.475(1-0.475)}{3006} + \frac{0.603(1-0.603)}{3006}}$$

$$-0.128 \pm 0.030$$

$$-0.158 \text{ to } -0.098$$

(e) $E = 0.030$ which is the same as that required in part (c).

17. Using Minitab, choose **Stat ▶ Basic statistics ▶ 1 Proportion...**, select the **Summarized data** option button, click in the **Number of trials** text box and type 1218, click in the **Number of successes** text box and type 733, click the **Options...** button, click in the **Confidence level** text box and type 95, click **OK**, and click **OK**. The resulting output is

Test of p = 0.5 vs p not = 0.5

Sample	X	N	Sample p	Exact 95.0 % CI	P-Value
1	733	1218	0.601806	(0.573685, 0.629434)	0.000

18. Using Minitab, choose **Stat ▶ Basic statistics ▶ 1 Proportion...,** select the **Summarized data** option button, click in the **Number of trials** text box and type 2512, click in the **Number of successes** text box and type 578, click the **Options...** button, click in the **Test proportion** text box and type 0.25, click the arrow button at the right of the **Alternative** drop-down list box and select **less than,** click **OK,** and click **OK.** The resulting output is

```
Test of p = 0.25 vs p < 0.25

                                                              Exact
Sample        X      N  Sample p          95.0 % CI         P-Value
1           578   2512  0.230096  (0.213759, 0.247063)        0.011
```

19. Using Minitab, choose **Calc ▶ Basic statistics ▶ 2 Proportions...,** select the **Summarized data** option button, click in the **Trials** text box for **First sample** and type 600, click in the **Successes** text box for **First sample** and type 288, click in the **Trials** text box for **Second sample** and type 600, click in the **Successes** text box for **Second sample** and type 360, click the **Options...** button, click in the **Confidence level** text box and type 98, click in the **Test difference** text box and type 0, click the arrow button at the right of the **Alternative** drop-down list box and select **less than,** select the **Use pooled estimate of p for test** check box, click **OK,** and click **OK.** The resulting output is

```
Sample        X      N  Sample p
1           288    600  0.480000
2           360    600  0.600000

Estimate for p(1) - p(2):  -0.12
98% CI for p(1) - p(2):  (-0.186454, -0.0535462)
Test for p(1) - p(2) = 0 (vs < 0):  Z = -4.17  P-Value = 0.000
```

CHAPTER 13 ANSWERS

Exercises 13.1

13.1 A variable has a chi-square distribution if its distribution has the shape of right-skewed curve, called a chi-square curve.

13.3 The χ^2-curve with 20 degrees of freedom more closely resembles a normal curve. This follows from Property 4 of Key Fact 13.1, "As the number of degrees of freedom becomes larger, χ^2-curves look increasingly like normal curves."

13.5 (a) $\chi^2_{0.025} = 32.852$ (b) $\chi^2_{0.95} = 10.117$

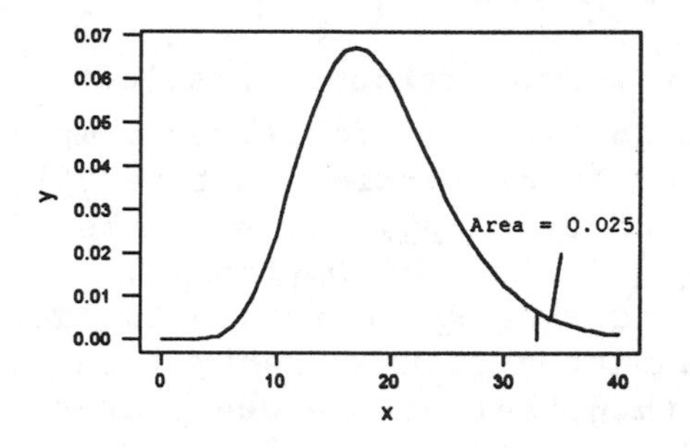

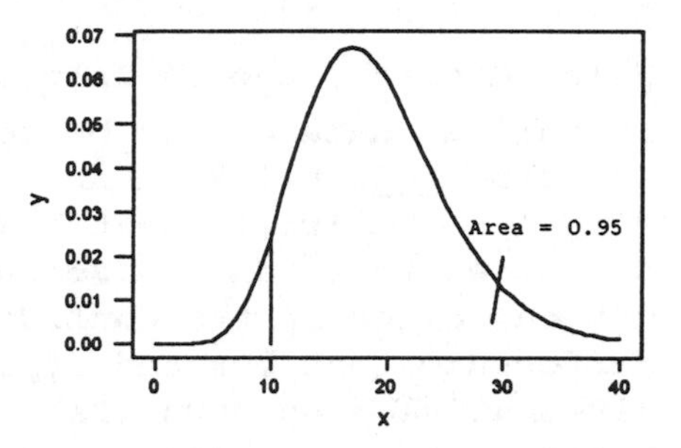

13.7 (a) $\chi^2_{0.05} = 18.307$ (b) $\chi^2_{0.975} = 3.247$

13.9 The χ^2-value having area 0.05 to its left has 0.95 to its right. Table VII gives values with specified areas to their right. If df = 26, $\chi^2_{0.95} = 15.379$.

Exercises 13.2

13.11 The term "goodness-of-fit" is used to describe the type of hypothesis test considered in this section because the test is carried out by determining how well the observed frequencies match or fit the expected frequencies.

13.13 (a) The assumptions are satisfied. The expected frequencies are np = 65, 30, and 5. All are 1 or more, and none are less than 5.

(b) The assumptions are not satisfied. The expected frequencies are np = 32.5, 15, and 2.5. All are 1 or more, but more than 20% (33.3%) are less than 5.

(c) The assumptions are satisfied. The expected frequencies are np = 10, 10, 12.5, 15, and 2.5. All are 1 or more, and exactly 20% are less than 5.

(d) The assumptions are satisfied. The expected frequencies are np = 11, 10.5, 12.5, 15, and 1. All are 1 or more, and exactly 20% are less than 5.

(e) The assumptions are not satisfied. The expected frequencies are np = 11, 11, 12.5, 15, and 0.5. One of them is not 1 or more.

(f) The assumptions are not satisfied. The expected frequencies are np = 44, 25, 30, and 1. All are 1 or more, but 25% are less than 5.

13.15 (a) The population consists of all prisoners in the U.S. sentenced to death in 1998. The variable under consideration is their level of education.

(b)

Education	O	p	E = np	$(O - E)^2/E$
8th grade or less	18	0.257	32.90	6.748
9th-11th grade	48	0.370	47.36	0.009
High school grad/GED	49	0.295	37.76	3.346
Any college	13	0.078	9.98	0.914
	128		128.00	11.017

Step 1: H_0: The distribution of education level for 1998 prisoners on death row is the same as the 1980 distribution.

H_a: The distribution of education level for 1998 prisoners on death row is different from the 1980 distribution.

Step 2: Expected frequencies are presented in column 4 of the table.

Step 3: Assumptions 1 and 2 are satisfied since all expected frequencies are at least 5.

Step 4: $\alpha = 0.05$

Step 5: $\chi^2 = 11.017$ (See column 5 of the table.)

Step 6: df = 3; From Table VII, critical value = 7.815

Step 7: Since 11.017 > 7.815, reject H_0.

Step 8: At the 5% significance level, the data do provide sufficient evidence to conclude that the distribution of education level for 1998 prisoners on death row is different from the 1980 distribution.

For the P-value approach, $0.01 < P(\chi^2 > 11.017) < 0.025$. Since the P-value is smaller than the significance level, reject H_0.

(a) If $\alpha = 0.01$, the critical value is 11.345, and since 11.017 < 11.345, do not reject H_0. At the 1% significance level, the data do not provide sufficient evidence to conclude that the distribution of education level for 1998 prisoners on death row is different from the 1980 distribution.

13.17

Color	O	p	E = np	$(O - E)^2/E$
Brown	152	0.3	152.7	0.003
Yellow	114	0.2	101.8	1.462
Red	106	0.2	101.8	0.173
Orange	51	0.1	50.9	0.000
Green	43	0.1	50.9	1.226
Blue	43	0.1	50.9	1.226
	509		509.0	4.090

Step 1: H_0: The color distribution of M&Ms is the same as that reported by M&M/Mars consumer affairs.

H_a: The color distribution of M&Ms is different from that reported by M&M/Mars consumer affairs.

Step 2: Expected frequencies are presented in column 4 of the table.

Step 3: Assumptions 1 and 2 are satisfied since all of the expected frequencies are at least 5.

Step 4: $\alpha = 0.05$

Step 5: $\chi^2 = 4.090$ (See column 5 of the table.)

Step 6: df = 5; From Table VII, the critical value = 11.070

Step 7: Since $4.090 < 11.070$, do not reject H_0.

Step 8: There is not sufficient evidence to conclude that ehe color distribution of M&Ms is different from that reported by M&M/Mars consumer affairs.

For the P-value approach, $P(\chi^2 > 4.090) > 0.10$. Since the P-value is larger than the significance level, do not reject H_0.

13.19 (a) The observed frequencies and the expected frequencies should both sum to n. By definition, n is the total number of observed frequencies. If we let p_i and E_i be the probability and expected frequency for category i, then $\sum E_i = \sum np_i = n\sum p_i = n \cdot 1 = n$.

(b) The sum of the differences between each observed and expected frequency should equal zero.

(c) From part (a), the sums of the observed and expected frequencies must be the same. If they are not the same (except for possible round-off error), you can conclude that you have made an error either in finding the expected frequencies or in summing them.

(d) No. It is possible (though admittedly not very likely) that you made two or more compensating errors in finding the expected frequencies and that they still sum to the correct number.

13.21 Using Minitab, click in the Session window, choose **Editor ▶ Enable Command Language** if it is not already enabled, and type in the Session window after the MTB> prompt, a percent sign (%) followed by the path for *fittest.mac*. If the *WeissStats* CD is in drive D, we type %D:\IS6\Minitab\macro\fittest.mac and press the ENTER key. Then proceed as follows: Type 3 and press the ENTER key in response to Enter the number of possible values for the variable under consideration; type 0.257 0.370 0.295 0.078 and press the ENTER key in response to Enter the relative frequencies (or probabilities) for the null hypothesis; and type 18 48 49 13 and press the ENTER key in response to Enter the observed frequencies. The resulting output is

```
Chi-square goodness-of-fit test

  Row      n      k     ChiSq      P-value

    1    128      4   11.0108    0.0116678
```

13.23 Using Minitab, click in the Session window, choose **Editor ▶ Enable Command Language** if it is not already enabled, and type in the Session window after the MTB> prompt, a percent sign (%) followed by the path for *fittest.mac*. If the *WeissStats* CD is in drive D, we type %d:\IS6\Minitab\macro\fittest.mac and press the ENTER key. Then proceed as follows: Type 4 and press the ENTER key in response to Enter the number of possible values for the variable under consideration; type 0.28 0.33 0.21 0.18 and press the ENTER key in response to Enter the relative frequencies (or probabilities) for the null hypothesis; and type 25 29 26 29 and press the ENTER key in response to Enter the observed frequencies. The resulting output is

```
Chi-square goodness-of-fit test

  Row      n      k     ChiSq      P-value

    1    109      4   7.25594    0.0641724
```

The null hypothesis is that the income distribution of Internet users is the same as that of credit card applicants, and the alternative hypothesis is that it is different. Since the p-value of 0.0641724 > 0.05, we do not reject the null hypothesis. There is not sufficient evidence to conclude that the income distribution of Internet users differs from that of credit card applicants.

Exercises 13.3

13.25 An example of univariate data arises if we record the religious affiliation of those in a sample. An example of bivariate data arises if we record the dominant eye and dominant hand of those in the sample. Answers will vary.

13.27 Cells

13.29 To obtain the total number of observations of bivariate data in a continency table, one can sum the individual cell frequencies, sum the row subtotals, or sum the column subtotals.

13.31 Yes. If there were no association between the gender of the physician and specialty of the physician, then the same percentage of male and female physicians would choose internal medicine. Since different percentages of male and female physicians chose internal medicine, there is an association between the variables "sex" and "specialty."

13.33 (a)

	M	F	Total
BUS	2	7	9
ENG	10	2	12
LIB	3	1	4
Total	15	10	25

(b)

	BUS	ENG	LIB	Total
M	0.222	0.833	0.750	0.600
F	0.778	0.167	0.250	0.400
Total	1.000	1.000	1.000	1.000

(c)

	M	F	Total
BUS	0.133	0.700	0.360
ENG	0.667	0.200	0.480
LIB	0.200	0.100	0.160
Total	1.000	1.000	1.000

(d) Yes. The conditional distributions of sex are different within each college.

13.35 (a)

	Fresh	Soph	Jun	Sen	Total
Dem	2	6	8	4	20
Rep	3	9	12	6	30
Other	1	3	4	2	10
Total	6	18	24	12	60

(b)

	Fresh	Soph	Jun	Sen
Dem	0.333	0.333	0.333	0.333
Rep	0.500	0.500	0.500	0.500
Other	0.167	0.167	0.167	0.167
Total	1.000	1.000	1.000	1.000

(c) There is no association between party affiliation and class level. All of the conditional distributions of political party within class level are identical.

(d) The marginal distribution of party affiliation will be identical to each of the conditional distributions, that is

Party	Frequency
Dem	0.333
Rep	0.500
Other	0.167
Total	1.000

(e) True. Since party affiliation and class level are not associated, all of the conditional distributions of class level within political party will be identical and will be the same as the marginal distribution of class level.

13.37 (a) 8

(b) First complete the first row, then the first column total, then the third row total, then the grand total.

	Male	Female	Total
White	12855	1924	14779
Black	14946	6784	21730
Hispanic	7019	1948	8967
Other	439	103	542
Total	35259	10759	46018

(c) 46,018 (d) 8967 (e) 35,259 (f) 1924

13.39 (a) 73,970 (b) 15,540 (c) 12,328

(d) 73970 + 15540 - 12328 = 77,182

(e) 12,225 (f) 6,734 (g) 103,601 - 25,901 = 77,700

13.41 The table from Exercise 13.37 was first transposed so that the columns became the rows and vice versa. Then each cell entry was divided by the column total to produce the table below.

	White	**Black**	**Hispanic**	**Other**	**Total**
Male	0.870	0.688	0.783	0.810	0.766
Female	0.130	0.312	0.217	0.190	0.234
Total	1.000	1.000	1.000	1.000	1.000

(a) The conditional distributions of gender within each race are given in columns 2, 3, 4, and 5 of the above table.

(b) The marginal distribution of gender is given by the last column of the above table.

(c) Yes. The conditional distributions for gender are different for the four race categories.

(d) 23.4% of the AIDS cases were females.

(e) 13.0% of the AIDS cases among whites were females.

(f) True. Since there is an association between gender and race category, the conditional distributions of race by gender cannot be identical (If they were identical, there would be no association between the two variables.).

(g) Directly from the table in Exercise 13.37, divide each cell entry by the column total below it to obtain the table below.

	Male	**Female**	**Total**
White	0.365	0.179	0.321
Black	0.424	0.631	0.472
Hispanic	0.199	0.181	0.195
Other	0.012	0.010	0.012
Total	1.000	1.000	1.000

The conditional distributions of race by gender are given in columns 2 and 3 of the table. The marginal distribution of race is given in the last column of the table. The conditional distributions of race by gender indicate that the black population has the largest percentage of males with AIDS and the largest percentage of females with AIDS. Other interpretations are possible as well.

13.43 (a)

	Office	Hospital	Other	Total
General Surgery	0.326	0.472	0.445	0.367
Obstetrics/gynecology	0.326	0.260	0.306	0.309
Orthopedics	0.181	0.164	0.111	0.174
Ophthalmology	0.167	0.104	0.139	0.150
Total	1.000	1.000	1.000	1.000

(b) Yes. The conditional distributions of specialty within the base-of-practice categories (columns 2, 3, and 4 of the table in part a) are not identical.

(c) The marginal distribution of specialty is given in the last column of the table in part (a).

(d)

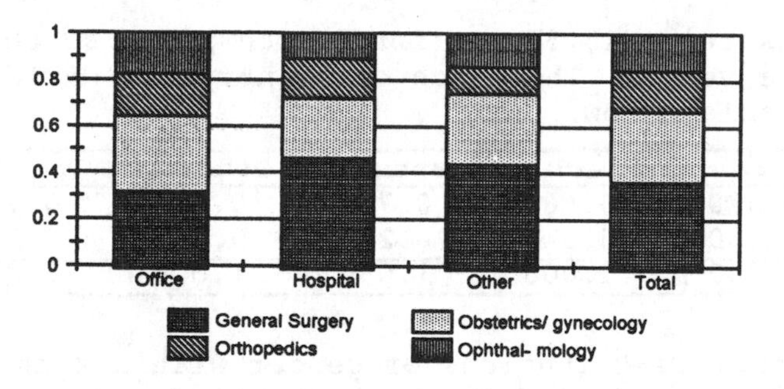

If the conditional distributions of specialty within the base-of-practice categories (first three bars) had been identical, each of the bars would have been segmented identically and would be identical to the fourth bar representing the marginal distribution of specialty. The fact that they are not segmented identically means that there is an association between specialty and base of practice.

(e) False. Since specialty and base of practice are associated, the conditional distributions of base-of-practice within specialty will be different.

(f) We interchanged the rows and columns of the table in Exercise 13.41 and then divided each cell entry by its associated column total to obtain the following table.

	General Surgery	Obstetrics/ gynecology	Orthopedics	Ophthal- mology	Total
Office	0.635	0.754	0.741	0.793	0.714
Hospital	0.322	0.210	0.236	0.173	0.250
Other	0.044	0.036	0.023	0.033	0.036
Total	1.000	1.000	1.000	1.000	1.000

The conditional distributions of base-of-practice within specialty are given in columns 2, 3, 4, and 5. The marginal distribution of base-of-practice is given by the last column.

(g) From the table in part (f), 25.0% of the surgeons are hospital based.

(h) From the table in part (f), 21.0% of the OB/GYNs are hospital based.

(i) From the table in part (a), 26.0% of the hospital-based surgeons are OB/GYNs.

13.45 (a) No. Every conditional distribution of y within x is identical.

(b) The marginal distribution of y is the same as each of the conditional distributions of y within x. That is,

y	Frequency
0	0.316
1	0.422
2	0.211
3	0.047
4	0.004
Total	1.000

(c) No. To determine the marginal distribution of x, the actual cell counts are needed. These could be determined from the cell percentages and the A, B, and C column total counts if those counts were known. Since the total counts for the three columns are not known, there is no way to obtain the marginal distribution of x.

13.47 (a) Part (a) of Exercise 13.32

With the data from Table 13.11 in three columns of Minitab named SEX, CLASS, and COLLEGE, choose **Stat ▶ Tables ▶ Cross tabulation...**, specify SEX and CLASS in the **Classification variables** text box, select the **Counts** check box in the **Display** list, and click **OK**. The resulting printout is

```
Rows: SEX     Columns: CLASS

      Junior   Senior     Soph      All
 F         5        3        2       10
 M         8        1        6       15
 All      13        4        8       25
  Cell Contents --
                    Count
```

Part (b) of Exercise 13.32

To determine the conditional distribution of SEX within CLASS and the marginal distribution of SEX, we proceed as in part (a) except that we select the **Column Percents** check box instead of the **Counts** check box (and unselect the **Counts** check box). The results are shown in the following table.

```
Rows: SEX     Columns: CLASS
      Junior   Senior     Soph      All
 F     38.46    75.00    25.00    40.00
 M     61.54    25.00    75.00    60.00
 All  100.00   100.00   100.00   100.00
  Cell Contents --
                    % of Col
```

Part (c) of Exercise 13.32

To determine the conditional distribution of CLASS within SEX and the marginal distribution of CLASS, we proceed as in part (b) except that we select the **Row Percents** check box instead of the **Column Percents** check box (and unselect the **Column Percents** check box). The results are shown in the following table.

Rows: SEX Columns: CLASS

	Junior	Senior	Soph	All
F	50.00	30.00	20.00	100.00
M	53.33	6.67	40.00	100.00
All	52.00	16.00	32.00	100.00

Cell Contents --

% of Row

(b) Part (a) of Exercise 13.33

With the data from Table 13.11 in three columns of Minitab named SEX, CLASS, and COLLEGE, choose **Stat ▶ Tables ▶ Cross tabulation...,** specify SEX and COLLEGE in the **Classification variables** text box, select the **Counts** check box in the **Display** list, and click **OK.** The resulting printout is

Rows: SEX Columns: COLLEGE

	BUS	ENG	LIB	All
F	7	2	1	10
M	2	10	3	15
All	9	12	4	25

Cell Contents --

Count

Part (b) of Exercise 13.33

To determine the conditional distribution of SEX within COLLEGE and the marginal distribution of SEX, we proceed as in part (a) except that we select the **Column Percents** check box instead of the **Counts** check box (and unselect the **Counts** check box). The results are shown in the following table.

	BUS	ENG	LIB	All
F	77.78	16.67	25.00	40.00
M	22.22	83.33	75.00	60.00
All	100.00	100.00	100.00	100.00

Cell Contents --

% of Col

Part (c) of Exercise 13.33

To determine the conditional distribution of COLLEGE within SEX and the marginal distribution of COLLEGE, we proceed as in part (b) except that we select the **Row Percents** check box instead of the **Column Percents** check box (and unselect the **Column Percents** check box). The results are shown in the following table.

	BUS	ENG	LIB	All
F	70.00	20.00	10.00	100.00
M	13.33	66.67	20.00	100.00
All	36.00	48.00	16.00	100.00

Cell Contents --

% of Row

Part (a) of Exercise 13.34

With the data from Table 13.11 in three columns of Minitab named SEX, CLASS, and COLLEGE, click anywhere in the CLASS column, then choose **Editor ▶ Set Column ▶ Value Order...**, select the **User-specified order** option button; in the **Define an order (one value per line)** text box, edit the order of the possible classes so that it reads Soph, Junior, Senior, and click **OK**. Now choose **Stat ▶ Tables ▶ Cross tabulation...**, specify CLASS and COLLEGE in the **Classification variables** text box, select the **Counts** check box in the **Display** list, and click **OK**. The resulting printout is

	BUS	ENG	LIB	All
Soph	3	4	1	8
Junior	4	7	2	13
Senior	2	1	1	4
All	9	12	4	25

Cell Contents --

Count

Part (b) of Exercise 13.34

To determine the conditional distribution of CLASS within COLLEGE and the marginal distribution of CLASS, we proceed as in part (a) except that we select the **Column Percents** check box instead of the **Counts** check box (and unselect the **Counts** check box). The results are shown in the following table.

	BUS	ENG	LIB	All
Soph	33.33	33.33	25.00	32.00
Junior	44.44	58.33	50.00	52.00
Senior	22.22	8.33	25.00	16.00
All	100.00	100.00	100.00	100.00

Cell Contents --

% of Col

Part (c) of Exercise 13.34

To determine the conditional distribution of COLLEGE within CLASS and the marginal distribution of COLLEGE, we proceed as in part (b) except that we select the **Row Percents** check box instead of the **Column Percents** check box (and unselect the **Column Percents** check box). The results are shown in the following table.

	BUS	ENG	LIB	All
Soph	37.50	50.00	12.50	100.00
Junior	30.77	53.85	15.38	100.00
Senior	50.00	25.00	25.00	100.00
All	36.00	48.00	16.00	100.00

Cell Contents -

% of Row

Exercises 13.4

13.49 In most cases, data for an entire population are not available. Thus we must apply inferential methods to decide whether an association exists between two variables.

13.51 In Section 13.3, we learned that if there is no association between two variables, all of the conditional distributions for the first variable within the values of the other variable will be identical, and those conditional distributions will be the same as the marginal distribution of the first variable. The same statement is true if the order of the variables in the above statement is reversed.

13.53 The degrees of freedom equal $(r - 1)(c - 1) = (6 - 1)(4 - 1) = 15$.

13.55 If the variables did have a causal relationship, then they would be associated. If two variables are not associated, then they cannot possibly be causally related.

13.57 Step 1: H_0: Siskel's ratings and Ebert's ratings of movies are not associated.

H_a: Siskel's ratings and Ebert's ratings of movies are associated.

Step 2: Calculate the expected frequencies using the formula

E=RC/n where R = row total, C = column total, and n = sample size. The results are shown in the following table.

Ebert's rating

		Thumbs down	Mixed	Thumbs up	Total
Siskel's rating	Thumbs down	11.8	8.4	24.8	**45.0**
	Mixed	8.4	6.0	17.6	**32.0**
	Thumbs up	21.8	15.6	45.6	**83.0**
	Total	**42.0**	**30.0**	**88.0**	**160.0**

Step 3: All of the expected frequencies are greater than 5, so the assumptions for the chi-square test are met.

Step 4: $\alpha = 0.01$

Step 5: Compute the value of the test statistic $\chi^2 = \sum \frac{(O-E)^2}{E}$,

Where O and E represent the observed and expected frequencies respectively. We show the contributions to this sum from each of the cells of the contingency table in the table below.

	Thumbs down	Mixed	Thumbs up
Thumbs down	12.574	0.023	5.578
Mixed	0.019	8.167	2.475
Thumbs up	6.377	2.767	7.376

The total of the 9 table entries above is the value of the chi-square statistic, that is $\chi^2 = 45.357$. Depending on rounding, your answer could differ slightly.

Step 6: The degrees of freedom are (3 - 1)((3 - 1) = 4, so the critical value from Table VII is $\chi^2_{0.01} = 13.277$.

Step 7: Since 45.357 > 13.277, we reject the null hypothesis.

Step 8: We conclude that there is an association between Siskel's ratings and Ebert's ratings of movies.

13.59 The expected frequencies are shown below the observed frequencies in the following contingency table.

Political Affiliation	Good Idea	Poor Idea	No Opinion	Total
Republican	266 282.9	266 255.2	186 180.0	718
Democrat	308 289.2	250 260.8	176 184.0	734
Independent	28 29.9	27 27.0	21 19.0	76
Total	602	543	383	1528

The table below gives the contributions from each cell to the χ-square statistic.

Row, Column	O	E	$(O - E)^2/E$
1,1	266	282.9	1.010
1,2	266	255.2	0.457
1,3	186	180.0	0.200
2,1	308	289.2	1.222
2,2	250	260.8	0.447
2,3	176	184.0	0.348
3,1	28	29.9	0.121
3,2	27	27.0	0.000
3,3	21	19.0	0.211
	1528		4.016

Step 1: H_0: The feelings of adults on the issue of regional primaries are independent of political affiliation.

H_a: The feelings of adults on the issue of regional primaries are dependent on political affiliation.

Step 2: Observed and expected frequencies are presented in the frequency contingency table. Each expected frequency is placed below its corresponding observed frequency. Expected frequencies are calculated using the formula $E = (R \cdot C)/n$.

The same information about the Os and Es is presented in the table below the contingency table. Column 4 of this table is useful for Step 6.

Step 3: Assumptions 1 and 2 are satisfied since all expected frequencies are at least 5.

Step 4: $\alpha = 0.05$

Step 5: $\chi^2 = 4.016$ (See column 4 of the table below the contingency table.)

Step 6: Critical value = 9.488

Step 7: Since $4.016 < 9.488$, do not reject H_0.

Step 8: The data do not provide sufficient evidence to conclude that the feelings of adults on the issue of regional primaries are dependent on political affiliation.

For the P-value approach, $P(\chi^2 > 4.016) > 0.10$. Since the P-value is larger than the significance level, do not reject H_0.

13.61

Size of City

Status in Practice	Less than 250,000	250,000-499,999	500,000 or more	Total
Government	12 15.7	4 4.2	14 10.1	30
Judicial	8 5.8	1 1.5	2 3.7	11
Private Practice	122 116.4	31 31.1	69 74.5	222
Salaried	19 23.1	7 6.2	18 14.8	44
Total	161	43	103	307

Step 1: H_0: Size of city and status in practice for lawyers are independent.

H_a: Size of city and status in practice for lawyers are dependent.

Step 2: Observed and expected frequencies are presented in the frequency contingency table. Each expected frequency is placed below its corresponding observed frequency. Expected frequencies are calculated using the formula $E = (R \cdot C)/n$.

Step 3: Assumption 2 is violated since 25% (3/12) of the expected frequencies are less than 5. Thus, we do not proceed with the test.

13.63 Using Minitab, with the data in columns named 'THUMBS DOWN', 'MIXED', and

'THUMBS UP', choose **Stat ▶ Tables ▶ Chisquare test...**, select 'THUMBS DOWN', 'MIXED', and 'THUMBS UP' as the variables in the **Columns containing the table** text box, and click **OK**. The result is

Expected counts are printed below observed counts

	THUMBS D	MIXED	THUMBS U	Total
1	24	8	13	45
	11.81	8.44	24.75	
2	8	13	11	32
	8.40	6.00	17.60	
3	10	9	64	83
	21.79	15.56	45.65	
Total	42	30	88	160

```
Chi-Sq = 12.574 +  0.023 +  5.578 +
          0.019 +  8.167 +  2.475 +
          6.377 +  2.767 +  7.376 = 45.357
DF = 4, P-Value = 0.000
```

13.65 All of the data for this exercise are found on the *WeissStats* CD in one worksheet for Minitab. To work each part, we will copy the pertinent rows of data and paste them to new columns to do the analysis. This can be done by highlighting the appropriate cells with your mouse and using the **Edit-Copy** and **Edit-Paste** from the pull down menu. You will want to name the new columns 'ON JOB', 'OFF JOB', and DONTKNOW (leave out the space between 'DONT' and 'KNOW' so that the heading will be different from the original name in column C4.

(a) Copy the data from rows 1 and 2, columns C2, C3, and C4 to the new columns named ON JOB, OFF JOB, and DONTKNOW, choose **Stat ▶ Tables ▶ Chisquare test...**, select 'ON JOB', 'OFF JOB', and DONTKNOW as the variables in the **Columns containing the table** text box, and click **OK**. The result is

Expected counts are printed below observed counts

	ON JOB	OFF JOB	DONTKNOW	Total
1	77	263	28	368
	82.49	256.05	29.46	
2	77	215	27	319
	71.51	221.95	25.54	
Total	154	478	55	687

```
Chi-Sq =  0.366 +  0.189 +  0.072 +
          0.422 +  0.218 +  0.084 = 1.350
DF = 2, P-Value = 0.509
```

Since the p-value is greater than 0.05, we do not reject the null hypothesis. There is not sufficient evidence to conclude that there is an association between sex and response to the question "Which do you enjoy more, the hours when you are on your job, or the hours when you are not on your job?"

(b) Copy the data from rows 3-6, columns C2, C3, and C4 to the new columns named ON JOB, OFF JOB, and DONTKNOW, choose **Stat ▶ Tables ▶ Chisquare test...**, select 'ON JOB', 'OFF JOB', and DONTKNOW as the variables in the **Columns containing the table** text box, and click **OK**. The result is

```
Expected counts are printed below observed counts

         ON JOB  OFF JOB DONTKNOW    Total
    1        33      136        5      174
          39.12   121.16    13.72

    2        77      274       25      376
          84.53   261.83    29.64

    3        35       56       19      110
          24.73    76.60     8.67

    4         9       11        5       25
           5.62    17.41     1.97


Total       154      477       54      685

Chi-Sq =  0.957 +  1.816 +  5.539 +
          0.671 +  0.566 +  0.727 +
          4.265 +  5.539 + 12.302 +
          2.032 +  2.359 +  4.656 = 41.430
DF = 6, P-Value = 0.000
1 cell with expected count less than 5.0
```

The assumptions for the test are satisfied since no expected counts are less than 1 and only 1 out of twelve is less than five (8%). Since the p-value is less than 0.05, we reject the null hypothesis. There is sufficient evidence to conclude that there is an association between age and response to the question "Which do you enjoy more, the hours when you are on your job, or the hours when you are not on your job?"

(c) Copy the data from rows 7-9, columns C2, C3, and C4 to the new columns named ON JOB, OFF JOB, and DONTKNOW, choose **Stat ▶ Tables ▶ Chisquare test...**, select 'ON JOB', 'OFF JOB', and DONTKNOW as the variables in the **Columns containing the table** text box, and click **OK**. The result is

```
Expected counts are printed below observed counts

        ON JOB  OFF JOB DONTKNOW     Total
    1       62      197       14       273
         60.44   190.94    21.62

    2       47      171       25       243
         53.80   169.96    19.24

    3       42      109       15       166
         36.75   116.10    13.14


Total      151      477       54       682


Chi-Sq =  0.040 +  0.192 +  2.683 +
          0.860 +  0.006 +  1.724 +
          0.749 +  0.435 +  0.262 = 6.952
DF = 4, P-Value = 0.138
```

Since the p-value is greater than 0.05, we do not reject the null hypothesis. There is not sufficient evidence to conclude that there is an association between type of community and response to the question "Which do you enjoy more, the hours when you are on your job, or the hours when you are not on your job?"

(d) Copy the data from rows 10-13, columns C2, C3, and C4 to the new columns named ON JOB, OFF JOB, and DONTKNOW, choose **Stat ▶ Tables ▶ Chisquare test...**, select 'ON JOB', 'OFF JOB', and DONTKNOW as the variables in the **Columns containing the table** text box, and click **OK**. The result is

```
Expected counts are printed below observed counts

        ON JOB  OFF JOB DONTKNOW     Total
    1       23       51       10        84
         18.69    58.66     6.64
    2       41      126       18       185
         41.17   129.20    14.63
    3       20      108        5       133
         29.60    92.89    10.52
    4       68      192       21       281
         62.54   196.25    22.22


Total      152      477       54       683


Chi-Sq =  0.992 +  1.001 +  1.699 +
          0.001 +  0.079 +  0.778 +
          3.113 +  2.459 +  2.893 +
          0.477 +  0.092 +  0.067 = 13.651
DF = 6, P-Value = 0.034
```

Since the p-value is less than 0.05, we reject the null hypothesis. There is sufficient evidence to conclude that there is an association between amount of education and response to the question "Which do you enjoy more, the hours when you are on your job, or the hours when you are not on your job?"

(e) Copy the data from rows 14-17, columns C2, C3, and C4 to the new columns named ON JOB, OFF JOB, and DONTKNOW, choose **Stat ▶ Tables ▶ Chisquare test...**, select 'ON JOB', 'OFF JOB', and DONTKNOW as the variables in the **Columns containing the table** text box, and click **OK**. The result is

```
Expected counts are printed below observed counts

        ON JOB  OFF JOB DONTKNOW    Total
    1       40       80       11      131
         29.18    92.30     9.53

    2       32      116        7      155
         34.52   109.20    11.27

    3       41      131        8      180
         40.09   126.82    13.09

    4       34      138       22      194
         43.21   136.68    14.11


Total      147      465       48      660


Chi-Sq =  4.014 +  1.638 +  0.228 +
          0.184 +  0.423 +  1.620 +
          0.021 +  0.138 +  1.980 +
          1.963 +  0.013 +  4.413 = 16.634
DF = 6, P-Value = 0.011
```

Since the p-value is less than 0.05, we reject the null hypothesis. There is sufficient evidence to conclude that there is an association between income and response to the question "Which do you enjoy more, the hours when you are on your job, or the hours when you are not on your job?"

(f) Copy the data from rows 18-20, columns C2, C3, and C4 to the new columns named ON JOB, OFF JOB, and DONTKNOW, choose **Stat ▶ Tables ▶ Chisquare test...**, select 'ON JOB', 'OFF JOB', and DONTKNOW as the variables in the **Columns containing the table** text box, and click **OK**. The result is

```
Expected counts are printed below observed counts

        ON JOB  OFF JOB DONTKNOW    Total
    1       67      326       27      420
         93.26   294.62    32.12
    2       23       82       11      116
         25.76    81.37     8.87
    3       61       69       14      144
         31.98   101.01    11.01

Total      151      477       52      680
```

```
Chi-Sq =  7.397 +  3.343 +  0.815 +
          0.295 +  0.005 +  0.511 +
         26.343 + 10.145 +  0.811 = 49.665
DF = 4, P-Value = 0.000
```

Since the p-value is less than 0.05, we reject the null hypothesis. There is sufficient evidence to conclude that there is an association between type of employer and response to the question "Which do you enjoy more, the hours when you are on your job, or the hours when you are not on your job?"

REVIEW TEST FOR CHAPTER 13

1. The distributions and curves are distinguished by their degrees of freedom.

2. (a) zero (b) right skewed (c) normal curve

3. (a) No. The degrees of freedom for the chi-square goodness-of-fit test depends on the number of categories, not the number of observations.

(b) No. The degrees of freedom for the chi-square independence test is (r-1)(c-1) where r and c are the number of rows and columns, respectively, in the contingency table.

4. Values of the test statistic near zero arise when the observed and expected frequencies are in close agreement. It is only when these frequencies differ enough to produce large values of the test statistic that the null hypothesis is rejected. These values are in the right tail of the chi-square distribution.

5. The value would be zero since O - E = 0 for each cell.

6. (a) All expected frequencies are 1 or greater, and at most 20% of the expected frequencies are less than 5.

(b) Very important. If either of these assumptions are not met, the test should not be carried out by these procedures.

7. (a) 5.3%

(b) 5.3% of 58.5 million, or 3.1 million

(c) Since the observed number of American living in the West who use public transportation is not equal to the number expected if there were no association between means of transportation and area of residence, we conclude that there *is* an association between means of transportation and area of residence.

8. (a) Compare the conditional distributions of one of the variables within categories of the other variable. If all of the conditional distributions are identical, there is no association between the variables; if not, there is an association.

(b) No. Since the data are for an entire population, we are not making an inference from a sample to the population. The association (or non-association) is a fact.

9. (a) Perform a chi-square test of independence. If the null hypothesis (of non-association) is rejected, we conclude that there is an association between the variables.

(b) Yes. It is possible (with probability α) that we could reject the null hypothesis when it is, in fact, true. It is also possible, that, even though there is actually an association between the variables, the evidence is not strong enough to draw that conclusion. Either of these types of errors are due to randomness in selecting a sample which does not exactly reflect the characteristics of the population.

10. For df = 17:

(a) $\chi^2_{0.99} = 6.408$ (b) $\chi^2_{0.01} = 33.409$ (c) $\chi^2_{0.05} = 27.587$

(d) $\chi^2_{0.95} = 8.672$ (e) $\chi^2_{0.975} = 7.564$ and $\chi^2_{0.025} = 30.191$

11.

Highest level	O	p	E = np	$(O-E)^2/E$
Not HS graduate	86	0.248	124.0	11.6452
HS graduate	169	0.300	150.0	2.4067
Some college	86	0.187	93.5	0.6016
Associate's degree	37	0.062	31.0	1.1613
Bachelor's degree	82	0.131	65.5	4.1565
Advanced degree	40	0.072	36.0	0.4444
Total	500		500.0	20.4157

Step 1: H_0: The educational attainment distribution for adults 25 years old and over this year is the same as in 1990.

H_a: The educational attainment distribution for adults 25 years old and over this year differs from that of 1990.

Step 2: Expected frequencies are presented in column 4 of the table.

Step 3: Assumptions 1 and 2 are satisfied since all of the expected frequencies are at least 5.

Step 4: $\alpha = 0.05$

Step 5: $\chi^2 = 20.4157$ (See column 5 of the table.)

Step 6: Critical value = 11.070

Step 7: Since 20.4157 > 11.070, reject H_0.

Step 8: It appears that the educational attainment distribution for adults 25 years old and over this year differs from that of 1990.

(b) For the P-value approach, $P(\chi^2 > 20.4157) < 0.005$. Since the P-value is smaller than the significance level, reject H_0. The evidence against the null hypothesis is very strong.

12. (a)

	DEM	REP	IND	TOTAL
MW	3	8	1	12
NE	2	6	1	9
SO	7	9	0	16
WE	5	8	0	13
TOTAL	17	31	2	50

(b)

	DEM	REP	IND	TOTAL
MW	0.176	0.258	0.500	0.240
NE	0.118	0.194	0.500	0.180
SO	0.412	0.290	0.000	0.320
WE	0.294	0.258	0.000	0.260
TOTAL	1.000	1.000	1.000	1.000

The conditional distributions of region within party are given in columns 2,

3, and 4 of the above table. The marginal distribution of region is given in the last column of the table.

(c)

	MW	NE	SO	WE	TOTAL
DEM	0.250	0.222	0.438	0.385	0.340
REP	0.667	0.667	0.562	0.615	0.620
IND	0.083	0.111	0.000	0.000	0.040
TOTAL	1.000	1.000	1.000	1.000	1.000

The conditional distributions of party within region are given in columns 2, 3, 4, and 5 of the above table. The marginal distribution of party is given in the last column of the table.

(d) There is an association between region and party of governor for the states of the U.S. since the conditional distributions of party within the several regions are not identical.

(e) From the table in part (c), 62.0% of the states have Republican governors.

(f) If there were no association between region and party of governor, 62% of the Midwest states would have Republican governors.

(g) From the table in part (c), 66.7% of the Midwest states have Republican governors.

(h) From the table in part (b), 24.0% of the states are in the Midwest.

(i) If there were no association between region and party of governor, the percentage of states with Republican governors that would be in the Midwest would be the same as the percentage of states that are in the Midwest, i.e. 24.0%.

(j) In reality, from the table in part (b), 25.8% of the states with Republican governors are in the Midwest.

13. (a) 2046 (b) 737 (c) 266 (d) 3046 (e) 6580 - 1167 = 5413

(f) 5403 + 1167 - 660 = 5910

14. (a)

	General	Psychiatric	Chronic	Tuberculosis	Other	Total
GOV	0.314	0.361	0.808	0.750	0.144	0.311
PROP	0.122	0.486	0.038	0.000	0.361	0.177
NP	0.564	0.153	0.154	0.250	0.495	0.512
Total	1.000	1.000	1.000	1.000	1.000	1.000

The conditional distributions of control type with facility type are given in columns 2, 3, 4, 5, and 6 of the table.

(b) Yes. The conditional distributions of control type within facility type are not all identical.

(c) The marginal distribution of control type is given by the last column of the table above.

(d)

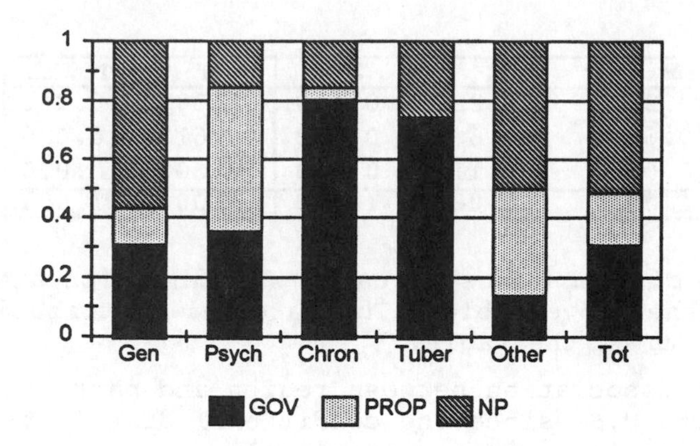

The conditional distributions of control type within facility type are shown by the first five bars of the graph. The marginal distribution of control type is given by the last bar. Since the bars are not identically shaded, control type and facility type are associated variables.

(e) False. Since we have established that facility type and control type are associated, the conditional distributions of facility type within control types will not be identical.

(f) After interchanging the rows and columns of the table given in Problem 13, we divided each cell entry by its associated column total to obtain the table below.

	GOV	PROP	NP	Total
General	0.829	0.566	0.905	0.821
Psychiatric	0.130	0.307	0.034	0.112
Chronic	0.010	0.001	0.001	0.004
Tuberculosis	0.001	0.000	0.000	0.001
Other	0.029	0.127	0.060	0.062
Total	1.000	1.000	1.000	1.000

The conditional distributions of facility type within control type are given in columns 2, 3, and 4 of the table. The marginal distribution of facility type is given by the last column of the table.

(g) From the table in part (a), 17.7% of the hospitals are under proprietary control.

(h) From the table in part (a), 48.6% of the psychiatric hospitals are under proprietary control.

(i) From the table in part (f), 30.7% of the hospitals under proprietary control are psychiatric hospitals.

15.

	Positive	Partial	None	Total
Lymphocyte depletion	18	10	44	72
Lymphocyte dominance	74	18	12	104
Mixed cellularity	154	54	58	266
Nodular sclerosis	68	16	12	96
Total	314	98	126	538

Row, Column	O	E	$(O - E)^2/E$
1,1	18	42.02	13.732
1,2	10	13.12	0.740
1,3	44	16.86	43.674
2,1	74	60.70	2.915
2,2	18	18.94	0.047
2,3	12	24.36	6.269
3,1	154	15.25	0.010
3,2	54	48.45	0.635
3,3	58	62.30	0.296
4,1	68	56.03	2.557
4,2	16	17.49	0.126
4,3	12	22.48	4.888
	538	538.00	75.889

Step 1: H_0: Treatment response and histological type are statistically independent.

H_a: Treatment response and histological type are statistically dependent.

Step 2: Observed frequencies are presented in the frequency contingency table. Expected frequencies are calculated using the formula $E = (R \cdot C)/n$ and are included in the third column of the second table. Column 4 of this table is useful for Step 6.

Step 3: Assumptions 1 and 2 are satisfied since all expected frequencies are at least 5.

Step 4: $\alpha = 0.01$

Step 5: $\chi^2 = 75.889$ (See column 4 of the table below the contingency table.)

Note: Answers may vary slightly due to rounding.

Step 6: Critical value = 16.812

Step 7: Since 75.889 > 16.812, reject H_0.

Step 8: The data provide sufficient evidence to conclude that treatment response and histological type are associated.

For the P-value approach, $P(\chi^2 > 75.889) < 0.005$. Since the P-value is smaller than the significance level, reject H_0.

16. Using Minitab, click in the Session window, choose **Editor ▶ Enable Command Language** if it is not already enabled, and type in the Session window after the MTB> prompt, a percent sign (%) followed by the path for *fittest.mac*. If the *WeissStats* CD is in drive d, we type %d:\IS6\Minitab\macro\fittest.mac and press the ENTER key. Then proceed as follows: type 6 and press the ENTER key in response to Enter the number of possible values for the variable under consideration; type 0.248 0.300 0.187 0.062 0.131 0.072 and press the ENTER

key in response to Enter the relative frequencies (or probabilities) for the null hypothesis; and type 86 169 86 37 82 40 and press the ENTER key in response to Enter the observed frequencies. The resulting output is

Chi-square goodness-of-fit test

Row	n	k	ChiSq	P-value
1	500	6	20.4157	0.0010440

17. (a) With the data from Problem 12 in three columns of Minitab named STATE, REGION, and PARTY, choose **Stat ▶ Tables ▶ Cross tabulation...**, specify REGION and PARTY in the **Classification variables** text box, select the **Counts** check box in the **Display** list, and click **OK**. The resulting printout is

Rows: REGION   Columns: PARTY

	Dem	Ind	Rep	All
MW	3	1	8	12
NE	2	1	6	9
SO	7	0	9	16
WE	5	0	8	13
All	**17**	**2**	**31**	**50**

Cell Contents -

Count

(b) To determine the conditional distribution of REGION within PARTY and the marginal distribution of REGION, we proceed as in part (a) except that we select the **Column Percents** check box instead of the **Counts** check box (and unselect the **Counts** check box). The results are shown in the following table.

	Dem	Ind	Rep	All
MW	17.65	50.00	25.81	24.00
NE	11.76	50.00	19.35	18.00
SO	41.18	--	29.03	32.00
WE	29.41	--	25.81	26.00
All	100.00	100.00	100.00	100.00

Cell Contents --

% of Col

(c) To determine the conditional distribution of PARTY within REGION and the marginal distribution of PARTY, we proceed as in part (b) except that we select the **Row Percents** check box instead of the **Column Percents** check box (and unselect the **Column Percents** check box). The results are shown in the following table.

	Dem	Ind	Rep	All
MW	25.00	8.33	66.67	100.00
NE	22.22	11.11	66.67	100.00
SO	43.75	--	56.25	100.00
WE	38.46	--	61.54	100.00
All	34.00	4.00	62.00	100.00

18. With the data in columns named POSITIVE, PARTIAL, and NONE, choose **Stat ▶ Tables ▶ Chisquare test...**, select POSITIVE, PARTIAL, and NONE as the variables in the **Columns containing the table** text box, and click **OK.** The result is

```
Expected counts are printed below observed counts

        POSITIVE  PARTIAL      NONE    Total
    1         18       10        44       72
           42.02    13.12     16.86

    2         74       18        12      104
           60.70    18.94     24.36

    3        154       54        58      266
          155.25    48.45     62.30

    4         68       16        12       96
           56.03    17.49     22.48

Total        314       98       126      538

Chi-Sq = 13.732 +  0.740 + 43.674 +
          2.915 +  0.047 +  6.269 +
          0.010 +  0.635 +  0.296 +
          2.557 +  0.126 +  4.888 = 75.890
DF = 6, P-Value = 0.000
```

CHAPTER 14 ANSWERS

Exercises 14.1

14.1 (a) $y = b_0 + b_1x$ (b) Constants are b_0, b_1; variables are x, y.

(c) The independent variable is x, and the dependent variable is y.

14.3 (a) b_0 is the y-intercept; it is the value of y where the line crosses the y-axis.

(b) b_1 is the slope; it indicates the change in the value of y for every 1 unit increase in the value of x.

14.5 (a) $y = 120.00 + 0.25x$ (b) $b_0 = 120.00$, $b_1 = 0.25$

(c) (d)

Miles x	Cost ($) y
50	120.00 + 0.25(50) = 132.50
100	120.00 + 0.25(100)= 145.00
250	120.00 + 0.25(250)= 182.50

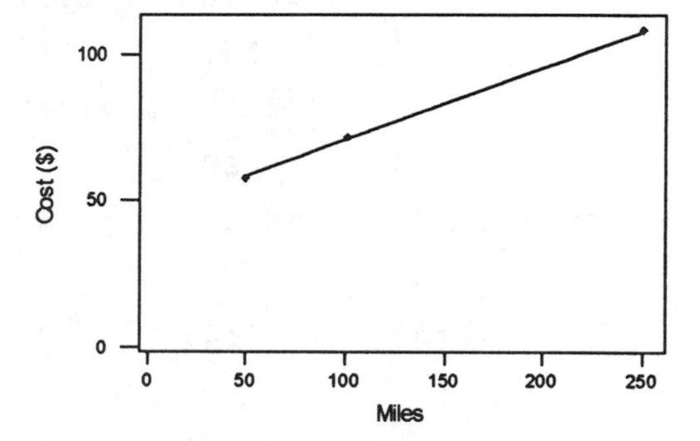

(e) Using the graph, the estimate of the cost of driving the car 150 miles is about $157. The exact cost is

$y = 120.00 + 0.25(150) = 157.50.$

14.7 (a) $b_0 = 32$, $b_1 = 1.8$

(b) (c)

x(°C)	y(°F)
-40	32 + 1.8(-40) = -40
0	32 + 1.8(0) = 32
20	32 + 1.8(20) = 68
100	32 + 1.8(100) = 212

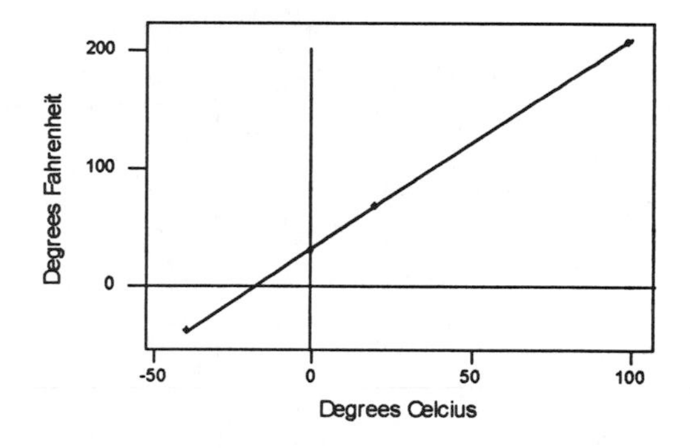

(d) Using the graph, the estimate of the Fahrenheit temperature corresponding to a Celsius temperature of 28° is about 80°F. The exact temperature is $y = 32 + 1.8(28) = 82.4$°F.

14.9 (a) $b_0 = 120.00$, $b_1 = 0.25$

(b) The y-intercept $b_0 = 120.00$ gives the y-value at which the straight line $y = 120.00 + 0.25x$ intersects the y-axis. The slope $b_1 = 0.25$ indicates that the y-value increases by 0.25 units for every increase in x of one unit.

(c) The y-intercept $b_0 = 120.00$ is the cost (in dollars) for driving the car zero miles. The slope $b_1 = 0.25$ represents the fact that the cost per mile is \$0.25; it is the amount the total cost increases for each additional mile driven.

14.11 (a) $b_0 = 32$, $b_1 = 1.8$

(b) The y-intercept $b_0 = 32$ gives the y-value at which the straight line $y = 32 + 1.8x$ intersects the y-axis. The slope $b_1 = 1.8$ indicates that the y-value increases by 1.8 units for every increase in x of one unit.

(c) The y-intercept $b_0 = 32$ is the Fahrenheit temperature corresponding to 0°C. The slope $b_1 = 1.8$ represents the fact that Fahrenheit temperature increases by 1.8° for every increase of the Celsius temperature of 1°.

14.13 (a) $b_0 = 3$, $b_1 = 4$

(b) slopes upward

(c)

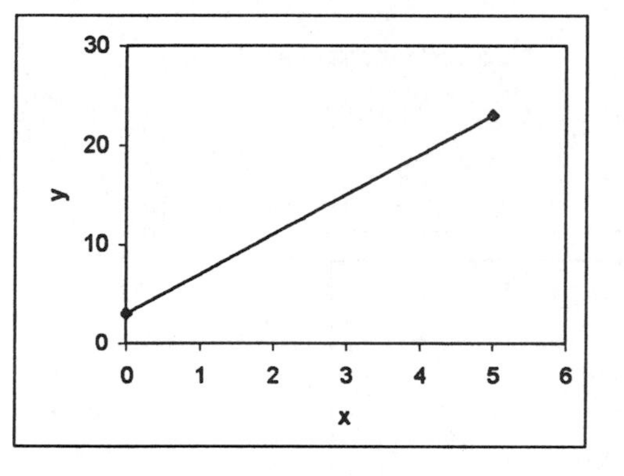

14.15 (a) $b_0 = 6$, $b_1 = -7$

(b) slopes downward

(c)

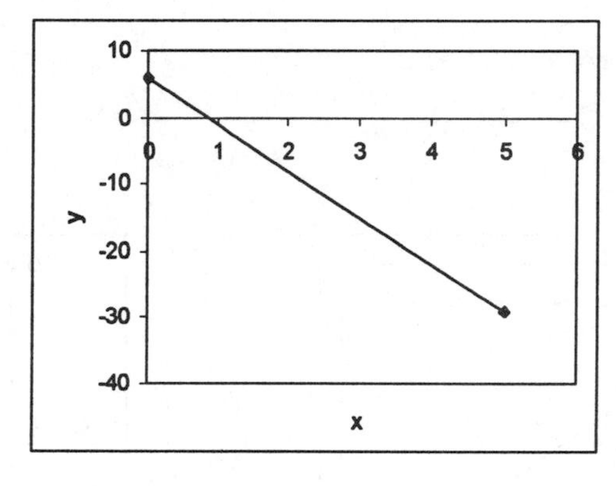

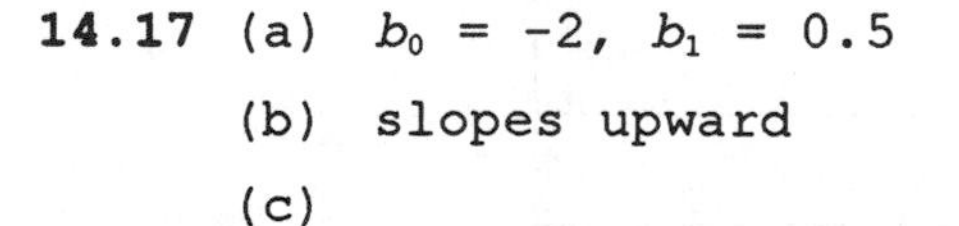

14.17 (a) $b_0 = -2$, $b_1 = 0.5$

(b) slopes upward

(c)

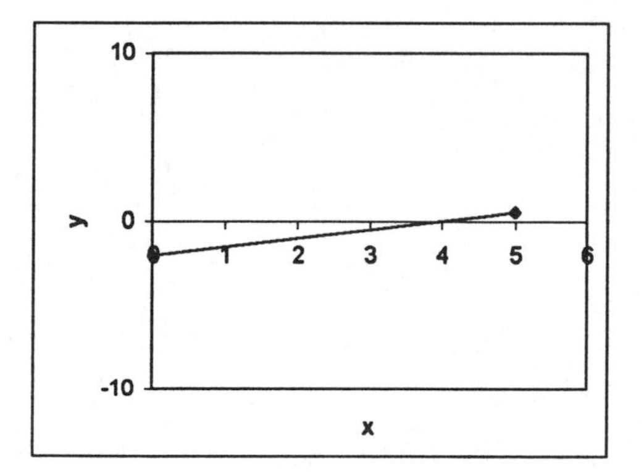

14.19 (a) $b_0 = 2$, $b_1 = 0$

(b) horizontal

(c)

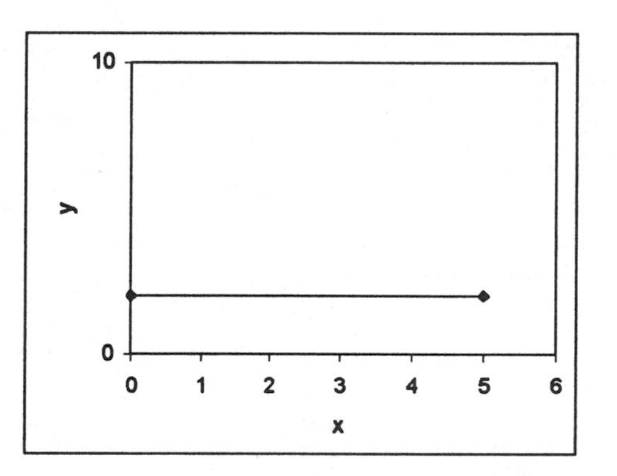

14.21 (a) $b_0 = 0$, $b_1 = 1.5$

(b) slopes upward

(c)

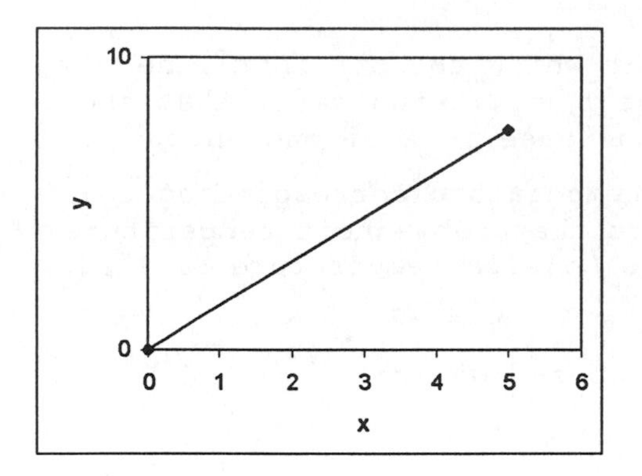

14.23 (a) slopes upward

(b) $y = 5 + 2x$

(c)

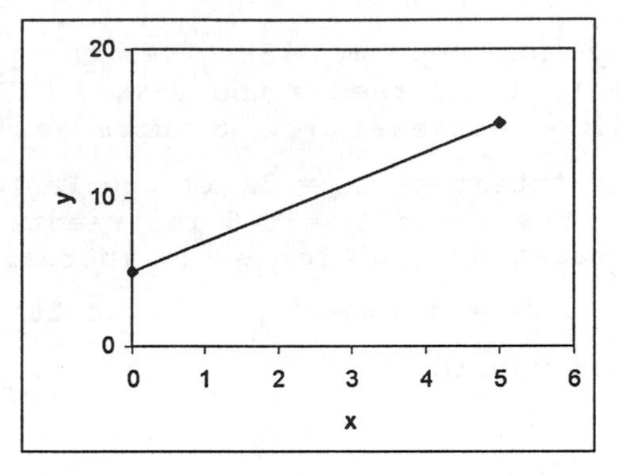

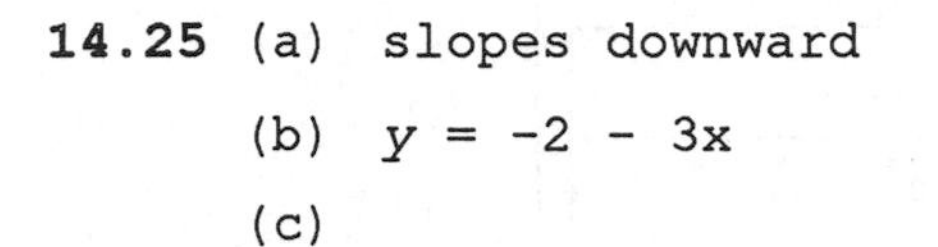

14.25 (a) slopes downward

(b) $y = -2 - 3x$

(c)

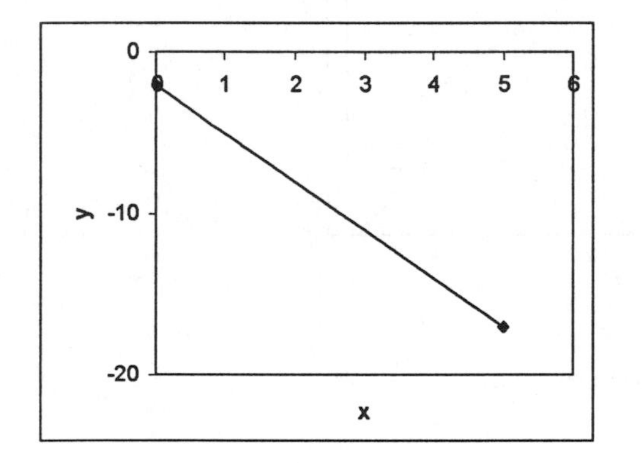

14.27 (a) slopes downward

(b) $y = -0.5x$

(c)

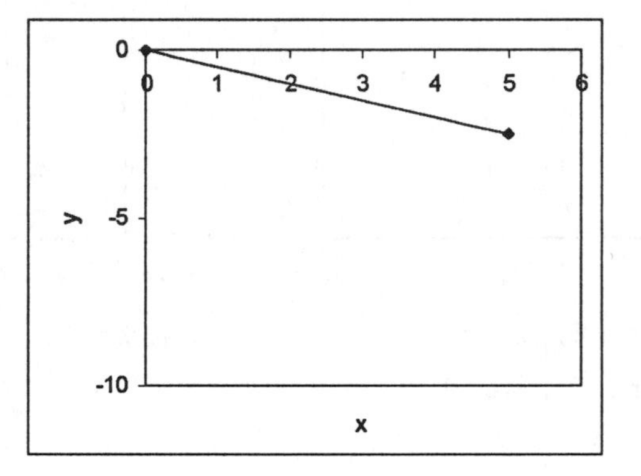

14.29 (a) horizontal

(b) $y = 3$

(c)

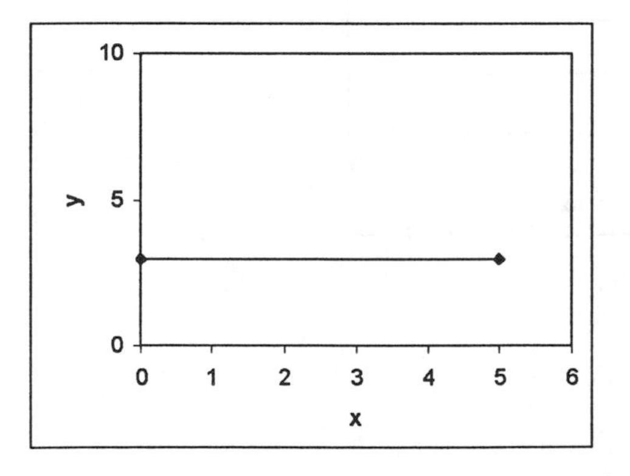

14.31 (a) If we can express a straight line in the form $y = b_0 + b_1x$, then there will be one and only one y-value corresponding to each x-value. However, that is not the case for a vertical straight line; one value of x corresponds to an infinite number of y-values.

(b) The form of the equation of a vertical straight line is $x = x_0$, where x_0 is the x-coordinate of the vertical straight line.

(c) For a linear equation, the slope indicates how much the y-value on the straight line increases (or decreases) when the x-value increases by one unit. We cannot apply this concept to a vertical straight line, since the x-value is *not* permitted to change. Thus, a vertical straight line has no slope.

Exercises 14.2

14.33 (a) The criterion used to decide on the line that best fits a set of data points is called the least squares criterion.

(b) The criterion is that the straight line that best fits a set of data points is the one that has the smallest possible sum of the squares of the errors (errors are the differences between and actual and predicted y values).

14.35 (a) The dependent variable is called the response variable.

(b) The independent variable is called the predictor variable or the explanatory variable.

14.37 (a) In the context of regression, an outlier is a data point that lies far from the regression line, relative to the other data points.

(b) In regression analysis, an influential observation is a data point whose removal causes the regression equation to change considerably.

14.39 (a) Line A: $y = 3 - 0.6x$ Line B: $y = 4 - x$

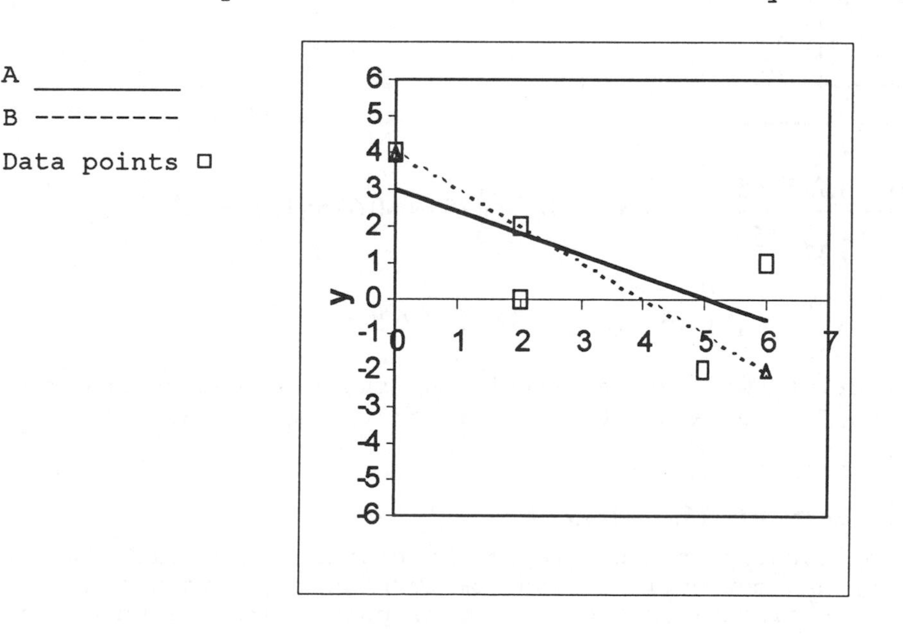

(b)

Line A: $y = 3 - 0.6x$

x	y	ŷ	e	e^2
0	4	3.0	1.0	1.00
2	2	1.8	0.2	0.04
2	0	1.8	-1.8	3.24
5	-2	0.0	-2.0	4.00
6	1	-0.6	1.6	2.56
				10.84

Line B: $y = 4 - x$

x	y	ŷ	e	e^2
0	4	4	0	0
2	2	2	0	0
2	0	2	-2	4
5	-2	-1	-1	1
6	1	-2	3	9
				14

(c) According to the least-squares criterion, Line A fits the set of data points better than Line B. This is because the sum of squared errors, Σe^2, is smaller for Line A than for Line B.

14.41 (a) Formulas for the slope (b_1) and intercept (b_0) of the regression equation are, respectively:

$$b_1 = \frac{\sum xy - \sum x \sum y / n}{\sum x^2 - (\sum x)^2 / n} \qquad b_0 = \frac{1}{n}(\sum y - b_1 \sum x)$$

To compute b_0 and b_1, construct a table of values for x, y, xy, x^2, and their sums:

x	y	xy	x^2
0	4	0	0
2	2	4	4
2	0	0	4
5	-2	-10	25
6	1	6	36
15	5	0	69

Thus: $b_1 = \frac{0-(15)(5)/5}{69-15^2/5} = -0.625 \qquad b_0 = \frac{1}{5}(5-(-0.625)(15)) = 2.875$

and the regression equation is $\hat{y} = 2.875 - 0.625x$.

(b) Begin by selecting two *x*-values within the range of the *x*-data. For the *x*-values 0 and 6, the calculated values for *y* are, respectively:

$$\hat{y} = 2.875 - 0.625(0) = 2.875$$

$$\hat{y} = 2.875 - 0.625(6) = -0.875$$

The regression equation can be graphed by plotting the pairs (0, 2.875) and (6,-0.875) and connecting these points with a straight line. This equation and the original set of five data points are presented as follows:

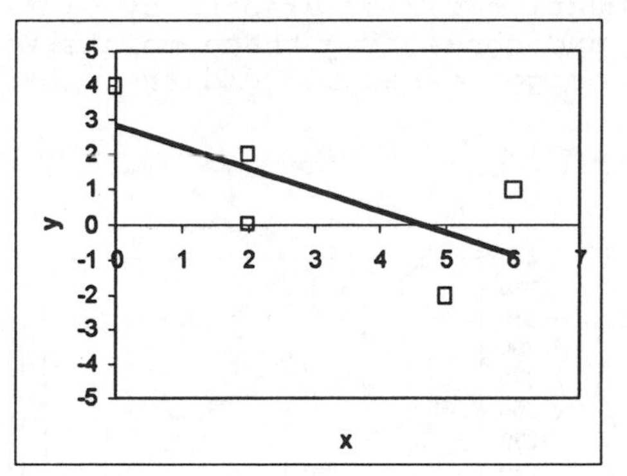

14.43 (a) Formulas for the slope (b_1) and intercept (b_0) of the regression equation are, respectively:

$$b_1 = \frac{\sum xy - \sum x \sum y / n}{\sum x^2 - (\sum x)^2 / n} \qquad b_0 = \frac{1}{n}(\sum y - b_1 \sum x)$$

To compute b_0 and b_1, construct a table of values for x, y, xy, x^2, and their sums:

x	y	xy	x^2
6	205	1230	36
6	195	1170	36
6	210	1260	36
2	340	680	4
2	299	598	4
5	230	1150	25
4	270	1080	16
5	243	1215	25
1	340	340	1
4	240	960	16
41	2572	9683	199

Thus:

$$b_1 = \frac{9683 - (41)(2572)/10}{199 - 41^2/10} = -27.9029 \qquad b_0 = \frac{1}{10}(2572 - (-27.9029)(41)) = 371.602$$

and the regression equation is $\hat{y} = 371.602 - 27.9029x$.

(b) Begin by selecting two *x*-values within the range of the *x*-data. For the *x*-values 1 and 6, the calculated values for *y* are, respectively:

$$\hat{y} = 371.602 - 27.9029(1) = 343.699$$
$$\hat{y} = 371.602 - 27.9029(6) = 204.185$$

The regression equation can be graphed by plotting the pairs (1,343.699) and (6, 204.185) and connecting these points with a straight line. This equation and the original set of 10 data points are presented as follows:

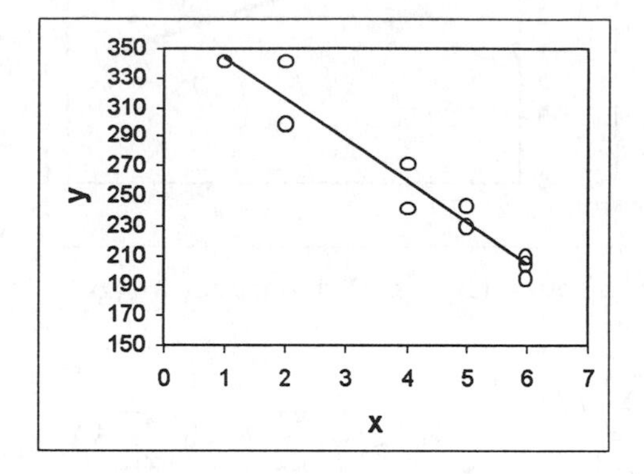

(c) Price tends to decrease as age increases.

(d) Corvettes depreciate an estimated $2,790.29 per year.

(e) Price of two-year old Corvette: $\hat{y} = 371.602 - 27.9029(2) = 315.7962 = \$31{,}579.62$

Price of three-year old Corvette:
$\hat{y} = 371.602 - 27.9029(3) = 287.8933 = \$28{,}789.33$

(f) Predictor variable is age; response variable is price (in $hundreds).

(g) There are no outliers or potential influential observations.

14.45 (a) Formulas for the slope (b_1) and intercept (b_0) of the regression equation are, respectively:

$$b_1 = \frac{\sum xy - \sum x \sum y / n}{\sum x^2 - (\sum x)^2 / n} \qquad b_0 = \frac{1}{n}(\sum y - b_1 \sum x)$$

To compute b_0 and b_1, construct a table of values for x, y, xy, x^2, and their sums:

x	y	xy	x^2
57	8.0	456.0	3249
85	22.0	1870.0	7225
57	10.5	598.5	3249
65	22.5	1462.5	4225
52	12.0	624.0	2704
67	11.5	770.5	4489
62	7.5	465.0	3844
80	13.0	1040.0	6400
77	16.5	1270.5	5929
53	21.0	1113.0	2809
68	12.0	816.0	4624
723	156.5	10486.0	48747

Thus,

$$b_1 = \frac{10486 - (723)(156.5)/11}{48747 - 723^2/11} = 0.16285 \qquad b_0 = \frac{1}{11}(156.5 - 0.16285(723)) = 3.52369$$

and the regression equation is $\hat{y} = 3.524 + 0.163x$.

(b) Begin by selecting two *x*-values within the range of the *x*-data. For the *x*-values 52 and 85, the predicted values for *y* are, respectively:

$$\hat{y} = 3.524 + 0.163(52) = 12.000$$
$$\hat{y} = 3.524 + 0.163(85) = 17.379$$

The regression equation can be graphed by plotting the pairs (52,12.000) and (85, 17.379) and connecting these points with a straight line. This equation and the original set of 11 data points are presented as follows:

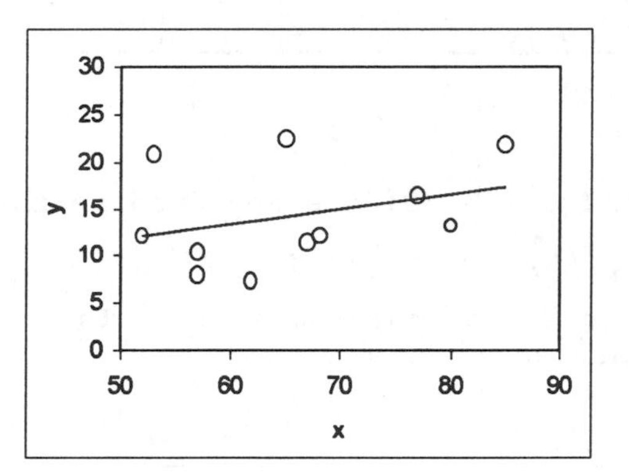

(c) The quantity of volatile compounds emitted tends to increase as plant weight increases.

(d) The quantity of volatile compounds emitted increases by an estimated 0.163 hundred nanograms for each increase in plant weight of one gram.

(e) The quantity of volatile compounds emitted by a 75 gram plant: $\hat{y} = 3.524 + 0.163(75) = 15.749$ hundred nanograms.

(f) The predictor variable is plant weight. The response variable is the quantity of volatile compounds emitted by the plant.

(g) There are no outliers or potential influential observations.

14.47 The idea behind finding a regression line is based on the assumption that the data points are actually scattered about a straight line. Only the second data set appears to be scattered about a straight line. Thus, it is reasonable to determine a regression line only for the second set of data.

14.49 (a) It is acceptable to use the regression equation to predict the price of a four-year-old Corvette since that age lies within the range of the ages in the sample data. It is not acceptable (and would be extrapolation) to use the regression equation to predict the price of a 10-year-old Corvette since that age lies outside the range of the ages in the sample data.

(b) It is reasonable to use the regression equation to predict price for cars of ages between one and six years, inclusive.

14.51 (a) We first construct a table with the necessary sums. Since n=5, we see that the means of x and y are 3 and 1, respectively, using the totals at the bottom of the first two columns. We then subtract 3 from each x value to get the values in the third column and subtract 1 from each y value to get the values in the fourth column. The numbers in the fifth column are the products of the corresponding numbers in the third and fourth columns. The sixth column containing the squares of the numbers in column 3 will be used in part (b).

x	y	$x-\bar{x}$	$y-\bar{y}$	$(x-\bar{x})(y-\bar{y})$	$(x-\bar{x})^2$
0	4	-3	3	-9	9
2	2	-1	1	-1	1
2	0	-1	-1	1	1
5	-2	2	-3	-6	4
6	1	3	0	0	9
15	5	0	0	-15	24

$$s_{xy} = \frac{\sum(x-\bar{x})(y-\bar{y})}{n-1} = \frac{-15}{4} = -3.75$$

(b) The equations in Formula (2) are repeated as follows:

$$b_1 = s_{xy} / s_x^2 \qquad b_0 = \bar{y} - b_1\bar{x}$$

The equation for s_{xy} is found in Formula (1). This and the (familiar) equation for s_x^2 are presented as follows:

$$s_{xy} = \frac{\sum(x-\bar{x})(y-\bar{y})}{n-1} \qquad s_x^2 = \frac{\sum(x-\bar{x})^2}{n-1}$$

The column manipulations required to calculate s_{xy} for the data in Exercise 14.39 were presented in part (a) where we found that $s_{xy} = -3.75.$. From the sixth column of the table in part (a), we find that $s_x^2 = \frac{24}{4} = 6.$

Substituting these last two calculations into the equation for b_1 presented in Formula (2), we get $b_1 = -3.75/6 = -0.625$. Finally, substituting the calculations for b_1, $\bar{x}$, and $\bar{y}$ into the equation for b_0 presented in Formula (2), we get $b_0 = 1 - (-0.625)(3) = 2.875$. Thus, the regression equation using the equations in Formula (2) is

$$\hat{y} = 2.875 - 0.625x$$

This is the same as the result obtained in part (a) of Exercise 14.41.

14.53 (a) Using Minitab, with the data in columns named AGE and %FAT, choose **Graph ▶ Plot...**, select %FAT for the **Y** variable for Graph **1** and AGE for the **X** variable, and click **OK**. The result is

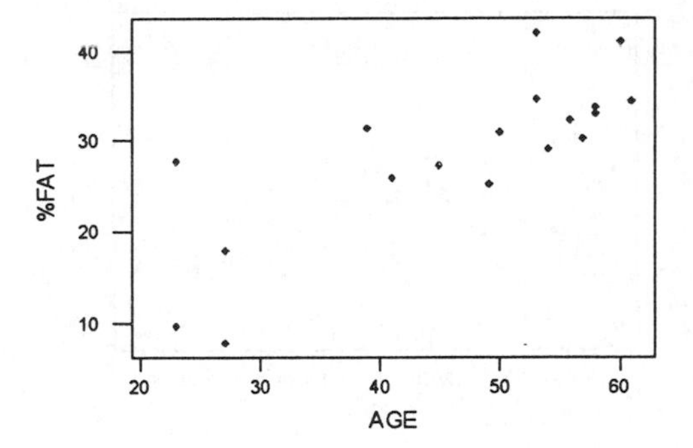

(b) The data appear to follow a linear pattern, so it is reasonable to find a regression line for the data.

(c) We choose **Stat ▶ Regression ▶ Regression...**, select %FAT in the **Response** text box, select AGE in the **Predictors** text box, and click **OK**. The results are

```
The regression equation is
%FAT = 3.22 + 0.548 AGE

Predictor         Coef        StDev          T         P
Constant         3.221        5.076       0.63     0.535
AGE             0.5480       0.1056       5.19     0.000

S = 5.754        R-Sq = 62.7%       R-Sq(adj) = 60.4%


Analysis of Variance
Source           DF          SS          MS          F         P
Regression        1      891.87      891.87      26.94     0.000
Residual Error   16      529.66       33.10
Total            17     1421.54

Unusual Observations
Obs       AGE       %FAT         Fit    StDev Fit    Residual    St Resid
  2      23.0      27.90       15.82         2.81       12.08       2.41R

R denotes an observation with a large standardized residual
```

The regression equation is $\hat{y} = 3.221 + 0.548x$. This indicates that the percent of body fat increases a little more than 0.5% for each one year increase in age.

(d) From part (a), the data points appear to be scattered about a straight line and, from part (b), there is one potential outlier (23.0, 27.90) and no potential influential observations.

14.55 (a) Using Minitab, with the data in columns named INCOME and BEER, choose **Graph ▶ Plot...**, select BEER for the **Y** variable for Graph **1** and INCOME for the **X** variable, and click **OK**. The result is

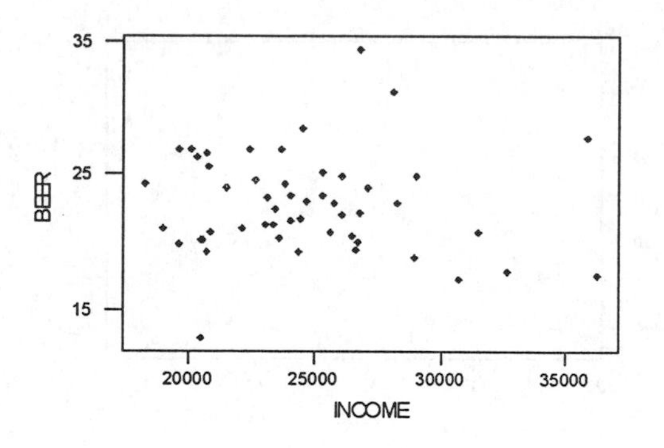

(b) There is no linear pattern in these data, so it is inappropriate to carry out a linear regression. Parts (c)-(d) are omitted.

14.57 (a) Using Minitab, with the data in columns named ESTRIOL and WEIGHT, choose **Graph ▶ Plot...**, select WEIGHT for the **Y** variable for Graph **1** and ESTRIOL for the **X** variable, and click **OK**. The result is

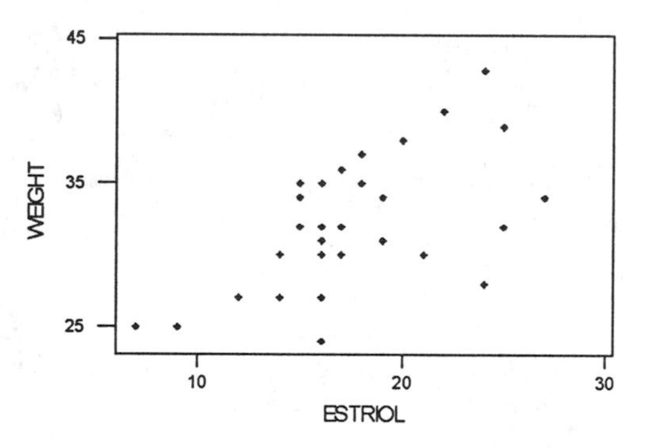

(b) There appears to be a (weak) linear pattern in these data, so it is reasonable to find a regression line for the data.

(c) We choose **Stat ▶ Regression ▶ Regression...**, select WEIGHT in the **Response** text box, select ESTRIOL in the **Predictors** text box, and click **OK**. The results are

```
The regression equation is
WEIGHT = 21.5 + 0.608 ESTRIOL

Predictor        Coef       StDev          T        P
Constant       21.523       2.620       8.21    0.000
ESTRIOL        0.6082      0.1468       4.14    0.000

S = 3.821        R-Sq = 37.2%      R-Sq(adj) = 35.0%
```

Analysis of Variance

Source	DF	SS	MS	F	P
Regression	1	250.57	250.57	17.16	0.000
Residual Error	29	423.43	14.60		
Total	30	674.00			

Unusual Observations

Obs	ESTRIOL	WEIGHT	Fit	StDev Fit	Residual	St Resid
14	24.0	28.000	36.120	1.208	-8.120	-2.24R

R denotes an observation with a large standardized residual

Thus the regression line is $\hat{y} = 21.523 + 0.6082x$. This indicates that birth weight tends to increase about 0.6 hectograms for each increase of one mg/24 hr in estriol level.

(d) There is one outlier, (24.0, 28.0), indicated by Minitab and there are no influential observations.

Exercises 14.3

14.59 (a) The coefficient of determination is a descriptive measure of the utility of a regression equation for making predictions. The symbol for the coefficient of determination is r^2.

(b) Two interpretations of the coefficient of determination are:

(i) It represents the percentage reduction obtained in the total squared error by using the regression equation to predict the observed values, instead of simply using the mean $\bar{y}$.

(ii) It represents the percentage of variation in the observed y-values that is explained by the regression.

14.61 (a) The coefficient of determination is r^2 = SSR/SST = 7626.6/8291.0 = 0.9199. 91.99% of the variation in the observed values of the response variable is explained by the regression. The fact that r^2 is close to 1 indicates that the regression equation is extremely useful for making predictions.

(b) SSE = SST - SSR = 8291.0 - 7626.6 = 664.4

14.63 To use the defining formulas, we begin with the following table.

x	y	$(y-\bar{y})$	$(y-\bar{y})^2$	$\hat{y}$	$(\hat{y}-\bar{y})$	$(\hat{y}-\bar{y})^2$	$(y-\hat{y})$	$(y-\hat{y})^2$
0	4	3	9	2.875	1.875	3.51563	1.125	1.26563
2	2	1	1	1.625	0.625	0.39063	0.375	0.14063
2	0	-1	1	1.625	0.625	0.39063	-1.625	2.64062
5	-2	-3	9	-0.250	-1.250	1.56250	-1.750	3.06250
6	1	0	0	-0.875	-1.875	3.51563	1.875	3.51563
15	5	0	20		0	9.375	0	10.625

Each $\hat{y}$ value is obtained by substituting the respective value of x into the regression equation $\hat{y} = 2.875 - 0.625x$. (This equation was derived in Exercise 14.41).

(a) $SST = \sum (y-\bar{y})^2 = 20$ $SSR = \sum (\hat{y}-\bar{y})^2 = 9.375$ $SSE = \sum (y-\hat{y})^2 = 10.625$

(b) 20 = 9.375 + 10.625

(c) $r^2 = 1 - \frac{SSE}{SST} = 1 - \frac{10.625}{20} = 0.46875$ or $r^2 = \frac{SSR}{SST} = \frac{9.375}{20} = 0.46875$

The percentage of variation in the observed *y*-values that is explained by the regression is 46.875%.

(d) Based on the answer in part (c), the regression equation appears to be moderately useful for making predictions.

4.65 To use the computing formulas, we begin with the following table. Notice that columns 1-4 are presented in the solution to part (a) of Exercise 14.43, so that only the column for y^2 needs to be calculated.

x	y	xy	x^2	y^2
6	205	1230	36	42,025
6	195	1170	36	38,025
6	210	1260	36	44,100
2	340	680	4	115,600
2	299	598	4	89,401
5	230	1150	25	52,900
4	270	1080	16	72,900
5	243	1215	25	59,049
1	340	340	1	115,600
4	240	960	16	57,600
41	2572	9683	199	687,200

(a) Using the last row of the table and Formula 14.2 of the text, we obtain the three sums of squares as follows.

$$SST = S_{yy} = \sum y^2 - (\sum y)^2 / n = 687{,}200 - 2572^2 / 10 = 25{,}681.6$$

$$SSR = \frac{S_{xy}^2}{S_{xx}} = \frac{[\sum xy - (\sum x)(\sum y)/n]^2}{\sum x^2 - (\sum x)^2 / n} = \frac{[9683 - (41)(2572)/10]^2}{199 - 41^2/10} = 24{,}057.9$$

$$SSE = S_{yy} - \frac{S_{xy}^2}{S_{xx}} = 25{,}681.6 - 24{,}057.9 = 1623.7$$

(b) $r^2 = \frac{SSR}{SST} = \frac{24{,}057.9}{25{,}681.6} = 0.9368$

(c) The percentage of variation in the observed *y*-values that is explained by the regression is 93.68% In other words, 93.68% of the variation in the price data is explained by the age data.

(d) Based on the answers to parts (b) and (c), the regression equation appears to be extremely useful for making predictions.

14.67 To use the computing formulas, we begin with the following table. Notice that columns 1-4 are presented in the solution to part (a) of Exercise 14.45, so that only the column for y^2 needs to be calculated.

x	y	xy	x^2	y^2
57	8.0	456.0	3249	64.00
85	22.0	1870.0	7225	484.00
57	10.5	598.5	3249	110.25
65	22.5	1462.5	4225	506.25
52	12.0	624.0	2704	144.00
67	11.5	770.5	4489	132.25
62	7.5	465.0	3844	56.25
80	13.0	1040.0	6400	169.00
77	16.5	1270.5	5929	272.25
53	21.0	1113.0	2809	441.00
68	12.0	816.0	4624	144.00
723	156.5	10486.0	48747	2523.25

(a) Using the last row of the table and Formula 14.2 of the text, we obtain the three sums of squares as follows.

$$SST = S_{yy} = \sum y^2 - (\sum y)^2 / n = 2523.25 - 156.5^2 / 11 = 296.68$$

$$SSR = \frac{S_{xy}^2}{S_{xx}} = \frac{[\sum xy - (\sum x)(\sum y)/n]^2}{\sum x^2 - (\sum x)^2 / n} = \frac{[10{,}486 - (723)(156.5)/11]^2}{48{,}747 - 723^2/11} = 32.52$$

$$SSE = S_{yy} - \frac{S_{xy}^2}{S_{xx}} = 296.68 - 32.52 = 264.16$$

(b) $r^2 = \frac{SSR}{SST} = \frac{32.52}{296.68} = 0.1096$

(c) The percentage of variation in the observed y-values that is explained by the regression is 10.96%. In other words, only 10.96% of the variation in the emissions data is explained by plant weight.

(d) Based on the answers to parts (b) and (c), the regression equation appears to be useless for making predictions.

14.69 (a) $r^2 = 1 - SSE/SST = (SST - SSE)/SST$. If the mean were used to predict the observed values of the response variable, the total squared error would be SST. By using the regression line to predict the observed values of the response variable, the sum of squares of the differences between the predicted values and the mean is SSR = SST - SSE. This is a reduction in the error sum of squares. Dividing this quantity by SST (and converting to a percentage) gives us the percentage reduction in the squared error when we use the regression equation instead of the mean to predict the observed values of the response variable.

(b) From Exercise 14.65, $r^2 = 0.9368$, so the percentage reduction obtained in the total squared error by using the regression equation instead of the mean of the observed prices to predict the observed prices is 93.68%.

14.71 Using Minitab, with the data in columns named AGE and %FAT, we choose **Stat ▶ Regression ▶ Regression...**, select %FAT in the **Response** text box, select AGE in the **Predictors** text box, and click **OK.** The results are

```
The regression equation is
%FAT = 3.22 + 0.548 AGE
```

Predictor	Coef	StDev	T	P
Constant	3.221	5.076	0.63	0.535
AGE	0.5480	0.1056	5.19	0.000

S = 5.754 R-Sq = 62.7% R-Sq(adj) = 60.4%

Analysis of Variance

Source	DF	SS	MS	F	P
Regression	1	891.87	891.87	26.94	0.000
Residual Error	16	529.66	33.10		
Total	17	1421.54			

(a) Thus the coefficient of determination is $r^2 = 0.627$.

(b) 62.7% of the variation in the observed values of percent body fat is explained by a linear relationship with the predictor variable, age.

(c) The regression equation is moderately useful for making predictions.

14.73 Using Minitab, with the data in columns named INCOME and BEER, we choose **Stat ▶ Regression ▶ Regression...**, select BEER in the **Response** text box, select INCOME in the **Predictors** text box, and click **OK**. The results are

The regression equation is

BEER = 24.4 -0.000064 INCOME

Predictor	Coef	StDev	T	P
Constant	24.415	3.280	7.44	0.000
INCOME	-0.0000641	0.0001315	-0.49	0.628

S = 3.766 R-Sq = 0.5% R-Sq(adj) = 0.0%

Analysis of Variance

Source	DF	SS	MS	F	P
Regression	1	3.37	3.37	0.24	0.628
Residual Error	49	695.03	14.18		
Total	50	698.40			

(a) Thus the coefficient of determination is $r^2 = 0.005$.

(b) Only 0.5% of the variation in the observed values of per capita beer consumption is explained by a linear relationship with the predictor variable, per capita income.

(c) The regression equation is totally useless for making predictions.

14.75 Using Minitab, with the data in columns named ESTRIOL and WEIGHT, we choose **Stat ▶ Regression ▶ Regression...**, select WEIGHT in the **Response** text box, select ESTRIOL in the **Predictors** text box, and click **OK**. The results are

The regression equation is

WEIGHT = 21.5 + 0.608 ESTRIOL

Predictor	Coef	StDev	T	P
Constant	21.523	2.620	8.21	0.000
ESTRIOL	0.6082	0.1468	4.14	0.000

S = 3.821   R-Sq = 37.2%   R-Sq(adj) = 35.0%

Analysis of Variance

Source	DF	SS	MS	F	P
Regression	1	250.57	250.57	17.16	0.000
Residual Error	29	423.43	14.60		
Total	30	674.00			

(a) Thus the coefficient of determination is $r^2 = 0.372$.

(b) Only 37.2% of the variation in the observed values of birth weight is explained by a linear relationship with the predictor variable, estriol level.

(c) Based solely on the coefficient of determination, the regression equation is not very useful for making predictions.

Exercises 14.4

14.77 Pearson product moment correlation coefficient

14.79 (a) ± 1 (b) not very useful

14.81 False. It is possible that both variables are associated with a third variable.

14.83 The signs of the slope and of r are always the same. This can be seen from

$$r = \frac{S_{xy}}{\sqrt{S_{xx}S_{yy}}} = \frac{S_{xy}}{S_{xx}} \cdot \frac{\sqrt{S_{xx}}}{\sqrt{S_{yy}}} = b_1 \cdot \frac{\sqrt{S_{xx}}}{\sqrt{S_{yy}}} .$$

Since the ratio of square roots in the last term is always positive, r will always have the same sign as b_1. Since the slope of the regression line is -3.58, r will also be negative. Therefore, $r = -\sqrt{r^2} = -\sqrt{0.709} = -0.842$.

14.85 To compute the linear correlation coefficient, begin with the following table.

x	y	xy	x^2	y^2
0	4	0	0	16
2	2	4	4	4
2	0	0	4	0
5	-2	-10	25	4
6	1	6	36	1
15	5	0	69	25

The linear correlation coefficient r is computed using the computing formula in Definition 14.6 of the text:

$$r = \frac{S_{xy}}{\sqrt{S_{xx}S_{yy}}} = \frac{\sum xy - (\sum x)(\sum y)/n}{\sqrt{[\sum x^2 - (\sum x)^2/n][\sum y^2 - (\sum y)^2/n]}}$$

$$= \frac{0 - (15)(5)/5}{\sqrt{[69 - 15^2/5][25 - 5^2/5]}} = -0.684653$$

14.87 To compute the linear correlation coefficient, return to the table presented at the beginning of the solution to Exercise 14.65. Use the last row of this table to perform the calculations in part (a).

(a) The linear correlation coefficient r is computed using the formula in Definition 14.6 of the text:

$$r = \frac{S_{xy}}{\sqrt{S_{xx}S_{yy}}} = \frac{\sum xy - (\sum x)(\sum y)/n}{\sqrt{[\sum x^2 - (\sum x)^2/n][\sum y^2 - (\sum y)^2/n]}}$$

$$= \frac{9683 - (41)(2572)/10}{\sqrt{[199 - 41^2/10][687200 - 2572^2/10]}} = -0.967872$$

(b) The value of r in part (a) suggests a strong negative linear correlation.

(c) Data points are clustered closely about the regression line.

(d) $r^2 = (-0.967872)^2 = 0.9368$. This matches the coefficient of determination that was calculated in part (b) of Exercise 14.65.

14.89 To compute the linear correlation coefficient, return to the table presented at the beginning of the solution to Exercise 14.67. Use the last row of this table to perform the calculations in part (a).

(a) The linear correlation coefficient r is computed using the formula in Definition 14.6 of the text:

$$r = \frac{S_{xy}}{\sqrt{S_{xx}S_{yy}}} = \frac{\sum xy - (\sum x)(\sum y)/n}{\sqrt{[\sum x^2 - (\sum x)^2/n][\sum y^2 - (\sum y)^2/n]}}$$

$$= \frac{10{,}486 - (723)(156.5)/11}{\sqrt{[48{,}747 - 723^2/11][2523.25 - 156.5^2/11]}} = 0.331067$$

(b) The value of r in part (a) suggests a weak positive linear correlation.

(c) Data points are clustered very loosely about the regression line.

(d) $r^2 = (0.331067)^2 = 0.1096$. This matches the coefficient of determination that was calculated in part (b) of Exercise 14.67.

14.91 (a) We will need the totals from the following table:

x	y	xy	x^2	y^2
-3	9	-27	9	81
-2	4	-8	4	16
-1	1	-1	1	1
0	0	0	0	0
1	1	1	1	1
2	4	8	4	16
3	9	27	9	81
0	28	0	28	196

r is computed using the formula in Definition 14.6 of the text:

$$r = \frac{S_{xy}}{\sqrt{S_{xx}S_{yy}}} = \frac{\sum xy - (\sum x)(\sum y)/n}{\sqrt{[\sum x^2 - (\sum x)^2/n][\sum y^2 - (\sum y)^2/n]}}$$

$$= \frac{0-(0)(28)/7}{\sqrt{[28-0^2/7][196-28^2/7]}} = 0.0$$

(b) We cannot conclude from the result in part (a) that x and y are unrelated. We can conclude only that there is no *linear* relationship between x and y.

(c) Graph for part (e)

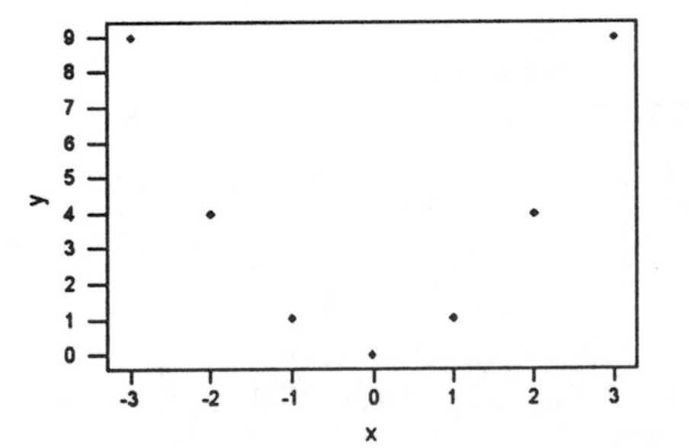

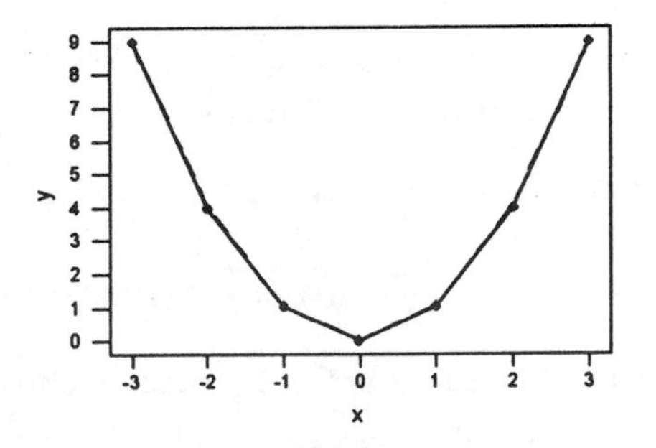

(d) It is not appropriate to use the linear correlation coefficient as a descriptive measure for the data because the data points are not scattered about a straight line.

(e) For each data point (x, y), we have $y = x^2$. (See columns 1 and 2 of the previous table.) See the graph above at the right.

(f) We will need the following totals:

$$\sum x = 0;\ \sum y = 0;\ \sum xy = 196;\ \sum x^2 = 28;\ \sum y^2 = 1588$$

Then $r = \dfrac{S_{xy}}{\sqrt{S_{xx}S_{yy}}} = \dfrac{196-(0)(0)/7}{\sqrt{[28-0^2/7][1588-0^2/7]}} = 0.929505$

(g) It is tempting to conclude that x and y are linearly related, but the scatterplot below shows that, although the points fall close to a straight line, they are not randomly scattered about that line. This illustrates the danger of drawing a conclusion about the linearity of the data without looking at a scatterplot of the data.

(h) Graph for part (j)

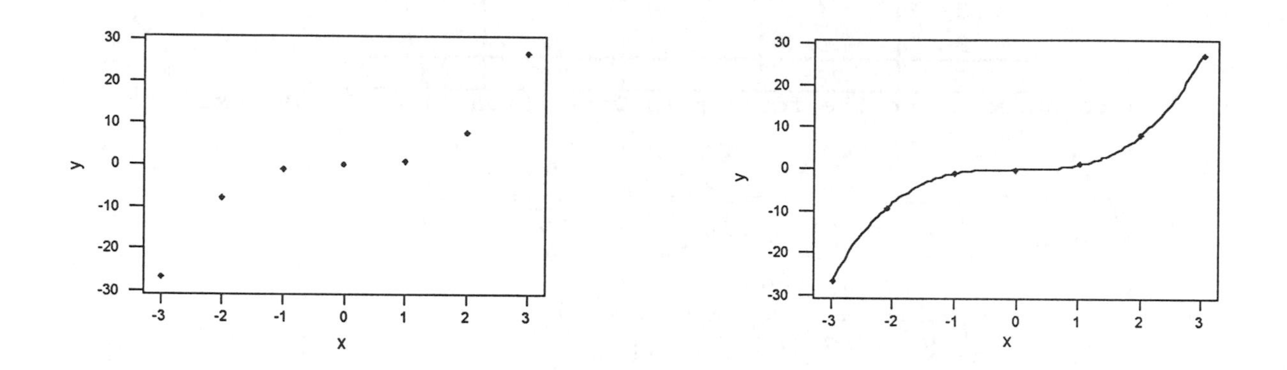

(i) No. As mentioned above, the points follow a distinct non-linear pattern and are not scattered randomly about a straight line.

(j) See the graph above at the right for the equation $y = x^3$.

14.93 (a) No. We only know that the linear correlation coefficient is the square root of the coefficient of determination or it is the negative of that square root.

(b) No. The slope is positive if r is positive and negative if r is negative, but we cannot determine the sign of r.

(c) Yes. $r = -\sqrt{0.716} = -0.846$

(d) Yes. $r = \sqrt{0.716} = 0.846$

14.95 (a) Using Minitab, with the data in columns named AVERAGE and RUNS, we choose **Stat ▶ Basic Statistics ▶ Correlation...**, select AVERAGE and RUNS in the **Variables** text box, and click **OK**. The result is

Correlation of AVERAGE and RUNS = 0.865, P-Value = 0.000

(b) There is a strong positive linear relationship between AVERAGE and RUNS. The data points should be clustered quite closely about the regression line.

14.97 (a) Using Minitab, with the data in columns named PCB and THICKNESS, we choose **Stat ▶ Basic Statistics ▶ Correlation...**, select PCB and THICKNESS in the **Variables** text box, and click **OK**. The result is

Correlation of PCB and THICKNESS = -0.185, P-Value = 0.157

Alternatively, if the data were entered in Excel in cells A1 to A65 for PCB and B1 to B65 for THICKNESS, enter the formula =CORREL(A1:A65,B1:B65) in any other cell and the value of the correlation coefficient will appear in that cell as -0.18516.

(b) There is a very weak negative linear relationship between PCB concentration and shell thickness. The data points will be clustered very loosely about the regression line.

14.99 (a) Using Minitab, with the data in columns named MPG and DISP, we choose **Stat ▶ Basic Statistics ▶ Correlation...**, select MPG and DISP in the **Variables** text box, and click **OK**. The result is

Correlation of DISP and MPG = -0.842, P-Value = 0.000

(b) There is a moderately strong negative linear relationship between miles per gallon and engine displacement. The data points will be quite closely clustered about the regression line.

REVIEW TEST FOR CHAPTER 13

1. (a) x (b) y (c) b_1 (d) b_0

2. (a) It intersects the y-axis when x = 0. Therefore y = 4.

(b) It intersects the y-axis when x = 0.

(c) slope = -3

(d) The y-value decreases by 3 units when x increases by 1 unit.

(e) The y-value increases by 6 units when x decreases by 2 units.

3. (a) True. The y-intercept is represented by b_0 and that value is independent of b_1, the slope.

(b) False. A horizontal line has a slope of zero.

(c) True. If the slope is positive, the x-values and y-values increase and decrease together.

4. Scatterplot or scatter diagram

5. A regression equation can be used to predict the response variable for values of the predictor variable within the range of the observed values of the predictor variable.

6. (a) predictor variable or explanatory variable

(b) response variable

7. (a) Based on the least-squares criterion, the line that best fits a set of data points is the one having the smallest possible sum of squared errors.

(b) The line that best fits a set of data points according to the least-squares criterion is called the regression line.

(c) Using a regression equation to make predictions for values of the predictor variable outside the range of the observed values of the predictor variable is called extrapolation.

8. (a) An outlier is a data point that lies far from the regression line relative to the other data points.

(b) An influential observation is a data point whose removal causes the regression equation to change considerably. Often this is a data point which lies considerably to the left or right of the rest of the data points.

9. The coefficient of determination represents the percentage of the total variation in the y-values that is explained by the regression equation.

10. (a) SST is the total sum of squares and measures the variation in the observed values of the response variable.

(b) SSR is the regression sum of squares and measures the variation in the observed values of the response variable that is explained by the regression. It can also be thought of as the variation in the predicted values of the response variable corresponding to the observed x-values.

(c) SSE is the error sum of squares and measures the variation in the observed values of the response variable that is not explained by the regression.

11. (a) One use of the linear correlation coefficient is as a descriptive measure of the strength of the linear relationship between two variables.

(b) A positive linear relationship between two variables means that one variable tends to increase linearly as the other increases.

(c) A value of r close to −1 suggests a strong negative linear relationship between the variables.

(d) A value of r close to zero suggests at most a weak linear relationship between the variables.

12. True. It is quite possible that both variables are strongly affected by one (or more) other variables (called lurking variables).

13. (a) $y = 72 - 12x$ (b) $b_0 = 72$, $b_1 = -12$

(c) The line slopes downward since $b_1 < 0$.

(d) After two years: $y = 72 - 12(2) = \$48$ hundred $= \$4800$

After five years: $y = 72 - 12(5) = \$12$ hundred $= \$1200$.

(e)

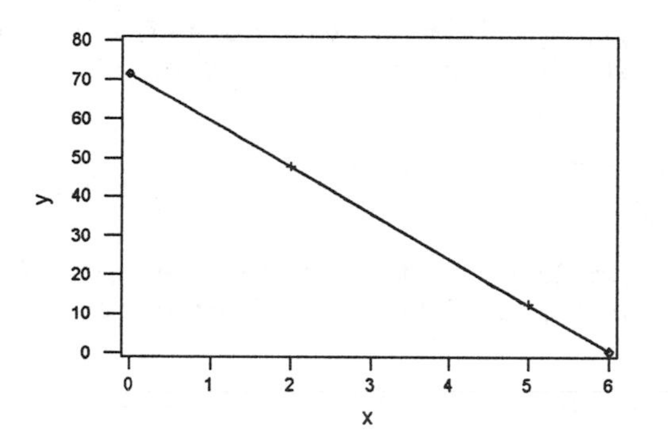

(f) From the graph, we estimate the value to be about \$2500 after 4 years. The actual value is $y = 7200 - 1200(4) = \$2400$.

14. (a)

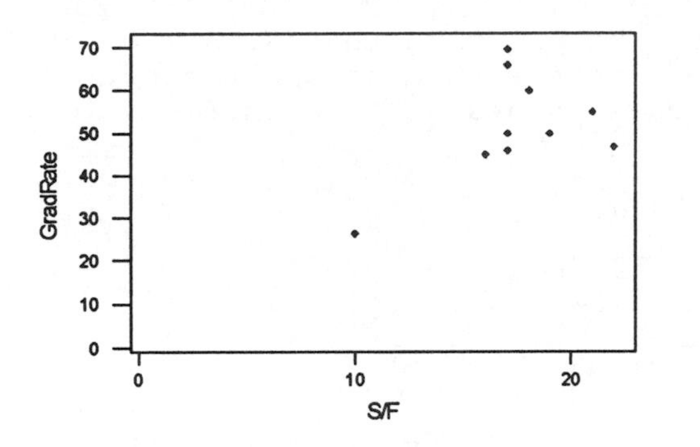

(b) It is moderately reasonable to find a regression line for the data because the data points appear to be scattered about a straight line. This perception is, however, heavily influenced by the single data point at x = 10.

(c) The regression equation can be determined by calculating its slope and intercept. Formulas for the slope (b_1) and intercept (b_0) of the regression equation are, respectively:

$$b_1 = \frac{\sum xy - \sum x \sum y / n}{\sum x^2 - (\sum x)^2 / n} \qquad b_0 = \frac{1}{n}(\sum y - b_1 \sum x)$$

To compute b_0 and b_1, construct a table of values for x, y, xy, x^2, and their sums. (Note: A column for y^2 is also presented. This will be used in Problems 15 and 16.)

x	y	xy	x^2	y^2
16	45	720	256	2,025
20	55	1,100	400	3,025
17	70	1,190	289	4,900
19	50	950	361	2,500
22	47	1,034	484	2,209
17	46	782	289	2,116
17	50	850	289	2,500
17	66	1,122	289	4,356
10	26	260	100	676
18	60	1,080	324	3,600
173	515	9,088	3,081	27,907

Thus,

$$b_1 = \frac{9088 - (173)(515)/10}{3081 - 173^2/10} = 2.02611 \qquad b_0 = \frac{1}{10}(515 - 2.02611(173)) = 16.448$$

and the regression equation is: $\hat{y} = 16.448 + 2.02611x$.

To graph the regression equation, begin by selecting two *x*-values within the range of the *x*-data. For the *x*-values 10 and 22, the predicted values for *y* are, respectively:

$$\hat{y} = 16.448 + 2.02611(10) = 36.71$$
$$\hat{y} = 16.448 + 2.02611(22) = 61.02$$

The regression equation can be graphed by plotting the pairs (10, 36.71) and (22, 61.02) and connecting these points with a straight line. This equation and the original set of 10 data points are presented as follows:

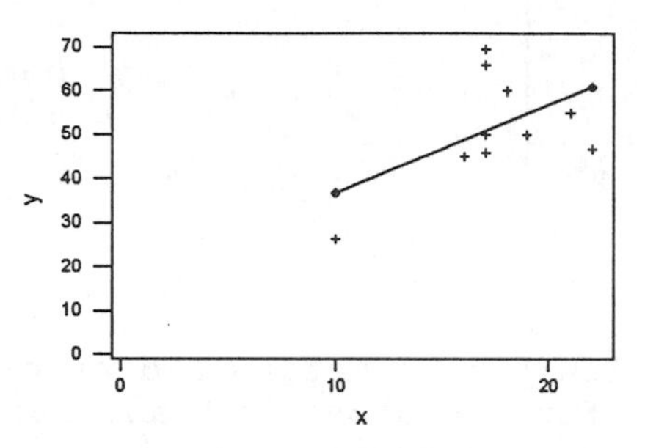

(d) Graduation rate tends to increase as the student-to-faculty ratio increases.

(e) Graduation rate increases an estimated 2.026% for each additional 1 unit increase in the student-to-faculty ratio.

(f) The predicted graduation rate for a university with a student-to-faculty ratio of 17 is 16.448 + 2.0261(17) = 50.89%.

(g) There is one potential influential observation, (10, 26) and there are no outliers. Looking at the scatterplot in part (c), we suspect that there will be little relationship between the student-to-faculty ratio and the graduation rate if the influential observation is removed from the data.

15. (a) To compute SST, SSR, and SSE using the computing formulas, begin with the table presented in Problem 14(c). Using the last row of this table and the formula in Definition 14.6 of the text, we obtain the three sums of squares as follows.

$$SST = S_{yy} = \sum y^2 - (\sum y)^2 / n = 27{,}907 - 515^2 / 10 = 1384.5$$

$$SSR = \frac{S_{xy}^2}{S_{xx}} = \frac{[\sum xy - (\sum x)(\sum y)/n]^2}{\sum x^2 - (\sum x)^2 / n} = \frac{[9088 - (173)(515)/10]^2}{3081 - 173^2/10} = 361.66$$

$$SSE = S_{yy} - \frac{S_{xy}^2}{S_{xx}} = 1384.50 - 361.66 = 1022.84$$

$$r^2 = \frac{SSR}{SST} = \frac{361.66}{1384.50} = 0.261$$

(b) The percentage reduction obtained in the total squared error by using the regression equation, instead of the sample mean $\bar{y}$, to predict the observed graduation rates is 26.1%.

(c) The percentage of the variation in the observed graduation rates that is explained by the student-to-faculty ratio is 26.1%.

(d) The regression equation is not very useful for making predictions.

16. (a) To compute the linear correlation coefficient, begin with the table presented in Problem 14(c). Using the last row of this table and the formula in Definition 14.6 of the text, we get

$$r = \frac{S_{xy}}{\sqrt{S_{xx}S_{yy}}} = \frac{\sum xy - (\sum x)(\sum y)/n}{\sqrt{[\sum x^2 - (\sum x)^2/n][\sum y^2 - (\sum y)^2/n]}}$$

$$= \frac{9088 - (173)(515)/10}{\sqrt{[3081 - 173^2/10][27{,}907 - 515^2/10]}} = 0.511$$

(b) The value of r suggests a weak to moderate positive linear correlation.

(c) Data points are clustered about the regression line, but not very closely.

(d) $r^2 = (0.511)^2 = 0.261$

17. (a) Using Minitab, with the data in two columns named S/F and GRADRATE, we choose **Graph ▶ Plot...**, select GRADRATE for the **Y** variable for **Graph 1** and S/F for the **X** variable for **Graph 1**, and click **OK.**

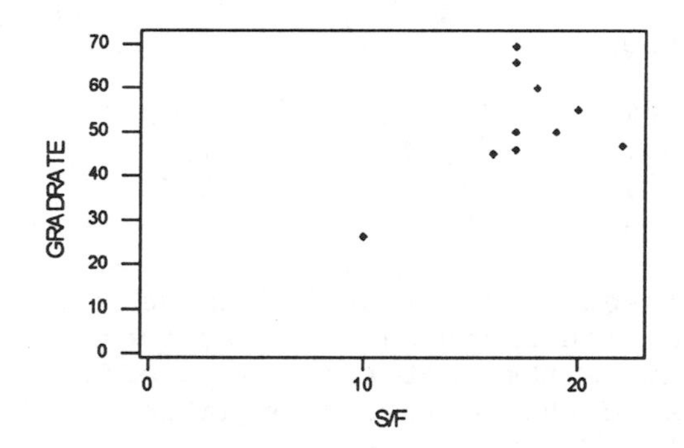

(b) We choose **Stat ▶ Regression ▶ Regression...**, select GRADRATE in the **Response** text box, select S/F in the **Predictors** text box, and click **OK.** The result is

```
The regression equation is
GRADRATE = 16.4 + 2.03 S/F

Predictor        Coef       StDev          T         P
Constant        16.45       21.15       0.78     0.459
S/F             2.026       1.205       1.68     0.131

S = 11.31        R-Sq = 26.1%      R-Sq(adj) = 16.9%

Analysis of Variance

Source            DF          SS          MS          F          P
Regression         1       361.7       361.7       2.83      0.131
Residual Error     8      1022.8       127.9
Total              9      1384.5
```

```
Unusual Observations
Obs       S/F   GRADRATE          Fit    StDev Fit    Residual     St Resid
  9      10.0      26.00        36.71         9.49      -10.71      -1.74 X
```

X denotes an observation whose X value gives it large influence.

(c) From the computer output, r^2 = 26.1%, SST = 1384.5, SSR = 361.7, and SSE = 1022.8.

(d) There is one potential influential observation, (10, 26).

(e) Click on the Data window and move the cursor to the value of 10 in the S/F column. Press the DELETE key. Move the cursor to the value of 26 in the GRADRATE column and press the DELETE key. Then choose **Stat ▶ Regression ▶ Regression...**, select GRADRATE in the **Response** text box, select S/F in the **Predictors** text box, and click **OK**. The result is

```
The regression equation is
GRADRATE = 72.1 - 0.98 S/F

Predictor          Coef         StDev           T          P
Constant          72.10         32.23        2.24      0.060
S/F              -0.981         1.771       -0.55      0.597

S = 9.518        R-Sq = 4.2%       R-Sq(adj) = 0.0%

Analysis of Variance

Source           DF           SS           MS          F         P
Regression        1        27.79        27.79       0.31     0.597
Residual Error    7       634.21        90.60
Total             8       662.00
```

(f) The potential influential observation was very influential. For example, the regression equation slope has changed from positive to negative. Even more important is the fact that the coefficient of determination is now only 4.2%, making the regression equation useless for making any predictions at all.

18. We choose **Stat ▶ Basic Statistics ▶ Correlation...**, select S/F and GRADRATE in the **Variables** text box, and click **OK**. The result is

```
Correlation of S/F and GRADRATE = 0.511, P-Value = 0.131
```

CHAPTER 15 ANSWERS

Exercises 15.1

15.1 conditional distribution, conditional mean, and conditional standard deviation

15.3 (a) population regression line

(b) σ

(c) normal, $\beta_0 + 6\ \beta_1$, σ

15.5 The sample regression line is the best estimate of the population regression line.

15.7 residual

15.9 The plot of the residuals against the values of the predictor variable provides the same information as a scatter diagram of the data points. However, it has the advantage of making it easier to spot patterns such as curvature and non-constant standard deviation.

15.11 If the assumptions for regression inferences are satisfied for a model relating a Corvette's age to its price, this means that there are constants β_0, β_1, and σ such that, for each age x, the prices for Corvettes of that age are normally distributed with mean $\beta_0 + \beta_1 x$ and standard deviation σ.

15.13 If the assumptions for regression inferences are satisfied for a model relating the volume of plant emissions of volatile compounds to the weight of the plant, this means that there are constants β_0, β_1, and σ such that, for each weight x, the volumes of emissions y are normally distributed with mean $\beta_0 + \beta_1 x$ and standard deviation σ.

15.15 To compute the standard error of the estimate, first retrieve the computation for the error sum of squares (SSE) in part (a) of Exercise 14.65 and then apply the formula for s_e in Definition 15.1 of the text.

(a) In part (a) of Exercise 14.65, n = 10 and SSE was computed as 1,623.7. Applying Definition 15.1, the standard error of the estimate is

$$s_e = \sqrt{\frac{SSE}{n-2}} = \sqrt{\frac{1623.7}{10-2}} = 14.2464$$

On average, roughly speaking, the predicted price differs from the observed price by about $1425.

(b) Presuming that the variables age (x) and price (y) for Corvettes satisfy Assumptions (1) - (3) for regression inferences, the standard error of the estimate s_e = $1424.64 provides an estimate for the common population standard deviation σ of prices for all Corvettes of any given age.

(c)

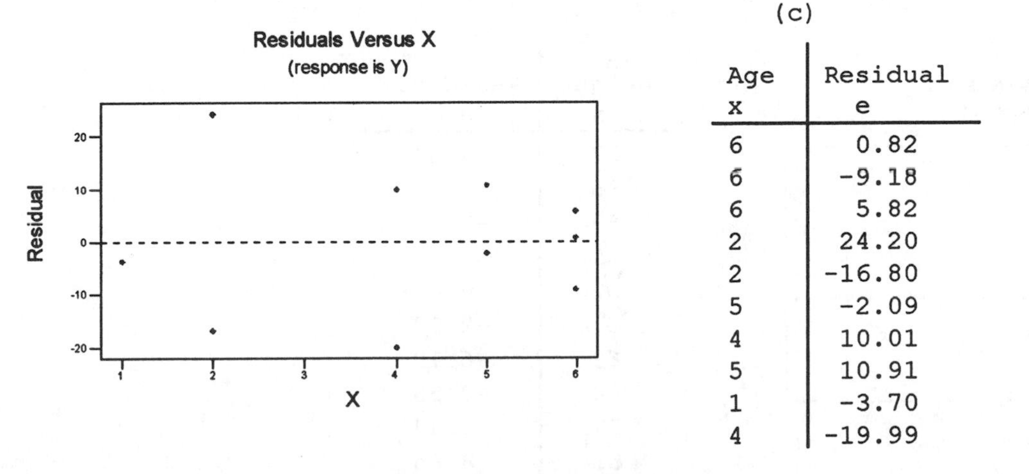

Age x	Residual e
6	0.82
6	-9.18
6	5.82
2	24.20
2	-16.80
5	-2.09
4	10.01
5	10.91
1	-3.70
4	-19.99

Normal Probability Plot of the Residuals
(response is Y)

Residual e	Normal score n
-19.99	-1.55
-16.80	-1.00
-9.18	-0.65
-3.70	-0.37
-2.09	-0.12
0.82	0.12
5.82	0.37
10.01	0.65
10.91	1.00
24.20	1.55

(d) Taking into account the small sample size, we can say that the residuals fall roughly in a horizontal band centered and symmetric about the x-axis. We can also say that the normal probability plot for residuals is very roughly linear. Therefore, it appears reasonable to consider the assumptions for regression inferences for the variables age and price of Corvettes to be met.

15.17 To compute the standard error of the estimate, first retrieve the computation for the error sum of squares (SSE) in part (a) of Exercise 14.67 and then apply the formula for s_e in Definition 15.1 of the text.

(a) In part (a) of Exercise 14.67, n = 10 and SSE was computed as 88.5. Applying Definition 15.1, the standard error of the estimate is

$$s_e = \sqrt{\frac{SSE}{n-2}} = \sqrt{\frac{264.16}{11-2}} = 5.4177$$

On average, the predicted quantity of volatile compounds emitted by a potato plant in the sample differs from the observed quantity by about 542 nanograms.

(b) Presuming that the weight (x) of the potato plants *Solanum tubersom* and volume of volatile emissions (y) from the plants satisfy Assumptions (1) - (3) for regression inferences, the standard error of the estimate s_e = 5.4177 provides an estimate for the common population standard deviation σ of emission volumes for all plants of any particular weight.

(c)

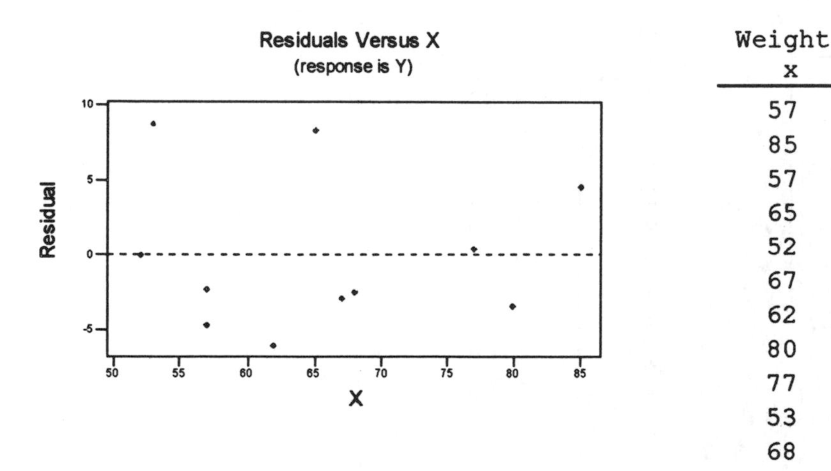

Weight x	Residual e
57	-4.81
85	4.63
57	-2.31
65	8.39
52	0.01
67	-2.93
62	-6.12
80	-3.55
77	0.44
53	8.85
68	-2.60

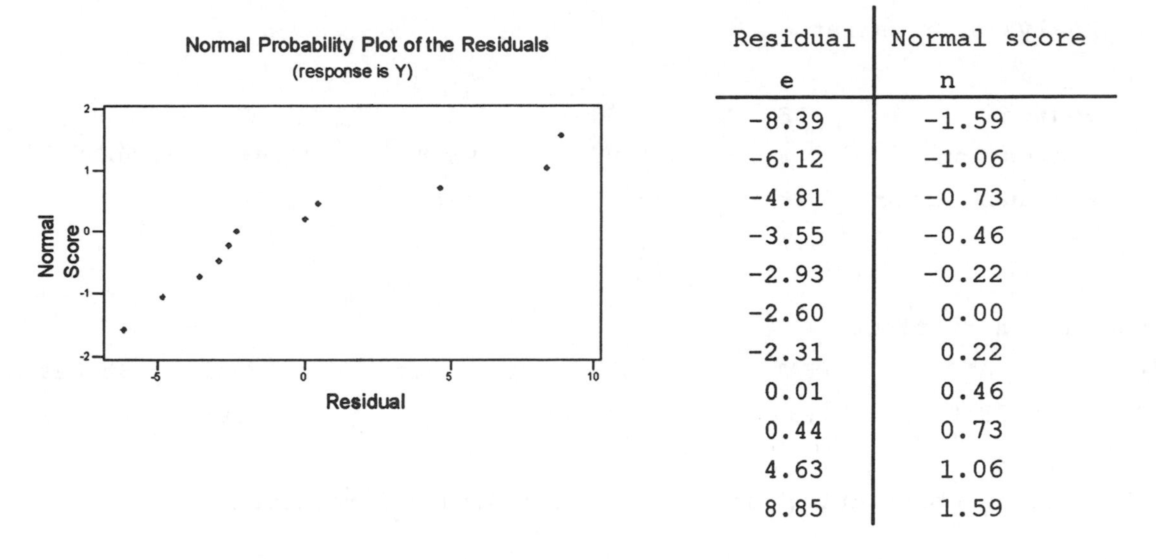

Residual e	Normal score n
-8.39	-1.59
-6.12	-1.06
-4.81	-0.73
-3.55	-0.46
-2.93	-0.22
-2.60	0.00
-2.31	0.22
0.01	0.46
0.44	0.73
4.63	1.06
8.85	1.59

(d) Taking into account the small sample size, we can say that the residuals fall roughly in a horizontal band centered and symmetric about the x-axis. We can also say that the normal probability plot for residuals is approximately linear. Therefore, based on the sample data, there are no obvious violations of the assumptions for regression inferences for the variables plant weight and volume of volatile emissions.

15.19 (a) The assumption of linearity (Assumption 1) may be violated since the band is not horizontal, as may the assumption of equal standard deviations (Assumption 2) since there is more variation in the residuals for small x than for large x.

(b) It appears that the standard deviation does not remain constant; thus, Assumption 2 is violated.

(c) The graph does not suggest violation of one or more of the assumptions for regression inferences.

(d) The normal probability plot appears to be more curved than linear; thus, the assumption of normality is violated.

15.21 Using Minitab, with the data in columns named AGE and %FAT, we choose **Stat ▶ Regression ▶ Regression...**, select %FAT in the **Response** text box, select AGE in the **Predictors** text box, select **Residuals** from the **Storage** check-box list. Click the **Graphs...** button, select the **Regular** option button from the **Residuals for Plots** list, select the **Normal plot of residuals** check box from the **Residual Plots** list, click in the **Residuals versus the variables** text box and specify AGE, click **OK**, and click **OK**. The results are

(a) The regression equation is

%FAT = 3.22 + 0.548 AGE

Predictor	Coef	StDev	T	P
Constant	3.221	5.076	0.63	0.535
AGE	0.5480	0.1056	5.19	0.000

S = 5.754 R-Sq = 62.7% R-Sq(adj) = 60.4%

Analysis of Variance

Source	DF	SS	MS	F	P
Regression	1	891.87	891.87	26.94	0.000
Residual Error	16	529.66	33.10		
Total	17	1421.54			

Unusual Observations

Obs	AGE	%FAT	Fit	StDev Fit	Residual	St Resid
2	23.0	27.90	15.82	2.81	12.08	2.41R

R denotes an observation with a large standardized residual

The standard error of the estimate is the first entry in the sixth line of the computer output. It is reported as s = 5.754. Presuming that the variables AGE and %FAT satisfy the assumptions for regression inferences, the standard error of the estimate, 5.754, provides an estimate for the common population standard deviation, σ, of percent body fat for all individuals of a particular age.

(b) The two graphs which result are shown below.

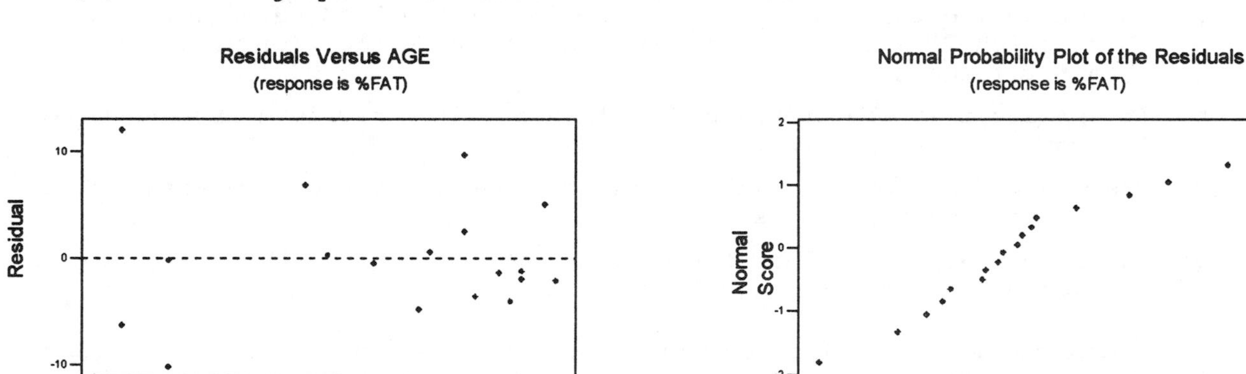

(c) The residual plots do not give any indication that Assumptions 1-3 are being violated, so it is reasonable to assume that those assumptions are met.

15.23 Using Minitab, with the data in columns named DISP and MPG, we choose **Stat ▶ Regression ▶ Regression...**, select DISP in the **Response** text box, select MPG in the **Predictors** text box, select **Residuals** from the **Storage** check-box list. Click the **Graphs...** button, select the **Regular** option button from the **Residuals for Plots** list, select the **Normal plot of residuals** check box from the **Residual Plots** list, click in the **Residuals versus the variables** text box and specify DISP, click **OK**, and click **OK**. The results are

(a) The regression equation is
MPG = 32.3 - 3.58 DISP

```
Predictor        Coef      StDev          T        P
Constant      32.2732     0.6704      48.14    0.000
DISP          -3.5762     0.2099     -17.03    0.000

S = 2.248       R-Sq = 70.9%     R-Sq(adj) = 70.7%

Analysis of Variance

Source            DF         SS          MS          F        P
Regression         1     1465.8      1465.8     290.18    0.000
Residual Error   119      601.1         5.1
Total            120     2067.0

Unusual Observations
Obs       DISP        MPG          Fit    StDev Fit      Residual    St Resid
  1       1.80     31.000       25.836        0.331         5.164      2.32R
 18       5.70     20.000       11.889        0.594         8.111      3.74RX
 21       1.80     31.000       25.836        0.331         5.164      2.32R
 23       5.70     13.000       11.889        0.594         1.111      0.51 X
 49       5.70     13.000       11.889        0.594         1.111      0.51 X
 53       1.60     31.000       26.551        0.365         4.449      2.01R
 87       3.30     15.000       20.472        0.211        -5.472     -2.45R

R denotes an observation with a large standardized residual
X denotes an observation whose X value gives it large influence.
```

The standard error of the estimate is the first entry in the sixth line of the computer output. It is reported as s = 2.248. Presuming that the variables DISP and MPG satisfy the assumptions for regression inferences, the standard error of the estimate, 2.248, provides an estimate for the common population standard deviation, σ, of miles per gallon for all cars with a particular engine displacement.

(b) The two graphs which result follow.

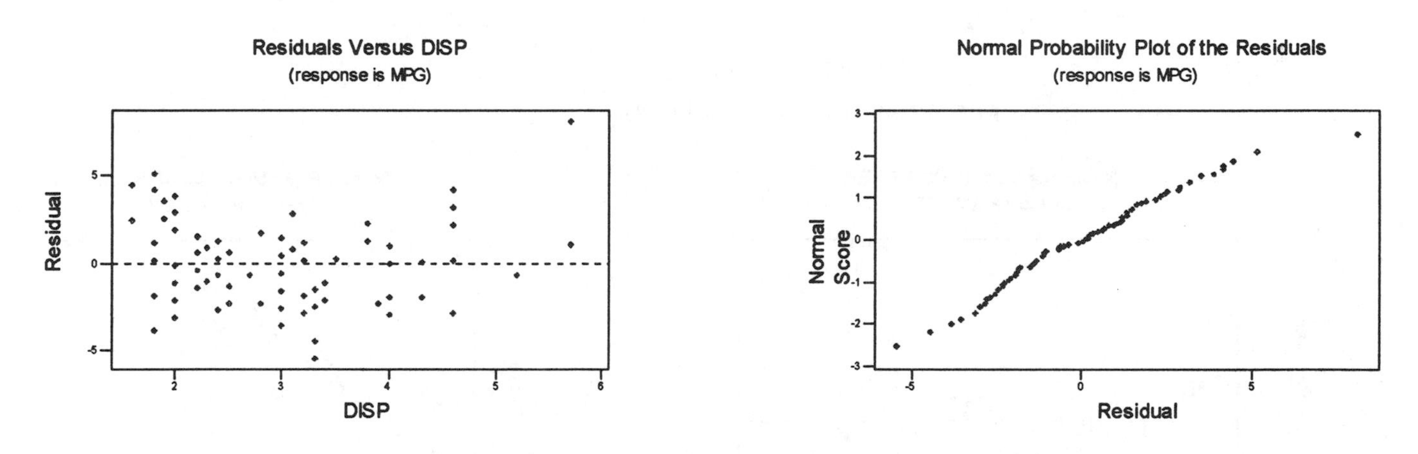

(c) The residual plotted against engine displacement display a concave upward curve, indicating that the linear model is not appropriate for the data. Thus Assumption 1 is violated and the statement made in part (a) interpreting the meaning of the standard error does not hold.

15.25 Using Minitab, with the data in columns named DIAMETER and VOLUME, we choose

Stat ▶ Regression ▶ Regression..., select VOLUME in the **Response** text box, select DIAMETER in the **Predictors** text box, select **Residuals** from the **Storage** check-box list. Click the **Graphs...** button, select the **Regular** option button from the **Residuals for Plots** list, select the **Normal plot of residuals** check box from the **Residual Plots** list, click in the **Residuals versus the variables** text box and specify DIAMETER, click **OK**, and click **OK**. The results are

(a) The regression equation is

VOLUME = - 41.6 + 6.84 DIAMETER

Predictor	Coef	StDev	T	P
Constant	-41.568	3.427	-12.13	0.000
DIAMETER	6.8367	0.2877	23.77	0.000

S = 9.875 R-Sq = 89.3% R-Sq(adj) = 89.1%

Analysis of Variance

Source	DF	SS	MS	F	P
Regression	1	55083	55083	564.88	0.000
Residual Error	68	6631	98		
Total	69	61714			

Unusual Observations

Obs	DIAMETER	VOLUME	Fit	StDev Fit	Residual	St Resid
70	23.4	163.50	118.41	3.71	45.09	4.93RX

R denotes an observation with a large standardized residual
X denotes an observation whose X value gives it large influence.

The standard error of the estimate is the first entry in the sixth line of the computer output. It is reported as s = 9.875. Presuming that the variables VOLUME and DIAMETER satisfy the assumptions for regression inferences, the standard error of the estimate, 9.875, provides an estimate for the common population standard deviation, σ, of tree volumes for all trees having a particular diameter at breast height.

(b) The two graphs which result follow.

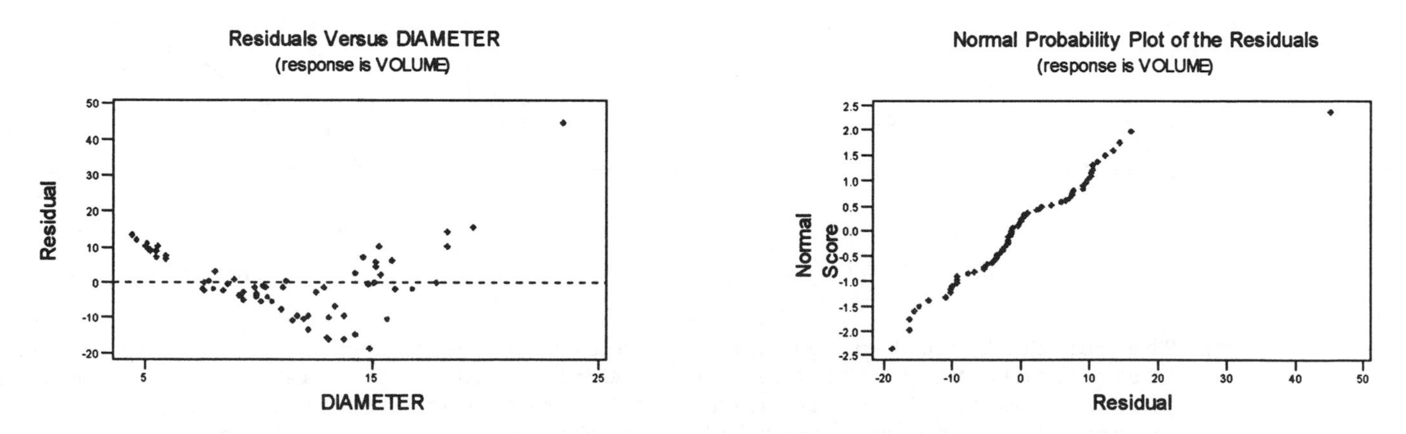

(c) The residuals plotted against diameter are displayed in a curved concave upward pattern, indicating that the linear model is not appropriate. This is a violation of Assumption 1. In addition, both plots indicate the presence of an outlier. Finally, it appears that there is more variability in the center of the first graph than at the left side, so Assumption 2 is also violated.

Removal of the outlier will not change the curved pattern of the other residuals or the unequal variation in the residuals, so this data should not be analyzed using a straight line model.

Exercises 15.2

15.27 normal, $\beta_1 = -3.5$

15.29 We can also use the coefficient of determination, r^2, and the linear correlation coefficient, r, as a basis for a test to decide whether a regression equation is useful for prediction.

15.31 From Exercise 14.43, $\Sigma x = 41$, $\Sigma x^2 = 199$, and $b_1 = -27.9029$. From Exercise 15.15, $s_e = 14.2464$.

Step 1: H_0: $\beta_1 = 0$, H_a: $\beta_1 \neq 0$

Step 2: $\alpha = 0.10$

Step 3: $$t = \frac{b_1}{s_e / \sqrt{\sum x^2 - (\sum x)^2 / n}} = \frac{-27.9029}{14.2464 / \sqrt{199 - 41^2 / 10}} = -10.887$$

Step 4: df = n - 2 = 8; critical values = ±1.860

Step 5: Since -10.887 < -1.860, reject H_0.

Step 6: The data provide sufficient evidence to conclude that the slope of the population regression line is not zero and, hence, that age is useful as a predictor of price for Corvettes.

For the P-value approach, P < 0.01. Therefore, because the P-value is less than the significance level of 0.10, we can reject H_0.

15.33 From Exercise 14.45, $\Sigma x = 723$, $\Sigma x^2 = 48747$, and $b_1 = 0.16285$. From Exercise 15.17, $s_e = 5.418$.

Step 1: H_0: $\beta_1 = 0$, H_a: $\beta_1 \neq 0$

Step 2: $\alpha = 0.05$

Step 3: $$t = \frac{b_1}{s_e / \sqrt{\sum x^2 - (\sum x)^2 / n}} = \frac{0.16285}{5.418 / \sqrt{48747 - 723^2 / 11}} = 1.053$$

Step 4: df = n - 2 = 9; critical values = ±2.262

Step 5: Since 1.053 < 2.262, do not reject H_0.

Step 6: Evidently, plant weight is not useful as a predictor of volume of volatile emissions.

For the P-value approach, P > 0.20. Therefore, because the P-value is greater than the significance level of 0.05, we can not reject H_0.

15.35 From Exercise 14.43, $\Sigma x = 41$, $\Sigma x^2 = 199$, and $b_1 = -27.9029$. From Exercise 15.15, $s_e = 14.2464$.

(a) Step 1: For a 90% confidence interval, $\alpha = 0.10$. With df = n - 2 = 8, $t_{\alpha/2} = t_{0.05} = 1.860$.

Step 2: The endpoints of the confidence interval for β_1 are

$$b_1 \pm t_{\alpha/2} \cdot s_e / \sqrt{\sum x^2 - (\sum x)^2 / n}$$

$$-27.9029 \pm 1.860 \cdot 14.2464 / \sqrt{199 - 41^2 / 10}$$

$$-27.9029 \pm 4.7669$$

$$-32.6698 \text{ to } -23.1360$$

(b) We can be 90% confident that the yearly decrease in mean price for Corvettes is somewhere between $2314 and $3267.

15.37 From Exercise 14.45, $\Sigma x = 723$, $\Sigma x^2 = 48747$, and $b_1 = 0.16285$. From Exercise 15.17, $s_e = 5.4177$.

(a) Step 1: For a 95% confidence interval, $\alpha = 0.05$. With df = n - 2 = 9, $t_{\alpha/2} = t_{0.025} = 2.262$.

Step 2: The endpoints of the confidence interval for β_1 are

$$b_1 \pm t_{\alpha/2} \cdot s_e / \sqrt{\sum x^2 - (\sum x)^2 / n}$$

$$0.16285 \pm 2.262 \cdot 5.4177 / \sqrt{48747 - 723^2 / 11}$$

$$0.16285 \pm 0.34997$$

$$-0.187 \text{ to } 0.513$$

(b) We can be 95% confident that the increase in mean volatile plant emissions per one gram increase in weight is somewhere between -0.187 and 0.513 hundred nanograms.

15.39 (a) From the fifth line of the Minitab computer output shown in Exercise 15.21, t = 5.19 and the associated P-value is 0.000. Since the P-value is less than the significance level of 0.05, we reject the null hypothesis that $\beta_1 = 0$ and conclude that the regression equation is useful for making predictions.

(b) Minitab identified the data point (23.0, 27.90) as a potential outlier. After removing that point from the data set and following the same procedure as in Exercise 15.21, the result is

```
The regression equation is
   %FAT = - 3.44 + 0.673 AGE

   Predictor         Coef        StDev           T          P
   Constant        -3.436        4.770       -0.72      0.482
   AGE            0.67263      0.09704        6.93      0.000

   S = 4.748        R-Sq = 76.2%      R-Sq(adj) = 74.6%

   Analysis of Variance

   Source            DF           SS          MS          F          P
   Regression         1       1082.9      1082.9      48.05      0.000
   Residual Error    15        338.1        22.5
   Total             16       1421.0

Unusual Observations
Obs        AGE        %FAT          Fit    StDev Fit     Residual    St Resid
 10       53.0       42.00        32.21         1.26         9.79       2.14R
R denotes an observation with a large standardized residual
```

(c) There is now one new potential outlier indicated although the standardized residual is 2.14, barely over the threshold of 2.00 for earning that distinction. The value of b_1 has changed to 0.67263 (from 0.5480) and its associated t value is now 6.93 (instead of 5.19) with a p-value of 0.000. Since the p-value is less than 0.05, we still conclude that the regression equation is useful for making predictions within the range of the values of the ages, 23 to 61.

15.41 (a) From the fifth line of the Minitab computer output shown in Exercise 15.23, t = -17.03 and the associated P-value is 0.000. Since the P-value is less than the significance level of 0.05, we reject the null hypothesis that $\beta_1 = 0$ and conclude that the regression equation is useful for making predictions.

(b) Minitab identified the four data points, (1.8, 31), (1.8, 31), (1.6, 31), and (3.3, 15), as potential outliers, the two data points (5.7, 13) and (5.7, 13) as influential, and the data point (5.7, 20) as both a potential outlier and influential. After removing those seven points from the data set and following the same procedure as in Exercise 15.23, the result is

```
The regression equation is
MPG = 32.4 - 3.66 DISP

Predictor        Coef       StDev         T        P
Constant      32.3592      0.6503     49.76    0.000
DISP          -3.6622      0.2078    -17.62    0.000

S = 1.950        R-Sq = 73.5%      R-Sq(adj) = 73.3%

Analysis of Variance

Source            DF          SS          MS          F        P
Regression         1      1180.5      1180.5     310.54    0.000
Residual Error   112       425.8         3.8
Total            113      1606.3

Unusual Observations
Obs      DISP        MPG        Fit   StDev Fit    Residual   St Resid
 13      4.60     20.000     15.513       0.379       4.487      2.35R
 29      5.20     13.000     13.316       0.492      -0.316     -0.17 X
 32      5.20     13.000     13.316       0.492      -0.316     -0.17 X
 53      3.30     16.000     20.274       0.193      -4.274     -2.20R
107      1.80     30.000     25.767       0.310       4.233      2.20R
112      2.00     29.000     25.035       0.277       3.965      2.05R

R denotes an observation with a large standardized residual
X denotes an observation whose X value gives it large influence.
```

(c) There are now four new potential outliers indicated, none of them extremely large, and two new influential observations, both at 5.20 displacement. The value of b_1 has changed to -3.622 (from -3.576 and its associated t value is now -17.62 (instead of -17.03) with a p-value of 0.000. Since the p-value is less than 0.05, we could conclude that the regression equation is useful for making predictions within the range of the values of the displacement, 1.6 to 5.2. Recall that previously we had concluded from the residual plot that the linear model was not appropriate for the full set of data even though the t value was significant and the coefficient of determination was moderately large. The coefficient of determination has increased slightly with the deletion of the seven data points, the t value is about the same, the standard error has decreased to 1.950 from 2.248, and if you look at a scatter plot of the data and/or a residual plot, you will find that a straight line model is now appropriate for the reduced data set.

Exercises 15.3

15.43 \$11,443

15.45 From Exercise 14.42, $\hat{y} = 371.602 - 27.9029x$, $\Sigma x = 41$, and $\Sigma x^2 = 199$. From Exercise 15.16, $s_e = 14.2464$.

(a) $\hat{y}_p = 371.602 - 27.9029(4) = 259.9904 = \$25,999.$

(b) Step 1: For a 90% confidence interval, $\alpha = 0.10$.

With df = n - 2 = 8, $t_{\alpha/2} = t_{0.05} = 1.860$.

Step 2: $\hat{y}_p = 259.9904$

Step 3: The endpoints of the confidence interval are

$$\hat{y}_p \pm t_{\alpha/2} \cdot s_e \cdot \sqrt{\frac{1}{n} + \frac{(x_p - \sum x/n)^2}{\sum x^2 - (\sum x)^2/n}}$$

$$= 259.9904 \pm 1.860 \cdot 14.2464 \cdot \sqrt{\frac{1}{10} + \frac{(4-41/10)^2}{199 - 41^2/10}}$$

$$= 259.9904 \pm 8.3930$$

$$= (251.5974,\ 268.3834)$$

The interpretation of this interval is as follows: We can be 90% confident that the mean price of all four-year-old Corvettes is somewhere between \$25,160 and \$26,838.

(c) This is the same as the answer in part (a): $\hat{y}_p = 259.9904$.

(d) For a 90% prediction interval, Steps 1 and 2 are the same as Steps 1 and 2, respectively, in part (b). Thus, they are not repeated here. Only Step 3 is presented.

Step 3: The endpoints of the prediction interval are

$$\hat{y}_p \pm t_{\alpha/2} \cdot s_e \cdot \sqrt{1 + \frac{1}{n} + \frac{(x_p - \sum x/n)^2}{\sum x^2 - (\sum x)^2/n}}$$

$$= 259.9904 \pm 1.860 \cdot 14.2464 \cdot \sqrt{1 + \frac{1}{10} + \frac{(4-41/10)^2}{199 - 41^2/10}}$$

$$= 259.9904 \pm 27.7957$$

$$= (232.1947,\ 287.7861)$$

The interpretation of this interval is as follows: We can be 90% certain that the price of a randomly selected four-year-old Corvette will be somewhere between \$23,219 and \$28,779.

(e)

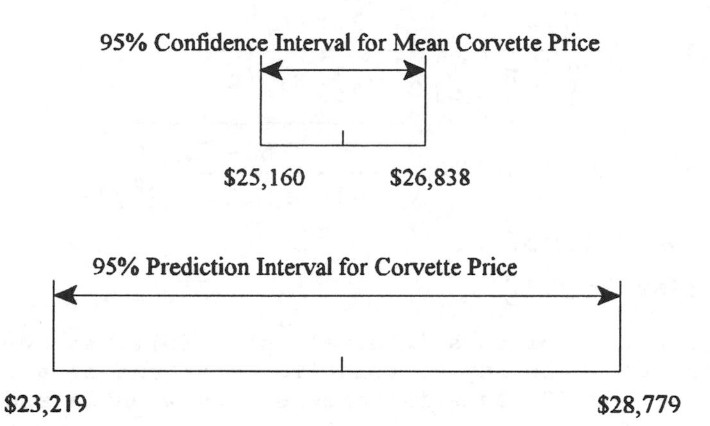

(f) The error in the estimate of the mean price of four-year-old Corvettes is due only to the fact that the population regression line is being estimated by a sample regression line; whereas, the error in the prediction of the price of a randomly selected four-year-old Corvette is due to that fact plus the variation in prices for four-year-old Corvettes.

15.47 From Exercise 14.45, $\hat{y} = 3.523688 + 0.162848x$, $\Sigma x = 723$, and $\Sigma x^2 = 48747$. From Exercise 15.17, $s_e = 5.4177$.

(a) $\hat{y}_p = 3.523688 + 0.162848(60) = 13.2946$

(b) Step 1: For a 95% confidence interval, $\alpha = 0.05$.

With df = n - 2 = 9, $t_{\alpha/2} = t_{0.025} = 2.262$.

Step 2: $\hat{y}_p = 13.2946$

Step 3: The endpoints of the confidence interval are

$$\hat{y}_p \pm t_{\alpha/2} \cdot s_e \cdot \sqrt{\frac{1}{n} + \frac{(x_p - \sum x/n)^2}{\sum x^2 - (\sum x)^2/n}}$$

$$= 13.2946 \pm 2.262 \cdot 5.4177 \cdot \sqrt{\frac{1}{11} + \frac{(60 - 723/11)^2}{48747 - 723^2/11}}$$

$$= 13.2946 \pm 4.2036$$

$$= (9.0910,\ 17.4982)$$

The interpretation of this interval is as follows: We can be 95% confident that the mean quantity of volatile emissions of all plants that weigh 60 grams is somewhere between 909 and 1750 nanograms.

(c) This is the same as the answer in part (a): $\hat{y}_p = 13.2946$.

(d) For a 95% prediction interval, Steps 1 and 2 are the same as Steps 1 and 2, respectively, in part (b). Thus, they are not repeated here. Only Step 3 is presented.

Step 3: The endpoints of the prediction interval are

$$\hat{y}_p \pm t_{\alpha/2} \cdot s_e \cdot \sqrt{1 + \frac{1}{n} + \frac{(x_p - \sum x/n)^2}{\sum x^2 - (\sum x)^2/n}}$$

$$= 13.2946 \pm 2.262 \cdot 5.4177 \cdot \sqrt{1 + \frac{1}{11} + \frac{(60 - 723/11)^2}{48747 - 723^2/11}}$$

$$= 13.2946 \pm 12.9557$$

$$= (0.3389, 26.2503)$$

The interpretation of this interval is as follows: We can be 95% certain that the quantity of volatile emissions of a randomly selected plant that weighs 60 grams is somewhere between 34 and 2625 nanograms.

15.49 (a) The confidence interval formula for the conditional mean of the response variable is

$$\hat{y}_p \pm t_{\alpha/2} \cdot s_e \cdot \sqrt{\frac{1}{n} + \frac{(x_p - \sum x/n)^2}{\sum x^2 - (\sum x)^2/n}}.$$

The margin of error term to the right of the $\pm$ sign contains the term $(x_p - \sum x/n)^2 = (x_p - \bar{x})^2$. As the value of the predictor variable moves farther from the mean of the predictor variable in either direction, this squared term increases in size, thereby increasing the size of the entire term for the margin of error.

(b) The prediction interval formula for the predicted value of the response variable is

$$\hat{y}_p \pm t_{\alpha/2} \cdot s_e \cdot \sqrt{1 + \frac{1}{n} + \frac{(x_p - \sum x/n)^2}{\sum x^2 - (\sum x)^2/n}}.$$

The margin of error term to the right of the $\pm$ sign contains the term $(x_p - \sum x/n)^2 = (x_p - \bar{x})^2$. As the value of the predictor variable moves farther from the mean of the predictor variable in either direction, this squared term increases in size, thereby increasing the size of the entire term for the margin of error.

15.51 Using Minitab, with the data in columns named AGE and %FAT, to obtain both confidence and prediction intervals, we choose **Stat ▶ Regression ▶ Regression...**, select %FAT in the **Response** text box, select AGE in the **Predictors** text box, click on the **Options** button, type 30 in the **Prediction intervals for new observations** text box, click on the check-boxes for **Confidence limits** and **Prediction limits**, click **OK** and click **OK**. Those parts of the results needed for parts (a)-(d) are

```
Predicted Values
   Fit  StDev Fit          95.0% CI              95.0% PI
 19.66       2.19    (  15.01,    24.31)  (    6.61,    32.71)
```

(a) 19.66

(b) 15.01 to 24.31 is the 95% confidence interval.

(c) 19.66

(d) 6.61 to 32.71 is the 95% prediction interval.

15.53 Using Minitab, with the data in columns named DISP and MPG, to obtain both confidence and prediction intervals, we choose **Stat ▶ Regression ▶ Regression...**, select MPG in the **Response** text box, select DISP in the **Predictors** text box, click on the **Options** button, type <u>3.0</u> in the **Prediction intervals for new observations** text box, click on the check-boxes for **Confidence limits** and **Prediction limits**, click **OK** and click **OK**. Those parts of the results needed for parts (a)-(d) are

```
Predicted Values

    Fit  StDev Fit          95.0% CI             95.0% PI
 21.544      0.205   (  21.140,  21.949)  (  17.076,  26.013)
```

(a) 21.140 to 21.949 is the 95% confidence interval.

(b) 17.076 to 26.013 is the 95% prediction interval.

(c) Both intervals are centered at the point estimate 21.544 for MPG for a car with a 3.0 liter displacement. The confidence interval for the mean miles per gallon of all cars with a 3.0 liter displacement is shorter than the prediction interval for the miles per gallon of a randomly selected car with a 3.0 liter displacement due to the additional variation in individual MPG values over that experienced by a sample mean.

<u>**Exercises 15.4**</u>

15.55 r

15.57 (a) uncorrelated

(b) increases

(c) negatively

15.59 From Exercise 14.87, $r = -0.96783$ and $n = 10$.

Step 1: H_0: $\rho = 0$ H_a: $\rho < 0$

Step 2: $\alpha = 0.05$

Step 3: $$t = \frac{r}{\sqrt{\frac{1-r^2}{n-2}}} = \frac{-0.96783}{\sqrt{\frac{1-(-0.96783)^2}{10-2}}} = -10.8873$$

Step 4: The critical value for $n - 2 = 8$ df is -1.860.

Step 5: Since $-10.8873 < -1.860$, reject H_0 and conclude that $\rho < 0$.

For the p-value approach, $P < 0.005$. Since $P < 0.05$, reject H_0 and conclude that $\rho < 0$.

15.61 From Exercise 14.89, $r = 0.33107$ and $n = 11$.

Step 1: H_0: $\rho = 0$ H_a: $\rho \neq 0$

Step 2: $\alpha = 0.05$

Step 3: $$t = \frac{r}{\sqrt{\frac{1-r^2}{n-2}}} = \frac{0.33107}{\sqrt{\frac{1-(0.33107)^2}{11-2}}} = 1.0526$$

Step 4: The critical values for n - 2 = 9 df are ±2.262.

Step 5: Since $-2.262 < 1.0526 < 2.262$, do not reject H_0 and conclude that $\rho = 0$ is reasonable.

For the p-value approach, $P > 0.200$. Since $P > 0.05$, do not reject H_0 and conclude that $\rho = 0$ is reasonable.

15.63 The population linear correlation coefficient ρ is a parameter (constant) that measures the linear correlation between the population of all data points. The sample linear correlation coefficient *r* is a statistic (random variable); it measures the linear correlation between a sample of data points, and so its value depends on chance, namely, on which data points are obtained from sampling.

15.65 (a) Using Minitab, with the data in columns named AGE and %FAT, we choose **Stat ▶ Basic Statistics ▶ Correlation..**, enter AGE and %FAT in the **Variables:** box, click to put a ✓ in the **Display p-values** box, and click **OK.** The result is

Correlation of AGE and %FAT = 0.792, P-Value = 0.000

We note that the p-value in Minitab is for a two-tailed test of $\rho = 0$. In the case of a one-tailed test, if the correlation is in the direction of the alternative hypothesis, the p-value is one-half of that shown. Since this is a right-tailed test, the p-value is 0.000/2 = 0.000 which is less than 0.025. Therefore we reject H_0 and conclude that percent body fat and age are positively linearly correlated for adults.

(b) After deleting the data point (23, 27.90), the result is

Correlation of AGE and %FAT = 0.873, P-Value = 0.000

(c) In this case, the value of r has increased, and the p-value is still 0.000. Our conclusion is the same after removing the potential outlier.

15.67 Using Minitab, with the data in columns named DISP and MPG, we choose **Stat ▶ Basic Statistics ▶ Correlation..**, enter DISP and MPG in the **Variables:** box, click to put a ✓ in the **Display p-values** box, and click **OK.** The result is

Correlation of DISP and MPG = -0.842, P-Value = 0.000

We note that the p-value in Minitab is for a two-tailed test of $\rho = 0$. Since this is a left-tailed test, the p-value is 0.000/2 = 0.000 which is less than 0.05. Therefore we reject H_0. There is sufficient evidence to conclude that engine displacement and gas mileage are negatively linearly correlated.

Exercises 15.5

15.69 (a) A normal probability plot is a plot of normal scores against sample data.

(b) An important use of such plots is to help assess the normality of a variable.

(c) If the sample data come from a normal distribution, the plot should be roughly linear. Therefore, if the plot is roughly linear, we accept as reasonable that the variable is normally distributed; if the plot shows systematic deviations from a straight line, then conclude that the variable probably is not normally distributed.

(d) The method in (c) is subjective because what constitutes "roughly linear" is a matter of opinion.

15.71 If the population under consideration is normally distributed, then the correlation between the sample data and its normal scores should be near 1. Note that since large normal scores are associated with large data values and vice versa, the correlation between the sample data and its normal scores cannot be negative. Thus, the correlation test for normality is always left-tailed because if the correlation (the test statistic of interest) is significantly smaller than 1, the null hypothesis that the population is normally distributed is rejected.

15.73 Step 1: H_0: The population is normally distributed.

H_a: The population is not normally distributed.

Step 2: $\alpha = 0.05$

Step 3:

Exam score x	Normal score w	xw	x^2	w^2
34	-1.87	-63.58	1156	3.4969
39	-1.40	-54.60	1521	1.9600
63	-1.13	-71.19	3969	1.2769
64	-0.92	-58.88	4096	0.8464
67	-0.74	-49.58	4489	0.5476
70	-0.59	-41.30	4900	0.3481
75	-0.45	-33.75	5625	0.2025
76	-0.31	-23.56	5776	0.0961
81	-0.19	-15.39	6561	0.0361
82	-0.06	-4.92	6724	0.0036
84	0.06	5.04	7056	0.0036
85	0.19	16.15	7225	0.0361
86	0.31	26.66	7396	0.0961
88	0.45	39.60	7744	0.2025
89	0.59	52.51	7921	0.3481
90	0.74	66.60	8100	0.5476
90	0.92	82.80	8100	0.8464
96	1.13	108.48	9216	1.2769
96	1.40	134.40	9216	1.9600
100	1.87	187.00	10000	3.4969
1555	0.00	302.49	126,791	17.6284

$$R_p = \frac{\sum xw}{\sqrt{[\sum x^2 - (\sum x)^2 / n][\sum w^2]}}$$

$$= \frac{302.49}{\sqrt{[126791 - (1555)^2 / 20][17.6284]}} = 0.939$$

Step 4: From Table IX, the critical value is = 0.951.

Step 5: From Step 4 the value of the test statistic is $R_p = 0.939$, which is less than 0.952 and therefore falls in the rejection region. Hence we reject H_0.

The test results are statistically significant at the 5% level, that is, at the 5% significance level, the data provide sufficient evidence to conclude that final exam scores are not normally distributed.

15.75 Step 1: H_0: The population is normally distributed.

H_a: The population is not normally distributed.

Step 2: $\alpha = 0.10$ Step 3:

Miles	Normal score			
x	w	xw	x^2	w^2
6.3	-1.74	-10.962	39.69	3.0276
8.7	-1.24	-10.788	75.69	1.5376
9.6	-0.94	-9.024	92.16	0.8836
10.7	-0.71	-7.957	114.49	0.5041
11.3	-0.51	-5.763	127.69	0.2601
11.6	-0.33	-3.828	134.56	0.1089
11.9	-0.16	-1.904	141.61	0.0256
12.2	0.00	0.000	148.84	0.0256
13.2	0.16	2.112	174.24	0.0256
13.3	0.33	4.389	176.89	0.1089
13.6	0.51	6.936	184.96	0.2601
14.8	0.71	10.508	219.04	0.5041
15.0	0.94	14.100	225.00	0.8836
15.7	1.24	19.468	246.49	1.5376
16.7	1.74	29.058	278.89	3.0276
184.6	0.00	36.705	2380.24	12.6950

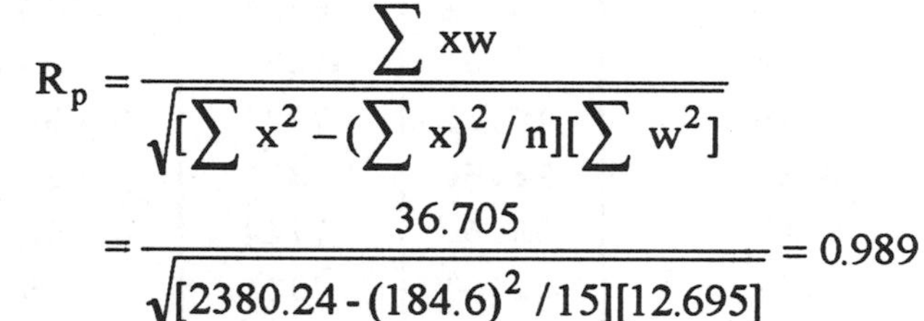

$$R_p = \frac{\sum xw}{\sqrt{[\sum x^2 - (\sum x)^2/n][\sum w^2]}}$$

$$= \frac{36.705}{\sqrt{[2380.24 - (184.6)^2/15][12.695]}} = 0.989$$

Step 4: From Table IX, the critical value is = 0.951.

Step 5: From Step 4 the value of the test statistic is $R_p = 0.989$, which does not fall in the rejection region. Hence we do not reject H_0.

Step 6: The test results are not statistically significant at the 10% level; that is, at the 10% significance level, the data do not provide sufficient evidence to conclude that the number of miles cars are driven are not normally distributed.

15.77 Using Minitab with the data in a column named SCORES, we choose **Stat ▶ Basic statistics ▶ Normality test...**, select SCORES in the **Variable** text box, select the **Ryan-Joiner** option button from the **Tests for Normality** field, and click **OK**. The result is shown at the right. The P-value shown in the lower right is .0321. Since this is smaller than the 0.05 significance level, we reject the null hypothesis of normality.

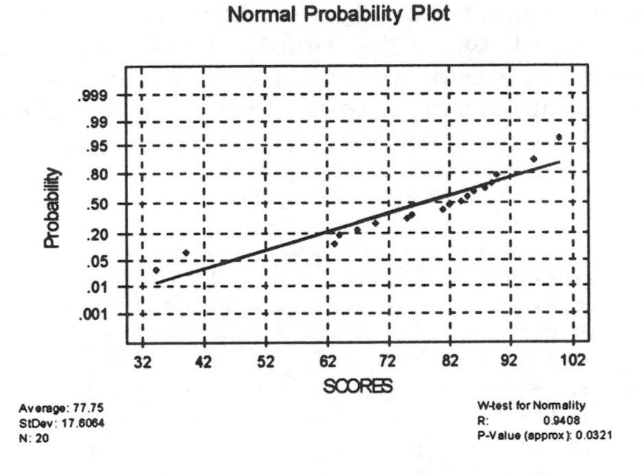

15.79 Using Minitab with the data in a column named FAT, we choose **Stat ▶ Basic Statistics ▶ Normality test...**, select FAT in the **Variable** text box, select the **Ryan-Joiner** option button from the **Tests for Normality** field, and click **OK.** The result is shown following. The P-value shown in the lower right is > 0.100. Since this is larger than the 0.05 significance level, we do not reject the null hypothesis of normality.

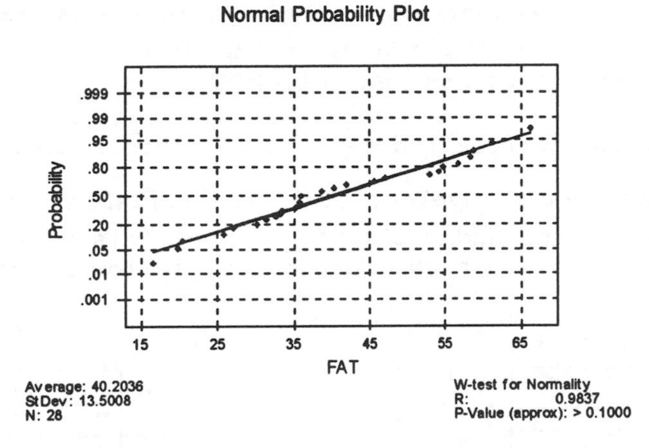

15.81 Minitab does not have the capability of performing a normality test using grouped data. However, it does have an easy way to enter repeated data values so that every value occurs in the column as often as its frequency dictates. First, name one of the columns LENGTH. Then, in the Session Window, following the MTB > prompt, type the command SET 'LENGTH'. A new prompt, DATA> will appear. Following this prompt, enter each data value in parentheses preceded by its frequency. The number 9.8 with its frequency of 4 is entered as 4(9.8). Put a space or a comma before entering the next number. You may hit the enter key at any time and continue the data on the next line. When you have entered the last data values, type END. Once you have named one column LENGTH, the entire data entry process will look like this:

```
MTB > SET 'LENGTH'
DATA> 9.5 4(9.8) 24(10.1) 67(10.4) 193(10.7) 417(11.0) 575(11.3)
DATA> 691(11.6) 509(11.9) 306(12.2) 131(12.5) 63(12.8) 16(13.1) 3(13.4)
DATA> END
```

Now, we choose **Stat ▶ Basic Statistics ▶ Normality test...**, select LENGTH in the **Variable** text box, select the **Ryan-Joiner** option button from the **Tests for Normality** field, and click **OK**. The result is shown following. The value of r is 0.9998 and the P-value shown in the lower right is > 0.100. Since this is larger than the 0.05 significance level, we do not reject the null hypothesis of normality.

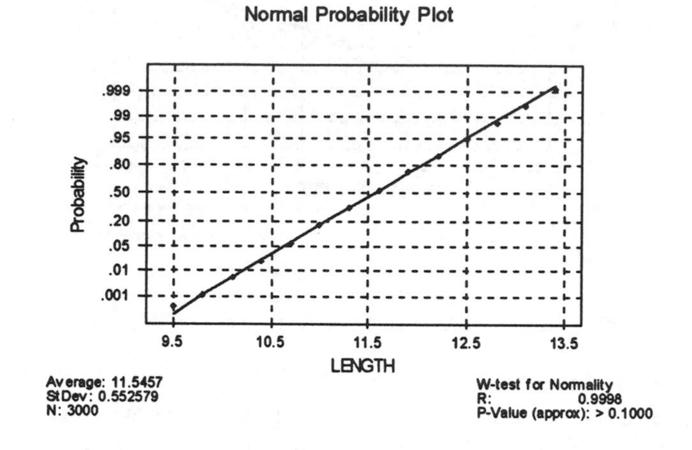

15.83 (a) In Minitab, name four columns T1, T2, T3, and T4. Then choose **Calc ▶ Random data ▶ Exponential...**, type 75 in the **Generate rows of data** text box, select T1, T2, T3, and T4 in the **Store in column(s):** text box, type 8.7 in the **Mean** text box, and click **OK**.

(b) To perform the correlation test on T1, choose **Stat ▶ Basic statistics ▶ Normality test...**, select T1 in the **Variable** text box, click on the **Ryan-Joiner** button and click **OK**. Repeat this process for T2, T3, and T4. The results are shown in the four following graphs.

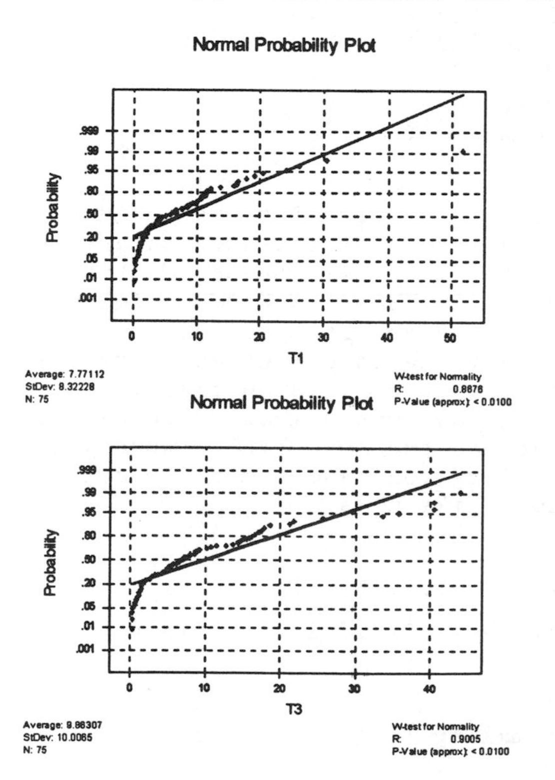

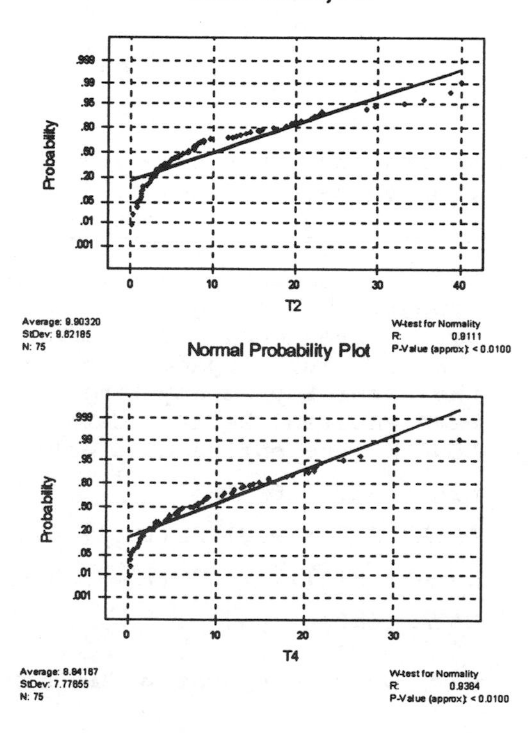

The four values of R_p are 0.8676, 0.9111, 0.9005, and 0.9384. Their P-values are all less than 0.0100. Thus all of them are significant at the 0.05 significance level.

(c) Since the samples were generated from a non-normal (exponential) distribution and we expect that samples will reflect the properties of the population, the results in (b) are what we should have expected.

REVIEW TEST FOR CHAPTER 15

1. (a) conditional

   (b) The four assumptions for regression inferences are:

   (1) *Population regression line:* There is a straight line $y = \beta_0 + \beta_1 x$ such that, for each x-value, the mean of the corresponding population of y-values lies on that straight line.

   (2) *Equal standard deviations:* The standard deviation σ of the population of y-values corresponding to a particular x-value is the same, regardless of the x-value.

   (3) *Normality:* For each x-value, the corresponding population of y-values is normally distributed.

   (4) *Independence:* The observations of the response variable are independent of one another.

2. (a) The slope of the sample regression line, b_1

   (b) The y-intercept of the sample regression line, b_0

   (c) s_e

3. We used a plot of the residuals against the values of the predictor variable x and a normal probability plot of the residuals. In the first plot, the residuals should lie in a horizontal band centered on and symmetric about the x-axis. In the second plot, the points should lie roughly in a straight line.

4 (a) A residual plot showing curvature indicates that the first assumption, that of linearity, is probably not valid.

   (b) This type of plot indicates that the second assumption, that of constant standard deviation, is probably not valid.

   (c) A normal probability plot with extreme curvature indicates that the third assumption, that the conditional distribution of the response variable is normally distributed, is not valid.

   (d) A normal probability plot that is roughly linear, but shows outliers may be indicating that: the linear model is appropriate for most values of x, but not for all; or, that the standard deviation is not constant for all values of x, allowing for a few y values to lie far from the regression line; or, that a few data values are 'faulty', that is, the experimental conditions represented by the value of the x variable were not as they should have been or that the y value was in error.

5. If we reject the null hypothesis, we are claiming that β_1 is not zero. This means that different values of x will lead to different values of y. Hence, the regression equation is useful for making predictions.

6. b_1 (or t), r, r^2

7. No. The best estimate of conditional mean of the response variable and the best prediction of a single future value of y are the same.

8. A confidence interval estimates the value of a parameter; a prediction interval is used to predict a future value of a random variable.

9. ρ

10. (a) If $\rho > 0$, the variables are positively correlated, that is, there is a tendency for one variable to increase as the other one increases.

(b) If $\rho = 0$, the two variables are linearly uncorrelated, that is, there is no straight line relationship between them.

(c) If $\rho < 0$, the variables are negatively correlated, that is, there is a tendency for one variable to decrease as the other one increases.

11. If the regression assumptions are satisfied, then there is a linear relationship between the student/faculty ratio and the graduation rate, the conditional standard deviation of the graduation rate is the same for all values of the student/faculty ratio, the conditional distribution of the graduation rate is a normal distribution with mean $\beta_0 + \beta_1 x$ and standard deviation σ for all values x of the student/faculty ratio, and the values of the graduation rate are independent of each other.

12. (a) To determine b_0 and b_1 for the regression line, construct a table of values for x, y, x^2, xy and their sums. A column for y^2 is also presented for later use.

x	y	x^2	xy	y^2
16	45	256	720	2025
20	55	400	1100	3025
17	70	289	1190	4900
19	50	361	950	2500
22	47	484	1034	2209
17	46	289	782	2116
17	50	289	850	2500
17	66	289	1122	4356
10	26	100	260	676
18	60	324	1080	3600
173	515	3081	9088	27907

$S_{xx} = 3081 - 173^2/10 = 88.10$

$S_{xy} = 9088 - (173)(515)/10 = 178.50$

$b_1 = 178.50/88.10 = 2.0261$

$b_0 = 515/10 - 2.0261(173/10) = 16.4484$

$\hat{y}_p = 16.448 + 2.026x$ is the equation of the regression line.

(b) $S_{yy} = 27907 - 515^2/10 = 1384.50$

$SSE = S_{yy} - S^2_{xy}/S_{xx} = 1384.50 - 178.50^2/88.10 = 1022.8400$

$$s_e = \sqrt{\frac{SSE}{n-2}} = \sqrt{\frac{1022.8400}{8}} = 11.3073$$

This value of s_e indicates that, roughly speaking, the predicted values of y differ from the observed values of y by about 11.31.

(c) Presuming that the variables Student/Faculty ratio and Graduation rate satisfy the assumptions for regression inferences, the standard error of the estimate, $s_e = 11.31\%$, provides an estimate for the common population standard deviation, σ, of graduation rates of entering freshmen at universities with any particular student/faculty ratio.

13. For each value of x, we compute $e = y - \hat{y}$ in the following table and plot e against x.

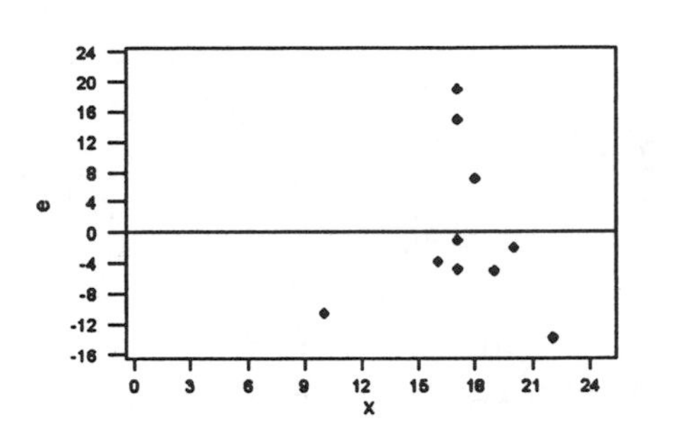

x	e
16	-3.87
20	-1.97
17	19.11
19	-4.94
22	-14.02
17	-4.89
17	-0.89
17	15.11
10	-10.71
18	7.08

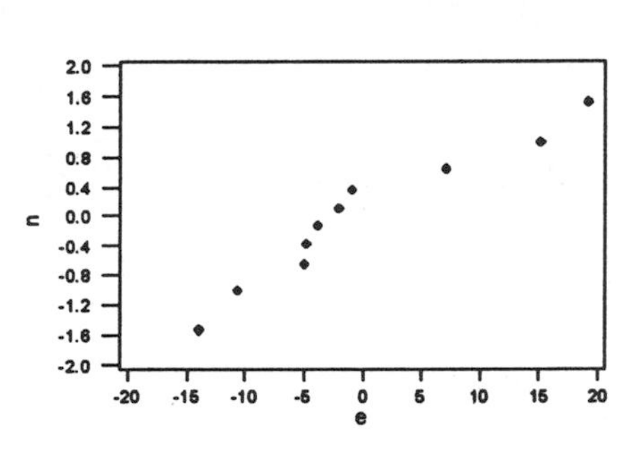

Residual	Normal score
-14.02	-1.55
-10.71	-1.00
-4.94	-0.65
-4.89	-0.37
-3.87	-0.12
-1.97	0.12
-0.89	0.37
7.08	0.65
15.11	1.00
19.11	1.55

The small sample size makes it difficult to evaluate the plot of e against x. While there are no obvious patterns in the first plot, there are two points (in the lower left and right corners of the plot) which are cause for concern. The normal probability plot is reasonably linear.

14. (a) From Review Problem 12, $\Sigma x = 173$, $\Sigma x^2 = 3,081$, $b_1 = 2.0261$, and $s_e = 11.3073$.

Step 1: H_0: $\beta_1 = 0$

H_a: $\beta_1 \neq 0$

Step 2: $\alpha = 0.05$

Step 3:
$$t = \frac{b_1}{s_e\Big/\sqrt{\sum x^2 - (\sum x)^2 / n}} = \frac{2.0261}{11.3073\Big/\sqrt{3081 - \frac{173^2}{10}}} = 1.682$$

Step 4: df = n - 2 = 8; critical values = ±2.306

Step 5: Since 1.682 < 2.306, do not reject the null hypothesis; at the 5% significance level.

Step 6: The data do not provide sufficient evidence to conclude that the student-to-faculty ratio is useful as a predictor of graduation rate. For the P-value approach, note that 0.10 < P < 0.20. Since

$P > \alpha$, do not reject the null hypothesis.

(b) Step 1: For a 95% confidence interval, $\alpha = 0.05$. With df = n - 2 = 8, $t_{\alpha/2} = t_{0.025} = 2.306$.

Step 2: The endpoints of the confidence interval for β_1 are

$$b_1 \pm t_{\alpha/2} \cdot s_e / \sqrt{\sum x^2 - (\sum x)^2 / n}$$

$$\text{or } 2.0261 \pm 2.306 \cdot 11.3073 / \sqrt{3081 - 173^2 / 10}$$

$$\text{or } 2.0261 \pm 2.7780$$

$$\text{or } -0.7519 \text{ to } 4.8041$$

We can be 95% confident that the change in graduation rate for universities per 1 unit increase in the student/faculty ratio is somewhere between -0.7519% and 4.8041%.

15. From Review Exercise 12, $\hat{y} = 16.4484 + 2.0261x$, $\Sigma x = 173$, $\Sigma x^2 = 3,081$, and $s_e = 11.3073$.

(a) $\hat{y}_p = 16.4484 + 2.0261(17) = 50.89$

(b) Step 1: For a 95% confidence interval, $\alpha = 0.05$.

With df = n - 2 = 8, $t_{\alpha/2} = t_{0.025} = 2.306$.

Step 2: $\hat{y}_p = 50.89$

Step 3: The endpoints of the confidence interval are:

$$\hat{y}_p \pm t_{\alpha/2} \cdot s_e \cdot \sqrt{\frac{1}{n} + \frac{(x_p - \sum x / n)^2}{\sum x^2 - (\sum x)^2 / n}}$$

$$= 50.89 \pm 2.306 \cdot 11.3073 \cdot \sqrt{\frac{1}{10} + \frac{(17 - 173/10)^2}{3081 - 173^2 / 10}}$$

$$= 50.89 \pm 8.29$$

$$= (42.60, 59.18)$$

The interpretation of this interval is as follows: We can be 95% confident that the mean graduation rate of universities with a student/faculty ratio of 17 is somewhere between 42.60% and 59.18%.

(c) This is the same as the answer in part (a): $\hat{y}_p = 50.89$.

(d) For a 95% prediction interval, Steps 1 and 2 are the same as Steps 1 and 2, respectively, in part (b). Thus, they are not repeated here. Only Step 3 is presented.

Step 3: The endpoints of the prediction interval are:

$$\hat{y}_p \pm t_{\alpha/2} \cdot s_e \cdot \sqrt{1+\frac{1}{n}+\frac{(x_p-\sum x/n)^2}{\sum x^2-(\sum x)^2/n}}$$

$$= 50.89 \pm 2.306 \cdot 11.3073 \cdot \sqrt{1+\frac{1}{10}+\frac{(17-173/10)^2}{3081-173^2/10}}$$

$$= 50.89 \pm 27.36$$

$$= (23.53,\ 78.25)$$

The interpretation of this interval is as follows: We can be 95% certain that the graduation rate of a randomly selected university with a student/faculty ratio of 17 will be somewhere between 23.53% and 78.25%.

(e) The error in the estimate of the mean graduation rate for universities with a student/faculty ratio of 17 is due only to the fact that the population regression line is being estimated by a sample regression line. The error in the prediction of the graduation rate of a randomly chosen university with a student/faculty ratio is due to the estimation error mentioned above plus the variation in graduation rates of universities with a student/faculty ratio of 17.

16. From Review Problem 11,

S_{xx} = 88.10

S_{xy} = 178.50

S_{yy} = 1384.50

$$r = \frac{S_{xy}}{\sqrt{S_{xx}S_{yy}}} = \frac{178.50}{\sqrt{(88.10)(1384.50)}} = 0.5111$$

Step 1: H_0: $\rho = 0$, H_a: $\rho > 0$

Step 2: $\alpha = 0.025$

Step 3: $$t = \frac{r}{\sqrt{\frac{1-r^2}{n-2}}} = \frac{0.5111}{\sqrt{\frac{1-0.5111^2}{10-2}}} = 1.682$$

Step 4: df = n - 2 = 8; critical value = 2.306

Step 5: Since 1.682 < 2.306, do not reject H_0.

Step 6: The data do not provide sufficient evidence to conclude that graduation rate and student /faculty ratio are positively linearly correlated.

For the P-value approach, $0.05 < P < 0.10$. Therefore, because the P-value is larger than the significance level of 0.025, we can not reject H_0.

17. normal scores

18. Step 1: H_0: The population is normally distributed.

H_a: The population is not normally distributed.

Step 2: $\alpha = 0.05$

Step 3:

Mileage x	Normal score w	xw	x^2	w^2
25.9	-1.74	-45.066	670.81	3.0276
27.3	-1.24	-33.852	745.29	1.5376
27.3	-0.94	-25.662	745.29	0.8836
27.6	-0.71	-19.596	761.76	0.5041
27.8	-0.51	-14.178	772.84	0.2601
27.8	-0.33	-9.174	772.84	0.1089
28.5	-0.16	-4.560	812.25	0.0256
28.6	0.00	0.000	817.96	0.0000
28.8	0.16	4.608	829.44	0.0256
28.9	0.33	9.537	835.21	0.1089
29.4	0.51	14.994	864.36	0.2601
29.7	0.71	21.087	882.09	0.5041
30.9	0.94	29.046	954.81	0.8836
31.2	1.24	38.688	973.44	1.5376
31.6	1.74	54.984	998.56	3.0276
431.3	0.00	20.856	12,436.95	12.6950

$$R_p = \frac{\sum xw}{\sqrt{[\sum x^2 - (\sum x)^2/n][\sum w^2]}}$$

$$= \frac{20.856}{\sqrt{[12436.95 - 431.3^2/15][12.6950]}} = 0.981$$

Step 4: The critical value is = 0.938.

Step 5: From Step 3 the value of the test statistic is $R_p = 0.981$, which does not fall in the rejection region. Hence we do not reject H_0.

Step 6: The test results are not statistically significant at the 5% level, that is, at the 5% significance level, the data do not provide sufficient evidence to conclude that the gas mileages for this model are not normally distributed.

19. Using Minitab, with the data in columns named S/F and GRADRATE, we choose **Stat ▶ Regression ▶ Regression...**,select GRADRATE in the **Response:** text box, select 'S/F' in the **Predictors:** text box, click on the Graphs button, check the **Normal plot of residuals** box, click in the **Residuals versus the variables** text box and select 'S/F', and click **OK.** Looking ahead to Review Problems 21,22 and 24, click on the **Options...** button, type 17 in the **Prediction intervals for new observations:** text box, type 95 in the **Confidence level:** text box, check the **Confidence limits** and **Prediction limits** boxes, and click **OK.** Click on the **Storage...** button, check the **Residuals** box, click **OK,** and click **OK.** The conclusions are the same as for Review Problem 13.

20. Following the procedure in Review Problem 19, the regression output is

```
The regression equation is
GRADRATE = 16.4 + 2.03 S/F

Predictor        Coef       StDev          T        P
Constant        16.45       21.15       0.78    0.459
S/F             2.026       1.205       1.68    0.131

S = 11.31       R-Sq = 26.1%     R-Sq(adj) = 16.9%

Analysis of Variance

Source          DF         SS          MS         F        P
Regression       1      361.7       361.7      2.83    0.131
Residual Error   8     1022.8       127.9
Total            9     1384.5

Predicted Values

    Fit  StDev Fit          95.0% CI               95.0% PI
  50.89       3.59    (   42.60,    59.18)  (   23.53,    78.25)
```

(a) The regression equation is shown at the top of the output:

GRADRATE = 16.4 + 2.03 S/F

(b) The standard error of the estimate is shown in the sixth line of output as S = 11.31.

21. (a) Referring to the output in Review Problem 21, the fifth line of the output shows a t-value of 1.68 with a P-value of 0.131 associated with the regression parameter for the S/F variable. Since .131 > 0.05, the null hypothesis that $\beta_1 = 0$ cannot be rejected. Thus there is not sufficient evidence to conclude that the S/F ratio is useful as a predictor of graduation rate.

(b) The last line of the output gives the 95% confidence interval for the mean graduation rate when S/F = 17 as 42.60 to 59.18 and the prediction interval for a randomly chosen university with an S/F ratio of 17 as 23.53 to 78.25.

22. In Review Problem 19, checking the Residuals box after clicking on the **Options...** button resulted in the residuals being stored in a column named RESI1. To perform the correlation test for normality, we now choose **Stat ▶ Basic statistics ▶ Correlation,** select S/F and GRADRATE in the **Variables:** text box, check the **Display p-values** box, and click **OK.** The results are shown below.

```
Correlation of S/F and GRADRATE = 0.511, P-Value = 0.131
```

Since Minitab reports the P-value for a two-tailed test and we wish to test whether the correlation is positive, the actual P-value is 0.131/2 or 0.0655. This is greater than the significance level of 0.025, so we do not reject the null hypothesis that the student/faculty ratio and the graduation rate are uncorrelated. There is insufficient evidence to claim that the variables are positively correlated.

23. We choose **Stat** ▶ **Basic statistics** ▶

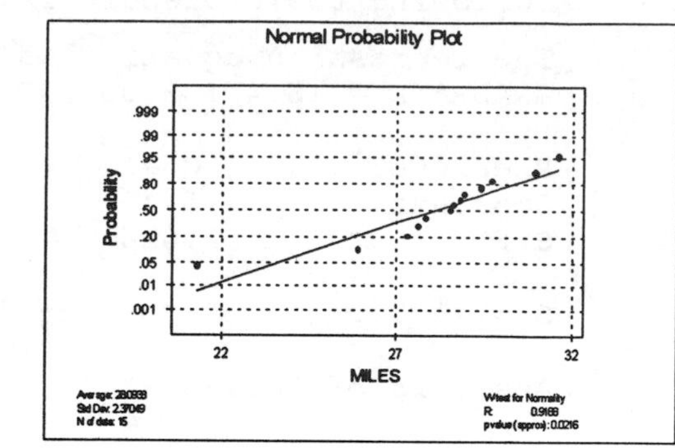

Normality test..., select MILES in the **Variable** text box, select the **Ryan-Joiner** option button from the **Tests for Normality** field, and click **OK**. The P-value for the normality test is greater than 0.1000. Since this is larger than the 0.025 significance level for the test, we do not reject the null hypothesis of normality. The correlation between MILES and NSCORE = 0.9832.

CHAPTER 16 ANSWERS

Exercises 16.1

16.1 We state the two numbers of degrees of freedom.

16.3 $F_{0.05}$, $F_{0.025}$, F_{α}

16.5 (a) The first number in parentheses (12) is the number of degrees of freedom for the numerator.

(b) The second number in parentheses (7) is the number of degrees of freedom for the denominator.

16.7 (a) $F_{0.05} = 1.89$ (b) $F_{0.01} = 2.47$ (c) $F_{0.025} = 2.14$

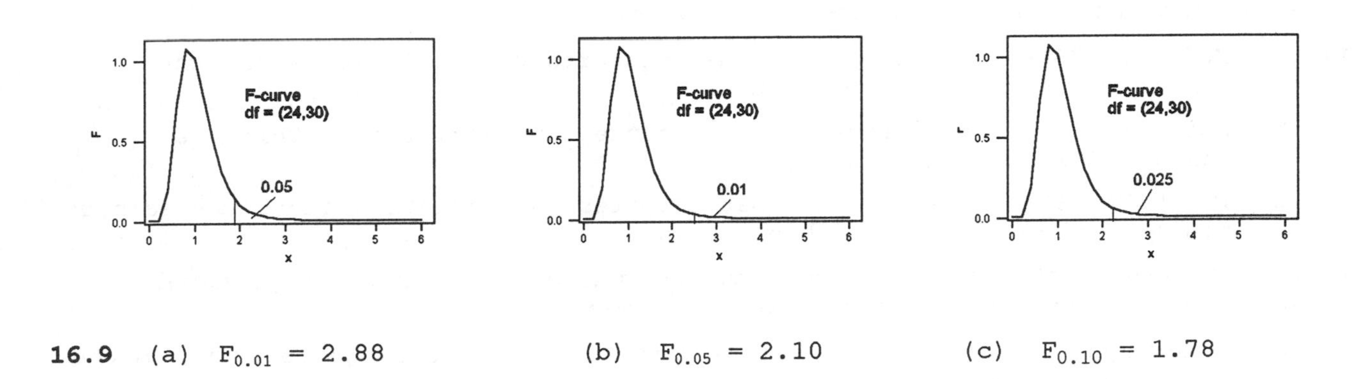

16.9 (a) $F_{0.01} = 2.88$ (b) $F_{0.05} = 2.10$ (c) $F_{0.10} = 1.78$

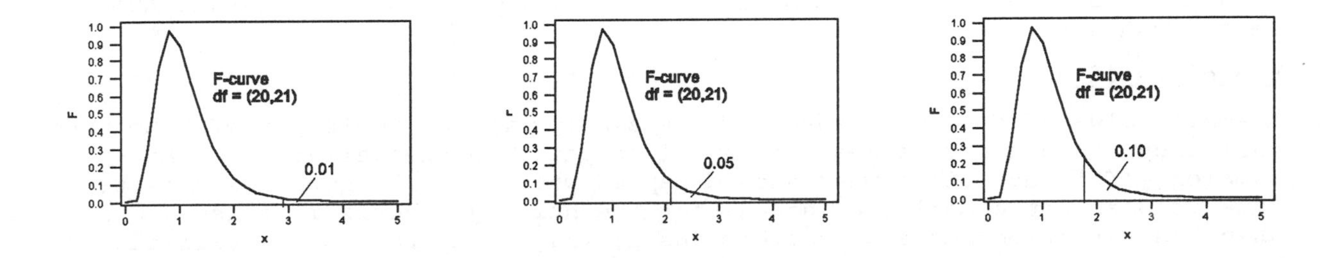

16.11 A straightforward method for finding $F_{0.05}$ for df = (25, 20) using Table VIII is by interpolation. Specifically, proceed along the top row of the table until locating the numbers 24 and 30, between which is 25, the desired number of degrees of freedom for the numerator. Notice that 25 is not reported in this row but is 1/6 of the way in moving from 24 to 30; i.e., (25 - 24)/(30 - 24) = 1/6.

The outside columns of the table give the degrees of freedom for the denominator, which is 20 in this case. Go down either of the outside columns to the row labeled "20." Then go across that row until under the columns headed "24" and "30." The numbers in the body of the table intersecting these row and column positions are the F-values 2.08 and 2.04. Thus, 24 is matched with 2.08, and 30 is matched with 2.04.

Now, proceed with interpolation. With 25 known to be 1/6 of the distance between 24 and 30, we likewise want to find the F-value that is 1/6 of the distance between 2.08 and 2.04. We do this by taking (1/6) · (2.04 - 2.08) = -0.0066. Adding -0.0066 to 2.08 gives us the desired F-value, which is

2.0734, or 2.07.

Thus, an approximation to $F_{0.05}$ for df = (25, 20) using Table VIII is 2.07. The limitation of this approximation is that it uses a linear technique on values that are related in a nonlinear fashion. However, because the difference between 2.08 and 2.04 is so small in the first place, the approximation errors will likewise be small.

Exercises 16.2

16.13 The pooled t-procedure (Procedure 10.1 in Section 10.2) is a method for comparing the means of two populations. One-way ANOVA is a procedure for comparing the means of several populations. Thus, one-way ANOVA is a generalization of the pooled t-procedure.

16.15 The reason for the word "variance" in the phrase "analysis of variance" is because the analysis-of-variance procedure for comparing means involves analyzing the *variation* in the sample data.

16.17 (a) MSTR (or SSTR) is a statistic that measures the variation among the sample means for a one-way ANOVA.

(b) MSE (or SSE) is a statistic that measures the variation within the samples for a one-way ANOVA.

(c) F = MSTR/MSE is a statistic that compares the variation among the sample means to the variation within the samples.

16.19 It signifies that each sample data value is classified in one way, namely, according to the population from which it was sampled.

16.21 No, because the variation among the sample means is not large relative to the variation within the samples.

16.23 If the hypothesis test situation abides by the characteristics outlined in this exercise, we can use the pooled t-test or we can use the one-way ANOVA test discussed in this section.

Exercises 16.3

16.25 A small value of F results when SSTR is small compared to SSE, i.e., when the variation between sample means is small compared to the variation within samples. This describes what should happen when the null hypothesis is true, thus it does not comprise evidence that the null hypothesis is false. Only when the variation between sample means is large compared to the variation within samples, i.e., when F is large, do we have evidence that the null hypothesis is not true.

16.27 SST = SSTR + SSE; this means that the total variation can be partitioned into a component representing variation among the sample means and another component representing variation within the samples.

16.29 Since SSTR/2 = MSTR, we have SSTR = 2(21.652) = 43.304.

Then SST = SSTR + SSE = 43.304 + 84.400 = 127.704.

Since df (Total) = df(Treatment) + df(Error), we have df(Error) = 12.

Then MSE = SSE/12 = 84.400/12 = 7.033

Finally, F = MSTR/MSE = 21.652/7.033 = 3.079. Thus the completed table is

Source	df	SS	MS=S/df	F-statistic
Treatment	2	43.304	21.652	3.079
Error	12	84.400	7.033	
Total	14	127.704		

16.31 The total number of populations being sampled is $k = 3$. Let the subscripts 1, 2, and 3 refer to A, B, and C, respectively. The total number of sample data values is $n = 10$. Also,

$n_1 = 2$, $n_2 = 5$, $n_3 = 3$. The following statistics for each sample are:

$\bar{x}_1 = 5$, $\bar{x}_2 = 3$, and $\bar{x}_3 = 5$. Also, $s_1 = 5.657$, $s_2 = 1.581$, and $s_3 = 3.000$. Note, the mean of all the sample data is $\bar{x} = 4$. We use this information as follows

(a) $SST = \Sigma(x - \bar{x})^2 = (1 - 4)^2 + \ldots + (5 - 4)^2 = 70.0$

$SSTR = n_1(\bar{x}_1 - \bar{x})^2 + n_2(\bar{x}_2 - \bar{x})^2 + n_3(\bar{x}_3 - \bar{x})^2$

$= 2(5 - 4)^2 + 5(3 - 4)^2 + 3(5 -4)^2 = 10.0$

$SSE = (n_1 - 1)s_1^2 + (n_2 - 1)s_2^2 + (n_3 - 1)s_3^2$

$= (2 - 1)(5.657)^2 + (5 - 1)(1.581)^2 + (3 - 1)(3.000)^2 = 60.0$

(b) $SST = SSTR + SSE$ since $70.0 = 10.0 + 60.0$

(c) Let T_1, T_2, and T_3 refer to the sum of the data values in each of the three samples, respectively. Thus

$T_1 = 10 \quad T_2 = 15 \quad T_3 = 15.$

Also, the sum of all the data values is $\Sigma x = 40$, and their sum of squares is $\sum x^2 = 230$.

Consequently, $SST = \sum x^2 - \frac{(\sum x)^2}{n} = 230 - \frac{40^2}{10} = 70$

$$SSTR = \frac{T_1^2}{n_1} + \frac{T_2^2}{n_2} + \frac{T_3^2}{n_3} - \frac{(\sum x)^2}{n} = \frac{10^2}{2} + \frac{15^2}{5} + \frac{15^2}{3} - \frac{40^2}{10} = 10$$

and

$SSE = SST - SSTR = 70 - 10 = 60$.

The two methods of computing yield the same results.

16.33 The total number of populations being sampled is $k = 3$. Let the subscripts 1, 2, and 3 refer to Hank, Joseph, and Susan, respectively. The total number of pieces of sample data is $n = 15$. Also,

$n_1 = n_2 = n_3 = 5$. The following statistics for each individual are:

$\bar{x}_1 = 9.6$, $\bar{x}_2 = 8.8$, and $\bar{x}_3 = 9.8$. Also, $s_1 = 1.14$, $s_2 = 0.837$, and $s_3 = 0.837$. Note, the mean of all the sample data is $\bar{x} = 9.4$. We use this information as follows:

(i) $SSTR = n_1(\bar{x}_1 - \bar{x})^2 + n_2(\bar{x}_2 - \bar{x})^2 + n_3(\bar{x}_3 - \bar{x})^2$

$= 5(9.6 - 9.4)^2 + 5(8.8 - 9.4)^2 + 5(9.8 - 9.4)^2 = 2.8$

(ii) SSE $= (n_1 - 1)s_1^2 + (n_2 - 1)s_2^2 + (n_3 - 1)s_3^2$

$= (5 - 1)(1.14)^2 + (5 - 1)(0.837)^2 + (5 - 1)(0.837)^2 = 10.8$

(iii) SST $= \Sigma(x - \bar{x})^2 = (8 - 9.4)^2 + \ldots + (9 - 9.4)^2 = 13.6$

(iv) $\text{MSTR} = \dfrac{\text{SSTR}}{k-1} = \dfrac{2.8}{3-1} = 1.4$

(v) $\text{MSE} = \dfrac{\text{SSE}}{n-k} = \dfrac{10.8}{15-3} = 0.9$

The one-way ANOVA table for the data is

Source	df	SS	MS = SS/df	F-statistic
Treatment	2	2.8	1.4	1.56
Error	12	10.8	0.9	
Total	14	13.6		

With the exception of the F-statistic, every value in the table above has been calculated using (i)-(v). The F-statistic is defined and calculated as

$$F = \frac{\text{MSTR}}{\text{MSE}} = \frac{1.4}{0.9} = 1.56.$$

16.35 The total number of populations being sampled is $k = 3$. Let the subscripts 1, 2, and 3 refer to diatoms, bacteria, and macroalgae, respectively. The total number of sample data values is $n = 12$. Also, $n_1 = 4$, $n_2 = 4$, and $n_3 = 4$.

Step 1: H_0: $\mu_1 = \mu_2 = \mu_3$ (population means are equal)

H_a: not all population means are equal

Step 2: $\alpha = 0.05$

Step 3: Let T_1, T_2 and T_3 refer to the sum of the data values in each of the three samples, respectively. Thus:

$T_1 = 1828$ $\quad T_2 = 1225$ $\quad T_3 = 1175.$

Also, the sum of all the data values is $\Sigma x = 4228$, and their sum of squares is $\Sigma x^2 = 1{,}561{,}154$. Then,

$$\text{SST} = \sum x^2 - \frac{(\sum x)^2}{n} = 1{,}561{,}154 - \frac{4228^2}{12} = 71{,}488.67$$

$$\text{SSTR} = \frac{T_1^2}{n_1} + \frac{T_2^2}{n_2} + \frac{T_3^2}{n_3} - \frac{(\sum x)^2}{n} = \frac{1828^2}{4} + \frac{12255^2}{4} + \frac{1175^2}{4} - \frac{4228^2}{12} = 66{,}043.17$$

and SSE = SST − SSTR = 71488.67 − 66043.17 = 5445.50

Step 4: MSTR = SSTR/(k − 1) = 66043.17/(3 − 1) = 33021.585

MSE = SSE/(n − k) = 5445.50/(12 − 3) = 605.056

F = MSTR/MSE = 33021.585/605.056 = 54.58

The one-way ANOVA table is

Source	df	SS	MS = SS/df	F-statistic
Treatment	2	66043.17	33021.585	54.58
Error	9	5445.50	605.056	
Total	11	71488.67		

Step 5: df = (k - 1, n - k) = (2, 9); critical value = 4.26

Step 6: Since 54.58 > 4.26, we reject the null hypothesis.

Step 7: At the 5% level, the data provide sufficient evidence to conclude that there is a difference in the mean number of copepods among the three different diets. For the p-value approach, $P(F > 54.58) < 0.005$. Since $P < 0.01$, we reject the null hypothesis.

16.37 The total number of populations sampled is k = 5. Let the subscripts 1, 2, 3, 4, and 5 refer to Transp. and Pub. util.; Wholesale trade; Retail trade; Finance, Insurance, Real Estate; and Services, respectively. The total number of sample data values is n = 27. Also, $n_1 = 6$, $n_2 = 5$, $n_3 = 6$, $n_4 = 4$, $n_5 = 6$.

Step 1: H_0: $\mu_1 = \mu_2 = \mu_3 = \mu_4 = \mu_5$ (mean earnings are equal)

H_a: Not all the means are equal.

Step 2: $\alpha = 0.05$

Step 3: Let T_1, T_2, T_3, T_4, and T_5 refer to the sum of the data values in each of the five samples, respectively. Thus:

$T_1 = 3459$ $T_2 = 2462$ $T_3 = 1380$ $T_4 = 1840$ $T_5 = 2295$

Also, the sum of all the data values is $\Sigma x = 11436$, and their sum of squares is $\Sigma x^2 = 5{,}290{,}870$. Consequently,

$$SST = \sum x^2 - \frac{(\sum x)^2}{n} = 5{,}290{,}870 - \frac{11436^2}{27} = 447{,}088.667$$

$$SSTR = \frac{T_1^2}{n_1} + \frac{T_2^2}{n_2} + \frac{T_3^2}{n_3} + \frac{T_4^2}{n_4} + \frac{T_5^2}{n_5} - \frac{(\sum x)^2}{n}$$

$$= \frac{2459^2}{6} + \frac{2462^2}{5} + \frac{1380^2}{6} + \frac{1840^2}{4} + \frac{2295^2}{6} - \frac{11436^2}{27} = 404{,}258.467$$

and

SSE = SST - SSTR = 447,088.667 - 404,258.467 = 42,830.200.

Step 4: MSTR = SSTR/(k - 1) = 404,258.467/(5 - 1) = 101,064.617

MSE = SSE/(n - k) = 42,830.200/(27 - 5) = 1946.827

F = MSTR/MSE = 101,064.617/1946.827 = 51.91

The one-way ANOVA table is

Source	df	SS	MS = SS/df	F-statistic
Treatment	4	404,258.467	101,064.617	51.91
Error	22	42,830.200	1946.827	
Total	26	447,088.667		

Step 5: df = (k - 1, n - k) = (4, 22); critical value = 2.82

Step 6: From Step 4, F = 51.91. From Step 5, $F_{0.05}$ = 2.82. Since 51.91 > 2.82, reject H_0.

Step 7: At the 5% significance level, the data provide sufficient evidence to conclude that there is a difference in the mean weekly earnings among nonsupervisory workers in the five industries.

For the P-value approach, P(F > 51.91) < 0.005. Therefore, since the P-value is smaller than the significance level, reject H_0.

16.39 The total number of populations being sampled is k = 3. Let the subscripts 1, 2, and 3 refer to Chronic PTSD, Remitted PTSD, and None, respectively. The total number of sample data values is n = 81. Also, n_1 = 32, n_2 = 20, and n_3 = 29.

Step 1: H_0: $\mu_1 = \mu_2 = \mu_3$ (mean earnings are equal)

H_a: Not all the means are equal.

Step 2: $\alpha = 0.01$

Step 3: Let T_1, T_2, and T_3 refer to the sum of the data values in each of the three samples, respectively. Then $T_i = n_i\bar{x}_i$. Thus

T_1 = 32(25.8) = 825.6 T_2 = 20(22.1) = 442.0 T_3 = 29(26.6) = 771.4

Also, the sum of all the data values is $\Sigma x = T_1 + T_2 + T_3 = 2039$ and $\bar{x}$ = 2039/81 = 25.2.

$$SSTR = \frac{T_1^2}{n_1} + \frac{T_2^2}{n_2} + \frac{T_3^2}{n_3} - \frac{(\sum x)^2}{n} = \frac{825.6^2}{32} + \frac{442.0^2}{20} + \frac{771.4^2}{29} - \frac{2039^2}{81} = 260.50$$

$$SSE = \sum (n_i - 1)s_i^2 = 31(9.2)^2 + 19(5.7)^2 + 28(9.6)^2 = 5821.63$$

SST = SSTR + SSE = 260.50 + 5821.63 = 6082.13

Step 4: MSTR = SSTR/(k - 1) = 260.50/(3 - 1) = 130.25

MSE = SSE/(n - k) = 5821.63/(81 - 3) = 74.64

F = MSTR/MSE = 130.25/74.64 = 1.745

The one-way ANOVA table is

Source	df	SS	MS = SS/df	F-statistic
Treatment	2	260.50	130.25	1.745
Error	78	5821.63	74.64	
Total	80	6082.13		

Step 5: df = (k - 1, n - k) = (2, 78); critical value = 4.98

Step 6: From Step 4, F = 1.745. From Step 5, $F_{0.01}$ = 4.98. Since 1.745 < 4.98, do not reject H_0.

Step 7: At the 1% significance level, the data do not provide sufficient evidence to conclude that there is a difference in the mean age at time of arrest among the three types of former prisoners.

For the P-value approach, P(F > 1.745) > 0.10. Therefore, since the P-value is larger than the significance level, do not reject H_0.

16.41 Suppose that we define the sample events A and B as follows:

A: the interval constructed around the difference $\mu_1 - \mu_2$

B: the interval constructed around the difference $\mu_1 - \mu_3$.

The 99% confidence interval for each event above is defined as:

$$P(A) = 0.99 \text{ and } P(B) = 0.99.$$

The probability of both A and B occurring simultaneously is written

P(A and B). Since A and B are realistically not independent, the general multiplication rule applies; i.e., P(A and B) = P(A) · P(B|A).

A difficulty arises in calculating a precise number for P(A and B) because we need additional information about P(B|A), which we do not have. However, P(B|A) is by no means equal to 1.00, which results in the product of P(A) and P(B|A) being less than 0.99 (because 0.99 times a probability less than 1.00 is clearly less than 0.99). Thus, the probability of both A and B occurring simultaneously is not 0.99.

16.43 (a) Using Minitab, with the data in three columns named High, Medium, and Low, we choose **Calc ▶ Calculator...**, select High in the **Input column** text box and type <u>NSCOREH</u> in the **Store result in variable** text box, click in the **Expression** text box, select **Normal scores** from the function list, double click on High to replace **number** in the NSCOR function, and click **OK.** Then repeat this process to create, respectively, the normal scores columns Medium and Low. To obtain the normal probability plots, we choose **Graph ▶ Plot...**, select NSCOREH as the **Y** variable and High as the **X** variable for **Graph 1,** select NSCOREM as the **Y** variable and Medium as the **X** variable for **Graph 2,** select NSCOREL as the **Y** variable and Low as the **X** variable for **Graph 3,** and click **OK.** The results are

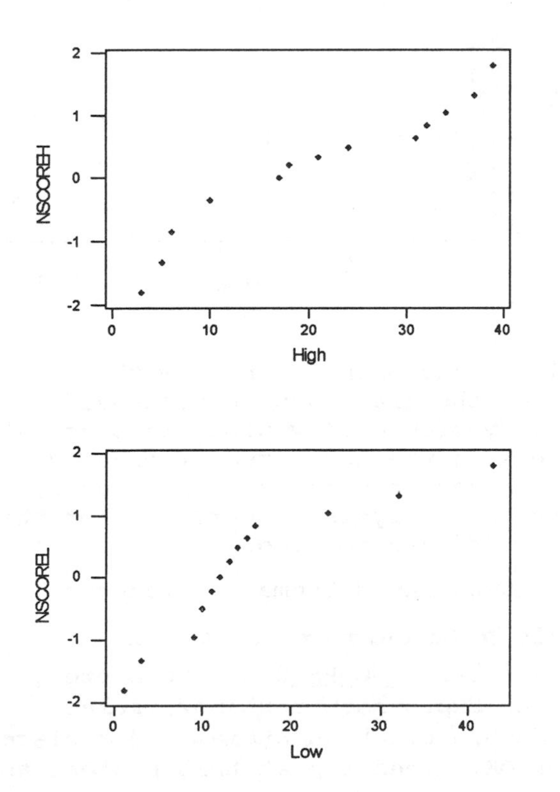

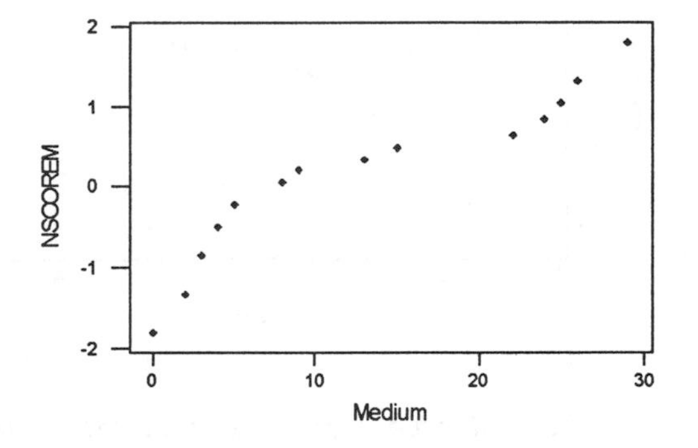

None of the normal probability plots are very linear and the plot for the Low category of data exhibits three outliers on the right side of the graph. A boxplot of the data will also show another outlier on the left side of the graph.

To get the standard deviations, we choose **Stat ▶ Column Statistics...**, select the **Standard deviation** button, select High in the **Input variable** text box, and click **OK**. Repeat this process for the other two variables. The results are

Standard deviation of High = 12.097

Standard deviation of Medium = 9.7574

Standard deviation of Low = 9.9280

(b) To carry out the Analysis of variance and residual analysis, use the data in a single column which is named WORDS as provided on the Weiss Stats CD. In the next column, which is named EDLEVEL, are the levels of each of the magazines corresponding to each data value in WORDS.

The residual analysis consists of plotting the residuals against the means (or fits) and constructing a normal probability plot. This is done at the same time as the analysis of variance in Minitab, but the results must be examined before accepting the results of the analysis of variance. To do this, we choose **Stat ▶ Anova ▶One-way...**, select WORDS for the **Response:** text box and EDLEVEL in the **Factor:** text box. Then click on the **Graphs** button and click to place check marks in the boxes for **Normal plot of residuals** and **Residuals versus fits**, and click **OK**. The graphic results are

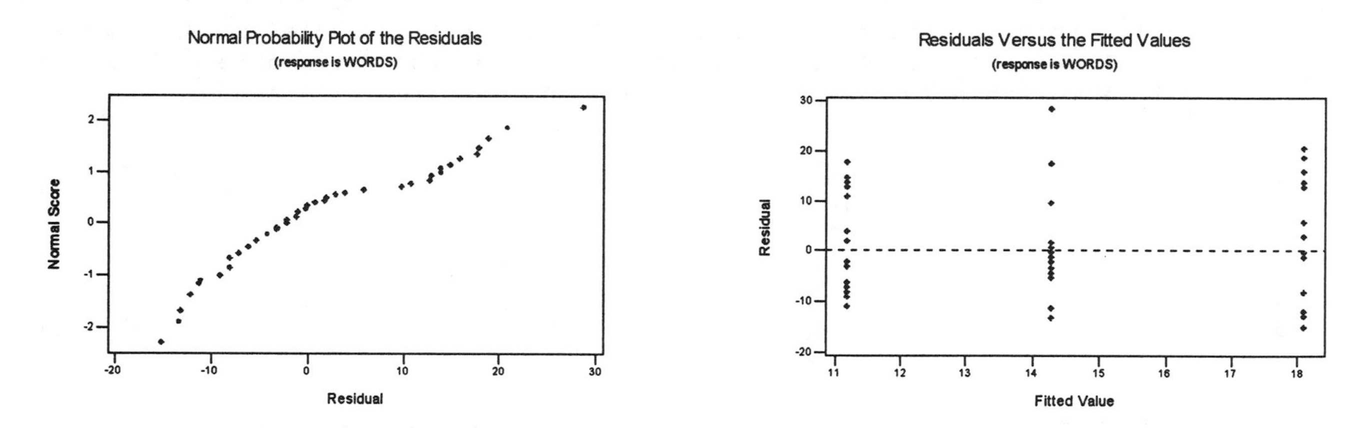

(c) While the overall plot of the residuals is reasonably linear with possibly one outlier on the right side of the graph and the standard deviations are very similar, the normality probability plots in part (a) indicate the presence of several outliers in the Low category of data. Thus the assumption of normality for each set of data is questionable, and we do not recommend proceeding with the Analysis of Variance for the comparison of means. Thus parts (d) and (e) are omitted.

16.45 (a) Using Minitab, with the data in five columns named Stomach, Bronchus, Colon, Ovary, and Breast, we choose **Calc ▶ Calculator...**, select Bronchus in the **Input column** text box and type <u>NSCORSTO</u> in the **Store result in variable** text box, click in the **Expression** text box, select **Normal scores** from the function list, double click on Stomach to replace **number** in the NSCOR function, and click **OK**. Then repeat this process to create, respectively, the normal scores columns NSCORSTO, NSCORCOL, NSCOROV, and NSCORBRS. To obtain the normal probability plots, we choose **Graph ▶ Plot...**, select NSCORSTO as the **Y** variable and Stomach as the **X** variable for **Graph 1**, select NSCORBRN as the **Y** variable and Bronchus as the **X** variable for **Graph 2** select NSCORCOL as the **Y** variable and Colon as the **X** variable for **Graph 3**, select NSCOROV as the **Y** variable and Ovary as the **X** variable for **Graph 4**, select NSCORBRT as the **Y** variable and Breast as the **X** variable for **Graph 5**, and click **OK**. The results are

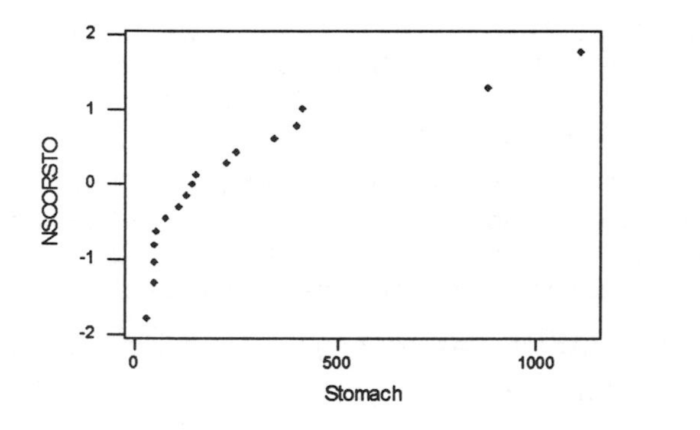

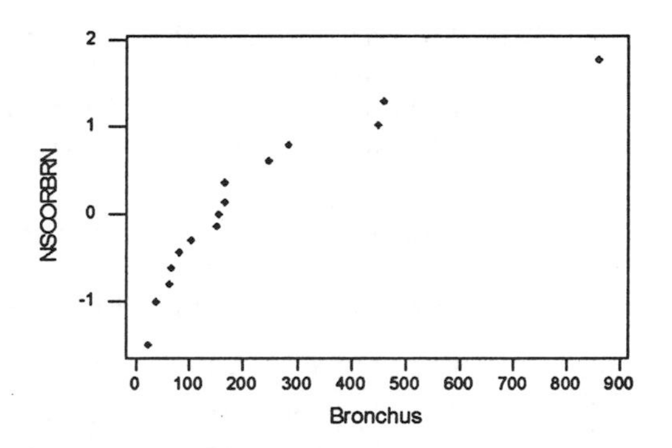

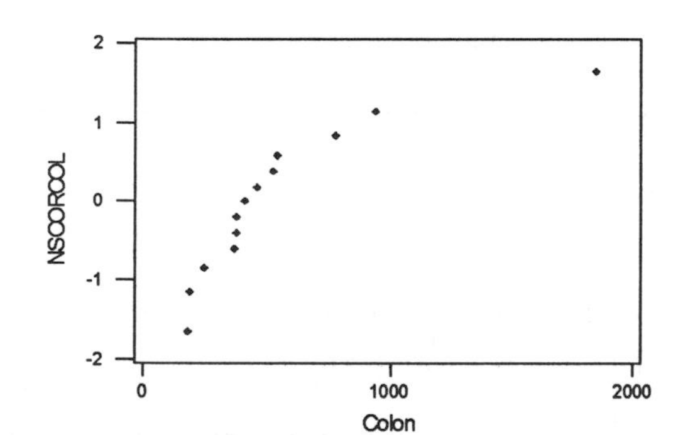

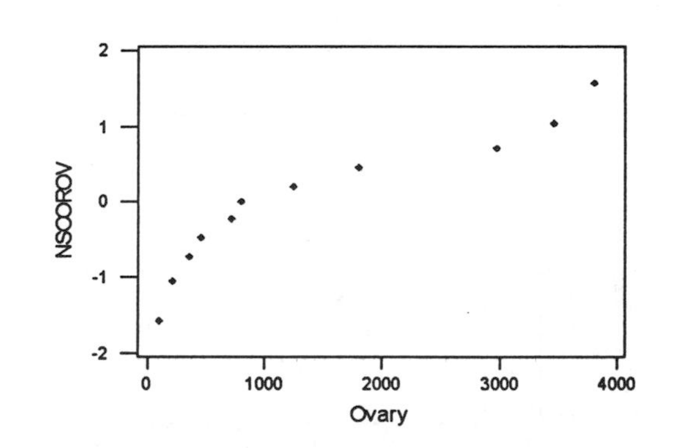

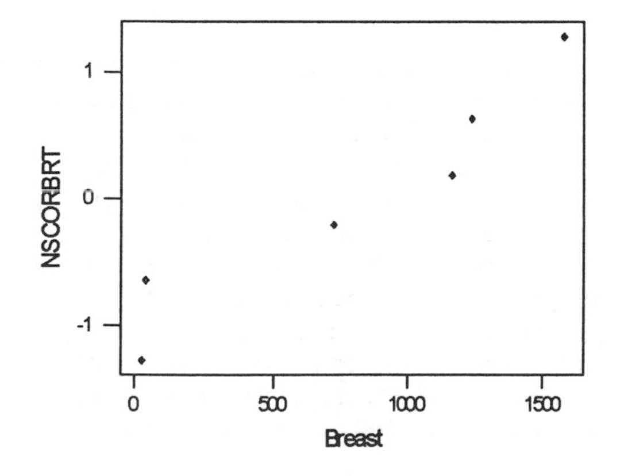

To get the standard deviations, we choose **Stat ▶ Column Statistics...**, select the **Standard deviation** button, select Stomach in the **Input variable** text box, and click **OK.** Repeat this process for the other four variables. The results are

Standard deviation of Stomach = 306.16

Standard deviation of Bronchus = 214.21

Standard deviation of Colon = 443.61

Standard deviation of Ovary = 1365.6

Standard deviation of Breast = 650.86

(b) To carry out the Analysis of variance and residual analysis, we will use the data in a single column which is named TIME. This is provided on the Weiss Stats CD. In the next column, which is named TYPE, are the types of cancer corresponding to each data value in TIME.

The residual analysis consists of plotting the residuals against the means (or fits) and constructing a normal probability plot. This is done at the same time as the analysis of variance in Minitab, but the results must be examined before accepting the results of the Analysis of variance. To do this, we choose **Stat ▶ Anova ▶One-way...**, select TIME for the **Response:** text box and TYPE in the **Factor:** text box. Then click on the **Graphs** button and click to place check marks in the boxes for **Normal plot of residuals** and **Residuals versus fits**, and click **OK.** The graphic results are

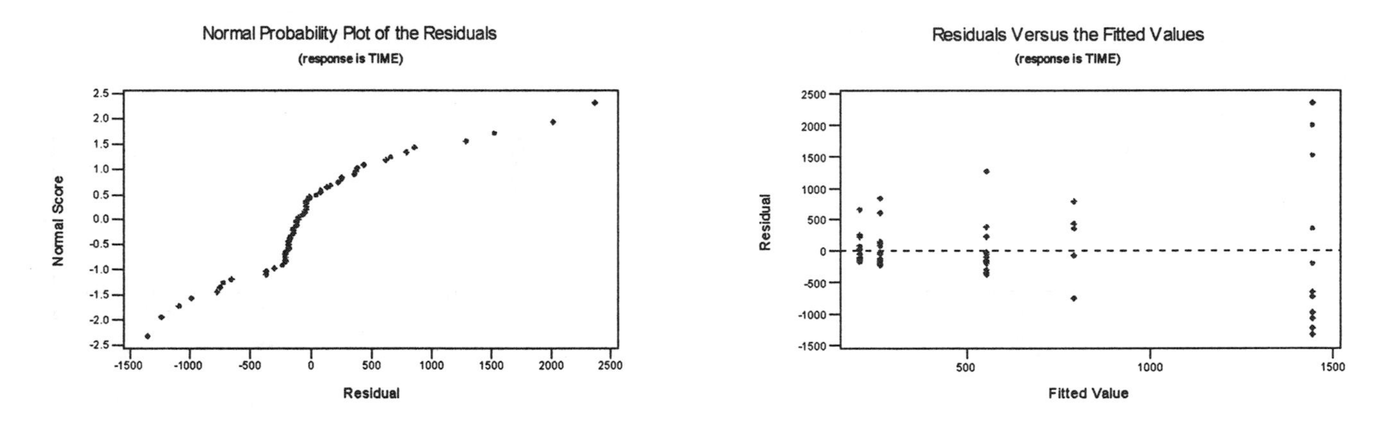

(c) The individual group normal probability plots in part(a) and the residual normal probability plot in part (b) exhibit considerable non-normality. Boxplots would also reveal outliers in three of the five groups of data. The calculation of the group standard deviations in part (a) and the plot of residuals versus fitted values in part (b) reveal a great disparity in the standard deviations of the data. The ratio of the largest to smallest standard deviation is 1365.6/214.21 = 6.375. This is much larger than the rule of thumb value of 2 or less to consider the assumption of equal standard deviation to be met. Since this data appears to not satisfy two of the three assumptions for carrying out an analysis of variance, we do not recommend the use of analysis for the comparison of means for this data. Parts (d) and (e) are omitted.

Exercises 16.4

16.47 zero

16.49 (a) The family confidence level, because the family confidence level is the confidence we have that all the confidence intervals contain the true differences between the corresponding population means. On the other hand, the individual confidence level pertains to the confidence we have that any particular confidence interval contains the true difference between the corresponding population means.

(b) They are the same since there is only one difference in the family.

16.51 $\nu = n - k$, the degrees of freedom for the denominator in the F-distribution.

16.53 (a) 4.69 (b) 5.98

16.55 Step 1: Family confidence level = 0.95.

Step 2: $\kappa = 3$ and $\nu = n - k = 12 - 3 = 9$. Consulting Table XI, we find that $q_{0.05} = 3.95$.

Step 3: Before obtaining all possible confidence intervals for $\mu_i - \mu_j$, we construct a table giving the sample means and sample sizes.

j	1	2	3
$\bar{x}_j$	457.00	306.25	293.75
n_j	4	4	4

In Exercise 16.35, we found that MSE = 605.056. Now we are ready to obtain the required confidence intervals.

The confidence interval for $\mu_1 - \mu_2$ is

$$457.00 - 306.25 \pm \frac{3.95}{\sqrt{2}} \cdot \sqrt{605.056} \cdot \sqrt{\frac{1}{4} + \frac{1}{4}}$$

$$150.75 \pm 48.58$$

$$102.17 \text{ to } 199.33$$

The confidence interval for $\mu_1 - \mu_3$ is

$$457.00 - 293.75 \pm \frac{3.95}{\sqrt{2}} \cdot \sqrt{605.056} \cdot \sqrt{\frac{1}{4} + \frac{1}{4}}$$

$$163.25 \pm 48.58$$

$$114.67 \text{ to } 211.83$$

The confidence interval for $\mu_2 - \mu_3$ is

$$306.25 - 293.75 \pm \frac{3.95}{\sqrt{2}} \cdot \sqrt{605.056} \cdot \sqrt{\frac{1}{4} + \frac{1}{4}}$$

$$12.50 \pm 48.58$$

$$-36.08 \text{ to } 61.08$$

Step 4: Based on the confidence intervals in Step 3, μ_1 is different from μ_2, and μ_1 is different from μ_3; μ_2 and μ_3 can not be declared different.

Step 5: We summarize the results with the following diagram.

Microalgae	Bacteria	Diatoms
(3)	(2)	(1)
293.75	306.25	457.00

(In the diagram, 293.75 and 306.25 are joined by one underline.)

Interpreting this diagram, we conclude with 95% confidence that μ_1 is different from μ_2, and μ_1 is different from μ_3.

16.57 Step 1: Family confidence level = 0.95.

Step 2: $\kappa = 5$ and $\nu = n - k = 27 - 5 = 22$. Consulting Table XI, we take the mean of 4.23 and 4.17 to get $q_{0.05} = 4.20$.

Step 3: Before obtaining all possible confidence intervals for $\mu_i - \mu_j$, we construct a table giving the sample means and sample sizes.

j	1	2	3	4	5
$\bar{x}_j$	576.5	492.4	230.0	460.0	382.5
n_j	6	5	6	4	6

In Exercise 16.37, we found that MSE = 1946.8. Now we are ready to obtain the required confidence intervals.

The confidence interval for $\mu_1 - \mu_2$ is

$$(576.5 - 492.4) \pm \frac{4.20}{\sqrt{2}} \cdot \sqrt{1946.8}\sqrt{\frac{1}{6} + \frac{1}{5}}$$

or

4.8 *to* 163.4

The confidence interval for $\mu_1 - \mu_3$ is

$$(576.5 - 230.0) \pm \frac{4.20}{\sqrt{2}} \cdot \sqrt{1946.8}\sqrt{\frac{1}{6} + \frac{1}{6}}$$

or

270.8 *to* 422.2

The confidence interval for $\mu_1 - \mu_4$ is

$$(576.5 - 460.0) \pm \frac{4.20}{\sqrt{2}} \cdot \sqrt{1946.8}\sqrt{\frac{1}{6} + \frac{1}{4}}$$

or

31.9 *to* 201.1

The confidence interval for $\mu_1 - \mu_5$ is

$$(576.5 - 382.5) \pm \frac{4.20}{\sqrt{2}} \cdot \sqrt{1946.8}\sqrt{\frac{1}{6} + \frac{1}{6}}$$

or

118.3 *to* 269.7

The confidence interval for $\mu_2 - \mu_3$ is

$$(492.4 - 230.0) \pm \frac{4.20}{\sqrt{2}} \cdot \sqrt{1946.8}\sqrt{\frac{1}{5} + \frac{1}{6}}$$

or

183.1 *to* 341.7

The confidence interval for $\mu_2 - \mu_4$ is

$$(492.4 - 460.0) \pm \frac{4.20}{\sqrt{2}} \cdot \sqrt{1946.8}\sqrt{\frac{1}{5} + \frac{1}{4}}$$

or

-55.5 *to* 120.3

The confidence interval for $\mu_2 - \mu_5$ is

$$(492.4 - 382.5) \pm \frac{4.20}{\sqrt{2}} \cdot \sqrt{1946.8}\sqrt{\frac{1}{5} + \frac{1}{6}}$$

or

30.6 *to* 189.2

The confidence interval for $\mu_3 - \mu_4$ is

$$(230.0 - 460.0) \pm \frac{4.20}{\sqrt{2}} \cdot \sqrt{1946.8}\sqrt{\frac{1}{6} + \frac{1}{4}}$$

or

-314.6 *to* -145.4

The confidence interval for $\mu_3 - \mu_5$ is

$$(230.0 - 382.5) \pm \frac{4.20}{\sqrt{2}} \cdot \sqrt{1946.8}\sqrt{\frac{1}{6} + \frac{1}{6}}$$

or

-228.2 *to* -76.8

The confidence interval for $\mu_4 - \mu_5$ is

$$(460.0 - 382.5) \pm \frac{4.20}{\sqrt{2}} \cdot \sqrt{1946.8}\sqrt{\frac{1}{4} + \frac{1}{6}}$$

or

-7.1 *to* 162.1

Step 4: Based on the confidence intervals in Step 3, we declare the following means different: μ_1 and μ_2, μ_1 and μ_3, μ_1 and μ_4, μ_1 and μ_5, μ_2 and μ_3,

μ_2 and μ_5, μ_3 and μ_4, μ_3 and μ_5. The other two pairs of means are not declared different.

Step 5: We summarize the results with the following diagram.

Retail Trade	Services	Finance, Insurance, Real Estate	Wholesale Trade	Transp. and Pub. util.
(3)	(5)	(4)	(2)	(1)
230.0	382.5	460.0	492.4	576.5

Interpreting this diagram, we conclude with 95% confidence that the mean weekly earnings of transportation/public-utility workers exceeds those of the other four industries; the mean weekly earnings of retail-trade workers is less than those of the other four industries; the mean weekly earnings of service workers is less than those of wholesale trade workers; no other means can be declared different.

16.59 Step 1: Family confidence level = 0.99.

Step 2: $\kappa = 3$ and $\nu = n - k = 81 - 3 = 78$. Consulting Table X, we find that $q_{0.01} = 4.28$.

Step 3: Before obtaining all possible confidence intervals for $\mu_i - \mu_j$, we construct a table giving the sample means and sample sizes.

j	1	2	3
$\bar{x}_j$	25.8	22.1	26.6
n_j	32	20	29

In Exercise 16.39, we found that MSE = 74.64. Now we are ready to obtain the required confidence intervals.

The confidence interval for $\mu_1 - \mu_2$ is

$$(25.8 - 22.1) \pm \frac{4.28}{\sqrt{2}} \cdot \sqrt{74.64}\sqrt{\frac{1}{32} + \frac{1}{20}}$$

or

-3.8 *to* 11.2

The confidence interval for $\mu_1 - \mu_3$ is

$$(25.8 - 26.6) \pm \frac{4.28}{\sqrt{2}} \cdot \sqrt{74.64}\sqrt{\frac{1}{32} + \frac{1}{29}}$$

or

-7.5 *to* 5.9

The confidence interval for $\mu_2 - \mu_3$ is

$$(22.1 - 26.6) \pm \frac{4.28}{\sqrt{2}} \cdot \sqrt{74.64} \sqrt{\frac{1}{20} + \frac{1}{29}}$$

or

-12.3 *to* 3.1

Step 4: Based on the confidence intervals in Step 3, we declare none of the means different.

Step 5: We summarize the results with the following diagram.

Remitted	Chronic	None
(2)	(1)	(3)
22.1	25.8	26.6

Interpreting this diagram, we conclude with 99% confidence that there is no difference in the mean ages at time of arrest among the three groups of former East Germany political prisoners classified by the current status relative to posttraumatic stress disorder.

16.61 (a) If $i > j$, then we obtain the confidence interval for $\mu_i - \mu_j$, by taking the negative of the confidence interval for $\mu_j - \mu_i$.

(b) The confidence intervals are as follows:

$\mu_2 - \mu_1$ is from -2.43 to 5.43

$\mu_3 - \mu_1$ is from -7.36 to 1.36

$\mu_4 - \mu_1$ is from -7.91 to 0.31

$\mu_3 - \mu_2$ is from -8.69 to -0.31

$\mu_4 - \mu_2$ is from -9.23 to -1.37

$\mu_4 - \mu_3$ is from -5.16 to 3.56.

16.63 In Exercise 16.43, we recommended not proceeding with the analysis of variance due to violation of the assumptions. For those who felt the violations were not significant enough to cause concern, we provide the entire analysis of variance here. Using Minitab, with all of the data in a column named WORDS and the magazine educational level in a column named EDLEVEL, we choose **Stat ▶ ANOVA ▶ Oneway...**, select WORDS in the **Response** text box and EDLEVEL in the **Factor** text box, click on the **Comparisons** button, click on **Tukey's, family error rate** so that an X shows in its check-box, type 5 in its text box, and click **OK**.

Analysis of Variance for WORDS

Source	DF	SS	MS	F	P
EDLEVEL	2	436	218	1.92	0.157
Error	51	5782	113		
Total	53	6217			

```
                                        Individual 95% CIs For Mean
                                        Based on Pooled StDev
Level       N      Mean     StDev   --------+---------+---------+--------
High       18     18.11     12.10                 (---------*---------)
Low        18     14.28      9.93           (----------*---------)
Medium     18     11.17      9.76   (---------*---------)
                                    --------+---------+---------+--------
Pooled StDev =    10.65                    10.0      15.0      20.0
```

```
Tukey's pairwise comparisons
    Family error rate = 0.0500
Individual error rate = 0.0195
Critical value = 3.41
Intervals for (column level mean) - (row level mean)
                High        Low
  Low          -4.72
               12.39
  Medium       -1.61      -5.45
               15.50      11.67
```

Since all of the confidence intervals contain zero, we conclude at the family confidence level of 0.95, that there are no differences in the mean number of words of three syllables or more in the ads at different educational levels.

16.65 The analysis of variance procedure was not recommended in Exercise 16.45 due to violations of assumptions. Therefore, no Tukey multiple comparison based on an analysis of variance should be done.

Exercises 16.5

16.67 The conditions required for using the Kruskal-Wallis test are:

(1) Independent samples
(2) Same-shape populations
(3) All sample sizes are 5 or greater.

16.69 equal

16.71 H has approximately a chi-square distribution with k - 1 degrees of freedom, so for five populations, we use critical values from the right hand side of the chi-square distribution with 4 degrees of freedom.

16.73 The total number of populations being sampled is k = 3. Let the subscripts 1, 2, and 3 refer to 1980, 1990, and 1997, respectively. The total number of sample data values is n = 24. Also, $n_1 = 8$, $n_2 = 7$, and $n_3 = 9$.

Step 1: H_0: $\mu_1 = \mu_2 = \mu_3$ (mean consumption of low-fat milk are equal)

H_a: Not all the means are equal.

Step 2: $\alpha = 0.01$

Step 3:

Sample 1	Rank	Sample 2	Rank	Sample 3	Rank
8.3	1	8.8	3	12.6	10
8.6	2	12.0	9	12.8	11.5
9.2	4	12.8	11.5	14.1	16
9.4	5	13.3	13	14.8	18
10.7	6	13.4	14	15.3	20
11.1	7	13.5	15	16.0	21
11.6	8	14.4	17	16.6	22
15.1	19			18.5	23
				18.8	24
	52		82.5		165.5

Step 4:

$$H = \frac{12}{n(n+1)} \sum \frac{R_j^2}{n_j} - 3(n+1)$$

$$= \frac{12}{24(24+1)}\left(\frac{52^2}{8} + \frac{82.5^2}{7} + \frac{165.5^2}{9}\right) - 3(24+1)$$

$$= 12.074$$

Step 5: df = k - 1 = 2; critical value = 9.210

Step 6: Since 12.074 > 9.210, reject H_0.

Step 7: At the 1% significance level, the data provide sufficient evidence to conclude that there is a difference in mean consumption of low-fat milk for 1980, 1990, and 1997.

For the P-value approach, $P(\chi^2 > 12.074) < 0.005$. Therefore, because the P-value is smaller than the significance level, reject H_0.

16.75 The total number of populations being sampled is k = 4. Let the subscripts 1, 2, 3, and 4 refer to Northeast, Midwest, South, and West, respectively. The total number of sample data values is n = 32. Also, $n_1 = n_2 = n_3 = n_4 = 8$.

Step 1: H_0: $\eta_1 = \eta_2 = \eta_3 = \eta_4$ (median asking rents are equal)

H_a: Not all the medians are equal.

Step 2: $\alpha = 0.05$

Step 3:

Sample 1	Rank	Sample 2	Rank	Sample 3	Rank	Sample 4	Rank
1293	4	1605	11	642	1	694	2
1581	9	1639	12.5	722	3	1345	5
1781	18	1655	15.5	1354	6	1565	8
2130	23	1691	17	1513	7	1649	14
2149	25	2058	20	1591	10	1655	15.5
2286	27	2115	22	1639	12.5	2068	21
2989	30	2413	28	1982	19	2203	26
3182	31	3361	32	2135	24	2789	29
	167		158		82.5		120.5

Step 4:

$$H = \frac{12}{n(n+1)} \sum \frac{R_j^2}{n_j} - 3(n+1)$$

$$= \frac{12}{32(32+1)}\left(\frac{167^2}{8} + \frac{158^2}{8} + \frac{82.5^2}{8} + \frac{120.5^2}{8}\right) - 3(32+1)$$

$$= 6.369$$

Step 5: df = k - 1 = 3; critical value = 7.815

Step 6: Since 6.369 < 7.815, do not reject H_0.

Step 7: At the 5% significance level, the data do not provide sufficient evidence to conclude that a difference exists among the median square footage of single-family detached homes in the four U.S. regions.

For the P-value approach, $0.05 < P(\chi^2 > 6.369) < 0.10$. Therefore, because the P-value is larger than the significance level, do not reject H_0.

16.77 (a) Because the populations have the same shape, use the Kruskal-Wallis test.

(b) Because the populations are normally distributed and have the same shape, use the one-way ANOVA test.

16.79 (a) The defining formula and the computing formula for H are equivalent as long as there are no ties in the data. The computing formula uses the facts that the sum of the first n integers is n(n+1)/2 and that the sum of the squares of the first n integers is n(n+1)(2n+1)/6. Thus it assumes that all of the ranks are distinct integers. The discrepancy between the formulas results, as in this case, when there are ties in the ranks, invalidating the formula for the sum of squares.

(b) No. Both values are greater than the critical value of 9.91, so the null hypothesis is rejected in both cases.

(c) Using technology, the P-values associated with 9.930 and 9.923 are 0.006978 and 0.007002 respectively. Since our estimate of the P-value is 0.007 in both cases, the difference in values does not affect our estimate of the P-value.

16.81 (a) The assumptions for Kruskal-Wallis test are satisfied. The samples are independent; although the populations are not normal, the probability plots in Exercise 16.43 have the same shape indicating that the populations have the same shape; and the sample sizes are all at least five.

(b) Using Minitab, with all of the data in one column named WORDS and magazine educational levels in a column named EDLEVEL, we choose **Stat ▶ Nonparametrics ▶ Kruskal-Wallis...**, select WORDS in the **Response** text box, select EDLEVEL in the **Factor** text box, and click **OK**. The result is

Kruskal-Wallis Test on WORDS

EDLEVEL	N	Median	Ave Rank	Z
High	18	17.000	32.4	1.62
Low	18	12.000	28.5	0.32
Medium	18	6.500	21.6	-1.95
Overall	54		27.5	

H = 4.35 DF = 2 P = 0.114
H = 4.36 DF = 2 P = 0.113 (adjusted for ties)

(c) The p-value of 0.114 (or 0.113) is greater than the significance level 0.05, and therefore we do not reject the null hypothesis of equal means. There is not sufficient evidence to conclude that there are differences in the mean number of words of three syllables or more in the ads at the three educational levels.

(d) For those who considered the violations of ANOVA assumptions not to be of concern, we provided the ANOVA results in Exercise 16.63. The p-value for that test was 0.157, just slightly greater than that for the Kruskal-Wallis test. Thus the two analyses result in identical conclusions.

16.83 (a) The assumptions for Kruskal-Wallis test are satisfied. The samples are independent; although the populations are not normal, they do appear to be the same shape; and the sample sizes are all at least five.

(b) Using Minitab, with all of the data in one column named TIME and cancer types in a column named TYPE, we choose **Stat ▶ Nonparametrics ▶ Kruskal-Wallis...**, select TIME in the **Response** text box, select TYPE in the **Factor** text box, and click **OK**. The result is

Kruskal-Wallis Test on TIME

TYPE	N	Median	Ave Rank	Z
Breast	6	946.5	38.5	0.83
Bronchus	17	155.0	22.3	-2.64
Colon	13	406.0	41.3	1.91
Ovary	11	791.0	47.9	3.02
Stomach	17	138.0	23.9	-2.23
Overall	64		32.5	

H = 19.82 DF = 4 P = 0.001

H = 19.82 DF = 4 P = 0.001 (adjusted for ties)

(c) Since the p-value of 0.001 is less than the significance level of 0.05, we reject the null hypothesis of equal means and conclude that there is sufficient evidence to conclude that there are differences in the mean survival times of patients given a Vitamin C supplement who were in advanced stages of cancer of five different types.

(d) No ANOVA was carried out in Exercise 16.45.

REVIEW TEST FOR CHAPTER 16

1. One-way ANOVA is used to compare means of a variable for populations that result from classification by one other variable.

2. (i) Independent samples; check by studying the way the sampling was done.

   (ii) Normal populations; check with normal probability plots, histograms, dotplots.

   (iii) All populations have equal standard deviations; this is a reasonable assumption if the ratio of the largest sample standard deviation to the smallest one is less than 2.

3. F distribution

4. There are n = 17 observations and k = 3 samples. The degrees of freedom are (k - 1, n - k) = (2, 14).

5. (a) Variation among sample means is measured by the mean square for treatments, MSTR = SSTR/(k - 1).

   (b) The variation within samples is measured by the error mean square, MSE = SSE/(n - k).

6. (a) SST is the total sum of squares. It measures the total variation among all of the sample data. $SST = \sum (x - \bar{x})^2$

   SSTR is the treatment sum of squares. It measures the variation among the sample means. $SSTR = \sum n_i(\bar{x}_i - \bar{x})^2$

   SSE is the error sum of squares. It measures the variation within the samples. $SSE = \sum (x - \bar{x}_i)^2 = \sum (n_i - 1)s_i^2$

   (b) SST = SSTR + SSE. This means that the total variation in the sample can be broken down into two components, one representing the variation between the sample means and one representing the variation within the samples.

7. (a) One purpose of a one-way ANOVA table is to organize and summarize the quantities required for ANOVA.

   (b)

Source	df	SS	MS=SS/df	F-statistic
Treatment	k - 1	SSTR	MSTR=SSTR/(k - 1)	F=MSTR/MSE
Error	n - k	SSE	MSE=SSE/(n - k)	
Total	n - 1	SST		

8. If the null hypothesis is rejected, a multiple comparison is done to determine which means are different.

9. The individual confidence level gives the confidence that we have that any particular confidence interval will contain the population quantity being estimated. The family confidence level gives the confidence that we have that all of the confidence intervals will contain all of the population quantities being estimated. The family confidence level is appropriate for multiple comparisons because we are interested in all of the possible comparisons.

10. Tukey's multiple-comparison procedure is based upon the Studentized Range distribution or q-distribution.

11. Larger. One has to be less confident about the truth of several statements at once than about the truth of a single statement. For example, if one were 99% confident about a single statement, the confidence that two statements were both true must be smaller since there is no way to have 100% confidence in the second statement. Similarly, each time a statement is added to the list, the overall confidence that all of them are true must decrease.

12. The parameters for the q-curve are $\kappa = k = 3$, and $\nu = n - k = 17 - 3 = 14$. [k = number of samples and n = total number of observations.]

13. Kruskal-Wallis test

14. Chi-square distribution with k - 1 degrees of freedom [k = number of samples]

15. If the null hypothesis of equal population means is true, then the means of the ranks of the k samples should be about equal. If the variation in the means of the ranks for the k samples is too large, then we have evidence against the null hypothesis.

16. Use the Kruskal-Wallis test. The outliers will have a greater effect on the ANOVA than on the Kruskal-Wallis test since an outlier will be replaced by its rank in the Kruskal-Wallis test and the rank of the most distant outlier is either 1 or n regardless of how large or small the actual data value is. In other words, the Kruskal-Wallis test is more robust to outliers than is the ANOVA.

17. (a) 2 (b) 14 (c) 3.74 (d) 6.51 (e) 3.74

18. (a) The total number of populations being sampled is k = 3. Let the subscripts 1, 2, and 3 refer to A, B, and C, respectively. The total number of sample data values is n = 12. Also,

$n_1 = 3$, $n_2 = 5$, $n_3 = 4$. The following statistics for each sample are:

$\bar{x}_1 = 3$, $\bar{x}_2 = 3$, and $\bar{x}_3 = 6$. Also, $s_1 = 2.000$, $s_2 = 2.449$, and $s_3 = 4.243$. Note, the mean of all the sample data is $\bar{x} = 4$. We use this information as follows:

(b) $SST = \Sigma(x - \bar{x})^2 = (1 - 4)^2 + \ldots + (3 - 4)^2 = 110.0$

$SSTR = n_1(\bar{x}_1 - \bar{x})^2 + n_2(\bar{x}_2 - \bar{x})^2 + n_3(\bar{x}_3 - \bar{x})^2$

$= 3(3 - 4)^2 + 5(3 - 4)^2 + 4(6 - 4)^2 = 24.0$

$SSE = (n_1 - 1)s_1^2 + (n_2 - 1)s_2^2 + (n_3 - 1)s_3^2$

$= (3 - 1)(2.000)^2 + (5 - 1)(2.449)^2 + (4 - 1)(4.243)^2 = 86.0$

SST = SSTR + SSE since 110.0 = 24.0 + 86.0

(c) Let T_1, T_2, and T_3 refer to the sum of the data values in each of the three samples, respectively. Thus:

$T_1 = 9 \quad T_2 = 15 \quad T_3 = 24.$

Also, the sum of all the data values is $\Sigma x = 48$, and their sum of squares is $\Sigma x^2 = 302$.

Consequently:

$$SST = \Sigma x^2 - \frac{(\Sigma x)^2}{n} = 302 - \frac{(48)^2}{12} = 110 ,$$

$$SSTR = \left(\frac{T_1^2}{n_1} + \frac{T_2^2}{n_2} + \frac{T_3^2}{n_3} \right) - \frac{(\Sigma x)^2}{n} = \left(\frac{9^2}{3} + \frac{15^2}{5} + \frac{24^2}{4} \right) - \frac{(48)^2}{12} = 24 ,$$

and

$SSE = SST - SSTR = 110 - 24 = 86$.

(d)

Source	df	SS	MS=SS/df	F-statistic
Treatment	2	24	12	1.255
Error	9	86	9.556	
Total	11	110		

19. (a) MSTR is a measure of the variation between the sample mean losses for highway robberies, gas station robberies, and convenience store robberies.

(b) MSE is a measure of the variation within the three samples.

(c) The three assumptions for one-way ANOVA, given in Key Fact 16.2: independent samples, normal populations, and equal standard deviations. Assumption 1 on independent samples is absolutely essential to the one-way ANOVA procedure. Assumption 2 on normality is not too critical as long as the populations are not too far from being normally distributed. Assumption 3 on equal standard deviations is also not very critical provided the sample sizes are roughly equal.

20. The total number of populations being sampled is $k = 3$. Let the subscripts 1, 2, and 3 refer to population 1, population 2, and population 3, respectively. The total number of pieces of sample data is $n = 17$. Also, $n_1 = 5$, $n_2 = n_3 = 6$.

Step 1: H_0: $\mu_1 = \mu_2 = \mu_3$ (population means are equal)

H_a: Not all the means are equal.

Step 2: $\alpha = 0.05$

Step 3: The sums of squares and mean squares have been calculated in Problem 4.

Step 4: The one-way ANOVA table is:

Source	df	SS	MS = SS/df	F-statistic
Treatment	2	160,601.416	80,300.708	5.34
Error	14	210,540.467	15,038.605	
	16	371,141.882		

The F-statistic is defined and calculated as

$$F = \frac{MSTR}{MSE} = \frac{80,300.708}{15,038.605} = 5.3$$

Step 5: df = (k - 1, n - k) = (2, 14); critical value = 3.74

Step 6: From Step 4, F = 5.34. From Step 5, $F_{0.05} = 3.74$. Since 5.34 > 3.74, reject H_0.

Step 7: At the 5% significance level, the data provide sufficient evidence to conclude that a difference in mean losses exists among the three types of robberies.

For the P-value approach, $0.01 < P(F > 5.34) < 0.025$. Therefore, since the P-value is smaller than the significance level, reject H_0.

21. (a) $q_{0.05} = 3.70$ (b) 4.89

22. (a) Step 1: Family confidence level = 0.95.

Step 2: $\kappa = 3$ and $\nu = n - k = 17 - 3 = 14$. From Exercise 21(a), we find that $q_{0.05} = 3.70$.

Step 3: Before obtaining all possible confidence intervals for $\mu_i - \mu_j$, we construct a table giving the sample means and sample sizes.

j	1	2	3
$\bar{x}_j$	635.8	506.8	393.2
n_j	5	6	6

In Problem 19, we found that MSE = 15,039. Now we are ready to obtain the required confidence intervals.

The confidence interval for $\mu_1 - \mu_2$ is

$$(635.8 - 506.8) \pm \frac{3.70}{\sqrt{2}} \cdot \sqrt{15,039}\sqrt{\frac{1}{5} + \frac{1}{6}}$$

-65.3 *to* 323.3

The confidence interval for $\mu_1 - \mu_3$ is

$$(635.8 - 393.2) \pm \frac{3.70}{\sqrt{2}} \cdot \sqrt{15,039}\sqrt{\frac{1}{5} + \frac{1}{6}}$$

48.3 *to* 436.9

The confidence interval for $\mu_2 - \mu_3$ is

$$(506.8 - 393.2) \pm \frac{3.70}{\sqrt{2}} \cdot \sqrt{15,039}\sqrt{\frac{1}{6} + \frac{1}{6}}$$

-71.6 *to* 298.8

Step 4: Based on the confidence intervals in Step 3, we declare means μ_1 and μ_3 different. All other pairs of means are not declared different.

Step 5: We summarize the results with the following diagram.

Convenience store (3)	Gas station (2)	Highway (1)
393.17	506.83	635.80

(b) Interpreting this diagram, we conclude with 95% confidence that the mean loss due to convenience-store robberies is less than that due to highway robberies; no other means can be declared different.

23. (a) The total number of populations being sampled is $k = 3$. Let the subscripts 1, 2, and 3 refer to highway, gas station, and convenience store, respectively. The total number of pieces of sample data is $n = 17$. Also, $n_1 = 5$, $n_2 = n_3 = 6$.

Step 1: H_0: $\mu_1 = \mu_2 = \mu_3$ (mean losses are equal)

H_a: Not all the means are equal.

Step 2: $\alpha = 0.05$

Step 3:

Sample 1	Rank	Sample 2	Rank	Sample 3	Rank
495	7	291	3	234	1
608	12	451	5	246	2
652	15	512	8.5	338	4
680	16	533	10	476	6
744	17	618	13	512	8.5
		636	14	553	11
	67		53.5		32.5

Step 4:

$$H = \frac{12}{n(n+1)} \sum \frac{R_j^2}{n_j} - 3(n+1)$$

$$= \frac{12}{17(17+1)}\left(\frac{67^2}{5} + \frac{53.5^2}{6} + \frac{32.5^2}{6}\right) - 3(17+1)$$

$$= 6.819$$

Step 5: df = $k - 1 = 2$; critical value = 5.991

Step 6: Since $6.819 > 5.991$, reject H_0.

Step 7: At the 5% significance level, the data provide sufficient evidence to conclude that a difference exists in mean losses among the three types of robberies.

For the P-value approach, $0.025 < P(\chi^2 > 6.819) < 0.05$. Therefore, because the P-value is smaller than the significance level, reject H_0.

(b) It is permissible to perform the Kruskal-Wallis test because normal populations having equal standard deviations have the same shape. It is better to use the one-way ANOVA test because when the assumptions for that test are met, it is more powerful than the Kruskal-Wallis test.

24. (a) With the data in three columns named HIGHWAY, GAS, and STORE we choose **Calc ▶ Calculator...**, select HIGHWAY in the **Input column** text box and type NSCOREH in the **Store result in variable** text box, click in the **Expression** text box, select **Normal scores** from the function list, double click on HIGHWAY to replace **number** in the NSCOR function, and click **OK.** Then repeat this process to create, respectively, the normal scores columns NSCOREG and NSCORES. To obtain the normal probability plots, we choose **Graph ▶ Plot...**, select NSCOREH as the **Y** variable and HIGHWAY as the **X** variable for **Graph 1**, select NSCOREG as the **Y** variable and GAS as the **X** variable for **Graph 2**, select NSCORES as the **Y** variable and STORE as the **X** variable for **Graph 3**, and click **OK.** The results are

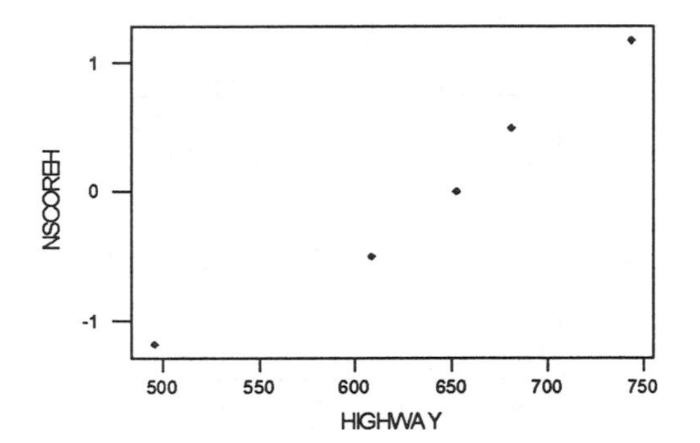

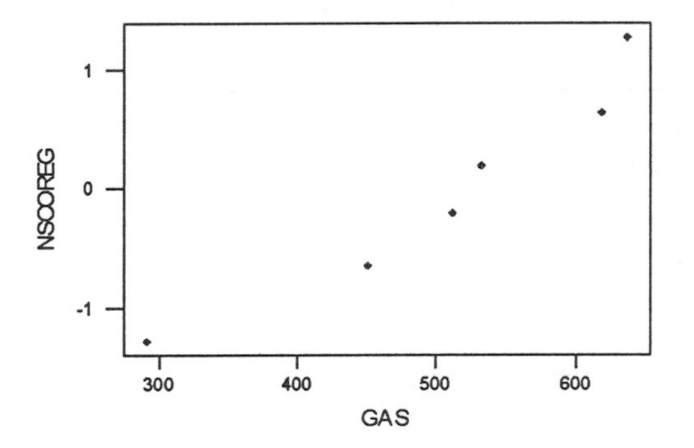

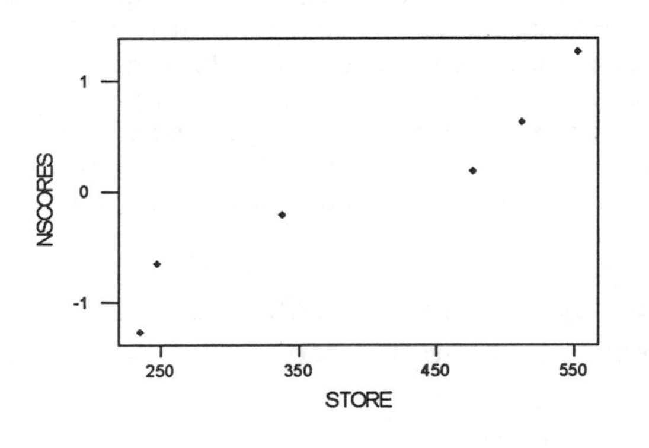

(b) To get the standard deviations, we choose **Stat ▶ Column Statistics...**, select the **Standard deviation** button, select HIGHWAY in the **Input variable** text box, and click **OK.** Repeat this process for the other two variables. The results are

Standard deviation of HIGHWAY = 92.899

Standard deviation of GAS = 126.06

Standard deviation of STORE = 138.97

To carry out the Analysis of variance and residual analysis, we will use the data in a single column which is named LOSS. This is provided on the Weiss Stats CD. In the next column, which is named TYPE, are the types of robberies corresponding to each data value in LOSS.

The residual analysis consists of plotting the residuals against the means (or fits) and constructing a normal probability plot. This is done at the same time as the analysis of variance in Minitab, but the results must be examined before accepting the results of the Analysis of variance. To do this, we choose **Stat ▶ Anova ▶One-way...**, select LOSS for the **Response:** text box and TYPE in the **Factor:** text box. Then click on the **Graphs** button and click to place check marks in the boxes for **Normal plot of residuals** and **Residuals versus fits**, and click **OK**. The graphic results are

(c) Based on the graphics in part (a) for the independent samples, the normality assumption appears to be met, and the ratio of the largest and smallest sample standard deviation is less than two, so Assumption 3 is met. Additionally, from the residual analysis in part (b), the normal probability plot of (all) the residuals is roughly linear with no obvious outliers. Also, the plot of the residuals against the sample means shows that the points fall roughly in a horizontal band centered and symmetric about the horizontal axis. Thus, the use of the one-way ANOVA appears reasonable.

25. Using Minitab, we choose **Stat ▶ ANOVA ▶ Oneway...**, select LOSS, in the **Response:** text box, and TYPE in **Factor:** text box and click **OK**. The result is

Analysis of Variance

Source	DF	SS	MS	F	P
Factor	2	160601	80301	5.34	0.019
Error	14	210540	15039		
Total	16	371142			

```
                                       Individual 95% CIs For Mean
                                       Based on Pooled StDev
Level          N      Mean      StDev  -+---------+---------+---------+-----
HIGHWAY        5     635.8       92.9                 (------*-------)
GAS            6     506.8      126.1          (------*------)
STORE          6     393.2      139.0  (------*------)
                                       -+---------+---------+---------+-----
Pooled StDev =       122.6            300       450       600       750
```

26. With the data in a single column named LOSS and the type of loss HIGHWAY, GAS, and STORE in a column named TYPE, we choose **Stat ▶ ANOVA ▶ Oneway...**, select LOSS in the **Response** text box and TYPE in the **Factor** text box, click on the **Comparisons** button, select **Tukey's (family error rate)**, type 5 in its text box, and click **OK** twice. The first part of the output will be the same as that given in Problem 20 of the Chapter Test. The remaining output is

```
Tukey's pairwise comparisons

    Family error rate = 0.0500
Individual error rate = 0.0203

Critical value = 3.70

Intervals for (column level mean) - (row level mean)

                 1         2

     2         -65
               323

     3          48       -72
               437       299
```

27. We choose **Stat ▶ Nonparametrics ▶ Kruskal-Wallis...**, select LOSS in the **Response** text box and TYPE in the **Factor** text box, and click OK. The result is

```
LEVEL     NOBS    MEDIAN  AVE. RANK   Z VALUE
    1        5     652.0       13.4      2.32
    2        6     522.5        8.9     -0.05
    3        6     407.0        5.4     -2.16
OVERALL     17                  9.0

H = 6.82  df = 2  p = 0.033
H = 6.83  df = 2  p = 0.033 (adjusted for ties)
```

SUPPLEMENTARY EXERCISE ANSWERS

CHAPTER 1 SUPPLEMENTARY EXERCISES

S1.1 Descriptive

S1.3 (a) Inferential

(b) Descriptive

(c) Descriptive

(d) Inferential

(e) Inferential

(f) Inferential

S1.5 Use Table I to obtain a list of 25 random numbers between 1 and 685 as follows. First, pick a random starting point by closing your eyes and putting your finger down on the table.

Suppose your finger falls on the three digits located at the intersection of line number 16 with columns 07, 08, and 09. The selected digits are 552. This is your starting point.

Now go down the table and record the three-digit numbers appearing directly beneath 552 which are between 1 and 685 only, throwing out 000 and numbers between 686 and 999, inclusive.

When you reach the bottom of the table, move directly rightward to the adjacent column of three-digit numbers and go up. Our final list is

552	593	670	407	163
155	667	001	047	378
008	452	581	422	596
016	432	577	293	428
534	594	408	182	242

S1.7 (a) Set a range of 1 to 685 integers and have a random-number generator generate 25 numbers in this range. Match these numbers to a numbered list of the 685 employees.

(b) Answers will vary.

S1.9 (a) Answers will vary, but here is the procedure: (1) Divide the population size, 685, by the sample size, 25, and round down to the nearest whole number; this gives 27. (2) Use a table of random numbers (or a similar device) to select a number between 1 and 27, call it k. (3) List every 27th number, starting with k, until 25 numbers are obtained; thus the first number on the required list of 25 numbers is k, the second is $k+27$, the third is $k+54$, and so forth (e.g., if $k=6$, then the numbers on the list are 6, 33, 60, ...).

(b) Systematic random sampling is easier.

(c) Yes, unless there is some kind of cyclical pattern in the listing of the employees.

S1.11 Observational study.

S1.13 (a) Experimental units: the 18 stores

(b) Response variable: one-month sales figures

(c) Factors: one factor - advertising policy

(d) Levels of each factor: The three different advertising policies

(e) Treatments: The three different advertising policies

S1.15 The "traditional" family of the 1950s was one in which the husband was the breadwinner and wife stayed at home with the children. Many things are different in our society now from what they were in the 1950s. Two-earner families are common now; they weren't then. Given the many changes that have taken place, it would probably be difficult to change back to the 1950s in just one area. It may be that the conclusion that returning to the traditional family of the 1950s would return wives and mothers to a psychologically disadvantaged position in which husbands have much better mental health than wives is justified, but it is difficult to determine what kind of data from the 1990s would allow one to reach that conclusion.

S1.17 Descriptive study.

S1.19 Descriptive study.

S1.21 Inferential study.

S1.23 (a)

AH,RL,SM	AH,RL,CR	AH,RL,LL	AH,SM,CR	AH,SM,LL
AH,CR,LL	RL,SM,CR	RL,SM,LL	RL,CR,LL	SM,CR,LL

(b) 1/10, 1/10, 1/10

S1.25 (a)

MS, FS	MS, JS	FS, BI	LG, BI	BI, JS
MS, LG	MS, JC	FS, JS	LG, JS	BI, JC
MS, BI	FS, LG	FS, JC	LG, JC	JS, JC

(b) One procedure for taking a random sample of two representatives from the six is to write the initials of the representatives on six separate ieces of paper, place the six slips of paper into a box, and then, while blindfolded, pick two of the slips of paper.

(c) P(MS and FS) = 1/15; P(LG and JC) = 1/15

S1.27 (a)

MS, FS, LG	MS, LG, JS	FS, LG, BI	FS, JS, JC
MS, FS, BI	MS, LG, JC	FS, LG, JS	LG, BI, JS
MS, FS, JS	MS, BI, JS	FS, LG, JC	LG, BI, JC
MS, FS, JC	MS, BI, JC	FS, BI, JS	LG, JS, JC
MS, LG, BI	MS, JS, JC	FS, BI, JC	BI, JS, JC

(b) One procedure for taking a random sample of three representatives from the six is to number the representatives 1-6, and use a table of random numbers or a random-number generator to select three different numbers between 1 and 6.

(c) P(MS, FS, and LG) = 1/20; P(LG, JS, and JC) = 1/20

S1.29 (a) Divide the population size, 7246, by the sample size, 50, and round down to the nearest whole number; this gives 144. (2) Use a table of random numbers (or a similar device) to select a number between 1 and 144, call it k. (3) List every 144th number, starting with k, until 50 numbers are obtained. If the first number chosen is 87, then the sample consists of voters numbered 87, 231, 375, 519, ..., 7143.

(b) If the list of voters is alphabetical, systematic sampling should give results comparable to simple random sampling in this case.

S1.31 Observational study.

S1.33 Inferential study.

CHAPTER 2 SUPPLEMENTARY EXERCISES

S2.1 quantitative, discrete data.

S2.3 (a) quantitative, discrete data.

(b) quantitative, discrete data.

(c) qualitative data.

S2.5 (a) quantitative, continuous data.

(b) quantitative, discrete data.

(c) Classifying a baseball player as right-handed or left-handed would result in the collection of *qualitative* data. Using this classification to count the number of right-handed and left-handed players would result in the collection of *quantitative, discrete* data.

(d) quantitative, continuous data (since estimating means measuring dollar amounts).

(e) Classifying an individual as Democrat or Republican would result in the collection of *qualitative* data. Using this classification to count the number in each group would result in the collection of *quantitative, discrete* data.

(f) Finding the number of men and women participating in varsity sports would result in the collection of *quantitative, discrete* data. Finding out how much money was spent on men's sports and on women's sports would result in the collection of *quantitative, continuous* data.

S2.7 quantitative, continuous data

S2.9 quantitative, discrete data.

S2.11 quantitative, discrete data.

S2.13

Iron intake (mg)	Frequency	Relative frequency	Midpoint
6<8	1	0.022	7
8<10	1	0.022	9
10<12	7	0.156	11
12<14	9	0.200	13
14<16	9	0.200	15
16<18	9	0.200	17
18<20	8	0.178	19
20<22	1	0.022	21
	45	1.000	

S2.15

Iron intake (mg)	Frequency	Relative frequency	Midpoint
6.0-7.9	1	0.022	7
8.0-9.9	1	0.022	9
10.0-11.9	7	0.156	11
12.0-13.9	9	0.200	13
14.0-15.9	9	0.200	15
16.0-17.9	9	0.200	17
18.0-19.9	8	0.178	19
20.0-21.9	1	0.022	21
	45	1.000	

S2.17

Champion	Frequency	Relative frequency
Oklahoma	1	0.033
Oklahoma State	5	0.167
Iowa State	6	0.200
Iowa	17	0.567
Arizona State	1	0.033
	30	1.000

S2.19

Starting salary ($thousands)	Frequency	Relative frequency	Midpoint
25<26	3	0.086	25.5
26<27	3	0.086	26.5
27<28	5	0.143	27.5
28<29	9	0.257	28.5
29<30	9	0.257	29.5
30<31	4	0.114	30.5
31<32	1	0.029	31.5
32<33	1	0.029	32.5
	35	1.001	

S2.21

Age (yrs)	Frequency	Relative frequency	Midpoint
0<10	1	0.029	5
10<20	1	0.029	15
20<30	2	0.057	25
30<40	2	0.057	35
40<50	7	0.200	45
50<60	6	0.171	55
60<70	7	0.200	65
70<80	6	0.171	75
80<90	3	0.086	85
	35	1.000	

S2.23

Fee ($1000)	Frequency	Relative frequency	Midpoint
0<5	10	0.40	2.5
5<10	4	0.16	7.5
10<15	4	0.26	12.5
15<20	5	0.20	17.5
20<25	1	0.04	22.5
25<30	1	0.04	27.5
	25	1.00	

S2.25

Color	Frequency	Relative frequency
M/D Green	10	0.250
Black	8	0.200
White	6	0.150
M Red	5	0.125
L Brown	4	0.100
B Red	3	0.075
M/D Blue	2	0.050
Brown	2	0.050
	40	1.000

S2.27 (a)

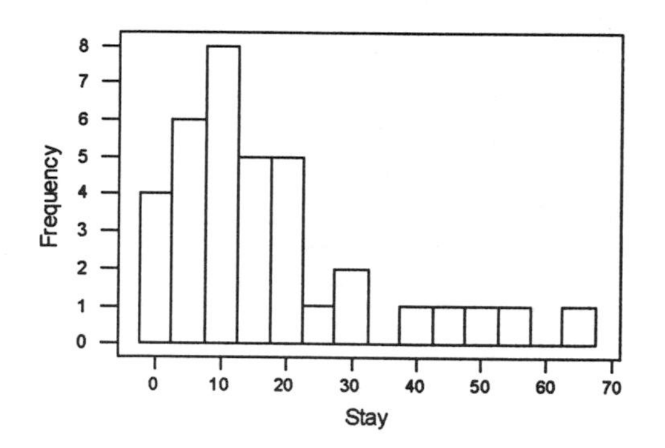

(b)

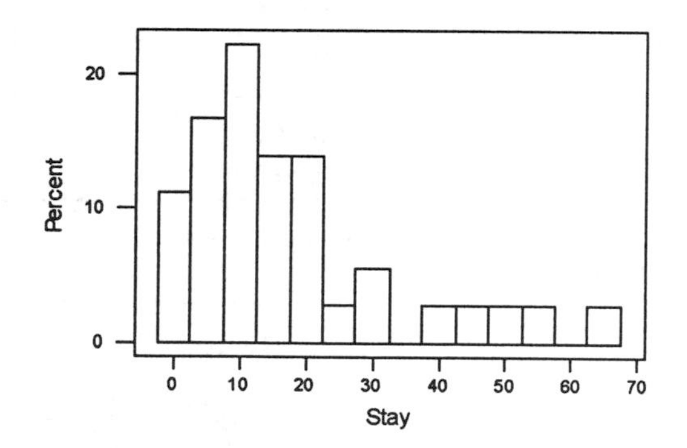

S2.29 (a) (b)

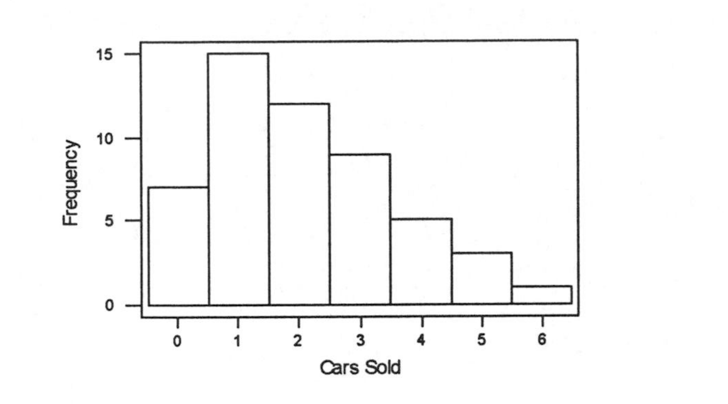

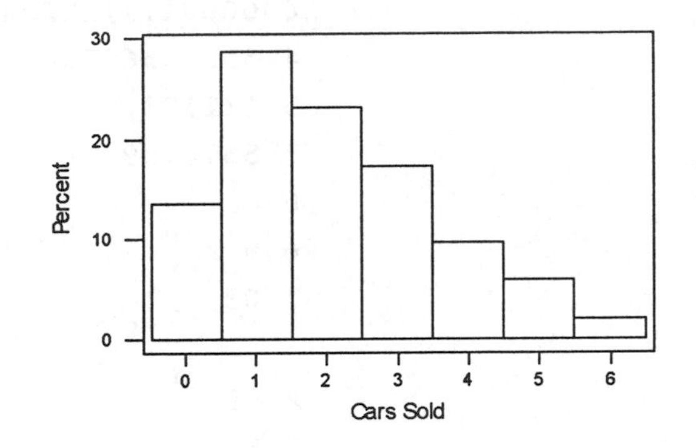

S2.31

```
                                 .   .
   .       .   .       :   :   :       .   .       :
---+---------+---------+---------+---------+---------+---Bushels
55.0      57.5      60.0      62.5      65.0      67.5
```

S2.33 (a)

```
0 11123335568
1 0001222345678
2 01117
3 12
4 148
5 6
6 4
```

(b)

```
0 1112333
0 5568
1 000122234
1 5678
2 0111
2 7
3 12
3
4 14
4 8
5
5 6
6 4
```

S2.35 (a)

```
2 99
3 1233334
3 55567789999
4 00001111222344444
4 55555567788899999
5 111123
5 5577789
6
6 9
7 03
```

(b)

```
2 99
3 1
3 23333
3 4555
3 677
3 89999
4 00001111
4 2223
4 44444 555555
4 677
4 88899999
5 1111
5 23
5 55
5 777
5 89
6
6
6
6
6 9
7 0
7 3
```

S2.37 (a) right skewed

(b) right skewed

S2.39 (a) left skewed

(b) left skewed

S2.41 (a)

Cars Sold	Frequency	Relative	Midpoint
100<150	7	0.35	125
150<200	3	0.15	175
200<250	3	0.15	225
250<300	2	0.10	275
300<350	3	0.15	325
350<400	2	0.10	375
	20	1.00	

(b)

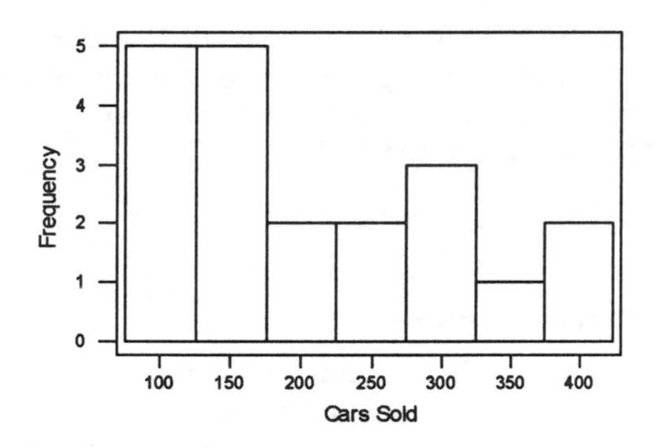

(c)

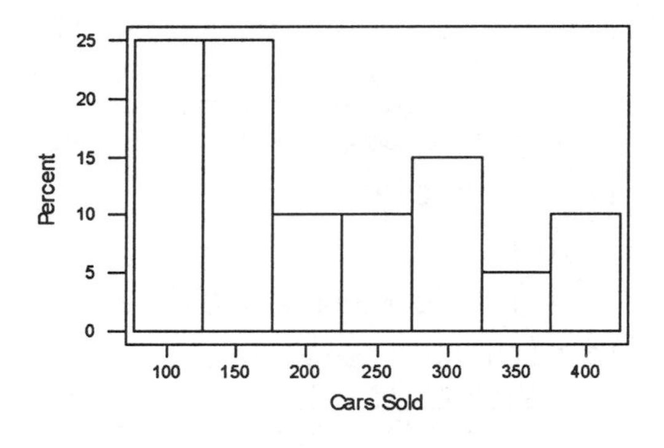

S2.43 (a) Ordinal

(b) Qualitative

(c) Quantitative Discrete

CHAPTER 3 SUPPLEMENTARY EXERCISES

S3.1 (a) 33.5 years

(b) 34.5 years

(c) 24, 28, and 37 years.

S3.3 (a) $17859.5

(b) 18452.5

(c) No mode

S3.5 (a) 13.86

(b) 4

(c) The median is the best measure of center for these data.

S3.7 34 years

S3.9 As a measure of central tendency, the midrange has the advantage of being relatively easy to compute; it has the disadvantage of ignoring a great deal of pertinent information--only the largest and smallest data values are considered, whereas the remainder of the data is disregarded.

S3.11 (a) 210-214.

(b) 210

(c) The mode 210 is contained in the modal class 210-214.

S3.13 With the data in cells A1 to A20 of Excel (or other spreadsheet), type =AVERAGE(A1:A20) in any other cell and the mean will be displayed in that cell as 13.723. Type =MEDIAN(A1:A20) in another cell and it will be displayed in that cell as 14.885.

S3.15 (a) With the data in cells A1 to A51 of Excel (or other spreadsheet), type =AVERAGE(A1:A51) in any other cell and the mean will be displayed in that cell as $25,370.

(b) Type =MEDIAN(A1:A51) in another cell and it will be displayed in that cell as $24,957.

(c) The mean is a little larger than the median. This is due to the fact that the data is slightly skewed to the right. The larger data values have the effect of increasing the mean, but they do not affect the median.

S3.17 (a) 1965

(b) 12

(c) 163.8

S3.19 (a) 19109

(b) 8

(c) 2388.6

S3.21 (a) 431.3

(b) 15

(c) 28.75

S3.23 (a) The range is $1163 - $582 = $581.

(b)

x	$x-\bar{x}$	$(x-\bar{x})^2$	x^2
792	-240.8	57984.64	627264
1146	113.2	12814.24	1313316
1257	224.2	50265.64	1580049
909	-123.8	15326.44	826281
939	-93.8	8798.44	881721
1176	143.2	20506.24	1382976
1146	113.2	12814.24	1313316
972	-60.8	3696.64	944784
705	-327.8	107452.80	497025
1286	253.2	64110.24	1653796
10328	0.0	353769.60	11020528

$\bar{x} = \Sigma x/n = 10{,}328/10 = \$1032.8.$

$$s = \sqrt{\frac{353769.60}{10-1}} = \$198.3$$

(c) $$s = \sqrt{\frac{11020528 - 10328^2/10}{10-1}} = \$198.3$$

(d) The computing formula was easier to use. It required both fewer and easier column manipulations.

S3.25

x	$\lvert x-\bar{x} \rvert$
37	3.5
28	5.5
36	2.5
33	0.5
37	3.5
43	9.5
41	7.5
28	5.5
24	9.5
44	10.5
27	6.5
24	9.5
402	74.0

$\bar{x} = 402/12 = 33.5$

MAD = 74.0/12 = 6.17

S3.27 Advantages: The MAD makes use of all data and is easy to interpret as the average distance that observations are from the mean.

Disadvantages: There are no computing formulas for the MAD, meaning that even when n is large, difference between x and $\overline{x}$ must still be found. Generally speaking, the absolute value function makes it very difficult, if not impossible, to develop theory that would make it useful in statistical inference situations.

S3.29 (a) Nine of the ten, or 90%, of the observations in Figure 3.6 lie within 2 standard deviations of the mean.

(b) Ten of the ten, or 100%, of the observations in Figure 3.6 lie within 3 standard deviations of the mean.

(c) Nine of the ten, or 90%, of the observations in Figure 3.7 lie within 2 standard deviations of the mean.

Ten of the ten, or 100%, of the observations in Figure 3.7 lie within 3 standard deviations of the mean.

(d) Chebychev's Rule is important because it applies to all data distributions regardless of the shape of the distribution. It is thus more general than the Empirical Rule which applies only to bell-shaped distributions. It also enables us to make a statement about the data when all we know is the mean and standard deviation.

S3.31 (a) Since 30 out of 40 is 75%, we compute $53.75 - 2($10.42) = $32.91 and $53.75 + 2($10.42) = 74.59. Thus at least 30 of the 40 sociology books cost between <u>$32.91</u> and <u>$74.59</u>.

(b) Since $53.75 - 22.49 = $31.26 and this is 3 standard deviations (as is $85.01 - $53.75), Chebychev's Rule applies with k = 3. 89% of 40 books is 35.6 or 36. Thus, at least <u>36</u> of the 40 sociology books cost between $22.49 and $85.01.

S3.33 (a) According to the empirical rule, approximately 68% of the observations should lie between 35.08 and 59.08, approximately 95% between 23.08 and 71.08, and approximately 99.7% between 11.08 and 83.08.

(b) Thirty-three of the 50 (66%) lie within one standard deviation of the mean, 48 of the 50 (96%) lie within two standard deviations of the mean and all 50 (100%) lie within three standard deviations of the mean.

(c) The actual values are close to those provided by the empirical rule.

(d) Although the stem-and-leaf diagram in Exercise 2.117 is slightly right-skewed, the skewness does not appear to be great enough to make approximations from the empirical rule be greatly incorrect.

(e) The skewness is not sufficient to invalidate the use of the empirical rule. The largest difference (about 2%) between the actual and empirical rule percentages is for one standard deviation either side of the mean, and that is not where skewness would normally have the greatest effect.

S3.35 (a) Thirty-eight out of forty is 95%, so application of the empirical rule to this data yields an estimate that 38 of the 40 sociology text books cost between 53.75 - 2(10.42) = $32.91 and 53.75 + 2(10.42) = $74.59.

(b) The interval from $22.49 to $85.01 is three standard deviations either side of the mean. The empirical rule states that approximately 99.7% (or 39.88) of the 40 costs should fall in this interval. Since the number of costs must be an integer, our best estimate is that all 40 of the costs should be between $22.49 and $85.01.

S3.37 Using Minitab, with the data in a column named HEIGHTS, we choose **Calc ▶ Column Statistics...**, select the **Range** option button from the **Statistic** field, click in the **Input variable** text box and specify HEIGHTS, and click **OK**. Then choose **Calc ▶ Column Statistics...**, select the **Standard Deviation** option button from the **Statistic** field, click in the **Input variable** text box and specify HEIGHTS, and click **OK**.

The resulting output in the Session Window is

Range of HEIGHTS = 13.000

Standard deviation of HEIGHTS = 3.3916

Alternatively, one could enter the 20 data values in rows 1-20 of Column A of a spreadsheet like Excel, Lotus, or Quattro.

Using Excel, in cell A22, enter the formula **=MAX(A1:A20)-MIN(A1:A20)**. The result shown in the cell will be 13.00, the range.

In cell A23, enter the formula, **=STDEV(A1:A20)**. The result shown in the cell will be 3.391553, the sample standard deviation.

S3.39 Median = 70.0, Q_1 = 64.5, Q_3 = 81.5

S3.41 Median = 1247.0, Q_1 = 1168.0, Q_3 = 1393.0

S3.43 (a) From Exercise S3.38, recall Q_1 = 68.5 and Q_3 = 89.5. So the interquartile range (IQR) is given by: IQR = $Q_3 - Q_1$ = 89.5 - 68.5 = 21. Thus, the middle 50% of the exam scores has a range of 21 points.

(b) Min = 34, Q_1 = 68.5, Q_2 = 83, Q_3 = 89.5, Max = 100.

(c) Lower limit = Q_1 - 1.5(IQR) = 68.5 - 1.5(21) = 37.0

Upper limit = Q_3 + 1.5(IQR) = 89.5 + 1.5(21) = 121.0

Since 34 is below the lower limit, it is a potential outlier.

(d) Boxplot — Modified boxplot

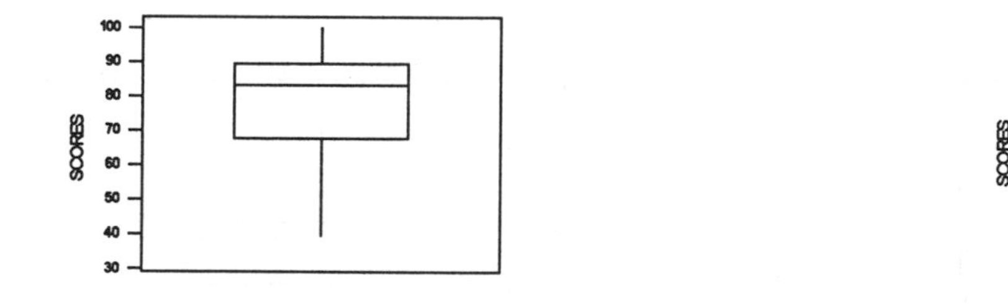

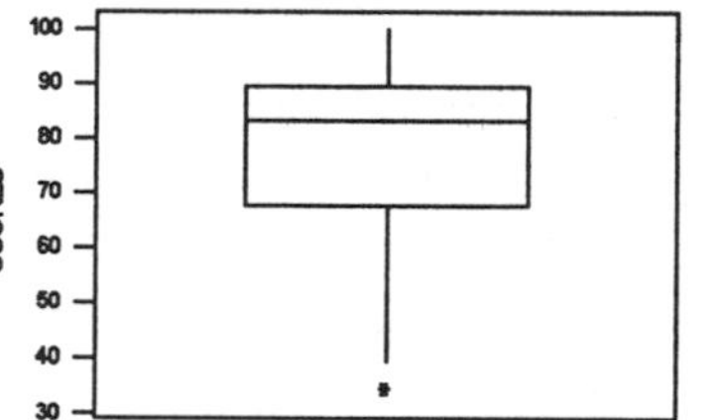

Note that the two boxes in the boxplot indicate the spread of the two middle quarters of the data and that the two whiskers indicate the spread of the first and fourth quarters. Thus, we see that there is less variation in the top two quarters of the exam score data than in the bottom two, and that the first quarter has the greatest variation of all. The (ii) modified boxplot indicates the potential outlier of 34.

S3.45 (a) From Exercise S3.40 recall Q_1 = 96.0 and Q_3 = 115.0. So the interquartile range (IQR) is given by: IQR = $Q_3 - Q_1$ = 115.0 - 96.0 = 19. Thus, the middle 50% of the IQ scores has a range of 19 points.

(b) Min = 66, Q_1 = 96.0, Q_2 = 102, Q_3 = 115.0, Max = 129.

(c) Lower limit = Q_1 - 1.5(IQR) = 96.0- 1.5(19) = 67.5
Upper limit = Q_3 + 1.5(IQR) = 115.0 + 1.5(19) = 143.5
The data value 66 lies just outside the lower limit and is a potential outlier.

(d) Boxplot Modified Boxplot

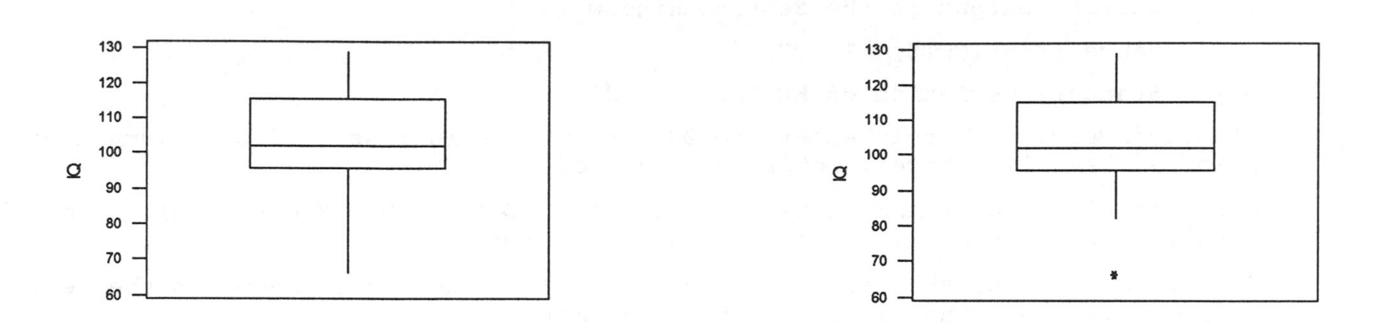

S3.47 (a) From Exercise S3.42 recall Q_1 = 22610.0 and Q_3 = 25997.5. So the interquartile range (IQR) is given by: IQR = Q_3 - Q_1 = 25997.5 - 22610.0 = 3387.5. Thus, the middle 50% of the prices has a range of $3387.5.

(b) Min = 14995, Q_1 = 22610.0, Q_2 = 24900.0, Q_3 = 25997.5, Max = 33900.

(c) Lower limit = Q_1 - 1.5(IQR) = 22610.0 - 1.5(3387.5) = 17528.75

Upper limit = Q_3 + 1.5(IQR) = 25997.5 + 1.5(3387.5) = 31078.75

The data values $14,995, $32,680 and $33,900 lie outside these limits, so there are three potential outliers.

(d) Boxplot Modified Boxplot

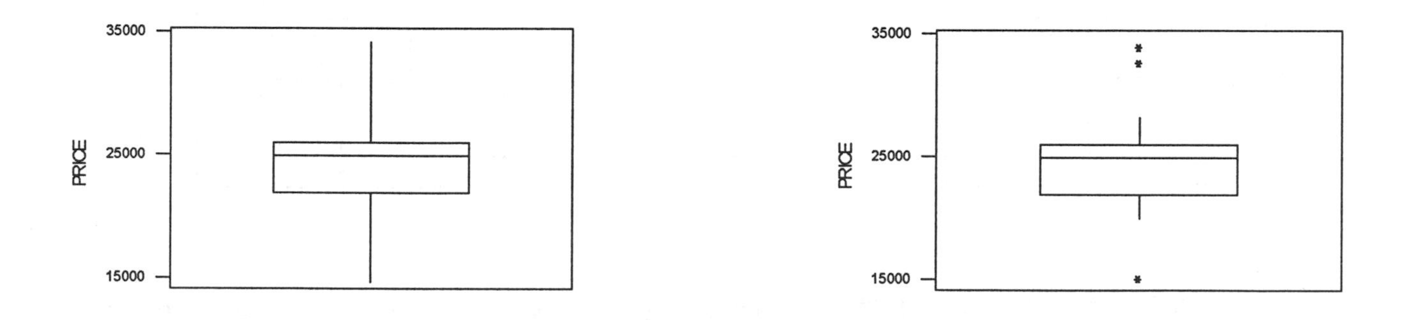

S3.49 (a) Using Minitab, with the temperature data in a column named TEMP, to obtain a modified boxplot, we choose **Graphs ▶ Boxplot...**, select TEMP in the **Y** text box for **Graph 1** and click **OK.**

(b) To determine the smallest and largest data values and the quartiles of the data, we choose **Stat ▶ Basic Statistics ▶ Display Descriptive**

Statistics..., select TEMP in the **Variables** text box, and click **OK**.

The output for parts (a) and (b) are, respectively:

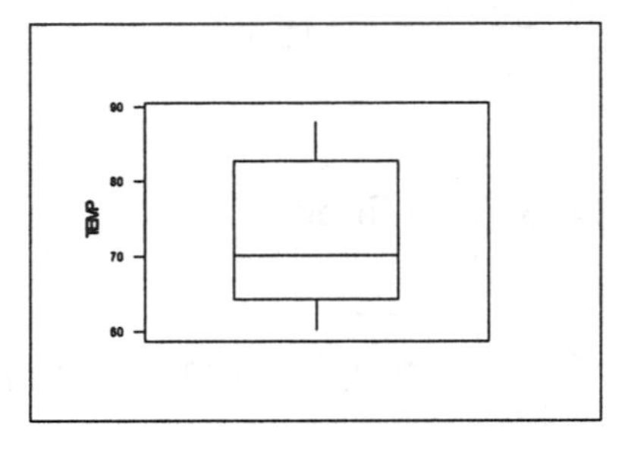

	N	MEAN	MEDIAN	TRMEAN	STDEV	SEMEAN
TEMP	24	72.13	70.00	71.95	9.43	1.92

	MIN	MAX	Q1	Q3
TEMP	60.00	88.00	64.25	82.75

Thus, the smallest and largest data values are 60.0 and 88.0, respectively. The first, second, and third quartiles are 64.25, 70.0, and 82.75, respectively. Note that the quartiles shown differ slightly from those obtained in S3.39 since Minitab uses a slightly different procedure to obtain them.

S3.51 (a) Using Minitab, with the height data in a column named HEIGHTS, to obtain a modified boxplot, we choose **Graphs ▶ Boxplot...**, select HEIGHTS in the **Y** text box for **Graph 1**, and click **OK**.

(b) To determine the five-number summary of the data, we choose **Stat ▶ Basic Statistics ▶ Display Descriptive Statistics...**, select HEIGHTS in the **Variables** text box, and click **OK**.

The output for parts (a) and (b) are, respectively:

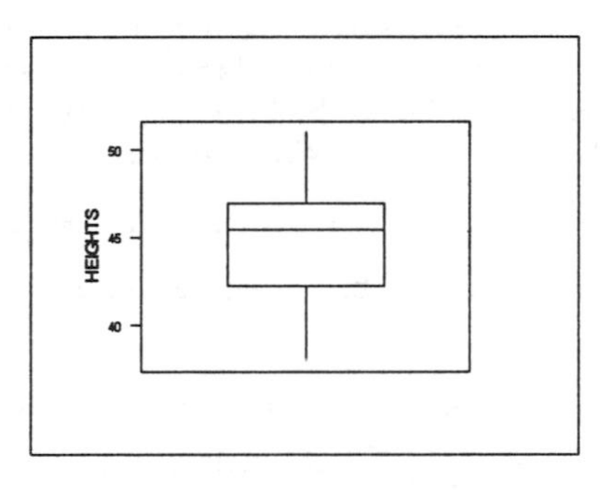

Variable	N	Mean	Median	TrMean	StDev	SEMean
HEIGHTS	20	44.850	45.500	44.889	3.392	0.758

Variable	Min	Max	Q1	Q3
HEIGHTS	38.000	51.000	42.250	47.000

The five number summary consists, in order, of Min, Q1, Median, Q3, Max.

S3.53 (a) $\mu = \sum x / n = 1280/12 = \$106.67$

(b) $\sigma = \sqrt{\dfrac{\sum (x-\mu)^2}{N}} = \sqrt{\dfrac{21384.67}{12}} = \$42.2$

S3.55 (a) $\mu = \sum x / n = 604/12 = \$50.3 \text{ million}$

(b) $\sigma = \sqrt{\dfrac{\sum x^2}{N} - \mu^2} = \sqrt{\dfrac{51780}{12} - 50.33^2} = \$42.2 \text{ million}$

S3.57 We are given μ = 14 oz, σ = 0.4 oz, and x = 17.28 oz.

(a) z = (17.28 - 14)/0.4 = 8.2

Let k = |z| = 8.2. At least $1 - 1/k^2 = 1 - 1/8.2^2 = 0.985$ of the weights lie between -8.2 and +8.2 standard deviations from the mean. Therefore, at least 98.5% of the weights are less than 17.28 ounces, i.e, a can weighing 17.28 oz is heavier than at least 98.5% of all cans.

(b) The quality-control engineer should be concerned that the true mean weight is not 14 oz. If the 17.28 oz can is a representative weight, the true mean weight is probably much higher than 14 oz.

S3.59 We are given μ = \$120,258, σ = \$5237, and x = \$105,500. Thus

z = (105500 - 120258)/5237 = -2.82. Let k = |z| = 2.82. At least $1 - 1/k^2 = 1 - 1/2.82^2 = 0.874$ of the prices lie between -2.82 and +2.82 standard deviations from the mean. Therefore, at least 87.4% of the prices are greater than \$105,500, i.e, a home priced at \$105,500 is priced lower than at least 87.4% of all comparable homes in the area. It does appear that this home is a bargain.

S3.61 After entering the data in cells A1-A12 of the Excel spreadsheet, in A13, enter the formula <u>=AVERAGE(A1:A12)</u>, and in A14, enter the formula <u>=STDEVP(A1:A12)</u>. The result shown in the cells will be 50.33 and 42.20848, respectively for the population mean and standard deviation.

S3.63 (a) $\bar{x}$ = 139/16 = 8.6875; Median = 9; Mode = 10

The median is the best measure of center for these data. Clearly the mode is not at the center. The data is highly skewed to the left. For skewed data, the median is a better measure of center than the mean which is lowered by the left-skewness.

S3.65 (a) The standardized version of y is z = (y - 356)/1.63.

(b) The mean and standard deviation of z are 0 and 1 respectively.

(c) For y = 352, the z score is (352 - 356)/1.63 = -2.45

For x = 361, the z score is (361 - 356)/1.63 = 3.07

(d) The value 352 is 2.45 standard deviations below the mean 356.

The value 361 is 3.07 standard deviations above the mean 356.

(e)

$\bar{x}-3s$	$\bar{x}-2s$	$\bar{x}-s$	$\bar{x}$	$\bar{x}+s$	$\bar{x}+2s$	$\bar{x}+3s$	
351.11	352.74	354.37	356.00	357.63	359.26	360.89	x
-3	-2	-1	0	1	2	3	z

Chapter 4 Supplementary Exercises

S4.1 (a) 0.405 (b) 0.360 (c) 0.640 (d) 0 (e) 1

S4.3 (a) 0.730 (b) 0.929 (c) 0.199

S4.5 The event in part (d), that the family has one person, is impossible. The event in part (e), that the family has at least one person, is a certainty.

S4.7 When tossing a balanced coin twice and observing the total number of heads, there are four possible equally-likely outcomes, not three. The probability of getting two heads is 1/4, not 1/3.

S4.9 54 to 46.

S4.11 4 to 1.

S4.13 3 to 2

S4.15 A = {HHTT, HTHT, HTTH, THHT, THTH, TTHH}

B = {TTHH, TTHT, TTTH, TTTT}

C = {HHHH, HHHT, HHTH, HHTT, HTHH, HTHT, HTTH, HTTT}

D = {HHHH, TTTT}

S4.17 (a) (not B) = {HHHH, HHHT, HHTH, HHTT, HTHH, HTHT, HTTH, HTTT, THHH, THHT, THTH, THTT}

The event that at least one of the first two tosses is heads.

(b) (A & B) = {TTHH}

The event that the first two tosses are tails and the last two are heads.

(c) (C or D) = {HHHH, HHHT, HHTH, HHTT, HTHH, HTHT, HTTH, HTTT, TTTT}

The event that the first toss is a head or all four tosses are tails.

S4.19 (a) (not B) is the event that the family has less than three members, i.e., two members. There are 28,722 (thousand) such families.

(b) (C&D) is the event that the family has between 4 and 6 members and has at least 5 members, i.e., has 5 or 6 members. There are 6,972 + 2,195 = 9,167 (thousand) such families.

(c) (A or D) is the event that the family has at most 5 members or has at least 5 members. Every family is included in A or D. Therefore the number of such families is the sum of all of the listed frequencies, or 70,879 (thousand).

S4.21 (a) (A or B) = event the primary format is rock or country or adult contemporary. There are 3955 such stations.

(b) (Not C) = event the primary format **is** news. There are 1356 such stations.

(c) (C & D) = event the primary format is not news and is not oldies and classic hits. There are 8049 such stations.

S4.23 (a) not mutually exclusive (b) mutually exclusive

(c) not mutually exclusive (d) not mutually exclusive

S4.25 P(E) = 0.2.

S4.27 (a) 0.106 (b) 0.602 (c) 0.398

(d) (i) 10.6% of U.S. adults aged 25 years old and over have at most an elementary-school education.

(ii) 60.2% of U.S. adults aged 25 years old and over have at most a high-school education.

(iii) 39.8% of U.S. adults aged 25 years old and over have completed at least one year of college.

S4.29 (a) 0.199 (b) 0.911

S4.31 (a) 0.786 (b) 0.938.

S4.33 (a) P(W) = 0.565; P(M) = 0.940; P(W & M) = 0.535.

(b) P(W or M) = 0.970.

97% of jail inmates are either white or male.

(c) P(F) = 0.060.

S4.35 P(A or B or C or D) = P(A) + P(B) + P (C) + P(D) - P(A&B) - P(A&C) - P(A&D) - P(B&C) - P(B&D) - P(C&D) + P(A&B&C) + P(A&B&D) + P(A&C&D) + P(B&C&D) - P(A&B&C&D)

S4.37 (a) 8 (b) 3274 (c) 863 (d) 1471 (e) 502

S4.39 (a) 73,970 (b) 15.540 (c) 12,328

(d) 77,182 (e) 12,225 (f) 6,734 (g) 77,700

S4.41 (a) The missing entries in the first, third, and sixth rows are, respectively, 460, 565, 169, 36, 182, and 1913.

(b) 15 (c) 565 thousand (d) 191 thousand (e) 103 thousand

(f) 765 thousand (g) 90 thousand

S4.43 (a) T_2: the institution selected is private;

R_3: the institution selected is in the South;

(T_1 & R_4): the institution selected is a public school in the West.

(b) $P(T_2) = 0.551$; $P(R_3) = 0.316$;

$P(T_1 \& R_4) = 0.096$.

The interpretation of each item above is: 55.1% of institutions of higher education are private; 31.6% are in the South; 9.6% are public schools in the West.

(c)

	Type		
Region	Public T_1	Private T_2	$P(R_i)$
Northeast R_1	0.081	0.170	0.251
Midwest R_2	0.110	0.154	0.264
South R_3	0.163	0.153	0.316
West R_4	0.096	0.074	0.170
$P(T_j)$	0.449	0.551	1.000

(d) Begin with the table in part (c). Summing the cell entries in each row results in the marginal probability in the respective row. Summing the cell entries in each column results in the marginal probability in the respective column.

S4.45 (a) B_1: the base of practice for the surgeon is an office;

S_3: the surgeon's specialty is orthopedics;

$(B_1 \& S_3)$: the surgeon has a specialty in orthopedics and is based in an office.

(b) $P(B_1) = 0.714$; $P(S_3) = 0.174$; $P(B_1 \& S_3) = 0.129$.

The interpretation of each item above is: 71.4% of surgeons base their practice in an office; 17.4% of surgeons have a specialty in orthopedics; 12.9% of surgeons specialize in orthopedics and are based in an office.

(a) $P(B_1 \text{ or } S_3) = 0.759$

(b) $P(B_1 \text{ or } S_3) = 0.759$

(e) Base of Practice

	Office B_1	Hospital B_2	Other B_3	$P(S_i)$
General Surgery S_1	0.233	0.118	0.016	0.367
Obstetrics/ gynecology S_2	0.233	0.065	0.011	0.309
Orthopedics S_3	0.129	0.041	0.004	0.174
Ophthalmology S_4	0.119	0.026	0.005	0.150
$P(B_j)$	0.714	0.250	0.036	1.000

S4.47 (a) (i) A_3: the farm selected has between 180 and 500 acres, inclusive.

(b) T_2: the farm selected is part-owner operated;

(ii $(T_1 \& A_5)$: the farm selected is full-owner operated with at least 1,000 acres.

(b) (i) $P(A_3) = 0.211$;

(ii) $P(T_2) = 0.300$;

(iii) $P(T_1 \& A_5) = 0.021$.

(c) Tenure of operator

Acreage		Full Owner T_1	Part Owner T_2	Tenant T_3	Total
Under 50	A_1	24.0	3.0	2.5	29.5
50-179	A_2	21.4	6.8	2.8	31.0
180-499	A_3	9.9	8.8	2.4	21.1
500-999	A_4	2.6	5.4	1.2	9.2
1000+	A_5	2.1	6.0	1.2	9.2
Total		69.0	30.0	10.0	100.0

S4.49 (a) Conditional probability is the probability that an event will occur given that another event has occurred.

(b) In the notation $P(B|A)$, the given event is A.

S4.51 (a) 0.100 (b) 0.119 (c) 0.548

(d) (i) 10.0% of the states selected have populations between two and three million;

(ii of those states with a population of at least one million, 11.9% have populations between two and three million;

(iii) of those states with a population of at least one million, 54.8% have populations less than five million.

S4.53 (a) 0.383 (b) 0.375 (c) 0.637 (d) 0.624.

(e) (i) 38.3% of all vehicles are under six years old;

(ii) 37.5% of all cars are under six years old;

(iii) 63.7% of all vehicles are cars;

(iv) 62.4% of all vehicles under six years old are cars.

S4.55 (a) $P(H_1) = 0.8211$ (b) $P(H_1 \& B_3) = 0.5406$

(c) $P(B_3|H_1) = 0.6583$ (d) $P(B_3|H_1) = 0.6584$

(e) (i) the probability is 0.8211 that a hospital is a general hospital;

(ii) the probability is 0.5406 that a hospital is a general hospital with at least 75 beds;

(iii) of those that are general hospitals, the probability is 0.6583 that this type of hospital will have at least 75 beds.

S4.57 (a) 0.471 (b) 0.108 (c) 0.017

(d) 0.157 (e) 0.036

(f) (i) 47.1% of all engineers and scientists are engineers;

(ii) 10.8% of all engineers and scientists have doctorates;

(iii) 1.7% of all engineers and scientists are engineers with a doctorate;

(iv) 15.7% of all engineers and scientists with doctorates are engineers;

(v) 3.6% of all engineers have doctorates.

S4.59 (a)

Age (yrs)		Type: Car V_1	Truck V_2	$P(A_i)$
Under 6	A_1	0.239	0.144	0.383
6-8	A_2	0.139	0.068	0.207
9-11	A_3	0.120	0.055	0.176
12 & over	A_4	0.139	0.096	0.235
$P(V_j)$		0.637	0.363	1.000

(b) If each entry in column 2, i.e., the car column, of the table in part (a) is divided by 0.637, the resulting column of figures together with the information presented in column 1 comprises the probability distribution of age of cars in use. This distribution is presented below.

Car Age (yrs)	Probability
under 6	0.375
6-8	0.218
9-11	0.188
12 & over	0.218

(c) If each entry in the 6-8 row in part (a) is divided by 0.207, the resulting row of figures together with the information presented at the very top of the table comprises the probability distribution for type of vehicles that are 6-8 years old. Written in column form, this distribution is presented below.

Type (6-8 yrs)	Probability
Car	0.6725
Truck	0.3275

(d) Two other conditional probability distributions are presented: (i) one of age for trucks in use; and (ii) another for type of vehicles 9-11 years old.

(i)

Truck Age (yrs)	Probability
under 6	0.396
6-8	0.187
9-11	0.152
12 & over	0.265

(ii)

Type (9-11 yrs)	Probability
Car	0.685
Truck	0.315

S4.61 22.88%

S4.63 (a) 0.1 (b) 1/9 or 0.111 (c) 0.011 (d) 2/11 or 0.222 .

S4.65 (a) 0.896 (b) 0.968

(c) not independent (d) not independent

S4.67 (a) $P(P_1) = 0.478$; $P(C_2) = 0.187$; $P(P_1 \& C_2) = 0.084$.

(b) not independent.

S4.69 (a) 0.083 (b) 0.5

S4.71 0.9506 or 95.06%

S4.73 (a) 0.013 (b) 0.015

S4.75 Four events are exhaustive if one or more of them must occur.

S4.77 (a) 0.342 (b) 0.29 (c) 0.283

S4.79 (a) 0.011655 or 1.2% (b) 0.229

S4.81 (a) 900 (b) 9,000,000 (c) 8,100,000,000

S4.83 (a) ${}_4P_3 = 24$ (b) ${}_{15}P_4 = 32,760$ (c) ${}_6P_2 = 30$

(d) ${}_{10}P_0 = 1$ (e) ${}_8P_8 = 40,320$

S4.85 5,040

S4.87 8,145,060

S4.89 (a) 0.48 (b) 0.527 (c) 0.685 (d) 0.624

(e) 48% of the women surveyed answered 'no' to the question; 52.7% of the people surveyed answered 'no' to the question; 68.5% of the people surveyed were women; 62.4% of the people who answered 'no' to the question were women.

(f) The probabilities in parts (b) and (c) are prior; those in parts (a) and (d) are posterior.

CHAPTER 5 SUPPLEMENTARY EXERCISES

S5.1 (a) X =1, 2, 3, 4, 5, 6, 7

(b) {X=5}

(c) P(X=5) = 0.073

7.3% of U.S. households consist of exactly five people.

(d)

Number of persons x	Probability P(X=x)
1	0.232
2	0.317
3	0.175
4	0.154
5	0.073
6	0.030
7	0.019

(e)

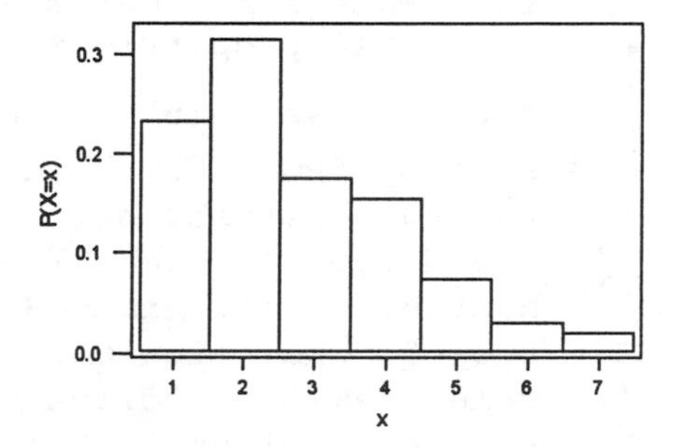

S5.3 (a) X = 1, 2, 3, 4, 5, 6

(b) {X = 4}

(c) P(X = 4) = 7/36 = 0.194

(d)

Larger number x	Probability P(X=x)
1	1/36
2	1/12
3	5/36
4	7/36
5	1/4
6	11/36

(e)

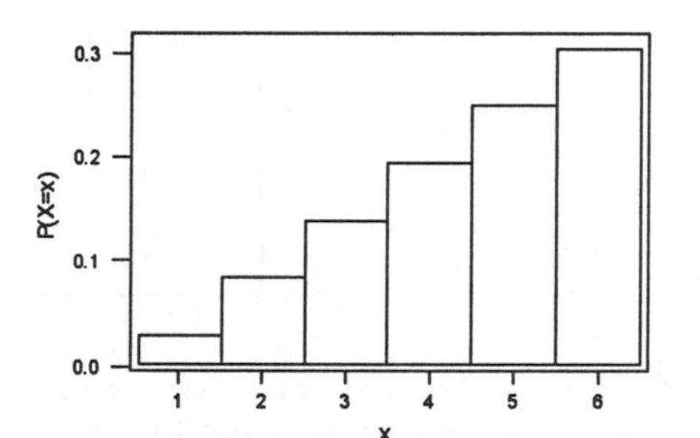

S5.5 (a) After storing the probability distribution from Table 5.2 in two columns named x and P(X=x), choose **Calc ▶ Random data ▶ Discrete...** , type 2000 in the **Generate rows of data** text box, click in the **Store in column(s)** text box and type NUMSIBS, click in the **Values in** text box and specify x, click in the **Probabilities in** text box and specify "P(X=x)', and click **OK.** This will store the numbers of siblings for 2000 observations of a randomly chosen student.

(b) Now choose **Stat ▶ Tables ▶ Tally...,** specify NUMSIBS in the **Variables** text box, select **Counts** and **Percents** from the list of display check boxes, and click **OK.** Our results are

NUMSIBS	Count	Percent
0	409	20.45
1	822	41.10
2	577	28.85
3	154	7.70
4	38	1.90
N=	2000	

The percentages are very close to those of the probability distribution.

(c) To create a histogram of the proportions, name a new column PROP, and enter the proportions from your output for 0, 1, 2, 3, and 4 siblings.

Then choose **Graph** ▶ **Chart...**, click in the **Y** text box for **Graph 1** and specify PROP, click in the **X** text box for **Graph 1** and specify x, click the **Edit attributes...** button, click in the **Bar Width** text box for **Graph 1** and type 1, and click **OK**. Click the **Frame** stand-alone pop-up-menu button, select **Min and Max...**, click in the **Minimum for Y** text box and type 0, and click **OK**. Click the **Frame** stand-alone pop-up-menu button, select **Axis...**, click in the **Label** text box for **1** and type Number of siblings, click in the **Label** text box for **2** and type Probability, click **OK**, and click **OK**. The result is

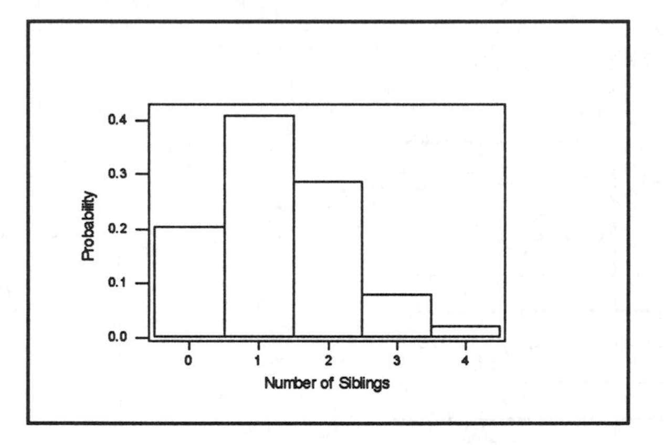

(d) Parts (b) and (c) illustrate that the proportions of times each possible value occurs will approximate the probability distribution itself, and the histogram of proportions will approximate the probability histogram for X.

S5.7 The required calculations are:

x	P(X=x)	xP(X=x)	x^2	x^2 P(X=x)
9	0.301	2.709	81	24.381
10	0.263	2.630	100	26.300
11	0.232	2.552	121	28.072
12	0.204	2.448	144	29.376
		10.339		108.129

(a) μ_x = 10.339. The average grade level of secondary school students is about 10.339.

(b) 1.111

(c)

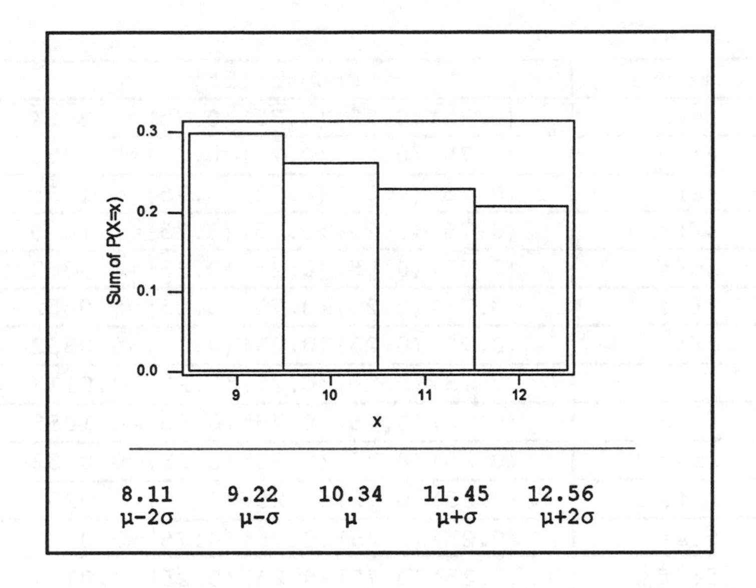

S5.9 (a) 2.002

(b) 100 cars.

S5.11 (a) 1 (b) 2 (c) 24 (d) 720

S5.13 (a) 3 (b) 1 (c) 1 (d) 35

S5.15 (a) p = 0.75

(b)

Outcome	Probability
ssss	(0.75)(0.75)(0.75)(0.75)=0.3164
sssf	(0.75)(0.75)(0.75)(0.25)=0.1055
ssfs	(0.75)(0.75)(0.25)(0.75)=0.1055
sfss	(0.75)(0.25)(0.75)(0.75)=0.1055
ssff	(0.75)(0.75)(0.25)(0.25)=0.0352
sfsf	(0.75)(0.25)(0.75)(0.25)=0.0352
sffs	(0.75)(0.25)(0.25)(0.75)=0.0352
sfff	(0.75)(0.25)(0.25)(0.25)=0.0117
fsss	(0.25)(0.75)(0.75)(0.75)=0.1055
fssf	(0.25)(0.75)(0.75)(0.25)=0.0352
fsfs	(0.25)(0.75)(0.25)(0.75)=0.0352
ffss	(0.25)(0.25)(0.75)(0.75)=0.0352
fsff	(0.25)(0.75)(0.25)(0.25)=0.0117
ffsf	(0.25)(0.25)(0.75)(0.25)=0.0117
fffs	(0.25)(0.25)(0.25)(0.75)=0.0117
ffff	(0.25)(0.25)(0.25)(0.25)=0.0039

(c)

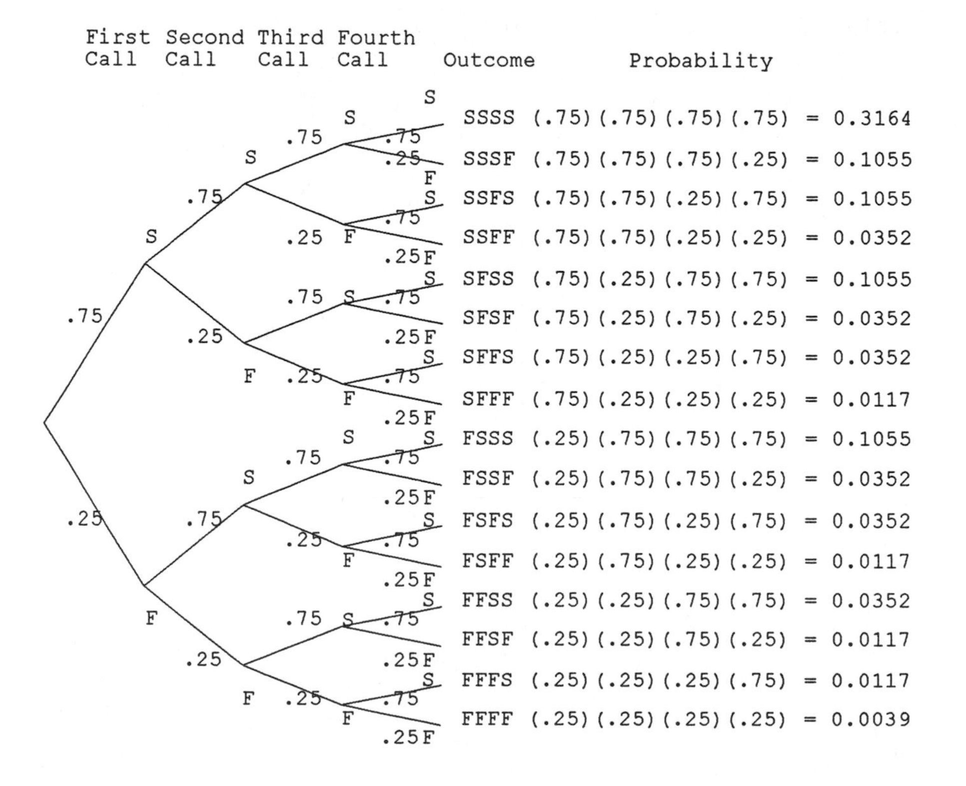

(d) The outcomes in which exactly two of the four calls last at most 3.8 minutes are ssff, sfsf, sffs, fssf, fsfs, ffss.

(e) Each outcome in part (d) has probability 0.0352.

(f) 0.2112

(g) P(exactly zero calls last at most 3.8 minutes) = 0.0039

P(exactly one call lasts at most 3.8 minutes) = 0.0468

P(exactly three calls last at most 3.8 minutes) = 0.4220

P(exactly four calls last at most 3.8 minutes) = 0.3164

Thus

x	0	1	2	3	4
P(X=x)	0.0039	0.0468	0.2112	0.4220	0.3164

Note: The probabilities in the table do not sum to 1 due to round-off error.

S5.17 Step 1: A success is that a call lasts less than 3.8 minutes.

Step 2: The success probability is p = 0.25.

Step 3: The number of trials is n = 4.

Step 4: The formula for y successes is

$P(Y=y)=\binom{4}{y}(.25)^{y}(.75)^{4-y}$. For y = 0, 1, 2, 3, and 4, the probabilities are

$$P(Y=0)=\binom{4}{0}(.25)^{0}(.75)^{4-0}=\frac{4!}{0!4!}(.25)^{0}(.75)^{4}=0.3164$$

$$P(Y=1)=\binom{4}{1}(.25)^{1}(.75)^{4-1}=\frac{4!}{1!3!}(.25)^{1}(.75)^{3}=0.4219$$

$$P(Y=2)=\binom{4}{2}(.25)^{2}(.75)^{4-2}=\frac{4!}{2!2!}(.25)^{2}(.75)^{2}=0.2109$$

$$P(Y=3)=\binom{4}{3}(.25)^{3}(.75)^{4-3}=\frac{4!}{3!1!}(.25)^{3}(.75)^{1}=0.0469$$

$$P(Y=4)=\binom{4}{4}(.25)^{4}(.75)^{4-4}=\frac{4!}{4!0!}(.25)^{4}(.75)^{0}=0.0039$$

S5.19 (a) Step 1: A success is that a home buyer will buy a new home.

Step 2: The success probability is p = 0.227.

Step 3: The number of trials is n = 4.

Step 4: The formula for x successes is

$$P(X=x)=\binom{4}{x}(.227)^{x}(.773)^{4-x}.$$

(a) 0.0362 (b) 0.1847 (c) 0.2236 (d) 0.2209

(e)

x	0	1	2	3	4
P(X=x)	0.3570	0.4194	0.1847	0.0362	0.0027

(f) right-skewed.

(g)

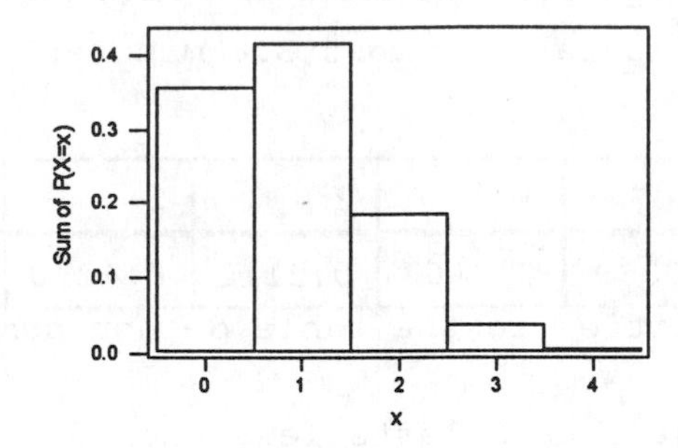

(h)

x	P(X=x)	xP(X=x)	x^2	x^2P(X=x)
0	0.3570	0.0000	0	0.0000
1	0.4194	0.4194	1	0.4194
2	0.1847	0.3694	4	0.7388
3	0.0362	0.1085	9	0.3249
4	0.0027	0.0108	16	0.0432
		0.9080		1.5263

$\mu = 0.9080$

$\sigma^2 = 1.5263 - 0.9080^2 = 0.701836$; $\sigma = \sqrt{0.701836} = 0.8378$

(i) $\mu = np = 4(0.227) = 0.908$

$\sigma^2 = np(1-p) = 4(0.227)(0.773) = 0.701884$

$\sigma = \sqrt{0.701884} = 0.8378$

(j) Out of every four home-buyers, an average of 0.908 will buy a new home.

S5.21 n = 10; p = 0.60

(a) P(5) = 0.201 (b) $P(5 \le X \le 7) = 0.667$

(c) P(over 80%) = $P(X > 8) = 0.046$ (d) $P(X < 9) = 0.954$

S5.23 (a) 0.3275 (b) 0.6096 (c) 0.7180

S5.25 0.962

S5.27 (a) 0.1806 (b) 0.1744

(c) The answers in (a) and (b) are close, but not equal.

(d) With replacement, 0.1806; without replacement, 0.1800

(e) There is less difference between sampling with and without replacement in the latter case where the population size is 400. This is because reducing the population by one male out of 400 does not change the probability of a male on the second selection as much as does reducing the population by one male out of 40. In terms of proportions, the population for the second selection is more like the population for the first selection when the population size is 400 than when it is 40.

S5.29 (a) 0.174 (b) 0.052 (c) 0.848

(d) 4.7 (e) 2.168

S5.31 (a) 0.261 (b) 0.430

S5.33 (a)

x	P(X=x)	x	P(X=x)
0	0.091	6	0.024
1	0.218	7	0.008
2	0.261	8	0.002
3	0.209	9	0.001
4	0.125	10	0.000
5	0.060		

(b)

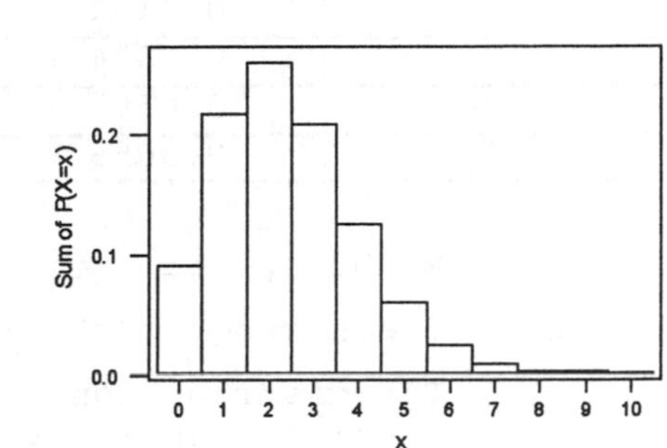

S5.35 (a) 0.479 (b) 0.832 (c) 0.168

S5.37 In Excel, enter 0 through 5 in cells A2 to A7. Then, in B2, enter the formula, =POISSON(A2,3.87,0). Finally copy this formula into B3 through B7 to get the probabilities of X= 0 through X = 5. From these probabilities, get the probabilities previously obtained in S5.30.

S5.39 Using Minitab, we obtain

ROW	x	BIN_P(x)	POI_P(x)
1	0	0.135065	0.135335
2	1	0.270670	0.270671
3	2	0.270942	0.270671
4	3	0.180628	0.180447
5	4	0.090223	0.090224
6	5	0.036017	0.036089
7	6	0.011970	0.012030
8	7	0.003406	0.003437
9	8	0.000847	0.000859
10	9	0.000187	0.000191
11	10	0.000037	0.000038

Excel could also have used, utilizing the worksheet functions BINOMDIST and POISSON.

S5.41 (a) $P(3) = 0.4194$

(b) $P(X \leq 1) = 0.6972$ (c) $P(X \geq 1) = 0.5806$

(d)

Number of Hindu x	Probability P(X=x)
0	0.2778
1	0.4194
2	0.2374
3	0.0597
4	0.0056

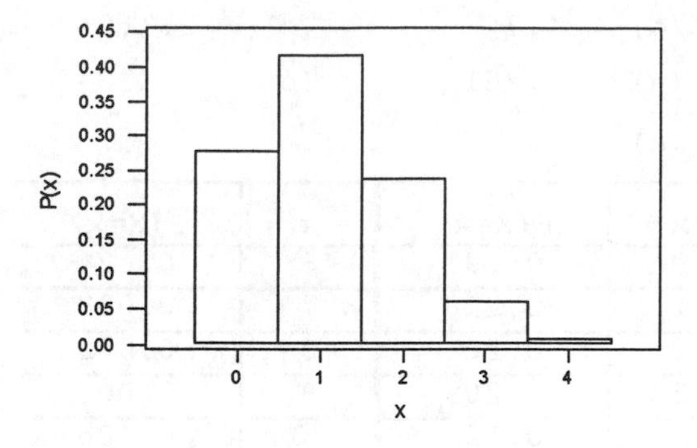

(e) Right skewed, since $p < 0.5$.

(f) See histogram at right.

(g) The distribution is only approximate for several reasons: the actual distribution is hypergeometric, based on sampling without replacement; and the success probability p = 0.274 may be based on a sample, or even if it is a population figure, it would have been obtained at a particular point in time and may become slightly inaccurate as time elapses.

(h) $\mu = np = 4(.274) = 1.096$; On the average, 1.096 out of 4 Surinamese are Hindu.

(i) $\sigma^2 = np(1-p) = 4(0.274)(0.726) = 0.795696$; $\sigma = \sqrt{0.795696} = 0.892$

S5.43 Enter the numbers 0 through 10 in cells A2 through A12 of Excel. Then, in B2, enter the formula =BINOMDIST(A2,10,0.49,0) and copy the formula to cells B3 through B12. The result is the table

x	P(X=x)
0	0.0012
1	0.0114
2	0.0494
3	0.1267
4	0.2130
5	0.2456
6	0.1966
7	0.1080
8	0.0389
9	0.0083
10	0.0008

CHAPTER 6 SUPPLEMENTARY EXERCISES

S6.1

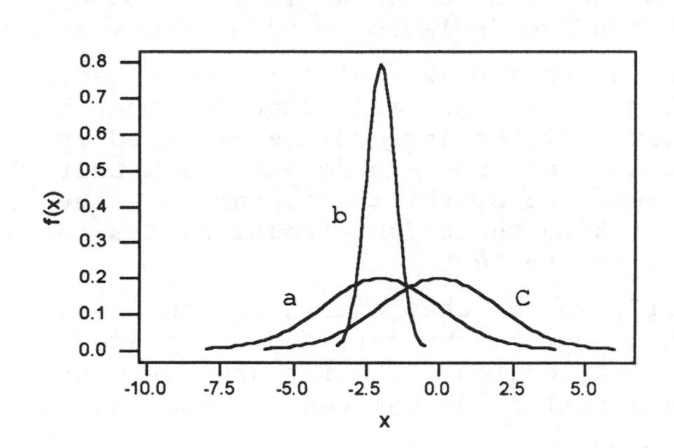

S6.3 (a)

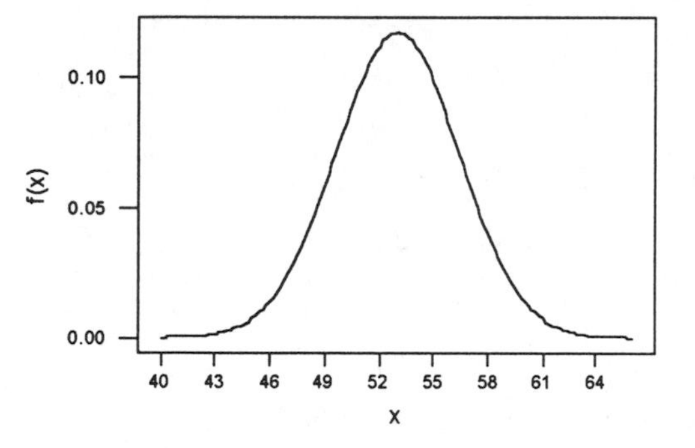

(b) $z = (x - 53)/3.4$ (b) Standard normal

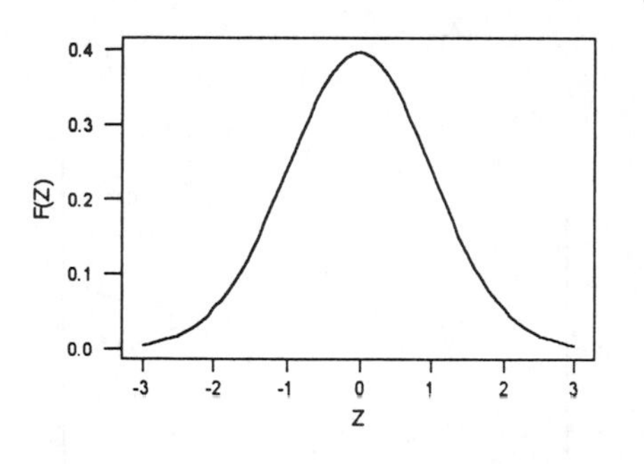

(d) -3.82 and -0.88 (e) left of -2.94 or to the right of +2.94

S6.5 (a) The inequality $\mu + a\sigma < x < b < \mu + b\sigma$ is equivalent to

$a\sigma < x - \mu < b\sigma$ which is equivalent to

$a < (x - \mu)/\sigma < b$ which is the same as

$a < z < b$.

It follows that the percentage of all possible observations of z between a and b equals the percentage of all observations of x that lie between $\mu + a\sigma$ and $\mu + b\sigma$.

(b) The integral shown in the text represents the area under a normal curve (the integrand is the function shown in the footnote for a normal curve) with mean μ and standard deviation σ between $\mu + a\sigma$ and $\mu + b\sigma$.

(c) Making the substitution $z = (x - \mu)/\sigma$ in the integrand is equivalent to replacing x with $\mu + \sigma z$. This also requires that dx be replaced by σdz, that the upper limit of the integral be replaced by the corresponding value of z which is $([\mu + b\sigma] - \mu)/\sigma = b$, and that the lower limit of the integral be replaced by the corresponding value of z which is $([\mu + a\sigma] - \mu)/\sigma = a$. Making these four substitutions results in the integral shown in part (c) in the text.

(d) From Exercise 6.17, we see that the integrand in part (c) is like the one in part (b) with μ replaced by zero and σ replaced by 1, and thus z has a standard normal distribution. The integral in part (c) equals the area under a standard normal curve between the two values *a* and *b*.

S6.7 (a) 0.0217 (b) 0.7123 (c) 0.0000

S6.9 (a) 0.1814 (b) 0.8474

S6.11 0.84

S6.13 2.17

S6.15 -2.58 and +2.58

S6.17 (a) 0.6943 = 69.43% (b) 0.9726 = 97.26%

S6.19 (a) 0.1361 = 13.61% (b) 0.0367 = 3.67%

S6.21 (a) 0.0668

(b) 0.1585

S6.23 (a) 68.26% (b) 95.44% (c) 99.74%

S6.25 (a) \$139.30 and \$173.70 (b) \$122.10 and \$190.90

(c) \$104.90 and \$208.10

(d)

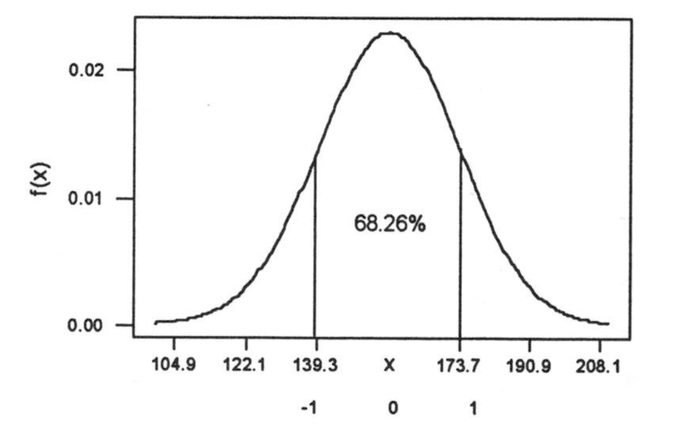

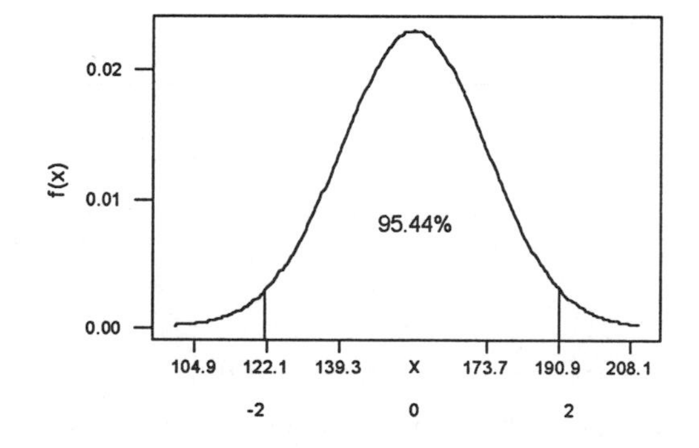

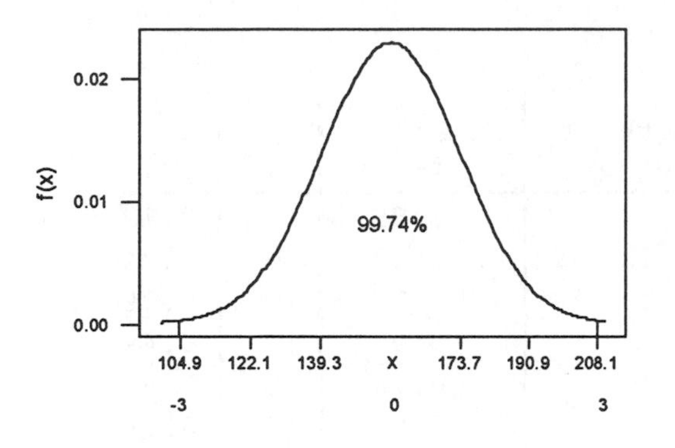

S6.27 (a) P_{82} = 0.299 (b) P_{10} = 0.230

(c) Q_1 = 0.249 Q_2 = 0.270 Q_3 = 0.291

S6.29 (a) 1.96 (b) 1.645

S6.31 For S6.20(a), using Excel, in any cell enter =NORMDIST(.250,.270,.031,1)-NORMDIST (.225,.270,.031,1). The result is 0.1861, which is close to the previous answer. The difference is due to round-off error in the first answer.

For S6.20(b), using Excel, in any cell enter =1-NORMDIST (.300,.270,.031,1). The result is 0.1666, which is close to the previous answer. The difference is due to round-off error in the first answer.

For S6.27(a), using Excel, in any cell enter =NORMINV(0.82,0.27,0.031). The result is 0.298, which is close to the previous answer. The difference is due to round-off error in the first answer.

For S6.27(b), using Excel, for Q2 in any cell enter =NORMINV(0.25,0.27,0.031). The result is 0.249, which is the same as the previous answer. For Q2, use 0.5 for the first number in the formula. The result is 0.270. For Q3, use 0.75 for the first number in the formula. The result is 0.291. These are also the same.

For S6.27(c), using Excel, in any cell enter =NORMINV(0.10,0.27,0.031). The result is 0.230, which is the same as the previous answer.

S6.33 (a)

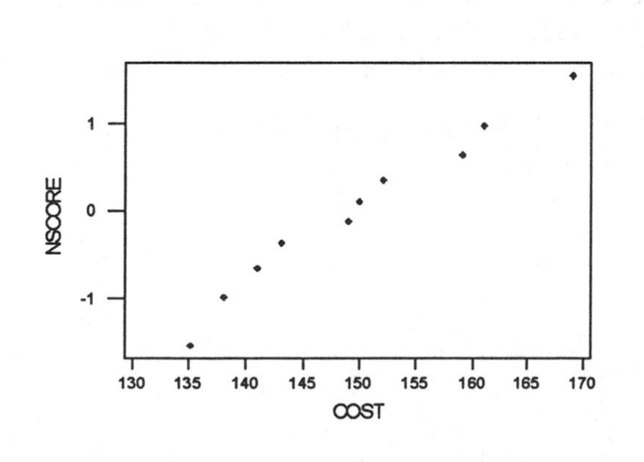

Food cost x	Normal Score y
135	-1.55
138	-1.00
141	-0.65
143	-0.37
149	-0.12
150	0.12
152	0.37
159	0.65
161	1.00
169	1.55

(b) Based on the probability plot, there do not appear to be any outliers in the sample.

(c) Based on the probability plot, the sample appears to come from an approximately normally distributed population.

S6.35 (a)

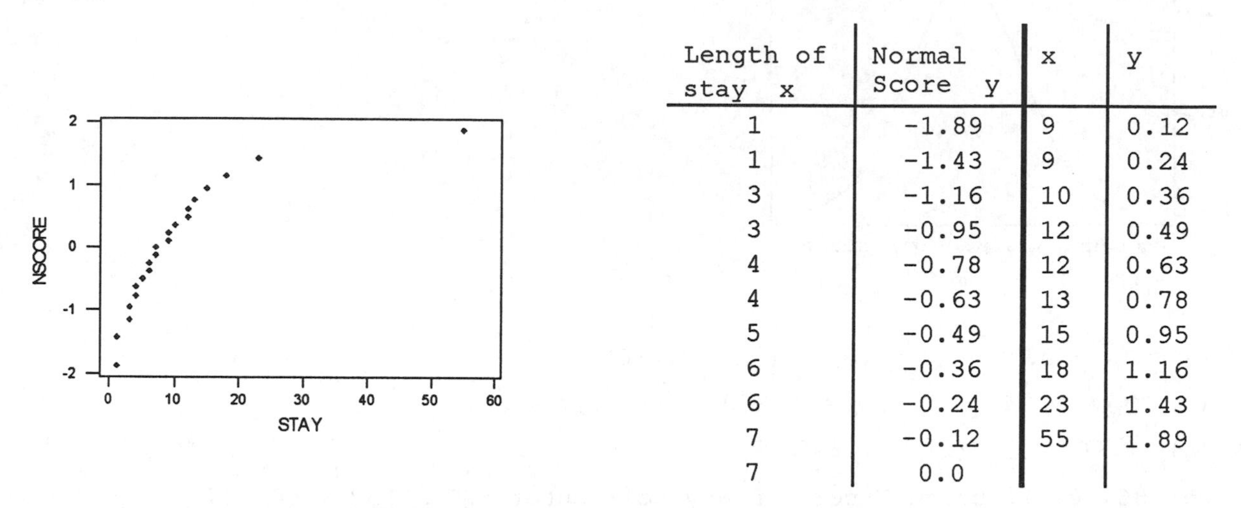

Length of stay x	Normal Score y	x	y
1	-1.89	9	0.12
1	-1.43	9	0.24
3	-1.16	10	0.36
3	-0.95	12	0.49
4	-0.78	12	0.63
4	-0.63	13	0.78
5	-0.49	15	0.95
6	-0.36	18	1.16
6	-0.24	23	1.43
7	-0.12	55	1.89
7	0.0		

(b) Based on the probability plot, there appears to be one possible outlier in the sample: 55.

(c) Based on the probability plot, the sample does not appear to be from an approximately normally distributed population.

S6.37 We will enter the data in Minitab. With the cursor in the Session Window, type Set C1 after the MTB > prompt. Then after the DATA > prompt, start typing the data in the format "frequency(data value)" separated by spaces or commas. You can hit the ENTER key at any time and continue on the next line. When you have finished, hit the ENTER key and type END on a new data line and hit the ENTER key. When you get done, your input should look like

```
MTB > SET C1
DATA> 1(1) 2(2) 2(3) 6(4) 7(5) 8(6) 16(7) 18(8) 18(9) 34(10) 55(11)
DATA> 45(12) 52(13) 35(14) 37(15) 20(16) 10(17) 5(18) 2(19) 4(20) 1(21)
DATA> END
```

This will put all of the data in column C1 as single observations. Name the column SIZE. Now, we choose **Calc ▶ Calculator...**, type NSCORES in the **Store result in variable** text box, scroll down to **Normal scores** in the **Functions** list box, click on the **Select** button, specify SIZE for **number** in the **Expression** text box by double-clicking on it, and click **OK**. Now choose **Graph ▶ Plot...**, select NSCORES for the **Y** variable for **Graph 1** and SIZE for the **X** variable for **Graph 1**, and click **OK**. The result is

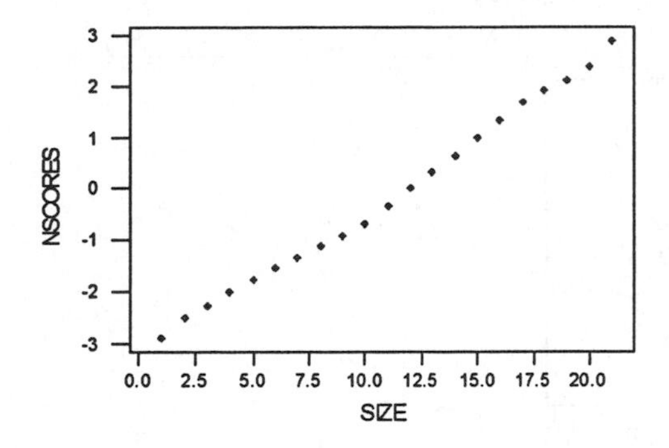

(b) There do not appear be any outliers.

(c) Normality seems to be very reasonable for this data.

S6.39 If $n = 25$ and p remains 0.5, $\mu = np = 12.5$ and $\sigma = 2.5$

Thus, the normal curve used to approximate probabilities for the number of correct guesses is that with parameters $\mu = 12.5$ and $\sigma = 2.5$.

S6.41 For parts (a), (b), and (c), steps 1-3 are as follows:

Step 1: $n = 500$; $p = 0.383$

Step 2: $np = 191.5$; $n(1 - p) = 308.5$. Since both np and $n(1 - p)$ are at least 5, the normal approximation can be used.

Step 3: $\mu = np = 191.5$ $\sigma = 10.87$

(a) 0.0263 (b) 0.8242 (c) 0.9991

S6.43 For parts (a), (b), and (c), steps 1-3 are as follows:

Step 1: $n = 4000$; $p = 0.423$

Step 2: $np = 1692$; $n(1 - p) = 2308$. Since both np and $n(1 - p)$ are at least 5, the normal approximation can be used.

Step 3: $\mu = np = 1692$ $\sigma = 31.25$

(a) 42.3% of 4000 = 1692 $P(X = 1692) \sim 0.0160$ (using $z = \pm 0.02$)

(b) 0.5080 (c) 0.5080

S6.45 (a)

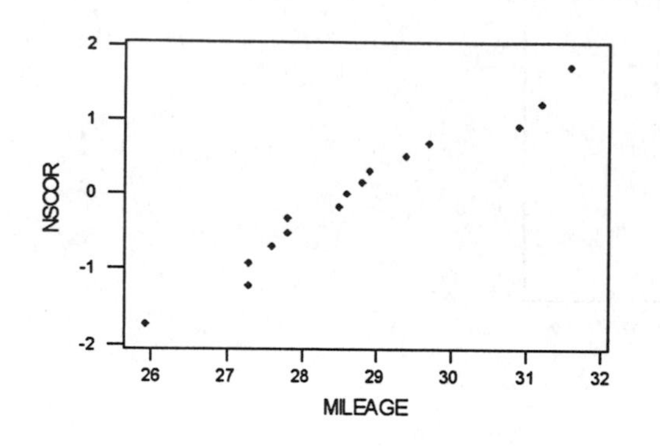

Mileage x	Normal Score y
25.9	-1.74
27.3	-1.24
27.3	-0.94
27.6	-0.71
27.8	-0.51
27.8	-0.33
28.5	-0.16
28.6	0.0
28.8	0.16
28.9	0.33
29.4	0.51
29.7	0.71
30.9	0.94
31.2	1.24
31.6	1.74

(b) Based on the probability plot, there do not appear to be any outliers in the sample.

(c) Based on the probability plot, the sample appears to be from an approximately normally distributed population.

CHAPTER 7 SUPPLEMENTARY EXERCISES

S7.1 (a) $\mu = \Sigma x/N = 322/5 = \$64.4$ thousand.

(b)

Sample	Salaries	$\overline{x}$
G,L	70, 63	66.5
G,S	70, 44	57.0
G,A	70, 75	72.5
G,T	70, 70	70.0
L,S	63, 44	53.5
L,A	63, 75	69.0
L,T	63, 70	66.5
S,A	44, 75	59.5
S,T	44, 70	57.0
A,T	75, 70	72.5

(c)

```
                          o                  o           o

                   o      o    o             o    o o    o

+-------+-------+-------+-------+-------+-------+-------+-------+

44      48      52      56      60      64      68      72      76
```

(d) $P(\overline{x} = \mu) = P(\overline{x} = 64.4) = 0.0$

(e) $P(64.4 - 4 \leq \overline{x} \leq 64.4 + 4) = P(66.5) = 0.2$

If we take a random sample of two salaries, there is a 20% chance that the mean of the sample selected will be within four (that is, $4,000) of the population mean.

S7.3 (b)

Sample	Salaries	$\overline{x}$
G,L,S	70,63,44	59.00
G,L,A	70,63,75	69.33
G,L,T	70,63,70	67.67
G,S,A	70,44,75	63.00
G,S,T	70,44,70	61.33
G,A,T	70,75,70	71.67
L,S,A	63,44,75	60.67
L,S,T	63,44,70	59.00
L,A,T	63,75,70	69.33
S,A,T	44,75,70	63.00

(c)

```
                                   o         o              o
                                   o    oo   o         o    o      o

+-------+-------+-------+-------+-------+-------+-------+-------+
44      48      52      56      60      64      68      72      76
```

(d) $P(\bar{x} = \mu) = P(\bar{x} = 64.4) = 0.0$

(e) $P(64.4 - 4 \leq \bar{x} \leq 64.4 + 4) = 0.5$

If we take a random sample of three salaries, there is a 50% chance that the mean of the sample selected will be within four (i.e., $4,000) of the population mean.

S7.5 (b)

Sample	Salaries	$\bar{x}$
G,L,S,A,T	70,63,44,75,70	64.40

(c)

```
                                             o

+-------+-------+-------+-------+-------+-------+-------+-------+
44      48      52      56      60      64      68      72      76
```

(d) $P(\bar{x} = \mu) = P(\bar{x} = 64.4) = 1.0$

(e) $P(64.4 - 4 \leq \bar{x} \leq 64.4 + 4) = P(64.40) = 1.0$

If we take a random sample of five salaries, there is a 100% chance that the mean of the sample selected will be within four (i.e., $4,000) of the population mean.

S7.7 (a) $\mu = \Sigma x/N = 90/6 = 15$ cm

(b)

Sample	Lengths	$\bar{x}$
A,B	19, 14	16.5
A,C	19, 15	17.0
A,D	19, 9	14.0
A,E	19, 16	17.5
A,F	19, 17	18.0
B,C	14, 15	14.5
B,D	14, 9	11.5
B,E	14, 16	15.0
B,F	14, 17	15.5
C,D	15, 9	12.0
C,E	15, 16	15.5
C,F	15, 17	16.0
D,E	9, 16	12.5
D,F	9, 17	13.0
E,F	16, 17	16.5

(c)

```
                                      o     o
               o  o  o  o     o  o  o o  o  o  o  o  o
+-----+-----+-----+-----+-----+-----+-----+-----+-----+-----+
9     10    11    12    13    14    15    16    17    18    19
```

(d) $P(\overline{x} = \mu) = P(\overline{x} = 15) = 1/15 = 0.067$

(e) $P(15 - 1 \le \overline{x} \le 15 + 1) = 0.4$

If we take a random sample of two bullfrogs, there is a 40% chance that their mean length will be within one cm of the population mean length.

S7.9 (b)

Sample	Lengths	$\overline{x}$
A,B,C	19, 14, 15	16.0
A,B,D	19, 14, 9	14.0
A,B,E	19, 14, 16	16.3
A,B,F	19, 14, 17	16.7
A,C,D	19, 15, 9	14.3
A,C,E	19, 15, 16	16.7
A,C,F	19, 15, 17	17.0
A,D,E	19, 9, 16	14.7
A,D,F	19, 9, 17	15.0
A,E,F	19, 16, 17	17.3
B,C,D	14, 15, 9	12.7
B,C,E	14, 15, 16	15.0
B,C,F	14, 15, 17	15.3
B,D,E	14, 9, 16	13.0
B,D,F	14, 9, 17	13.3
B,E,F	14, 16, 17	15.7
C,D,E	15, 9, 16	13.3
C,D,F	15, 9, 17	13.7
C,E,F	15, 16, 17	16.0
D,E,F	9, 16, 17	14.0

(c)

```
                          o   o     o     o  o
                      o o o o o o o oo o  oo o o o
+-----+-----+-----+-----+-----+-----+-----+-----+-----+-----+
9     10    11    12    13    14    15    16    17    18    19
```

(d) $P(\overline{x} = \mu) = P(\overline{x} = 15) = 2/20 = 0.10$

(e) $P(15 - 1 \le \overline{x} \le 15 + 1) = P(14 \le \overline{x} \le 16) = 0.50$

If we take a random sample of three bullfrogs, there is a 50% chance that their mean length will be within one cm of the population mean length.

S7.11 (b)

Sample	Lengths	$\bar{x}$
A,B,C,D,E	19, 14, 15, 9, 16	14.6
A,B,C,D,F	19, 14, 15, 9, 17	14.8
A,B,C,E,F	19, 14, 15, 16, 17	16.2
A,B,D,E,F	19, 14, 9, 16, 17	15.0
A,C,D,E,F	19, 15, 9, 16, 17	15.2
B,C,D,E,F	14, 15, 9, 16, 17	14.2

(c)

```
                                    o  o o o o      o

+-----+-----+-----+-----+-----+-----+-----+-----+-----+-----+

9     10    11    12    13    14    15    16    17    18    19
```

(d) $P(\bar{x} = \mu) = P(\bar{x} = 15) = 1/6 = 0.167$

(e) $P(15 - 1 \le \bar{x} \le 15 + 1) = P(14 \le \bar{x} \le 16) = 5/6 = 0.833$

If we take a random sample of five bullfrogs, there is an 83.3% chance that their mean length will be within one cm of the population mean length.

S7.13 Increasing the sample size tends to reduce the sampling error.

S7.15 (a) If n = 1, then $\sigma_{\bar{x}} = \sqrt{\frac{N-1}{N-1}} \cdot \frac{\sigma}{\sqrt{n}} = \frac{\sigma}{\sqrt{n}}$.

(a) If n=1, then $\bar{x} = x$, so $\sigma_{\bar{x}} = \sigma_x$.

(b) If a sample consists of the entire population (n = N), there is only one value of the sample mean possible, so there is no variation and $\sigma_{\bar{x}} = 0$.

(c) If n = N, then $\sigma_{\bar{x}} = \sqrt{\frac{N-N}{N-1}} \cdot \frac{\sigma}{\sqrt{n}} = \sqrt{\frac{0}{N-1}} \cdot \frac{\sigma}{\sqrt{n}} = 0.$

S7.17 (b)

$\bar{x}$	$P(\bar{x})$	$\bar{x}P(\bar{x})$
44	0.2	8.80
63	0.2	12.60
70	0.4	28.00
75	0.2	15.00
		64.4

From the third column, $\mu_{\bar{x}} = \Sigma \bar{x}P(\bar{x}) = 64.4$.

(c) $\mu_{\bar{x}} = \mu = 64.4$

S7.19 (b)

$\bar{x}$	$P(\bar{x})$	$\bar{x}P(\bar{x})$
61.75	0.2	12.35
63.00	0.4	25.20
64.75	0.2	12.95
69.50	0.2	13.90
		64.4

From the third column, $\mu_{\bar{x}} = \Sigma\bar{x}P(\bar{x}) = 64.4$.

(c) $\mu_{\bar{x}} = \mu = 64.4$

S7.21 (b) $\mu_{\bar{x}} = \mu = 8.5$ years $\quad \sigma_{\bar{x}} = \sigma/\sqrt{n} = 2.6/\sqrt{50} = 0.37$

(c) $\mu_{\bar{x}} = \mu = 8.5$ years $\quad \sigma_{\bar{x}} = \sigma/\sqrt{n} = 2.6/\sqrt{200} = 0.18$

S7.23 (a) (i) $\sigma_{\bar{x}} = \sqrt{\frac{5-1}{5-1}} \cdot \frac{3.41}{\sqrt{1}} = 3.41$ (ii) $\sigma_{\bar{x}} = \sqrt{\frac{5-2}{5-1}} \cdot \frac{3.41}{\sqrt{2}} = 2.09$

(iii) $\sigma_{\bar{x}} = \sqrt{\frac{5-3}{5-1}} \cdot \frac{3.41}{\sqrt{3}} = 1.39$ (iv) $\sigma_{\bar{x}} = \sqrt{\frac{5-4}{5-1}} \cdot \frac{3.41}{\sqrt{4}} = 0.85$

(v) $\sigma_{\bar{x}} = \sqrt{\frac{5-5}{5-1}} \cdot \frac{3.41}{\sqrt{5}} = 0.00$

These results are the same as those in Example 7.5 of the text.

(b) (i) $\sigma_{\bar{x}} = 3.41/\sqrt{1} = 3.41$ (ii) $\sigma_{\bar{x}} = 3.41/\sqrt{2} = 2.41$

(iii) $\sigma_{\bar{x}} = 3.41/\sqrt{3} = 1.97$ (iv) $\sigma_{\bar{x}} = 3.41/\sqrt{4} = 1.71$

(v) $\sigma_{\bar{x}} = 3.41/\sqrt{5} = 1.52$

Formula (2) yields such poor results because, in each case, the sample size is not small relative to the population size.

(c) (i) 1/5 = 20% (ii) 2/5 = 40% (iii) 3/5 = 60%

(iv) 4/5 = 80% (v) 5/5 = 100%

S7.25 (b) The procedure and result are identical to those presented in part (a) of Exercise S7.24; that is, $\sigma_{\bar{x}} = 10.89$.

(c) Both formulas are appropriate here since, for a sample of size n = 1, there is no difference between sampling with and without replacement.

(d) $\sigma_{\bar{x}} = \sqrt{\frac{5-1}{5-1}} \cdot \frac{10.89}{\sqrt{1}} = 10.89$

This is identical to the result in part (b).

(e) $\sigma_{\bar{x}} = 10.89/\sqrt{1} = 10.89$, same as in part (b)

S7.27 (b)

$\bar{x}$	$P(\bar{x})$	$\bar{x}P(\bar{x})$	$\bar{x}^2P(\bar{x})$
61.75	0.2	12.35	762.6125
63.00	0.4	25.20	1587.6000
64.75	0.2	12.95	838.5125
69.50	0.2	13.90	966.0500
		64.4	4154.775

$$\sigma_x = \sqrt{x^2P(\bar{x}) - \mu_{\bar{x}}^2} = \sqrt{4154.755 - 64.4^2} = 2.72$$

(c) Formula (1) is appropriate here because the sample size is not small relative to the population size. The sample size is 80% of the population size. By rule of thumb, the correction factor cannot be ignored if the sample size is larger than 5% of the population size.

(d) $\sigma_{\bar{x}} = \sqrt{\frac{5-4}{5-1}} \cdot \frac{10.89}{\sqrt{4}} = 2.72$

This is identical to the result in part (b).

(e) $\sigma_{\bar{x}} = 10.89 / \sqrt{4} = 5.44$

(f) Formula (2) yields such a poor approximation because the sample size is not small relative to the population size.

S7.29 (a) Since n $\geq$ 1, N - n $\leq$ N - 1. Also, if n $\leq$ 0.05N,

then N - n $\geq$ N - 0.05N = 0.95N. Therefore,

$$\sqrt{\frac{N-n}{N-1}} \leq \sqrt{\frac{N-1}{N-1}} = 1$$

and if n $\leq$ 0.05N,

$$\sqrt{\frac{N-n}{N-1}} \geq \sqrt{\frac{0.95N}{N-1}} \geq \sqrt{\frac{0.95N}{N}} = \sqrt{0.95} = 0.97$$

Consequently, if n $\leq$ 0.05N, $0.97 \leq \sqrt{\frac{N-n}{N-1}} \leq 1$.

(b) If n $\leq$ 0.05N, then by part (a), $0.97 \cdot \frac{\sigma}{\sqrt{n}} \leq \sqrt{\frac{N-n}{N-1}} \cdot \frac{\sigma}{\sqrt{n}} \leq 1 \cdot \frac{\sigma}{\sqrt{n}}$.

This shows that there is very little difference in the values given by Formulas (1) and (2) when the sample size is no larger than 5% of the population size.

(c) From the result in part(b), since the difference between equation (1) and equation (2) is small when n is small relative to N, we can ignore the finite population correction factor in that situation.

S7.31 (a) Normal distribution with mean 67.4 and standard deviation 2.615.

(b) Normal distribution with mean 67.4 and standard deviation 1.046.

(c)

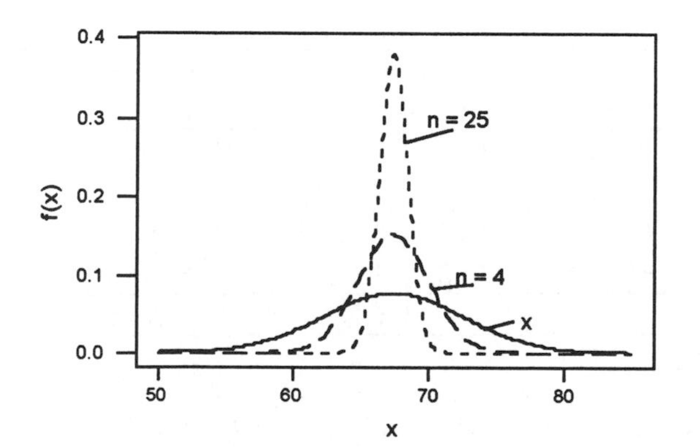

S7.33 (a) 0.5528

(b) 0.9438

S7.35 (a) 0.2877

(b) If $\bar{x}$ does equal \$1145, this *does not* provide substantial evidence that the 1997 mean was more than the 1984 mean of \$1122.17, even though \$1145 is greater than \$1122.17. Part (a) illustrates that we can expect a (fairly high) 28.77% chance that the mean of a random sample of 25 annual electric bills will be \$1145 or greater, *if* in fact the mean annual electric bill for *all* customers is \$1122.17.

(c) 0.0384

If $\bar{x}$ does equal \$1145, this *does* provide substantial evidence that the 1997 mean was more than the 1984 mean of \$1122.17. *If* the mean annual electric bill for *all* customers is \$1122.17, there is only a 3.84% chance that the mean of a random sample of 250 annual electric bills will be \$1145 or greater.

(d) It is not necessary to assume that the annual electric bills are normally distributed because the sample size is greater than 30.

S7.37 (a) False. By the central limit theorem, the random variable $\bar{x}$ is approximately normally distributed. Furthermore, $\mu_{\bar{x}} = 40$ and $\sigma_{\bar{x}} = \sigma/\sqrt{n} = 10/\sqrt{100} = 1$. Thus, $P(30 \leq \bar{x} \leq 50)$ equals the area under the normal curve with mean 40 and standard deviation 1 that lies between 30 and 50. Applying the usual techniques, we find that area to be 1.0000 to four decimal places. Hence, there is almost a 100% chance that the mean of the sample will be between 30 and 50.

(b) This is not possible to tell, since we do not know the distribution of the population.

(c) True. Referring to part (a), we see that $P(39 \leq \bar{x} \leq 41)$ equals the area under the normal curve with mean 40 and standard deviation 1 that lies between 39 and 41. Applying the usual techniques, we find that area to be 0.6826. Thus, there is about a 68.26% chance that the mean of the sample will be between 39 and 41.

S7.39 (a) The graphs for parts (a), (b), and (c) are combined for comparison purposes in part (c).

(b) The random variable $\bar{x}$ has a normal distribution with mean \$237.95 and standard deviation \$15.76 when n = 5.

(c) The random variable $\bar{x}$ has a normal distribution with mean \$237.95 and standard deviation \$11.15 when n = 10.

CHAPTER 8 SUPPLEMENTARY EXERCISES

S8.1 (a) $\overline{x}$ = 1640/20 = \$82.00

(b) it is unlikely that the sample mean is exactly equal the population mean μ since some sampling error is expected.

S8.3 $\overline{x}$ = 240.3/35 = 6.87 lb

S8.5 (a) \$74.84 to \$89.16

(b) We can be 95.44% confident that the mean price μ of all science books is somewhere between \$74.84 and \$89.16.

(c) The true population price may or may not lie in the confidence interval, but we can be 95.44% confident that it does.

S8.7 (a)6.22 to 7.21

(b) We can be 95.44% confident that the mean weight μ of all newborns is somewhere between 6.22 lbs and 7.51 lbs.

(c) This confidence interval is not exact because the sampling distribution of the mean $\overline{x}$ is not exactly normal.

S8.9 (a) Confidence level = 0.85; α = 0.15

(b) Confidence level = 0.95; α = 0.05

S8.11 (a) 15.94 to 16.68 oz.

(b) We can be 99% confident that the mean weight μ of bags of potato chips is somewhere between 15.94 and 16.08 oz.

S8.13 (a) \$12.30 to \$15.14

(b) We can be 95% confident that the mean hourly earnings μ of all persons employed in the aircraft industry is somewhere between \$12.30 and \$15.14.

S8.15 3.75 to 3.85 minutes

S8.17 (a) \$12.79 to \$14.65

(b) The confidence interval in part (a) is shorter than the one in Exercise S8.13 because we have changed the confidence level from 95% in Exercise S8.13 to 80% in this exercise. Notice that decreasing the confidence level from 95% to 80% decreases the $z_{\alpha/2}$-value from 1.96 to 1.28. The smaller z-value, in turn, results in a shorter interval.

(c)

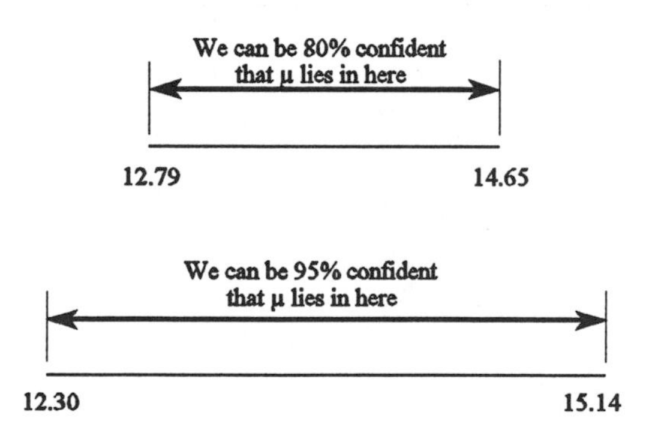

(d) The 80% confidence interval is shorter and therefore provides a more concise estimate of μ.

S8.19 (a) E = (16.08 - 15.94)/2 = .07

(b) $E = 2.575 \cdot (0.1)/\sqrt{12} = 0.074$

S8.21 (a) E = (15.15 - 12.30)/2 = 1.425

(b) We can be 95% confident that the maximum error made in using $\overline{x}$ to estimate μ is $1.43.

(c)

$$n = \left[\frac{z_{\alpha/2} \cdot \sigma}{E}\right]^2 = \left[\frac{1.96 \cdot 3.25}{0.5}\right]^2 = 162.3 \text{ or } 163$$

(d) $13.37 to $14.37

S8.23 (a) 50.1 to 62.9

(b) It does appear that the farmer can get a better mean yield than the national average by using the new fertilizer because the confidence interval does not contain, and is to the right of, the national average of 58.4 bushels per acre.

S8.25 (a) 43.3 to 46.4 inches

(b) We can be 95% confident that the mean height μ of all six-year-old girls is somewhere between 43.3 and 46.4 inches.

S8.27 (a) $56.22 to $61.58

(b) We can be 90% confident that the mean μ for monthly fuel expenditure for all household vehicles is somewhere between $56.22 and $61.58.

S8.29 (a) Since no formula for the t curves has been given in the text, software is required which already has the properties of the t-distributions. Minitab has that feature and can generate the needed curves. We require a set of x values in C1 over the same range for all of the curves. We can set values from -3.5 to 3.5 at .1 intervals in C1 by selecting **Calc ▶ Set patterned data...**, then type x in the **Store result in column:** text box, -3.5 in the **Start at:** box, 3.5 in the **End at:** box, and 0.1 in the **Increment:** box. Click **OK.** Then Choose **Calc ▶ Probability Distributions ▶ Normal...**, click on **Probability density**, select x in the **Input column** and z in the **Optional storage** box, and click **OK.** For the t distribution with 1 degree of freedom, choose **Calc ▶ Probability Distributions ▶ T...**, click on **Probability density**, type 1 in the **Degrees of freedom** text box, select x in the **Input column** box, and type t1 in the first **Optional storage** box. Repeat this last procedure using 2 and t2, 5 and t5, 10 and t10, and 20 and t20 as the degrees of freedom and names of storage columns. To ensure that all plots are on the same scale, select **Graph ▶ Plot...**, then select z as the **Y** variable for **Graph1**, and x as the **X** variable, t1 as the **Y** variable for **Graph2**, and x as the **X** variable, ..., t20 as the **Y** variable for **Graph6** and x as the **X** variable. Click **OK.** The graphs follow.

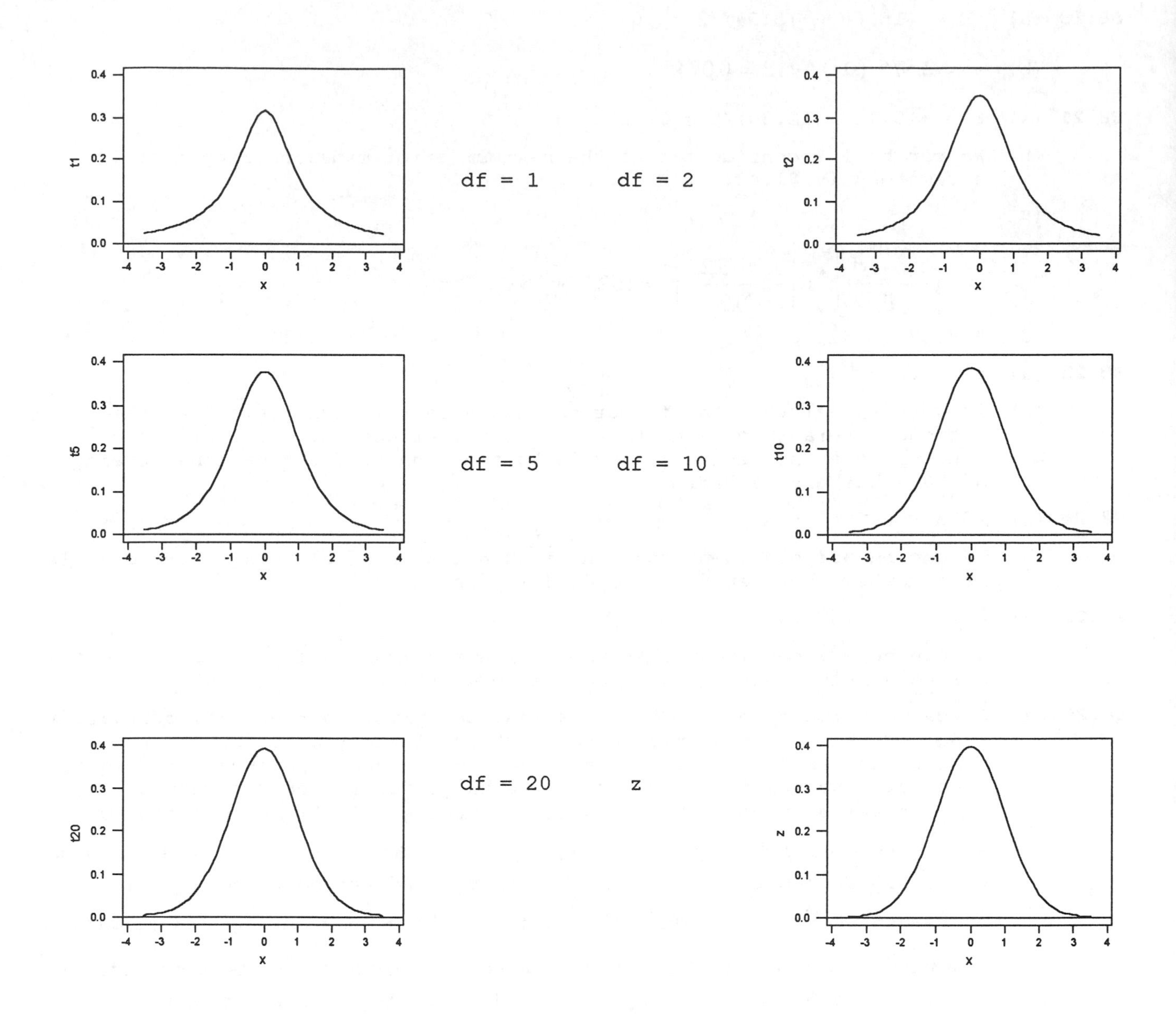

(b) All of the curves are symmetric about zero. As the degrees of freedom increases, the tails of the distributions become "thinner" and the distributions look more and more like the z curve in the lower right.

S8.31 (a) 57.8 to 62.4 hours

(b) We can be 99% confident that the mean battery life μ is somewhere between 57.8 and 62.4 hours.

(c) Since the sample size is not particularly large, the normal probability plot should be roughly linear and not indicate the presence of any outliers.

S8.33 (a) 6.88 to 8.54 hours

(b) We can be 95% confident that the mean daily viewing time μ of all American households is somewhere between 6.88 and 8.54 hours.

(c) The result in part (a) does not provide evidence of an increase in average daily viewing time because the 1992 average of seven hours and four minutes does not lie completely to the left of the confidence interval in part (a).

CHAPTER 9 SUPPLEMENTARY EXERCISES

S9.1 Let μ denote last year's mean amount telephone expenditure per consumer.

(a) H_0: μ = \$809 (b) H_a: μ > \$809 (c) right-tailed test

S9.3 Let μ denote this year's mean travel time to work for all North Dakota residents.

(a) H_0: μ = 13 minutes (b) H_a: $\mu \neq$ 13 minutes

(c) two-tailed test

S9.5 (a) If the mean weight $\bar{x}$ of the 50 bags of pretzels sampled is more than one standard deviation away from 454 grams, then reject the null hypothesis that μ = 454 grams and conclude that the alternative hypothesis, which is $\mu \neq$ 454 grams, is true. Otherwise, do not reject the null hypothesis.

Graphically, the decision criterion looks like:

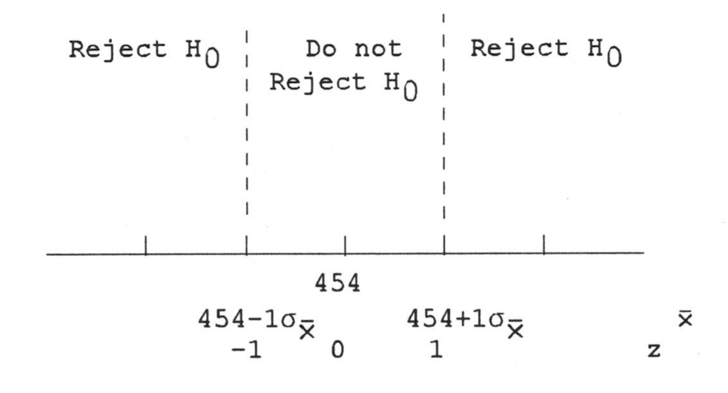

(b)

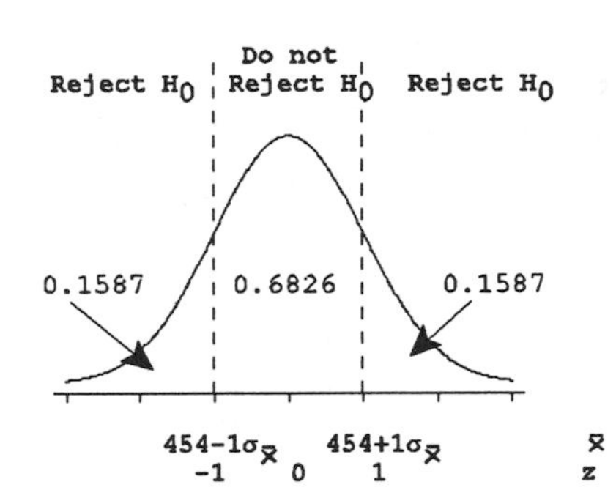

The figure at the right shows that, using our decision criterion, the probability is 0.3174 (= 0.1587 + 0.1587) of rejecting the null hypothesis if it is in fact true.

(c) We have σ = 7.8, n = 25, $\bar{x}$ = 450, and μ = 454 if H_0 is true. Thus, $z = (450 - 454)/(7.8/\sqrt{25}) = -2.56$. The sample mean $\bar{x}$ is 2.56 standard deviations below the null hypothesis mean of 454 grams. Since the mean weight $\bar{x}$ of 25 bags of pretzels sampled is more than one standard deviation away from 454 grams, we reject the null hypothesis that μ = 454 grams and conclude that the alternative hypothesis, which is $\mu \neq$ 454 grams, is true. In other words, the data provide sufficient evidence to conclude that the packaging machine is not working properly.

S9.7 (a) A Type I error would occur if, in fact, μ = \$809, but the results of the sampling lead to the conclusion that μ > \$809.

(b) A Type II error would occur if, in fact, μ > \$809, but the results of the sampling fail to lead to that conclusion.

(c) A correct decision would occur if, in fact, μ = \$809 and the results of the sampling do not lead to the rejection of that fact; or if, in fact, μ > \$809 and the results of the sampling lead to that conclusion.

(d) If, in fact, last year's mean telephone expenditure per consumer is equal to the 1997 mean of \$809, and we do not reject the null hypothesis that μ

= \$809, we made a correct decision.

(e) If, in fact, last year's mean telephone expenditure per consumer is greater than the 1997 mean of \$809, and we do not reject the null hypothesis that μ = \$809, we made a Type II error.

S9.9 (a) A Type I error would occur if, in fact, μ = 13 minutes, but the results of the sampling lead to the conclusion that $\mu \neq$ 13 minutes.

(b) A Type II error would occur if, in fact, $\mu \neq$ 13 minutes, but the results of the sampling fail to lead to that conclusion.

(c) A correct decision would occur if, in fact, μ = 13 minutes and the results of the sampling do not lead to the rejection of that fact; or if, in fact, $\mu \neq$ 13 minutes and the results of the sampling lead to that conclusion.

(d) If, in fact, this year's mean travel time to work has not changed from the 1990 mean of 13 minutes, and we do not reject the null hypothesis that μ = 13 minutes, we made a correct decision.

(e) If, in fact, this year's mean travel time to work has changed from the 1990 mean of 13 minutes, and we do not reject the null hypothesis that μ = 13 minutes, we made a Type II error.

S9.11 Critical value: $-z_{0.10} = -1.28$

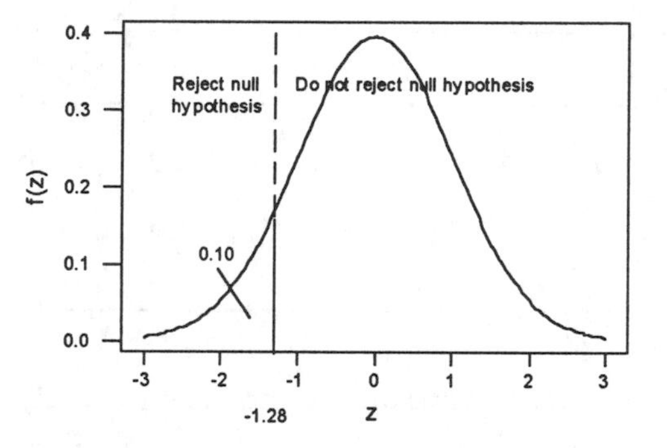

S9.13 Critical value = 1.645; z = 0.26; do not reject H_0.

At the 5% significance level, the data do not provide sufficient evidence to conclude that last year's mean amount μ of telephone expenditures per consumer unit has increased over the 1997 mean of \$809.

S9.15 Critical values = ±1.96; z = 0.53; do not reject H_0.

At the 5% significance level, the data do not provide sufficient evidence to indicate that this year's mean travel time to work μ for North Dakota residents has changed from the 1990 mean of 13 minutes.

S9.17 (a) Reject H_0 if $\bar{x} \leq 15.9$; otherwise do not reject H_0.
(b) $\alpha = 0.10$

(c)

True mean μ	z-score	P(Type II error) β	Power 1 - β
15.70	3.13	0.0009	0.9991
15.75	2.35	0.0094	0.9906
15.80	1.57	0.0582	0.9418
15.85	0.78	0.2177	0.7823
15.90	0.00	0.5000	0.5000
15.95	-0.78	0.7823	0.2177

(d)

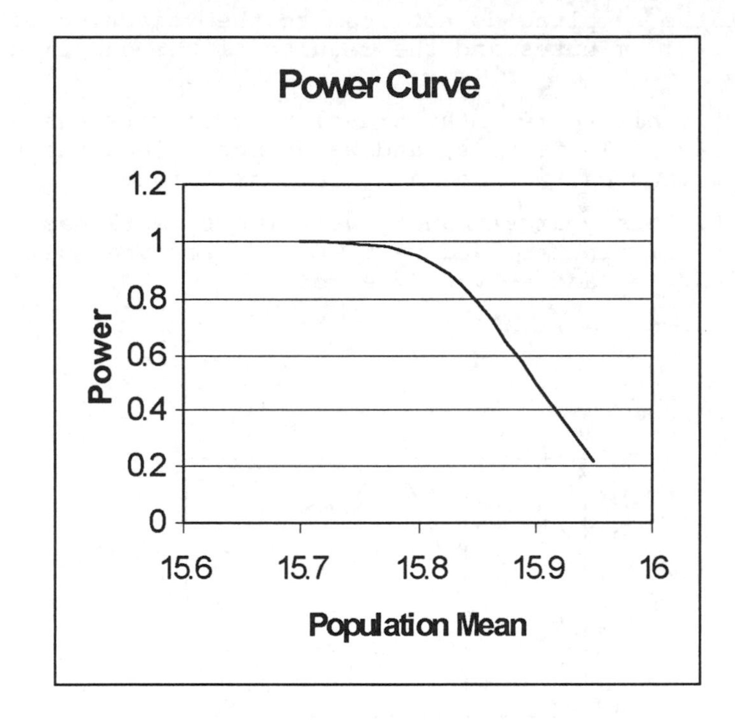

S9.19 (a) Reject H_0 if $\bar{x} \geq 754.4$; otherwise do not reject H_0.
(b) $\alpha = 0.05$
(c)

True mean μ	z-score	P(Type II error) β	Power 1 - β
839	0.88	0.8106	0.1894
869	0.11	0.5438	0.4562
899	-0.65	0.2578	0.7422
929	-1.42	0.0778	0.9222
959	-2.19	0.0143	0.9857
989	-2.95	0.0016	0.9984
1019	-3.72	0.0001	0.9999
1049	-4.49	0.0000	1.0000

(d)

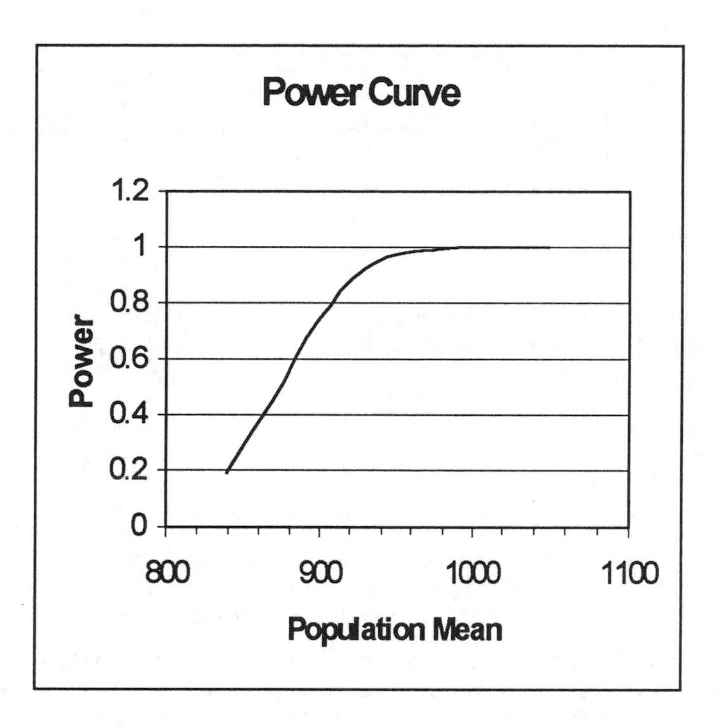

Comparing the power curves, we can see that the principle which seems to be illustrated is that increasing the sample size for a hypothesis test without changing the significance level increases the power of the test.

S9.21 (a) $z = -0.74$, P-value = 0.2296

(b) $z = 1.16$, P-value = 0.8770

S9.23 P-value = $P(z \geq 0.26) = 1.0000 - 0.6026 = 0.3974$

Since $0.3974 > 0.05$, do not reject H_0.

At the 5% significance level, the data do not provide sufficient evidence to conclude that last year's mean amount μ of telephone expenditure per consumer unit has increased over the 1997 mean of $809.

Using Table 9.12, we classify the strength of evidence against the null hypothesis as weak or none because $P > 0.10$.

S9.25 P-value = $P(z \leq -0.53 \text{ or } z \geq 0.53) = 2(0.2981) = 0.5962$

Since $0.5962 > 0.05$, do not reject H_0.

At the 5% significance level, the data do not provide sufficient evidence to indicate that this year's mean travel time to work μ for North Dakota residents has changed from the 1990 mean of 13 minutes.

Using Table 9.12, we classify the strength of evidence against the null hypothesis as weak or none because $P > 0.10$.

S9.27 (a) We used Minitab to produce the boxplot below. With the data in a column named YIELD, choose **Graph ▶ Boxplot...**, select YIELD for the **Y** variable for **Graph 1**. Click **OK**. No observations are identified as potential outliers.

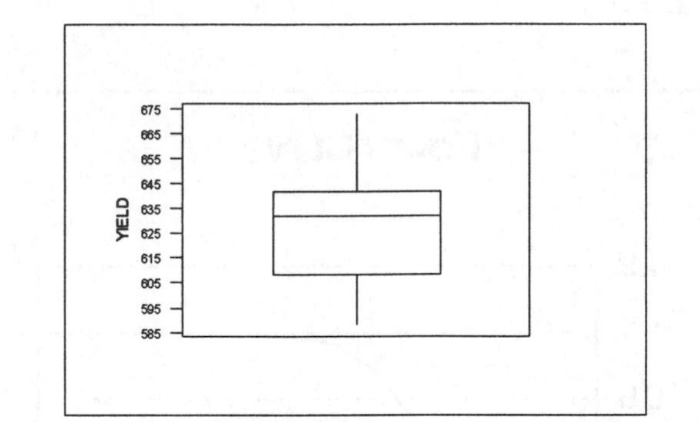

(b) Step 1: H_0: μ = 623 lb/acre, H_a: μ > 623 lb/acre

Step 2: $\alpha = 0.10$

Step 3: $z = 0.92$

Step 4: P-value = $P(z \geq 0.92) = 1.0000 - 0.8212 = 0.1788$

Step 5: Since 0.1788 > 0.10, do not reject H_0.

Step 6: At the 10% significance level, the data do not provide sufficient evidence to conclude that the new fertilizer increases the mean yield of cotton on the farmer's land.

Using Table 9.12, we classify the strength of evidence against the null hypothesis as weak or none because P > 0.10. If the new fertilizer is more expensive, the farmer has no reason to buy it. If the cost is the same or lower, it appears that he can get the approximately the same yield and it might be worth the cost savings.

S9.29 Critical value = 1.729; t = 1.386; Do not reject H_0. Note: For the P-value approach, 0.05 < p-value < 0.10. So, since the p-value > α, do not reject H_0.

At the 5% significance level, the data do not provide sufficient evidence to conclude that the mean drying time μ is greater than the manufacturer's claim of 120 minutes.

S9.31 Critical value = -1.796; t = -2.794; Reject H_0. Note: For the p-value approach, 0.005 < p-value < 0.01. So, since the p-value < α, reject H_0.

At the 5% significance level, it appears that Atlas Fishing Line's 10-lb test line is not up to specifications. The practical significance of this result is minimal. It takes a fairly large freshwater fish (more than 10 lbs) to break either a 10-lb or 9.75-lb test line. Most fish caught with 10-lb test line are considerably smaller than 10 lb.

S9.33 (a) Critical value = 2.821; t = 2.413; Do not reject H_0. Note: For the P-value approach, 0.010 < P-value < 0.025. So, since P-value > α, do not reject H_0.

At the 1% significance level, the data do not provide sufficient evidence to conclude that the new bulbs will outlast the old bulbs.

(b) (i) If z were used instead of t, the critical value of z would be 2.33.

(ii) The actual critical value of t used was 2.821.

(iii) The mistaken use of a z critical value, when a t critical value should be used, makes it more likely that the null hypothesis will be rejected. Particularly for small sample sizes, the critical values of t are much larger in absolute value (for given α-levels) than critical values of z, thus making rejection of H_0 less probable. We see this occurring directly above. Using z, we have 2.41 > 2.33, so we reject H_0. Using t, we have 2.41 < 2.821, so we do not reject H_0.

S9.35 (a) If t were mistakenly used instead of z, the critical value of t would be 1.761. The critical value of z that should have been used is 1.645 with a corresponding significance level of 0.05. The actual significance level that corresponds with the critical value 1.761 is found by consulting the z table. A z-value of 1.761 results in a tail area (i.e., a significance level) of 0.0392. This is lower than the desired significance level of 0.05.

(b) In the situation described, if the t-table is mistakenly used instead of the z-table to obtain the critical value(s), the actual significance level of the resulting test will be lower than α. This is demonstrated in part (a).

S9.37 Critical value = 26; W = sum of the + ranks = 20.5; since W < 26, reject H_0.

At the 5% significance level, the data do provide sufficient evidence to conclude that the new antacid tablet works faster.

S9.39 Critical values = ±2.145; t =-0.600; since -2.145 < -0.600 < 2.145, do not reject H_0.

At the 5% significance level, the data do not provide sufficient evidence to conclude the company's report was incorrect.

(b) t = -0.600; P > 0.20; Since the P-value > 0.05, do not reject H_0.

At the 5% significance level, the data do not provide sufficient evidence to conclude that the company's report was incorrect.

(c) Weak or none.

CHAPTER 10 SUPPLEMENTARY EXERCISES

S10.1 (a) Critical value = 1.96; z = 0.78; Do not reject H_0.

There is not sufficient evidence to conclude that there is a difference in the mean prices for Frigidaire and GE refrigerators.

(b) -$17.64 to $17.80

S10.3 s_p = 162.98; df = 64; Critical values = ±2.000; t = 6.304; Reject H_0.

At the 5% significance level, the data provide sufficient evidence to conclude that last year's mean annual fuel expenditure for households using natural gas is different from that for households using only electricity.

For the P-value approach, 2{P(t > 6.304)} = 0.0000 (to four decimal places). Therefore, because the P-value is smaller than the significance level, reject H_0.

S10.5 (a) -1.66 to -0.54 seconds

(b) We can be 90% confident that the difference, $\mu_1 - \mu_2$, between the mean time it takes the new machine to pack 10 cartons and the mean time it takes the present machine to pack 10 cartons is somewhere between -1.66 and -0.54 seconds.

S10.7 (a) 6.24 to 12.52 bushels

(b) We can be 98% confident that the difference, $\mu_1 - \mu_2$, between the yield of corn using an insecticide and the yield using sterilized male insects of an insect pest is somewhere between 6.24 and 12.52 bushels.

S10.9 Δ = 26.65, df =26; Critical value = 1.708; t = 0.443; do not reject H_0.

At the 5% significance level, the data do not provide sufficient evidence to conclude that college-bound males outperform college-bound females on the mathematics portion of the ACT test.

For the P-value approach, P(t>0.443) > 0.10. Therefore, since the P-value is larger than the significance level, do not reject H_0.

S10.11 (a) Δ = 27.84, df =27; Critical values = -2.473; t = -3.210; reject H_0.

At the 1% significance level, the data provide sufficient evidence to conclude that Mirror-sheen has a longer effectiveness time than Sureglow.

For the P-value approach, P(t < -3.210) < 0.005. Therefore, since the P-value is smaller than the significance level, reject H_0.

(b) Yes. Since the hypothesis test was performed at the 0.01 level of significance, there is only a 1% chance that we would conclude that Mirror-sheen outlasts Sureglow, on the average, when in fact it does not.

(c) The study is a designed experiment. The researcher assigned which cars would receive Sureglow and which would receive Mirror-sheen.

S10.13 Δ = 20.77, df =20; Critical values = ±2.086; t = -5.690; reject H_0.

At the 5% significance level, the data provide sufficient evidence to conclude that there is a difference between the mean LMA ratio of hybrid and *Q. turbinella* trees.

For the P-value approach, P(|t| > 5.690) < 0.01. Therefore, since the P-value is smaller than the significance level, reject H_0.

S10.15 (a) -3.42 to 5.82

(b) We can be 90% confident that the difference, $\mu_1 - \mu_2$, between this year's mean mathematics ACT score for males and females is somewhere between -3.42 and 5.82.

S10.17 (a) −7.2 to −0.9 days

(b) We can be 98% confident that the difference, $\mu_1 - \mu_2$, between the mean effectiveness times of Sureglow and Mirror-sheen is somewhere between −7.2 and −0.9 days.

S10.19 Paired t-test; df = 9; Critical value = 1.833; t = 2.213; reject H_0.

At the 5% significance level, the data provide sufficient evidence to conclude that the mean age of married men is greater than the mean age of married women.

S10.21 (a) 0.6 to 6.0 years

(b) 0.6 and 6.0 years.

S10.23 Critical value, $W_r = 44$; W = 45: reject H_0.

At the 5% significance level, the data do provide enough evidence to conclude that the mean age of married men is greater than the mean age of married women.

S10.25 (a) The pooled t-test is appropriate since the populations are normally distributed with approximately equal standard deviations.

(b) df = 57; critical values = ±2.665; $s_p = 27.5$; t = −1.58; do not reject H_0. For the p-value approach, 0.10 < p-value < 0.20, so do not reject H_0.

S10.27 Δ = 21.82, df = 21; critical value = −.1.721; t = −2.740; reject H_0.

At the 5% significance level, the data provide sufficient evidence to conclude that last year the average German consumed less fish than the average Russian.

For the P-value approach, $0.005 < P(t < -2.74) < 0.01$. Therefore, because the P-value is smaller than the significance level, reject H_0.

S10.29 (a) Choose the nonpooled t-test because the standard deviations are quite different.

(b) Normality is not critical for this data since the sample sizes are very large.

CHAPTER 11 SUPPLEMENTARY EXERCISES

S11.1 0.118 to 0.225 fl oz.

S11.3 df = (9,14); critical value = 4.03; F = 5.56; reject H_0.

There is sufficient evidence at the 0.01 significance level to claim that the variation in miles driven by trucks is greater than that for cars.

S11.5 (a) Using Minitab, with the data in columns named PUBLIC and PRIVATE, using the *WeissStats* CD in drive D, we type in the Sessions Window at the MTB> prompt,

```
%D:\IS6\Minitab\Macro\2stdev.mac 'PUBLIC' 'PRIVATE'
```

and press the ENTER key. Proceed as follows

1 In response to do you want to perform a hypothesis test (Y/N)?, type Y and press the ENTER key.

2 In response to Enter 0, 1, or -1, respectively, for a two-tailed, right-tailed, or left-tailed test., type 0 and press the ENTER key. The output is

F-Test of sigma1 = sigma2 (vs not =)

Row	Variable	n	StDev	F	P
1	PUBLIC	30	23.953	1.16	0.677
2	PRIVATE	35	22.261		

Since 0.677 > 0.05, we do not reject the null hypothesis. The is insufficient evidence to conclude that there is a difference in variation of faculty salaries between public and private institutions.

(b) We choose **Calc ▶ Calculator...**, type NPUBLIC in the **Store result in variable** text box, select the function NSCOR from the **Function** list, select PUBLIC to replace **number** in the **Expression** text box, and click **OK**. Then choose **Graph ▶ Plot...**, select NPUBLIC in the **Y** column for **Graph1** and PUBLIC in the **X** column, and click **OK**. Repeat this process for PRIVATE and NPRIVATE. The resulting graphs are

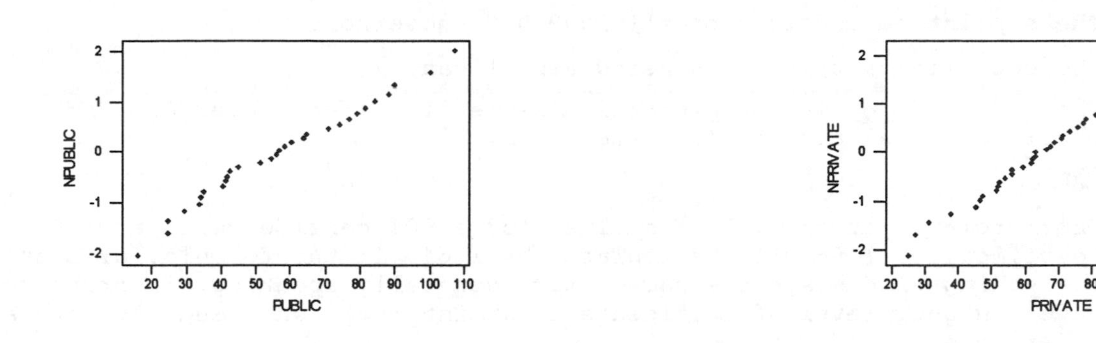

(c) Both of the plots are very linear, so it does seem reasonable to assume normal distributions for both variables. Hence the procedure in part (a) is justified.

S11.7 Using Minitab, we obtained normal probability plots for the Florida and Virginia data. Shown below, both plots seem to be reasonably linear (there may be a little left-skewness in the Florida plot). The normality assumption seems to be valid, and thus it seems reasonable to use an F-test to compare the variation in litter size of cottonmouths in the two states.

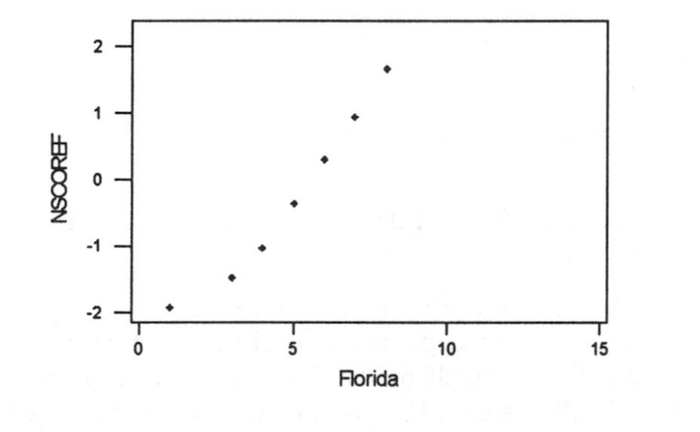

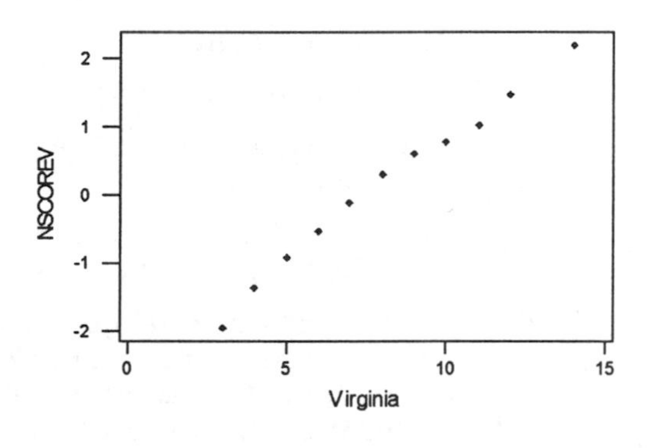

CHAPTER 12 SUPPLEMENTARY EXERCISES

S12.1 (a) The population consists of all 1999 U.S. governors.

(b) The specified attribute is being Republican.

(c) The 61% is a population proportion since all of the governors and their political affiliations are known.

S12.3 (a) E = 0.0347

(b) The margin of error will be smaller for a 90% confidence interval. Specifically, 1.96 will be replaced by 1.645 in the formula for E and everything else stays the same. More generally speaking, in order to have a higher level of confidence in an interval, one needs to have a wider interval.

S12.5 (a) E = 0.097

(b) E = 0.097

S12.7 (a) 78.4% to 83.6%

(b) We can be 99% confident that the percentage of adult Americans who are in favor of "right to die" laws is somewhere between 78.4% and 83.6%.

S12.9 73.2% to 82.8%

S12.11 31.6% to 36.4%

S12.13 (a) E = (83.6% - 78.4%)/2 = 2.6%.

(b) n = 16,567

(c) 0.817 to 0.833

(d) The margin of error for the estimate is 0.008, which is less than what is required in part (b).

(e) n = 12432; confidence interval is 0.816 to 0.834; E = 0.009, which is less than what is specified in part (b).

(f) By employing the guess for $\hat{p}$ in part (d) we can reduce the required sample size (from 16,577 to 12,433), saving considerable time and money. Moreover, the margin of error only rises from 0.008 to 0.009. The risk of using the guess 0.75 for $\hat{p}$ is that if the actual value of $\hat{p}$ turns out to be less than 0.75 (but not less than 0.25) then the achieved margin of error will exceed the specified 0.01.

S12.15 Critical value = 1.28; z = 0.65; do not reject H_0.

There is not sufficient evidence to conclude that more than one quarter of the physicians in the Cleveland area are dissatisfied with HMOs.

S12.17 (a) Critical value = 1.645; z = 11.45; reject H_0.

(b) Critical value = 1.645; z = 2.02; reject H_0.

The data provide sufficient evidence to conclude that a majority of college-aged adults from divorced families believe that equal residential time shared between parents is best for children, and sufficient evidence to conclude that more than 2/3 of them believe that equal residential time shared between parents is best for children.

S12.19 Critical value = 1.645; z = 9.01; reject H_0.

There is sufficient evidence to conclude that more than 2/3 of Americans believe that then-President clinton should get approval from congress before committing the troops.

S12.21 Critical values = ±1.96; $z = 0.58$; do not reject H_0.

The data do not provide sufficient evidence at the 0.05 level to conclude that there is a difference in labor force participation rates between American and Canadian women.

S12.23 Critical values = ±1.96; $z = 4.62$; reject H_0.

The data do provide evidence at the 0.05 level to conclude that the percentage of employed workers who have registered to vote differs from the percentage of unemployed workers who have registered to vote.

S12.25

(a) Critical values = ±1.96; $z = 1.932$; do not reject H_0.

The data do not provide evidence at the 0.05 level that a difference exists in the incidence of pharyngitis between patients who take Nasonex and those who take a placebo.

(b) Critical values = ±1.645; $z = 1.932$; do not reject H_0.

The data do provide evidence at the 0.10 level that a difference exists in the incidence of pharyngitis between patients who take Nasonex and those who take a placebo.

S12.27

(a) -0.055 to 0.101

(b) We can be 95% confident that the difference $p_1 - p_2$ between the labor force participation rates of American and Canadian women is somewhere between -0.055 and 0.101.

S12.29

(a) 0.091 to 0.223

(b) We can be 95% confident that the difference $p_1 - p_2$ between the proportions of employed and unemployed workers who have registered to vote is somewhere between 0.091 and 0.223.

S12.31

(a) Washing their vehicle at least once a month

(b) Car owners

(c) Proportion of all car owners who wash their car at least once a month

(d) Proportion of car owners in the sample who wash their car at least once a month

(e) It is a sample proportion. USA Today does not have the resources to take a census of all car owners, and even if it did, it would not make sense to spend the amount of money required to get the perfect answer to this question.

S12.33

(a) $E = (0.461 - 0.399)/2 = 0.031$.

(b) $n = 2401$

(c) 0.396 to .0436

(d) The margin of error for the estimate is 0.02, the same as what is required in part (b).

(e) $n = 2377$; confidence interval is 0.396 to 0.437; $E = 0.02$, which is the same as what is specified in part (b).

(f) By employing the guess for $\hat{p}$ in part (d) we can reduce the required sample size (from 2401 to 2377), saving a little time and money. Moreover, the margin of error stays the same. The risk of using the guess 0.45 for $\hat{p}$ is that if the actual value of $\hat{p}$ turns out to be larger than .45 (but not more than .55), then the achieved margin of error will exceed the specified 0.02.

S12.35 Critical value = -2.33; $z = -4.560$; reject H_0.

The data do provide sufficient evidence at the 0.01 level to conclude that the refusal rate in mortgage lending was high for minority applicants than for white applicants.

CHAPTER 13 SUPPLEMENTARY EXERCISES

S13.1 The basic idea behind the chi-square goodness-of-fit test is to compare the observed frequencies with the frequencies that would be expected if the null hypothesis were true. If the observed and expected frequencies match up well, then we do not reject the null hypothesis; if they match up poorly, we reject the null hypothesis.

S13.3 H_0: Last year's type-of-buyer distribution for U.S. cars is the same as the 1997 distribution. H_a: Last year's type-of-buyer distribution for U.S. cars is different from the 1997 distribution. Assumptions 1 and 2 are satisfied since all expected frequencies are 5 or greater. $\alpha = 0.05$; critical value = 5.991; $\chi^2 = 1.956$; do not reject H_0; at the 5% significance level, the data do not provide sufficient evidence to conclude that last year's type-of-buyer distribution for U.S. cars is different from the 1997 distribution. For the P-value approach, $P(\chi^2 > 1.956) > 0.10$.

S13.5 H_0: The die is not loaded. H_a: The die is loaded. Assumptions 1 and 2 are satisfied since all expected frequencies are at least 5. $\alpha = 0.05$; critical value = 11.070; $\chi^2 = 2.48$; do not reject H_0; at the 5% significance level, the data do not provide sufficient evidence to conclude that the die is loaded. For the P-value approach, $P(\chi^2 > 2.48) > 0.10$.

S13.7 (a)

	PP	LA	ED	AE	BU	Total
FR	0	2	0	0	0	2
SO	2	3	1	0	2	8
JU	2	5	0	0	0	7
SR	1	5	1	1	0	8
Total	5	15	2	1	2	25

(b)

	PP	LA	ED	AE	BU	Total
FR	0.00	0.13	0.00	0.00	0.00	0.08
SO	0.40	0.20	0.50	0.00	1.00	0.32
JU	0.40	0.33	0.00	0.00	0.00	0.28
SR	0.20	0.33	0.50	1.00	0.00	0.32
Total	1.00	1.00	1.00	1.00	1.00	1.00

The conditional distributions of class level within each college are in columns 2 through 6 and the marginal distribution of class level is in the last column.

(c)

	PP	LA	ED	AE	BU	Total
FR	0.00	1.00	0.00	0.00	0.00	1.00
SO	0.25	0.38	0.12	0.00	0.25	1.00
JU	0.29	0.71	0.00	0.00	0.00	1.00
SR	0.12	0.62	0.12	0.12	0.00	1.00
Total	0.20	0.60	0.08	0.04	0.08	1.00

The conditional distributions of college with each class level are in rows 2 through 5 and the marginal distribution of college is in the last row.

(d) Yes. Since the conditional distributions of college with each class level are not the same for each class level, there is an association between college and class level.

S13.9 (a) 24,270 (b) 25,795 (c) 17,799 (d) 32,266

(e) 482 (f) 520 (g) 4473

S13.11 (a)

	In-state	Out-of-state	Total
1-6	0.149	0.054	0.123
7-11	0.118	0.058	0.101
12+	0.733	0.889	0.775
Total	1.000	1.001	0.999

The conditional distributions of number of credit hours by residency status are in columns 1 and 2 of the above table.

(b) The marginal distribution of number of credit hours is in the last column of the above table.

(c) Yes. The conditional distributions of number of credit hours by residency status are not the same.

(d) 10.1%

(e) 11.8%

(f) True. If they were identical, residency status and number of credit hours would not be associated, but we know from part(c) that they are associated.

(g)

	In-state	Out-of-state	Total
1-6	0.882	0.118	1.000
7-11	0.846	0.154	1.000
12+	0.690	0.310	1.000
Total	0.730	0.270	1.000

The conditional distributions of residency status by number of credit hours are in rows 2, 3, and 4 of the above table.

The marginal distribution of residency status is in the last row of the above table.

S13.13 H_0: Accident circumstance and gender in this city are associated.

H_a: Accident circumstance and gender in this city are not associated. Assumptions 1 and 2 are satisfied since all expected frequencies are at least 1, and only 12.5% (1/8) of the expected frequencies are less than 5. $\alpha = 0.05$; critical value = 7.815; $\chi^2 = 8.665$; reject H_0. At the 5% significance level, the data provide sufficient evidence to conclude that there is an association between accident circumstance and gender in this city. For the P-value approach, $P(\chi^2 > 8.665) < 0.05$.

S13.15 H_0: Net worth and marital status for top wealthholders are statistically independent. H_a: Net worth and marital status for top wealthholders are statistically dependent. Assumption 2 is violated since 25% (3/12) of the expected frequencies are less than 5. Thus, we do not proceed with the test.

S13.17 H_0: Response and educational level are statistically independent.

H_a: Response and educational level are statistically dependent. Assumptions 1 and 2 are satisfied since all expected frequencies are at least 5. $\alpha = 0.01$; critical value = 16.812; $\chi^2 = 77.693$; reject H_0. The data provide sufficient evidence to conclude that response and educational level are associated. For the P-value approach, $P(\chi^2 > 77.693) < 0.005$.

CHAPTER 14 SUPPLEMENTARY EXERCISES

S14.1 (a) $\hat{y} = -174.49 + 4.83631x$

(b)

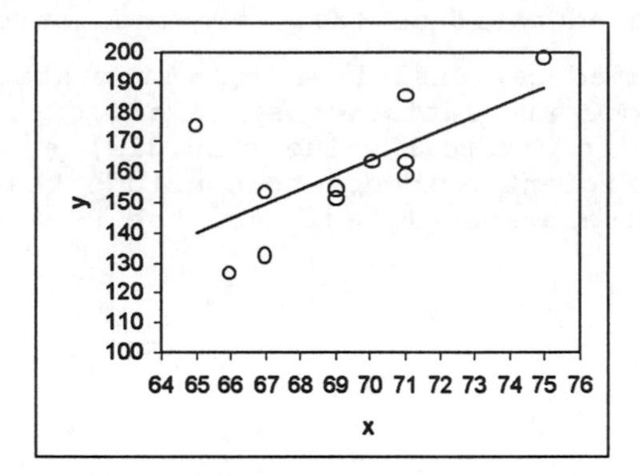

(c) Weight tends to increase as height increases.

(d) The weights of 18-24 year-old males increase an estimated 4.84 lb for each increase in height of one inch.

(e) Weight of 67-inch male: $\hat{y} = -174.49 + 4.83631(67) = 149.539$ lbs.

Weight of 73-inch male: $\hat{y} = -174.49 + 4.83631(73) = 178.557$ lbs.

(f) The predictor variable is height. The response variable is weight.

(g) The observation (65, 175) is an outlier; (75, 198) is a potential influential observation.

S14.3 (a) $\hat{y} = 94.867 - 0.845606x$

(b)

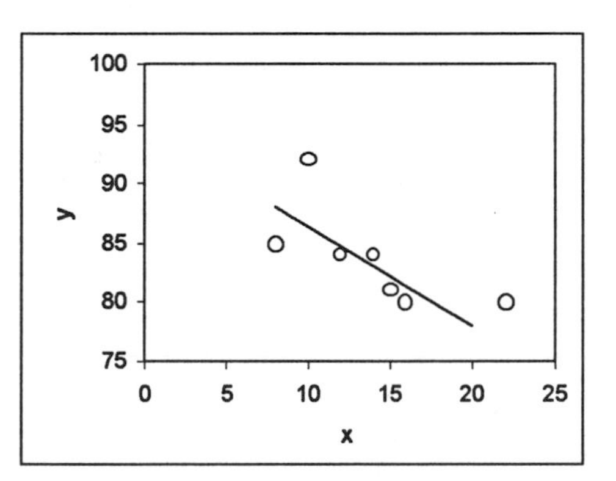

(c) Test score tends to decrease as study time increases. Yes.

(d) Test score decreases an estimated 0.85 for each additional hour of study.

(e) Test score of a student who studies 15 hours:
$\hat{y} = 222.271 - 1.1405(15) = 82.1829$.

(f) The predictor variable is total hours studied. The response variable is test score.

(g) There are no outliers or potential influential observations.

S14.5 (a) $\hat{y} = 12.8625 + 1.2137x$.

(b)

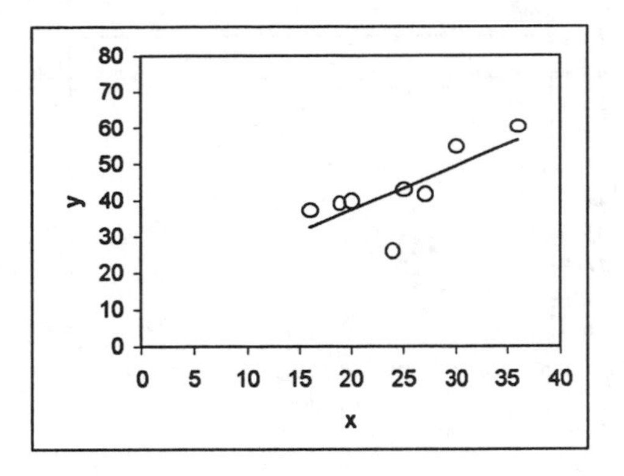

(c) Annual food expenditure tends to increase as disposable income increases.

(d) Annual food expenditures increase an estimated $121.37 (1.2137 hundred dollars) for each increase in disposable income of $1000.

(e) Annual food expenditure of a family with a disposable income of $25,000:

$$\hat{y} = 12.8625 + 1.2137(25) = 43.2051 = \$4,320.51.$$

(f) The predictor variable is disposable income. The response variable is annual food expenditure.

(g) The observation (24, 26) is a potential outlier; there are no potential influential observations.

S14.7 (a)

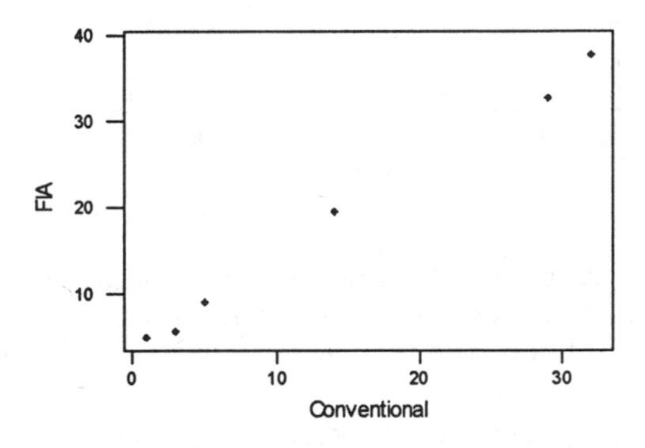

(b) $\hat{y} = 3.53 + 1.06x$ where y = FIA and x = Conventional

(c) Yes. The points fall very close to being in a straight line, so there is a linear relationship between the two measuring methods.

S14.9 (a)

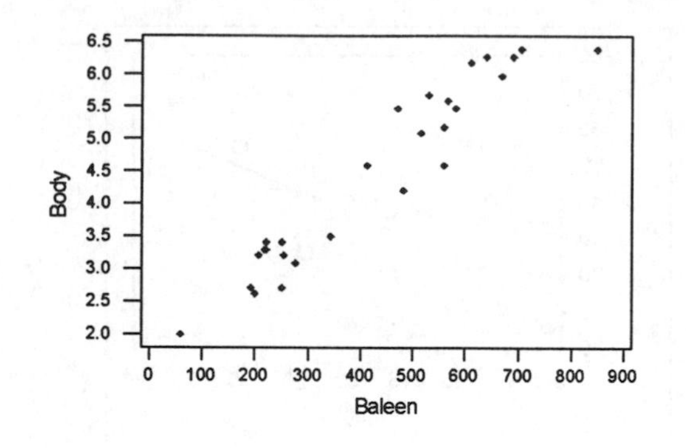

(b) The plot displays a linear relationship, so it is reasonable to find a regression line for the data.

(c) $\hat{y} = 1.64 + 0.00658x$ where y = Body and x = Baleen. The equation shows that the body length is increases as the baleen length increases.

(d) (850,6.4)is a potential outlier.

S14.11 (a)

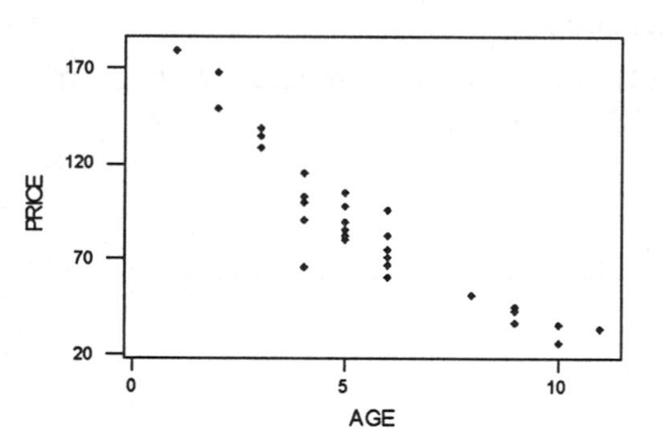

Although there is a distinctly decreasing relationship between the age and price of the Orions over the age range of 1 to 11 years, it does not appear to be linear after the 6th year. Thus a linear regression is not advised.

(b) In Example 14.4, the ages ranged from 1 to 8 years, over which range the relationship did appear to be linear. It is probably the case that after a certain length of time, the price of an experienced car is more dependent on other factors, such as body condition and mileage, than on age. Also, only the older cars which are in better condition are likely to find their way onto a used car lot and are more likely to keep their value.

S14.13 (a) SST = 79,444.9 SSR = 54,562.4 SSE = 24,882.5

(b) r^2 = 0.6868

(c) 68.68% of the variation in the peak heart rates is explained by age.

(d) Based on the answers to parts (b) and (c), the regression equation appears to be moderately useful for making predictions.

S14.15

(a) SST = 783.50 SSR = 429.95 SSE = 353.55

(b) $r^2 = 0.5488$

(c) 54.48% of the variation in the annual food expenditures is explained by disposable income.

(d) Based on the answers to parts (b) and (c), the regression equation appears to be moderately useful for making predictions.

S14.17

(a) SST = 1032.8 SSR = 1028.0 SSE = 4.8

(b) $r^2 = 0.995$

(c) 99.5% of the variation in the FIA method measurement is explained by the conventional method measurement.

(d) The regression equation seems to be extremely useful for making predictions.

S14.19

(a) $r^2 = 0.920$

(b) 92.0% of the variation in the body length of the whales is explained by the length of the baleen.

(c) The regression equation seems to be very useful for making predictions.

S14.21

(a) $r = -0.928536$

(b) The value of r in part (a) suggests a strong negative linear correlation.

(c) Data points are clustered closely about the regression line.

(d) $r^2 = (-0.928536)^2 = 0.86217$. This matches the coefficient of determination that was calculated in part (b) of Exercise S14.13.

S14.23

(a) $r = 0.740785$

(b) The value of r in part (a) suggests a moderately strong positive linear correlation.

(c) Data points are clustered quite closely about the regression line.

(d) $r^2 = (0.740785)^2 = 0.5488$. This matches the coefficient of determination that was calculated in part (b) of Exercise S14.15.

S14.25

(a) $r = 0.9975$

(b) The FIA measurements and the conventional measurements are very highly correlated, i.e., there is a very strong linear relationship between them.

(c) The data points fall very close to a straight line as shown in Exercise S14.7.

(d) $r^2 = 0.995$, the same value as obtained in Exercise S14.17.

S14.27

(a) $r = 0.9592$

(b) The body lengths and the baleen lengths are very highly correlated, i.e., there is a very strong linear relationship between them.

(c) The data points fall very close to a straight line as shown in Exercise S14.9.

(d) $r^2 = 0.920$, the same value as obtained in Exercise S14.19.

S14.29

(a) downward; the slope has the same sign as the correlation coefficient.

(b) $r^2 = 0.599$

CHAPTER 15 SUPPLEMENTARY EXERCISES

S15.1 If the assumptions for regression inferences are satisfied for a model relating an 18-24 year-old male's height to his weight, this means that there are constants β_0, β_1, and σ such that, for each height x, the weights of 18-24 year-old males of that height are normally distributed with mean $\beta_0 + \beta_1 x$ and standard deviation σ.

S15.3 If the assumptions for regression inferences are satisfied for a model relating a calculus student's study time to that person's test score, this means that there are constants β_0, β_1, and σ such that, for each amount of time studied x, the test scores for students who study that amount of time are normally distributed with mean $\beta_0 + \beta_1 x$ and standard deviation σ.

S15.5 If the assumptions for regression inferences are satisfied for a model relating the number of shark attacks to the size of the population where they occurred, this means that there are constants β_0, β_1, and σ such that, for each population size x, the numbers of shark attacks where that population resides are normally distributed with mean $\beta_0 + \beta_1 x$ and standard deviation σ.

S15.7 (a) $s_e = 3.326$ and is a measure of the variability of peak heart rates about the regression line.

(b) Presuming that the variables age (x) and peak heart rate (y) for individuals satisfy Assumptions (1) - (3) for regression inferences, the standard error of the estimate $s_e = 3.326$ provides an estimate for the common population standard deviation σ of peak heart rates for all individuals of any particular age.

(c)

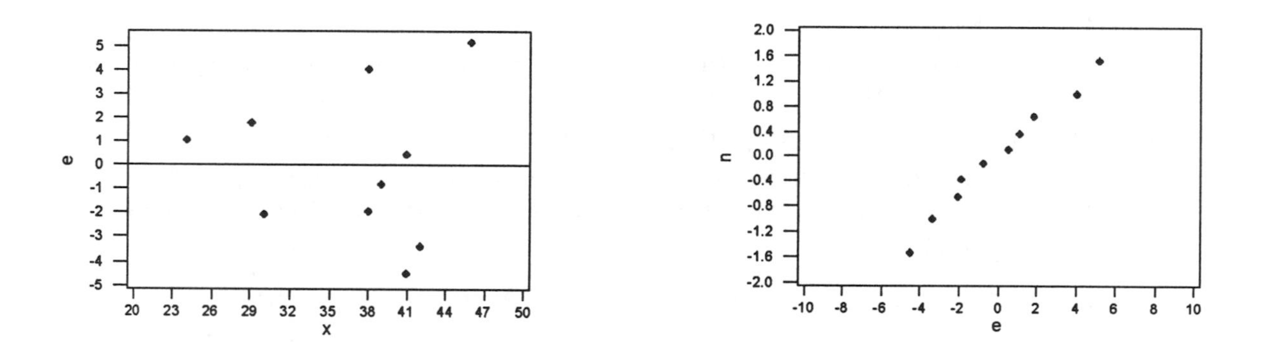

(d) Taking into account the small sample size, we can say that the residuals fall roughly in a horizontal band centered and symmetric about the x-axis. However, the residual plot casts some doubt on the assumption of equal standard deviations. We can also say that the normal probability plot for residuals is approximately linear. Therefore, based on the sample data, there are no obvious violations of the assumptions for regression inferences for the variables age and peak heart rate.

S15.9 (a) $s_e = 7.6763$ and is a measure of the variability of annual food expenditures about the regression line.

(b) Presuming that the variables disposable income (x) and annual food expenditure (y) for middle-income families of the same size satisfy Assumptions (1) - (3) for regression inferences, the standard error of the estimate $s_e = 7.6763$ (\$767.63) provides an estimate for the common population standard deviation σ of annual food expenditures for all middle-income families of the same size with any particular disposable income.

(c)

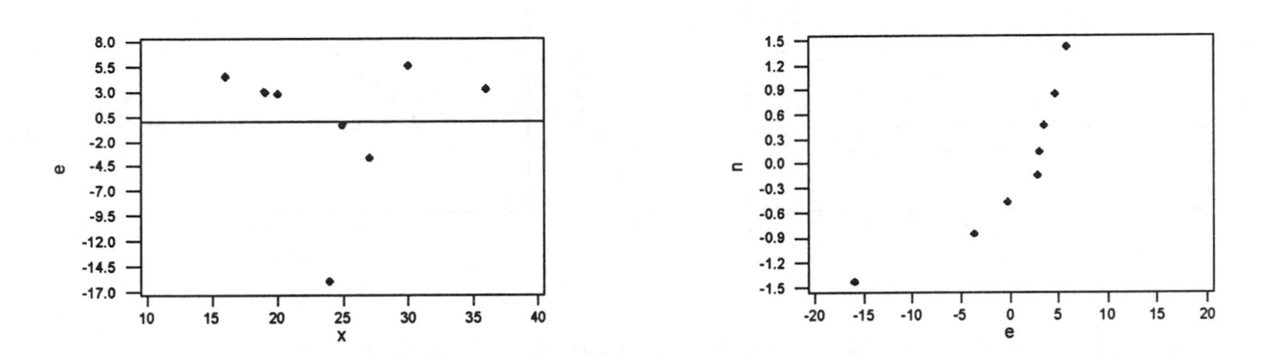

(d) If the outlier, (24,26), is a legitimate data point, then the assumptions for regression inferences may very well be violated by the variables under consideration; if the outlier is a recording error or can be removed for some other valid reason, then the resulting data reveal no obvious violations of the assumptions for regression inferences (as can be seen by constructing a residual plot and normal probability plot of the residuals for the abridged data).

S15.11 (a) s_e = 9.878 and measures the variability of the heights of the seedlings about the regression line.

(b)

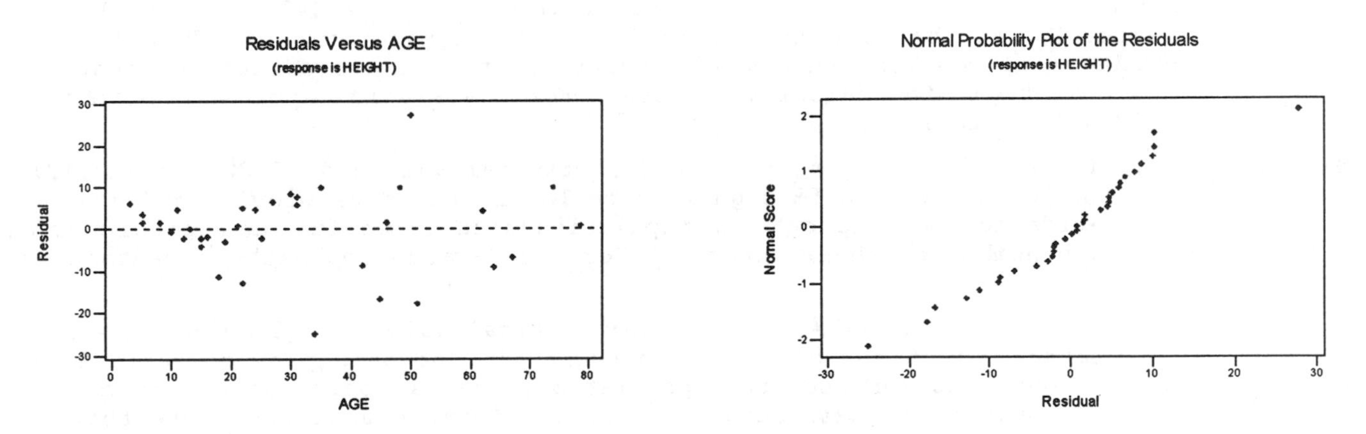

(c) The normal probability plot is close to linear with the exception of the one point in the upper right hand corner of the graph originating from the data point (50,108) and one in the lower left hand corner originating from the data point (34,28) which are potential outliers. The residual plot seems to show that the variation of the residuals about zero is not constant for all ages; it is smaller at the low ages than it is for the ages in the middle of the graph. Thus Assumption 2 for regression inferences may not be satisfied.

S15.13 (a) s_e = 0.04308 and measures the variation of mortality rates about the regression line.

(b)

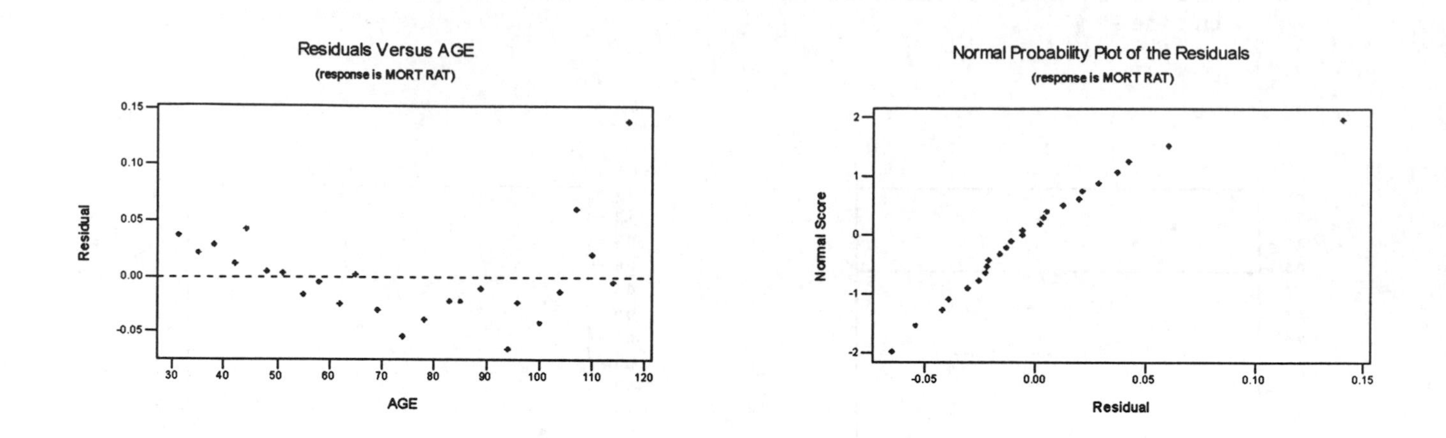

(c) The plot of residuals demonstrates that the linear model is not appropriate for this data. The residuals are positive at both ends of the graph and negative in the middle, indicating that there is concave upward curvature in the data points. Thus Assumption 1 for regression inferences is not satisfied. There is also a potential outlier at (117,0.585), although without the outlier, normality appears to be a reasonable assumption. Regression inferences should not be made based on this model.

S15.15 H_0: $\beta_1 = 0$, H_a: $\beta_1 \neq 0$; $\alpha = 0.10$; critical values = ± 1.833; t = 2.652; reject H0; at the 10% significance level, the data provide sufficient evidence to conclude that the slope of the population regression line is not 0 and, hence, that height is useful as a predictor of weight for 18-24 year-old males. For the P-value approach, note that $0.02 < P < 0.05$.

S15.17 H_0: $\beta_1 = 0$, H_a: $\beta_1 \neq 0$; $\alpha = 0.05$; critical values = ± 2.447; t = -3.003; reject H_0; at the 5% significance level, the data provide sufficient evidence to conclude that study time is useful as a predictor of test score in beginning calculus courses. For the P-value approach, note that $0.02 < P < 0.05$.

S15.19 (a) H_0: $\beta_1 = 0$, H_a: $\beta_1 \neq 0$; $\alpha = 0.05$; critical values = ± 2.306; t = 9.12; reject H_0; at the 5% significance level, the data provide sufficient evidence to conclude that population size is useful as a predictor of the number of shark attacks. For the P-value approach, note that $P < 0.01$.

(b) H_0: $\beta_1 = 0$, H_a: $\beta_1 \neq 0$; $\alpha = 0.05$; critical values = ± 2.365; t = 4.15; reject H_0; at the 5% significance level, the data provide sufficient evidence to conclude that population size is useful as a predictor of the number of shark attacks. For the P-value approach, note that $P < 0.01$.

(c) Although the value of t is reduced by eliminating the influential data point (600,45), at the 1% significance level, the data are still useful for predicting the number of shark attacks based on the population size.

S15.21 (a) -1.51 to - 0.77

(b) We can be 95% confident that the decrease in mean peak heart rate per one year increase in age is somewhere between 0.7687 and 1.5123.

S15.23 (a) -0.4519 to 2.8793

(b) We can be 99% confident that, for middle-income families with a father, mother, and two children, the change in mean annual food expenditure per $1,000 increase in family disposable income is somewhere between -$45.19 and $287.93.

S15.25

(a) H_0: $\beta_1 = 0$, H_a: $\beta_1 \neq 0$; $\alpha = 0.05$; critical values = ± 2.035; $t = 20.73$; reject H_0; at the 5% significance level, the data provide sufficient evidence to conclude that age is useful as a predictor of the height of the seedlings. For the P-value approach, note that $P < 0.01$.

(b) H_0: $\beta_1 = 0$, H_a: $\beta_1 \neq 0$; $\alpha = 0.05$; critical values = ± 2.042; $t = 23.21$; reject H_0; at the 5% significance level, the data provide sufficient evidence to conclude that age is useful as a predictor of the height of the seedlings. For the P-value approach, note that $P < 0.01$.

(c) After removing the observations (34,28), (79,130), and (50,108), the value of t is even greater than prior to their removal. It should be noted that there are now two new potential outliers and one new influential observation.

S15.27

(a) 164.048 lb

(b) 154.54 to 173.56 lb

(c) 164.048 lb

(d) 132.38 to 195.71

(e)

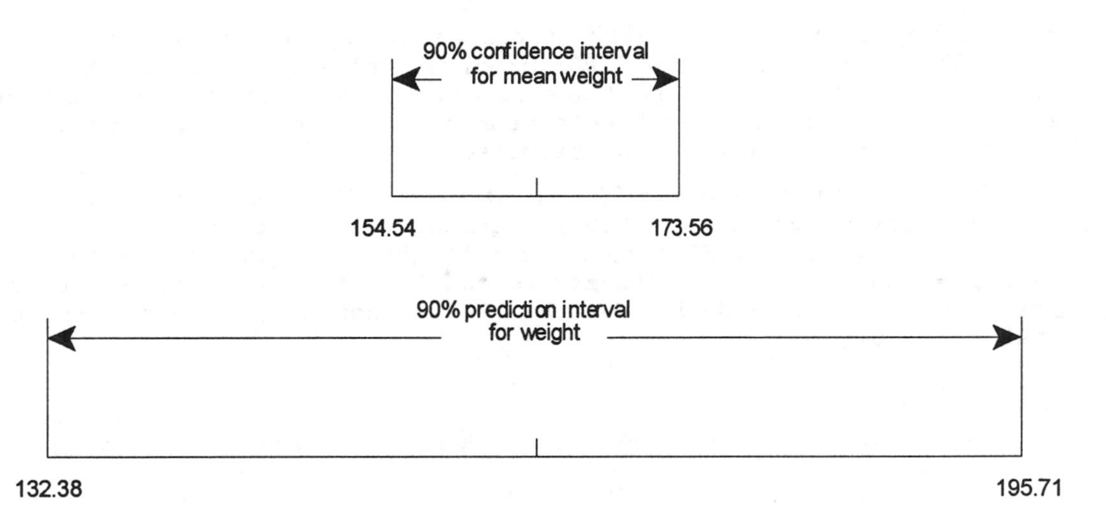

(f) The error in the estimate of the mean weight of all 18-24 year-old males who are 70 inches tall is due only to the fact that the population regression line is being estimated by a sample regression line; whereas, the error in the prediction of the weight of a randomly selected 18-24 year-old male who is 70 inches tall is due to that fact plus the variation in weights of such males.

S15.29

(a) 79.11 to 85.25

(b) 73.00 to 91.37

S15.31

(a) 3.18 to 9.93

(b) -3.54 to 16.64 (Note that the number of shark attacks cannot actually be negative.)

S15.33 (a) 4.1069 to 4.4348

(b) 3.4102 to 5.1315

S15.35 H_0: $\rho = 0$, H_a: $\rho < 0$; $\alpha = 0.025$; critical value = −2.306; t = −7.074; reject H_0; at the 2.5% significance level, the data provide sufficient evidence to conclude that age and peak heart rate are negatively linearly correlated. For the P-value approach, $P < 0.005$.

S15.37 H_0: $\rho = 0$, H_a: $\rho \neq 0$; $\alpha = 0.01$; critical values = ± 3.707; t = 2.701; do not reject H_0; at the 1% significance level, the data do not provide sufficient evidence to conclude that family disposable income and annual food expenditure are linearly correlated for middle-income families with a father, mother, and two children. For the P-value approach, $0.02 < P < 0.05$.

S15.39 H_0: $\rho = 0$, H_a: $\rho > 0$; $\alpha = 0.025$; critical value = 2.035; t = 10.208; reject H_0; at the 2.5% significance level, the data provide sufficient evidence to conclude that the age and height of the seedlings are positively linearly correlated. For the P-value approach, $P < 0.005$.

S15.41 H_0: The population is normally distributed. H_a: The population is not normally distributed. $\alpha = 0.10$; critical value is = 0.935; $R_p = 0.987$; do not reject H_0; at the 10% significance level, the data do not provide sufficient evidence to conclude that the weekly food costs for Kansas families of four having an intermediate budget are not normally distributed.

S15.43 H_0: The population is normally distributed. H_a: The population is not normally distributed. $\alpha = 0.05$; critical value is = 0.952; $R_p = 0.803$; reject H_0; at the 5% significance level, the data provide sufficient evidence to conclude that the lengths of stays by patients in short-term hospitals are not normally distributed.

S15.45 H_0: The population is normally distributed. H_a: The population is not normally distributed. $\alpha = 0.05$; critical value = 0.9958 (interpolating for n = 379); $R_p = 0.9947$; reject H_0; at the 5% significance level, the data provide sufficient evidence to conclude that pig litter sizes are not normally distributed. For the P-value approach, Minitab indicates that $p < 0.01$.

CHAPTER 16 SUPPLEMENTARY EXERCISES

S16.1 (a) For each sample, $\bar{x}_i = \frac{\sum x}{n_i}$, so $\sum x = n_i\bar{x}_i$. It follows then that

$$\bar{x} = \frac{\sum x}{n} = \frac{\sum x_1 + \sum x_2 + \ldots + \sum x_k}{n_1 + n_2 + \ldots + n_k} = \frac{n_1\bar{x}_1 + n_2\bar{x}_2 + \ldots + n_k\bar{x}_k}{n_1 + n_2 + \ldots + n_k}$$

(b) If all k of the sample sizes are equal, say to m, then

$$\bar{x} = \frac{n_1\bar{x}_1 + n_2\bar{x}_2 + \ldots + n_k\bar{x}_k}{n_1 + n_2 + \ldots + n_k} = \frac{m\bar{x}_1 + m\bar{x}_2 + \ldots + m\bar{x}_k}{m + m + \ldots + m} = \frac{m(\bar{x}_1 + \bar{x}_2 + \ldots + \bar{x}_k)}{mk} = \frac{(\bar{x}_1 + \bar{x}_2 + \ldots + \bar{x}_k)}{k}$$

which shows that $\bar{x}$ is simply the mean of the sample means.

S16.3

Source	df	SS	MS = SS/df	F-statistic
Treatment	3	132508.2	44169.40	7.37
Error	16	95877.6	5992.35	
Total	19	228385.8		

S16.5 H_0: $\mu_1 = \mu_2 = \mu_3$ (mean monthly sales are equal). H_a: Not all the means are equal. $\alpha = 0.01$; critical value = 6.36; SST = 216.28. SSTR = 115.11, SSE = 101.17; F = 8.53; reject H_0; at the 1% significance level, the data provide sufficient evidence to conclude that there is a difference in mean monthly sales among the three policies. For the P-value approach, note that $P < 0.005$.

S16.7 H_0: $\mu_1 = \mu_2 = \mu_3 = \mu_4$ (mean annual starting salaries are equal). H_a: Not all the means are equal. $\alpha = 0.05$; critical value = 2.68; SSTR = 2530.487; SSE = 1126.150; SST =3656.637 ; F = 89.88; reject H_0; at the 5% significance level, the data provide sufficient evidence to conclude that a difference exists in the mean annual starting salaries among the four majors. For the P-value approach, note that $P < 0.005$.

S16.9 Suppose that we define two events A and B as follows:

A: the interval constructed around the difference $\mu_1 - \mu_4$

B: the interval constructed around the difference $\mu_3 - \mu_2$.

The 90% confidence interval for each event above is defined as:

$$P(A) = 0.90 \text{ and } P(B) = 0.90.$$

The probability of both A and B occurring simultaneously is written

P(A and B). Since A and B are realistically not independent, the general multiplication rule applies; i.e., $P(A \text{ and } B) = P(A) \cdot P(B|A)$.

A difficulty arises in calculating a precise number for P(A and B) because we need additional information about $P(B|A)$, which we do not have. However, $P(B|A)$ is by no means equal to 1.00, which results in the product of P(A) and $P(B|A)$ being less than 0.90 (because 0.90 times a probability less than 1.00 is clearly less than 0.90). Thus, the probability of both A and B occurring simultaneously is not 0.90, and our confidence of both results occurring simultaneously is something less than 90%.

S16.11 Family confidence level = 0.99; $q_{0.01}$ = 4.83; simultaneous 99% confidence intervals are as follows:

Means difference	Confidence Interval
$\mu_1 - \mu_2$	-5.79 to 4.45
$\mu_1 - \mu_3$	-10.79 to -0.55
$\mu_2 - \mu_3$	-10.12 to 0.12

The table above shows that μ_1 and μ_3 can be declared different. The other two pairs of means are not declared different. This is summarized in the following diagram.

Policy 1	Policy 2	Policy 3
(1)	(2)	(3)
22.5	23.167	28.167

S16.13 Family confidence level = 0.95; $q_{0.05}$ = 3.68; simultaneous 95% confidence intervals follow:

Means difference	Confidence Interval
$\mu_1 - \mu_2$	-7.19 to -3.01
$\mu_1 - \mu_3$	0.82 to 4.78
$\mu_1 - \mu_4$	-10.62 to -6.78
$\mu_2 - \mu_3$	5.74 to 10.06
$\mu_2 - \mu_4$	-5.70 to -1.50
$\mu_3 - \mu_4$	-13.50 to -9.50

The above table shows that the following means can be declared different: μ_1 and μ_2, μ_1 and μ_3, μ_1 and μ_4, μ_2 and μ_3, μ_2 and μ_4, μ_3 and μ_4. This is summarized in the following diagram:

Hum	Market	Math	CompSci
(3)	(1)	(2)	(4)
23.9	26.7	31.8	35.4

Interpreting this diagram, we conclude with 95% confidence that the mean annual starting salary for computer science exceeds the mean annual starting salaries for all three of the others; also, the mean annual starting salary for mathematics exceeds the mean annual starting salaries for both humanities and marketing; and the mean annual starting salary for marketing exceeds the mean salary for humanities.